Cornish Today

Cornish Today

An examination of the revived language

Third edition

by

Nicholas Williams

MA PhD DipCeltStud FLS ITIA
Bard of the Gorsedd of Cornwall
Associate Professor in Celtic Languages
University College, Dublin

evertype
2006

Published by / *Dyllys gans* Evertype, Cnoc Sceichín, Leac an Anfa, Cathair na Mart, Co. Mhaigh Eo, Éire / *Wordhen. www.evertype.com.*

Third edition 2006. Reprinted with corrections January 2011.
Tressa dyllans 2006. Daspryntys gans ewnansow Genver 2011.

© 2006 Nicholas Williams.

Editor / *Penscrefer*: Michael Everson.

Y kefyr covath rolyans rag an lyver-ma dhyworth an Lyverva Vretennek.
A catalogue record for this book is available from dhe British Library.

ISBN-10 1-904808-07-7
ISBN-13 978-1-904808-07-7

Typeset in Palatino by Michael Everson.
Olsettys yn Palatino gans Michael Everson.

Cover / *Cudhlen*: Michael Everson

Printed by / *Pryntys gans* LightningSource.

CONTENTS

FOREWORD TO THE FIRST AND SECOND EDITIONS

Cornish, the Celtic language of Cornwall, is now extinct. Like Welsh and Breton, Cornish was a development of the language of the Ancient Britons, who lived in Britain before, during and after the Roman Conquest. Cornish was vigorous until the end of the Middle Ages, when for a number of reasons it went into a rapid decline. By 1700 Cornish was spoken only in the most westerly parts of Cornwall and within two generations the language was to all intents and purposes dead. Dolly Pentreath (?1692-?1777) of Mousehole is said to have been the last native-speaker of Cornish. There is good evidence, however, that her younger contemporary and neighbour, William Bodinar (1711-1789), had a native command of the language.

A first attempt at collecting phrases and expressions that were still found in Cornish English was made in the 1870s but it was not until the beginning of the twentieth century that anyone thought seriously of resuscitating the language. The revival began with the publication in 1904 of Henry Jenner's *Handbook of the Cornish Language*. Because Cornish had no native-speakers and because a variety of spelling-systems had been used for the traditional language at various stages in its history, the spelling and orthography of revived Cornish presented a problem.

Jenner's spelling was superseded in the 1920s by that of R. Morton Nance. Known as Unified Cornish, Nance's form of the language was the only variety of Cornish in use by revivalists until the 1980s. Dissatisfaction with Unified Cornish in the late 1980s led Ken George to develop his avowedly phonemic orthography. This system is known as *Kernewek Kemmyn* or "Common Cornish". After some hesitation Common Cornish was adopted in 1987 by the Cornish Language Board, the main body concerned with the teaching and publishing of Cornish. Both Unified and Common Cornish are based upon the medieval language. Also in the 1980s Richard Gendall began to promote a third variety of Cornish, *Curnoack* or Revived Late Cornish, based for the most part on the later stages of the language.

None of the three systems is satisfactory from an academic point of view. The present work offers a critique of the three forms of Cornish currently in use and suggests how the revival might eventually reunite around one generally accepted form of the language. The very warm welcome given to the first printing of this book leads me to believe that many revivalists are looking for a way out of the present unhappy impasse.

My thanks are due to many people who gave me advice and support while I was working on the present book. In particular I should like to thank Professor Glanville Price and K. E. P. Williams. I am especially indebted to †P. A. S. Pool, Richard Gendall and Dr Philip Payton for sending me items not available in Dublin. Ray Edwards also provided me with many invaluable documents, to say nothing of his countless helpful comments and suggestions. My debt to him is enormous. I am grateful also to Patricia Smyth for having saved me from innumerable stylistic infelicities.

Regrettably there were a number of typographical errors and errors of punctuation in the first printing of this book. I am grateful to Harry Woodhouse, Keith Syed and †Dr D. Balhatchet for having provided invaluable lists of *errata*. I hope that the majority of such mistakes will have been eliminated in this second printing. For all remaining imperfections in the book I am solely responsible.

Nicholas Williams
Dublin, 1995

FOREWORD TO THIS EDITION

In this edition of *Cornish Today* I have revised my arguments in a number of places. This I have done either in the body of the text itself or by the addition of footnotes. The changes were necessary, because further examination of evidence has convinced me that in the first and second editions I was mistaken about some important questions, namely, whether Middle Cornish had more than one long *o* (it did not), the development of the vowel in *prys* 'time', *bys* 'world' and *byth* 'will be', for example, and the pronunciation of unstressed final <eth> (Old Cornish *ed*).

In the first two editions of *Cornish Today* (13.00-39) I published a critique of Ken George's *Kernowek Kemyn*. I am disappointed that there has still been no proper response to these criticisms. In 1997 George and Dunbar published *Kernewek Kemmyn: Cornish for the Twenty-First Century*. This work is in the form of a dialogue between the master (George) and the pupil (Dunbar). It is marred throughout by gratuitous and rather childish insults against me. There are three far more serious faults in the work, however:

A George claims that Middle Cornish did not have its own scribal tradition, but that the various scribes wrote Cornish in their own individual manner, each of them basing his orthography on the English spelling of his own day. George does not attempt to prove this assertion by reference to the texts; he merely takes it for granted. To say that Middle Cornish had no scribal tradition is tantamount to saying that the mature and cultivated language of the mystery plays was without a literary tradition as well—which is clearly absurd. Indeed one is tempted to ask a number of questions: if Middle Cornish had no scribal tradition, what possible purpose was served by the scriptorium in Glasney priory? George claims that Middle Cornish was spelt according to English spelling conventions. It is generally agreed that Late Cornish was indeed spelt according to the orthographical conventions of English. Why then are the spelling-systems of Middle Cornish and Late Cornish so very different? The answer is that Middle Cornish had a strong scribal tradition, and Late Cornish did not.

B George does not actually cite the forms upon which his arguments are based. The reader has to take his "spelling profiles" on trust. Unfortunately, any such trust would be misplaced. As I have shown in my detailed review of his *Gerlyver Kernewek Kemmyn*, George's database is extremely inaccurate—something which George himself has reluctantly admitted.

C George does not attempt to dismiss my criticisms structurally. He does not, by citing forms in the texts, challenge my basic contention that the new prosodic system came into being before the Middle Cornish period. Nowhere does he oppose this view of mine head-on. Rather he attempts *seriatim* to answer some of my criticisms of Kernowek Kemyn. In so doing he lands himself in difficulties. He claims, for example, that the Prosodic Shift did not occur until the middle of the seventeenth century, by which time Cornish was extinct in east- and mid-Cornwall and moribund in the west. He claims (remarkably) that the Prosodic Shift lengthened some half-long vowels while shortening other half-long vowels; he does not explain why the Shift should work in two opposite directions. He asserts, for example, that the stressed vowel in the common prepositional pronoun *theso* 'to thee' was a half-long high front /i·/. He denies that *du* 'black' and *Du* 'God' had the same vowel and were therefore pronounced the same, for such an admission would mean admitting that the Prosodic Shift was a *fait accompli* in Middle Cornish. The following doublets also indicate that the Prosodic Shift had already operated: *gu/gew* 'woe', *gu/gew* 'spear', *glew/glu*, *pew/pu* 'who', *plew/plu* 'parish', *tru/trew* 'sorrow' and *tu/tew* side'. George cannot explain them except to say that the scribes "were sometimes confused". In order to show that unstressed vowels were kept separate George invents an entirely new metrical system with "perfect rhymes" and "imperfect rhymes" and "rhyming ensembles", all of which are entirely without parallel in either Welsh or Breton. A close examination of the Middle Cornish texts shows that George's prosody is fantasy.

I have dealt with George and Dunbar's *Kernewek Kemmyn: Cornish for the Twenty-First Century* in *Towards Authentic Cornish*, which is being published at the same time as this third edition of *Cornish Today*. None of George's assertions can bear scrutiny and I have had little difficulty in dismissing them all. I regret therefore that no proper answer to my critique of Kernowek Kemyn has yet been published. I conclude that no such refutation has been produced, because my criticisms of Kernowek Kemyn are valid and no such refutation can be produced.

This edition contains 31 footnotes where it seemed prudent to me to indicate that my views on a particular point had changed, or to make other clarifications.

I am grateful to Craig Weatherhill for providing me with toponymic evidence for this edition and to Michael Everson for his meticulous typography.

Nicholas Williams
Dublin, 2006

INTRODUCTION

0.1 Cornish cannot be revived. When the last native-speakers died at the end of the eighteenth century, they took with them their ability to speak the traditional Celtic language of Cornwall. The language that is now in the process of revival is different from the speech of the last native-speakers and indeed of any native-speakers of traditional Cornish of any period. The revived language is not Cornish in the way that the language of Dolly Pentreath and William Bodinar was Cornish.

Glanville Price goes further, for he says, "'revived' Cornish is not real Cornish" (1984: 144) and he prefers to call the revived language Cornic (cf. Latin *Cornice*, French *cornique* 'Cornish'). *Cornic* means little to a speaker of English and I therefore use the more neutral *Neo-Cornish* when referring to the language of the revival. *Neo-Cornish* is comparable with such terms as *Neo-Latin*, *Neo-Hebrew* and *Neo-Melanesian*.

Although Price has now apparently abandoned the term "Cornic", he continues to insist that the revived language is not Cornish in any real sense. He writes:

> In fact 'revived' is a barely appropriate term as 'revived' Cornish is to no inconsiderable extent a nineteenth- and, more especially, a twentieth-century invention, in its orthography, its pronunciation, its vocabulary, and even in its grammar (1992: 311).

It should be noted in passing that Neo-Cornish is a twentieth-century phenomenon only, since the Cornish revival did not begin until the publication of HCL in 1904.

Latin is used in Vatican publications, where it is required to discuss modern notions like nuclear disarmament, economic development, and the mass media. In order to do so the vocabulary of Latin has to be extended by adaptation and by borrowing backwards from the Romance languages. Moreover when used as a spoken medium ecclesiastical Latin acquires some of the features of the speaker's native language, Italian, German, Polish or whatever. One wonders whether those who dismiss Neo-Cornish, would be prepared to say that the Latin of the Vatican was not the Latin of Caesar and Cicero and not therefore "real" Latin at all.

Price quoting Charles Thomas observes that revived Cornish is full of "assumptions, accretions and inaccuracies" (1984: 144). The same unfortunately can be said of much of the academic criticism levelled at the revival. Price asserts, for example, that John Tregear may not have been a native-speaker of Cornish (1984: 140). This observation suggests that Price has

x

not read Tregear with sufficient care. A thorough reading shows that the language of the homilies is idiomatic and colloquial Cornish. The large number of English borrowings are either a deliberate feature of homiletic style or a true reflection of native Cornish in the 1550s (16.2).

0.2 Although they do not always adequately distinguish them, critics use two separate and unrelated arguments against the revival of Cornish. In the first place they say that the revival is seeking to do the impossible; languages are natural growths and if they die, they cannot be revived; secondly critics assert, the remains of Cornish are so slight, that even if reviving a language were possible, there is not enough Cornish to render the revival practicable. This latter is Price's argument and is not, in my view, compelling.

The notion that languages cannot be revived is a legacy of the romantic movement and of the ideas of Social Darwinism. Languages were the embodiment of the folk. They were a manifestation of the genius of the community that spoke them. Language death was historically determined; one language ousted another because it was the vehicle of a superior culture. Linguists nowadays prefer to understand languages as social conventions rather than mystical emanations of the people. As a result they are more prepared to admit the possibility of revival—and even to make an academic study of it.

Although languages appear natural enough to their speakers, it must be remembered that they are by their very nature human constructs. In that sense all languages are artificial. Most languages show the marks of deliberate manipulation. Much of the vocabulary of English has had to be invented. How many of us realize as we speak that words like *quality, quantity, scapegoat* and *gas* are all deliberate coinages?

0.3 The idea that languages cannot be resuscitated was one with which the revivalists of Hebrew were familiar. Hebrew remained a liturgical and literary language among the Jews for more than two millennia until it again became a spoken language at the end of the nineteenth century. Even when Israeli Hebrew had become the native speech of tens of thousands of people, some scholars insisted that resurrecting a language was impossible. As late as 1956 Whatmough was insisting that the revival of Hebrew ran counter to historical principles and was therefore an "unsuccessful experiment" (Rosén 1977: 33 fn). Others grudgingly allowed that Hebrew was being spoken, but, like Price in the case of Cornish, they denied either that it was genuine Hebrew or that it was a real language. Since the 1950s linguists have studied the whole question of the Hebrew revival in depth and have drawn conclusions from their studies that should be of interest to Cornish revivalists.

Israeli Hebrew is less like the Hebrew of the scriptures than Neo-Cornish is like traditional Cornish. The phonology of Israeli Hebrew is very far removed indeed from the sound-system of biblical Hebrew. The distinctions between laryngeals and pharyngeals have been lost and the vowel system has been radically reshaped. The lexicon of Israeli Hebrew is at a superficial level based on the vocabulary of Biblical Hebrew, but the categories underlying the revived lexicon are very largely European, in particular Russian, Yiddish and German. Moreover words have been freely borrowed from Aramaic and Arabic, just as Neo-Cornish has borrowed from Welsh and Breton. The syntax of Israeli Hebrew is also largely de-Semitized and owes much to Russian and Yiddish.

0.4 As far as the phonology and inflection of Neo-Cornish are concerned, Price and other sceptics are too pessimistic. A close and attentive reading of the Cornish texts coupled with Lhuyd's phonetic renderings gives us an accurate picture of the sounds of Cornish, provided we approach the question intelligently and systematically. The phonology of Unified Cornish itself is incomparably closer to traditional Cornish than that of Israeli Hebrew is to the sound-system of Biblical Hebrew.

Price seeks to prove the artificial nature of Cornish morphology by showing that the revivalists have invented verbal paradigms. This invention he says began with Jenner. Jenner, for example, gives for the pluperfect/conditional of *mos* 'to go' a completely hypothetical paradigm (1984: 144, fn 17). Jenner himself describes it as "probable, but not found" (HCL: 143). In fact at least one form of Jenner's paradigm is attested: *galse* 'had gone' at PA 207b.

Price observes that the imperfect of *dos* 'to come' is cited by Lewis only in the second person singular *dues*, no other parts of the tense being attested (1946: 64). Nance on the other hand has reconstructed the entire tense as *den, des, do, den, deugh, dens* (Price 1984: 144, fn. 18). Lewis cites *dues*, presumably because that is the only form for the tense given by Norris (1859: ii 284), from OM 155 in fact, and Lewis did not trouble to create his own paradigms. The form *dues* at OM 155 is the 2nd person imperative not the imperfect. The imperfect of *dos* is attested in the 3rd plural *y tens* at PA 97d and in the third singular elsewhere as *y to*.

We have a large body of Cornish writing. The absence of certain persons in certain tenses is not an indication of the limited nature of the remains of Cornish; it is rather a reflection of the language itself. From the earliest texts onwards auxiliaries are used to create both imperfect and pluperfect. We therefore find such expressions as *pub ur fystene a wre* 'she always used to hurry' PA 171a; *hedre vons y ov plentye* 'while they were complaining' PA 33c (see further 21.7-11); *ny wrussen the guhuthas* 'I would not accuse thee' OM 163-64.

Reconstruction of paradigms may seem desirable on occasion, even though it is largely unnecessary. Nance ought to have made it clear that some of his paradigms in Nance 1949 were reconstructions. His predecessor, Jenner, was more careful in this respect. Price wants his readers to believe that much of Neo-Cornish inflection is invented. This is quite simply untrue. It is perfectly possible to speak and write idiomatic Neo-Cornish without using any inflected verbal form that is not attested in the texts. In order to do so it is necessary only to imitate the sources by using auxiliaries.

0.5 The surviving lexicon of Cornish is remarkably extensive, largely because Lhuyd records such a wide variety of items. Since the revival began it has been necessary to extend the senses of old words and to coin new ones on the basis of Welsh and/or Breton. There is no harm in so doing provided the matter is approached in a scholarly way. Other languages do likewise. When French invents a word, not infrequently Spanish and Italian translate it literally. French *coup d'état* and *essuie-main* 'towel', for example, have become Italian *golpe di stato* and *asciugamano* respectively. Welsh/Breton calques in Cornish are not dissimilar. When Welsh-speakers point to the artificiality of the Cornish lexicon, they should remember that a page from a modern Welsh newspaper or magazine would be unintelligible to Dafydd ap Gwilym, but that does not make the modern language any less Welsh.

0.6 Price describes the Cornish revival in the following terms:

> [It] is rather as if one were to attempt in our present century to create a form of spoken English on the basis of the fifteenth century York mystery plays and very little else (1984: 144).

Cornish literature in its entirety is longer than the York mystery plays. In order for the parallel to be a valid one, one would have also to include as sources the Chester Plays, *Everyman*, a long devotional poem, a collection of sermons, an Anglo-Saxon and a modern English glossary, an eighteenth-century grammar, a folk-tale in phonetic script, translations from scripture, various other verses and fragments and survivals and innumerable place-names.

From all these sources one could deduce a great deal about the phonology, accidence, syntax and lexicon of Late Middle and Early Modern English. One would soon realize that the language was very close to Frisian and Low Saxon and had borrowed extensively from Old Norse and Middle French. One would therefore have ample resources with which to fill any lacunae in the lexicon. In a short time Neo-English would become a viable system—exactly as is now the case with Neo-Cornish.

0.7 Price also says:

> [T]he present writer... holds to the view he has expressed on various occasions in the past that 'revived' Cornish is not authentic Cornish. It could perhaps be compared with a painting that has been so heavily restored as no longer to qualify as an authentic work by the artist, or to a piece of music found in fragmentary form and arranged some centuries later by another composer (1992: 313).

Paintings and pieces of music are artefacts, usually created at one particular time by one person. Languages on the other hand are systems of communication that exist in the minds and on the lips of speakers; languages are susceptible to rational planning and are in any case constantly changing. Price's analogy is therefore invalid. Nonetheless in the light of Price's criticism I take at random a very short passage of Neo-Cornish and examine how far it exhibits a reconstructed diction—whether it should be classified according to Price's criteria as a genuine painting or a modern restoration.

Here is a short passage in Unified Cornish on the death of the tin-mining industry in Cornwall:

> **Dywysygneth moldrys wosa try myl bledhen**: An 25es mys Me 1991 yn dan gel an bresel yn Persya 3000 bledhen a valya sten yn Kernow o moldrys gans an governans Sawsnek. Oll rag fowt a £1.6 mylvyl a lendyans

> [**An industry murdered after three thousand years**: On the 25th of May 1991 under the cover of the war in Iran 3000 years of mining tin in Cornwall were murdered by the English Government. All for the want of £1.6 million of loans] (*Carn* 74: 16).

First it should be pointed out that there is a grammatical error in the sentence after the headline: *o moldrys* 'had been murdered' should be *ve moldrys* 'was murdered'. Neither the headline nor the final sentence has a verb, but in this respect neither is any worse than much contemporary journalism in English.

Whether all the sentiments in the above passage would be intelligible to a sixteenth or seventeenth Cornish speaker is impossible to say. The lexical items in it, however, all have warrant in the texts or can be justified as authentic Cornish:

> **moldrys** – *moldra* 'murder' BM 1189; **wosa** – *wosa* 'after'(temporal) BM 104; **try myl** – *tremmyl* 'three thousand' BM 1539, *iii myl* BM 1612; **bledhen** – *blethen* 'year' BM 565, *bledhan* AB: 3a; **25ves** = *pymp warn ugansves* – cf. *dek warnugens* ' 30' PC 593, *pymp* 'five' PC 505, *iganzvath* '20th' AB; **mys Me** – *Mîz mê* AB: 84b; **yn dan gel** – *yn dan geyl* 'under cover of' BM 1439 (see CPNE: 46); **bresel** – *bresel* 'conflict' PA 238a; **sten** – *stean* 'tin' AB: 154b; **yn Kernow** – *yn ol kernow* 'in all Cornwall' PC 2712; **governans** – *governens* BM 256, *governans* 'government' TH 25; **Sawsnek** – *Sousenack* 'English' BF: 29; **rag** – *rag* 'for' BM 403; **fowt** – *fowt* 'lack, want' TH 13a; **mylvyl** – *myl vyl* 'million' RD 132.

The adjective **dywysyk** 'assiduous' occurs at RD 1370. This has formed the basis of Neo-Cornish **dywysygneth** 'assiduity' > 'industry' (in the economic sense). *Dywysyk / dywysygneth* is parallel with *medhec* 'doctor' – *medhecnaid* 'medicine' in OCV and *gowek* 'mendacious' RD 55 – *gowegneth* 'falsehood' RD 906.

Lendyans 'act of lending, loan' is Neo-Cornish, formed from the unattested *lendya* 'lend'; with *lendya* compare *forsakya* 'forsake', *blamya* 'blame', *attendia* 'attend', *decernya* 'discern', *spedya* 'speed', *amendia* 'emend' from BM and *comondya* 'command', *persevya* 'perceive', *lamentya* 'lament', *exaltia* 'exalt', *wrappya* 'wrap', *institutya* 'institute', *performya* 'perform' all from John Tregear. With *lendyans* < *lendya*, compare: *dysquethyans* 'demonstration' from CW and *gorthyans* 'glory', *megyans* 'nurture', *devethyans* 'origin' all from BM.

The term *balya 'to mine' is a Neo-Cornish derivative of the Cornish word *bal* 'mine', which is attested in many toponyms (see CPNE: 15-6). Other -*ya* verbs based on native/naturalized roots include *crowsya* 'crucify', *arethya* 'harangue' and *cledhya* 'excavate'.

Persya 'Persia' is not attested in traditional Cornish, but compare the following from Tregear: *Aphrica, Galacie, Cappadocia, Asia, Bithinia*.

There are errors in Neo-Cornish, but they are susceptible of correction. I discuss such corrections at 16.1-22.10 below. The present passage is perforce very short, but it is typical of the whole article. It contains—apart from one grammatical error—nothing in its orthography, morphology, syntax or lexicon that is not firmly rooted in traditional Cornish. The same could be said for almost any comparable passage of Neo-Cornish. Price's analogy of the restored painting or the arranged piece of music is highly questionable in itself. As far as the authenticity of Neo-Cornish is concerned it is very wide of the mark.

0.8 Neo-Cornish is not completely natural. Its phonology is to some degree conjectural, its lexicon is not entirely native and a very small part of its inflection is reconstructed. There are, however, several things that can be said in its favour. First, Neo-Cornish is based on traditional Cornish and is therefore closer to traditional Cornish than either Breton or Welsh is. However artificial its origins, Neo-Cornish belongs in and to Cornwall in a way that no other language does, dialectal English included. Secondly, traditional Cornish before 1780 must have been similar to Neo-Cornish to-day. A fluent speaker of Neo-Cornish and a speaker of traditional Cornish can never meet. If they could, they would probably experience a great degree of mutual comprehension. In which case, their respective idioms must be dialects of the same language.

Thirdly, and this is already implicit in my second point, Neo-Cornish is a viable language. There are people now who can speak Neo-Cornish with ease and their numbers are growing. Neo-Cornish actually is a native language for a few. Unified Cornish in particular has produced some fine writing in both prose and verse. In a word, the Cornish revival is a fact which is not going to disappear. The sooner Neo-Cornish is put on a sound academic basis the better. An attempt has already been made by Ken George to analyse the sounds of Middle Cornish systematically, but in my view the results are not satisfactory (13.39).

0.9 It is sometimes claimed that revived Middle Cornish is medieval, Catholic, pre-industrial and backward-looking, whereas Late Cornish is Protestant, industrial and modern. This argument is invalid. From the ideological point of view languages are completely neutral. People can have value-systems; the languages they speak cannot. In recent times German has been used by Nazi, Communist, and democratic states, but it is still the same language. The antiquity of a revived language is also irrelevant. Before it was revived a hundred years ago, Hebrew had not been a vernacular since the first centuries of our era.

The claimed superiority of Late Cornish over Middle Cornish as a medium for the revival is invalid for another reason. As I demonstrate at 14.3 there is nothing either in the sound-system or the grammar of Late Cornish that is not already present in the earlier language. Middle Cornish and Late Cornish are not versions of the same language; they are the same language. Richard Gendall's Revived Late Cornish is merely late Middle Cornish in an English-based spelling. Speakers of Unified cannot with ease read texts in Revived Late Cornish, but if such texts are respelt in a more traditional orthography, the difficulty disappears (see, for example 23.14). I believe that attempting to revive the "orthography" of Late Cornish is a serious mistake and I set out my reasons at 14.31-9 below.

0.10 The Cornish revival cannot afford the luxury of three competing systems, particularly since none of them is ideal. Already the dispute among the three forms of Cornish has begun to damage the revival seriously. The numbers of those taking Cornish examinations has begun to drop significantly since the arrival of Kernowek Kemyn in 1986 (Payton 1993: 277).

In the following pages I describe the phonology of Cornish as I understand it. Thereafter I attempt a fairly detailed critique of Kernowek Kemyn, Revived Late Cornish and Unified Cornish. There have been other forms of Neo-Cornish, Jenner's of 1904, for example, and Tim Saunders's system (see Saunders 1990 and 23.16 below). I deal with Kernowek Kemyn, Revived Late Cornish and Unified Cornish only, since these are the most widely used systems.

Henry Jenner was the best linguist among the earlier revivalists. It is not astonishing therefore that his Neo-Cornish was both sensible and scholarly. Jenner attempted to make intelligible the later language but borrowed freely from Middle Cornish. He explains his own orthography in the following terms:

> The present system is not the phonetic ideal of 'one sound to each symbol, and one symbol for each sound', but it aims at being fairly consistent with itself, not too difficult to understand, not too much encumbered with diacritical signs, and not too startlingly different from the spellings of earlier times, especially from

that of Lhuyd, whose system was constructed from living Cornish speakers (HCL: x).

Although his spelling was internally consistent, Jenner did not attempt to use one symbol for one sound. In modern terminology, he did not try to be "phonemic". Although Jenner based his orthography on Lhuyd, he replaced Lhuyd's idiosyncratic *k, ku, dzh, tshi* and *z* with the more traditional *c, qu, j, ch* and *s*. Jenner regularly wrote pre-occlusion in *pedn* 'head' and *cabm* 'bent' on the one hand, yet made wide use of Middle Cornish forms on the other.

Jenner rightly saw that the difference between Middle and Late Cornish was slight, being largely a matter of spelling:

> As for grammatical forms, it will be seen that the writer is of [the] opinion that the difference between Middle and Modern Cornish was more apparent than real, and that... the so-called 'corruptions' were to a great extent due to differences of spelling (HCL: x–xi).

It is a pity that Jenner's Cornish was not maintained and refined. Jenner's system was ultimately replaced by Unified Cornish, whose demerits lay chiefly in its tendency to the quaint and archaic. Even so, in my view, Unified Cornish is by far the least unsatisfactory of the three major systems being used today.

0.11 Since I believe that Unified Cornish is susceptible of revision in a way that the other two systems are not, I put forward in the third section of this book my proposed revision of Unified Cornish. My reforms embrace phonology and spelling, accidence, syntax and vocabulary. By revising Unified Cornish, I am, in a sense, adding to the varieties of Neo-Cornish. My revision, though extensive, is intended as a reformed version of Unified Cornish, not a new system.

I should like to stress here that what I propose below are recommendations only. They may perhaps be of assistance as a first step in the reuniting the speakers of Neo-Cornish. I hope the present work will be read carefully and my arguments judged on their merits. I offer this work to those seeking to revive *agan eyth ny*, not just as a professional student of the Celtic languages but also as a member of the family.

ABBREVIATIONS AND REFERENCES

AB = Edward Lhuyd, *Archæologia Britannica* (London 1707 [reprinted Shannon 1971])

ACB = William Pryce, *Archæologia Cornu-Britannica* (Sherborne 1790)

Bakere 1980 = J. Bakere, *The Cornish Ordinalia*. (Cardiff: University of Wales Press, 1980)

BBCS = *Bulletin of the Board of Celtic Studies*

BF = O. J. Padel, *The Cornish Writings of the Boson Family* (Redruth 1975)

Bice = Christopher Bice, *The Tregear Manuscript: Homilies in Cornish.* (n.d.) [Multigraphed typescript]

BM = Whitley Stokes (ed.), *Beunans Meriasek: the life of St Meriasek, Bishop and confessor, a Cornish drama* (London: Trübner and Co. 1872)

Borlase = William Borlase, *Antiquities of the County of Cornwall* (London 1754)

Campanile = E. Campanile, *Profilo etimologico del cornico antico* (Pisa, 1974)

Carn = *Carn: A link between the Celtic Nations* (Journal of the Celtic League)

CC = Common Celtic

CCCG = Henry Lewis, Holger Pedersen, *A Concise Comparative Celtic Grammar* (Göttingen 1961)

CF = *The Charter Fragment*, text from E. Campanile, "Un frammento scenico medio-cornico", *Studi e saggi linguistici* 60-80, supplement to *L'Italia Dialettale 26*

CG = Whitley Stokes, "A Cornish Glossary", *Transactions of the Philological Society* (1868-69) 137-250

Commission of the European Communities (1986) *Linguistic Minorities in Countries Belonging to the European Community*. Luxembourg.

CPNE = O. J. Padel, *Cornish Place-name Elements* (Nottingham 1985)

CS = Caradar [A.S.D. Smith], *Cornish Simplified* (1955) [reprinted Camborne 1972]

CW = Whitley Stokes (ed.), *Gwreans an Bys: the Creation of the World*, (London: Williams & Norgate 1864 [reprinted Kessinger Publishing 1987, ISBN 0-7661-8009-3])

ECD = F. W. P. Jago, *An English-Cornish Dictionary* (London 1887)

EDD = J. Wright, *English Dialect Dictionary*, 1-6 (Oxford 1961)

Edwards 1993 = Ray Edwards, *Pascon agan Arluth: Passhyon agan Arloedh* (Sutton Coldfield 1993)

Ellis 1974 = P. Berresford Ellis. *The Cornish Language and its Literature* (London and Boston, 1974)

Emery 1971 = F. Emery, *Edward Lhuyd FRS, 1660-1709* (Cardiff 1971)

Fowler 1961 = D. C. Fowler, "The Date of the Cornish 'Ordinalia'", in *Medieval Studies* 23, 91-125

Fudge 1982 = C. Fudge, *The Life of Cornish* (Redruth 1982)

Gendall 1993-94 = Richard Gendall, "Early Modern Cornish Literature: a perspective", *The Celtic Pen* vol. 1, 17-20.

George 1990 = Ken George, "Word-order in Middle Breton and Middle Cornish" in M.J. Ball, J. Fife, E. Poppe and J. Rowland, *Celtic Linguistics: Ieithyddiaeth Geltaidd* (Amsterdam and Philadelphia) 225-40

George 1992 = Ken George, "An delinyans pellder-termyn toul rag studhya an yeth kernewek" in G. Le Menn and J.-Y. Le Moing, *Bretagne et Pays Celtiques: Mélanges offerts à la mémoire de Léon Fleuriot* (Rennes & St Brieuc 1992)

Gilbert 1838 = Davies Gilbert, *Parochial History of Cornwall* i-iv (London 1838)

ABBREVIATIONS AND REFERENCES

GKK = Ken George, *Gerlyver Kernewek Kemmyn* ([s.l.], Cornish Language Board 1993)

GMC1 = Wella Brown, *A Grammar of Modern Cornish* (Saltash: Cornish Language Board 1984) [Unified Cornish]

GMC2 = Wella Brown, *A Grammar of Modern Cornish*, second edition ([s.l.]: Cornish Language Board 1993)

GMW = D. Simon Evans, *A Grammar of Middle Welsh* (Dublin 1964)

HCL = Henry Jenner, *A Handbook of the Cornish Language chiefly in its latest stages with some account of its history and literature* (London 1904)

HMSB = Roparz Hemon, *A Historical Morphology and Syntax of Breton* (Dublin 1984)

Hooper 1972 = E. G. R. Hooper, *Passyon agan Arluth* (Kesva an Tavas Kernewek 1972)

HPB = Kenneth Hurlstone Jackson, *A Historical Phonology of Breton* (Dublin 1967)

IE = Indo-European

Jago 1882 = Fred W. P. Jago, *The Ancient Language and Dialect of Cornwall* (Truro 1882)

JCH = "Jowan Chy an Horth: John of Chyanhor" [text from AB: 251-53 and BF: 14-19]

Jenner 1875-76 = Henry Jenner, "Traditional relics of the Cornish language in Mount's Bay in 1875", *Transactions of the Philological Society*, 533-42

JRIC = *Journal of the Royal Institution of Cornwall*

KB = Richard Gendall, *Kernewek Bew* (Cornish Language Board 1972)

KK = Kernowek Kemyn

KMP = Crysten Fudge, *Kernewek Mar Plek: A Second Course in Cornish* (Redruth [no date])

LCB = Robert Williams, *Lexicon Cornu-Britannicum* (Llandovery 1865)

LHEB = Kenneth Hurlstone Jackson, *Language and History in Early Britain* (Edinburgh 1953)

LlCC = Henry Lewis, *Llawlyfr Cernyweg Canol* (Cardiff 1946)

Longsworth 1967 = R. Longsworth, *The Cornish Ordinalia* (Cambridge 1967)

Loth 1897 = J. Loth, "Études corniques i", in *Revue Celtique*, 18, 410-24.

Loth 1900 = J. Loth, "Cornique moderne", in *Archiv für Celtische Lexicographie* (Halle): 224-29

Loth 1902 = J. Loth, "Études corniques ii, textes inedits en cornique moderne", in *Revue Celtique*, 23, 173-200.

Lyon 1984 = R. Lyon, *Everyday Cornish* (Redruth 1984)

MacLennan 1988 = MacLennan, G. W., *Proceedings of the First North American Congress of Celtic Studies* (Ottawa 1988)

Mills 1980 = Mills, M., *Kernow a's dynergh gans blejyow tek* ([s.l.] 1980)

Murdoch 1993 = B. Murdoch, *Cornish Literature* (Cambridge 1993)

Nance 1949 = R. Morton Nance, *Cornish for All: A Guide to Unified Cornish* (St Ives: James Lanham 1949)

Nance 1952 = R. Morton Nance, *An English-Cornish Dictionary* (Marazion 1952) [reprinted 1978]

Nance 1954 = R. Morton Nance, "Cornish Words in the Tregear MS", *Zeitschrift für Celtische Philologie* 24, 1-5

Nance 1955 = R. Morton Nance, *A Cornish-English Dictionary* (Marazion 1955) [reprinted 1978]

Nance 1967 = R. Morton Nance, *A Guide to Cornish Place-names* (Marazion 1967)

Norris 1859 = Edwin Norris, *The Ancient Cornish Drama* i-ii (London [reprinted New York/London, Benjamin Blom 1968])

OCV = "Old Cornish Vocabulary" [quoted from Norris 1859 ii: 311-435 and Campanile 1974]

CORNISH TODAY

OED = *Oxford English Dictionary*
OldC = *Old Cornwall*
Ó Luain 1983 = C. Ó Luain, *For a Celtic Future: A tribute to Alan Heusaff* (Dublin 1983)
OM = "Origo Mundi" in Norris (1859) i: 1-219
PA = Whitley Stokes, "*Pascon agan Arluth*: 'the Passion of our Lord'", *Transactions of the Philological Society* (1860-61 Appendix 1-100)
Payton 1993 = Philip Payton, *Cornwall since the War* (Redruth 1993)
PC = "Passio Domini Nostri Jhesu Christi" in Norris 1859 i 221-479
PN = personal name
PNWP = P. A. S. Pool, *The Place-names of West Penwith*, second edition (Penzance 1985)
Pool 1982 = P. A. S. Pool, *The death of Cornish* (Penzance 1982)
Pool 1995 = P. A. S. Pool, *The second death of Cornish* (Redruth 1995)
Price 1984 = Glanville Price, *The Languages of Britain* (London 1984)
Price 1992 = Glanville Price, *The Celtic Connection* (Gerrards Cross 1992)
PSRC = Ken George, *The Pronunciation and Spelling of Revived Cornish* ([s.l.]: Cornish Language Board 1986)
RC = *Revue Celtique*
RD = "Resurrexio Domini Nostri Jhesu Christi" in Norris 1859 ii 1-199
Rosén 1977 = Haiim B. Rosén, *Contemporary Hebrew* (The Hague and Paris 1977)
SA = *Sacrament an Alter* "Sacrament of the Altar" text quoted from an unpublished edition by D.H. Frost, *Sacrament an Alter: Part II* (St David's College 2003)
Saunders 1990 = Tim Saunders, *Geriadur Arnevez kernauek-brezhonek*, ([s.l.], Imbourc'h 1990)
SC = *Studia Celtica*
SDMC = Richard R. M. Gendall, *A Student's Dictionary of Modern Cornish* (Menheniot 1993)
SGMC = Richard R. M. Gendall, *A Student's Grammar of Modern Cornish* (Menheniot 1991)
SND = Grant, W. and Murison, D.D, *The Scottish National Dictionary* i-x (Edinburgh *c.* 1941-76)
Snell & Morris 1981 = J. A. N. Snell and W. A. Morris, *Cornish Dictionary Supplement: no. 1* (Cornish Language Board 1981)
Snell & Morris 1983 = J. A. N. Snell and W. A. Morris, *Cornish Dictionary Supplement: no 2* (Cornish Language Board 1983)
Statutes = *Irish Statutes 1310-1786* (Dublin 1786)
Stokes 1860 = Whitley Stokes, "Poem of Mount Calvary: Pascon agan Arluth" in *Transactions of the Philological Society*, 1860-61, Appendix, 1-100.
Stokes 1900 = Whitley Stokes, "A glossary to the Cornish drama *Beunans Meriasek*", *Archiv für Celtische Lexicographie* i 101-42 (Halle)
TAC = Nicholas Williams, *Towards Authentic Cornish* (Westport: Evertype 2006, ISBN 978-1-904808-09-1)
TH = John Tregear, *Homelyes xiii in Cornysche* (British Library Additional MS 46, 397) [text from a cyclostyled text published by Christopher Bice ([s.l.] 1969)]
Thomas 1984 = A. R. Thomas, "Cornish" in P. Trudgill, *Language in the British Isles*, 278-88 (Cambridge 1984)
Thomas & Thomas 1989 = B. Thomas & P. W. Thomas, *Cymraeg, Cymrâg, Cymrêg: cyflwyno'r tafodieithoedd.* (Cardiff 1989)
Thurneysen 1946 = Rudolf Thurneysen, *Old Irish Grammar* (Dublin: Institute for Advanced Studies 1946)

ABBREVIATIONS AND REFERENCES

Toorians 1991 = L. Toorians, *The Middle Cornish Charter Endorsement: The making of a marrage in medieval Cornwall* (Innsbruck 1991)
UC = Unified Cornish
UCR = Unified Cornish Revised
Wakelin 1975 = Martyn F. Wakelin, *Language and history in Cornwall* (Leicester: Leicester University Press 1975)
WG = J. Morris Jones, *A Welsh Grammar* (Oxford 1930)
Williams 2006a = "A problem in Cornish phonology" in Nicholas Williams, *Writings on Revived Cornish* (Westport: Evertype 2006, ISBN 978-1-904808-08-4), 1–25
WORC = Nicholas Williams, *Writings on Revived Cornish* (Westport: Evertype 2006, ISBN 978-1-904808-08-4)

Cornish Today

PART I: THE SOUNDS OF CORNISH

CHAPTER 1
General remarks

1.1 Although the following account of Cornish phonology is systematic, it is not exhaustive. The description of the sound-system of Cornish given below is intended as a necessary introduction to the analysis of the varieties of Neo-Cornish in Part II.

Until recently the only attempts at providing a phonemic description of Middle Cornish have been George's PSRC and a brief description of Cornish by A. R. Thomas (1984). Thomas's work is perspicacious. He believes, for example, that /i/ and /e/ were in free variation. Although this is not so, the opposition between them is insignificant in some contexts. Thomas has also elucidated several other features of Middle Cornish phonology: that long /a/ is raised to [æ:] and that the opposition between long and short vowels is also one of tenseness versus laxness.

There are a number of minor points in Thomas's analysis with which I would disagree. He believes for example that the Cornish for the name *Jhesu* had an initial /j/ and was pronounced /jesɨ/, as in Welsh. I disagree with Thomas on this point (see 8.20). The main defect of Thomas's description is, in my view, that he believes the system of vowel length was similar to that of Welsh. In the following pages I give my account of why I believe Cornish differed from Welsh in the matter of vocalic length and how the Cornish system of length affected other aspects of the phonology. Nonetheless Thomas's analysis of Cornish is a business-like account of the phonemes of Cornish by a professional Celticist.

CHAPTER 2
The New Quantity System, the Accent Shift, and the New Prosodic System

The New Quantity System
2.1 The three Brythonic languages, Welsh, Cornish and Breton, are all developments of the language of the Ancient Britons spoken in Britain before, during and after the Roman occupation. This language I will call British. The presence of the Romans in Britain had a considerable influence on British. One noticeable influence was on the vocabulary. Many Cornish words were borrowed into British from Latin. Obvious examples are *gwyn* 'wine' < Lat. *vinum, eglos* 'church' < *ecclesia, scryfa* 'write' < *scribo*. Less transparent examples are *mos* 'table' < *mensa, gol* 'festival' < *vigilia* and *cusca* 'sleep' < *quiesco*. Latin may have had other effects on British quite apart from vocabulary, as we shall see. It should also be noted that the overwhelming majority of words in Cornish are not borrowed from Latin or from English for that matter. They are inherited from Common Celtic.

Irish, Scottish Gaelic and Manx are also Celtic but the Brythonic languages differ from them among other things in one very important respect. Welsh, Cornish and Breton, unlike the Gaelic languages, have replaced their inherited system of vowel length with a system based on the nature of the syllable. In British if a stressed syllable was originally closed, i.e. if it originally ended in a double consonant or a group of consonants, the preceding vowel either remained short or was shortened. If on the other hand the stressed syllable ended in a single consonant, the vowel was lengthened. Thus for example, in British **mamma* 'mother' the stressed syllable is closed before the double *m* and thus the vowel remains short to give Welsh *mam* and Breton *mamm*. In the British **'tatos* 'father', on the other hand, the stressed syllable ended in a vowel **'ta-tos* and consequently lengthened to give Welsh *tad*, Breton *tad* and Cornish *tas*, all with a long vowel.

In British in closed syllables in words of more than one syllable the vowel remained short. In open syllables it became half-long. Thus the British plural **mam'mowes* 'mothers' gave Welsh *mammau* and Breton *mammoù* both with a short vowel, whereas the plural **ta'towes* 'fathers' gave Welsh *tadau*, Breton *tadoù*, both with a half-long vowel. It should also be noted that half-long and long are really varieties of long and as such are usually grouped together, not only by linguists, but unconsciously also by speakers of the language concerned.

This system of vowel quantity developed in Late British or very early or "Primitive" Welsh, Cornish and Breton. It is usually known as the New Quantity System and Jackson believed that it arose in the 7th century C.E. It is

2

now believed to be considerably earlier. The lengthening of open syllables is a feature of the Romance languages, French, Spanish, etc., as distinct from Classical Latin and the similarities between the Brythonic new quantity system and the comparable development in the languages that descend from spoken Latin has often been noted. It is possible that the new quantity system arose in Britain under the impact of spoken Latin. If so, it must have started during the Roman occupation. In this context one should note Sims-Williams' recent suggestion that the final stages of the new quantity system were in place by 550 C.E. (BBCS 38: 49).

The Accent Shift

2.2 British almost certainly had penultimate stress. When final syllables were lost, however, in the transition from British to Primitive Welsh, Cornish and Breton, the stressed penultimate became the stressed ultimate syllable. Thus for example the British name /karata:kos/ with a long penultimate by the new quantity system became Primitive Welsh *Cara'dawg* with long /a:/ giving *aw*. Later the accent shifted from the final to the new penultimate syllable and the long but now unstressed final syllable was shortened to *o* giving *Ca'radog*.

The accent shift occurred throughout the Brythonic languages except in the south-eastern part of the Breton speech-area. Jackson has dated the accent shift to the eleventh century (LHEB: 699) but it is probably much older than that. Since it occurs throughout the Brythonic world it is likely to have occurred when Welsh, Cornish and Breton were a cultural unity.

In the transition from British to Primitive Welsh the reflex of British /u/ and /i/ were reduced to /ə/ immediately before the accent. Thus British *litanos* 'broad' in Primitive Welsh became * lətanos* >*lə'dan*. Later when the accent shifted to the new penultimate syllable the schwa received the stress and appears in Modern Welsh spelt as <y> but pronounced /ə/: *llydan* 'broad'.

In stressed position the reflex of British short /i/ appears in Welsh as /ɨ/ or /ɨ:/ according to whether it occurred in a historically open or closed syllable. In either case it is in Modern Welsh orthography spelt as <y>. Thus Welsh has *bydd* 'will be' (3rd person singular) /bɨ:ð/ from British stressed /i/ in an open syllable, but *byddaf* 'I will be' /'bəðav/ from an originally unstressed /i/ that was reduced to /ə/ before receiving the stress again when the accent shifted.

The position is similar in originally closed syllables. Welsh *mynnaf* 'I wish' for example has /ə/ from a historically short /i/ that remained short in a closed syllable but was reduced to /ə/ before the accent only to receive the accent again after the accent shift. On the other hand the third singular *myn* 'wishes, will wish' has short /ɨ/ with a short vowel from a historically short /i/ in a closed syllable.

So far only Welsh examples have been cited. The alternation of *y* ~ *ə* also occurs in Cornish, however. In Cornish the result of British stressed *i* is either /ɪ/ or /ɪ:/ , whereas the unstressed vowel /ə/ gives Middle Cornish /e/, for

3

example, in *ledan* 'broad', *tevy* 'grow' (Welsh *tyfu*), *eva* 'drink' (Welsh *yfed*), *enys* 'island' (Welsh *ynys*). The alternation Welsh *y* with Cornish *e* was noticed by Lhuyd (AB: 19). In Cornish therefore the Welsh alternation *y* ~ *y* appears as *y* ~ *e* where *y* is either long or short. It is long for example in *byth* 'he will be' as against short *e* (< half-long) in *bethaf* 'I will be' and *gwyth* 'trees' as against *gwethen* 'tree'. It is short in both *mennaf* 'I wish' and *myn* 'he wishes'. In Middle Cornish long *y* /ɪ:/ tends to become long /e:/ and the alternation often ultimately disappears. The alternation also occurs in diphthongs, for example in *byw* 'alive' but *bewnans* 'life'. I discuss this whole question more fully below at 5.1-6 and 6.3-6.

2.3 In Cornish the vowel was long in monosyllables before an originally single consonant, as for example in *tas* 'father', *beth* 'grave' (where the <th> /ð/ counts as a single consonant), *gwyn* 'wine', *mos* 'go', etc. There is some evidence in Cornish that the groups /st/ and /sk/ may also have counted as a single consonant, as they do in northern Welsh. Lhuyd cites the word for 'bitch' as *gêst* where <ê> means a long /e:/. Yet the word historically has a short vowel, Welsh *gast* 'bitch' (short *a* in South Wales), Breton *gast* 'femme de mauvaise vie'. At BM 784 the word *west* 'west' is spelt <weyst> which seems to indicate that it has a long vowel /we:st/. Similarly *Crist* 'Christ' has almost certainly got a long vowel. It is also probable that loan-words like *dowst* /du:st/ have a long vowel before /st/. That /sk/ might be considered a single consonant seems likely from Lhuyd's *pêsk zal* 'salted fish' (AB: 143c).

It is possible also that on occasion vowels were lengthened in Cornish before original double /ll/ as though it were a single consonant. This is the case in some dialects of Welsh and explains Lhuyd's *ôl* 'all' < Middle Cornish *oll* (AB: 107a), but probably not *Tî a il* 'thou canst' < *gyll* (see 19.18).

The New Prosodic System
2.4 The New Quantity System is likely to have occurred in British before the language developed into Welsh, Cornish and Breton. By the eleventh century Cornish was already very different from Welsh and somewhat different from Breton. Our earliest Middle Cornish texts were probably originally composed in the late thirteenth or early fourteenth century. Already by that period, Cornish, I believe, had undergone another major shift in the system of vowel length. This new system, unknown in Welsh and Breton, I refer to as the New Prosodic System.

It appears firstly that the relatively light stress accent that Cornish shared with Welsh and Breton became reinforced. The result was that stressed syllables were more emphatically pronounced than previously. Correspondingly, however, they were reduced in length. It was as though stressed vowels acquired in intensity what they lost in duration. Unstressed syllables shed much of their intensity; their vowels began to weaken and to fall together as the neutral vowel schwa. This is the common reduced vowel of unstressed syllables in English. The second syllables of *mother, fasten, bustle, bigot* all contain schwa, /ə/. The reason for the New Prosodic System was almost certainly English in Cornwall and I discuss the question at 12.3 below.

The evidence for this prosodic shift is everywhere in Middle Cornish, for it had far-reaching effects not only on vowels and diphthongs but on aspects of the consonantal system as well. Cornish, like Welsh and Breton, almost certainly had originally a threefold opposition of long, half-long and short vowels. The new prosodic system, however, reduced the three-fold opposition to a simpler system of two differences rather than three. When describing a threefold opposition of vowel length one can reasonably posit the following schema: long = three units of length or morae; half-long = two morae; short = one mora. The two-fold opposition on the other hand can be analysed as long = two morae; short = one mora.

The loss of half-long quantity really involves a shortening of both long and half-long. Long takes the place of old half-long, while half-long falls together with short. All the evidence suggest that in Cornish long vowels were reduced from three morae to two morae, whereas historically half-long vowels were reduced from two morae to one. As vowels of only one mora originally half-long vowels were now short and indistinguishable therefore from vowels that had always been short. To put it another way, Cornish before the prosodic shift had three lengths: long as in *tas* 'father' (3 morae); half-long as in the stressed vowel of *tasow* 'fathers' (2 morae); short (one mora) as in *mam* 'mother' and the stressed vowel in *mammow* 'mothers'. When the new prosodic system had taken effect the vowels were: new long in *tas* (2 morae); short (one mora) in *tasow, mam* and *mammow*.

We noticed above that by the Brythonic new quantity system vowels before doubled consonants remained short, whereas vowels before single consonants became long or half-long. In English spelling doubling a consonant does not actually affect the consonant itself. It is merely a trick of spelling. In some etyma in Middle Cornish, the double consonant (*nn*, for example) was actually longer than the single one. With most consonants there was no difference between a single and a double. Nonetheless it was the case in Cornish that a doubled consonant was a way of writing a short vowel.

2.5 If the new prosodic system in Middle Cornish were a reality, we might expect to find historically half-long vowels written as though they were short, that is to say, followed by a double consonant. This is exactly what we do find.

One of the best examples is the word for 'goodness', *dader*. This is historically the word *da* 'good' < **dago-* + the abstract suffix *-ter, -der. Da* by itself ends in a vowel because the original consonant *-g-* has been lost. When the abstract suffix was added, the vowel became half-long; compare *tas* long but *tasow* half-long. This word not infrequently appears therefore in the historically expected form <dader>. Often however it is written <dadder>

with a double <d> . <Dadder> can only mean /dader/ with a short stressed vowel for earlier /da.der/ with a half-long. Notice the following:

y thadder 'his goodness' PC 3097, BM 4271
dre y thadder 'through his goodness' RD 1224
dre y ʒadder 'through his goodness' PA 3c
mur a ʒadder 'much goodness' BM 189
dadder 'goodness' BM 485, 499, 2229, 3173, TH 11, 30a
mur thadder 'much goodness' BM 528
daddar 'goodness' TH 11a, 12
hay thaddar 'and his goodness' TH 14

In fact Tregear has so many examples of <dadder>, <daddar>, that I have not troubled to count them all. If the Cornish of the texts really preserved half-length in vowels, then the spellings listed above are unintelligible. If on the other hand half-long vowels have become short vowels, these spellings make perfect sense.

The result of the shift half-long > short is seen in other words as well. In the *Ordinalia* one finds such phrases as *yn chymma* 'in this house' PC 667, 1207, *alemma* 'hence' PC 699, *yn dre-mme* 'in this town' OM 2284. These can best be explained by assuming as we have done that half-long had become short. In the first of these phrases the original expression would have been *y'n chy ma* with a long /iː/ in *chy*. As the three words became fused into a single accentual unit, *chy* as the stressed open syllable of a trisyllable would have shortened its vowel to half-long /anʹtʃiˑma/. After the prosodic shift half-long would have become short and the syllable was now closed. The only way of showing this in writing was by doubling the consonant: *an chymma* /anʹtʃɪma/.

Among other examples from the Middle Cornish texts of consonants doubled unhistorically one could cite the following:

tassow 'fathers' OM 1409
assaf, assas 'I leave, he left' OM 1489, TH 24
yssel 'low' OM 1515
cossow 'woods' OM 2558
fossow 'walls' OM 2450, 2454
essof 'I am' RD 2145
essa 'was' TH 12a, 13
assow 'ribs' TH 15a
marrov, marrow 'dead' OM 2702, BM 3524
gorre 'hay' OM 1058
connan 'Conan' (personal name) BM 223
ingynnys 'engines' BM 3376
aswannas 'recognized' TH 7a
aswonna 'recognized' TH 39a
ennoc 'Enoch' (personal name) RD 197
thyallas 'punished' RD 1966

prenna, prennas, prennys 'buy, bought' BM 868, 885, PC 767, 922, RD 62, 147, 165,
   PA 7a, 9b, 196d
gocky, wokky 'foolish' (< ME *goky, gawky*) PC 1290, 2043, 2897, RD 87, 989, 1273
gweller 'is seen' BM 1571
gwellas 'to see' TH 6, 8a, 32a
powessens 'they were resting' PA 254a
drogkolleth 'evil' TH 3, 10a, 11a
esylly 'members TH 35a
eddryggys 'penitent' TH 40a
y gilla 'one another' TH 22
besitthis 'baptized' TH 37a.

There are many other examples not listed above. It is noticeable that the
doubling is commoner in the later texts BM and TH than in the *Ordinalia* (OM,
PC, RD). Given the conservatism of the scribal tradition, it is remarkable that
unetymological gemination occurs at all. We can be quite sure that in all the
words in the above list half-length had already been lost before our earliest
texts. If half-length had disappeared from all these words, it must have
disappeared even where the disappearance is not apparent from the spelling.[1]

2.6 Vowels are not infrequently described as 'tense' or 'lax'. These terms are
relative only. When a vowel is 'tense' it is pronounced with the tongue higher
in the mouth and with a greater amount of energy than its 'lax' equivalent.
Short vowels are usually less tense than their half-long and long counterparts.
It is for this reason that in Cornish previously half-long vowels when they
were shortened became more open, that is to say the tongue was lowered and
the articulatory organs relaxed slightly. Historically half-long /i/, for example
when it shortened became /ɪ/ or /e/. Thus in the texts the word *tryg* 'dwells'
has a long vowel /triːg/ and is always spelt with a <y>. The disyllabic form
tryga 'dwell' on the other hand had a half-long vowel that later became short.
When it had shortened under the new prosodic system it was lax and opened
to /ɪ/ or /e/. It is for this reason *tryga* is more often than not spelt as <trega>
in the texts. The new prosodic system was also the reason that the inherited
diphthongs /iw/ and /ɪw/ fell together as /ɪw/ (see 6.2). We can also ascribe
to the new prosodic system the diphthongization of /iː/ > /ej/, a phenomenon
most noticeable in Late Cornish, but clearly already present in the earlier
language. The developement /yː/ > /ɪw/ that gives rise to the common
spelling <du> 'God' is also a result of the new prosodic system (see 3.13; 6.4).

2.7 One of the most important results of the new prosody was the tendency of
all unstressed syllables to weaken. The Cornish poets had inherited a metrical
system that involved rhyming unstressed syllables. In English *hen* rhymes

---

1   A much fuller discussion of the gemination of historically single consonants in
   Middle Cornish orthography can now be found in TAC 6.00-6.07.

with *pen* but not with *open*. In Cornish on the other hand *pen* 'head' rhymes with *cren* 'shakes' but also with *benen* 'woman' and *mynsen* 'I should wish'. Unstressed vowels tended to become /ə/. As a result *benen* was /'benən/ and *mynsen* was /'mınsən/. Yet the poets continued to rhyme unstressed vowels as though they were proper vowels and not just a neutral schwa. They therefore attempted to give their rhyming vowels at least the appearance of colour according to the stressed vowels with which they rhymed. It is for this reason that one finds the same word spelt with a variety of unstressed vowels simply to give the appearance of rhyme. The word *colon* 'heart' has etymological *o* in the second syllable. As well as <colon> it is spelt <colan>, <colen> and <colyn> for the sake of rhyme. The whole question of unstressed syllables is discussed at 7.1-15 below.

Another direct result of the new prosodic system is the phenomenon known as pre-occlusion. This is the curious process by which historically long *n* becomes *dn*: *gwyn* 'white' > *gwydn, gwidden*. Because this is such an important development and one that is of dialectal significance in Cornish, I discuss it at length at 9.1-6.

CHAPTER 3
The long vowels

3.1 When discussing the effects of the loss of half-length on long vowels and diphthongs, I assume that in all cases the vowel/diphthong originally was three morae in duration. I also analyse long vowels and diphthongs as consisting of two separate elements, a half-long nucleus and a short coda. In the case of /iː/ for example the coda I take to be /j/, the whole vowel being /iˑj/, that is to say, a half-long /i/ followed by a semivocalic coda. Similarly /uː/ I analyse as /uˑw/. In the case of the long vowels /ɪː/, /oː/, /yː/ I assume that the nucleus was a half-long variety of the vowel and the coda was a less coloured variety of the vowel, which for simplicity's sake I will describe as schwa /ə/. There are parallels for such an analysis. The long *a*-vowel of Glamorganshire Welsh, for example, is often written <æə> by phonologists. Similarly the long vowels in the Irish of Connaught in words like *tá* 'is' and *bó* 'cow' are frequently [ɑːə], [oːə]. One might on the other hand analyse long /oː/, for instance, as /oˑo/ before the prosodic shift, where the coda is more or less identical with the nucleus as far as quality is concerned. This would not materially affect our understanding of the phonological processes involved in the prosodic shift.

3.2 Long stressed /iː/ in Middle Cornish had several sources including Common Celtic long /iː/ as in *gwyr* /gwiːr/ 'true' < CC */wiːros/; CC /uː/ in final position as for example in *ky* /kiː/ 'dog' < CC */kuː/ and Lat. /iː/ as for example in *gwyn* /gwiːn/ 'wine' < Latin *vinum* /wiːnum/. Cornish /iː/ occurs in stressed monosyllables as in the above examples. It can also occur in words of more than one syllable if the final syllable is open and stressed, as for example in *ogasty* /ogəsˈtiː/ 'nearly', *whywhy* /ʍəˈʍiː/ 'you' (pl. emphatic).

3.3 There is some evidence that /iː/ before /g/ is shortened to /i/ in Tudor Cornish. *Sacrament an Alter* regularly writes *kyg* /kiːg/ 'flesh' as <kigg>, for example. Notice also the place-name *Trigg Rocks* in Breage. The etymon is *trig* 'maris recessus'. This is probably related to Welsh *trai* 'ebb' but has been contaminated with the word *tryg* 'dwell', i.e. 'where the land remains'.

3.4 It seems that Cornish abhorred any high front vowel other than /i(ː)/ in final position. The British for 'house' must have been **tego-*. This developed as **tigo-*, whence Welsh *tŷ*. In Cornish the word has /iː/ because Cornish seems not to allow anything but /iː/ in absolute final. This is an important point for the following reason: if Cornish tolerated /iː/ in final position but not /ɪː/, then *my* /mɪː/ 'I' and *ty* /tɪː/ in Kernowek Kemyn are mistaken (13.23).

9

3.5 Frequently though not universally in Cornish /i:/ in final position was diphthongized to /ej/. Thus Lhuyd cites *kei* 'dog' (AB: 46a), for example, and *trei* 'three' (AB: 251a). The diphthongization of /i:/ > /ej/ was a direct consequence of the new prosodic system. Originally /i:/ had had three morae and could have been analysed as /i·j/. When half-length disappeared from Cornish, /i·j/ would have become /ij/. The first element, because it was no longer half-long but short, was correspondingly untensed to /ɪ/. As a result speakers would have felt that their /ij/ was now [ɪj]. In /i·j/ nucleus and coda are at the same height in the mouth. When the nucleus became /ɪ/ it was lower than /j/. In absolute final where the long vowel was unprotected by any consonant, the two elements in /ɪj/ continued to move apart. The result was /ej/, written <ei>, <oy> in Late Cornish.

There is good evidence from the texts that /i:/ had already become /ej/ in final position in Middle Cornish. PA 21 rhymes *otry* 'outrage' /o'tri:/ and *dry* 'bring' /dri:/ with *pray* /prej/, /praj/ 'prey' and *ioy* /dʒoj/ 'joy'. These rhymes already present in the early fourteenth century at the latest, would not have worked unless /i:/ could be pronounced as a diphthong. Other texts show many similar rhymes. I have space here for only a few examples:

ny 'we'	rhymes with	*joy* 'joy' OM 555-58
ty 'thou'	rhymes with	*moy* 'more' OM 946-48
deffry 'indeed' /də'frej/	rhymes with	*ioy* 'joy' OM 1374-78
rey 'to give'	rhymes with	*moy* 'more' PC 536-37
dry 'to bring'	rhymes with	*fey* 'faith' PC 1993-96
vy 'my' (enclitic)	rhymes with	*vay* 'kiss' BM 507-08
ny 'we'	rhymes with	*moy* 'more' BM 1874-77.

Cf also *ny vannaf vye* 'I (emphatic) do not wish' at CW 1380 which rhymes with *oye* 'egg'. Here *vye*, spelt like English *stye*, would have been pronounced /vej/ and would have made an adequate rhyme with /oj/.

It is quite apparent, then, that the diphthongization of /i:/ was already an accomplished fact in the earliest texts, and was used as a metrical resource by the poets. It should also be noted that Tregear spells *why* 'you' as *whay* at 33a. Similarly Andrew Borde has *tray kans myle dere* for 'three hundred miles' (Loth 1900: 226), implying that he heard *try* 'three' pronounced /trej/ or /traj/ *c.* 1542.

Since the development /i:/ > /ej/ can be neatly explained by reference to the new prosodic system, we have further evidence that half-length did not exist in Middle Cornish.

3.6 British short /i/ was more lax than /i:/. When it lengthened as a result of the new quantity system in Cornish it became /ɪ:/. This would have been similar to the vowel in standard English *hit, bin, wig* but lengthened. In Breton the reflex of British short /i/ when lengthened was /e:/; in Welsh it became a centralized vowel /ɨ:/ written <y>. British *bitu-* 'world' thus became *bys, beys*

10

/bɪːz/ in Cornish, *bed* /beːd/ in Breton and *byd* /bɨːd/ in Welsh. Eventually in Cornish, however, the vowel /ɪː/ fell together with /eː/ and one finds *bes* 'world' in Late Cornish. The change /ɪː/ > /eː/ I assume to be a direct result of the new prosodic system.

The original vowel /ɪː/ would have had three morae and could be analysed as /ɪˑə/, that is to say a half-long onset [ɪˑ] followed by a slightly lower coda [ə]. When half-length disappeared, the first element in the diphthong was shortened and consequently untensed: [eə]. I assume then that the first element because of its increased intensity absorbed the coda and the resulting complex fell together with /eː/ from other sources.

Although the transition /ɪː/ > /eː/ was probably accomplished soon after the prosodic shift, scribal practice lagged well behind. The 3rd singular future of bos and the 2nd singular imperative would both have been *byth* /bɪːð/ before the prosodic shift and /beːð/ after it (I am assuming for simplicity's sake that the final segment here is /ð/). In most of the texts, however, <byth> is commoner than <beth>. PA, for example, has 9 instances of *byth* as against only one of *veth*. PC has no examples of *beth* at all. Of all the Cornish texts only BM regularly writes *beth* rather than *byth*. For *byth/beth* see 5.2 below.

Even though *byth* is overall more frequent than *beth* in all the Middle Cornish texts put together, we can be sure that the word was pronounced /beːð/, because this was the regular form in Late Cornish, for example, *uelkom ti a vêdh* (JCH: §15); *el guz dethiow beth pel* 'so your days may be long' (BF: 55).

As well as the spelling <byth> and the variant <beth>, the texts also exhibit a variant *beyth*. This occurs at OM 324 and 405. <ey> here is probably just a way of writing /eː/ in the same way that <oy> and <ay> are frequently used as graphs for /oː/ and /aː/ respectively. <ey> may also represent /ɪː/ (5.1-5.3).

There are many other etyma that had /ɪː/ > /eː/. I list some of them below together with the variant spellings found in the texts. For the sake of brevity only one instance of any spelling is listed:

'world'	*bys* OM 1042	*beys* OM 6	[*bes* BF: 13]
'strong'	*cryff* PA 105d	*creif* CW 1422	*cref* RD 118
'day'	*dyth* OM 17	*deyth* RD 45	*deth* BM 1772
'faith'	*fyth* RD 373	*feyth* PC 1469	*feth* PA 49d
'trees'	*gwyth* CW 93	*gveyth* OM 28	*gweth* PA 16b
'reptile'	*prif* CW 1055	*preyf* CW 1919	*pref* PA 122c
'time, meal'	*prys* OM 1414	*preys* BM 1843	[*prêz* AB: 161c]
'drink! drinks'	*yyf* OM 1916	*eyf* OM 2294	—.

It will be seen from these examples that forms with <e> alone are not common, even though in the period of the Middle Cornish texts all the etyma could be pronounced with /eː/.[2]

---

2 Since writing 3.6 I have changed my views on this question. There can be no doubt that /ɪː/ did become /eː/ in words like *dyth* 'day' and *gwyth* 'trees' in some varieties

3.7 There seems to be some evidence that inherited /ɪː/ and /eː/ alike became /iː/ in some forms of Late Cornish. Rowe, for example, writes *preeve* 'serpent', *deeth* 'day', *wheeze* 'sweat' all with historic /ɪː/ as well as *wreeg* 'wife', *treeth* 'between', *neeve* 'heaven' with inherited /eː/ (RC 23: 174ff). This may be the same phenomenon as the raising of /œː/ > /yː/, for example, in *dîz* 'come' < *dues*, etc. (3.14) in stressed monosyllables, or it may be analogical (see footnote 2 above).

Long vowels in monosyllables had probably been lengthened by the Late Cornish period from two to three morae (12.5). Such lengthened vowels would have been very tense. As a result in stressed monosyllables /eː/ from whatever source sometimes became /iː/.

James Jenkins in his poem beginning *Ma leiaz gwreage* rhymes *gwreage* 'woman, wife' with *zeage* 'brewer's grains', where both words have Middle Cornish /eː/. On the other hand, he rhymes *beaze* 'world' < early Middle Cornish /bɪːz/ with *teez* 'men, husbands' < Middle Cornish /tyːz/ (ACB). This would seem to imply that in his speech original /ɪː/ in the word *bys* 'world' became /iː/, whereas original /eː/ remained as /eː/. Similarly Lhuyd's spelling <îz> 'corn' implies that in Late Cornish the word was /iːz/ as well as /eːz/. Two things should be noticed in these examples. First, that in both /iː/ rather than /eː/ as the reflex of /ɪː/ occurs before /z/, which may be significant factor; and secondly, that *bys* /biːz/ 'world', *ys* /iːz/ 'corn', etc. in Unified Cornish are not without justification (15.8).

3.8 We have just seen that as a result of the prosodic shift /ɪː/ fell together with /eː/. Symmetry would lead us to expect something similar in the back vowels. We should perhaps posit a threefold series /uː/, /ʊː/, /oː/, reducing to a two-member series /uː/, /oː/. In fact this theoretical picture is almost certainly correct. In order however, to conform to the conventions established by George, I shall refer to the two series as /uː/, /oː/, /ɔː/ and /uː/, /ɔː/ respectively.

Long /oː/ in pre-shifted Cornish was normally the reflex of Old Cornish /ui/, as for example in Old Cornish *cuit* 'wood' > Middle Cornish *coys*, Old Cornish *scuid* 'shoulder' > Middle Cornish *scoth* /skoːð/, Old Cornish *guit* 'blood' > Middle Cornish *goys* /goːs/, Old Cornish *guit* 'goose' > Middle

---

of Middle Cornish. It seems, however, that in other forms of Cornish analogy with very common alternation, for example, in *tryg* 'dwells' ~ *trega* 'to dwell', *gwyth* 'keeps' but *gwetha* 'to keep' affected the shift of *dyth* > *deth* and *gwyth* > *gweth*. As a result *dyth* 'day' ~ *dethyow* 'days' and *gwyth* 'trees' ~ *gwethen* 'tree' did not become *deth* ~ *dethyow* and *gweth* ~ *gwethen* respectively. Rather, an opposition in the stressed vowel was maintained between the monosyllable (*dyth*, *gwyth*) and the disyllable (*dethyow*, *gwethen*). It is for this reason that we find both the expected *deth* 'day' and *gweth* 'trees' in the Middle Cornish texts and also the analogically-motivated *dyth* and *gwyth*. I discuss this whole question in greater detail in TAC 11.00–11.05.

Cornish *goyth* /goːð/. Some words that have /oː/ < *ui* in Middle Cornish appear with /uː/ in Late Cornish, for example, *gûdzh* 'blood', *lûdzh* 'grey', *ûz* 'age', Middle Cornish *oys*. It has been suggested that Late Cornish /uː/ is the result of a shift in late Middle Cornish of /oː/ > /uː/ (PSRC: 129). This seems unlikely, since it would mean that /ui/ was lowered to /oː/ c. 1250 and was raised again before the Late Cornish period. There are, moreover, several examples of /uː/ < Old Cornish /ui/ in Middle Cornish itself.

It must be remembered that our remains of Late Cornish are exclusively western, whereas standard written Middle Cornish originated further east in Cornwall. Given that Old Cornish /ui/ in *guit* 'blood' appears as /uː/ in Late Cornish *gûdzh*, I assume that western Cornish monophthongized Old Cornish /ui/ > /uː/ but did not lower it to /oː/. Eastern Cornish, the origin of the literary standard, on the other hand, monophthongized Old Cornish /ui/ and simultaneously lowered it to /oː/ (see 3.10 below). Long /uː/ in Late Cornish is confined to some reflexes of Old Cornish /ui/ and does not occur in etyma with inherited /ɔː/. Therefore /uː/ cannot owe its origin to the tensing of long stressed vowels noticed above (3.7).

Inherited long /uː/ is not common in Middle Cornish. Most examples are English and French borrowings, as for example in *tour* /tuːr/ 'tower', *chambour* /tʃamˈbuːr/ 'chamber', etc. Among native words that had /uː/ one must include *gour* 'husband' /guːr/, cf. Welsh *gŵr*. Two etyma that had probably had /uː/ before the prosodic shift were *plu* 'parish' < Lat. *pleb(em)* and **cun* 'dogs' (Welsh *cwn*, Breton *koun*). In these two words, however, the /uː/ did not survive the shift and it is to their development that we now turn.[3]

3.9 We saw at 3.5 above that /iː/ in absolute final position was dipthongized to /əj/, /ej/ in the Middle Cornish period as a result of the new prosodic system. Something similar appears to have happened with inherited /uː/ as well. The only example of /uː/ in final position known to me is the word *plu* 'parish', Breton *plou*, Welsh *plwyf*. It would seem in the unprotected final position that the vowel broke into two parts and ultimately became /ew/. Notice, for example, the rhyme *plu* with *dev* 'God' at RD 247-48; the rhyme *plu* ~ *gu* 'spear' at RD 2584-8 (There is good reason to believe that *gu* was /gɪw/ or /gew/; see 3.14 below) and the spelling <plew> at TH 25a. Tregear's form

---

3   I followed George too closely here on the questsion of the varieties of long *o* in Middle Cornish. George believes that Middle Cornish had two such vowels, one open [ɔː] and one closed [oː] I now realize that this view was mistaken. Middle Cornish had only one long *o*. Old Cornish /ui/ was in standard Middle Cornish lowered to /oi/, written <oy>. This monophthongized to /oː/ by the middle of the fifteenth centiry, at the latest, though it was still often written <oy>. In more westerly dialects, that is, those that lay behind the remains of Late Cornish, /ui/ remained and monophthongized to /uː/. This is why 'wood' in Middle Cornish is *coys* or *cos* but appears in Late (that is, western) Cornish as *kûz*. I discuss this whole question in greater detail in TAC 7.00–7.32.

is corroborated by two sixteenth-century place-names with *plew* for *plu: Plewe-Golen* (< *plu Colan*) from 1501 and *Plewgolom* < *plu Golom*, (= ?St Columb Major) from 1543 (CPNE: 295); compare also Lhuyd's *plêu* 'parochia' ['parish'] (AB: 113b).

I assume that before the new prosodic system *plu* was [plu·w] with three morae. After the loss of half-length the word became [plʊw] where the first element was the short equivalent of half-long /u·/. The weakened first element appears to have been differentiated still further from the second element by lowering and centralizing to [ǫ]. The new [ǫu] then fell together in pronunciation with /ew/. The place-name *Plewe-Golen* is clear indication that the shift /plu:/ > /plew/ was already in place by the end of the fifteenth century.[4]

Something similar may also have happened to /u:/ in the word for 'dogs'. In British this was probably **kunes*, which appears in Welsh as *cwn* and in Breton as *koun*. In Cornish one would have expected **<coun>* /ku:n/. This may have been the form of the etymon before the new prosodic system. Thereafter, however, it appears that the vowel broke as it did in absolute final position. Probably the final *n* was sufficiently sonorous to allow diphthongization. At all events, I assume that /ku:n/ [ku·un] developed after the loss of half-length as [kʊun]. This then developed as [kǫun]. At that point, however, the /n/ appears to have absorbed the high back second element and the vowel fell together with /œ:/ from other sources. It is for this reason that the regular Middle Cornish word for 'dogs' is /kœ:n/ as for example *ov huen* rhyming with *luen* 'full' at BM 3913 and *kepar ha kuen* 'like dogs' rhyming with *fuen* 'we were' at RD 172.

The Welsh for 'water' is *dwfr* or *dŵr* with /u:/. The corresponding etymon in Breton is *dour* /du:r/. One might therefore expect the Cornish *dour* 'water' to contain /u:/ also. Yet at RD 2255 it rhymes with *our* 'gold', which has /ow/. Moreover Lhuyd spells the Cornish for 'water' as <doṵr> [with a point under the *u* to indicate its semivocalic status] at AB: 3b and again at AB: 83a. Similarly the Welsh for 'deep' is *dwfn* and the Breton is *don*. The Cornish is *doun*, where the graph <ou> represents the diphthong /ow/; cf. Lhuyd's *doṵn* [with semivocalic u] (AB: 129c). The diphthongization in *dour* and *doun* in Cornish is a result of the loss of the following /v/ and is not related to the shift /ku:n/ > /kœ:n/. Presumably in the pre-forms of *dour* and *doun* /uv/ before a sonant

---

4 My explanation for the spelling <plew> here is ingenious but mistaken. The Latin word *plēb(em)* would quite regularly give Late British **pluif*; cf. Welsh *plwyf* 'parish'. This appears with the loss of the final spirant as *plui* in Old Cornish. The diphthong of *plui* was metathesized to **pliu*, which appears in Middle Cornish as *plew*. This metathesis is identical with Middle Cornish *yw/ew* 'is' from earlier **ui* < Proto-Celtic **ĕsti*. The spelling *plu* is merely graphemic for /plew/. For the question of the orthographic alternation <ew> ~ <u> see now TAC 13.00–13.09.

first became /uw/. Since stressed /u/ and /o/ tended to alternate (4.4), /uw/ was indistinguishable from /ow/.

3.10 As has been mentioned above, the distribution of etyma with Old Cornish /ui/ among the members /u:/ and /o:/ probably varied between eastern Cornish, with a tendency to forms in /o:/, and western dialects, that had a tendency to prefer /u:/. Given that standard Middle Cornish is largely eastern in spelling, such variation in distribution is not for the most part apparent from the texts, though there are some hints.

I have suggested elsewhere that I believe PC may be of relatively western origin. This seems be borne out by its treatment of Old Cornish /ui/ which is not infrequently /u:/ in the text rather than the more usual /o:/. Note for example, *scouth* 'shoulder' at PC 658. This spelling represents /sku:ð/; cf. *tour* 'tower' /tu:r/ and *chammbour* /tʃam'bu:r/ at OM 2110. *Scouth* occurs again at PC 2623-26 where it rhymes with *gouth* 'falls' /gu:ð/. Notice further *glovs* /glu:z/ 'pang' at PC 1147 and *trous* /tru:z/ 'foot' at PC 1223. The phrase *a'y yvs* 'ever, always till now' occurs at PC 786 where it rhymes with *tus* /ty:z/ or /tju:z/ 'people'; *yvs* /u:z/ is for the more usual *oys* /o:z/ 'age'.

Twice in CW the word *goyth, goeth* 'behoves' rhymes with the English word *forsothe* 'forsooth' (CW 1435-40, 1890-91). By the time of CW or its early sixteenth-century exemplar *forsothe* in English must have been /for'su:θ/. It is probable therefore that *goyth, goeth* < Middle Cornish unlenited *coth* /ko:ð/ 'behoves' was pronounced /gu:ð/ by the scribe of CW. CW is a western text, having been written in Helston in 1611. The scribe, however, was not the author. It is likely, nonetheless, that *goeth* had /u:/ in the dialect of CW's exemplar and that it too was of western provenance.

The Cornish word *cos* /ko:z/ 'wood' has developed from Old Cornish *cuit*. In Western Cornish one would expect the word to appear as /ku:z/. This is indeed the case. Not only does *Carrek Glas yn Cos* 'St Michael's Mount' appear as *Garrack Glas en Kûz* in Late Cornish (BF: 44), but the three place-names *Cusvey* (Gwennap), *Cusgarne* (Gwennap) and *Cusveorth* (Kea) have original /u:/ and are all west of Truro. In the far east of Cornwall Middle Cornish 'wood' appers as *cos* in *Coskallow Wood* (South Hill).

The toponym *Carrick Lûz* < *carrek los* 'grey rock' in St Keverne is of significance here. It exhibits /lu:z/ 'grey' and yet has *-ick* < *-ek* rather than the later *-ack*. Since *-ack* does not normally occur before the 16th century, we have to assume that in the area of St Keverne *los* 'grey' was pronounced /lu:z/ before the sixteenth century and that the name preserves Middle Cornish forms. In which case /lu:z/ 'grey' was already present in western Middle Cornish. *Lûz* 'grey' for *los* cannot be a Late Cornish phenomenon.

Although western texts on occasion exhibit /u:/ as a reflex of Old Cornish /ui/, this is not an invariable rule. PC writes *oan* 'lamb' at 697, a spelling that suggests [ɔ:] < earlier [o:]. In Lhuyd's Late Cornish *ô* not infrequently occurs

15

where *û* might have been expected. Note for example *ôan* 'lamb' (AB: 2a); *kôn* 'dinner' (AB: 48c); *skodh* 'shoulder' (AB: 242b).

3.11 As well as /o:/ Middle Cornish in all dialects also had a long open *o* /ɔ:/ which was usually the reflex of short *o* lengthened by the new quantity system. This originally contrasted with /o:/. In Cornish before the prosodic shift **ros* /rɔ:z/ 'promontory' Welsh *rhos*, and Cornish *roys* /ro:z/ 'net', Welsh *rhwyd*, were a minimal pair. Since the two vowels /o:/ and /ɔ:/ were different, it is not astonishing that some texts are careful not to rhyme them. PA for example rhymes *oys* /o:z/ 'age', *poys* /po:z/ 'heavy', *woys* /wo:z/ 'blood' and *boys* /bo:z/ 'food' together at stanza 10 and *ros* /rɔ:z/ 'gave' and *nos* /nɔ:z/ 'night' at 250. Rhymes of /o:/ with /ɔ:/ are not forthcoming in PA.

Although the reflex of Old Cornish /ui/ is sometimes /u:/ in PC and RD, more often than not Old Cornish /ui/ appears as /o:/ in both plays. On occasion this /o:/ rhymes with /ɔ:/. Note, for example, *coth* 'behoves' /ko:ð/ at PC 2488 rhyming with *both* 'wish' /bɔ:ð/ at 2485 and *uos* 'blood' at RD 860 rhyming with *bos* 'be' at RD 859.

BM also has a marked tendency to rhyme /o:/ and /ɔ:/ (the form with /ɔ:/ occurs after the diagonal stroke): *woys* 'blood' /*mois* 'go' 130-31; *goth* 'behoves' / *voth* 'wish' 584-85; *goys* 'blood' / *boys* 'be' 1599-1603; *loys* 'grey' / *boys* 'be' 2168-71; *boys* 'food' / *moys* 'go' 3927-29; *poys* 'heavy' / *moys* 'go' 4092-94; *loys* 'grey' / *voys* 'be' 4415-18; *loys* 'grey' / *toys* 'come' 4476-77.

In spite of their conservatism, then, the texts give us ample evidence that in standard Middle Cornish the two inherited phonemes /o:/ and /ɔ:/ were no longer distinct, but were falling together as /ɔ:/ or had already fallen together.[5] The development /o:/ > /ɔ:/ is only to have been expected. After all /ɪ:/ was falling together with /e:/ at the same period and the shift of /ɪ:/ > /e:/ is exactly comparable with /o:/ > /ɔ:/. One important difference would have been that /ɪ:/ > /e:/ was almost universal, whereas /o:/ > /ɔ:/ was more restricted in scope in western dialects where /o:/ had never arisen in many words. These had /u:/ < Old Cornish /ui/ which emerges into full view in the Late Cornish period.

If /o:/ and /ɔ:/ did fall together in Middle Cornish it was almost certainly as a result of the new prosodic system. I assume that as with /ɪ:/ described above original /o:/ was /o·ə/, or the like, that is to say a half-long element followed by a short coda. When the vowel lost one mora, the nucleus was untensed to /ɔ/ giving /ɔə/. The second element then was absorbed into the nucleus and the vowel became [ɔ:] with two morae.

3.12 Middle Cornish had two central vowels /œ:/ and /y:/. /œ:/ corresponds to Breton /œ:/ and Welsh /aw/ as for example in *brues* 'judgment', Breton

---

5   I would now prefer to say that /oj/ and /o:/ fell together (rather than /o:/ and /ɔ:/). See footnote 3 above.

breud, Welsh *brawd*; Cornish *due* 'comes' with Breton *deu*, Welsh *daw*. There was a tendency from the period of the earliest Middle Cornish texts for /œ:/ to fall together with its unrounded equivalent /e:/. Thus *due* /dœ:/ 'comes' is often written <de> and rhymes with words in /e:/. Note also the following: *mer* 'great' for *meur, mur* PC 684, 718, 2601; *bres, vres* 'judgment' for *breus, brus*, PC 515, 2504, PA 98b; *lef, leff, leyff* 'hand' for *leuf*, OM 421, PA 136d, 138a, 178a; *nymbes, na'm bes* for *ny'm bus, na'm bes* OM 171, 1884; *nyns es* for *nyns us* OM 1236. By the period of CW and Late Cornish /œ:/ had probably unrounded to /e:/ everywhere.

Middle Cornish also had /y:/ usually written <u>. This was the exact equivalent of Breton /y:/ <u> and Welsh /ɨ/ < /y:/, as for example, in Middle Cornish *tus* 'people' Breton *tud*; Middle Cornish *ruth* /ry:ð/ 'red', Breton *ruzh*, Welsh *rhudd*. /y:/ is usually written <u> throughout the Middle Cornish period, but it is clear from Late Cornish that it has become /i:/, for example, Nicholas Boson's <Teez> for earlier *tus* 'people'.

3.13 That /y:/ persisted longer in Middle Cornish than did /œ:/ is seen from the way in which it survived the prosodic shift long enough to be diphthongized. When long in absolute final position /y:/ seems to have fallen together with /ɪw/ from other sources. Before the rise of the new prosodic system /y:/ in the word *du* 'black', for example, could have been analysed as [y·y]. When half-length was lost from Cornish, the first element of the long vowel would have been shortened and untensed to a lower variety of [y] which I will write as <ø>. The new vowel was thus [øy]. The first element seems to have lost its rounding and was fronted to /e/ along with the phonetically similar /œ/ from other sources. Simultaneously it seems that the second element of [øy] by compensation reinforced its rounding but lost its front quality. It thus became [u] or [w]. As a result original /y:/ in final position having gone through the stages [y·y] > [øy] > [øu] > [eu] > [ew] was indistinguishable from the diphthong /ɪw/, /ew/. It is for this reason that Lhuyd cites the word for 'black' as *diu* (AB: 44a).

When original /y:/ had diphthongized it rhymed freely with /ɪw/, /ew/. Note, for example, *tru* 'pity, alas!' /trɪw/ < /try:/ (Middle Breton, Middle Welsh *tru*) rhyming with *hythev* 'today' (Breton *hiziv*, Welsh *heddiw*) at RD 732 and with *glev* 'clear' at PC 2088-89; and *tu* 'side' /tɪw/ < /ty:/ (Welsh *tu*) rhyming with *glv* (for *glew*) 'clear' at OM 2061-62.

Since original /y:/ in auslaut was after the prosodic shift indistinguishable from /ɪw/, /ew/, these diphthongs themselves are often written as <u>. Thus <du> is a common spelling of *dev* 'God' in PC, PA, BM and TH. We find *du* 'God' rhyming with *glu* 'clear' (for *glew*) at BM 764-65. Notice also *pv, pu* for *pyv* 'who' PA 42d, 253d; *dule* for *dywle* 'two hands' PC 583, 2499, 2677 and *gusel* for *gewsel*, lenited form of *kewsel* 'speak' PA 127a.

Bugh 'cow' was probably /by:x/ before the prosodic shift; cf. Middle Welsh *buch*. The final /x/ was weakened early with the result that the vowel was effectively in auslaut. As a result diphthongization took place and the word became /bɪw/; this is what is meant by Lhuyd's *byuh, biuh* (AB: 60c, 168c). Since, however, <u> in Middle Cornish could represent /ɪw/, the word is spelt <bugh> at OM 123. The spelling <bewgh> at CW 403 makes it certain that the vowel was a diphthong.

3.14 The word for 'spear' is attested in OCV in the compound *hochwuyu* 'boar-spear'. With the simplex **guyu* compare the Old Breton plural *guugoiuou*. The British form is apparently a compound **wogaiso-* of **wo-* and **gaiso-* 'spear', cf. Irish *ga* 'spear'. The Breton form points to an Old Breton simplex **gwoiw*. This is virtually identical with the Old Cornish which I understand as **gwuiw*. This gave **/giw/* by dissimilation of the labials. With the vowel shortened by the prosodic shift this appears in Middle Cornish as /gɪw/: *gyw* PA 219b, 221a, *giu* PC 3010, *guv* PC 2917, RD 432, 1015. In Middle Cornish the diphthong /ɪw/, however, is not distinct from /ew/ and thus the word is also attested as <gew>, for example, at PA 217c. Moreover /ɪw/, /ew/ are as we have seen frequently written <u>. Hence the spellings <gu>, <gv> at PC 1130 (rhymes with *dev* 'God') and RD 491, 1117, 1245, 2603.

AT PC 2924 we read *hag a'n gy evn th'y golon* 'and the spear right to his heart'. A second hand has emended *gy* to *gye*. The original *gy* is quite intelligible. The word was pronounced /gɪw/ but before the following diphthong with /ew/ dissimilation has occurred: /gɪw ewn/ > /gɪ ewn/ > /gi: ewn/. The spelling of the word for 'spear' as <gy> at this point merely corroborates the view that its vowel had been diphthongized.

I suggested above that the long /u:/ in Cornish **/ku:n/* 'dogs' was diphthongized before the sonant /n/ and then simplified to /œ:/. It seems that on occasion /y:/ also diphthongized before the phoneme /l/. The verbal noun of the verb 'to do' was originally /gy:l/. The vowel behaved first as it did in *du* 'black' and became **/gɪwl/*. This is the form which lies behind Borde's *gewel* 'do' in *me e uyden gewel ages commaundement* 'I will do your command-ment' (Loth 1900: 226). /gɪwl/ was then apparently metathesized to /gwɪl/. This is probably what is intended by such spellings as <gwell> (SA: 59, 59a) and <gwiell> (SA 62, 62) for *gul* 'to do'. Notice also Nicholas Boson's: *an hagar auall iggeva gweell* 'the bad weather he makes' (BF: 9).

3.15 When long in a closed syllable /œ:/ was on occasion unrounded not to /e:/ but to /i:/ as though it were /y:/ and not /œ:/. Thus *dys* 'come!' at PC 1233 is probably to be interpreted as /di:z/ for more usual *deus* /dœ:z/. This is identical with *Dîz* 'come' in JCH § 20. Compare *ny a thy* 'we come' for *ny a thue* at PC 1654; *meer* 'great' for *muer* SA 59a; *marsees* 'if there is' for *mars ues* SA 62a.

We have noted above that the difference between long and short vowels is also one of tenseness versus laxness. The long vowel /œ:/ when it unrounded may have been sufficiently close to /iː/ to fall together with it rather than with the expected /eː/. And /eː/ itself sometimes develops as /iː/ (3.7).

3.16 Cornish long vowels were more tense than their short equivalents. Short /a/, for example in *mam* 'mother' or *cam* 'bent', was [a]. Its long equivalent would naturally have tended to be tenser than [aː]. Since, however, [a] is pronounced with the tongue in the mid-low position, that is to say as low in the mouth as is possible, any tensing of the long vowel would entail raising the tongue forward or backward as well as upward. Middle Cornish long /aː/ would of necessity be closer than /a/ to either /oː/ or /eː/. In a word Cornish /aː/ would either be [ɑː] or [æː]. In fact both varieties are attested. Let us look at [ɑː] first.

The best attested example of /aː/ as [ɑː] is in the word *bras* 'big'. Here the tensing has occurred in the direction of the back of the mouth because of the rounding effect of the preceding labial even before the following [aː] was tensed. The retracted pronunciation of *bras* is guaranteed by a number of Late Cornish spellings: for example, *broas* (BF: 9); *brosse* (BF: 38); *broaz* (BF: 43). It is apparent that the retraction of the vowel in *bras* occurred in the Middle Cornish period for the following reason. When [brɑːz] 'big' occurred in disyllables the long vowel was shortened by the new prosodic system. The resulting short vowel was sufficiently different from /a/ that it fell together with the nearest short vowel: /o/. As a result one finds such Middle Cornish spellings as *brosyen* 'important people' BM 3215; *brossa* 'greater' SA 65; *broster* 'firmament' CW 81.

/aː/ appears to have been pronounced [ɑː] in some other environments, in particular before /l/. In Late Cornish the word for 'cliff', *als*, is written <aules>, <awles> (BF: 9, 12) which seems to imply a pronunciation [ɑːlz]. The word for 'forehead; brow; front' is *tal*. In place-names this often appears as <tol>, as for example in *Tolponds* < *tal pons*, *Tolgullow* < *tal golow* and *Tolvadden* < *tal va(d)n*. <Tol> /tol/ in these names is to be understood as a shortened variety of [tɑːl].

3.17 Before examining the evidence for a raised allophone [æː] of /aː/ some general points are in order. In the first place one shoud note that Lhuyd spells Late Cornish /aː/ phonetically as <â>. It has been suggested that this is proof that Cornish /aː/ was [aː] and not [æː]. This argument has little force, however. [æː] for [aː] is the normal pronunciation of long *a* in the Welsh of Mid-Wales from Harlech in the west to the border with English in the east (Thomas and Thomas 1989: 37). Lhuyd was born in Llanforda near Oswestry *c.* 1660 (Emery 1971: 10-1) when the area was still strongly Welsh . To Lhuyd, then, Welsh /aː/ was almost certainly [æː] as well as [aː]. At all events Lhuyd's phonetics are not in themselves sufficient evidence against [æː] for /aː/ in Cornish.

It should also be remembered that [æː] for /aː/ is attested not only in Mid Wales but also in a wide area in Glamorgan, a region which was at one time probably contiguous with the area of Primitive Cornish (Thomas and Thomas 1989: 37). It is also worthy of note that in Irish /aː/ is in Southern and Western dialects pronounced as [ɑː] but in Ulster as [æː]. Although the two varieties of /aː/ do not occur together in any known dialect, they may well have done when Irish was more widely spoken. At any rate there is every theoretical probability that Cornish realized /aː/ as both [æː] and [ɑː].

To return to the evidence for Cornish [æː]. In the first place it is difficult not to conclude that [æː] is intended by in the spellings of the Middle Cornish texts themselves. Thus *baal* 'spade', *graas* 'grace', *taal* 'forehead', *haal* 'marsh' at OM 380, 422, 2705, 2708 respectively are surely indicative of something more than [aː]. Note also *taan* 'fire' rhyming with *certan* at OM 1314. Some spellings in CW are probably also not without significance in this matter. CW spells Middle Cornish *plas* 'place' as <place> (CW 361, 364), *gras* 'grace, thanks' as <grace> (CW 1234), Cornish *dal* (lenited) 'is worth' as <dale> (CW 484) , *saf* 'stand' as <save> (CW 351) and Cornish *cas* 'case' as <case> (CW 130). William Jordan's spelling is heavily influenced by English and it is likely that he pronounced all these words similarly to their English homographs. Since he would have pronounced the English words as something like [plæːs] or [plɛːs], [græːs], [dæːl], etc., it is likely that he pronounced the Cornish words in the same way.

The normal spelling of the Cornish word for 'face' is <fas> or even <face> because it is a borrowing from Middle English *face* < Old French *face*. On two occasions, however, PC rhymes the word with *bythqueth* 'ever' and spells it <feth> (PC 1240, 1413). The alternation of <s> with <th> is not uncommon in Middle Cornish texts. The rhyme was possible, since the vowel of *fas* was [æː] or [ɛː] and though long was considered sufficiently similar to that of the second syllable of *bythqueth* /ˈbɪθkweθ/ to allow a rhyme.

Further evidence for /aː/ as [æː] is to be found in the word for 'bitch'. This is cited by Lhuyd as *gêst*, plural *gesti* (AB: 46a s.v. *canis*). One would expect <a> not <e> in the singular in view of Welsh *gast*. The *e*-form of the Cornish singular is not difficult to explain, however. In nouns like *tas* 'father' the singular/plural paradigm would have been [tæːz] ~ [ˈtazow]. The unfronted short *a* in the plural would serve to remind speakers that the underlying vowel of the singular was /aː/. Original */gaːst/ would have been pronounced [gæːst]. Since the plural had /e/ < /a/ by *i*-affection, the paradigm was [gæːst], [ˈgesti]. Naturally enough the singular was re-interpreted as /geːst/ not /gaːst/.

A similar case is the plural of *haal* 'marsh' to which we have alluded. Since the Welsh congener of *haal* is *hal*, there can be no doubt that the word had a long *a* as root vowel. The plural occurs at BM 3411 where it is spelt *hellov*. This form can only be explained by assuming that the simplex was [hæːl] or [hɛːl], where the vowel was so close to /eː/ that it fell together with it. It was on the basis of **hel* 'marsh' that the plural *hellov* was formed.

THE LONG VOWELS

One of the most compelling reasons for thinking that /aː/ was [æː] in Cornish is the evidence from place-names. There are numerous local names in west Cornwall that have -glaze < glas 'green, grey' as their second element. Such names include Creeglase, Cruglaze, Menaglaze, Carn Glaze, Polglaze, Penglaze, Porthglaze and Pentireglaze (CPNE: 104). These would all have [ɛː] or [ei] in the local pronunciation. Further place-names contain the element pras 'meadow' (cf. OM 1137), for example Praze, Praze-an-Beeble, Prazeruth, Prazegooth, Chypraze and Penpraze (CPNE: 193). It is difficult to see how names in -glaze or (-)praze could have come about had the vowel in Cornish not already been [æː] or [ɛː]. If for example glas had been [glaːz], it is difficult to see why Creeglaze, Cruglaze, and the rest do not appear in English as *Creeglass, *Cruglass, etc.

Padel also cites an earlier name Presthilleck which may be for Pras helig 'the meadow of the willows'. If so one should note that the long [æː] or [ɛː] has been shortened in the quasi-compound and has become [e]. Such a development could arise only if the vowel in pras had originally been fronted to [æː].

To sum up then, there is good evidence that Middle Cornish and Late Cornish /aː/ had two realizations: [ɑː] in the word bras 'great' and sometimes before /l/; and [æː] elsewhere.

CHAPTER 4
The short stressed vowels

4.1 Middle Cornish has a marked tendency to alternate stressed /ɪ/ and /e/. Note the closed monosyllable, *bez*, *bes* for *bys* 'towards' CW 1495, 1560, 1827, 1903 and the open syllables: *speris*, *sperys* for *spyrys* 'spirit' at PA 1a, 3c, 18a, OM 62, BM 2631, 2643, 2657, 2739, CW 2457; *teller*, *tellar* for *tyller* 'place' PA 206d, OM 939, 1823, 1909, 2275, 2795, BM 677, 1145, 2922, CW 871, TH 2, 7a, 19, 32a; *thellos* for *thyllas* 'released' PC 1200; *teby* for *tyby* 'consider' BM 3350. Given that the alternation of /ɪ/ and /e/ is particularly common in the presence of an adjacent labial or following /r/ or /l/, it is likely that we are dealing with phonetic reality rather than simply with graphemic practice. I assume that /ɪ/ and /e/ remained phonemically distinct but that in certain environments the two tended to fall together as /e/.

4.2 Not only does /ɪ/ frequently appear as <e> in short stressed syllables, but so does historic /i/. Indeed the variants with <e> for <y> are so common in some Middle Cornish texts as to be the customary form. Since it is impossible to examine all the examples I will take the reflexes of five etyma that have historic /i/ in their root: 1. *tryga* 'dwell' (Welsh *trigo*); 2. *whylas* 'search' (Breton *c'hwilian*, Welsh *chwilo*); 3. *scryfa* 'write' (Breton *skrivan*; cf. Welsh *ysgrifennu*); 4. *myras* 'watch, look' (Breton *mirout*); 5. *kyle* 'fellow, other one' (Breton *kile*, Welsh *cilydd*). This last usually appears with the poss. pronoun in the expression *y gyle* 'the other one'. I have noticed the following examples from the Middle Cornish texts:

1. *trege* PA 37b, 214c, OM 566, 1711, BM 947, 1344; *trega* OM 2190, 2665, BM 4348, CW 981, 1722, TH 2, 39a; *tregys* BM 687, 816, 1963, CW 246, TH 39a; *tregis* PA 46c, 84a, 85d, 89d, 93c, 255d; *treges* BM 4338; *drega* BM 3183, CW 334, TH 36a, 46a; *dregas* PA 213d; *tregough* OM 1893; *tregans* CW 1700
2. *whela* PA 21c, CW 483; *whelaf* CW 1695; *whelaff* TH 22a; *wheleugh* PA 68b; *weleugh* PA 69b; *whelas* PA 90a, 145d, 156b, 257b, 257d, OM 1139, CW 1691, TH 8a, 18a, 30a, 36a; *wheles* TH 27a; *whele* OM 1106; *welas* PA 94d, 257d, OM 378
3. *screffa* TH 19, 27a, 33; *screfa* TH 48; *screfys* PA 188d, 188d, BM 2766; *screfis* BM 394; *screffes* TH 43a; *screfas* TH 48a, 52a, 52a
4. *merough* PA 125c, CW 1550; *merowgh* TH 49a, CW 736, 736; *merow* TH 28a; *merogh* TH 36a; *merugh* BM 1577; *meras* PA 215d, TH 49a, 50a; *veras* PA 168b, OM 2325, BM 4074, TH 2, 3a, 7, 9; *veres* BM 4351; *verys* PC 1257; *verays* BM 4433
5. *gela* BM 1267, 2072, TH 16a, 17, 24a, 27a, CW 1063; *gele* 179c, 199a.

It is unlikely that <e> in these spellings is a mere graph intended to represent /i/. In the first place, when monosyllabic forms occur, because they have a long vowel, they are always spelt with <y> /iː/, as for example in *dryk* PA 212d, *tryg* OM 1104, *dryg* OM 2112, TH 39a; *myr* BM 935, 1805, 3194, 3229, 3270, 3656. In the second place *e*-forms survived into Late Cornish, e.g. *dho trega* 'dwell' (AB: 64c); *mero* 'behold!' (BF: 53), *meraz* 'to look' (BF: 58); *screfa* (BF: 46), *skrepha* (AB: 146c).

<e> occurs in many other words both native and borrowed that have etymological /i/, for example, in the following: *thefen, defen* for *dyfen* 'prohibition' OM 280, 922; *pebough* for *pibeugh* 'pipe!' (pl.) OM 2846; *teryov* for *tyryow* 'lands' (cf. Welsh *tiroedd*) BM 385, 2594; *besyon* for *bisyon* 'vision' BM 984; *streppyough* for *stryppyough* 'strip!' BM 1929; *delles* for *dillas* 'clothes' BM 1965; *bete* (len.) for *pite* 'pity' PA 47a; *belat* (len.) for *Pilat* 'Pilate' PA 115a, 146a; *velen* (len.) for *bilen* 'villain' (Breton *bilen*) PA 183b and cf. *belan* BM 2295; *preson/presan* for *prison* 'prison' PA 124a, 124d, BM 3675, 3713; *ȝeseria(s)* for *ȝesyria(s)* 'desire' PA 4a, 9d; *levyaw* for *lyvyow* 'floods' CW 2164; *ȝerevas, derevas* for *deryvas* 'recount' PA 1c, 79c.

In the phenomenon /i/ > /e/ we are again seeing a result of the new prosodic system. Originally the two forms *tryg* 'dwell' and *tryge* 'to dwell', for example, would have been /triːg/ and /triˑge/, where the monosyllable had a long vowel and the disyllable a half-long vowel; compare Welsh *trig* /triːg/ but *trigo* /triˑgo/. When half-length disappeared from Cornish *tryg, tryge* would have become /triːg/ and /trige/ respectively. /i/, when short, would have been less tense than its long counterpart and would consequently have been realized as [ɪ]. It is this lowered [ɪ] that alternates with /e/ and is often written as <e>.

The common spellings like *trega, screfa, whela, merough*, etc., are by themselves sufficient evidence that Middle Cornish had only long and short vowels and that the three-fold distinction of long, half-long and short had disappeared from the language.

4.3 Before the new prosodic system Cornish had both long /iː/ and half-long /iˑ/ as well as long /ɪː/ and half-long /ɪˑ/. Thus *tryg* 'dwell!' would have been /triːg/ with long /iː/ and *tryge* 'to dwell' would have been /triˑge/ with half-long /iˑ/. *Bys* 'world' would have been /bɪːz/ with long /ɪː/ and *myn* 'wishes' would have been /mɪn/ with short /ɪ/. After the prosodic shift *tryg* would have been /triːg/ but *tryga* (< *tryge*) /trɪgə/. Similarly *bys* would have become /beːz/ while *myn* would have remained /mɪn/. The result would have been that /ɪː/ disappeared and /ɪ/ became the short equivalent of /iː/. Or to put it another way: after the prosodic shift the opposition long ~ short in /iː/ ~ /ɪ/ was simultaneously one of tenseness ~ laxness. This is an important point because it means that Neo-Cornish needs a distinction of length only in the *i*-vowels (as is the case in Unified Cornish) not one of length and tenseness (as is the case in Kernowek Kemyn). See further 12.2 below.

4.4 Just as in the front vowels in Middle Cornish there is no longer any /i/ and /ɪ/ alternates with /e/, so with the back vowels, short /u/ is [ʊ] not [u] and it alternates with /o/ particularly before sonants.

Thus in the verb *tulle* 'deceive' (Welsh *twyllo*, Breton *touellan*) one finds both <u> and <o>: *tullas* OM 252, *tulle* OM 278 but *tolle* OM 294, PC 1885; *dolle* OM 2731, *tholle* OM 286, *tolste* OM 302, *tollys* PC 19, 604. One finds a similar variation in the verb *scullya* 'shed, pour' (Breton *skuilhet*): *skulye* PC 260, *scullye* PC 476, 2142, *skullye* PC 534, 2370, *skullys* PC 825, *scullyas* RD 333 but *scollye* PC 341, *scollyas* PC 547. Note also *umma* 'here' OM 102, 244, 350, 885 as against *omma* OM 1059, 1589, 1605, 2408, 2515.

The vowels *u* and *o* also seem to be in free variation in the verb 'to sleep': *cuske* OM 2047, *guskens* PA 241c; *guskas* PA 243a / *coske*, OM 1780, 1905, 1920, PA 51a, 55c; *coskeugh* PC 1093, *koscough* PA 61b.

4.5 The product of British short /u/ in historically pretonic syllables was /e/ in Cornish as for example in *degaf* 'I carry' as against the imperative *dog* 'carry!'. In the transition from /u/ > /e/ the vowel passed through a stage /œ/. Before a nasal it would seem that the vowel /œ/ was not unrounded but remained in Middle Cornish. It is for this reason, for example, that one finds such forms as *cuntell* 'collect' Welsh *cynull* < *kun-tull-*, where the <u> in Cornish represents /œ/.

Another striking example of the same phenomenon is to be seen in the almost universal spelling of the preposition *the* 'to' and *re* 'by' (in oaths) and the perfective particle *re*. The first of these was probably *do* which developed in Middle Cornish as /ðe/ <the> via a stage */ðǫ/. This development was identical with that of unstressed syllables. This is not astonishing since both *the* 'to', *re* 'by' and perfective *re*, were all used as unstressed proclitics, closely bound to the following accented word. The lenited initial /ð/ of *the* need not concern us here—it probably developed by analogy from the third singular masculine prepositional pronoun *thotho* /ðoðo/. Before the possessive 'm 'my' the vowel of *the* 'to' is almost always written as <u>. Note the following examples: *thu'm lauarow* 'to my words' OM 174, *thu'm wolcumme* 'to welcome me' OM 258, *thu'm fas* 'to my face' OM 418. The vowel in <thu'm> can only mean /œ/. It would seem that at the stage */do/ the vowel did not unround because of the following *m* but remained as /œ/.

The preposition *re* 'by' in oaths was probably only a particularized form of the particle *re* < *ro* < *pro* 'before, in the sight of' that is also seen in the perfective *re*. In the Middle Cornish texts 'by' (in oaths) is regularly *re*, as for example in *renothas* 'by my father' at RD 405, 1839. Before the possessive 'm 'my', however, *re* almost invariably appears as <ru'm> /rœm/. Note the following examples: *ru'm lowte, ru'm leute* 'by my loyalty' OM 611, PC 3065, *ru'm soul* 'by my soul' PC 2919, *ru'm fey* 'by my faith' OM 2041.

Similarly with the perfective particle. This is in origin IE *pro > CC *ro. In Cornish it usually appears as *re* < *rœ* < *ro*; cf. Welsh *rhy*. Note for example *ty* *re duth* 'thou hast come' PC 1107. Before the infixed pronoun *'m* 'me', however, it appears that the vowel of **rœ* was not unrounded and (as was the case with *the* and the *re* in oaths) fell together with *œ* from other sources. Thus *re + m* is almost invariably <ru'm> /rœm/ in the texts. Note the following examples: *ru'm gorre* 'may he send me' OM 532, *ru'm tullas* 'has deceived me' OM 252, *ru'm kemeres* 'has taken me' RD 512, *ru'm guerthas* 'has sold me' PC 737, *ru'm gruk* 'has made me' OM 88.

The nasal /m/ did not always prevent the unrounding of /œ/ > /e/ however. Take for example the personal and local names, *Walter Kembro, Chykembro, Hayle Kimbro Pool* and *Richard Kembre* (CPNE: 48). These would all suggest that pretonic British /u/ < earlier /o/ in **Kom'brogos, *Kom'brogi* 'Welshman, Welshmen' became /e/ via < /œ/.

Eventually /œ/ disappeared from Cornish having become /e/ in exactly the same way that the long equivalent /œ:/ became /e:/. In the vicinity of labials and nasals however /œ/ seems to have been unfronted to /o/. It is for this reason that one finds <o> in *3om cara* 'to accuse me' PA 75b, *3om sensy* 'to hold me' PA 75b, *tho'm face* 'to my face' OM 2337, *tho'm care* 'to love me' PC 530; *ro'm laute* 'by my troth' PC 94, *rom growntyas* 'has granted me' PA 75c, where *tho'm* /ðom/, *ro'm* /rom/ are the later reflexes of *thu'm* /ðœm/, *ru'm* /rœm/.

4.6 /y/ in Middle Cornish was the reflex of Old Cornish /y/ in such words as *dewlugy* 'devilment'. It also arose spontaneously from the rounding of /i/ in the vicinity of a labial. This is analogous with /œ/ before /n/ and /m/. Note for example the following: *kunda, gunde* 'kind' OM 989, 1459, 1950; *tumbyr* 'timber' OM 2484; *trubit* 'tribute' PC 1575. The most significant example is the native word *cumyas* 'permission'. This is the exact equivalent of Breton *kimiad* 'farewell' and occurs with as <kymmyas>, i.e., with /ɪ/ as the stressed vowel at OM 79. Elsewhere however the word is usually written <cummyas> with <u> /y/, as for example at OM 375, 376, 410, 750, 792, PC 3139, 3146.

Bruttall CW 452, *brotall* CW 614 'brittle' are not instances of Cornish /ɪ/ > /y/ > /u/, since the word has /y/ in Old English. In the western dialects of Middle English *brytel* developed regularly as *bruttel* or *brottel*. These are reflected in the forms in CW.

4.7 On occasion, short /y/ in stressed syllables when no labial or nasal was present was unrounded not to the expected /ɪ/ but to /e/. In the verb *gruthyl* for example disyllabic forms are not infrequently spelt with an <e>, as for example: *we3yll* PA 68d, 70c, 75d; *wresse* PA 119d, *wressa* PA 213b. Notice also *venys* for *vunys* 'tiny' (cf. Breton *munud*) OM 2720; *gesul* for *cusyl* 'counsel' (Breton *kuzul*) at PC 1543; *begel* for *bugel* 'shepherd' (cf Breton *bugel* 'child') at PA 48c; *myserough* 'measure! (pl.) for *musurough* (cf. Breton *muzulian*) at PC 2740; *barthesek* 'miraculous' for *barthusek* (cf. Middle Breton *berzudec*) at RD 109; *y tefenas* for *y tyfunas* 'he awoke' (cf. Breton *dihunañ*) at PA 244a.

We have to assume that inherited vocalic quality in the central vowels was to some degree replaced by quality according to length. As a result short central vowels tended to /œ/ > /e/ whereas the long equivalents tended to /y:/ > /i:/ (see 3.15 above).

4.8 There is one notable exception to the tendencies just enuntiated. When short (< half-long) /œ/ stood immediately before /ɪ/ < /i/ in the next syllable, it was raised to /y/ and subsequently unrounded to /ɪ/. Examples of this secondary *i*-affection include: *usy*, *ugy* 'is', Late Cornish *igge*, as against *ues* /œ:z/ 'is'; **fusyk* 'happy' < Old Cornish *fodic* (<o> = /œ/) in the toponym *Nanphysick*; Breton *beuziñ* 'drown', Welsh *boddi* 'drown', but Late Cornish *bidhyz* 'drowned' (AB: 248b) < **budhys*. *Bethys* at CW 2315 is probably for **bythys* < **buthys*; had the word had /œ/, one would expect **buthys*, **bothys* in CW; *buthes* 'drowned' OM 984 may represent /'bœðəz/. It is more probably /'bʊðəz/ < **/'bɪðəz/.

4.9 In Middle Cornish stressed /e/ seems to have had a lowered allophone [æ] immediately before /n/. I know of no comparable phenomenon in Middle Breton, but *y* and *a* alternate in Middle Welsh before a nasal in unaccented syllables and occasionally in accented syllables also (GMW: 2). The lowering of /e/ > /a/ before nasals in Cornish is reflected particularly in the verb *mynnes*. Properly speaking the verb should have /e/ in disyllabic forms like *mennaf* 'I wish', *mennyth* 'thou wishest' and /ɪ/ in the monosyllable *myn*; see 5.6 below. In the first person singular the /a/ in the unstressed second syllable appears to have lowered the allophonic [æ] in the first syllable to [a] where it fell together with the phoneme /a/. The shift of *mennaf* ['mæn:av] > /'manaf/ must have been early, for it predates the shift of /a/ > /ə/ in unstressed syllables.

At first it appears that *mannaf* for *mennaf* was not socially acceptable. The first recorded instance of *mannaf* occurs at PA 155d. The blacksmith is refusing to make nails with which to crucify Christ. The leaders of the Jews, anxious that Christ should be put to death, threaten the blacksmith and say, *gorȝewyth te an prenvyth... yn ethom ȝyn mar fyllyth* 'once and for all you will pay for it... if you fail us in the hour of need'. The smith replies: *ny vannaff aga guȝyll war ow fyth* 'I will not make them by my faith'. The smith, though clearly a man of high moral character, is a manual worker. Into his mouth is put the only instance of the 1st singular of this verb in PA and it contains /a/ and not /e/. The only example of the 1st person of the verb in the Charter Fragment, on the other hand, has /e/: *byȝ ny venna* (RC 4: 259). I assume that at the time of writing of PA, *mannaf* was considered slightly substandard.

PC has three examples of *mynnaf*, one of *mennaf* and none of *mannaf*. RD has six examples of *mynnaf*, one of *mennaf* and none of *mannaf*. Later on, however, *mannaf* for *mennaf* becomes normal. BM has no examples of *mynnaf*, one of *mennaf* and no fewer than 31 instances of *mannaf*. Similarly CW has one example of *mynnaf* and 15 of *mannaf*. If we add all the instances of the 1st singular pres.-fut. of *mynnes* in Middle Cornish together we get: *mynnaf* 17; *mennaf* 12; *mannaf* 47. Forms in /ɪ/ survive until the Late Cornish period, for example, in the sentence preserved by Carew from 1602 : *Meea nauidna cowza sawsneck* (Jago 1882: 5).

4.10 An etymon that exhibits *e* > *a* regularly before *n*, though not universally is *benneth, bennath* 'blessing' < Lat. *benedictio*. The distribution of forms in Middle Cornish is as follows (the *a*-forms are cited after the diagonal stroke): OM 1/15; PC 11/0; RD 5/0; BM 9/19; CW 1/3. The shift of /e/ > /a/ in *bennath* > *bannath* (though probably not in *mannaf*) is almost certainly as a result of the new prosodic system. Before the loss of half-length the two words 'woman' and 'blessing', for example, would have been doubly distinct in their first syllables. They would have had both differing vowel lengths, half-long ~ short, and differing medial consonants long ~ short: /'be·nen/ and /'ben:eθ/. Some dialects of Cornish, however, had probably already lost the distinction between /n/ and /n:/. The only indication in these dialects that the consonant of *bennath* had once been long would have been the lowered allophone of the vowel: ['bæneθ]. When half-length disappeared the allophonic [æ] became fully phonemic: /'banəθ/. In those dialects that maintained the distinction /n/ ~ /n:/, /n:/ was pre-occluded to /'be^dnəθ/. It is significant that BM writes *bedneth* with /e/ as a stressed vowel at 198, 224 and 225 and *bannath* with /a/ at 211, 217, 506, etc. This seems to indicate that /e/ > /a/ before /n/ and pre-occlusion do not occur together. BM is the work of two different scribes and I assume that the scribe who wrote *bedneth* spoke a different dialect from the hand that preferred *banneth*. For pre-occlusion as a dialect marker see 9.5-6.

CHAPTER 5
Vocalic alternation

5.1 In Welsh the alternation seen in *bydd ~ byddaf* is audible in speech but invisible in writing, because the reflexes of British stressed /i/ and unstressed /i/ > /ə/ are in Welsh both spelt <y> (see 2.2). In Cornish and Breton pretonic British short /i/ was lowered to [ɪ] but not retracted and thus fell together in both languages with /e/ from British /e/ (and /o/ and /a/ with *i*-affection). In both Middle Cornish and Middle Breton /e/ was spelt <e>. In Breton moreover the reflex of British stressed /i/ also became /e/, as a result of which the alternation between the reflexes of British tonic and pretonic /ɪ/ was entirely lost in the language. Thus the exact equivalents of Welsh *bydd, byddaf* are Middle Breton *bez, bezaff* with long and half-long varieties of the same vowel.

The stressed long reflex of British /i/ originally became [iː] in Old Cornish, where it is variously spelt <y>, <ey> and <i>. Thus the two reflexes of British short /i/ were both pronounced and spelt differently. As examples of /e/ <e> as the reflex of pretonic British short /i/ in Cornish one might cite *ledan* 'wide' OM 2261, Welsh *llydan; enys* 'island' OM 2592, Welsh *ynys*. As examples of /iː/, the reflex of British stressed /i/, spelt <y>, <ey>, one could cite *beys, bys* 'world' OM 6, 1042, Welsh *byd; preys* 'time' OM 316, Welsh *pryd; eys* 'corn' OM 1058, Welsh *yd*.

If the paradigmatic alternation seen for example in Welsh *bydd ~ byddaf* were attested in Middle Cornish, we would expect to see <y>, <ey> in monosyllables alternating with <e> in disyllables. This is precisely what we do find. Because we have so little Cornish, the examples of the alternation *y ~ e* are of necessity limited. The two etyma in which vocalic alternation are best attested in Cornish are the *byth, beth-* stem of *bos* 'to be' and the word *gwethen* 'tree'. These I will deal with at some length.

5.2 The 3rd sg. future of *bos* 'to be' is most commonly *byth* in its unmutated form; it is also written on occasion as <beyth>. We can be fairly certain that the 3rd sg. of the future was originally pronounced /biːð/. Identical in form with the 3rd sg. future is the 2nd sg. imperative <byth>.

The other persons and the passive of the future and the imperative are all disyllabic and are most frequently written in the texts with <e>. The past habitual is also disyllabic and exhibits <e>. Here I take the pronunciation to be /beð-/.

The evidence of the texts is as follows. The monosyllabic forms are listed under A, the disyllables under B:

VOCALIC ALTERNATION

PA

A. *vyth* 17d, 44c, 125c, 126c, 259c ; *fyth* 48c, 72b, 169c, 259d; *veth* 49a

B *beʒens* 55b, 57d, 113c, 126d, 128c, 185c, 188c; *beʒans* 149d; *veʒens* 148b; *veʒyth* 46c; *veʒough* 255a; *feʒaff* 93c; *fethyth* 6d

OM:

A. *vyth* 35, 53, 134, 189, 431, 433, 886, 1286, 1288, 1502, 1907, 2032, 2066, 2126, 2137, 2162, 2178, 2276, 2382, 2390, 2522, 2729; *vyt* 2, 678, 1064, 1226, 1256; *fyth* 314, 676, 1244, 2123, 2548; *veyth* 324, 405; *veth* 2396; *feth* 1934, 1949

B. *bethens* 8, 21, 954, 1297, 2262; *vethens* (read *bethens*) 1434, 1576, 2560; *vethaf* 596, 1910, 2111; *vethyth* 597, 1465; *vethyn* 1655; *vethons* 1589, 1644; *fethe* 290; *fethons* 342, 1515, 2307; *fether* 46; *pethaf* 1349, 2386; *fythe* 1327; *fythyn* 1606

PC

A. *byth* 2307, 2310; *vyth* 9, 450, 568, 772, 789, 825, 891, 1030, 1644, 2460, 2533, 2910, 3134; *vyt* 734; *uyth* 1946; *fyth* 75, 295, 716, 1097, 2453; *pyth* 1938, 1961, 2371; *feyth* 529

B. *bethens* 842, 1040, 2164, 2374, 2518, 2828; *bethough* 879; *bethyth* (read *vethyth*) 3130; *vethe* 919; *vethons* 2698; *fethaf* 1429; *pethe* 1344, 2729; *pethyn* 2305; *bythens* 794, 2742; *bytheugh* 767; *vythyth* 858, *vythons* 2732; *fythons* 3093; *fythyth* 3233

RD

A. *vyth* 48, 636, 678, 1110, 1400, 1701, 1842, 1946, 2157, 2313, 2367, 2468; *uyth* 348; *fyth* 354, 572, 702, 1109, 1113, 1478, 1700, 1866, 1903, 2166; *pyth* 1958

B. *betheugh* 2276; *bytheugh* 1679; *bythyth* 2454; *fythyth* 2349

BM

A. *byth* 2201; *vyth* 37, 89, 141, 1073, 4263; *beth* 840; *veth passim* (I have noted 53 instances); *feth* 304, 725, 1218, 1298, 1466, 1570, 1631, 1700, 2529, 2828, 3236, 3872, 4299; *peth* 422, 2315, 2839, 3612, 4301

B. *bethens* 274, 1517, 1614, 1637, 2984, 3299, 3870; *bethugh* 292, 1460, 2350, 2747, 4262, 4312; *bethe* 2130; *bethen* 1341, 3945; *betheth* 531; *veʒaf* 109; *vethe* 769, 771, 2382, 2859, 4448; *vetha* 4462; *vethen* 3245; *vethugh* 1492, 2729, 3238, 4567; *vethy* 3745; *fethe* 3351; *fetheth* 1242; *fethen* 1731; *fethugh* 1513; *fethogh* 2352; *pethen* 420, 2159

TH

A. *vyth* 3a; *vith* 3a, 3a, 3a, 5, 5, 5, 10a, 16, 17, 20, 22a, 23a, 27, 27, 28a, 28a, 30a, 31a, 34, 36a, 38a, 38a, 39a, 39a, 39a, 39a, 41, 41, 41a, 44, 44, 44, 44, 44, 44a, 45a, 47a, 52, 55; *pith* 37; *peth* 14, 42. Notice also *veth* at 60a in SA

B. *bethow* 19a; *vetha* 6a, 13, 33a, 37a, 52, 52, 52, 53; *vethans* 33a, 33a; *petha* 53a *pethans* 25a, 25a; *vethyn* 26

CW

A. *byth* 371, 521, 1235; *bith* 100; *vyth* 35, 40, 89, 244, 246, 492, 514, 525, 572, 626, 653, 663, 717, 796, 815, 820, 842, 848, 1348, 1407, 1745, 1935, 1938, 2025, 2027, 2120, 2140, 2162, 2183; *vyt* 793; *vythe* 20, 28, 264, 733, 1500, 2204, 2375; *vith* 253, 489, 2076; *vithe* 38, 2407; *fyth* 1405, 1590, 1934, 2152, 2163, 2165, 2289, 2500; *fythe* 14, 25, 1496, 1555, 2230; *fithe* 51; *pyth* 491; *veth* 163

B. *bethowgh* 2367; *bethowh* 2517; *bethans* 979, 1854; *bethance* 2259; [*b*]*ethis* 2115; *vethaf* 532, 824, 1176, 1368, 1516; *vethys* 523, 1178; *vethis* 1183; *fethan* 890, 1637; *fetha* 1002, 1642; *fethe* (disyllable) 2277; *fethow* 67.

[For what it is worth one should notice that Lhuyd gives the future of the verb 'to be' as follows: 1 sg *bedhav*; 2 sg *bedhi*; 1pl *bedhon*; 2 pl *bedhoh*; 3 pl *bedhanz* all with <e> but 3 sg *bŷdh* with <y> (AB: 245c)]

In PC and RD there seems to be a tendency to replace <e> forms with forms in <y>. In PA, OM, CW and TH the alternation between long <y> and short <e> is clear and unmistakable although an occasional <beth> or <veth> replaces <byth> or <vyth> in these texts. Nonetheless the opposition *y ~ e* is still firmly in place. BM on the other hand is very much given to monosyllabic forms in <e>. There are a few instances of <vyth> at the beginning of the play in particular, but for the most part <y> has throughout been replaced by <e>. I assume that <beth> in BM and elsewhere means /beːð/ and that the word is identical in pronunciation with <beth> 'grave'.

5.3 *Gwethen/gweyth*: the alternation here is between the singular *(g)wethen* /gweðen/ and the collective/ plural *gweyth/gwyth* /gwiːð/. The word *gwethen* is *guithen* in Old Cornish. This is presumably a spelling inherited from British which does not reflect the shift of originally pretonic short /i/ > /e/ in Cornish and Breton. The alternation *y ~ e* is unmistakable in the Middle Cornish texts, however:

OM
A *gveyth* 28, 37, 51,1128
B *gvethen* 29, 775, 828; *guethen* 797; *gwethen* 186; *wethen* 167, 176, 184, 201, 216, 230, 240, 284, 755, 800, 804, 837

TH
A. *gwyth* 9
B. *gwethan* 3a; *wethan* 2a, 3a, 4a, 39a

CW
A *gwyth* 93
B. *gwethan* 365, 372, 376, 1808, 1856, 1899, 1916, 1935; *wethan* 375, 620, 751, 827, 1811, 1825, 1834, 1841, 1926; *weathan* 759, 762.

Note also *gweth* 'trees' PA 16b. I have noted no instances of this word in either singular or plural in PC, RD or BM.

Placenames in Cornwall containing the word *gwethen* frequently appear in English with <i> and not <e>, for example: *Burnwithen* (< *bron gwethen*), *Manywithan* (< *meneth gwethen*), *Trewithen* (< *tre wethen*). In the light of the evidence from the texts one might expect <e> not <i> in such names; cf.

Trewethack < *tre *wethek* 'the wooded settlement'. It must be borne in mind that a) Cornish <e> frequently appears as <i> in placenames: *Lellisick* < *lann *wlesyk, Cligga Head* < **cleger* + Eng. *head, Illiswilgig* < *enys gwelsek*, for example; b) many of the *within* names may have come into English before the development of Old Cornish /ɪ/ > Middle Cornish /e/ was complete.

5.4 It is quite apparent from the above examples that the alternation *y ~ e* was firmly rooted in Middle Cornish scribal practice. The <y> or <ey> however represented /ɪː/ which as we have seen became /eː/ in the Middle Cornish period. Instances, then, of <beth> for <byth> 'be, will be' are not anomalous in the texts. They rather represent the phonetic reality of Cornish after the prosodic shift. <y> ~ <e> /ɪː/ ~ /e/ gives way to <e> ~ <e> /eː/ ~ /e/, even though the Middle Cornish scribes because of their conservatism continued to write <y> for /eː/.

Apart from *byth/bethaf* and *gwyth/gwethen* there are a number of words in the texts that appear to show the alternation we have been discussing. They include *dyth/dethyow, pryf/prevyon* 'reptile', *prys/pregyow* 'meals', *tyf/tevy* 'grow', *yf/evaf* 'drink'. The evidence from the texts is not sufficient to give a clear picture of all these items. Note the following short selection of examples:

preys 'time' BM 4269	*preggyov* 'meals' BM 1972
dyth 'day' CW 92	*dethyow* 'days' CW 1850
preyf 'serpent' CW 1919	*prevas* 'serpents' CW 497
eyf 'drink!' OM 2294	*eve* 'to drink' OM 1901
teyf 'grows' CW 366	*tevy* 'to grow' CW 1827.

Since <y> gives way to <ey> and <e> in such words, as with *byth* and *gwyth* the alternation is already disappearing in the texts.

5.5 The alternation in *byth/bethaf* is one of long vowel versus short vowel. The variation in vowel length is because by the Brythonic quantity system *byth* is long since <th> /ð/ is a single consonant. The vowel in *byth* was originally therefore in an open syllable: /bɪːð/ < */biðed/. If the final consonant of a verbal stem was originally a long /nː/, the preceding vowel would have remained short. The alternation *y* in monosyllables ~ *e* in polysyllables should be apparent in the texts, but in both cases the vowel would be short.

There are two verbs that fall into the category of short British /i/ before geminate /nː/ and they are *mynnes* 'to wish' and *tenna* 'to pull'. I shall start with *mynnes* because it is by far the better attested. The commonest form in the texts is *mannaf* and this is by vocalic harmony < *mennaf* (4.9). *Mennaf* is the etymological form and is also common; it occurs at OM 233, 486, 624, 1581, 1976, PC 232, 485, 1612, 1677, etc.

5.6 The *e*-vowel is also frequent in other disyllabic forms of the verb:

may fenne PA 41c
y fenne PA 91b
y fense PA 188c
fennas OM 432
mennyth PC 128
mennas PC 378
menne PC 1816
vennyth BM 487
vensen BM 1042, 1044
mensen BM 1368, etc.

The third singular of the present future is *myn* virtually everywhere. This is the expected form, since it contains /ɪ/ < British stressed /i/. In Late Cornish, however, the usual form is *medn/vedn*. This has come about by analogy with the *e*-forms in the rest of the paradigm. *Men* for *myn* is already present in Tudor Cornish. I have noticed three examples: *gul gueres dymo mar men* 'if he will help me' BM 734; *gasa crystyen byv ny ven* 'will not leave a Christian alive' BM 1327; *mar men an cristonnyan* 'if Christians wish' TH 19a. We should include as possible instances of *men* the following: *agys pesy me a vyen* 'I will pray you' rhyming with *na ven* 'that I be not' at BM 2998-99 and *me a vyn* 'I wish' rhyming with *flehys vyan* 'small children' at BM 1671-76. It is probable that the scribes were reluctant to write <men> for <myn> because it was considered substandard.

We saw that *bennath* tended to become *banneth* in those varieties of Cornish that did not have pre-occlusion. It seems that the vulgar form *men* similarly became *man* when pre-occlusion did not occur. We have only one instance. The imprecation *mar man dev* 'if God wills' occurs at OM 2620. The remark is uttered by the Jewish bishop shortly before he orders Maximilla to be tortured to death for her faith. Since the bishop is bibulous, cruel and foul-mouthed (*thow harlot for goddys bloud* at line 2671 is typical of him), we can assume that the author intends him to be thought of as plebeian, for all that he is a bishop. *Men* for *myn* was probably substandard. *Man* for *men* was probably even more so, it is thus highly appropriate in the "bishop's" mouth.

It is also interesting to note that Late Cornish has pre-occlusion in this word and /e/ as the root vowel: *vedden, vedn* (BF: 31). Pre-occlusion and /e/ > /a/ before /n/ are mutually exclusive (4.10). Since the scribe of OM has *man* < *men*, it is likely that he came from outside the area of pre-occlusion. He was probably, therefore, from east of Truro (9.6). This agrees with the opinion I have already expressed (Williams 1990: 267), that OM is of more easterly provenance than PC or RD.

5.7 In theory *tenna* 'to draw' should have developed similarly to *mynnes* 'to wish' since their roots apart from the initial consonant are identical. In Welsh their equivalents are *tynnu* and *mynnu* respectively. In fact the Cornish verb *tenna* has generalized the *e*-forms everywhere. Notice the following (I ignore initial mutation): *tenne* OM 2280, 2301, 2799, 2806, PA 134b; *tenna* PA 183b; *tennas* PA 71a; *tennys* PA 181d; *tensons* PA 182a. An example of the rare stem *tynn*- occurs at OM 2691: *Eugh! tynneugh an gasadow* 'go, yank the vile woman...'

We have just seen that the vowel of the 3rd singular present future *men* 'wishes' was lowered to *man*. The same also occurred with the 2nd singular imperative of *ten* > *tan*. This then gave rise to a plural form *tanneugh*. *Tan*, *tanneugh* are distinctively colloquial forms and have the sense 'take that, here you are' as, for example, *tan hemma war an challa* 'take that on the jaw!'; OM 540; *Tan atomma thys x puns* 'There you are; there's ten quid for you!' BM 1464; *tan dis dewes ha boys* 'grab some food and drink' BM 4243; *tannegh honthsel kyns sevel* 'have breakfast in bed!' (said ironically while belabouring the torturers) BM 960.

Nance 1955 makes *tan* a separate headword, for he does not connect it with *tenna*. Given that Unified Cornish is silent on *men, man, mannaf* as well, his failure to connect *tan* and *tenna* is not astonishing. GKK refers to *tann* (i.e. *tan*) as a 'defective verb'.

5.8 The word for 'spirit' is frequently *sperys, speris*, for example, at PA 1a. In TH, however, it appears invariably as *spuris*. It seems that the preceding /p/ rounded the /e/ to /œ/ written <u>. The same phenomenon occurred in the plural of *pysk* 'fish' < Latin *piscis*. It is not clear whether in Cornish the root vowel of 'fish' was long or short. On the one hand Lhuyd cites *pêsk zal* 'salted fish' with a long vowel /eː/ < /ɪː/ at AB: 143c. On the other he gives *pysg* 'fish' without lengthening at AB: 121a. At all events the length of the vowel is not crucial to the argument.

The plural of Welsh *pysg* is *pysgod*. This is a reflex of the Latin collective *piscat(us)*. Since the original /i/ in the plural was unstressed before the accent shift, it appears in Welsh as /ə/. In Cornish one would therefore expect /e/ by the alternation of *y* ~ *e* we have been discussing. In fact the Cornish plural is *puskes* OM 52, *puskas* CW 397, 2513, *puscas* TH 2. This can only mean /ˈpœskəs/. When /œ/ disappeared from the phonemic inventory of Cornish the vowel of *puskes* was not unrounded but unfronted (cf 4.5) giving *poskas* (BF: 52, § 26).

A similar rounding occurred in the word for 'finger'. The expected forms in Middle Cornish would have been, singular **bys* /biː/ > /beːz/, plural **besyas* /ˈbezjəz/. As far as I am aware the word is not attested in the Middle Cornish texts. Lhuyd, however, cites *Boz*, pl. *byzîas* (AB: 54c); *bozîaz* 'fingers' (AB: 243a). Lhuyd's singular *Boz* is probably a misprint for **bêz*. His plural /ˈbozjəz/ I take to be a Late Cornish reflex of earlier ** busyas* /ˈbœzjəz/, where the preceding labial has rounded the expected /e/ > /œ/.

The alternation *y* ~ *e* was also originally to be seen in the diphthongs *yw/ew* and this I discuss at 6.3-6 below.

5.9 In Primitive Cornish British short /u/ when stressed and lengthened appears in Middle Cornish as /oː/. If unlengthened because of a following consonant group or long consonant it appears as /o/ (spelt <o> or <u>). On the other hand British short /u/ in pretonic position appears to have been lowered and fronted to /œ/. This then was unrounded early and seems to have fallen together with short /e/. In Middle Cornish therefore the reflex of British pretonic short /u/ is /e/ (except before a nasal; see 4.5). In Welsh the equivalent vowels are /u/ <w> alternating with /ə/ <y>. The alternation /o(ː)/ ~ /e/ is not common in Middle Cornish. For the most part it appears that paradigmatic pressure has levelled out the alternation; as a result /o/ <o> or <u> only is found—as is the case in Breton. Contrast therefore Middle Cornish *cosk* 'sleep' and *cosca* 'sleep' (vn.) and Breton *kousk, kousket* on the one hand with Welsh *cwsg, cysgu* on the other.

One certain example, however, of the alternation <o> with <e> is *dog* 'carry', *degaf* 'I carry', cf. Welsh *dwg, dygaf*. There are of course many examples in Middle Cornish of the alternation /o/ ~ /e/, as in *porthaf, perthy; collaf, kelly; ancovas, ankevy*, for example. Such alternation is the result of the presence or absence of *i*-affection on British /o/, and is thus not relevant to the alternation /o/ ~ /e/. Nonetheless it would appear that *dog, degaf* was assimilated to the alternation /o/ ~ /e/ (by *i*-affection). As a result one finds pres. subj. *docko*, where the disyllabic form properly should have /e/ not /o/ in the root.

CHAPTER 6
Diphthongs

6.1 Nowhere has the loss of half-length had more impact than in the diphthongs of Cornish. Before the prosodic shift diphthongs had either a half-long or a short nucleus. The shortening of half-long vowels meant that after the shift no Cornish diphthong had anything other than a short nucleus. The resulting nuclei were both less tense and less high than before the new prosodic system arose.

6.2 There seems little doubt that Cornish like Welsh and Breton had originally three separate diphthongs /iw/, /ɪw/ and /ew/. In Primitive Breton the second and the third fell together when the distinction between /ɪ/ and /e/ was lost. In southern Welsh the first and the second are no longer different, since /i/ and /ɨ/ have fallen together. In northern Welsh the three are still separate as for example in *gwiw* 'worthy', *lliw* 'colour' ~ *byw* 'alive', *clyw* 'hear!' ~ *tew* 'fat', *rhew* 'frost'.[6]

In Cornish the new prosodic system reduced the three diphthongs /iw/, /ɪw/, /ew/ to two, for /iw/ and /ɪw/ fell together as /ɪw/. The diphthong /ɪw/ itself, moreover, is only partially distinct from /ew/ < /e·w/. That inherited /iw/ has fallen together with /ɪw/ (itself falling together with /ew/) by the period of the Middle Cornish texts is obvious from rhymes. If one examines the rhymes involving the words *gwyw* 'worthy' (Welsh *gwiw*) and *lyw* (Welsh *lliw*, Breton *liv*) that originally had /i·w/, one finds the following:

> *guyv* ~ *yv* /ɪw/ PC 283-84, 711-12, RD 783-86, 1004-05 2315-17;
> *guyv* ~ *blew* /blew/ 'hair' PC 481-84.
> *lyv* ~ *yv* PC 696-97, RD 2101-04;
> *lyv* ~ *bew, vew* /bew/ PC 1590-92, 3083-85.

Noteworthy also is *brew* 'wounded' (Welsh *briw*) rhyming with *wev* /wew/ 'lips' at PC 2085-86. On occasion /ew/ < /ɪw/ < /i·w/ becomes /ef/, for example, *gweff yw ʒe vonas leʒys* 'worthy he is to be killed' PA 95b and *gwef* rhyming with *greyf* /greːv/ 'strong' at CW 1633. There can be little doubt, therefore, that /i·w/ had by the time of the Middle Cornish texts fallen together with /ɪw/, /ew/.

---

6 Note, however, that the nucleus of North Welsh *byw* is a central vowel, not a front one: /bɨw/.

The line *du yw y lyw* 'black is his hue' at RD 2101 occurs in a slapstick passage, and was clearly meant to be comic with its double internal rhyme: /dıw ıw ı lıw/ (for *du* 'black' > /dıw/ see 3.13).

6.3 We have seen at 5.1-4 that in the earliest stratum of Middle Cornish the alternation *y ~ e* was still vigorous. This opposition was functional in the diphthongs also, as indeed it is still in Welsh. In Welsh for example *byw* 'alive' has /i/ or /ɨ/, whereas *bywyd* 'life'has /ə/ in the stressed syllable. In Middle Cornish one would expect /ıw/ < /ɪ·w/ in monosyllables to alternate with /ew/ in disyllables. This is indeed the case. The best attested instance of the alternation /ıw/ ~ /ew/ occurs in the alternation *byw* 'alive', *bewnans* 'life', *bewe* 'live'. I shall confine myself to examples of (A) *byw* and (B) *bewnans* only:

A   *byv, byw* OM 2349, PC 847, BM 354, 1327, 4352, RD 904; *yn fyv* BM 1784
B   *bevnans* OM 63, 89, 848, 985, 1834, 1886, PC 3216, RD 1586, 2446, BM 117, 389, 483, 1163, 1685, 2023, 2126, 2500, 2541, 2818, 3358, 3662, 3850, 4114; *bewnans* TH 6a, 41, 51, 51, 51a, 52, 53, SA 63a; *vewnans* RD 516, TH 44, CW 1927; *bewnens* PC 2876, RD 459; *bewnes* PC 66; *bewnas* TH 40.

It is apparent from these examples that **bywnans* (cf. 13.28) is entirely alien to Cornish and does not appear in the language at any period.

Although there is no disyllabic equivalent, the 3rd sing. of the verb 'to be' ought to exhibit /ıw/ spelt <yv>, <yw> (Welsh *yw*, Breton *ev*, *eo*). This is indeed so. Since instances are so frequent I cite merely from OM: *yv* 9, 15, 655, 687, 688, 733, 780, etc ; *yw* 93, 124, 142, 145, 266, 389, 476, 483, 657, 684, 753, 1127; *yu* 614, 618.

Already by the time of the *Ordinalia*, however, /ıw/ and /ew/ are tending to fall together as /ew/ <ew>. Thus one finds the following: *ew* 'is' OM 191, 943, 1012; *ev* 'is' OM 384, 619, 623, 737, 841, 848, 856, 868, 945, 967, 998; *eu* 'is' OM 2611; *bev* 'alive' OM 2386; *bew* 'alive' PC 846, RD 1048. TH seems only to use <ew> for 'is' and knows no other form. Rhymes corroborate this picture: *yw* 'is' rhymes with *deuw* 'two' RD 2113-16; *bleaw* (earlier *blew*) 'hair' (Welsh *blew*) rhymes with *ythew* 'it is' at CW 1508-10 and with *bew* 'alive' at CW 1605-08.

The verb *clewes* 'to hear' ought perhaps to provide instances of the alternation /ıw/ ~ /ew/. One might expect *clyw!* 'hear' but *clewes* 'to hear', *clewaf* 'I hear', etc. Apparently analogy has reshaped the monosyllabic forms to *clew*, for **clyw* is nowhere attested, as far as I am aware: *clew* 'hear!' OM 1619, RD 881; *klew* 'hear!' OM 1895; *glew* 'hears' OM 1658, 1783, 1776; *na glew* 'hears not' OM 2013.

6.4 The Proto-Celtic word for 'god' (later the Christian God) was */deːwos/ < IE */deiwos/. This would have given **duiw* in Primitive Cornish, which by dissimilation of labials developed as *duy* in Old Cornish; cf. Breton *doué*. By the Middle Cornish period the vowel had been metathesized to **dyw*. Oddly, this form is hardly attested, while <dev>, <dew> are common. Note, for example, *dev* OM 1188, 1190, 1193, 1196, 1198, 1200, 1201, 1260, etc., PC 3, 60, 71, 76, 81, 99, 104, etc.; RD 1498, *dew* PC 49. The only example I can find of the word with <yw> is *thyw* rhyming with *guv* 'spear' at RD 1018. Rhymes corroborate the pronunciation /dew/: *den ha dev* 'God and man' rhyming with *glev* 'sharp' RD 2580-62, for example.

If <dyw> is a rare spelling, there is a good reason. The word *du* 'black' was, as a result of the prosodic shift, pronounced /dıw/ (3.13). Thus /dıw/ 'God' is regularly written <du>, not <dyw>.

6.5 The rearrangement of the diphthongs /iw/, /ıw/, /ew/ was entirely a result of the new prosodic system. When half-length disappeared /i.w/ would have become /iw/, but since short /i/ was [ı], the transition /i·w/ > /iw/ meant the simultaneous shift to [ıw]. Similarly /ı·w/ became /ıw/ and because /ı/ and /e/ tended to alternate with each other, /ıw/ was in part indistinguishable from /ew/. Because /ıw/, unlike /iw/, still existed, however, the opposition /ıw/ ~ /ew/ did not disappear completely.

6.6 The diphthong /ew/ from earlier /e·w/ in monosyllables was shortened but otherwise remained in words like *tew* 'fat', *blew* 'hair', *rew* 'frost'. Original short /ew/ in disyllables on the other hand appears to have weakened to /ǫw/ and subsequently to have fallen together with /ow/ from other sources. It is probable therefore that the shift of /ew/ to /ow/ was already in progress before /e·w/ > /ew/ otherwise new /ew/ would have become /ow/. Indeed the shift /ew/ > /ow/ seems to have been early for we find examples of it in the *Ordinalia* and PA: for example, *ny glowys* 'was not heard' PC 2435; *del glowys* 'as I have heard' PC 2874; *dowȝek* 'twelve' PA 47a, 61a; *dovses* 'deity' RD 2454; *dowlyn* 'knees' PA 137a, 171c, 220b.

In Tudor and Late Cornish, therefore, one finds that the original alternation *byw* /bı·w/ ~ *bewnans* /bewnǝnz/ has become *bew* /bew/ ~ *bownans* /bownanz/; cf. Lhuyd's *bêu* 'vivus; alive' (AB: 175b) but *bounaz* 'vita; life' (AB: 175a). Disyllabic forms of *clewes* 'to hear' almost always have <ow> in the Tudor Cornish texts BM, TH and CW, for example, *ny clowys* BM 191, *re glowes* BM 527, 802, *pan glowe* BM 1030, *del glowas* BM 1160, *clowugh* BM 1890, *clowys* BM 2224, *ny glowys* BM 2238, *a glowes* BM 2394, *a glowas* TH 4a, 4a, 30, *clowas* TH 5, 41, *the glowes* TH 38a, *clowes* TH 41a, *a glowas* CW 140, *tha glowas* CW 637, *a glowses* CW 770, *pan glowa* CW 1136, 1205, *a glowaf* CW 1166; cf. *klouaz* 'to hear' (AB: 44a). The alternation /ew/ ~ /ow/ is also seen in *dew* 'God' / *douses* 'deity'; *eun* 'correct' / *ouna* 'to correct'; *deu* 'two' / *dowla* 'two hands'.

/ew/ < /e·w/ did not become /ow/. On the other hand /ew/ < /ı·w/ does become /ow/ occasionally in *yw*, *ew* 'is' which is <ow> at CW 962 and 1259. *Clow* 'hears, hear!' (CW 1580) is an analogical formation on the basis of *clowaf, clowes*, etc.

6.7 Original /ow/ < /oꞏw/ was also affected by the prosodic shift, for it appears to have fallen together with /aw/. This is apparent from the following doublets:

fout 'lack' BM 2560; *fowt* TH 4	*faut* AB: 56c; *fawt* TH 28a
jowle 'devil' CW 1768	*dzhiaul* AB: 54c
lour 'enough' TH 13a	*laur* AB: 144c
Sousenack 'English' BF: 25	*sawzneck* Jago 1882: 15
Sousen 'Englishmen' BF: 31	*Sausen* BF: 25
S Powle 'St Paul' TH 4a	*S Pawle* TH 4a
sow 'but' TH 1, 11a	*saw* TH 2
cowis 'to get' SA 60	*cawas* CW 1034
our 'gold' AB: 44b	*awr* RC 23: 197.

It is not apparent whether the shift /ow/ > /aw/ has been prompted by the desire to keep /ow/ distinct from the new /ow/ < /ew/ or whether it is the result of the prosodic shift: /oꞏw/ > /ɔw/ > /aw/. Probably the first reason is the valid one, since /ow/ < /ew/ is not lowered to /aw/. Neither apparently is /ow/ < /uv/ in *dowr* 'water', *down* 'deep' and *own* 'fear'.

Original /ow/ had a tendency to become /aw/ in unstressed syllables as well as stressed ones. This is apparent from such spellings as *canhasawe* 'messengers' CW 29; *sethaw* 'arrows' CW 1491; *levyaw* 'floods' CW 2164; *benaw* 'female' CW 2271, 2414, 2416; *gorrawe, gorawe* 'male' CW 2414, 2416; *taklawe* 'things', *derggawe* 'doors', *hannawe* 'name', *terwitheyaw* 'sometimes' BF: 39; *ganaw* 'mouth' RC: 23 186; *maraw* 'dead' RC 23: 300. Similarly Lhuyd observes that the plural ending *ou* is sometimes pronounced as if it were *au* and cites as examples: *Kêau* 'hedges', *Guelîau* 'beds' and *Breihau* 'arms' (AB: 242c).

6.8 The development of the diphthongs having /j/ as their second element is similar to that of the diphthongs in /w/. I analyse Cornish inherited /iː/ above as /iꞏj/. After the prosodic shift this became /ɪj/ and then /ej/. Similarly /eꞏj/ was shortened as a result of the shift and the second element was accordingly untensed to [æ]. The end result of inherited /eꞏj/ was therefore /aj/.

There is convincing evidence for the shift /eꞏj/ > /aj/ in Cornish. Middle Cornish had /ej/ in borrowings from Middle English. Middle English itself originally had two diphthongs /ej/ and /aj/ but these had fallen together as /aj/ by the fourteenth century. It seems probable that most of the Middle English borrowings in Cornish were already in the language before that, however. I assume that the Middle English word for 'pains' was borrowed into Cornish as /pejnəz/. This is written <peynys> at PA 6a, 66d, 86b, 168d but <paynys> at PA 70d, 182c. The variation in spelling suggests that it was pronounced /pajnəz/ in Middle Cornish. The free variation of the graphs <ei>, <ai> is noticeable in other etyma as well, for example, in *treytour* PA 119c, *traytour, traytor* PA 98c, 121a.

DIPHTHONGS

The Cornish word for 'to turn' is *trelya, treylya*. This is a borrowing from Middle English *treyle* < Old French *treyle* 'trail, turn', cf. Modern English *trail*. Although the Middle Cornish spelling would suggest that it was borrowed as /trejl/, in CW it is spelt both as <treyl> CW 350, 573, 926, 951, 2085 and as <trayl> CW 352, 739. This is further evidence that the two diphthongs /ej/ and /aj/ were not distinct. In Late Cornish the word is pronounced with /aj/ as is clear from Lhuyd's <trailia> at JCH §23.

CW spells the diphthong /ej/ in native words as <ey>, for example, in *dreyne* 'thorns' at CW 1091. *Gweyl* 'rods' is spelt <gwaile> at CW 1355, however, and the feminine form of 'three', which is *tyr, teyr* in Middle Cornish, is variously spelt <tayre>, <tayr>, <dayer> at CW 1845, 1923, 2087 respectively. This is further evidence for the shift /eˑj/ > /aj/. Place-names provide additional evidence. It is significant for example that *dreyn* 'thorns' appears as <drine> in the local names, *Trendrine, Landrine, Halldrine*, for example. Such spellings suggest a pronunciation /drajn/. Similarly *keyn* 'back' appears as <kine> in place-names, for example, *Carrack kine marh, Carrack Kine hoh*, which indicates the etymon was pronounced /kajn/.

One might be tempted to think that the diphthong /ej/ remained in some environments. Lhuyd cites 'seven' as <seith> (AB: 148c), for example. Given that he spells the obsolete word *gweyth* 'work' as *guaith* (AB: 108c), it is unlikely that he considered /ej/ and /aj/ to have been separate diphthongs in the Cornish of his own day.

Spellings like *whay* 'you' TH 33a, *tray* 'three' (Loth 1900: 226) might suggest that /ej/ < /iː/ became /aj/ in Tudor Cornish. On the other hand Lhuyd cites *trei* 'three' and *kei* 'dog' (3.5). I suspect that /ej/ as the product of /iː/ in absolute auslaut remained distinct from /aj/ < /ej/ for the most part, if not always.

CHAPTER 7
Unstressed vowels

7.1 Before the prosodic shift Cornish, like Welsh and Breton, must have had a variety of different vowels in unstressed syllables. When the new prosodic system became operative, however, it would seem that in Cornish most distinctions in the unstressed vowels were neutralized. Two unstressed vowels that can be shown to have existed after the shift were /ə/ and /ɪ/. These exist in unstressed syllables in English as for example in *spigot, bigot* with /ə/ and *wicket, picket* with /ɪ/. In Tudor and Late Cornish there was a tendency for both /ə/ and /ɪ/ to fall together as /ə/. The diphthong *-ow* of the plural and of 2nd plural verbal endings also survived the prosodic shift in Cornish and it is likely that it was pronounced as /ow/ or /aw/ (6.7) in deliberate speech. In rapid speech it was probably pronounced as some kind of rounded neutral vowel. This latter had a tendency to fall together with /ə/.

7.2 George has drawn attention to the way in which *-e* and *-a* are kept separate in the *Ordinalia* (PSRC: 120). He cites PC 431-42 to exemplify his point:

ihesu pendar leuerta
    a'n fleghys vs ov cane
yowynkes menogh a wra
    yn yowynkneth mur notye

yn lyfryow scryfys yma
    bos collenwys lowene
a ganow a'n fleghys da
    ha'n re mvnys ow tene

ny amont travyth hemma
    cayphas ny yllyn spedye
yma ol tus a'n bys-ma
    yn certan worth y sywe

[Jesus, what dost thou say
    of the children that are singing?
The young frequently
    in their youth do much of note

It is written in the scriptures
    that joy is fulfilled
from the mouth of good children
    and from babes at the breast

Nothing here is of avail,
  Caiaphas, we cannot succeed.
All the people of the world
  assuredly are following him].

It can hardly be doubted that in those lines and indeed elsewhere in PC a distinction was maintained between final unstressed -*e* and final unstressed -*a*. If one looks a little more closely at the spellings and rhymes of PC, however, the position is not quite as clear-cut as appears at first sight.

The enclitic masculine pronoun after vowels is -*ve* < **efef*. This appears at PC 1460 in *kyn feue* 'though he were' and at 2969 in *a peue* 'if he were' both with <e>. Yet it has <a> in *a peua* 'if he were' at PC 690 and in *mara qureva* 'if he does' at PC 2882. The second person enclitic pronoun is -*se*, -*ge*, which is an assibilated form of the pronoun *te* 'thou'. It occurs with <e> at PC 2867 in *maras ose* 'if thou art', at PC 2891 in *mars oge* 'if thou art', at PC 2897 in *as oge* 'how... thou art'. Forms with <a> occur however at PC 1720 *mars osa* 'if thou art', at PC 732 *del osa* 'as thou art' and PC 2179 *a pile osa* 'whence art thou?' (rhyming with *da* 'good').

The superlative of adjectives in Middle Cornish ends in -*a* < **af* (cf. Welsh -*af*), for example, in *brassa* 'greatest' at PC 778. At PC 773, however, the same word occurs as *brasse* with an unexpected final <e>. The same hesitation of final *a/e* is seen in the word *kensa* 'first' (Welsh *cyntaf*) at PC 795 but *kynse* at PC 2947. The comparative is identical with the superlative in Middle Cornish and normally ends in <a>. Note, however, *lowenne* 'more joyful(ly)' for **lowenna* at PC 3158.

The word *arte* 'again' (cf. Breton *adarre*) is regularly spelt with an <e>, at PC 346, 758, 1156, 1795, 2532 and 2863, for example. At PC 2442, however, it is spelt with final <a>: *arta*. The third person plural of the prepositional pronouns usually ends in -*e* in PC, for example in *ganse* 'with them' PC 694, 702, 2850. Yet at PC 1431 the word is *gansa* with final <a>. The first person singular of the prepositional pronoun *a* 'from' is usually *ahanaf* 'from me' as for example at RD 1614. On occasion the final *f* is dropped to give *ahana*. At PC 2907, however, 'from me' is <ahane> and rhymes with the past subjunctive *pysse* 'should pray'.

One of the most frequent instances of final <e> in PC is that of the ending of the verbal noun, as for example, *sywe* 'to follow' PC 442, *amme* 'to kiss' PC 480, *lettye* 'to prevent' PC 1969, *spedye* 'to hurry' PC 440, *tryge* 'to dwell' PC 542, etc. The -*e* here is a reflex of British **-ima* with *a*-affection of the /i/. Occasionally in PC the <e> is replaced by <a>. Note, for example, *yth il cotha* 'it can fall' rhyming with *yn tor-ma* 'on this occasion' at PC 2295-96; *ymassaya* 'to attempt' rhyming with *leverys da* 'well said' at PC 2301-02 ; *trystya* 'trust' at PC 1439.

The same hesitation between <e> and <a> is to be seen in RD. The superlative is frequently in <e> rather than in the expected <a>, as for example

41

whekke 'sweetest' RD 144, *hagkre, hakcre, haccre, hacre* 'most dreadful' at RD 1972, 2005, 2033, 2072 and *gokye* 'most foolish' RD 1454.

The enclitic second person pronoun has both <e>, *asoge* RD 971, *essoge* RD 983, *nynsose* RD 1261 and <a>, *osa* RD 675, *assosa* RD 953. Similarly the enclitic third person pronoun has both <e>, *ottefe* RD 1901, *yth ofe* RD 2121 and <a>, *ny wrefa* RD 2473. Notice also *ot omme* 'behold here!' RD 1803 but *ot omma* RD 2177; *ple ma* 'where is?' RD 646, 849, 856 but *ple me* 'where is?' RD 46. Noteworthy also is *haga* 'and their' at RD 1452 but *yge* 'in their' at RD 886.

Adam's wife is known in OM as *eua* < Latin *Eva*. See, for example, OM 149, 159, 166, 179. At RD 2634, however, she is called *eue* and her name rhymes with *fue* /fe:/ 'was' and *lowene* 'joy'. Notice also the variation in the verbal nouns: *orth the greffye* 'grieving thee' RD 488, *orth ow greffye* 'grieving me' RD 502 but *orth ow greffya* RD 484; *the laddre* 'to steal' RD 370 but *laddra* RD 23, 35.

7.3 The hesitation between <e> and <a> is more pronounced in OM than in either PC or RD. Note for example the comparatives *tekke* 'fairer' OM 1177, 1730, *lelle* 'more faithful' OM 1111 where final <a> would have been expected. Significant also are such spellings as *y dre-mme* (with *-mme* for *-mma*) 'this town' OM 2284, *bare* 'bread' for *bara* OM 2186 and *a'n par-ne* 'of that kind' with *-ne* for *-na* OM 2182. One also sees variation in *ny gemeraf* OM 1234 'I will not take' OM but *ny gemere* 'id' OM 1208; *maga ta* 'as well' OM 995, 1182, but *mage ta* OM 972. Compare also *temple* 'temple' at OM 1259 but *templa* rhyming with *guella* 'best' at OM 2621.

Verbal nouns in *-a* rather than *-e* are commonplace in OM, for example, *lafurrya* 'to travel' (rhyming with *alemma*) OM 1268; *offrynna* 'to offer' rhyming with *alemma* OM 1307; *ow tewraga* 'flowing' OM 1084; *compressa* 'to oppress' rhyming with *ena* 'there' OM 1424; *sywa* 'to follow' rhyming with *gorra* 'to put' OM 1693-94 (spelt <sywe> at OM 1630); *scapya* 'to escape' OM 1656; *lettya* 'to hinder' rhyming with *servya* 'to serve' and *y'n tor-ma* 'now' at OM 1495-97; *repryfa* 'to reprove' OM 1500; *tryga* 'to dwell' OM 1599 and the variant *trega* rhyming with *amma* 'to kiss' OM 2190-91 and with *tressa* 'third' at OM 2665; *ov peve* 'living' rhyming with *hemma* and *awartha* OM 1030, but *bewa* rhyming with *thetha* 'to them' and *bynytha* 'ever' at 2833; *cole, gole* 'harken' at OM 323, 626 but *gola* at OM 293.

In spite of their conservatism the scribes of the *Ordinalia* were unable to maintain the difference between final unstressed *e* and final unstressed *a*.

7.4 The hesitation between final unstressed vowels in the *Ordinalia* is not just confined to <e> and <a>, but extends to historic /o/ as well. Not infrequently, for example, the third singular present subjunctive has <e> or <a> rather than the expected <o>, for example *re'm gorre* 'may he put me' OM 858, *re'n sawye* 'may he save him' OM 1088; *erna'n prenne* 'till he buy it' OM 2152; *re'th ordene* 'may he ordain thee' PC 685; *byth na scapye* 'may he never escape' PC 1888; *na wrella dampnye* 'may he not condemn him' PC 1958; *may farwe an thew vylen* 'so the two villains may die' PC 2827; *na potre* 'that it may not rot' PC 3200; *byth na schapye* 'that he may never escape' RD 2270; *kemmys na greysa* 'whoever believes not' RD 176; *a lauarre* 'who might say' PD 422; *methek a'n sawya* 'a doctor who might save him' RD 1648. On occasion words that should end in <e> or <a> have a final <o> instead. Notice, for example, *kynso* 'first' for *kynsa* rhyming with *rollo* 'may give' at OM 2162-63.

The implications of this hesitation between <e>, <a> and <o> in the *Ordinalia* are, I think, quite clear. The authors of the plays clearly learned to write Cornish as though unstressed /e/, /a/ and /o/ were all distinct. That is to say they learnt the standard orthography of Middle Cornish, which had been devised before the full operation of the new prosodic system. In their own speech, however, which postdated the new prosody, the three vowels when in unstressed final position were falling together, if they had not fallen together already. This is why we find confusion of the three vowels in their rhymes. We can be confident, I think, that at the latest by the date of the composition of the *Ordinalia* in the later fourteenth century final inherited /e/, /a/ and /o/ were all /ə/.

7.5 Confusion of the three unstressed vowels /e/, /a/ and /o/ occurs in the rhymes of PA, which indicates that the three vowels had fallen together as /ə/ already in the author's speech.

Notice the following rhymes of *-e* with *-a: olva* 'weeping' with final etymological /a/ at PA 4b *-a* rhyming with *a ʒeserya* 'desired', *dijskynna* 'would descend' and *perna* 'to redeem' all with original *-e; a calla* 'if he could' with original *-e* at 21d rhyming with *yma* 'is', *da* 'good', *whela* 'seeks'; *a lene* 'thence' with etymological *-a* at 30d rhyming with *lowene* 'joy'; *dre* 'town' with etymological *-e* and *the* 'comes' with /œː/; *ʒeʒa* for *ʒeʒe* 'to them' at 54c rhyming with *yn vrna* 'at that time', *henna* 'that', *yn ketelma* 'thus'.

PA may be earlier than the *Ordinalia*, yet its rhymes clearly indicate that final unstressed /e/ and final unstressed /a/ have fallen together as /ə/.

There are no examples in PA of *-o* rhyming with *-a* or *-e*. At 72b the spelling *veughe* for *vewo*, the third singular of the pres. subjunctive, rhyming with *ro* 'row', *ʒymmo* 'to me', is graphemic only and reflects the scribe's dialect, not that of the author. It is likely nonetheless that final /o/ as well as final /e/ and /a/ had also been reduced to schwa in the author's speech.

7.6 In BM the confusion between original final *-e, -a* and *-o* is very marked indeed. The verbal nouns that have etymological *-ye* and *-e* are generally spelt with <ya> and <a> and rhyme with historic *-a: rekna* 'to reckon' BM 799 rhymes with *alemma* 'hence'; *attendya* 'to attend' BM 848 rhymes with *genegygva* 'birth'; *gorthya* 'to worship' BM 901 rhymes with *honna* 'that' (fem.); *sewagya* 'assuage' at BM 1004 rhymes with *plasma* 'this place', etc.

Not infrequently <e> is written for etymological *-a: gorte* 'waits' BM 2435; *na felle* 'no longer' BM 2488; *na gerte* 'that thou lovest not' BM 2569; *an bysme* 'this world' BM 3030; *ome* 'here' BM 3335; *nesse* 'nearest' BM 175; *varye* 'Mary' BM 133.

In BM <e>, <a> are frequently written for etymological *-o: dotha* 'to him' BM 2854, 3614, 466; *dothe* 'to him' BM 2934; *theorta* 'from him' BM 3837; *warnotha* 'upon him' BM 4554; *annotha, anotha* 'from him' BM 188, 2578; *dore* 'bring' BM 3685; *na relle* 'that she do not' BM 4005, 4139; *may welle* 'that... may see' BM 4006'; *ren tala* 'may he repay it' BM 3082; *reth gedya* 'may he guide thee' BM 3015; *re werese* 'may he help' BM 3822; *rum gueresa* 'may he help me' BM 2536; *na gemerre* 'let him not take' BM 405. Rarely also <o> is written for etymological *-a, -e*, for example in *venytho* 'ever' BM 4267.

BM as we have it was written in 1504. The confusion in the text between final unstressed /e/, /a/ and /o/ is total. This should not astonish us. All three vowels had probably been reduced to schwa by the fourteenth century if not before.

7.7 Inherited /e/, /a/ and /o/ had fallen together as schwa in absolute final position by the fourteenth century at the latest. They had also fallen together as schwa when they were protected by a final consonant. This can clearly be seen by the way in which the graphs <e>, <a>, and <o> and <y> alternate with one another in closed post-tonic syllables. I will take a handful of etyma from OM, PC, RD, PA, BM and TH to demonstrate the point. For simplicity's sake I ignore initial mutation and quote the form with its unmutated initial.

'one' (original /a/): *onan* OM 3, 12, 99, 1192; *onen* OM 57, 2099, 2308; *onon* PC 772, PA 25b, 89c, 124d; *onyn* TH 7a, 7a

'self' (original /a/): *honan* OM 16, 94, 2248, 2650; *honon* PA 25d, 37d, 81c, 101b; *honyn* BM 3641, TH 1, 1a, 4, 7a

'heart' (original /o/): *colan* OM 357, TH 20a; *colen* OM 365, 428, PA 115c, BM 2049, 2408; *colon* OM 527, 1264, 1376; *colyn* BM 628, 1804

'certain' (original /a/): *certan* OM 14, 93, 494, 1313, TH 3; *certen* OM 918, BM 2034, 2067, 2073; *certyn* BM 1744, 2515, 4471; *certeyn* BM 3006

'to see' (original /e/): *guelas, gwelas* OM 1452, 378, 2840, PA 172c; *gveles, gueles* OM 351, 794, 2007, 2103

'to know' (original /o/): *gothfos, gothvos* OM 751, 821, 2098, BM 1987; *gothfes* BM 2273, 2701, 3259, TH 2a, 3a; *gothfas* TH 11, 14, 14

'to wait' (original /o/): *gortes* OM 1718, BM 3655; *gortos* PA 250d; *gurtas* TH 13a; *gortays* BM 2472

'children' (original /e/): *flehas* OM 1159, 975, 1031, BM 1782, 3153; *flehes* OM 1036, BM 2014, TH 7a; *fleghys, flehys* OM 1588, 1611, 1623, PA 149d; *flehis* TH 23a

'ship' (original /e/): *gorhal* OM 1050; *gorhel* OM 950, 1146, 1158, BM 467; *gorhyl* OM 1040, 1047, 1124

'people' (original /e/): *pobal* OM 1843; *pobel* OM 1543, 1557, 1564, 1574; *pobyl* OM 1803, 1832, PA 6b, BM 2022, 2324, TH 4.

The high degree of confusion is striking. As with final unstressed vowels, so with unstressed vowels before a final consonant: /e/, /a/, /o/ have fallen together. The spellings with <y> suggest moreover that inherited unstressed /ɪ/ before a final consonant has also become /ə/. This indeed appears to be the case and it is worthwhile examining the matter a little more closely.

7.8 /ɪ/ > /ə/ is particularly frequent in the past participle, as, for example, in the following: *hynwes* 'named' OM 962; *buthes* 'drowned' OM 984; *senges* 'held' PC 773; *gylles* 'gone' BM 4412; *senses* 'held' BM 716; *serres* 'angered' BM 1943; *towles* 'thrown' CW 329; *confethes* 'understood' CW 532; *gweskes* 'worn' CW 979; *treyles* 'turned' CW 951; *tulles* 'deceived' 1003; *kyffes* 'got' TH 1; *kewses*, *kowses* 'spoken' TH 1, 1; *scriffes*, *skryffes* 'written' TH 2, 3, 6; etc.

The spelling <e> for <y> is common in the first person of prepositional pronouns. Note for example: *ortheff* BM 1356, 2542, 3126; *theworthef* OM 206; *theortheff* BM 2577, 4143; *thyworthef* PC 1217. Such spellings imply /ðə'worθəv/, etc.

Although it must have been pronounced with a final /əz/ there is nonetheless a slight reluctance on the part of scribes to write the past participle with anything other than <y>. Two etyma are exceptions to this rule however. They are *benyges* 'blessed' and *melyges* 'accursed'. They are virtually always spelt with <es> or <as> rather than <ys>. Note the following selection of examples:

> *bynyges*: OM 831, 938 PC 230, 253, 283, 418, 489, 769, 817, 1045, 1073; *byneges* OM 1067; *beneges* OM 1407, 1792, 1812, 1837, 1851, 2023; *benygas* BM 3406; *benegas* PA 30b, 244d, TH 6, 6a, 8, 8a, 18, 18a, 19a, 30; CW 396
>
> *myleges*: OM 311, 610; *mylleges* OM 580, 582; *mylyges* PC 2552; *vylyges* PC 2553; *melegas* CW 283; *malegas* CW 901, 1004, 1007, 1160, 1345, 1716, 1751; *melagas* CW 305, 1613.

The reason for the almost universal spelling of these two etyma with final <es>, <as> is probably the following. These two words were not merely past participles, but were used also as nominalized adjectives in such expressions as *ty, velyges!* 'thou accursed one'. As a result they were no longer felt to be parts of a verb and could be spelt as nouns and not as past participles in <ys>.

7.9 Just as unstressed /ɪ/ became /ə/, so inherited unstressed /i/ after the prosodic shift became /ɪ/. Except in absolute final position this new /ɪ/ like original /ɪ/ frequently became /ə/. This is apparent in both pretonic and post-tonic syllables. The preposition *dyworth, (a)thyworth* has etymological /i/ in the pretonic syllable; cf. Welsh *diworth*, Breton *diouz*. In Middle Cornish, however, more often than not, the <y> in *dyworth, (a)thyworth* appears as <e>. This I take to be a spelling /ə/. Note the following examples: *ʒeworto* PA 23d; *ʒeworth* PA 88a, 150b; *theworthyf* OM 503, 2131; *theworth* OM 575, 843;

theworthys OM 1405; *theworthyn* OM 2065; *theortheff* BM 2577, 4143; *theworth* BM 1958; *theworto, theworta* TH 3a, TH 4; *theworth* TH 4, 10, 11, 14, 15a, etc.; *theworthan* TH 16. The spellings *thaworth* CW 1524; *ȝawarta* CW 266 make it quite clear that the initial vowel in *thyworth* is /ə/.

Etymological pretonic /i/ also appears as <e> /ə/ in the following: *deveth* 'shameless' PA 242d; *ȝestrewy* 'destroy' PA 26d, *destrowy* CW 2388; *debertheys, deberthys* 'separated' BM 3108, 3130, *dyberthis, debyrthys* TH 25a, 40a (cf. *deberthva* CW 84); *seluester* for *Silvester* BM 1798, 1793, 1859.

7.10 Middle Cornish has preterites whose 3rd singular ends in *-ys*, for example *kewsys* 'he spoke', *leverys* 'he said' and *sevys* 'he stood'. The Middle Welsh equivalent of such preterites end in /is/, for example, *gelwis* 'called', *seuis* 'stood', *erchis* 'asked' (GMW 122-23). If the comparison with Welsh is valid, *kewsys, leverys*, etc., originally ended in /is/. Moreover if our contention above is correct, namely that unstressed /i/ before *a* gave /ɪ/ in Middle Cornish, then Middle Cornish *kewsys, leverys* by the Middle Cornish period were on occasion pronounced with final /əz/. There is convincing evidence that this was indeed the case.

Some of our best evidence for /is/ > /əz/ is to be found in PA. At 165d for example the text has <y clamderis> for *clamderas* 'she fainted'. This is not a slip on the scribe's part, because the word rhymes with *dygtis, curunys* and *gorris*. It must be that in the scribe's dialect final *-ys* in verbs and final *-as* in verbs were falling together as /əz/ and as a result he wrote the incorrect <is> for the expected <as>.

A comparable verbal form is seen at BM 888 where the preterite of *kemeres* 'take' is written *kemereys* rather than the expected *kemeras*. This cannot be a mere slip, since it rhymes with *concevijs* 'conceived' and *devsys* 'godhead'. It can only be that the author of BM pronounced the ending of the 3rd singular preterite in <ys> and the 3rd singular preterite in <as> identically, and as a result he sought to rhyme final <as> with final <ys>. Or to put it another way, in his dialect final <ys> of the preterite might be pronounced /əz/.

The verb *kewsel* 'to speak' has a regular 3rd singular preterite *kewsys*. This in the lenited form *gewsys* is attested in PA fourteen times, at PA 14a, 66a, 74a, 92c, 93a, 104a, 105a, 107a, 111c, 141a, 143a, 214b, 240a, 247a. Once the word is written <gwesys> (102d) and once as <gowsys> (50d). On nine occasions the scribe writes <gowsas>, i.e. at 68a, 80d, 84d, 92a, 94b, 126c, 147c, 201c, 246a. This latter form is not a different word from *gewsys*, I think, but a regular phonetic development of it. /ew/ in Middle Cornish became /ow/ in stressed disyllables (see 6.6). Such a shift gave rise to *gowsys* recorded at PA 50d. The final syllable /is/ became first /ɪz/ and then /əz/. Of course <gowsas> had every appearance of being a new preterite in *-as* and has been taken as such by modern scholars. That *gowsas* was rather a reflex of *gewsys* with a lowered final vowel seems assured by other instances of the word in later texts. Tregear, who is a very conservative speller, usually writes the preterite of 'speak' with <ow>

and <ys>, <is>, for example, *gowsis* TH 23, *gowsys* TH 43, *cowsys* TH 44. At 43, however, he writes: *nena eff a gowses thotha arata* 'then he spoke to them again' where his preterite ends in *-es* rather than *-ys*. Compare further *cowses* 'he spoke' at CW 828, 1533 and 1538. In all cases we are probably dealing with /ˈkowzəz/.

Among other examples of /is/ > /əz/ in the preterites of verbs one can include the following: *denes* at BM 251 as against *denys* at BM 295; *te a fylles* for **te a fyllys* 'thou hast failed' CW 1343; *ny synges* for **ny syngys* 'he did not consider' CW 2051. Notice also that *eff agen gelwys* 'he called us' at BM 4428 rhymes with *a comondyas*, which indicates that the <ys> in *gelwys* was pronounced /əz/. Similarly the third sing. pret. *y trehevys* at BM 4431 rhymes with *verays* 'looked' and *creyays* 'cried', where the final <ays> is a variant spelling for more normal <as>. It is likely also that Tregear's *debbras* TH 3a, *thebbras* TH 3a for *debrys* 'ate' (cf. *dybrys* OM 824) is not an analogical *-as* preterite but a direct phonetic development: *debrys* > **debres* > *debras*.

There is corroborative evidence from Middle English borrowings, that unstressed final /is/ became /əz/ in some words. The English word *promise* would have been borrowed into Middle Cornish from Middle English as /promis/. The word appears as *promes* at BM 2594 and CW 1539, where it is clear that /i/ has become /ɪ/ or /e/. At CW 776 the lenited form of the word is spelt <bromas>, suggesting that it was pronounced /brɔməz/. A comparable development is seen in Middle English *covetise* > Cornish *coveytes* rhyming with *poyntyes* at CW 1000. If Middle English *promise* became Cornish *promes*, *promas* and Middle English *coveytise* became Cornish *coveytes*, then there is nothing inherently implausible in the development of Middle Cornish *gowsys* > *gowsas*, *debrys* > *debras*.

The first person of the pret. verbs in *-ys* and *-as* in the 3rd singular has the ending <ys> in Middle Cornish. To judge by such forms as Middle Breton *guilis* 'I saw', *liuiris* 'I spoke' (HMSB: 174), this <ys> probably before the prosodic shift in Cornish was /is/. Thereafter it became /ɪz/ > /əz/. First singular preterites are poorly attested in the texts, and I have no example of the first sing. pret. in <ys> spelt as <es> or <as> anywhere. Note however *gampollys* 'I mentioned' at BM 2791 rhyming with *bollys* 'papal bulls'. *Bollys* is obviously a borrowing from Middle English *bolles* /ˈboləz/. If this is a perfect rhyme, as seems likely, then *gampollys* can only mean /gamˈpoləz/. Similarly *wylys* 'I saw' rhymes with *bys* /beːz/ 'world' at OM 766.

7.11 There are no examples at all of **leveres*, **leveras* in the Middle Cornish texts. This, I assume, is because the word was pronounced /ləˈverɪz/ rather than /ləˈverəz/. At PA 36 *leverys* rhymes with the past part. *gwerthys* 'sold' and *bys* 'world' which must have been either /biːz/ or /beːz/. *Leverys* also rhymes with three separate past participles at PA 48 and again at PA 61, just as *leferis* 'he said' at BM 4422 rhymes with the past participle *tuchys*. In all these cases, I assume that a pronunciation /ləˈverɪz/ is intended. It is probable also that the preceding high front vowel contributed to the maintenance of the high unstressed /ɪ/ rather than /ə/.

In the more advanced text CW *Y leverys* 'said' at line 1374 rhymes with *warnas* 'upon thee' which suggests that the scribe of CW pronounced *leverys* as /le'verəz/. It is interesting even so that he writes <leverys> and not *<leveras>. It is not until the Late Cornish period that instances of the word are found actually spelt with final <as>, <az>. Note, for example the eight occurrences of *laveraz* in BF: 51-2. Late Cornish *laveraz* is unlikely to be an analogical preterite on the basis of the imperative *lavar*, because the stressed *e* makes it apparent that the stem was originally *lever-* with *i*-affection.

In the light of *leverys* perhaps one should make a further observation about final <ys> in the Middle Cornish texts in general. Although other reduced spellings with <es>, <as> do occur, it is undeniably the case that the past participle, the 1st singular preterite and the 3rd singular preterite of verbs in -*ys* are more commonly spelt <ys> than in any other way. In part no doubt this is the result of scribal conservatism. In part it must be that such endings could be pronounced as /ɪz/ rather than /əz/.

7.12 Final unstressed <y> /ɪ/ is common in the Middle Cornish texts. It is likely that /i/ became /ɪ/ in absolute final position at the same time as the comparable shift of /i/ > /ɪ/ in closed final syllables, but that in absolute final position the ensuing /ɪ/ was only sporadically reduced to /ə/.

Lhuyd discusses the spelling of final *y* and he recommends writing <i> for <y>. He says, 'The Letter y differing so very little from i, especially in the Terminations of words of more than one Syllable, may be in this Infinitive spar'd: and such words written constantly with an i: As Deski (not desky) To learn...' (AB: 245b). Although he compares final *i/y* in Cornish with its equivalents in Welsh and Breton, nowhere does Lhuyd specify the pronunciation of final *i/y*. Indeed his concern seems orthographical rather than phonetic. There is no reason to deduce from Lhuyd's observations that /ɪ/ was still [i]. Indeed after the operation of the new prosodic system it could hardly have been.

At PA 114 the 3rd singular imperfect of *kewsel*, i.e. *ny gewsy*, rhymes with *scornye*, *ʒeʒe* and *laʒe*. This can only mean that the author on occasion pronounced *kewsy* as /'kewzə/ or more probably /'kowzə/. At line 919 the scribe of BM writes *nahy* for *naha* 'deny'. This suggests that he on occasion pronounced final <y> as /ə/ and here wrote <a> as <y> by hypercorrection. Tregear's customary spelling for 'to believe' is *cresy*, *cregy*. At TH 19 however he writes *ow crege*, a spelling which suggests that he pronounced the word as /'kredʒə/. Similarly Tregear writes *vsa* for his more normal *vsy* at TH 54. SA normally writes the 3rd singular definite of the long form of bos as *vgy* (cf. SA 59a); at SA 59, 61 *bis* and 62a, however, the word is written *vge*, a spelling which suggests /ɪdʒə/.

The conclusion to be drawn from all this evidence would seem to be the following. In Middle Cornish inherited unstressed /a/, /e/ and /o/ had as a result of the prosodic shift fallen together as /ə/. Inherited unstressed /i/ also became /ə/ in some contexts. For the most part, however, unstressed /i/ was lowered to /ɪ/ and fell together with original unstressed /ɪ/, but /ɪ/ was not reduced any further (see also 7.15).

7.13 Something similar may have happened with the high back vowels /u/ and /o/ in unstressed syllables. It seems that they may have survived as a reduced but rounded vowel which I will write as <ǫ>.

In Cornish the most frequent plural marker is /ow/. Although unstressed this formant is preserved for the most part, as indeed the /ow/ in English *fellow, window* is preserved though unstressed. Middle Cornish /ow/ survives into Late Cornish in such forms as *taklou* /taklow/ 'things' (BF: 52), *tazow* 'fathers' (BF: 55), etc. /ow/ also occurs in Cornish in the second plural ending, for example in /beðowx/ 'be!' and /gezowx/ 'allow!'. It also occurs in the related second plural prepositional pronouns like /genowx/ 'with you' and /ə'hanowx/ 'from you'. Not infrequently /ow/ in the second plural is reduced to /ǫ/, which in BM is spelt <ogh> or <ugh>: *vynnogh* BM 113, *wethugh* BM 276; *esethugh* BM 283; *bethugh* BM 292; *omgersyogh* BM 296; *drethogh* BM 315; *aragogh* BM 323; *na govsogh* BM 340. Notice also such Late Cornish plural imperatives as *preezyo* 'praise' /pre:zjǫ/ (BF: 39), *beniggo* 'bless' /benIgǫ/ (BF: 39); *keno* 'sing' /kenǫ/ (BF: 39). Compare also *aso why* 'how... you are' RD 87. The plural marker /ow/ is also sometimes written <ogh> implying that /owx/ and /ow/ had fallen together. Note, for example <pehosogh> 'sins' for *pehosow* TH 39.

The ending /ow/ is sometimes reduced still further to /ə/, as can be seen from such spellings as *levra* 'books' (BF: 48), *gerria* 'words' (BF: 55); *medha* < *medhow* 'drunk' (AB: 107a). Compare also the place-names *Retanna* (< *res tanow*), *Goldstanna* (< *cos tanow*) and *Crig-a-Tana* (< *crugow tanow*) that may all contain *tanow* 'thin, narrow' (CPNE: 215). Pool also cites *Regia* as an early version of *Ridgeo* (< *rysyow* 'fords'); see PNWP: 66.

The diphthong /ɪw/ could also stand in unstressed syllables, for example, in *hethyw* 'today' /'heðɪw/. Spellings like Tregear's *hethow* TH 37, 48 and Lhuyd's *hidhu* (AB: 65c) however, indicate that final unstressed /ɪw/ tended to fall together with /ow/ as /ǫ/.

7.14 Normally before /s/, /θ/ and other consonants, post-tonic /u/ and /o/ [ɔ] were reduced to schwa. Take, for example, the two etyma *profus* 'prophet' Old Cornish *profuit*, Welsh *proffwyd* and *compes* 'even, level', Welsh *cymwys*. These two both had unstressed /ui/ in Old Cornish and this would have developed as /u/ or /o/ before the operation of the new prosodic system. Thereafter the final vowel was reduced to schwa, as can seen from the various Middle Cornish spellings of the two etyma:

profus: OM 1799, PC 325, 489, 1465, 2197, 2672, 2884, RD 1264. 1485, 1680, 1805
profos: PC 2672, RD 66, 1686
profes: PC 562; *profeth*: PC 1895
profys: PC 1923

compos: OM 2442, 2485
compes: OM 2472, 2494, 2510, CW 492
compys: OM 2455, 2531, 2536, PC 1206, 2736, TH 8a, 25a
compis: TH 21, 26a, 26a
compas: CW 1743.

Place-names in *compes* exhibit a very reduced final vowel: *Goon Gumpas, Woon Gumpus Common* (<us> = /əs/) and *Ventongimps*, where the syllable has been lost altogether.

Some words, however, that had original unstressed /ui/ are most frequently written in Middle Cornish with <u> or <o> in their unstressed syllable. I can think of four such etyma: *eglos* 'church', *arluth* 'lord', *gallus* 'power; to be able' and *cafus* 'to get'. *Eglos* is attested in Old Cornish as *eglos* but the Welsh cognate *eglwys* < *ecclesia*, indicates that the final vowel must originally have been /ui/. *Arluth* is attested in OCV as *arluit*. *Gallus* is not attested in Old Cornish but Middle Cornish *gallosek* 'powerful' occurs in OCV as *galluidoc*. The ending of both *gallus* and *cafus* should probably be connected with the endings of such Middle Welsh verbal nouns as *dywedwyt* 'say', *catwyt* 'keep' and *kyscwyt* 'sleep'.

The four Cornish etyma are attested in the texts in the following forms:

eglos: PC 333, BM 723, 1320, 1876, 2826, 2983, 3790, 4462, 4470, 4488, PA 13d, TH
    17 x 5, 39
egglos: TH x 150; SA 64 x 3
egglys: SA 59a

arluth: *passim* in all texts
arloth: OM 105, 172, 2595, 2685, PC 2189

gallus: OM 2149, 2287, RD 426, PA 70b, 75b, 113d, 116a, BM 553, 2032, 2557, 2759,
    3596, 4022, 4029, 4040, 4105, 4397, CW 356, TH 3a, 21, 21a, SA 59, 62a x 3, 63,
    64
galus: TH 56
gallos: OM 1155, 1214, PC 21, 44, 53, 788, 793, 1601, 2182, 2184, 2185, 2187, RD
    331, 834, 966, 1183, 2569, PA 22c, BM 2675
galloys: PA 135c, 224c, BM 233, 282, 2062, 2387, 3217, 3305, 4244
galles: PC 3194

caffus, kaffus: OM 1835, RD 1875, 2170
caffos: PC 2068

cafus kafus: OM 553, 2071, 2467, 2482, PC 588, 594, 678, 594, 985, 1178, 1214, 1404, 1498, 1531, RD 183, 189, 540; BM 426, 841, 1053, 1251, 2067, 2728, 2814, 2853, 2867, 2977, 3029, 3069, TH 3, 13a, 14a, 16a, 19, 21a, 24, 24a, 24a, 39a, etc.

cafos: PC 2455, PA 38b, 39b, 121b, 164c, 174d, 234b, 251c

cavos: CW 1515

cafes: OM 391, 454

cafys: OM 432

kafas: TH 11, 36, SA 65

couis: SA 60

cawys: RD 1957

cawas: BM 85, 255, CW 205, 808, 959, 1034, 1081, 1133, 1221, 2141.

There can be no doubt that in *eglos, cafus* and *gallus* the final unstressed vowel was frequently schwa in the spoken language. This can be deduced from such spellings as <egglys>, <galles> and <cafes>, <cafys>, <cawys>. Notice moreover that at PA 257b the preterite *cafas* 'got' /'kafəz/ is spelt <cafos>, which suggests that <cafos> in the verbal noun may also have meant /'kafəz/. Nonetheless, until the period of TH and SA in the second half of the sixteenth century, these words are spelt as though on occasion their unstressed syllable had a rounded vowel. I assume that this was the same vowel as we have noted in such words as *leverogh, betho* above, i.e. /ǫ/.

The first question to answer is why *eglos* should have had <o> while the others for the most part had <u>. I think we must allow that the dialectal variation in the treatment of /ui/ > /uː/ or /oː/ that we noticed in the stressed vowels, must also have operated in the unstressed vowels, though it is curious that *eglos* already has <o> in OCV. At all events *eglos* regularly has <o> while the other etyma have <o> sporadically only. <eglos> on the one hand and <cafus>, <gallus> on the other are spellings that originated before the prosodic shift. They imply that before the shift occurred a high back vowel /ʊ/ and a mid back vowel /ɔ/ were distinguished in unstressed syllables.

After the prosodic shift and in our earliest Middle Cornish texts, therefore, the two unstressed back vowels /ʊ/ and /ɔ/ fell together as /ǫ/ (and indeed had a tendency to become /ə/). If the unstressed vowels of *eglos, arluth, cafus/cafos* and *gallus* were ever rounded in Middle Cornish speech, I think we can be fairly certain it was the same vowel /ǫ/ in them all.

The second question is why these four words should have had a rounded unstressed vowel at all. *Arluth, eglos* and *gallus* (cf. *gallosek* 'mighty' as an epithet of God) were all associated with religious language, with preaching and the religious drama. Since such discourse was the domain of clerics who were literate, it would have tended to an elevated and formal style. We should not be astonished therefore if an archaizing spelling and pronunciation were to survive in these words in certain contexts.

When *arluth, eglos* and *gallus* were used in less formal contexts, however, they would almost certainly have been pronounced with /ə/ in the unstressed syllable; cf. the spelling <galles> in PC and <egglys> in SA. It is the more colloquial pronunciation which lies behind Late Cornish spellings: *egles* (BF: 41, 57; RC 23: 187); *eglez* (BF: 27); *egliz* (BF: 56, 60). Compare also such place-names as *Eglarooze* < *eglos ros*, *Foregles* and *Treviglas* that all indicate /ə/ in the final syllable; and *arleth* (BF: 39 x 2, 55 x 6, 56, 60; RC 23: 174, 178 x 3, 179, 180, 183 x 2, 184, 187, 188, 189), *arlith* (BF: 41 x 5), *arlyth* (BF: 29).

Cafus is a special case, because the word has no apparent religious connotations. I suspect that in speech from the fourteenth century onwards the word was /ˈkafəz/ or /ˈkawəz/ and that this pronunciation is what lies behind the Middle Cornish spellings <cafes>, <cafys>, <cawys> and <cawas>. Alongside these colloquial pronunciations there may well have been a more elevated /ˈkaɸọz/ with a bilabial articulation of the *f*. This pronunciation with marked rounding might well have prevented the complete unrounding of /ọ/ to /ə/. The difference between /ˈkawəz/ and /ˈkaɸọz/ would have been one of register and/or social standing. The variant /ˈkawəz/ would have been quotidian and plebeian, whereas the more etymological /ˈkaɸọz/ would have been formal and elevated. Late Cornish has the colloquial form only: *cavas* (BF: 29); *gawaz* (BF: 31); *gavas* (RC 23: 196).

7.15 In Late Cornish there is considerable variation in the way final inherited /ɪ/ < /i/ is written. Compare for example the following doublets: *tivi* 'grow' (AB: 245a)/ *teva* (AB: 52b), *tivia* (AB: 245a); *midzhi* 'reap' (AB: 90a) / *medge* (ACB Ff2); *pizi* 'pray' (AB: 250b) / *pidzha* (AB: 127c); *debri* 'eat' (AB: 85a), *a tebry* 'eating' (AB: 248a) / *debre* (RC 23, 174, 175, 176); *deski* 'teach' (AB: 245b) / *desga* (AB: 55a), *deske* (RC 23: 192). It would seem that unstressed /ɪ/ in auslaut has become /ə/.

In Late Cornish also it appears that unstressed vowels may have *o*-colouring on occasion. Nicholas Boson writes *Curnooack* 'Cornish' and *Sousenack* 'English' with <a> (BF: 25) but *Frenkock* 'French' with <o> (BF: 29). With this latter contrast Lhuyd's *Vrinkak* 'French' (AB: 62c). Middle Cornish -*el* appears in Late Cornish with <o> in *leverol* 'say' (BF: 31), *derevoll* 'raise' (BF: 9) and *chattol* 'cattle' (BF: 52), with <a> in *lenal* 'fill (BF: 53) and *hanwall* 'name' (BF: 41) but with <e> in *gueskel* 'strike' (BF: 16), *chattell* 'cattle' (BF: 55).

There is also evidence that in absolute final position /ə/ in Late Cornish was pronounced as [a]. This is guaranteed for instance by such late spellings as *garah* 'to leave', *magah* 'to rear' (SGMC: 83). This is not a survival, I think, of any quality in the vowel but rather a phonetic development of schwa itself. Such a development is common in some dialects of English. Cockney speech in London, for example, pronounces final /ə/ as [a], for example in [ˈrɪjta frəm ˈmɔːta] *Rita from Malta*.

Lhuyd says of the pronunciation of the ending of the past participle:

[T]hey generally end it in *ez*, Saying *Kreiez*, Called; *Trehez*, Cut; *Miskemerez*, Mistaken; *Dylîez*, Revenged; *Guerhez*, Sold, &c. and sometimes in *az*: As *Ledhaz*,

Slain; *Kyrtaz*, Delayed; *Guesgaz*, Worn; tho' not seldom also in *yz*: As *Devydhyz*, Quenched, *Bidhyz*, Drowned; *Kelmyz*, Bound; *Huedhyz*, Swoln (AB: 248b).

I assume that by *ez* Lhuyd means [əz] and by *yz* he means [ɪz]. His observations are corroborated by the spelling of Late Cornish writers, since <az>, <iz> and <ez> are all attested as endings of the past participle: *trigaz* < *trygys* (JCH § 1); *comeraz* < *kemerys, tormentyaz* < *tormentyes* (RC 23: 193); *kavas* < *cafys* 'found' (BF: 46) but *sendzhyz* < *sengys* (JCH §20); *guelyz* < *gwelys* (JCH § 35); *kregyz* < *cregys* (JCH § 36); *prevez* < *prevys* (JCH § 35); *kameres* < *kemerys* (BF: 43); *gennes* < *genys* (BF: 41); *denethes* < *denythys* (BF: 41); *creages* < *cregys* (BF: 41); *umclithes* < *ancledhys* (BF: 41); *kellez* < *kellys* (BF: 46); *deskes* < *dyskys* (BF: 49); *screffez* < *scryfys* (RC 23: 188).

I would from this evidence draw the following tentative conclusions. Early Middle Cornish had three unstressed vowels: /ə/, /ɪ/ and /o̞/. By the seventeenth century, if not before, /ɪ/ and /o̞/ seem to have become allophones of /ə/ with which they are in free variation. Moreover, in absolute final position Late Cornish /ə/ has a fourth allophone: [a].

CHAPTER 8
Consonants

8.1 It is possible, indeed likely, that most consonants were marked for length before the operation of the new prosodic system. It is probable, for example, that *poppo* 'may bake' and *popa* 'puffin' were distinguished by vocalic and consonantal length alike: /pop:o/ ~ /po·pa/. Similarly *gwelaf* 'I see' and *gwella* (< *gwellaf*) 'best' would have been /gwe·la/ and /gwel:a/ respectively. Whether there was ever a distinction between the medial segments in *seghe* 'to dry' /'se·xe/ and *segha* 'drier' */'sexxa/ is impossible to prove and seems unlikely.

Simple voiceless stops like /k/, /p/ or /t/ were uncommon in Cornish in medial position. This was because inherited /k/, /p/ and /t/ had been lenited to /g/, /b/ and /d/ in the transition from British to Primitive Cornish. Where /k/, /p/ and /t/ do occur it is either by internal provection, as for example in *poppo* 'may bake', *docco* 'may carry' or as borrowings for example in *pokkat* 'pocket' in JCH § 35. In this last word Gendall suggests (SDMC: xvii) that the medial consonant was /k:/, that is, a long variety of [k]. On theoretical grounds I find this difficult to believe, particularly since there is no evidence in Late Cornish for /p:/ or /t:/. I would prefer to understand Lhuyd's <pokkat> as a way of emphasizing the intensity and perhaps brevity of the vowel.

I believe that the prosodic shift was occasioned by an increase in intensity in the articulation of syllables and a decrease in their length. I assume that in the case of both /'gwe·la/ 'I see' and /'gwel:a/ 'best' the decrease in duration meant not only the reduction in vowel length in the first but also the reduction in consonantal length in the second. As a result both became /'gwelə/. The same kind of shortening would have affected all half-long vowels and all long consonants. The only exception would have been the long sonants /n:/ and [m:]. These acquired a partially plosive articulation. This phenomenon is known as pre-occlusion and I discuss it at 9.1-6 below.

The presence of pre-occlusion in later Middle Cornish is a clear indication that the opposition /n/ ~ /n:/ had been lost. If length had been lost in the sonants, it was very unlikely to have survived in the stops. This is corroborative evidence that long /p:/, /t:/, and /k:/ no longer existed after the prosodic shift. The loss of such long consonants is also guaranteed by the way scribes regularly wrote historically single consonants as geminates between vowels, a point that has been alluded to above (2.5).

8.2 In the texts <gh> frequently alternates with <h>: *flogh, pegh, nagh, golgh, myrgh* but *flehes, pehas, naha, golhy, myrhes*. This is not a mere scribal habit, but is almost certainly indicative of a phonetic difference. It seems that in final

54

position, whether after a vowel as in *pegh* or after a consonant as in *myrgh*, inherited /x/ remained. At the beginning of a syllable, however, /x/ was weakened to /h/: /pe-həs/, /na-hə/, /gol-hɪ/, etc. This should not astonish us. The initial spirantization of *p* and *t* produces /f/ and /θ/ respectively, for example in *pen* 'head', *ow fen* 'my head' and *tas* 'father', *ow thas* 'my father'. When initial *c/k* is spirantized the result is not /x/ but /h/: *colon* 'heart' but *ow holon* 'my heart'. The expected /x/ becomes /h/ at the beginning of a syllable. In the same way final /x/ in *nagh* 'deny!' becomes /h/ in syllable initial position *naha* /na-hə/ 'to deny'.

There are many striking examples of the alternation <gh> ~ <h> in the texts. The scribes are largely consistent in the matter. Note, for example, *kyrhys* 'fetched' OM 886 but *kyrgh* 'fetch' OM 887; *gerhes* 'to fetch' BM 660 but *kergh* 'fetch' BM 275, 1379, 1392. Similarly we find the following: *yagh* 'healthy' BM 711, 713 but *yehes* 'health' BM 701; *dynagh* 'deny!' BM 1230 but *denaha* 'to deny' BM 893; *flogh* 'child' BM 1550, 1554, 15561, 1569, 1574 but *flehys* 'children' BM 94, 116, 1321, 1593.

For further instances of A <gh> finally but B <h> at the beginning of a syllable compare the following spellings from BM:

A.
mergh 'daughter' BM 179
pegh 'sin' BM 882
warlergh 'according to' BM 391
ij vregh 'arms' BM 1187
trogh 'cut' BM 1279
brogh 'badger' BM 1280.

B.
perhennek 'owner' BM 16
bohosek 'poor' BM 438, 450
guirhas, guirhays, werhes, wyrhes 'virgin' BM 552, 631, 756, 1125
ehen 'kindred' BM 1159
laha 'law' BM 849
golhys 'washed' BM 1493, 1496.

It should be observed that before /s/ in verbal inflection the scribes write <gh> since /x/ is at the end of a syllable: *del yrghsys* PC 187.

If Neo-Cornish is to reflect the spelling and pronunciation of the texts, it would be advisable to spell <flogh> but <flehes>, <yagh> but <yehes>, etc.

8.3 Between vowels /h/ is frequently lost. Thus *byhan* 'small' (Welsh *bychan*) is often written without medial <h>: *byen* BM 1550, *byan* BM 1676, *bean* TH 5. The Old Cornish for 'right, south' is *dehou* (Welsh *dehau*, Breton *dehou*), which is attested only in the compound *dehoules* 'southernwood' in OCV. This had original /h/, not /x/, and it seems that the consonant was lost early, the ensuing hiatus being filled by yod, which raised the preceding vowel: *dehou* > */'de-ow/ > /'dejow/ > /'dɪjow/. It is /'dɪjow/ that I take to be represented by the Middle Cornish spellings *thyow* PC 2519 and *dyou* BM 1850, 4085. The <gh> in spellings like *ȝyghow* PA 97c,136d; *dyghow* PA 193a, 198a is graphemic only. *Thyghyow* at OM 421, 921 as well as having graphemic <gh> appears to indicate the intervocalic /j/ by <y>. Nowhere in Middle Cornish does *dyghow*, *dyow* appear with <e> rather than <y> as the stressed vowel. Lhuyd's *dehou* 'right' (AB: 54b) is a misprint on the basis of the Breton form; Lhuyd writes *dyhou* four lines later.

When intervocalic /h/ < /x/ is lost after a rounded vowel, the resulting hiatus is filled by /w/. One example is *ughel, uhel* 'high', which seems to have developed as follows: /'yˑxel/ > */'yhəl/ > */'y-əl/ > */'ywəl/ > /'ɪwəl/. /ɪwəl/ then alternates with /'ewəl/, a form represented by Lhuyd's *ehual* (AB: 2b).

Another example of /w/ in hiatus is the word for 'evening'. This probably developed as follows: /gorθ'yˑxer/ > */gorð'y-ər/ > /gorð'ywər/ > /go'ðywər/. What lies behind *gorȝewar* at BM 103 is /gorð'ywer/; the form /go'ðywər/ is represented by Lhuyd's *gydhihuar, gydhiuhar* (AB: 52b, 65b, 172c). For /rθ/ > /rð/ > /ð/ in this word see 8.6.

8.4 Cornish probably had /lː/, /rː/ and /nː/ originally. After the prosodic shift these all fell together with their short equivalents—except that /nː/ became /ᵈn/. As a result of later sound changes, however, Cornish developed a threefold series of voiceless sonants /lh/, /rh/ and /nh/.

/lh/ is presumably what is meant by such spellings as <pelha> 'further' in TH 4 and <na velha> 'no longer' JCH §11. *Pella* 'further' probably originally had a long medial consonant /lː/ while *gwelaf* 'I see' and *palas* 'to dig' had a short one /l/. After the prosodic shift the distinction was lost (8.1). It was then found necessary to recharacterize the comparative forms *gwella, pella*. Before the prosodic shift *gwlyb* 'wet' and *gwlyppa* 'wetter, wettest' would have been distinguished in their medial consonant by length and by voice: /gwlɪːb/ ~ /gwlɪpːa/. After the shift the distinction in the consonant would have been one of voice only: /gwleːb/ ~ /gwlipə/. As a result the superlative formant was taken to be devoicing + -ə, that is, /hə/ . This was then attached afresh to *pell-* /pel/ to reform the comparative/ superlative as /pelhə/ where /lh/ is a voiceless /l/.

In BM, TH and CW sonants are frequently written double before /j/ <y>; thus one finds such spellings as <myllyow> 'thousands', <tellyrryow> 'places', etc. Such spellings probably indicate the long variety of the sonant in question, which arose spontaneously before /j/. In most cases the long sonant fell together with the short variety when the distinction /l/ ~ /lː/ was lost. In the word *dellyow* 'leaves', however, the long /lː/ is replaced not by /l/ but /lh/. The ensuing */delhjow/ is then further strengthened to /delkjow/ in Late Cornish. Lhuyd gives *delkio* 'leaves' (AB: 242c). The replacement of /lː/ by

/lh/ seems also to have occurred elsewhere, for example in *collan* 'knife', spelt <kolhan> at TH 27, *telhar* 'place, palace' (AB: 111b). Rarely /lj/ is strengthened to /lgj/, for example, in *kysylgou* 'counsels' (AB: 242c) < *cusullyow*. The cluster /lg/ < /lj/ has been metathesized in *deragla* 'scold' (AB: 74b) < *deralga < *deraylya; cf. English *rail* 'scold'.

/lh/ also seems to occur in the word *flogh* 'child' after the definite article. Lhuyd says that 'the child', 'to the child' are *an hlôh* and *dhan hlôh* respectively (AB: 242a). It would seem that the fricative /f/ is reduced in articulation between the adjacent sonants, to such an extent that only its voicelessness remains.

Norden writing *c.* 1580 says that the Cornish pronounce the equivalent of Welsh *ll* 'with a kinde of reflecting of the tounge' (Jago 1882: 34). This not only corroborates the view that Cornish had a voiceless *l* but it also suggests that /lh/ was retroflexed [ɭ] and not lateral [ɬ] as in Welsh.

/nh/ is not common as far as one can see, though it does occur in verb in *-hé* like as *glanhe* 'cleanse' TH 8, and probably also in *gwanha* 'weaker' TH 4, *ynhy* 'in her' PA 182b, *unhy* 'in her' CW 1809.

/rh/ is commoner than either /lh/ or /nh/, since it is a reflex of earlier /rθ/, for example *gorthyb* 'answer' *perthy* 'bear'. These appear in Late Cornish as *gorryb, perry*. That /rθ/ gives /rh/ seems guaranteed by spellings like <Guerha> for *gwertha* 'sell' (BF: 44) and *harha* 'bark' < *hartha* (AB: 77a); cf. Welsh *cyfarth*.

On occasion /rh/ occurs in initial position, where it appears to be a reflex of inherited British unlenited /r/. Lhuyd says of the Cornish: 'I have frequently observed them to say *Rhag* [For] as well as *Rag*' (AB: 229a).

8.5 In some Cornish texts *wh* is frequently written as <w> (13.17), which seems to indicate that /ʍ/ was in some varieties of Cornish voiced to /w/. Symmetry would lead us to expect that /lh/, /nh/, /rh/ would also on occasion be voiced to /l/, /n/, /r/. This might explain why spellings with <lh>, <nh>, <rh> are relatively rare.

8.6 The shift /rθ/ > /rh/ occurs when the vowel preceding the consonant group bore the stress. If /rθ/ was immediately followed by the main stress, however, the cluster was first voiced to /rð/ before simplifying to the ordinary voiced sonant, /r/. The stage /rð/ is written <rdh> in the fourteenth-century place-names *Pordhunes, Pordhenes* (PNWP: 40, 65), both < *porth enys, with the primary stress on the second element. A further example of /rθ/ > /rð/ is provided by the Cornish word for 'evening', *gurthuwer* OCV, *gorȝewar* BM 103; *gydhihuar, gydhiuhar* (8.3). The word is a compound of *(g)orth* 'upon, against' and *ugher 'evening'. The second element is identical with Welsh *ucher* 'evening' < CC **wisker-* < IE **wesper-* (WG: 89) and indeed Norris had already connected the word with Welsh *ucher* as early as 1859 (ii 380). Lhuyd's spellings suggest that /rð/ was dissimilated to /ð/ before /r/ in the same word.

/rð/ is also written <rd>, for example in the toponyms *Pordmenster, Pordmur, Pordye* 'St Ives' (all early 14th century; PNWP: 65). This last develops regularly as *Poreeah* (BF: 25). *Orth* 'upon' appears as <ord> in the phrase *ord en grows* 'upon the cross' PA 179b. I take <ord> here to represent /orð/ < /orθ/ before the main stress in *grows.*

The shift /rð/ > /r/ is at least as early as the *Ordinalia*, as is clear from the spellings *for* PC 2418 for *forth* 'way', and *aber* RD 2108 for *aberth* 'within'. Presumably /rθ/ > /rh/ dates from the same period.

8.7 The development /rθ/ > /rh/, appears to have worked the other way on occasion. *Myrgh* 'daughter', *mergh* 'horses', and *yrgh* 'snow' are spelt by Tregear as <mirth> (21a), <merth> (56a), and <yrth> (56a) respectively. Similarly CW has <kerth> for *kergh* 'oats' at 1066 and <marth> for *margh* 'horse' at 406. This seems to imply that all three etyma had a final /θ/ in Tudor Cornish. The change /rx/ > /rθ/ is amply corroborated by place-names containing the word *margh, mergh* 'horse, horses': *Polmarth* (< *pol margh*), *Lemarth* (< ?*lyn margh*), *Goonamarth* (*gun an margh*), *Kilmarth* (< ?*kyl margh*), *Carn Marth* (< *carn margh*), *Trevarth* (*tre vargh*), *Carvarth* (< *ker vargh*); *Ventonveth* (*fenten vergh*), *Carveth* (< *ker vergh*), *Roseveth* (< *res vergh*). The place-names *Carnyorth* (< *carn yorgh* 'tor of the roe deer') and *Lanjeth* (< *nans yergh* 'valley of the roe deer' [pl.]) should also be mentioned here.

The change /x/ > /θ/ has taken place in final position after a stressed vowel. For example *pegh* 'sin' is spelt <peth> at CW 586, a spelling which implies a pronunciation /peːθ/. Similarly John Boson spells *segh* 'dry' as *zeth* (BF: 52), i.e. /zeːθ/. The shift /x/ > /θ/ in final position after a stressed vowel, though not universal in place-names, is well attested: *Polzeath* (< *pol segh*), *Ventonzeth* (< *fenten segh*), *Mellanzeath* (< *melyn segh*), *Roseath* (< *res segh*), *Goverseath* (< *gover segh*).

Notice incidentally that the shift /x/ > /θ/ is later than /rθ/ > /rð/ > /r/, otherwise all examples of *marth* would have become **mar'*. *Mar* for *margh* 'horse' is in fact attested in the Bilbao manuscript.

8.8 The question of historically voiced consonants in final position is difficult to answer unambiguously. Neither Welsh nor Breton seems to offer much of a parallel. In Welsh if a word has etymological final /v/, /ð/, /b/, /d/ or /g/, for example in *nef* 'heaven', *hedd* 'peace', *mab* 'son', *byd* 'world' and *mwg* 'smoke', the final segment remains voiced irrespective of position in the sentence. In Breton on the other hand words with final etymological /v/, /z/, /b/, /d/ or /g/ devoice the final segment in pausa and before a following voiceless consonant. Before a following vowel or voiced consonant, the consonant is voiced. Thus in Breton *beleg kozh* 'old priest' is /'beˑlek koːs/ and *beleg kozh eo* 'he is an old priest' is /'be·lek ko:z eu/. But *beleg mat eo* 'he is a good priest' is /'be·leg ma:d eu/.

It is possible that something like the Breton system once operated in Cornish. The rule in Tudor and Late Cornish, however, seems to have been as follows: if a word has an inherited final voiced obstruent, the segment is always voiced if preceded by a stressed vowel. If the preceding vowel is unstressed, however, the segment is voiceless.

The difference between the Breton and Cornish treatment of final voiced/unvoiced stops after a stressed vowel is apparent from Lhuyd. Here with their Latin head-words are some Cornish and Breton entries from his *Comparative Vocabulary* (AB ii):

Latin	C[ornish]	Ar[morican]
coram	*dyrag*	*dirak*
cur?	*prag?*	*perak?*
decem	*dêg*	*dêk*
enim	*rag*	*rak*
filius	*mâb*	*map*
impius	*drôg*	*drouk*
pix	*pêg*	*pek*
uxor	*gurêg*	*grek.*

8.9 The texts do not distinguish /ð/ from /θ/ inasmuch as both are written <th>. Moreover /v/ is almost always written <f> or even <ff> at the end of a word, though note *ev* 'he' for *ef* at RD 2017. We have, in addition, very few examples of /d/ in final position, since Old Cornish /d/ has been assibilated to /s/ by the time of our earliest Middle Cornish texts. Further, as late as BM the words for 'sweet' and 'fair', for example, are regularly written <whek>, <tek> respectively for the sake of rhyme.

If one examines the examples of the alternation g/k in final position from TH and SA, however, one obtains the following picture:

1) Tregear's *Homilies* (1-25a)

		g	k
STRESSED	*rag* 'for'	passim	0
	therag 'before	4	0
	(g)rug 'did'	passim	0
	kyg 'flesh'	9	0
	drog 'evil' (noun)	4	0
	gwreg 'wife'	2	0
	wheg 'sweet'	1	0
	teg 'fair'	1	0
UNSTRESSED			
	kerengeek 'loving'	0	6
	peswartrosek '4-footed'	0	1
	humbrak 'lead'	1	1

behosek 'poor'		0	1
gowak 'deceitful'		0	1
govenek 'hope'		0	1
methek 'ashamed'		0	1
galosek 'powerful'		0	2
kevrennek 'sharing in'		0	1
colonnek 'willing'		0	3
resak 'run'		0	3
kentrevak 'neighbour'		0	1
nownsag 'nineteen'		1	0
metheg 'doctor'		2	0

2) *Sacrament an Alter*

		g	k
STRESSED	*rag* 'for'	10	0
	derag 'before'	5	0
	kyg 'flesh'	27	0
UNSTRESSED			
	pensevik 'prince'	0	2
	galosak 'powerful'	0	1.

In SA *(w)rug* is normal but there are at least 8 instances of *(w)ruk*. This latter may well have come about when used with *del* 'as', since the phrase *del wrug* 'as he did' would have been one accentual unit: '*del rug* and unaccented syllable *rug* would therefore have tended to become *ruk*.

It is apparent from the above instances that final *g/k* when following a stressed vowel is almost always written <g>. When following an unstressed vowel it is usually written <k> though there are a few exceptions.

8.10 The alternation stressed vowel + *g* versus unstressed vowel + *k* is also apparent from place-names. Notice for example the following:

STRESSED VOWEL: *Trigg Rocks* < *tryg*; *Treweeg* < *tre wyg*; *Nanteague* < *nans teg*; *Brassteague* < *?pras teg*; *Vogue* < *fog*; *Chyvogue* < *chy fog*

UNSTRESSED VOWEL: *Adjawinjack* < *ajwy wynsak*; *Angarrack* < *an garrek*; *Boswednack* < *bos wynnek*; *Trelissick* < *tre *wlesyk*, etc.

Tregear spells 'nineteen' as *nownsag* and 'doctor' as *metheg*. Both probably had a final /k/ in speech. Lhuyd gives *noundzhak* 'nineteen' (AB: 176b) and *medhek* (AB: 47c). Notice also the place-name *Tremethick* < *tre methek* 'doctor's dwelling'. The alternation *g/k* is clearly related to whether the preceding vowel was stressed or not. The nature of what followed *g/k*, consonant, vowel or pause is not relevant. Cornish therefore is radically different from Breton in this respect.

CONSONANTS

8.11 Because Cornish assibilated final /d/ there are no native words that demonstrate the alternation *d/t*. On the other hand one should note that Tregear writes *fowt* 'fault' as <foude> at 2a and *David* as <Davit> at 1. He seems to be applying the rule stressed vowel + voiced ~ unstressed vowel + unvoiced to *d/t* in English borrowings. *David* is the English name, not the *Daveth, Davyth* of the *Ordinalia*.

8.12 The evidence for the alternation *b/p* is more ambiguous in TH and SA than for *g/k*. Tregear and SA alike almost invariably write *pub* 'every' and *mab* 'son'. As far as *b/p* after an unstressed vowel is concerned their practice is less consistent. Both write *gorryb* 'answer' with <b> only. SA has one example of *hevelep* and none of **heveleb*. Tregear has four examples with <b> as against two with <p>. Tregear has one example of *methewnep* 'drunkenness' with a <p>.

The alternation b/p is seen in place-names. Note the following with a stressed vowel: *Greeb < (an) gryb, Carn greeb < carn gryb*; and the following with an unstressed vowel: *Tretharrup < tre wortharap, Vorrap < morrep* 'sea-shore' (though *Morrab* also occurs).

8.13 The alternation stressed vowel + voiced consonant ~ unstressed vowel + voiceless consonant is noticeable also in CW. Although consonants are sometimes written voiceless after stressed consonants in such words as *cof* 'memory', *whek* 'sweet', more often than not they appear as voiced. On the other hand consonants are almost always voiceless after unstressed vowels.

Creation of the World

STRESSED SYLLABLES
mabe 'son' 9, 1056, 1164, 1252, 1254, 1323
neb 'some' 454

neve 'heaven' 23
preve 'serpent' 335, 498
have 'summer' 366
eve 'he' 1180
ove 'I am' 440, 1040, 1173, 1213
cove 'memory' 1215
skave 'light' 1198
clave 'sick' 1199

arage 'forth' 40, 53
prage 'why' 543, 1175
pleag 'pleases' 755
moog 'smoke' 1102
gwreag(e) 'wife' 834, 877, 966, 976

UNSTRESSED SYLLABLES
gorryb(e) 'answer' 1198, 1736, 1761

pensevicke 'prince' 120
lowenacke 'joyful' 546
eddrack 'regret' 717, 1506
tyack 'farmer' 920
crothacke 'carping' 1105
gwaracke 'bow' 1466, 1488
conycke 'cunning' 1406.

Again it would seem that *gorryb* has a voiced final. There are no examples of final /p/ after unstressed vowels. Examples of /f/ after unstressed vowels are also wanting. The alternation of stressed vowel + *g*: unstressed vowel + *k* is nonetheless remarkable. It should, however, be pointed out that CW has more examples of *yddrag* 'regret' with /g/ than with /k/. Variants with /g/ occur at CW 1290, 1306, 1685, 2043, 2048, 2339. Quite possibly *eddrack* 'regret' has been contaminated by *edrege* (< **edregeth*) with the result that the voiced final consonant has been generalized.

8.14 Lhuyd is another source of evidence for voice/voicelessness in final consonants. In his text of JCH, for example, Lhuyd agrees exactly with TH and SA as far as *g/k* is concerned, since he invariably has *gwreg* 'wife', *teg* 'fair', *ryg* 'did' with <g> but *tiack* 'farmer' with <k>. On the other hand he writes *meppig* 'little boy' at § 44. If this is not a slip, it may be explicable with reference to the preceding /p/. The voiceless stop /p/ may have caused the final voiceless /k/ to dissimilate to /g/. This could explain *gurryb* 'answer' in TH, SA and CW. The original form of the word for 'answer' was *gorthyp* /gorθɪp/. The internal /θ/ was weakened to /h/ and devoiced the /r/ (see 8.4 above). Quite possibly this devoiced /r/ was sufficient to dissimilate the voiceless /p/ to its voiced counterpart /b/: /gorθɪp/ > /gorhɪp/ > /gorhɪb/. A comparable dissimilation might explain the final /g/ in Lhuyd's *marhag* 'horseman' (AB: 57a).

Lhuyd expressly mentions the way in which final <k> is to be pronounced [g] for he makes the following two statements:

1. So in Cornish, *gurek* A wife is pronounced *Gureg* (AB: 227a)
2. For *kyk* [Flesh] must be read *kîg* (AB: 228a).

The alternation, stressed vowel + voiced stop ~ unstressed vowel + unvoiced stop, is seen in the following spellings from Lhuyd: *dêg* 'ten' (AB: 53c), *deg uar nigans* 'thirty' (AB: 166c), *padzhar iganz ha dêg* 'ninety' (AB: 100a) but *idnak* 'eleven' (AB: 176b), *tardhak, tredhek* 'thirteen' (AB: 166a), *pazuardhak* 'fourteen' (AB: 135a). The alternation *g* ~ *k* in Lhuyd is not just graphemic. Jenner heard exactly the same phenomenon in 1875 from when he collected Cornish survivals in Mount's Bay. His informants said *deg* 'ten' but *'ignak* 'eleven', *'daudhak* 'twelve', *'taudhak* 'thirteen', *bi'zwaudhak* 'fourteen' (Jenner 1875-76: 535).

8.15 As far as the continuants /ð/ and /z/ in JCH are concerned, it appears that there is a strong tendency to generalize the voiced form everywhere. Although Lhuyd writes *noueth* 'new' at § 6 and § 16 and *diuath* 'end' at § 13, he writes *duadh, diuadh, diuedh, diwadh* 'end' at §§ 3, 5, 7, 9, 29 and 46. The final segment in *medh* 'said' is <dh> throughout and in *vêdh* 'will be' at §§ 15, 20, 24.

If one looks at other spellings elsewhere in Lhuyd's *Cornish Grammar* (AB vi) one finds the following: *goruedh* 'lie' (250a), *dyhodzhedh* 'afternoon' (249a), *auêdh, enuêdh* 'also' (249a), *eledh* 'angels' (249b), *heruydh* 'according to' (249c), *hemladh* 'fight' (249c), *bedh* 'be!' (245c), *klêdh* 'ditch' (242b), *gurêdh* 'root' (242b), *blaidh* 'wolf' (241b), *menedh* 'mountain' (230c), *guragedh* 'wives' (243a), *brederedh* 'brothers' (243a), *abesteledh* 'apostles' (243a).

One might argue that Lhuyd was mistaken in hearing final /ð/ in *bedh, dedh,* etc., and that the analogy of Welsh led him astray. This is unlikely, I think. Lhuyd on a number of occasions makes it perfectly clear that what he heard on the lips of Cornish-speakers and what was written in Cornish manuscripts were at variance with one another. Lhuyd makes the following three statements:

1. '...for *deyth* [a day] must be read *dedh*' (AB: 227b)
2. 'For *Aflauar*, mute; *yn few*, alive, & *Ty a fyth*, Thou shalt be, must be read *avlavar, in vêu, tî a vydh*' (AB: 227c)
3. '*Th* supplied the use of *Dh* in the Cornish as in English. For *Daveth*, David; *Forth*, A way; *Deth*, A day; *Fyth*, Faith; *Ethen*, Birds; *Goith*, A goose, &c. should be read *Davydh, Fordh, Dêdh, Fydh, Ydhyn, Gûydh*' (AB: 229b).

Moreover it is clear that he distinguished carefully between /ð/ and /θ/ in the Cornish he heard spoken for he says of ancient Cornish manuscripts:

'For *Diwet*, an end, is pronounced *Diuedh*, and *Bitqueth*, Ever, should be read *Bithqueth...*' (AB: 229a).

8.16 It is apparent then that in the Cornish of Lhuyd's time the reflex of final /ð/ was /ð/ after stressed and unstressed syllables alike. This was the view taken by Williams in LCB. Whitley Stokes takes issue with Williams on this point for he says:

But I have invariably written *th* in auslaut. In this respect Mr. Williams has throughout his Lexicon been misled by Welsh analogy, and failed to see that at the end of a word an old *dh* (ð) has always been sharpened into *th* (þ). In the *Passion*, with the single exception of *molloʒ*, P. 66, 3, (ʒ = *dh*) never occurs as a final, but only a *th*. Moreover, words which, in Old Cornish, may have ended in *dh*, rhyme in the Middle Cornish poems with words which unquestionably end in *th*. See, for example, the *Passion*, stanza 49, 4, where *beth* 'erit' (W. *bydd*) and *feth* (W. *fydd* from *fides*) rhyme with *haneth* (W. *henoeth*, Ir. *innocht*) 'to-night' and *tergweth* (W. *teirgwaith*) 'thrice'. So in P. 52, 3 *aseth* (W. *eistedd*, O.W. *estid*) 'seat' rhymes with *haneth* (W. *henoeth*, Ir. *innocht*). I conclude from this that in all words ending, according to the MSS., in *th*, that combination was pronounced sharp, as in Welsh, and should be so printed (CG: 138).

I would suggest that both Stokes and Williams were right. Cornish originally devoiced final /ð/ in most positions and words in final etymological /ð/ could therefore be rhymed with words in final /θ/. As a result of the prosodic shift (see 8.19 below), however, final /ð/ was revoiced in those final positions where it had previously been devoiced. At first this revoicing may have applied only after stressed vowels. Later it was extended to unstressed vowels as well. The original devoicing, however, was allowed *metri gratia* in Middle Cornish verse long after it had ceased to reflect the spoken language.

We can sum up the position best by giving some examples. Before the prosodic shift: *cleth* 'ditch' was /kle:θ/ before consonants and in pausa and /kle:ð/ before vowels. *Meneth* 'mountain' was /'meneθ/ before consonants and in pausa and /'meneð/ before vowels. After the shift *cleth* was /kle:ð/ everywhere. *Meneth* had /θ/ in pausa and before consonants for a while, but eventually final /ð/ was generalized. Thus *meneth* became /'meneð/ everywhere also. The only indication that the generalization of final /ð/ was recent was the following: for the purposes of rhyme *cleth*, *meneth* could be treated as though ending in /θ/ rather than /ð/.

It should be noticed, however, that Lhuyd spells the word for 'truth' with a final <th>: *gwyroneth* (AB: 240c) although the Welsh cognate, *gwirionedd* has final /ð/. It seems that while *gwyroneth* was still pronounced with final /θ/ in pausa, the word was assimilated to other abstracts in -*eth* /eθ/ < *-akta*. Such abstract nouns in -*eth* (Welsh -*aeth*) include *skiantoleth* 'prudence', *gowegneth* 'fraud' (AB: 240c).[7]

8.17 Lhuyd's text of JCH is a useful source of evidence for the question of final /s/ ~ /z/. Historic /s/ is <z> after stressed vowels in '*gyz* 'your' § 2; *dhîz* 'to

---

7   A thorough examination of the evidence shows that Lhuyd did not really hear unstressed -*edh* as a plural termination. He says "The Fourth Plural Terminated formerly (as still in the Welsh) in *edh*; as *Brederedh*, Brothers; *Eledh*, Angels, *Abesteledh*, Apostles. Which pronunciation was more anciently expressed by *t*; as *Guraget*, Wives for *Geragedh*. It's at present changed into *es* according to their writing; but into *ez* according to their Pronunciation" AB: 243a. I think it likely that the variation stressed vowel + *b*, *g* ~ unstressed vowel + *p*, *k* (for example, *mab*, *gwreg* ~ *morrep*, *carrek*) also operated with ð and θ. I now, therefore, write *fedh* 'faith', *gwedh* 'trees', and *scodh* 'shoulder' but *eleth* 'angels', *bugeleth* 'shepherds', *deweth* 'end' and *gwyryoneth*, *gwyroneth* 'truth' in the vocabulary of UCR at the end of this book.

thee' § 5, 7, 8; *bez* 'but' §§ 5, 7, 9, 11; *doz* 'come' § 11; *tîz* 'people' § 20 and <z> after unstressed vowels also in *passiez* 'past' § 1; *trigaz* 'settled' § 1; *kydhaz* 'fell, became' § 2; *huillaz* 'seek' § 2; *bounaz* 'life' § 2;, *kibmiaz* 'leave' § 3; *kymeraz* 'took' § 3; *travaliaz* 'travelled' § 3; etc. The evidence from elsewhere in Lhuyd corroborates this picture: historic /s/ is everywhere [z] in final position.

There can be no doubt that the final segment in *tas, pras, glas* and the medial segment in *resek, casek* was before the prosodic shift a lenis /s/. That is to say, it was as weak in articulation as English /z/, but was voiceless like English /s/. Where place-names came into English before the full operation of the shift, the lenis /s/ was often heard as [s] and the Cornish consonant is spelt <ss> in English. After the prosodic shift the lenis /s/ was voiced and became indistinguishable from English /z/. In place-names that were adopted into English after the prosodic shift <z> is a common spelling.

It has often been noted that *s/z* alternates in some Cornish words with *g/j*. This is a separate matter and I deal with it at 10.1-5 below.

8.18 There is no evidence for *f/v* after unstressed vowels in JCH but after stressed vowels only <v> occurs, as for example, in *ev* 'he' § 3, 40, 43; *prev* 'prove' § 39 and *kav* 'will get' § 23. This agrees with the evidence we have from CW (8.13).

8.19 We can sum up our findings as follows. Tudor and Late Cornish exhibited a voiced/unvoiced alternation in inherited final *g* and *b*. After stressed vowels inherited final /g/ was /g/ but was replaced by /k/ after unstressed vowels. There was a similar though less consistent alternation between /b/ and /p/ in the case of the inherited labial plosive. After stressed vowels it was almost invariably /b/ and after unstressed vowels /p/. The alternation was not consistently applied, however, and /b/ is attested even after unstressed vowels.

There had also probably existed a similar alternation of voiced/unvoiced in the continuants *ð/θ, v/f* and *z/s*. By the Late Cornish period, however, this alternation has disappeared in the case of *z/s*, since only /z/ occurs in final position. Similarly final lenited *d* is /ð/ virtually everywhere.[8] We have no evidence for final /f/ after unstressed vowels. After stressed vowels only /v/ occurred.

The consonants we are dealing with here are the historically voiced stops and fricatives /b (d) g v ð z/. They were for the most part products of lenition and were therefore lenes. The final segment in /mab/ for example was the lenition product of /p/ in British */ma·pos/ > */mabos/ > /mab/. It is likely that the rule we have observed, namely stressed vowel + voiced: unstressed vowel + unvoiced, is a direct consequence of the new prosodic system. Before the prosodic shift historically voiced final consonants when in pausa were voiceless lenes. A lenis [p], for example, would have been weakly articulated

---

8   But see footnote 7 above.

like /b/ but it would still have been voiceless like /p/. When stressed vowels acquired an increased degree of intensity in their articulation during the prosodic shift, they became sufficiently strong to voice the following consonant. Unstressed vowels, however, lost intensity as the stressed vowels gained it. Unstressed vowels were accordingly quite unable to voice the following consonant. The voiceless lenes after unstressed vowels remained voiceless, therefore. Later when the opposition lenis ~ fortis disappeared such voiceless lenes fell together with the voiceless stops.

I have no doubt that in Cornish the alternation, stressed vowel + voiced stop ~ unstressed vowel + unvoiced stop, was present after the prosodic shift not only with *g/k* and *b/p* but also *d/t* (where they occurred—cf. *fowde, Dauit* above) and with the continuants *v/f*, *ð/θ* and *s/z*.

If these observations have any basis, then our pronunciation of Cornish will have to be revised radically. There can be no justification for such spellings as <whek>, <tek>, <gwrek>, <gwak>, <rak>, <prak>, <kyk>. These words will have to become <wheg>, <teg>, <gwreg>, <gwag>, <rag>, <prag>, <kyg>. Indeed such spellings with final <g> are common in Tudor Cornish. In addition items like *ef, nef, kyf, lef, scaf* will need to be pronounced with final /v/. More significantly perhaps, *lath* 'kill!', *coth* 'falls', *deth* 'day' will have to be pronounced with final /ð/. If Revised Cornish retains <dh> for /ð/, then such words will have to be spelt (as in LCB): *ladh, codh* and *dedh* (see 17.14 below). Revived Late Cornish already pronounces such words with final /ð/, even though it spells them with <th> (SGMC: xix).

8.20 Thomas believes that the initial segment in Middle Cornish *Ihesu(s), Jhesus, Jesus* is /j/ (1.1). This view was shared by Caradar who spells the name as *Yesu* in his translation of the gospel of St Mark. Indeed many revivalists continue to spell *Ihesus* as <Yesu>. In Old Cornish the name *Iesu* did indeed have an initial /j/ (see below), but this form was superseded in the Middle Cornish period by a variant in /dʒ/. The evidence for this later form is fourfold. In the first place one might expect initial /j/ on occasion to be spelt with <y>, as is the case with *yar* 'fowl' OM 129, *yagh* 'healthy' BM 713, *yeyn* 'cold' PC 1209, etc. **Yesus* is never attested in the Middle Cornish texts, however. Welsh *Iesu* 'Jesus' has an initial /j/. Not astonishingly the spellings <Yessu>, <Yiessu> are attested in Middle Welsh (WG: 27). The second reason for believing *Jhesus* to have initial /dʒ/ is related to the first. Initial inherited /j/ in Middle Cornish has a strong tendency to be lost. Examples include *ewnadow* 'desire' BM 30 for **yeunadow* as against *yenes* 'desire' OM 2125, PC 1046; *yethewon* 'Jews' PC 1252 but *eʒewon* PA 81a; **yeth* 'language' (Welsh *iaith*), which appears in Tregear as *eyth* TH 1. If the initial segment of *Jhesus* were /j/ one might expect **Esus* on occasion. This form is unattested in the Middle Cornish texts. Thirdly initial <I> or <J> as in *Jhesus, Ihesus* is customary in the Middle Cornish texts with the name *Johan, Jowan* 'John'. But in JCH Lhuyd spells the name *Jowan* as <Dzhuan>, that is to say as /dʒuən/. The fourth and most decisive reason is that Lhuyd spells the name *Jesu(s)* as <Dzeziu> (AB: 67b). This is presumably a spelling error for *Dzheziu* /'dʒeːzɪw/ and is unambiguous evidence that the name had initial /dʒ/. /'dʒezyz/ 'Jesus' in Cornish is almost certainly a borrowing from Breton.

Perhaps a digression is in order here on the nature of Cornish personal and local names. Welsh has a large number of proper names that have been inherited from British and/or Latin. Note, for example, the biblical names *Iesu* 'Jesus' < Lat. *Iesus*, *Mair* 'Mary' < Lat. *Maria*, *Iago* 'James' < Lat. *Iacobus*, *Ieuan* 'John' < *Iohannes*. Further Latin personal names in Welsh include *Tegid* < *Tacitus*, *Geraint* < *Gerontius* and *Emrys* < *Ambrosius*. Other Welsh place-names inherited from British/Latin include *Rhufain* 'Rome' < *Romania*, *Llydaw* 'Brittany' < *Letavia*, *Lloegr* 'England' < Proto-Celtic *(P)lesik-ro-* 'neighbouring land'. *Llundain* 'London' was borrowed early from Old English *Lunden*.

It is true that British/Latin names survive in Cornish for places outside Cornwall, for example, *Kembre* 'Wales' (CPNE: 48) and *Karesk* 'Exeter' (BF: 17). Early personal names survive in the language as well. Apart from saints' names one might mention *Casvelyn* 'Cassivellaunus' BM 1465, *Massen* 'Maximius' BM 3156 and *Pygys* BM 2463, a misreading for *Tygys* 'Tacitus'.[9] In many cases, however, British proper names seem to have been replaced in Middle Cornish by borrowings from Middle Breton, French and English: *Londres* 'London' (Loth 1900: 225); *Rome* BM 1344, TH 48; *Ynglonde*, *Englond* 'England' TH 51; *Bryten*, *Breton* 'Brittany' BM 1, 231; *Marya* 'Mary' PA 52a, etc. The reason for the loss of native names is not hard to find. From the ninth to the eleventh centuries Cornwall was dominated by Wessex and Cornish was under constant pressure from English. With the Norman invasion the influence of English declined but already many but the very commonest native names would have been lost. Gaps in the inventory of native names were naturally enough filled by French/Breton and English items. This is similar to the position in Ireland. Irish-speakers in County Galway, for example, know the Irish names for Galway and Dublin but use the English forms for the less common names, e.g. *Belfast*, *Donegal*, *Athlone* and *Westmeath*.

Middle and Tudor Cornish *Rome*, *Marya* and *Londres*, unlike their Welsh equivalents *Rhufain*, *Mair* and *Llundain*, are clearly not inherited from British or Anglo-Saxon but are later borrowings from Breton (< French) and Middle English. The same is therefore likely to be true of *Jhesus* and *Jowan*, etc., particularly since we know that the initial segment was /dʒ/ in later Cornish (see also 11.13). Initial /dʒ/ would have presented no problem to the Cornish, because they, unlike the Welsh, had a native phoneme /dʒ/ in initial position, for example, in *y gy* 'his house' and *yn jeves* 'he has' (see further 17.11).

Because personal names in Cornish can be either of British/Latin origin on the one hand or from Breton/French or Middle English on the other, the language sometimes exhibits variants of the same or related names in different

---

9 *Pygys* might also be a misreading for *Rygys* < *Ricatos* < *Rigicatos*.

guises. The names for *Jesus* and *John* in Cornish provide two such doublets. I know of three others and I list all five together below. The early forms (A) have initial /j/ or /∅/, while the later variants (B) have initial /dʒ/.

A. *Ponteisou* 'Bridge of Jesus' in parish of St Neot quoted in a document of 1241 (Hooper 1972: 4) < *pont* 'bridge' + *(I)esu* 'Jesus' < Latin *Iesu(s)*. This is the original form of the name *Panters Bridge*

B. *Dz[h]eziu* 'Jesus' (AB: 67b), *Ihesu* BM *passim*, *Jhesus* TH *passim*, *Jesus* SA 60a, 61a < Middle French *Jésus*, Middle Breton *Jesus*.

A. *Goluan* 'Midsummer, St John's Eve' (JRIC 1886: 11) < *gol* 'festival' < Latin *vigilia* 'vigil' + *(Y)owan* 'John' < Latin *Iohannes*; cf. *Leyowne* (Golant) < *Lann Yowan* 'Church of St John'

B. *Johann* PC 687, *Dzhuan* 'John' (AB: 251a), *Jooan* 'John' (BF: 15), *Jowan* TH 41a < Middle English and Middle French *Johan* < Latin *Iohannes*.

A. *deyow* PA 41c, *deow* SA 66, *De Ieu* (AB: 54c) 'Thursday'< Latin *dies Iouis* 'day of Jupiter/Jove' (Note: *J* in *Market Jew* 'Thursday market' is from the Old Cornish form *Marchadyow*; the Middle Cornish form is seen in *Marghas Yow* PC 2668)

B. *Iovyn* ' Jove' PC 1292, 1363, BM 3406 < Middle English *Jovine* < Latin **Iouinus* < *Iouis, Iouem*.

A. *St Yuste* 'St Just' (PNWP: 81); *Pluyust* (16th century; CPNE: 295), *pleu Yst* 'parish of St Just' (AB: 222); *Venton Ust* 'St Just's Well' (PNWP: 19); *Est* 'St Just' (AB: 249c); *Laneast* (parish) < Latin *Iustus*

B. *Justine* 'Justin' SA 64 < Latin *Iustinus* < *iustus* 'just'; cf. *Iustis* 'justice' PA 92a, *Justys* 'justice' TH 15 < Latin *iustitia* 'tribunal' < Latin *iustus* 'just'.

A. *Yethewon* 'Jews' RD 2406, *Eʒow* 'Jew' PA 182b, *Eʒewon* 'Jews' PA 63a, *Edheuon* 'Jews' (AB: 73c) < Latin *Iudaeus* 'Jew' < Hebrew *Yehudah* 'Judah'

B. *Jewys* 'Jews' TH 16a < Middle English *Jeue(s)* < Anglo-French *Geu* < Latin *Iudaeus* < Hebrew *Yehudah* 'Judah'; cf. *Iudy* 'Judaea' RD 10 < Middle English *Judy* < Latin *Iudaea* < Hebrew *Yehudah* 'Judah'.

The view that /j/ in Middle Cornish *Jesus, Jowan*, etc., became /dʒ/ in the later language is without foundation. In the first place /j/ has a tendency to weaken to zero in the Middle Cornish period (for example in *Yethewon* > *Ethewon*, *Yust* > *Ust* above), whereas the alleged shift /j/ > /dʒ/ would on the contrary have involved reinforcement not weakening. In the second place, if /j/ had become /dʒ/ in *Jesus* and *Jowan*, it would have become /dʒ/ in *yagh* 'healthy', *yeyn* 'cold', *younk* 'young', etc. Forms with /dʒ/ in such words would be spelt with initial <j>, <g> or <dzh> in Late Cornish. Such forms do not occur.

In sum: *Jowan, Jesus*, etc. were pronounced with initial /dʒ/ in Middle Cornish and should be so pronounced in the revived language.

8.21 There is some evidence that the initial segment of the word for 'January' is /dʒ/ in Late Cornish. Lhuyd writes <genver> with initial <g> for /dʒ/ (AB: 67a). See further SDMC: 54. The Cornish *Genver* itself is probably not derived directly from Latin *Ianuarius*, **Ienarius*, since that would have given something like **yener* in Cornish. It is more likely that *Genver* /'dʒenvər/ is borrowed from a dialectal Breton form with initial /dʒ/. Alternatively the initial segment in Cornish may have been contaminated by English *January*.

8.22 Metathesis of /r/ and /n/ is very common in later Cornish both in stressed and unstressed syllables. I have noticed the following examples: *perna* 'buy' (AB: 56c) < *prena*, *kerna* 'tremble' (AB: 166a) < *crena*; *leddarn* 'robbers' (BF: 17) < *ladron*; *yborn* 'sky' < *ebron* CW 82; *debarn* 'itch' (AB: 145a) < *debron*.

Such metathesis was probably made possible by the prosodic shift. The word *prena* 'buy' before the shift would have had a half-long vowel. It would therefore have been unlikely to metathesize the initial sonant, which would have been too far from the following one to be captured by it. After the shift the vowel in *prena* was short and as a result /r/ was close enough to /n/ to undergo metathesis.

The same kind of analysis can be used to explain *leddarn*, etc. After the shift the final unstressed sequence in such etyma would have become /rən/ or /ræn/ where syllabic onset and nucleus were difficult to distinguish. A metathesized spelling is symptomatic of such ambiguity.

CHAPTER 9
Pre-occlusion

9.1 In words like *pen* /pen:/ 'head', *cam* /kam/ 'bent', *benneth* /'ben:eθ/ 'blessing' and *omma* /oma/ 'here' the stressed vowel was short but the following nasal, /n:/ or /m/, was long. We can assume that the syllable in /pen:/ had three morae, the vowel being one mora in length and the long /n:/ two. When the prosodic shift occurred, stressed syllables gained in vigour. As a result /pen:/ did not become /pen/, since there was the risk that the loss of the opposition *n* ~ *n*: might render too many words too similar to one another. Instead relative duration was reinterpreted as relative intensity and the nasal acquired a partially stopped pronunciation: a homorganic stop appeared immediately before the nasal coda. The whole complex /en:/ > /eᵈn/ retained three morae but was articulated with greater emphasis than previously. This unexploded consonant can be represented as [ᵈn]. The [ᵈ] is not a full [d]. Contact is made between the tongue and the teeth-ridge but no air is expelled—as would be the case with a full plosive. As soon as the airflow is stopped, the nasal is coda articulated. The same thing occurred with *cam* /kam/ which acquired a unexploded [ᵇ] in front of it: [kaᵇm].

The phenomenon of the unexploded homorganic stop is known as pre-occlusion and is a distinctive feature of western Cornish. In more easterly Cornish it is probable that the opposition /n/ ~ /n:/ had already been lost before the prosodic shift. In consequence pre-occlusion could not occur (5.6 and 9.6).

Since pre-occlusion represents an increase in articulatory vigour, it can occur in stressed syllables only. It will normally arise only where /n:/ is historically long, as for example, in *pedn* < **pennos*, *gwydn* 'white' < **windos* (Old Irish *find*), *bedneth* < *ben'dict(io)*, *cabm* < **kambos*, etc. If a syllable had been shortened early by a following yod, pre-occlusion could occur: *vargidniaz* 'bargained' < *bargidnia* < *bargin:ja* < *barginya*. Pre-occlusion did not occur when the nasal was followed by a stop. Thus one finds *medn* 'he wishes' with pre-occlusion but *menta* 'thou wishest' without it.

The definite article /an/ has a historically long nasal < **(s)indos*, yet the article is never pre-occluded. This is because it is always in proclitic position and unstressed. The proclitic nature of the Cornish article is guaranteed by such forms as *an chy* < /an tʃi:/ where assibilation has occurred across word boundary. In Cornish the article was not a separate 'word' that could be pre-occluded but a unstressed particle attached to its following substantive.

The numeral *un* /y(:)n/ 'one' used with nouns, unlike the definite article does not appear to have been a proclitic. Historically *un* had a short /n/ and a long vowel < Common Celtic **oinos*, yet it is regularly pre-occluded in Cornish:

try person yn idn dewges 'three persons in one deity' CW 6; *comprehendys in vdn dew* 'comprehended in one God' CW 11. It is likely that the use of *un* with a following substantive caused the vowel to shorten early. As a result the nasal was lengthened and pre-occlusion could take place: /y:n dɪw/ > /yn: dɪw/ > /ɪᵈn dew/.

9.2 If a vowel before single /n/ was half-long until the prosodic shift, it shortened thereafter and the following /n/ was often written double as a way of showing the short vowel. Since the nasal was not historically long it was not pre-occluded. This is apparent from Late Cornish spelling. The following are examples of <nn> without pre-occlusion in late sources: *e vonnin* < *y honen* 'himself' (BF: 52, 53); *nabonnen* 'someone' < *nebonen* (JCH § 34); *bennen* < *benen* 'woman' (JCH § 1, BF: 43); *gennam* 'with me' < *genama* (BF: 53); *gennan* 'with us' < *genen* 'with us' (JCH § 14); *genn'o* 'with you' < *genough* (BF: 46); *enna* 'there' < *ena* (JCH §§ 13, 19, 22, 41); *hinneth* 'generation' < *henath* (BF: 55).

Similarly the etymon *amanen* 'butter' which has a short /n/ appears with <nn> in place-names but without pre-occlusion: *Enysmannen* < *enys amanen* (Sancreed), *Park-Mannin* < *park amanen* (Mabe). Note further the two place-names *Zennor* < personal name *Senarius*, *Sennen* < Old Irish personal name *Senán*, a derivative of *sen-* 'old'; cf. *hen*. These toponyms occur in the area of maximum pre-occlusion. They are both spelt with <nn> but neither shows pre-occlusion.

The opposition seen in /n/ ~ /n:/ is absent from the labial nasal /m/ and for the following reason: /m/ is equivalent to /n:/. Lenited or short *m* has already become /v/ by the Old Cornish period. Since /m/ wherever it occurs etymologically is the reflex of earlier /m:/ as in *mam* 'mother' < **mamma* or /mb/ as in *cam* 'bent' < **kambo-*, it is always likely to be pre-occluded after a short vowel in those dialects that have pre-occlusion.

9.3 GKK says of the word <alena> 'thence' s.v.: 'NB incorrectly spelled by Nance; the etymology indicates <n>, and if it had contained /nn/, it would have become **aledna* in LateC.' The criticism of Nance is unjustified. Although the spelling <alenna> is not attested in Middle Cornish, it does occur in the later period, for Rowe writes: *Ha moaze a lenna* 'and he went thence' (RC 23: 191). Rowe regularly indicates pre-occlusion in writing, for example, in *radn* 'part', *aprodnies* 'aprons', *pedn* 'head', *avednaz* < **(g)ovynas* 'asked'. It is apparent, therefore, that in this word <nn> and /ᵈn/ are not one and the same. Lhuyd cites *alene* from the Middle Cornish texts with a single *n* (AB: 227b). On the other hand he gives the related etyma *A dhenna* (< ** adhya ena*), *enna*, *nenna* all glossing *inde* 'thence' with double <nn> but without pre-occlusion (AB: 71a).

<Alena> with a single <n> is not mere scribal conservatism. It is the customary spelling in Middle Cornish because scribes did not wish to write <nn> lest it be thought that /ᵈn/ were intended. Nance was nonetheless

justified in spelling the word <alenna> in order to emphasize that the stressed vowel was short. In so doing he was following Jenner, who cites 'thence' as *alenna, en mes alenna* (HCL: 152). The view expressed in GKK that the stressed syllable in <alenna> would have been pre-occluded is mistaken. Two quite separate phenomena are being confused, namely pre-occlusion before historically long /nː/ and the gemination of <n> as a graphemic device to show a shortened vowel.

9.4 Since pre-occlusion is a direct result of the new prosodic system, it cannot be very much later. Pre-occlusion is not shown in writing until the sixteenth century, however. There are three instances of *bedneth* 'blessing' in BM at lines 198, 225 and 226. The first part of the text is in a different hand and later than the main body of the text written in 1504. Padel cites *Pednanpill* in Feock from 1597 (CPNE: 290). It is clear from the evidence given by Pool (PNWP) that pre-occlusion was often not written even until the seventeenth century. Pool gives *Boskennan* from 1570 but *Boskednan* from 1623, for example.

Incidentally the name *Boskednan* cannot contain either *kenen* 'reeds' or *conyn* 'rabbit', as Pool suggests, since neither etymon has a historic /nː/. I should prefer to derive it from *bos + cenin* 'wild garlic' (cf. Old Welsh *cennin* 'ramsons' and Ir *cainnenn* 'leek'). GKK says of *kenin* 'garlic, ramsons':

> Although W has <nn>, the C could not have contained /nn/, or the word would have had [dn] in LateC; but Lhuyd wrote *kinin* (GKK: 160-61).

If *Boskednan* is for *bos kennin* 'settlement of ramsons', GKK is mistaken, and the word could be spelt with <nn>.

9.5 I believe that the more easterly parts of Cornwall lost the opposition /n/ ~ /nː/ before the prosodic shift and as a result pre-occlusion could not occur there. I take pre-occlusion to be a western phenomenon. Pre-occlusion is well attested in Late Cornish which is by its very nature western in provenance. Moreover if we examine the place-name evidence closely we see that pre-occlusion is confined to the western part of Cornwall. Having collected all the certain examples of pre-occlusion from the index of CPNE, I have supplied them all with an etymology where possible and have put them in alphabetical order of the parish or town in which they occur. The result is as follows:

Chytodden < chy war an ton (Breage)
Pengwedna < pen ?Gwenna (Breage)
Chytodden < chy war an don (Camborne)
Pencobben < pen *comm (Camborne)
Chegwidden < chy gwyn (Constantine)
Crack-an-Godna < crak an godna (Constantine)
Park-an-Gubman < park an *goumman (Constantine)
Park-an-Toddan < park an ton (Constantine)

PRE-OCCLUSION

Park-Cabben < *park cam* (Constantine)
Park Tobma < *park tom* (Constantine)
Pedn Billy < *pen byly* (Constantine)
Penbothidnow < *pen + budinnow* (Constantine)
Polgwidden Cove < *poll gwyn* (Constantine)
The Ladden < *?glan* (Crowan)
Pednanpill Point < *pen an *pyll* (Feock)
Porthgwidden < *porth gwyn* (Feock)
Pednvadan < *pen tal van* (Gerrans)
Ingewidden < *hensy wyn* (Grade)
Polgwidden < *poll gwyn* (Grade)
Carnaquidden < *kernyk gwyn* (Gulval)
Cascadden < *casek gan* (Gwennap)
Menergwidden < *meneth gwyn* (Gwennap)
Tolvaddon < *tal van* (Illogan)
Landewednack < *lann to-Winnok* (Landewednack)
Kilcobben Cove < **kyl *comm* (Landewednack)
Peddenporperre < *pen + ?* (Landewednack)
The Gabmas < *camas* (Lelant)
Pedndrea < *pen an dre* (Lelant)
Porth Kidney Sands < *pol cumyas* (Lelant)
Menwidden < *men wyn* (Ludgvan)
Nangidnall < *gun aswy enyall* (Madron)
Pednpons < *pen pons* (Madron)
Pedn Venton < *pen-fenten* (Madron)
Todne Rosemoddress < *ton* + PN (Madron)
Trewidden < *tre wyn* (Madron)
Lo Cabm < *loch cam* (Mullion)
Pedn Crifton < *pen ?*crygh* (Mullion)
Crockagodna < *crak an gonna* (Mylor)
Park Tuban < *park tom* (Paul)
Pedn Bejuffin < *pen + mydzhovan* (Paul)
Pedn Tenjack < *pen denjack* (Paul)
Pedn y coanse < *pen an *cawns* (Paul)
Todden Coath < *ton coth* (Paul)
Street an Dudden < *stret an don* (Penzance)
Blankednick < *blyn + ?* (Perrananaworthal)
Codnidne < *conna yn* (Perranzabuloe)
Pedn-an-drea < *pen an dre* (Redruth)
Pednanvounder < *pen an vounder* (Ruan Major)
Chirgwidden < *chy gour gwyn* (Sancreed)
Codnagooth < *conna goth* (Sancreed)
Cudedno < *cudynnow* (Scilly)
Enys Dodnan < *enys don* (Sennen)
Pedden an wollas < *pen an wlas* (Sennen)
Croc-an-codna < *crak an gonna* (Sithney)
Cudno < *conna* (Sithney)
Pednavounder < *pen an vounder* (Sithney)
Prospidnack < **prys *pynnek* (Sithney)

Taban Denty < *tam denty* (Sithney)
Ventonvedna < *fenten *fenna* (Sithney)
Chytodden < *chy ton* (St Agnes)
Codna-coos < *conna cos* (St Agnes)
Godna < *conna* (St Anthony in Meneage)
Codna Willy < *conna whilan* (St Buryan)
Pridden < **pen-ryn* (St Buryan)
Parke an Clibmier < *park an colomyer* (St Erth)
Park Todden < *park ton* (St Ewe)
Brevadnack < *bre vannek* (St Hilary)
Tolvadden < *tal van* (St Hilary)
Pedn Olva < *pen guilva* (St Ives)
Porth Gwidden < *porth gwyn* (St Ives)
Balleswidden < *bal + ?* (St Just in Penwith)
Cargodna < *crak an gonna* (St Just in Penwith)
Cudna Reeth < *conna ruth* (St Just in Penwith)
Leswidden < *lys gwyn* (St Just in Penwith)
Marcradden < *men crom* (St Just in Roseland)
Chywednack < *chy wynnek* (St Keverne)
Frogabbin < *forth gam* (St Keverne)
Gull Gwidden < *gwel gwyn* (St Keverne)
Laddenvean < **lann vyghan* (St Keverne)
Pednavounder < *pen an vounder* (St Keverne)
Pedn-myin < *pen men* (St Keverne)
Pedn Tiere < *pen-tyr* (St Keverne)
Polpidnick < *pol *pennek* (St Keverne)
Pednvounder < *pen an vounder* (St Levan)
Carlidna < *kelennow* (St Mawgan in Meneage)
Carnwidden < *carn gwyn* (Stithians)
Amalwhidden < *amal gwyn* (Towednack)
Beagletodn < *begel tom* (Towednack)
Chytodden < *chy ton* (Towednack)
Park Gwidden < *park gwyn* (Towednack)
Skillywadden < *? + gwan* (Towednack)
Towednack < *to-Winnok* (Towednack)
Street Eden < *stret yn* (Truro)
Carn Pednathan < *carn pen ethen* (Veryan)
Calvadnack < *kal vannek* (Wendron)
Crackagodna < *crak an gonna* (Wendron)
Garlidna < *grelynyow* (Wendron)
Roselidden < *ros *lyn* (Wendron)
Boswednack < *bos wynnek* (Zennor)
Pedenleda < *pen lether* (Zennor)
Pedn Kei < *pen ky* (Zennor).

Apart from one stray each in Veryan, St Ewe and Perranzabuloe, none is further east than Truro. Moreover it is clear that the names with pre-occlusion are particularly numerous in the far west. This cannot simply be because

74

Cornish survived longer in the west than further east, since pre-occlusion is also recorded in Scilly, where the language died early, and it is also apparent that Cornish was spoken as far as the Tamar until the 15th century at least (see 11.1-5). Moreover the toponym *Polpidnick* in St Keverne < *pol pennek* shows pre-occlusion but not -*ack* < -*ek*. Since -*ack* does not normally occur in toponyms before the sixteenth century, we must assume that pre-occlusion is earlier than Tudor Cornish. In which case its absence from central and eastern Cornwall cannot be explained chronologically, for the language probably survived everywhere in Cornwall until the Reformation (11.6-15). It is much more likely that the presence or absence of pre-occlusion is a dialect feature (see also Map I, p. 330).

9.6 Stokes believed that BM in its entirety was written by the same hand. The scribe (if that is what he was) signs himself *Dominus Rad. Ton* and says that he finished the work in 1504. *Rad.Ton* may be for *Ricardus Ton*. There was a cleric of that name who was priest of Crowan near Camborne in 1537. The manuscript of BM has three examples of pre-occlusion in the first couple of hundred lines of the play.

CW was written in Helston by William Jordan in 1611. He was clearly copying from an earlier exemplar but much of the spelling may well be Jordan's own. CW has several examples of pre-occlusion. Here are some instances: *idn* 'one' 6, *vdn* 'one' 11 *pan vidnaf* 'when I will' 36, *pedn* 'head' 182, 916, 1090, *thybma* 'to me' 570, *na gybmar* 'take not' 692, *tabm* 'bit' 775.

BM written in 1504 has three examples of pre-occlusion. Jordan writing in Helston in 1611 has in 2548 lines about 25 examples. John Tregear's homilies were written *c.* 1555-60, that is to say, roughly in the same period as BM and CW. They are the longest single Cornish text we have and contain approximately 30,000 words. Yet not once does Tregear exhibit any example of pre-occlusion. It is likely therefore that Tregear came from the Cornish-speaking area where pre-occlusion did not occur, i.e. well to the east of Truro. It has been suggested that Tregear may have come from Newlyn East. His dialect certainly supports this view.

SA is relatively short yet it has one apparent instance of pre-occlusion: at 59 it has <mamb> for <mam> 'mother'. I take this spelling to represent [ma^{b}m]. If this view is correct, then the author of SA, unlike his contemporary John Tregear, was probably of westerly provenance.

Forms without pre-occlusion occur alongside those with pre-occlusion in Late and therefore western Cornish. I have mentioned above that dialects without pre-occlusion lowered /e/ > /a/ before /n/. We have an excellent example of the complementary distribution of [e^{d}n] and [an] in Lhuyd's *hana, hedda* (< *hedna*) 'that man, he' (AB: 73b).

CHAPTER 10
The alternation $s/z \sim g/j$

10.1 It has long been noticed that the spellings *crysy, crygy*, 'believe', *wose, woge* 'after', etc. alternate in Middle Cornish. There have been several attempts to explain such alternation. Lhuyd, and following him Jenner, believed that the /dʒ/ of *cregy* /ˈkredʒɪ/ was a "softening" of the earlier /z/, written <s>. It is unmistakeable that /dʒ/ is common in Late Cornish, whereas /z/ <s> seems to be the norm in the earlier language. This view was also held by Nance and has apparently been espoused by most observers until recently. By this view /z/ was Middle Cornish, /dʒ/ was "Late Cornish".

10.2 It is quite obvious, however, that the /dʒ/ in *cregy* 'believe' cannot possibly be a "softening" of /z/ and for two reasons. In the first place, if /z/ really did become /dʒ/ in the later language, one would expect every example of /z/ to become /dʒ/. *Sowznack* 'English' should be **Sowgnak, preezyo* 'praise' should be **preedzhyo*, etc. In the second place, the phonetic development /z/ > /dʒ/ is difficult, not to say impossible, to explain. There is no problem with /z/ > /ʒ/ and indeed such a shift is a regular occurrence in English. We say *erase* /ɪˈreiz/ but *erasure* /ɪˈreiʒə/. But /dʒ/ is an affricate, that is, a consonant cluster which begins as a plosive and ends as a continuant. It is difficult to see where the plosive element originated if in Cornish /z/ really did develop into /dʒ/.

10.3 George, taking up a suggestion made first by Loth, offered a different solution. He pointed out that variants like *wose/woge, ese/ege* were widespread in the texts. He suggested therefore that the graphs <s> and <g> or <i> (for <j>), which seemed to be in free variation, actually represented a sound that was neither /z/ nor /dʒ/ but rather a palatalized kind of *d* (perhaps [dʲ]). This he wrote as <dj> and suggested it be pronounced similarly to the *d + y* in groups like English *I bid you*. George also recommended introducing into Cornish a similar voiceless consonant <tj> (perhaps [tʲ]) which was to appear in words like *kerentja* 'love' and *an tji* 'the house'.

Now there are serious theoretical objections to this hypothesis of Loth that was adopted by George. I have set them out elsewhere (Williams 2006a) and do not wish to explain them all at length here. Three are enough. In the first place the graphs <s> and <g> are not in free variation in the texts. They overlap, but are nonetheless distinct in distribution. The second objection is this: in words in which *s/g* alternate in Cornish, Welsh and Breton have /d/. Cornish *wose/woge* 'after' is the exact equivalent of Welsh *wedi* and Breton *goude*. Similarly *gallosek/gallogek* 'powerful' is the same as Breton *galloudek*. In

76

final position original /d/ in Cornish has become /s/, as for example in Cornish *tas* 'father', Welsh *tad*, Breton *tad*; Cornish *cos* 'wood', W *coed*, Breton *koad*. The shift **wode* > *wose/woge* must be closely related to the shift *tad* > *tas*. Yet if the Loth-George hypothesis were correct, one would be /d/ > /dʲ/ and the other /d/ > /s/, two apparently unrelated changes.

There is a further objection to the Loth-George hypothesis: if George had been right, then *caswyth* 'thicket', *logosek* 'full of mice', *aswy* 'gap', **gwlesyk* 'chieftain' would have been **cadjwyth*, **logodjek*, **adjwa* and **gwledjek*. They would appear in place-names either with a medial /d/ or possibly /dʒ/. It is true that in west Cornwall forms with *j/g* in such etyma are attested. In more easterly place-names these etyma appear with <s> or <ss>, as in *Tregaswith*, *Trelogossick*, *Assawine* and *Trelissick*. /dʲ/ could not possibly have appeared in place-names as <s> or <ss>. To attempt to derive <s>, <ss> in English language place-names from Cornish **/dʲ/ is fruitless. The conclusion to be drawn from place-names with <s> or <ss> is that /dʲ/ does not occur in such place-names because it never existed in Cornish at all.

10.4 My own explanation for the alternation *s/g* is as follows. I assume that the shift of Old Cornish **tat* /tad/ > Middle Cornish *tas* and of Old Cornish *bochodoc* > Middle Cornish *boghosek/boghogek* were closely related. In early Middle Cornish at the end of syllables /d/ was affricated to /dz/. This is an intelligible phonetic shift. Something like it occurs English in the urban speech of Liverpool, for example, where *good and bad* is approximately /gʊdz ən baːdz/. In certain collocations division into syllables took place across word boundary. For this reason *an devan* 'the devil' became *an dzevan*. A similar phenomenon occurred with /n/ + /t/ in the expression *an ti* 'the house' which became *an tsi*.

In Cornish in final position the /dz/ was simplified to /z/ written <s>. Actually the /z/ was more of a lenis /s/ than /z/, but for our purposes here that is a detail. Internally /dz/ simplified to /z/ in some dialects of Cornish: this resulted in forms like /boˈxozek/ 'poor'. Others palatalized the second element of /dz/ to /dʒ/ before the group could simplify. As a result the group became /dʒ/ as in /boˈxodʒek/. Thus the two forms *boghosek* and *boghogek* were dialectal variants. *An dzevan* and *an tsi* seem to have palatalized everywhere to give /an ˈdʒevan/ *an gevan* 'the demon' and /an tʃiː/ *an chy* 'the house'.

10.5 There is good evidence that until the Reformation, i.e. the middle of the sixteenth century, Cornish was probably spoken as far as the Tamar (see 11.6-15 below). In this area the dialects that preferred *g/j* to *s/z* were the westerly ones. Since our remains of Late Cornish are exclusively western Late Cornish has a marked preference for *g/j* over *s/z*. Literary Cornish probably arose in central Cornwall and preferred *s/z* (written <s>). Thus the medieval texts have <s> where Late Cornish often has *d/g*. The opposition between *g/j* and *s/z* is not clear-cut. Late Cornish has plenty of examples in s/z and there are place-names quite far to the east of Cornish-speaking Cornwall that show g/j. Nonetheless the alternation can be used to establish two main dialect areas.

The patron saint of Camborne is of course Meriasek and in the play he is always known as *Meryasek* spelt with <s>. People who used to bathe in St Meriasek's Well in Camborne in the hope of being cured of their ailments were known as *Merrasicks* or *Merrasickers*. This name clearly contains the name of the saint. Yet such devotees of the saint were also known as *Moragicks* or *Mearagaks* and the inhabitants of Camborne themselves were called *Merry-geeks* or *Mera-jacks*. These forms are Anglicizations of the variant *Meryagek*. Since both *Meryasek* and *Meryagek* are associated with Camborne, it may be that the s-dialect and the g-dialect met in the Camborne area.

This seems likely on the basis of place-names. I have collected placenames containing five different etyma 1) *aswy* 'gap'; 2) **caswith* 'thicket'; 3) *logosen* 'mouse'/*logosek* 'place of mice'; 4) **gwelsek* 'grassy'; 5) the personal names *Cadoc, Madoc*. The place-names in question, which are all derived from CPNE, are as follows (I list the forms in g/j after the diagonal stroke):

1) *Assa Govrankowe* (Gwennap 1580), *Assawine* (Illogan? 1582) / *Adga Bullocke* (Lelant), *Adgewella* (Camborne), *Adgyan Frank* (Constantine 1649), *Adgaporth* (Madron 1614), *Adjawinjack* (Ruan Major), *Agahave* (Ruan Major), *Aja-Bullocke* (Perranuthnoe), *Aga-Gai* (Sennen), *Agareeth* (St Hilary 1665), *Nangidnall* (< *Goone Agga Idniall* 1670) (Madron)
2) *Tregaswith* (St Columb Major), *Rosecassa* (St Just in Roseland) / *Cadgwith* (Grade), *Trecadgwith* (St Buryan)
3) *Trelogossick* (Veryan), *Legossick* (St Issey) / *Parken Legagen* (St Keverne 1710)
4) *Carwalsick* (St Stephen in Brannel) / *Illiswilgig* (Scilly)
5) *Ventongassick* (St Just in Roseland), *Roscarrack* (< **Ros Casek*) (Budock), cf. *Polmassick* (< pons + Madoc) (St Ewe) / *Porth-cadjack Cove* (Illogan).

The consistency of the distribution is quite remarkable. Noteworthy also is the presence *Illiswilgig* < *gwelsek*/*gwelgek* 'grassy' in Scilly. Since Cornish died out in the sixteenth century in the islands, we have clear evidence that g/j is dialectal and has little to do with chronology.

The distribution is even more striking when seen on the relevant map (Map II, p. 330). There can, I think, be little doubt that we have here uncovered a significant dialect isogloss in Cornish. As we have seen, pre-occlusion provides us with another that likewise differentiates east from west (9.5).

More recently George has made an attempt to revise his original hypothesis concerning the alternation between s and j. It is to this I now turn.

CHAPTER 11
Cornish in eastern Cornwall

11.1 In April 1989 George gave a lecture in St Erth on dialect in Cornish as part of the 14th 'Cornish Weekend'. The event was reported in Welsh by Robat ap Tomos in *Carn* 66: 11, as follows:

Rhan arbennig o ddiddorol o'r penwythnos i mi oedd sgwrs gan y Dr. Ken George ynghylch tystiolaeth newydd sydd yn awgrymu bod rhai o'r gwahaniaethau rhwng Cernyweg Canol a Chernyweg Diweddar efallai yn ganlyniad i wahaniaethau mewn tafodieithoedd ardaloedd gwahanol yn hytrach na newidiau yn yr iaith dros amser. Er enghraifft mae rhai geiriau a sillefir gydag 's' (sain 'z') gan fwyaf yn y llenyddiaeth Gernyweg Canol e.e. crysy 'credu', yn cael eu sillafu â 'j', 'g', 'gg' (sain 'j') yng Nghernyweg Diweddar. Y golwg traddodiadol yw bod y sain wedi newid rhwng y cyfnod canol (tua 1500) a'r cyfnod diweddar (tua 1700), ac esbonir hyn gan gyfeirio at enwau lleoedd lle mae'r 'j' yn y gorllewin pell yn ardal Penzance yn cyfateb i 's' yn yr un elfennau mewn enwau yn ardal Truro lle diflannodd yr iaith cyn i'r newid ddigwydd. Ond ar ôl archwilio dosbarthiad yr 's' a'r 'j' mewn dramâu unigol gwelwyd mewn ambell ddrama ma 'j' (neu lythyren gyfatebol) a ddefnyddid bron bob amser yn y geiriau hyn, ond 's' a geir yn gyffredinol yn y rhan fwyaf o ddramâu. Mae awgrym yma bod rhai o'r dramâu wedi cael eu hysgrifennu gan bobl oedd yn seinio'r iaith ychydig yn wahanol, pobl oedd yn siarad tafodiaith wahanol efallai. A phan gyplysir hyn â'r amrywio rhwng 's' a 'j' mewn elfennau cyfatebol rhai enwau lleoedd sydd yn rhannu gorllewin Cernyw yn ddwy; gwelir peth tystiolaeth o blaid tafodieithoedd daearyddol yn y Gernyweg gyda datblygiadau gwahanol o 'd' hanesyddol. Ategir hyn gan y ffaith nad ydyw patrwm dosbarthiad yr 's/j' mewn enwau lleoedd yn cyfateb yn hollol i batrwm diflaniad yr iaith e.e. credir bod yr iaith wedi marw ar Ynysoedd Syllan (Scilly) yng nghyfnod Cernyweg Canol ond ceir enwau lleoedd yno sydd yn cynnwys seiniau nodweddiadol o Gernyweg Diweddar, e.e. Pednathise, Pednbrose, Rosevear, Illiswilgig, Melledgan. Mae llawer iawn o ymchil i'w wneud yn y maes yma eto.

[To me a particularly interesting part of the week-end was a talk by Dr Ken George about new evidence that suggests that some of the differences between Middle Cornish and Late Cornish are perhaps a result of variation in the dialects of different areas rather than changes in the language over time. For example some words that are spelt with 's' (pronounced 'z') for the most part in Middle Cornish literature, e.g. crysy 'believe', are spelt with 'j', 'g', 'gg' (pronounced 'j') in Late Cornish. The traditional view was that the sound had changed between the Middle period (*c.* 1500) and the Modern period (*c.* 1700), and this is explained by reference to the place-names where 'j' in the far west in the region of Penzance corresponds to 's' in the same elements in place-names in the Truro region, where the language disappeared before the change took place. But as a result of research on the distribution of 's' and 'j' in individual plays it was noticed that 'j' (or equivalent letter) was almost always used in these words, but 's' is found usually in the bulk of the plays. There is a suggestion here that some of the plays were written by people who spoke the language slightly differently, people who spoke a different dialect perhaps. And when this is linked with the variation between 's' and 'j' in equivalent place-names that divide western Cornwall in two parts, one sees a degree of evidence for geographical dialect in Cornish *vis à vis* the development of historic 'd'. This view is supported by the fact that the pattern of distribution of 's/j' in place-names does not correspond completely with the pattern of the disappearance of the language, e.g. it is believed that the language died out in Scilly in the Middle Cornish period but place-names are found there that contain distinctively Late Cornish sounds, for example, Pednathise, Pednbrose, Rosevear, Illiswilgig, Melledgan. There is much research to be done in this field.]

This account by Ap Tomos is lucidly written. It suggests that in April 1989 George, having read my then unpublished article (Williams 2006a), not only espoused my views on the *s/j* isogloss completely but was prepared to expound them publicly. Indeed he even added examples of his own from Scilly.

11.2 Since then George has changed his mind. He now believes that phonological differences in place-names are a function of the disappearance of Cornish from eastern and central Cornwall earlier than in the far west (George 1992). George would now divide Cornwall into three distinct areas. The most easterly is from the Tamar to a line runnning north-south from Boscastle to Looe. The second is from this imaginary line to another drawn from St Austell Bay to Newquay. The third is Cornwall to the west of this second line. In the first area, according to George, Cornish died out in the Old Cornish period, in the second in the Middle Cornish period, and in the third in recent times.

I believe George is right when he divides Cornwall into three toponymic areas, even though I would perhaps take issue slightly with the size and shape of his three regions. He is not right, I think, in believing that Cornish died out in the most easterly area in the Old Cornish period, i.e. before *c.* 1250. The evidence suggests to me that Cornish was spoken by a proportion of the population at least as far as the Tamar until the fifteenth century, if not until the Reformation. This view is not my own, for it was originally put forward by Henry Jenner.[10] Indeed Loth adduced evidence to suggest that Cornish was spoken in part of Devonshire as late as the fourteenth century (RC 34: 180-81).

---

10 "It is highly probable, from the number of places still retaining undoubtedly Celtic names, and retaining them in an undoubtedly Cornish form, that until at least the fifteenth century the Tamar awas the general boundary of English and Cornish." HCL: 11)

Jenner believed that Cornish was spoken as far east as the Tamar until the 15th century, because of the high incidence of Celtic place-names in Cornish form as far as the border with Devonshire. I have no doubt that Jenner was right in this matter. In the far east of Cornwall, however, in particular, toponyms usually exhibit Old Cornish unassibilated *-nt* for later *-ns*, (e.g. *Trewint* < *tre wint* 'windy settlement' in St Minver) and with *d*/*t* (e.g. *Trequite* < *tre cuit* 'settlement of the wood' in St Germans) for later *s*. This has led commentators to assume that Cornish died out in eastern Cornwall in the Old Cornish period. Such a view is in my opinion mistaken, as I hope to demonstrate below.

11.3 It is a common error of Anglophones to believe that the Celtic languages have always been in retreat. They find it difficult to credit that any Celtic language was ever in a position to expand and absorb other languages. Yet Gaelic in Scotland absorbed both Brythonic and Pictish. In Ireland by the fourteenth century Irish had almost swamped English completely. British underwent a revival after the departure of the Romans and later Welsh replaced English in the Anglian colonies of the north Welsh coast.

Similarly the idea of a continuous retreat of Cornish is quite misleading and does not correspond with the evidence we have. From the Norman Conquest to the Reformation there was no steady decline in Cornish. Quite the opposite. I believe that in the first century or so after the Conquest English was in decline in Cornwall and Cornish was in the ascendant. I have several reasons for this view.

We know from the Bodmin Manumissions that in the tenth and eleventh centuries the class of landowners in and around Bodmin were Saxons speaking Old English. Moreover Cornwall from the tenth century onwards was ecclesiastically part of Wessex. Cornwall's bishop and many of his clergy were English-speaking. By the thirteenth century, however, Cornwall was producing mystery plays on a large scale for a largely monoglot Cornish audience. Those who wrote, transcribed and staged these plays must have been clerics and must have been Cornish-speakers.

If we look at our surviving Cornish literature we can see that it is based on French and Breton models and owes little to Middle English. We can assume that in the generation or so after the conquest, Saxon landowners and Saxon clerics were replaced by French-speakers and more importantly by Bretons. There is good evidence for a large influx of Bretons into Cornwall after the Conquest. Indeed some speak not of the "Norman Invasion" but of the "Armorican return". William the Conqueror made the Breton, Robert earl of Mortain, ruler of Cornwall. Bretons appear as holders of manors already in the Domesday Survey. Among Bretons known to have received grants of land in Cornwall were the founders of the families of Bloyon and Montagne. Another was Gunnar, who held Dimelihoc and Wiluniow (Ellis: 30). There is good evidence for the presence in Cornwall of large numbers of Bretons until the Reformation (RC 32: 290-95).

Although the Breton nobility and the higher clergy would have spoken French, the lower Breton clergy would have known Breton and probably little else. It is likely that in the decades after the Conquest Bretons were given preferment to Cornish livings because they could undertand the local people. The result of the decline in the status of the English and their language, was, I believe, that many English-speakers in Cornwall began to speak Cornish. At first re-Celticized Cornishmen would have been bilingual. Within a generation or two many must have been monoglot Celtic speakers.

As well as being spoken in Cornwall, Wales and Brittany, Brythonic was also spoken in Cumbria. This territory stretched from the present county of that name to southern Scotland. The original capital of the Britons of the north-west was Dumbarton, 'fort of the Britons'. The Norman Conquest did not assist the Britons of Cumbria to maintain their language. The Cumbrians unlike the Cornish did not experience the re-establishment of links with British-speaking cousins over the sea. Cut off from their Welsh kinsmen to the south-west, they were condemned to cultural assimilation with the Anglo-Norse around them. As a result Cumbrian retreated very quickly and was extinct by the thirteenth century. The difference in fortunes between Cumbrian on the one hand and Cornish on the other is impossible to explain without reference to the strengthening of relations between Cornwall and Brittany after the Norman Conquest.

11.4 The Old Cornish Vocabulary is probably evidence of a Celtic resurgence in Cornwall. The OCV is in a language transitional between Old and Middle Cornish and was probably written in the first half of the twelfth century. It is based upon the Old English-Latin vocabulary of Ælfric of Cerne and contains almost a thousand Latin words and their Cornish equivalents.

OCV, then, was written about two generations after the Norman Conquest. It is based upon an Anglo-Saxon work and attempts to provide a basic vocabulary of Cornish. It was clearly written by someone familiar with Old English and Cornish who wished to assist others in learning the Celtic tongue.

11.5 There is good evidence for the strength of Cornish in central Cornwall in the later Middle Ages. In 1339 a licence was granted to J. Polmarke to help the vicar of St Merryn near Padstow in his cure of souls. One of his duties was to preach in Cornish. Presumably preaching in Cornish in St Merryn was necessary since the parishioners would not have understood English (Wakelin 1975: 88).

In 1354-55 two penitentiaries were appointed for the archdeaconry of Cornwall. One was Brother John, of the Franciscan friary at Bodmin, was to serve those who knew Cornish and English, whereas brother Roger, of the Dominican friary in Truro, was to hear the confessions of those who knew Cornish only (Wakelin 1975: 89). It would seem that in the middle of the fourteenth century in and around Truro Cornish was the only language commonly known, whereas in the Bodmin area some spoke Cornish and others English. Given that Bodmin was a larger town than Truro, this is not astonishing.

In 1349 the prior of Minster, near Boscastle, died from the Black Death. So many other clerics died that a chaplain could not be provided for the parish, since none of the survivors spoke Cornish (Wakelin 1975: 88-9). This implies that there were monoglot Cornish speakers near Boscastle in the mid fourteenth century. There is no reason to believe that Cornish declined immediately thereafter. It is likely, therefore, that Cornish was spoken in the area of Boscastle well into the fifteenth century if not longer.

11.6 Polwhele tells us that Dr John Moreman, vicar of Menheniot (1529-54) and a firm Catholic, was the first incumbent to teach his parishioners the Lord's Prayer, Creed and Ten Commandments in English (see HCL: 12-13). Nance believed that the language displaced at Menheniot was Latin, not Cornish. I do not think he was correct. Before the Reformation the language of popular piety (rather than the liturgy) was always the vernacular. Lay people knew the Pater, the Ave Maria and the Creed so that they could say the Rosary in their own language. Inded the Rosary was developed in order to help the illiterate laity, who knew no Latin, become familiar with the gospel story.

In 1537 Henry VIII's parliament in Ireland passed an "act for the English order, habit and language". Each parson was required "to learn, instruct and teach the English tongue", "to bid the beads in English and to preach in English if he could preach" (Statutes: 124). The language forbidden after 1537 in Ireland was certainly not Latin. It was Irish. Henry's legislation was of course completely unsuccessful. There are still plenty of older Irish Catholics who learnt the Paternoster, Ave and Creed in Irish before Vatican II, while the language of the liturgy was Latin. These lay people heard mass regularly in Latin but said their prayers in Irish only.

In English-speaking communities before Vatican II, Catholics learnt their prayers in English, not Latin. My own mother-in-law, who was born in County Armagh in Northern Ireland in the 1920s regularly heard mass in Latin until the change to the vernacular after the Second Vatican Council. She never, however, learnt her prayers in Latin. She can recite the Lord's Prayer, Hail Mary and Creed in English only, even though for the much of her life Latin was the language of the liturgy.

It is likely that the same state of affairs obtained in Catholic Cornwall as in Catholic Ireland—which in the sixteenth century was almost entirely Irish-speaking. Since Henry VIII tried unsuccessfully to effect a change from Irish to English in Ireland, the equivalent shift in Cornwall must have been from Cornish to English not from Latin to English. If the laity in a parish first learnt their prayers in English during the reign of Henry VIII, the language they used before must have been Cornish not Latin. It is likely therefore, *pace* Nance, that Cornish was in use in the parish of Menheniot until the incumbency of

Moreman. This means that Cornish was spoken further to the east than Nance believed. The difference between the language of the liturgy (Latin) and of lay piety (the vernacular, Irish, Cornish or whatever) was understood by Henry Jenner, a Tridentine Catholic. Nance on the other hand, who was not a Catholic, missed the point entirely. Jenner was, I believe, right in this matter and Nance was mistaken.

In fact we can probably date the change from Cornish to English in Menheniot quite accurately. Although he had broken with the Papacy Henry VIII remained a Catholic in theology. In 1539 his parliament passed the Six Articles aimed at preventing the spread of Protestant ideas. The articles affirmed transubstantiation, communion in one kind, celibacy of the clergy, monastic vows, private masses and auricular confession. In 1543 Henry published *A Necessary Doctrine and Erudition for any Christian Man*. This work, also known as the King's Primer, which had the full backing of parliament, expounded the Creed, Sacraments, Ten Commandments, Lord's Prayer and Ave Maria in a very Catholic fashion. Quite probably English was making inroads into eastern Cornwall at this period. Moreman realized that the language of religious controversy would be English and anxious to protect his flock from Protestant ideas, may well have decided when the King's Primer was published, that it was now time to teach his parishioners in English rather than Cornish.

Since I wrote this paragraph the Rev. Brian Coombes has kindly sent me the text of a note of his in the *Cornish Banner* (March 1980, page 22), in which he reaches the same conclusion as I (and 15 years earlier!), namely that the language-shift in the church in Menheniot in the time of Dr John Moreman was from Cornish to English not Latin to English.

11.7 As has been noted above, we have excellent evidence that Cornish was spoken as far east as Bodmin and Minster in the fourteenth and fifteenth centuries. On the other hand there are many places to the west of Bodmin that have names in which -*nt* and -*d* have remained unassibilated. Note, for example: *Penpont* (St Mawgan in Pydar) < *pont* 'bridge'; *Redallen* (Breage) < *red* 'ford'; *Boderlogan* (Wendron) < *bod* 'dwelling'; *Boderwennack* (Wendron) < *bod*; *Bodelva* (St Blazey); *Bodiggo* (Luxulyan) < *bod*; *Bodinnick* (St Stephen in Brannell) < *bod*; *Talskiddy* (St Columb Major) < *skes* 'shadow'; *Polgoda* (Luxulyan) < *gosa* 'bleed'; *Polridmouth* (Tywardreath) < *red* 'ford'; *Allet* (Kenwyn) < *aled*; *Caruggat* (Tywardreath) < *huel-gos* 'high wood'; *Bodruggan* (Gorran) < *bod* 'dwelling'; *Menmundy* (St Stephen in Brannel) < *mon-dy* 'mineral house'; *Crofthandy* (Gwennap) < *hen-dy* 'ruin'; *Redruth* < *red* 'ford'; *Lelant* < PN *Anta*; *Trenant* (Fowey) < *nant* 'valley'; *Penquite* (St Sampson) < *cuit* 'wood'; *Tremoddrett* (Roche) < PN *Modred*; *Lanivet* < **neved* 'sanctuary'.

Since these names have not assibilated Old Cornish -*nt* and -*d*, sound changes which took place in the later eleventh and twelfth centuries, we have to assume the places in question were colonized by West Saxons in the ninth, tenth and eleventh centuries, before the shift of -*nt*, -*d* > *nt*, *s*. The name *Boderwennack* (< *bod* + ?*meynek*) preserves Old Cornish -*d*, but it has final -*ack* < -*ek*. This latter sound change is a late Middle Cornish one. It is likely therefore that the descendants of the first Saxon settlers in Boderwennack became Cornish-speakers in the early Middle Cornish period, early enough for the name *Boderwennack* to have undergone the late Middle Cornish -*ek* > -*ak*, even though it had missed an early MC one: -*d* > -*s*.

11.8 Something similar appears to have happened on a much wider scale in Cornwall to the east of Bodmin. In western Cornwall most place-names exhibit -*ns* and -*s* and only a small percentage, like those listed above, maintain the Old Cornish unassibilated dentals. In the more easterly parts of Cornwall on the other hand most place-names exhibit Old Cornish -*d*, -*nt* rather than -*s* and -*ns*, as is normal further to the west. Thus, for example, one finds *Trewint* with -*wint* 'wind' in Advent, Altarnun, St Endellion, Menheniot, St Erney, St Minver and Poundstock, but *Trewince* with -*wins* 'wind' in Constantine, Gerrans, St Issey, St Columb Minor, Ladock, St Martin in Meneage, Probus and Stithians. There are other Middle Cornish features, however, that are widely distributed in eastern Cornish place-names.

The name *Redruth* in West Cornwall has /u:/ in the second syllable. This is the expected reflex of West Saxon /y:/ and shows that the form of the name in English is as old as the Old Cornish period. In later Middle Cornish /y:/ becomes /i:/ (see 3.12 above). Cornish /y:/ has developed as /i:/ in the following toponyms in eastern Cornwall: *Polpeer* < *pur* 'pure' (Tintagel), *Tencreek* (Menheniot), *Tencreek* (Talland), *Tencreeks* (St Veep), *Trencreek* (Blisland and St Gennys), all < *crug* 'hillock'.

Other Middle Cornish sound changes include the raising of /a:/ > /æ:/ and the voicing of final /s/ > /z/. These developments are to be seen in toponyms in eastern Cornwall. *Canaglaze* (Altarnun), *Polglaze* (St Mabyn and Altarnun), *Penglaze* (Lansallos) all contain *glas* 'grey, green'. The shift of /a:/ > /æ:/ and of /s/ > /z/ cannot have occurred inside English. *Pen glas*, had it been borrowed into English in the Anglo-Saxon period, would almost certainly have given *Pengles, *Pingles or something similar. The voicing of *z* has also occurred in *Eglarooze* in St Germans.

The Cornish for 'small' is *byghan*, *byhan*. In place-names in eastern Cornwall and indeed elswhere the medial /x/ has become a stop, for example, in *Barbican* (St Martin by Looe) and *Collibeacon* (St Winnow). In some eastern place-names, however, one finds the form *bean* for *byghan*: *Pollvean Wood* (near Duloe), for example. *Bean/byan* for *byghan*, *byhan* is Middle and not Old Cornish.

Another relatively modern feature of place-names in eastern Cornwall is that they maintain grammatical gender. Thus, for example, one finds *Venton Veor* (northwest of Liskeard). Old Cornish does not usually show the lenition of initial *m*, for instance in *caur march* 'camel', lit. 'giant horse' OCV 566 >

Middle Cornish *cawrfargh. One would expect therefore *Venton Mur* not *Venton Veor* from the Old Cornish period. Initial lenition of *bean* 'small' is seen in *Polvean Wood* cited above.

The shift of final /x/ > /θ/ is also a late one (8.7). It occurs in eastern Cornwall, for example, in *Polzeath* (St Minver) < *pol segh*.

11.9 George (1992) has drawn attention to the numerous place-names in eastern Cornwall that contain the adjectival suffix -*oc*. Since Old Cornish -*oc*, for example in *bochodoc* 'poor' in the OCV, becomes -*ek* in Middle Cornish, e.g. *bohosek* BM 1679, George believes that Cornish became extinct in eastern Cornwall before the shift -*oc* > -*ek* took place. Frequently, however, Old Cornish -*oc* appears as -*ick* in eastern place-names. This I take to be a development in English of Middle Cornish -*ek*. Indeed toponyms in -*ick* < -*ek* occur alongside place-names in -*oc* in eastern Cornwall, and they outnumber them as well.

I have noticed the following examples (where I do not know the parish I give the name of the nearest town):

Badharlick (between Egloskerry and Tregeare); *Bephillick* (near Herodsfoot); *Bodinnick Hall Farm* (Lanteglos); *Bohetherick* (near Calstock); *Botallick* (near Lanreath); *Bowithick* (near Altarnun); *Castick* (North Hill); *Coldrenick* (near Menheniot); *Drinnick Farm* (near S. Petherwin); *Great Gormellick* (near Liskeard); *Halwinnick Butts* (near Rilaton); *Hantergantick* (St Breward); *Hendersick Farm* (near W Looe); *Hendraburnick* (near Davidstow); *Killigorrick* (near Herodsfoot); *Landlizzick Wood* (Landulph); *Lanwarnick* (Duloe); *Larrick* (S. Petherwin); *Leburnick* (near Lawhitton); *Lewannick*; *Linnick* (S. Petherwin); *Molenick* (between Menheniot and Landrake); *Mornick* (South Hill); *Polbathic* (near St Germans); *Polinnick* (near S. Petherwin); *Pottinnick* (near S. Petherwin); *Trebetherick* (St Minver); *Trebinnick* (near St Neots); *Treblethick* (near St Mabyn); *Tredrissick* (St Minver); *Trefinnick* (South Hill); *Tregaddick* (Blisland); *Tregastick* (near Widegates); *Tregavithick* (near Lansallos); *Tregunnick* (near Seaton); *Trekennick* (near Altarnun); *Treleathick* (north-west of Liskeard); *Treludick* (near N. Petherwin); *Trenannick* (near Warbstow); *Trerithick* (near Polyphant); *Treskinnick Cross* (near Poundstock); *Treswithick* (Cardinham); *Trethick* (St Mabyn); *Trethinnick* (St Cleer); *Trevisick* (Poundstock); *Trevissick* (Blisland); *Trewinnick* (near Boscastle); *Trewithick* (St Stephen by Launceston); *Treworrick* (St Cleer); *Winnick* (near Lanreath).

Some of these names must contain -*yk* rather than -*ek* < -*oc*, and may not be relevant to our present purposes. Many of them are likely to contain -*ek* < -*oc*, however. Names in -*ack* also occur in eastern Cornwall: *Lantallack Cross* (near Landrake); *Lithiack* (near St Germans); *Tresallack* (near Treburley); *Trewethack* (St Endellion). -*ak* for -*ek* is a later Middle Cornish phenomenon and is not normally written in place-names much before the sixteenth century (see Map III, p. 331).

It should also be noticed incidentally that names in -*oc* are not uncommon in central Cornwall, where we know Cornish survived well beyond the Old

Cornish period, for example, in *Ladock, Ventonladdock, St Breock, Feock, Budock, Crantock, Lanhydrock* (see Map IV, p. 331).

11.10 Anglo-Saxon or Old English had initial stress in native words. It also assimilated borrowings to the native pattern. Thus Latin *can'dela* appears in Old English as *'candel*. In Middle English by the beginning of the fifteenth century final unstressed syllables had been lost in English and words like *colde, greate* had become *cold, great*. These two developments in English are of crucial importance when dealing with the representation of Cornish place-names in English.

Since Launceston was so near to the border with Devon it was always known to English-speakers and its name represents the regular development in English of *Lann Stephen*, that is *Lann Stephen > 'Lanstephen > Launceston*. Other names in *lann* in eastern Cornwall, however, do not show the same kind of development. If *Lansallos* had been borrowed into English before 1200, it might have been expected to appear as **Launsells*. Indeed *Launcells* is the name of a parish near Stratton. *Launcells* has been an English name since the tenth century. *Lansallos* could not have been an English name until the early fifteenth. Similarly *Lansugle* in South Hill ought to have developed as *Lantsygal > *'Lansygle > *Lanskell, *Launskill* or something of the kind.

Trisyllabic names in *-ek/-oc* could not possibly have survived intact in English from the Old Cornish period, for the accent would have been shifted to the first syllable and the unaccented second syllable would have been lost. *Treludick < tre* + personal name in *-oc* would by the Modern English period have become something like **Trillock* or similar. *Treswithick < red + *guithoc* would have given something like **Rettock* or **Trettock*. *Trewithick < tre + *guithoc* would by now be **Trewthock* or **Trowthock* or something similar.

There are a number of places called *Hendra* 'old dwelling' in eastern Cornwall. Instances include *Abbott's Hendra* (Davidstow), *Hendra* (Altarnun) and *Hendra* (between Polbathic and Downderry). *Hendra* was probably still *Hendref c.* 1200 (cf. *Trefrida*, Jacobstow, *< tref ridou*) and ought to have developed in English as **Hendriff*. If *Hendref* was already *Hendre, Hendra* by the late twelfth century, in English one would expect **Hender* just as Old French *rendre* gave English *render*.

The two names *Patrieda* (Linkinhorne) and *Pathada* (Menheniot) are believed to derive from an Old Cornish **pedreda* of uncertain meaning. If this element had been borrowed into English before 1200, one would expect it to have developed something like *pedreda > pe'dredə > *'pedredə > *perredə > *perred > parret*. *Parret* is indeed the form of this Celtic name attested in the two English river-names *Parret* in Dorset/Somerset and in Gloucestershire/ Worcestershire (CPNE: 176). The two trisyllabic names *Patrieda* and *Pathada* in Cornwall, however, must have been Cornish at least until the loss of unstressed syllables in English, that is to say until the beginning of the fifteenth century.

In South Petherwin there is a place called *Trevozah Barton*, which is about two and a half miles from the Tamar. Padel derives it from *tre fosow* 'settlement of dykes'. If *Tre Fosow* had ceased to be a Cornish name before 1200, it would perhaps have developed in English as *Tre fosow* > **'Trefəsow* > **Trefsow* > **Trefsə* > **Triffs* or possibly with the final *-ow* preserved as **Trefsoe, *Tresfsow*. The trisyllabic *Trevozah* with penultimate stress and final *-ah* < *-ow* could not possibly have been borrowed into English until the beginning of the fifteenth century at the earliest.

The toponym *Tresawson* in Lanreath, like *Trevozah* and the other names to which I have referred, is stressed on the second syllable. Had *Tresawson* been an English name since the 12th century, it would probably have developed into **Tressen* or **Trasson* or something similar. *Tresawson* is likely to have been a Cornish name until the late Middle English period at the earliest. Yet *Tresawson* means 'the settlement of the Englishmen', where Englishmen means English-speakers. It would seem, then, that in the late Middle English period the presence of English-speakers in the parish of Lanreath was noteworthy enough to be reflected in the toponymy of the district.

11.11 Although most toponyms east of Bodmin exhibit unassibilated *nt* and *d* there are some names that show assibilation, for example: *Brownsue* (St Minver) < *bren du*; *Coskallow Wood* (South Hill) < *cos* 'wood'; *Hensens* (St Minver 1315) < (?) *sans*; *Nancedeuy* (St Mabyn 1302) < *nans*; *Rezare* (Lezant) < *red* 'ford'; *Treslea* (Cardinham) < *red + legh*; *Trewins* (Trevalga); *Treweers* (Lansallos) < *gweras* [Welsh *gweryd*]; *Treweese* (Quethiock) < *gweras*; *Trezance* (Cardinham) < *sans* 'holy'; *Bosmaugan* near Fairy Cross < *bos* 'dwelling'; *Mouls* near Pentire < *mols* 'wether' (see Map V, p. 332).

Note incidentally that *Coskallow Wood* shows Middle Cornish /o:/ from Old Cornish /ui/.

11.12 We know from historical sources that Cornish was spoken in Bodmin and to the east of Bodmin in the later Middle Ages (11.5). The evidence of place-names seems to support this view. It is true that Old Cornish *-nt* and *-d* were not assibilitated for the most part in eastern Cornwall. This is almost certainly because of Saxon colonization. Yet place-names exhibit later Middle Cornish sound-changes, in particular *-oc* > *-ek* (later *-ick*) and even *-ak*; /a/ > /æ:/; /s/ > /z/; /y:/ > /i:/. This all suggests that Cornish was widely spoken in eastern Cornwall in the later Middle Ages.

The most potent reason for believing that Cornish survived late in eastern Cornwall is that so many place-names have escaped Middle English sound-changes completely. Names like *Trefinnik, Treludick, Trevozah*, etc., cannot possibly have been confined to English since the end of the eleventh century. They must rather have been Cornish until the fifteenth century at the very earliest. The Celtic toponymy of eastern Cornwall is Middle Cornish except for the assibilation of *nt* and *d*, and the monophthongization of /ui/ > /o:/ in *cuit* 'wood', etc. Since these two changes took place during the later Old Cornish period, we are compelled to conclude that eastern Cornwall was partially Anglicized while Old Cornish was spoken, and was re-Celticized in the twelfth and thirteenth centuries. This view is corroborated by the presence of so many names in -*ick* < -*ek* < -*oc* in the eastern part of the country. It is clear from OCV that assibilitation had already begun in the twelfth century, but that the vowel in -*oc* had not yet begun to unround. When eastern Cornwall was re-Celticized in the twelfth century, -*oc* in place-names developed into -*ek* > -*ick*. This explains the preponderance of -*ick* names over those in -*oc*.

When the Saxons conquered eastern Cornwall they could not have settled in very large numbers (apart from the area in the north-east near Bude and Stratton where the place-names are almost entirely English). Rather they became the land-owning elite. Many Cornish-speakers may have learnt English, though the majority probably did not. For more than a century, that is from *c.* 940 to *c.* 1080, the Saxons in eastern Cornwall, determined the names of places and continued to use the place-names they heard when they invaded, even though those same names were undergoing changes on the lips of the conquered. Such changes were ignored and the Celtic inhabitants would have been compelled to adopt the place-names of their masters, in the same way that hundreds of years later Nicholas Boson while speaking Cornish used the English names, *Redruth* and *Falmouth*. It would not have been until the end of the eleventh and the beginning of the twelfth century that the population of eastern Cornwall which was bilingual English and Cornish and possibly monoglot English in places, became increasingly Celtophone. At that point the place-names of the area started again to develop naturally within the Cornish language. We have incontestable evidence that the English forms of place-names sometimes maintain fossilized forms whereas the Cornish versions are more advanced. At OM 2463 we find the name *buthek* with Middle Cornish -*ek* < Old Cornish -*oc*. The present-day English name is *Budock* which preserves Old Cornish -*oc*. The twentieth-century English name is therefore more archaic than the medieval Cornish one.

Those scattered eastern place-names that do exhibit assibilation of -*nt* and -*d* indicate that there were areas in eastern Cornwall in which Cornish continued in full vigour throughout the tenth and eleventh centuries. If eastern Cornwall was indeed re-Celticized during the twelfth and thirteenth centuries, it was no doubt in part from these areas of strong Celtic speech.

Where -*nt*, and -*d* are unassibilated in eastern Cornwall it is likely that Cornish was in retreat during the Old Cornish period but underwent a renaissance after the Norman Conquest. Whoever inhabited the places with unassibilated dentals in the tenth and eleventh century, it is likely by the 13th century many such places were again in the possession of Cornish-speakers.

Although the Saxon conquest of the tenth and eleventh centuries and the influx of Bretons in the later twelfth century were disturbing factors in Cornwall, by the thirteenth century rural east Cornwall must have been relatively stable. It was the Reformation that began the decline and death of Cornish. Before the Reformation, however, the Celtophone communities in eastern Cornwall would have been in equilibrium. It is inherently likely therefore that Cornish survived in eastern Cornwall not merely into the fifteenth century but also until the Reformation in the first half of the sixteenth. Indeed we have good evidence that this was the case in Menheniot. The handful of eastern place-names in -*ack* corroborate this view.

11.13 I have suggested that there was a Celtic resurgence in Cornwall after the Norman Conquest and that the presence of Bretons in Cornwall was an important predisposing factor for such a turn of events. The Breton influence on medieval Cornwall and Middle Cornish is apparent in other ways.

I suggest at 8.20 that the Cornish name *Jhesu(s)* was pronounced with initial /dʒ/. The name was either /'dʒezɪw/ or /'dʒezəz/. Cornish almost certainly had a form of the name with initial /j/, cf. Welsh *Iesu*, but we must assume that this was lost as a result of Saxon domination in the tenth and eleventh centuries. The Middle Breton form is *Iesu* or *Iesus*, which was probably pronounced /dʒeˑzyz/, /dʒeˑzy/; cf. Modern Breton *Jezuz* /ʒeˑzyz/ (< Middle French /ʒezys/, earlier /dʒezys/). Forms with initial /dʒ/ in Cornish are almost certainly borrowings from Breton rather than from Middle English.

The inherited form of the name of the Blessed Virgin Mary in Cornish was probably similar to Welsh *Mair* < Lat. *Maria*. The name seems to have been lost from Cornish and has been replaced by the trisyllabic *Marya* /ma'riə/. This is probably a borrowing from Middle Breton *Maria, Marië*.

The influence of Breton on Cornish is noticeable also in a secular context. Padel has pointed out that the place-name *Croftenorgellous*, recorded from St Dennis in 1333, contains the Middle Breton word *orgouilhous* 'proud (man)' (CPNE: 174). Moreover Borde's Cornish dialogue from the early sixteenth century contains the question: *Pes myllder eus alemma de Londres* 'How many miles is it from here to London?' (Loth 1900: 229). The use of a foreign form of the name of England's capital city in a Cornish context is baffling, unless we assume that Cornish speech has been heavily influenced by Breton. Even today the Breton for 'London' is *Londrez* < French *Londres*.

11.14 The so-called Charter Fragment is a portion of a Middle Cornish play first discovered by Henry Jenner on the back of a charter connected with St Stephen in Brannel. The charter is from 1340 but the Cornish fragment may be slightly later, perhaps as late as 1400. In the fragment the speaker addresses a young man concerning his future bride. The text reads as follows:

Lemyn yȝ torn my as re
ha war an Greyȝ my an te
nag vs y far
an barȝ ma ȝe pons Tamar

CORNISH IN EASTERN CORNWALL

[Now I give her into thy hand
and by the holy Faith I swear
that she has no equal
from here to the Tamar bridge] (OldC. 2 (1932): 35)

The older man is saying to the younger man that the girl in question has no equal from where they are standing to the Tamar bridge. It is customary for the Middle Cornish dramatists to add local colour to their plays and to mention places in the immediate locality. The allusions to place-names in the *Ordinalia*, for example, enabled Fowler (1961) to localize the original composition of the trilogy to near Penryn. In the Charter Fragment the author is by implication saying something about central and eastern Cornwall.

The Charter Fragment was written on the back of a charter connected with St Stephen in Brannel. It is probable therefore that the piece itself originated in or near St Stephen and was intended to be performed in the vicinity. The older man in the fragment stresses the girl's beauty and qualities and assures the young man that she will make an ideal wife. Indeed he claims she has no equal from Mid-Cornwall to the Tamar. The young man whom he addresses is, like himself, a fictional character and not a real person, but as a character in a literary work the youth is probably similar to the young men among the listeners. He speaks Cornish as his first language and presumably knows no other. Let us remember here the monoglot Cornish-speakers near Boscastle in 1349 (11.5). Any potential bride for the young man must also speak Cornish as her first language. Otherwise she would be inherently unsuitable as a wife and the older man could not legitimately recommend her. Yet the older man compares the future bride favourably with all the other girls of marriageable age as far as the Tamar. The unspoken assumption, which the fragment takes for granted, is surely that all or most of such young women are likewise Cornish-speakers. The older man refers to the girl as very young (*rag flog yw* 'for she is a child' CF 23). This probably means that she was fifteen years of age or younger. It seems fair to assume, then, that in the mid-fourteenth century Cornish was spoken by those under twenty years of age from the vicinity of St Stephen in Brannel as far the Tamar. If the younger generation spoke Cornish, then the older generations probably did as well. In short, in the fourteenth century all central and eastern Cornwall was largely Celtophone.

Toorians (1991) has suggested that the fragment may not actually be part of a play at all, but a secular poem for recital at a wedding. Indeed he argues that the piece may be complete in itself and not a fragment. I remain completely unconvinced by either suggestion. An epithalamium of that kind presupposes two factors: lay patrons of Cornish literature and a secular literary class. There is no evidence for either in medieval Cornwall. I believe that the piece is indeed a dramatic fragment and is part of an early scene from a saint's life. The saint, who is the young man, is urged rather cynically to enter into a marriage. He refuses (as does St Meriasek in a comparable situation) and dedicates the rest of his life to the chaste service of God. One thing is certain: the Charter Fragment indicates that Cornish was the everyday vernacular in St Stephen in Brannel in and after 1340. The rest is speculation.

There are, however, further indications to suggest that Cornish was to be heard as far as the Tamar in the later Middle Ages. In the first place, as we have seen, modern place-names like *Trevozah* indicate that Cornish was spoken at least as late as the latter part of the fourteenth century to within three miles of the Tamar. In the second place, we have archaeological evidence of a *plen-an-gwary* or medieval theatre for Cornish plays in East Wivelshire, that is to say, within a few miles of the modern Tamar Bridge at Saltash (*Carn* 76: 21).

11.15 Our evidence is not unambiguous and we must not attempt to read into it more than is permissible. I should, therefore, interpret it as follows. Apart from a small area in the north-east corner of Cornwall between the river Ottery and the border with Devon, Cornish was spoken widely until the beginning of the sixteenth century. Yet Cornish-speaking was not uniform and we must distinguish three areas:

A. From the Tamar to a line drawn from Padstow to Fowey English was widely spoken in the Old Cornish period. English retreated in the twelfth and thirteenth centuries but by the early sixteenth century was in the ascendant again. Thereafter Cornish died out very rapidly and English became the sole language of the region, probably by the later sixteenth century
B. Further west Cornish was the dominant language everywhere until the Reformation. By the beginning of the seventeenth century, however, Cornish had ceased to be a community language from the area between the Padstow-Fowey line and Truro
C. From Truro westward Cornish remained a community language well into the seventeenth century and in some far western places until the eighteenth

Because English was widely spoken in region A, many place-names survive in the form in which they were first acquired by English speakers in or before the twelfth century. Place-names in area A, therefore, exhibit the Old Cornish absence of assibilation. This explains the preponderance of names in *quite/cut* < *cuit* 'wood', *gwint* 'wind', *nant* 'valley', *sant* 'holy' and *rid* 'ford' in this region. Nonetheless assibilation occurs in some names and other Middle Cornish developments are clearly visible in many other place-names. The bulk of the place-names show Cornish features, however, not Middle English ones.

In area B place-names appear in Middle Cornish form. In C on the other hand many place-names show Late Cornish features, in particular the shift of *e* to schwa (spelt <a>) in unstressed syllables. In both area B and area C as a result of Saxon colonization unassibilated -*nt* and -*d* are attested. There is good evidence however that the Saxon settlements were Celtophone before the later Middle Cornish period.

The place-names of area C also exhibit western dialect features: *g*/*j* for *s*/*z*, for example, pre-occlusion and /u:/ for Middle Cornish /o:/ < Old Cornish /ui/.

11.16 George no longer believes that the isogloss *s*/*j* is a dialect marker. He thinks that *d* assibilated to some kind of *s* about the year 1300 and remained unchanged throughout the Middle Cornish period. By about 1675, he believes, this assibilated *s* shifted to /dʒ/ in the area in which Cornish was still spoken. This, he believes, is why <j>, <g>, etc. are confined to place-names in the far west of Cornwall.

As I have explained above, I do not believe that Old Cornish -*d*- passed through a stage -*s*- before becoming /dʒ/. I believe rather that Old Cornish -*d*- became /dz/ everywhere and then moved to /dʒ/ in some words, particularly in the west, whereas in other cases /dz/ simplified to /z/, written <s>. I cannot agree with George that *d* assibilated everywhere to some kind of *s* and later became /dʒ/ throughout the much reduced area of Cornish speech.

George believes that the assibilation of Old Cornish *d* took place *c.* 1300. This is also Pedersen's view, though he gives no evidence. Kenneth Jackson has pointed out that the assibilation of final -*d* is already present in OCV in the word *chespar* 'spouse' and had begun therefore *c.* 1100 (LHEB: 398). It is likely to have been complete before *c.* 1200.

It is also impossible to accept George's opinion that /dʒ/ did not arise from *s* < Old Cornish /d/ until *c.* 1675. There is every indication that /dʒ/ < /d/ was already in place long before that. The word *hensy* 'ruin' is a compound of *hen* 'old' and Old Cornish *ti* 'house'. In place-names it occurs both with /z/: *Hensywassa* and /dʒ/: *Goonhingey*. Padel cites two early names with /dʒ/: *Hengyvghall* from 1586 and *Hyngy Espayne* from 1492 (CPNE: 271, 272). Clearly /dʒ/ in these toponyms is earlier than *c.* 1675. Note also *Park-an-Bowgy* [1649] < *bugh* 'cow' + *di* lenited form of *ti* 'house' (CPNE: 285).

If /dʒ/ from Old Cornish /d/ did not arise until *c.* 1675, it is difficult to explain the many instances of /dʒ/ in the Middle Cornish texts. Here are a few examples from the *Ordinalia* (*c.* 1450): *woge* 'after' OM 1427, PC 834, 850, 1327, 1755, RD 206, 955, 957, 993, 1194, 1268, 2599; *wege* 'after' OM 2828; *oge* 'thou art' OM 1767, PC 1234, 1769, PA 197b; *essoge, asoge* 'how thou art' RD 971, 983; *trege, tryge* 'third' RD 339, 452, 681, 691, 2605; *kerenge* 'love' OM 1207, 1231, RD 453, 471, 833, 2638; *ege* 'was' OM 796, RD 1095; *vryongen* 'throat' PC 1007. If /dʒ/ arose *c.* 1675, then *oydge* 'age' CW 2101 is also difficult to explain, given that CW was written in 1611.

Old Cornish final /d/ regularly gives /dʒ/ in the Cornish heard by Lhuyd (cf. *oydge* above), thus Lhuyd writes *gûdzh* 'blood' and *lûdzh* 'grey'. I have already pointed out above (10.2) that the shift *s*/*z* > *j* is illusory, since all instances of *s*/*z* would have become *j* and one would therefore find **preegyo*

93

'praise', *Sawgnek* 'English', etc. in Late Cornish. George might argue that the /s/ from Old Cornish /d/ was different from /z/ < Old Cornish /s/. If that were so, by George's late shift of *s* > *j* one might expect all instances of *s* < *d* to become *j* c. 1675. In Lhuyd, therefore, we should find **tadzh* 'father', **gadzh* 'leave', **madzh* 'good', **redzh* 'necessity', **beydzh* 'world', etc. Such forms do not occur.

In his first discussion of the question of the Middle Cornish alternation of <s> and <g/j> ("A computer analysis of Cornish orthography" in MacLennan 1988, 89-115) George lists all the occurrences of the various spellings in the Old, Middle and Late Cornish texts. He notes that in the *Ordinalia*, for example, spellings with <s> occur in 58% of the instances, whereas spellings with <g> or <j> are found in 37%. In Tregear the figures are <s> 76%, <g/j> 17%, while in CW the proportions are <s> 42% and <g/j> 27% (see George's figure 13 on page 113). George is fully aware, then, that <s> and <g/j> are contemporaneous with each other in Middle Cornish. His subsequent attempt to explain <g/j> as a late 17th century development of <s> would seem to be at variance with his own research. George now suggests that Middle Cornish <s> became /dʒ/ as late as 1675. If this were so, then the reflex of Old Cornish /d/ in the Middle and Tudor Cornish texts would everywhere be <s>, since /dʒ/ <g/j> had not yet arisen and therefore could not occur. Yet George's own statistics demonstrate conclusively that this is not so. According to his own analysis <g/j> is widespread in Middle and Tudor Cornish. George would appear now to be making two mutually exclusive assertions. His claim that the sound written <s> became /dʒ/ as late as 1675 contradicts his conclusion that <g/j> is widespread in Middle Cornish. The only solution to George's difficulty would be for him to admit that <s> /z/ and <g/j> /dʒ/ are dialectal variants, a view he supported publicly at the "Cornish Weekend" in April 1989.

11.17 George also claims that the shift of /s/ > /dʒ/ post-dates the change -*ek* > -*ak* in unstressed syllables, since he says there are no place-names that show -*jek* rather than -*jak*.

> Pella, y hwelsyn dre [sic] ensampel 1 bos *c.*1525 an termyn may trelys -*ek* > -*ack*. A pe an chanj *s* > *j* moy a-var [sic] es hemma, y kavsyn [sic] lies ensampel a **-jek*. Drefenn na's kevyn mann, y tiskwa bos *s* > *dzh* chanj diwedhes

> [Moreover, we saw by example 1 that *c.* 1525 was the time when -*ek* became -*ack*. Were the shift *s* > *j* earlier than that, we would get many examples of -**jek*. Since we do not get any at all, it shows that the shift *s* > *dzh* is a late one] (George 1992: 66).

By -*jek* George means names in /-dʒek/, usually spelt <-gek>. Place-names in -*jak* < -*jek* occur in the west where *j* is the western equivalent of -*ss*-. Since, however, Cornish also survived longer in the west than further east, the spelling of place-names in the west show Late Cornish <-ack> for Middle Cornish <-ek>. As a result in their modern forms place-names do not normally exhibit <-jek>. The only exception known to me is *Illiswilgig* in Scilly < *enys weljek* 'grassy island'. Because Cornish died out in the islands before the Late Cornish period the name contains -*wilgig* a reflex of Middle Cornish *(g)weljek* rather than a reflex of the Late Cornish equivalent *gweljack*.

The adjectival ending -*jek* is attested in the spelling *gallogek* 'powerful' at PC 2376. Moreover early forms of place-names do exhibit -*jek* for later -*jack*. Pool is a careful scholar and is at pains to give all the earlier forms of the name together with the dates of their occurrence. I have noted two certain instances of -*jek* for later -*jack* in PNWP:

> *Tregassack* < *tre* + PN *Carasek*, cf. Welsh *Caradog*. Poole cites the forms *Tregarasek* 1320, *Tregrasek* 1356 but *Tregaragek* 1326 (PNWP: 71)

> *Lescudjack* < *lan scosek* 'shielded'; Poole gives *Lanscoisek* 1302, *Lascossack* 1560, *Lescosack* 1628 but *Lanscoegek* 1327 (PNWP: 57).

Under *Kenidjack* (< *cunygek* 'place for fuel', Breton *keuneudek* 'abondant en bois à brûler') Poole gives *Kynysiek* 1322 but *Kenygyek* 1324, *Kynygiek* 1326 (PNWP: 55). We cannot include these here, since the original form may have been *cunidiek* rather than *cunidek* (the group *dy* /dj/ might have given /dʒ/ before the shift *d* > *s*). On the other hand Padel cites *Trevajegmur* and *Trevagecbyghan* from 1300 (CPNE: 22). These are subdivisions of *Trevassack* and are to be derived from *tre* + personal name *Masek* < *Madoc*. I have no doubt that an examination of the earlier forms of place-names in -*jack* from elsewhere in western Cornwall would bring to light other examples of spellings in -*gek* from the early 14th century onwards.

It is certain from *gallogek*, *Illiswilgig*, *Tregaragek*, *Lanscoegek* and *Trevagek/Trevajeg* that -*jek* does occur and that it is older than -*jak*. <g> in these items occurs as early as the 14th century, at a time when Cornish was spoken throughout most of Cornwall. The shift in spelling from -*ek* /ek/ > -*ak* /ək/ is a later one. Western -*jek* > -*jack* contrasts to some degree with more easterly -*sek*, for example, in *Carwalsick* < *ker welsek*, *Polmassick* < *pol* *Massek*, etc. Spellings in -*ack* in the far east of Cornwall (11.9) also tell heavily against George's hypothesis.

The toponym *Penjerrick* in Budock is also difficult to explain if George's hypothesis is correct. The first element is *pen nans* and the second element ends in -*ick* < -*ek*. George's hypothetical shift of *s* > *j* has occurred in the name, but -*ek* has not become -*ak*.

11.18 Although -*ock* is older than -*ick* < -*ek*, and -*ack* is younger still, all three endings can occur anywhere in Cornwall. Thus, for example, the toponyms *Quethiock*, *Sheviock* with -*oc*, *Poldrissick*, *Polbathic* with -*ic* < -*ek*, *Lantallack* and

Lithiack with *-ack* are all in the same region between Liskeard and the Tamar. In central Cornwall the place-names *Trefuttock Farm, Fentonladock* with *-ock, Trelassick, Domellick* with *-ick* < *-ek* and *Rostowrack Downs* and *Benallack* with *-ck* all occur in the area between St Denis, Indian Queens, Ladock and Mitchell. Similarly *Porthoustock, Zawn Vinoc* with *-ock, Polpidnick, Treglossick* with *-ick, Trewothack* and *Trevallack* with *-ack* are all in St Keverne, while *Rissick, Pordenack* and *Polostoc* are within four miles of one another in Penwith. Though not common in the far east of Cornwall, the assibilation of *nt* > *ns* and of *d* > *s* can, as we have noted, occur anywhere from the Tamar to Land's End.

It is apparent that *-oc/ek/ak* and assibilation in toponyms are chronological features. Their presence or absence can tell us only when any given place-name was first borrowed into English. They say nothing about regional dialect, since they all occur throughout Cornwall. Pre-occlusion on the other hand is very sparsely attested east of Truro. Similarly *-jack* < *-jek* is largely confined to Penwith and Kerrier. It is not possible, therefore, to explain either feature chronologically. Both must be dialect isoglosses. George's revised explanation of *-jek/jak* cannot be sustained.

11.19 In the same article (George 1992) George has drawn attention to the way in which initial <f> alternates with initial <v> in Cornish place-names. He posits three areas in Cornwall. In the most easterly area between the Tamar and a line from Boscastle to Looe initial <v> is commoner than <f>. To the west of this region almost as far as Truro <f> is commoner. Further west still <v> is far commoner than <f>.

George is certainly correct in assuming that initial <v> in the far east of Cornwall is a reflexion of the change /f/ > /v/ in western English. As far as the other two areas are concerned his explanation is as follows: in Cornish initial /f/ became /v/ *c.* 1575 and as a result the more westerly names prefer <v> whereas the eastern ones tend to have initial <f>.

I do not believe that George is correct in this matter. I believe (see 21.1 below) that the lenition of *an forth* > *an vorth* is as old as Middle Cornish itself. I understand the variation in spelling to be orthographical rather than phonetic. The area of central Cornwall that prefers initial <f> has adopted Middle Cornish spellings in toponyms. Middle Cornish did not show the lenition of initial /f/ in *an forth, an fenten*. Late Cornish and English ortho-graphy do of course distinguish initial /f/ and /v/. As a result the western parts of Cornwall where Cornish survived into the Late period, exhibit initial <v> rather than <f> in their toponyms. The phonetic reality of the initial segment is the same. The spelling only is different.

CHAPTER 12
The prosodic shift and its effects: summary

12.1 In the preceding chapters I have attempted to give an account of some aspects of Middle Cornish phonology. In particular I have discussed a number of phenomena that seem at first sight to be unrelated. On closer inspection they can all be convincingly ascribed to the new prosodic system. If we assume that at some time before the earliest Middle Cornish texts long vowels became half-long and half-long vowels became short, many apparently unrelated phenomena can be elegantly and cogently explained. Among such developments we can include the following:

1) spellings like *dadder* 'goodness', *yn chymma* 'in this house', *marrow* 'dead'
2) the diphthongization of /iː/ > /ej/
3) the diphthongization of /uː/ > /ew/ in *plu* 'parish' > /plew/ [11]
4) the diphthongization of /yː/ > /ɪw/ in *du* 'black' > /dɪw/
5) the development /kuːn/ 'dogs' > /kœːn/
6) the falling together of /ɪː/ and /eː/ as /eː/ [12]
7) the falling together of /ɔː/ and /oː/ as /oː/ [ɔː], written <o>, <oy> [13]
8) the lowering of short stressed /i/ > /ɪ/ or /e/ as in *trega, meras*, etc.
9) the reduction of the three diphthongs /iw/, /ɪw/, /ew/ to two /ɪw/, /ew/ and possibly one /ew/
10) the conflation of the two dipthongs /ej/, /aj/ as /aj/
11) the shift of stressed /ew/ in polysyllables > /ow/
12) the conflation of original /ow/ and /aw/ as /aw/
13) the reduction of unstressed /ɪ/, /e/, /a/ and /o/ to the neutral vowel /ə/ in all environments
14) the reduction of unstressed /i/ > /ɪ/ in pretonic and closed post-tonic syllables; and sporadically to /ə/ in unstressed final position
15) the phenomenon of voiced final stops after stressed vowels and voiceless stops after unstressed vowels
16) the shift of /e/ > /a/ before inherited /nː/ > /n/ in eastern Cornish
17) the pre-occlusion of inherited /nː/, /m/ in western Cornish > /ᵈn/ and /ᵇm/ respectively.

Some of the above processes are better attested than others and it is in the nature of things that we cannot be completely certain of some of them. Taken together, however, they seem to me to represent a very strong body of

---

11 See now footnote 4 on page 14 above.
12 Though in some cases /ɪː/ fell together with /iː/.
13 I should now prefer to write: "The falling together of /oː/ and /oj/ as [oː], written <o>, <oy>."

evidence. So strong indeed that I regard the basic question as settled: *by the time of our earliest medieval texts Cornish had replaced a threefold distinction of length with a binary one: long ~ short. There was no half-length in Middle Cornish.*

12.2 To illustrate my conclusions about the phonology of Middle Cornish I will set out what I consider to have been the vocalic phonemes of the language in tabular form. Before the operation of the new prosodic system, Cornish had the following vowels

i	y	u
ɪ	œ	o
e		ɔ
	a	

These could be long, half-long or short. The short members occurred in both stressed and unstressed syllables. Notice however that when long /aː/ was phonetically either [æː] or in some contexts [ɑː]. There were originally the following diphthongs /iw/, /ɪw/, /ew/, /ow/ and /aw/, /oj/ /aj/ /ej/.

After the operation of the new prosody in the period immediately before the major Middle Cornish texts the vocalic system underwent major restructuring:

	Long		Short	
iː		uː	ɪ	ʊ
eː		oː	ɛ	ɔ
	aː		a	

/aː/ was usually [æː] but [ɑː] in the word /braːz/ and before /l/ in some other words.

Long vowels:
/gwiːr/ 'true'; /guːr/ 'husband'; /beːð/ 'be!', /beːð/ 'grave'; / boːz/ 'to be'; /boːz/, /buːz/ (Western) 'food'; /taːz/ [tæːz] 'father'; /braːz/ [brɑːz] 'great'.

Short vowels:
Since there was no longer a difference of laxness between /iː/ and /ɪː/, it might be legitimate to write /ɪ/ as /i/. One might similarly write other short vowels with the same symbols as their long equivalents. I use the symbols for the lax vowels, however, to avoid any possible confusion.

/ɪ/ and /ɛ/ were quite definitely separate phonemes as is clear from such variants as /mɪn/ and /mɛn/ 'wishes'. Symmetry would lead us to expect that

/ʊ/, was different phonemically from /ɔ/, even though the two appear to have been in free variation in some words (see 4.4). I prefer to keep them separate here.

Examples of the short vowels include: /'skɪdʒow/ 'shoes'; /'bɛðə/ 'I will be'; /tʊbm/ 'hot'; /'kɔskə/ 'to sleep'; /mam/ 'mother'.

There were two unstressed vowels: /ɪ/, /ə/ as in /'gɪlɪz/ 'gone', /'gɔðvəz/ 'to know'. A third /ǫ/ may have existed for a while in such words as /'kaɸǫz/ 'to get'. Later all three fell together as allophones of /ə/.

Diphthongs

The diphthongs were reduced to: /ɪw/, /ew/, /ow/, /aw/, /oj/ and /aj/, as in /lɪw/ 'colour', /bew/ 'alive', /ew/ 'is', /'klowəz/ 'hear', /'bownanz/ 'life', /dʒawl/ 'devil', /saw/ 'but' /moj/ 'more', /'trajljə/ 'turn', /tajr/ 'three' (fem.). [Note: the exact height of the nucleus in the diphthong /ew/ is impossible to determine.] There was also a new diphthong /ej/, which arose by the diphthongization of /i:/ in absolute final position and which remained distinct from /aj/ to some degree.

It is probable that the central vowels /y(:)/ and /œ(:)/ both long and short survived in some forms of Cornish although they had been unrounded to the corresponding front vowels, /i:/, /ɪ/ and /e:/, /ɛ/.

The alternation *y ~ e* was vigorous before the prosodic shift in *bethaf, byth; dethyow, dyth; prevyon, pryf*. This was lost when /ɪ:/ fell together with /e:/. Thus /bɪ:ð/ ~ /'bɛðowx/ became /be:ð/ ~ /'bɛðowx/ ['bɛðǫx]. Similarly the alternation /bɪ:w/ ~ /'bewnanz/ became /bew/ ~ /'bownanz/. In some words the alternation *y ~ e* was *y ~ œ* before the prosodic shift, for example in /pɪsk/ (/pe:sk/) ~ /'pœskas/. This became later became /pɪsk/ ~ /'poskəz/.

12.3 The new prosodic system brought Cornish closer to English in its phonology than it had been previously. It is difficult not to see the influence of English on Cornish in the question of quantity. Modern English is essentially a language in which syllables are of short duration but of high intensity. The sound-changes of of Middle English would lead one to believe that Middle English was similar to Modern English in this respect.

It is unlikely that the influence of English on Cornish was simply the result of an increasing number of English-speakers in Cornwall. It is more likely, I think, that the English-speakers had themselves become Cornish-speaking and brought into their new vernacular their English speech-habits. I have suggested above that there is good evidence for a Celtic resurgence in Cornwall after the Norman Conquest. A man or woman whose grandparents would have been English monoglots and whose parents bilingual, might well have spoken Cornish only. Celtophone children of Anglophone parents would of necessity have spoken Cornish with English characteristics. In Cornwall the absolute number of original Celtic speakers was probably not large enough to swamp the Anglicized Cornish of the post-Norman period. As a result Anglicized phonological features persisted in the language.

Cornish had inherited from Old Cornish an orthography that went back to the British period and thus had much in common with Welsh and Breton spelling. In Cornwall as a result of Saxon dominance in the tenth and eleventh centuries the inherited orthography had become overlaid with some Anglo-Saxon spelling habits. This spelling system was adapted in the post-Norman period to conform with Norman French orthography. <gh> replaced <ch> for example and <th> replaced *thorn* and *eth*. The scribal tradition was extremely conservative, however, and vowels continued to be written according to historical conventions long after the sounds had changed. This is particularly true in Cornish of unstressed syllables and gives a misleading impression of the quality of such syllables. Only by a thorough examination of variants, rhymes and back-spellings can a true picture be acquired.

Late Cornish is fragmentary in scope and Anglicized in spelling. It has been believed until recently (except by Jenner; 0.10) that so-called Late Cornish is a very different language from Middle Cornish. According to this under-standing of the history of the language, Middle Cornish exhibited an inherited Brythonic phonology, whereas Late Cornish was heavily English in idiom and pronunciation and very unlike Middle Cornish. I do not myself subscribe to such a view. It must be remembered that Middle Cornish and Late Cornish merge into one another. CW was transcribed in 1611, though from an earlier original. Yet much of our Late Cornish dates from 1660-1730. There is therefore less than fifty years between our latest Middle Cornish and our earliest Late Cornish (see further 14.2).

If the view advanced here is correct, namely that the new prosodic system and its results should be dated to before our earliest Middle Cornish, then the distinction between Middle Cornish and Late Cornish becomes insignificant. Late Cornish is the same language as Middle Cornish, but in an English-based spelling, rather than the traditional one.

12.4 It would seem, then, that in Middle Cornish post-tonic vowels in closed syllables and in absolute final position were beginning to fall together as early as the composition of PA, that is in the earlier part of the fourteenth century. Since the weakening of final syllables is a symptom of the wider linguistic shift in Cornish that I have labelled the new prosodic system, it is perhaps reasonable to assume that the new prosodic system with all its various consequences began to appear in Middle Cornish texts in the first half of the fourteenth century. The conservatism of the Cornish scribal tradition was such, however, that the full effects of the shift are not obvious until *c.* 150–200 years later, in BM. Even there the strong literary tradition preserves a spelling that has been long at variance with the colloquial language.

The weakening of unstressed vowels to schwa had far-reaching effects. Before the weakening *a garaf* 'whom I love', *a gare* 'whom he used to love' and *a garro* 'whom he may love' would have been phonetically different. When final unstressed vowels fell together, the verb in each case would have been /'garə/. Similarly *clewys* 'I heard', *clewys* 'heard' and *clewes* 'to hear' would have been phonetically distinct before the new prosodic system had become fully operative. Thereafter all could be pronounced as /'klowəz/.

Later Middle Cornish, as exemplified in BM and TH, adopted several ways of maintaining distinctions in verbs that had been lost through the weakening of unstressed vowels. One obvious method was to affix a enclitic pronoun to an inflected form. Thus /ə/ < *af* of the first person of the present-future received an enclitic *-ma*, for example. This device is a common feature in BM: *marsama* 'if I go', *pendrama* < *pendra wrama* 'what shall I do', *ythama* 'I go', *ythoma* 'I am' (BM 3288, 727, 794, 1359). Not astonishingly it is widespread in CW also: *ythoma* 'I am', *avoydama* 'I will be off', *ythama* 'I shall go', *kynthoma* 'though I am' (CW 1225, 1292, 1598, 1690). This use of enclitic pronouns has become very common in Late Cornish, for example, in *Theram* 'I am' (BF: 56) < *yth esoma*; *na ellam* 'I cannot' (BF: 46) < *ny allama*; *piua glow vi* 'who do I hear?' (BF: 19) < *pyw a glowaf vy*?

The falling together of final *-o* and *-a* meant the loss of difference between the present and past subjunctive in the third person and as a result throughout the whole paradigm. From PA onwards the past subjunctive often replaces the present subjunctive (Edwards 1993: 14; and cf. 19.6 below).

The loss of the distinction between final *-e*, *-o* and *-a* also affected the prepositional pronouns. When *-e*, *-a*, *-o* had fallen together as schwa, forms like *gansa*, *thotha*, *warnotha* were no longer marked for number. Several devices were adopted to overcome the difficulty. One obvious solution was to append an enclitic pronoun. This is common in BM, TH and CW, notice for example, *dethy* < *detha y* 'to them' BM 3122, 4278; *thotheff* < *thotha eff* 'to him' TH 3a, 8a, 11, *anotheff* < *anotho eff* 'from him' TH 11, *theworth eff* 'from him' TH 15, *ganssy* 'with/by them' CW 1350, 1452. Another device was to give the third plural prepositional pronoun a verbal ending. This is common in TH, as for example, *ynnans* 'in them', *thethans* 'to them', *ragthans* 'for them' (TH 6a, 14, 23), etc.

12.5 It is apparent from Lhuyd's transcriptions and other Late Cornish texts that in some monosyllables the vowel had lengthened again, for example, in *gwreag* 'wife' [greːəg] and *choy* 'house' [tʃəːi] (SDMC: xii). This should not astonish us. Indeed it is very much what we might expect. It is a truism of historical linguistics that languages frequently undergo the same sound-change more than once in their history. This certainly seems to have been the case in Cornish. It would seem that the word for 'father' for example, began as */tatos/ with a short stressed vowel. The vowel lengthened in Late British to */taˑtos/ and when final syllables were lost it became *taːd* with a vowel of three morae. At the prosodic shift the reflex of /taːd/ was /taːz/ and it shortened to /taːz/ [tæˑz]. Later this was lengthened again to three morae /taːz/ [tæːz].

If indeed long monosyllables did have overlong vowels in the last stage of the language, then we can be quite certain that the prosodic shift was old. After all the half-long vowels /ta·zow/ 'fathers' could hardly have been losing duration while /ta·z/ was gaining it. The two processes must be quite widely separated in time. Since the prosodic shift was clearly in progress before the period of PA (late 14th century), I would tentatively place the beginnings of the new system in the previous century. I should say that Cornish began to undergo the prosodic shift *c.* 1250 C.E. or possibly earlier.

12.6 There is another feature of Middle Cornish phonology that may conceivably be a result of the Anglicization of Cornish after the Norman Conquest, even though it has nothing to do with the prosodic shift. I refer to the assibilation of /d/ > /s/ and /nt/ > /ns/.

Cornish, like Breton, originally probably distinguished fortes from lenes, that is to say vigorously pronounced consonants from less vigorous ones (see 8.19). The initial segment in *da* 'good' would have been a voiced fortis, whereas the final segment in *tat* 'father' would have been a lenis, voiceless or voiced according to position. Similarly the medial segment in **wode* 'after' would have been a voiced lenis.

The opposition fortis ~ lenis, which is one of articulatory vigour, was lacking in English. A different distinction of relative vigour is that of obstruence ~ continuance. I would suggest that when English-speakers learnt Cornish, they replaced the opposition fortis ~ lenis, which they lacked, by the opposition obstruence ~ continuance which was inherent in their English. In this way the initial segment of *da* 'good' remained a voiced stop, but the final segment of *tat* 'father' and the medial segment of **wode* 'after' acquired partial continuance to become the affricate /dz/. It was this /dz/ which developed in Middle Cornish as /z/ or /dʒ/. As a result Middle Cornish has *da* 'good', *tas* 'father' and either *wose* or *woge* 'after'.

Assibilation does not take place when either *n*, *l*, *r* or *w* occurs in the following syllable: *ledan* 'wide' OM 2261; *scudel* 'dish' PA 43c; *Peder* 'Peter' PC 855; *falladow* 'failure' OM 871. The sonorous continuants in the following syllable inhibited the affrication of /d/ by dissimilation. The following syllable already contained a continuant and as a result the plosive /d/ did not move towards a continuant pronunciation /dz/ but rather remained fully plosive: /d/.

Since the assibilation has already begun in OCV, we must assume that already by the time it was written, Anglophone Cornishmen were learning Cornish. This is likely in itself and indeed may be the chief reason that OCV was written in the first place. The usually accepted date for OCV is *c.* 1100, less than two generations after the Norman Conquest. I suspect this date may be rather too early, and that OCV may date from the middle of the twelfth century.

THE PROSODIC SHIFT AND ITS EFFECTS: SUMMARY

12.7 In the above discussion I have mentioned three features which I believe distinguished eastern Cornish, the standard language, from its more westerly varieties. Those features are as follows:

1) /u:/ as a reflex of Old Cornish /ui/ rather than /o:/. It is noteworthy that the last piece of traditional Cornish is William Bodinar's letter of 1775. Bodinar, who was from Mousehole, begins: *Bluth vee* 'my age' (JRIC N.S. 7: 234). *Bluth* /blu:ð/ for *bloth* is a distinctively western form.
2) /dʒ/ rather than /z/ in such words as *peswar, caswyth, bohosek*, etc. The /dʒ/ forms are normal to the west of Camborne-Illogan.
3) Pre-occlusion of /n:/ and /m:/ to /ᵈn/ and /ᵇm/ respectively. As we have seen this phenomenon was barely known to the west of Truro.

There may be a further dialect feature that distinguishes east from west. The standard verbal noun of the verb 'to obtain, to get' is *cafos, cafus*. This I take to mean /'kafəz/ < earlier /'kaɸǫz/. Alongside this literary form there existed another, *cawas* /'kawəz/. *Cawas* occurs regularly in CW from Helston. It is also attested in the early portion of BM that exhibits pre-occlusion, i.e. at lines 86 and 255. More interestingly it first occurs in RD at line 1957 where it is spelt <cawys>. RD and PC are given to <g> rather than <s> on occasion, a feature which leads me to believe that the scribe of both plays had a more westerly dialect than that of the scribe of OM (Williams 1990: 267). *Cawys* in RD may well be another western feature.

We saw when discussing pre-occlusion that the feature was entirely absent from John Tregear's writing. So is <cawas>, for Tregear writes <cafus>, <caffus>, <kafus> and <kafas> only. On the other hand there is evidence for pre-occlusion in the last sermon SA. SA has only one instance of the verbal noun 'to get' <gowis> at 60. This is clearly the same as *cawys, cawas* and is probably further evidence that SA is western.

PA writes *cafos* regularly but also confuses the preterite *cafas* with the verbal noun. It is likely therefore that in the scribe's dialect the verbal noun 'to get' was /'kafəz/. It is imprudent to base anything on a single form, but I believe it probable that the dialect of the scribe of PA was an eastern one. Notice that OM has the two spoken forms <cafes> and <cafys> at 391, 454 and 432 respectively. These spellings represent /'kafəz/ and would be consonant with an eastern dialect.

It is probable that much of our medieval literature including BM originated in Glasney. That is to say that the priory at Glasney was the school where clerics learnt to read and write Cornish. It is nonetheless likely that the authors came from all over Cornwall. I suspect that the author/scribe of *Origo Mundi* may well have come from east of Truro as did the scribe of PA. I believe that John Tregear himself probably came from east of Truro. On the other hand the scribe of PC and RD and the author of SA were all probably from considerably further west.

PART II: THE VARIETIES OF NEO-CORNISH

CHAPTER 13
Kernowek Kemyn

13.1 Kernowek Kemyn is an orthography for revived Cornish that was devised by Ken George. The outline of the system was first published in PSRC in 1986. Kernowek Kemyn seeks to represent the pronunciation of Middle Cornish and in particular BM, as clearly and unambiguously as possible. The orthography was so devised as to represent any one phoneme by a unique symbol or set of symbols. It is for this reason that Kernowek Kemyn is also known as "Phonemic Cornish". Kernowek Kemyn has been promoted by *Kesva an Taves Kernewek* or the Cornish Language Board since 1987. Its two most important publications are George's GKK and Brown's GMC2.

Although Kernowek Kemyn is, in my view, unsatisfactory, it has achieved something by its very existence. The Cornish Revival owes the proponents of Kernowek Kemyn a debt of gratitude. As a result of their efforts the whole question of an orthography for Cornish has been brought into the open and the infallibility of Unified Cornish has been shattered for good. With every dispute our understanding of Cornish progresses.

Nonetheless Kernowek Kemyn as it is constituted is mistaken. I deal below with some of the ways in which I believe it is defective. My objections fall into four classes: (1) general; (2) theoretical; (3) orthographical; (4) phonological. These I will deal with in turn.

General objections to Kernowek Kemyn
13.2 To draw up the phonemic inventory of a living language is a difficult affair, and the end result may well not satisfy other scholars in the field. To attempt to phonemicize a language that has no traditional speakers is an even more hazardous business, and requires exceptional linguistic expertise. It is not obvious that the devisers of Kernowek Kemyn satisfied these conditions. It should be noted incidentally that the devisers of Unified Cornish did not require such expert knowledge and skill. They after all were content for the most part to let their sources speak for themselves. They were mistaken in some respects but their system was very close to the texts. Kernowek Kemyn is a new orthography which has been imposed upon Middle Cornish according to avowedly academic criteria. If such criteria were incorrect, as I believe they were, then the imposed orthography was also wrong.

Under the heading 'phonological objections' I shall have something to say about Kernowek Kemyn's earlier phonemes /d^j/ and /t^j/. Fortunately these suppositious items have now been removed from Kernowek Kemyn but their original inclusion raises serious questions about methodology. The two phonemes were included in Kernowek Kemyn as a result of a computer analysis of the sounds of the language.

The earliest account of /dʲ/ by George was given in a paper, 'A computer analysis of Cornish orthography' to the Congress of Celtic Studies in Ottawa in March 1986. In the published version of his paper George says:

> 'The primary conclusion to be drawn from this particular example is that, in most phonetic environments OldC /-d-/ was palatalised in MidC, and the resulting alien sound was represented either by <s> or <g> (MacLennan 1988: 122).

If the phoneme /dʲ/ developed in Middle Cornish from Old Cornish /d/ between vowels, as is claimed, then it must have been a spontaneous and natural development. It could not be alien. George calls it "alien", probably because he himself is not convinced that it ever existed. It should never, therefore, have been included.

13.3 Since Cornish has no traditional speakers, we must rely for our knowledge of the language upon the evidence of the written texts, the place-names and survivals in the English of Cornwall. Of these three sources the texts are by far the most important. Anyone attempting to say anything significant about Middle Cornish should read them continuously. The devisers of Kernowek Kemyn are quite well aware of the importance of the Middle Cornish texts because we are told that they have made a computer database of the corpus of Middle Cornish literature. It is also apparent that this database is inadequate and, indeed, inaccurate, in what it contains and in how it is operated. Let me cite just a few examples.

In discussing vowel affection PSRC cites three pairs of words in Unified Cornish. One pair is *mousak* 'stinking'/*mousegy* 'to stink'. The author says, 'In the first word of each pair, Nance has taken a LateC form in *-ak* without back-dating it; the second word he has invented' (PSRC: 73). This is a serious accusation to level at Nance, and is quite misconceived. As we have noted above, final *-ak* and *-ek* were both pronounced /ak/ in Middle Cornish. In the case of *mousegy* the accusation is particularly unfair. Nance did not invent *mousegy*; he read it at RD 171, which says, *ow flerye ov mousegy* 'smelling, stinking'. It is the form suggested by the author of PSRC *mosogi* that is the unattested one.

GKK gives the word *cablys* (*kablys* in Kernowek Kemyn spelling) 'Maundy'. This is a derivative of Latin *capitilavium*, cf. Irish *caplaid*. A note to the entry *Kablys* says of the expression *De Yow Hablys* 'Maundy Thursday', 'N.B. Found in MidC as *duyow hamlos*' (GKK: 149). The dictionary is right in saying that *duyow hamlos* 'Maundy Thursday' occurs in Middle Cornish, for the word appears in this guise at PC 654. The more expected *hablys* occurs, however, in PA at 41c, *en gyth o deyow hablys* 'the day was Maundy Thursday' and in the final sermon in the Tregear manuscript, *Sacrament an Alter*, fol. 66 (page 46 in Bice's edition), *nyn gegy cowse vith a deow habblys* 'he does not speak at all of Maundy Thursday'. Of three occurrences in Middle Cornish two are *hablys* (Nance's form), one is *hamlos*. GKK mentions *duyow hamlos* only.

13.4 In a note on *arbennik* 'special' GKK says: "N.B. The suffix is -IK not -EK". It is likely, as we have seen, that by the later Middle Cornish period the two suffixes -*ik* and -*ek* would have been pronounced identically. The etymology of *arbennik* (Welsh *arbennig*, Breton *arbennig*) is not crucial from the phonetic point of view. After the head-word GKK has the code letter C which means "constructed by analogy with cognate words in Breton and/or in Welsh" (see GKK: 13). The dictionary fails to mention two points, however: 1) that the first person to do the constructing was Edward Lhuyd and 2) that Lhuyd spells the word with -*ek* and not -*ik*. In the preface to his Cornish grammar Lhuyd says: *aban nag yu hi por-reyzyz dhan Tîz a ôr pordhâ kouz Zouznak po 'n Tavas yu'n arbednek ha'n ydnek reyzyz lebmyn en an Glaskor nei* 'for it is not very necessary for the people who can speak English, since the language [i.e. Welsh] is specially and solely necessary in our country [i.e. Wales]' (AB: 224). Lhuyd does not provide the best Cornish there is (see 14.21), but he is important as a source of vocabulary. George's entry on the word *arbennik* takes no note of Lhuyd's preface.

GKK cites the verbal noun of the verb 'hope, expect, take care' as *gwaytya* and says, "N.B. The V[erbal] N[oun] is not attested" (GKK: 124). This is not so, however, for Tregear has two instances: *pana dra a ren ny gwettyas theworth du a lymma* 'what kind of thing can we expect from now on from God?' TH 15a and *fatell yllans gwetias favowre a thewleff aga thas a neff?* 'how can they expect favour from the hands of their heavenly father?' TH 55a. *Gwettyas, gwetias* is unmistakably the verbal noun of *gwaytyaf*. The verbal noun also occurs in Late Cornish where the initial consonant has acquired permanent provection, presumably because of frequent use with the provecting particle *ow*. Nicholas Boson writes: *uz na ellen skant quatiez the e wellaz crefhe arta* 'so that we can hardly expect to see it strengthen again' (BF: 25). A similar form *quachas* 'expect' is used by Tonkin (BF: 32).

Under the headword *o'ta* 'thou art' GKK says: "N.B. *osta* is not actually found in MidC." (GKK: 240). Nowhere does the compiler tell us exactly what he means by "Middle Cornish". One has to assume that CW is not Middle Cornish in his view, because *osta* occurs at least four times in the play: *dell osta* 'as thou art' CW 512; *pew osta-she* 'who art thou?' CW 548; *pew osta* 'who art thou?' CW 1593; *prag ythosta* 'why art thou?' CW1606. Elsewhere in GKK George implies that he does consider John Tregear to be Middle Cornish. Tregear uses *osta*, for example at § 44: *benegas osta ge Symon mab Joanna* 'blessed art thou, Simon son of Jona' TH 44.

When the Tregear manuscript was discovered Morton Nance published an article in which he listed all the new words that were to found in it (Nance 1954). One such completely new word listed by Nance was *seran* 'mass for the dead' < Latin *serena*, which occurs in *Sacrament an Alter*: *An keth [A]usten ma a leveris a seran rag e vam Monica* 'This same Augustine said the memorial mass for his mother Monica' SA: 66. *Seran* is not the most important word in the Cornish lexicon, but it should be in the dictionary—particularly so, when it had been noted by Nance and the dictionary claims to be "the full Cornish-English edition" (GKK: 9). I can find *seran* nowhere in GKK.[14]

Under the head-word *borlewenn* 'morning star, Venus' GKK mentions that the word is given by Lhuyd. Nowhere do we learn that it also occurs in Tregear: *why a ra da bys may teffa an jeth hag egery, han vurluan agery in agys colonow* 'you shall do good until the day shall break and the day-star open in your hearts' TH 18.

Under *treveth* 'occasion' GKK says the word is Late Cornish (Nicholas Boson). Yet the *trevath* 'time, occasion' is often used by John Tregear, for example: *An den gwyrryan a goth vii trevath in jeth* 'The just man sins seven times daily' TH 8; *me a vyn gull deweth rag an drevath ma* 'I will finish for the time being' TH 35; *nena eff a gowsys thotha an tryssa trevath* 'then he spoke to him a third time' TH 43. More astonishingly GKK fails to mention that *treveth* occurs in the *Ordinalia*: *ke weth tresse treveth thy* 'go yet a third time thither' OM 799; *lyes trefeth y'n clewys* 'many times I heard him' PC 1724.

13.5 Although GKK has a section on pronunciation nowhere is the reader told when vowels are to be pronounced long, "half-long" or short. On occasion a phonetic rendering makes the length in Kernowek Kemyn clear but this is infrequent.

GKK sets great store by the authenticity of the words it contains. It is always careful to cite from precisely which source the various items come. On page 14 of the work one finds a list of all the sources for Old, Middle and Late Cornish. Curiously *Pascon agan Arluth* is not mentioned in the list. This is odd for two reasons. Not only is it regarded by many as the finest surviving work in Middle Cornish, but it has also been published in a Kernowek Kemyn version by Ray Edwards that has gone into no fewer than three impressions.

13.6 Kernowek Kemyn is not afraid to invent new words on the basis of pre-existing roots. This is only sensible and the results are unobjectionable. Such words include: *plommwedhek* 'vertical'; *gorwelyek* 'horizontal'; *kettuek* 'parallel'; *ranndirel* 'regional'; *doronieth* 'geography'; *kresenn* 'centre'; *liesyethek* 'multilingual'; *korrdoner* 'microwave oven'.

---

14 David Frost informs me (personal communication) that *seran* is probably a misreading for *oferan* 'mass'.

One should, nonetheless, avoid the temptation to calque English closely. The term *delinyans pellder-termyn* has been used in Kernowek Kemyn to translate the English 'distance-time diagram' (George 1992). The expression is an unfortunate one. When three nouns are placed together in Cornish, each of the second two will be taken as qualifying genitivally the preceding noun. In the place-name *Lowerth-lavender-en-parson* (Veryan 1330; CPNE: 279) the definite noun-phrase *en parson* qualifies *lowerth lavender* and *lavender* qualifies *lowerth*; the whole means 'the parson's lavender garden'. Similarly *delinyans pellder termyn* can only mean 'a diagram of the remoteness of time'. Since the distance-time diagram is a graphic way of showing variables plotted along a vertical time-axis and a horizontal distance-axis, it might be better to translate in Cornish as *delinyans pellder ha termyn*.

Theoretical objections to Kernowek Kemyn

13.7 Under the word *dhis* 'to thee' for example, GKK says, 'The spelling of this word is not certain'. In fact the author of GKK cannot be referring to spelling, since he is himself the originator of his own orthography. He must surely be referring to the pronunciation of the word in Middle Cornish. He does not seem to realize that Middle Cornish *thys* 'to thee' had two forms; these I discuss at 18.8 below. Nor is his bafflement over *thys* an isolated example. The author says s.v. **guv* 'spear', "It is difficult to arrive at a satisfactory spelling for this word". Again he must mean "pronunciation" not "spelling". I have discussed this word at 3.14 above.

13.8 George claims that Cornish long /iː/ took part in the English Great Vowel Shift and was consequently diphthongized to /əi/ (PSRC: 110). Cornish /iː/ did certainly diphthongize but as a result of the new prosodic system in Cornish (3.5); it was nothing to do with the English sound change. How can one vowel in one language take part in the sound-changes of another albeit contiguous language? And if one vowel does take part in another language's sound-shift, why don't they all? Why doesn't Cornish long /uː/ become /aw/, as happened in English as a result of the Great Vowel Shift?

13.9 George's dating of his putative sound-changes is arbitrary. Let me take one example as typical. He says that the consonant group /rθ/ became /rh/ "*c.* 1625" (PSRC: 174). The sub-text of this statement is presumably that <rth> is still found in CW but is absent from Nicholas Boson and Lhuyd, ergo the shift of /rθ/ > /rh/ must have occurred at some point between them, say *c.* 1625.

George is mistaken in his dating, however, because *gorthyb* is spelt <gurryb> already in TH and SA (*c.* 1560). I have no doubt that the shift of internal /rθ/ > /rh/ and final /rθ/ > /rð/ > /r/ is actually much older than the middle of the 16th century. After all, both *for* 'way' (< *forth*) and *aber* 'within' (< *aberth*) occur in the *Ordinalia* (see 8.6 above). Moreover Pool cites a form *Porgorwothyu* for *Porthgorwithou* from 1485 (PNWP: 65). In any case it is unwise to base a rigid chronology on what little evidence we have. The Cornish scribal tradition is so conservative that forms continued to be written long after they had ceased to reflect the reality of the spoken language. One must also remember that Cornish was not uniform either across the area of Cornish-speaking Cornwall or as far as social class was concerned.

13.10 One of the most serious theoretical objections to Kernowek Kemyn is the way in which the term 'phonemic' is used to describe its orthography. A phoneme can be defined as the smallest unit of significant sound. /t/and /d/ are separate phonemes in English, because *to* and *do* are different words as are *tin* and *din*, *try* and *dry*, etc. The original intention of the devisers of Kernowek Kemyn was that its orthography should use one graph, that is, letter or combination of letters, for one phoneme. This aim is laudable but is not ultimately realized.

Kernowek Kemyn assumes in Middle Cornish the presence of two high front vowel phonemes /i/ and /ɪ/. These can be either, long, half-long or short. The short members can be either stressed or unstressed. Kernowek Kemyn is, I believe, mistaken on this point as I have made clear above, but I will accept it temporarily here simply for the sake of argument. The author of PSRC says of unstressed /i/:

> When unstressed, there was a tendency for the sound to become lowered to [-ɪ] or even lower' (PSRC: 110).

The author is talking about the phoneme /i/, yet he refers to it as 'a sound', and he says that this 'sound' [i] becomes [ɪ]. It seems unclear whether he is talking about sounds pure and simple (phonetics), or significant sounds/phonemes (phonology). If the latter, then clearly he believes that the phoneme /i/ has several members which alternate with one another according to environment: "this sound is lowered to [ɪ] and even further". By "even further" I take him to mean [e] or [ɛ].

If I may paraphrase, the author is here saying that the phoneme /i/ when unstressed is realized as [ɪ] or [e]. Elsewhere in PSRC, however, we are told that Middle Cornish has the short vowel phonemes /ɪ/ (PSRC: 113) and /e/ (PRSC: 116). In the present passage, however, we read that /i/ is when unstressed pronounced [ɪ] or [e]. But /ɪ/ and /e/ are phonemes in their own right, distinct from /i/. What in fact the author is saying is the following: in unstressed position the opposition between /i/, /ɪ/ and /e/ is neutralized. This is substantially correct (see 7.9 above).

If the opposition between /i/, /ɪ/ and /e/ disappears in unstressed syllables, this means that in unstressed syllables /i/, /ɪ/ and /e/ are not phonemically distinct. Therefore they cease to be separate phonemes. That means they need not, indeed they should not, be spelt differently. A truly phonemic spelling would spell them all the same. Yet Kernowek Kemyn spells them <i>, <y> or <e> according to etymology, as for example *kegin* 'kitchen' [kegɪn], *kelynn* 'holly' [kelɪn] and *estren* 'foreigner' [estrɪn]. Kernowek Kemyn has three different ways of spelling the identical phoneme. In short, at this point Kernowek Kemyn repudiates the very phonemic principle on which it claims to be based.

The same confusion is to be noted in the treatment of unstressed [y] spelt <u> in Kernowek Kemyn. In "Kernewek Kemmyn Up-Date" (*Carn* 68: 16) we read that when unstressed <u>, i.e. /y/, is to be pronounced [ɪ]. The users of Kernowek Kemyn are coming to realize that in Middle Cornish most unstressed vowels had fallen together as [ə] and/or [ɪ]. The phonetic facts are correct; the theoretical treatment is not. Compare the remarks in the more recent work, GKK. The compiler tells us that /i/ when unstressed is 'more like the i in English bit', /y/ when unstressed is 'more like the i in English bit' and /ɪ/ when short is 'as i in English bit'. Three separate 'phonemes' are to be pronounced identically. This is correct phonetically, but not from the phonemic point of view.

This elastic approach to phonemic theory runs like a thread throughout Kernowek Kemyn. The author of PSRC tells us that in final position /g/ is devoiced to /k/. It is for this reason that he spells *marghek* 'horseman' and *medhyk* 'doctor' with a final <k>. In the plural the underlying /g/ reappears: *marghogyon* and *medhygyon*. This seems a sensible approach to the problem of the alternation of final /k/ with internal /g/. Yet in stressed syllables the author insists that we spell final /k/ as <g> in, for example, *gwag* 'empty', *gwreg* 'wife' and *rag* 'for'. Despite this variation in orthographical practice GKK still claims to be phonemic and criticizes Nance for inconsistency. The dictionary says:

> Nance appeared undecided on the spelling, and gave both *rak* and *rag*. In Kernewek Kemmyn, *rag* is used in accordance with the phonemic principle in monosyllables (GKK: 267).

The phonemic principle operates in monosyllables only—in *gwag, gwreg* and *rag*, for example. Disyllables like *medhyk* and *marghek* on the other hand must be content to remain unphonemic. *Marghek* has a final [k] and is spelt with <k>. *Gwag* also with final [k] is spelt with <g> because it is a monosyllable and in monosyllables the "phonemic principle" allows (requires?) the phoneme /k/ to be spelt /g/.

The question of voiced/ voiceless stops is discussed at PSRC: 101. The author believes that the final phoneme in words like *gwag, rag, gwreg* is /g/ but that it is "realized" as [k] because voiced stops are devoiced in absolute auslaut. Similarly words with final /b/ and /d/ are "realized" with [p] and [t] respectively. As a statement of what the author believes of the phonetics this is unobjectionable. As far as phonemic theory is concerned it is confused. If phoneme x is realized identically with phoneme y, then it is phoneme y and not x. A more conventional analysis would say that /g/ and /k/ are different phonemes but that the opposition between them is neutralized in final position. To call /k/ a realization of /g/, when /k/ and /g/ are separate phonemes, is unsatisfactory phonology. Moreover the realization of /g/ as [k] is allowed only in monosyllables. In disyllables [k], the "realization" of /g/ in final position, is represented by <k>.

Ironically Kernowek Kemyn is, I believe, completely mistaken here over the nature of the alternation $g \sim k$ in final position. At 8.19 above I suggest that in Cornish after the prosodic shift historically voiced stops were always voiced following a stressed vowel but unvoiced after an unstressed one.

13.11 In GKK many of the entries are accompanied by phonetic representations. Were the orthography of Kernowek Kemyn really phonemic, the pronunciation of each headword would be immediately obvious. The mere fact that the compilers add pronunciation to many words indicates that they have less than total faith in their own spelling. Let me some examples.

GKK gives the Cornish word for 'aloes', which is spelt <aloes>. In Kernowek Kemyn /oe/ represents /oː/. In *aloes*, however, it is a disyllable for the dictionary gives the phonetic rendering [aˈlɔˑes] (GKK: 29). Yet if this spelling were phonemic, phonetic or even consistent that could only mean [ˈaloːs]. The same graph <oe> occurs in the Kernowek Kemyn word for 'Welshwoman': *Kembroes* (GKK: 159). The phonetic rendering given [kemˈbrɔˑes] indicates that <oe> here is not the Kernowek Kemyn graph for /oː/ but rather represents a disyllable, as was the case with *aloes*. Again Kernowek Kemyn is neither phonemic nor consistent.

The compiler adds after his entry on *Kembroes*: 'Nance's *Kembres* appears historically incorrect'. The word for 'Welshman' is attested traditionally in Cornish place-names, for example, in *Chykembro* and *Hayle Kimbro Pool* (CPNE: 48). Moreover the word for 'Wales' occurs in medieval Cornwall (fourteenth century) as an epithet, *Richard Kembre, John Kembre* (ibid.). *Kembro* 'Welshman' and *Kembre* 'Wales' come from singular **Kombrogos* and plural **Kombrogi* respectively, the local name 'Wales' being in origin the word for 'Welshmen'. Both items were originally stressed on the penultimate syllable. The Welsh word for 'Welsh' (language) is *Cymˈraeg* < **Kombrogika*, which was originally stressed on the penultimate syllable, -ˈik-, and is now stressed on the historically antepenultimate syllable. The Cornish for 'Welsh' is *Kembrack*, which is attested from Gwavas and Pender (SDMC s.v. *Welsh*). *Kembrack* appears from its spelling to have been pronounced [ˈkembrək], that is to say, as though the adjectival -*ack*, -*ek* had been added to the stem **Kembr-*. This can only mean that *Kembrack*, unlike Welsh *Cymraeg*, was stressed on the initial syllable. The Welsh for 'Welshwoman' is *Cymraes* which has final stress, as has *Cymraeg*. Since Cornish *Kembrack* has initial stress, one would expect the Cornish for 'Welshwoman' to have initial stress also, for it would have been

111

formed on the stem *Kembr-* by the addition of the feminine *-es* < *-issa* to give *Kembres*. Although *Kembres* is not attested in traditional Cornish it is identical with the word devised by Nance. GKK is, then, mistaken in describing Nance's *Kembres* as historically incorrect. It is *Kembroes* which is historically unjustified.

In the phonetic introduction to GKK we are told that <sh> is to be pronounced [ʃ], that is as *sh* in English *ship* (GKK: 22). Yet the body of the dictionary contains a number of words in which <sh> occurs but as two separate consonants, belonging to different syllables. On occasion a phonetic rendering is given to indicate that <sh> is not [ʃ], for example in the case of *eshe* 'facilitate', *kaleshe* 'harden', *neshe* 'approach'. In other cases no such assistance is given, e.g. with *leshanow* 'nickname', *leshenwel* 'to nickname', *leshwoer* 'half-sister', *neshevin* 'kinsmen'. Not only, therefore, is the orthography unphonemic in these items, the editorial policy of the dictionary is inconsistent as well.

GKK cites two Middle Cornish words *aperya* 'injure' and *apperya* 'appear'. The only difference in spelling between them is the <p> versus <pp> and one would expect according to "phonemic" principles of Kernowek Kemyn that *apperya* would have a short first vowel and *aperya* a long one. But that cannot be right, because the first syllable in both words is unstressed and must therefore be short. GKK says of *apperya* 'appear':

> Although <p> rather than <pp> was used in MidE, the word is spelled here with <pp>, to distinguish it from *aperya* 'to injure', and to reflect the origin Lat. *ap* + *parere* 'to come into view (GKK: 34).

Kernowek Kemyn then will spell words in order 1) to keep them different from words pronounced identically with them; 2) in order to show their etymology. Both may well be sound orthographical principles. Phonemic they are not.

13.12 GKK in its guide to pronunciation says nothing about the position of the accent. Such information is intended to be gleaned from the pronunciation that is included in many of the articles. In native words unless otherwise specified the stress is on the penultimate syllable. Thus *arloedh* 'lord' is to be stressed on the first syllable, but *arloedhes* 'lady' on the second. In the word *dadhel* 'argument' we are to assume, I think, that the stress is on the first syllable. In *dadhelva* a learner would naturally assume the accent to fall on the penultimate. The dictionary is no help in this matter because it does not give the pronunciation of this item. Presumably the reader is to deduce the pronunciation from the "phonemic" spelling. Yet we are told that *dadhelva* survives in Cornish dialect as *dalva*, which implies that the first syllable is stressed not the second. Why then is the anomalous stress not marked?

The word for the noun 'chase' is given as *chas*. Since it has a single <s>, we can assume the vowel is long. The word in Kernowek Kemyn for 'to chase, to hunt' is *chasya*. Here the vowel is presumably short, as it would also be, for example, in *passya* 'pass' and *passhyon* 'passion'. It is curious then that it is not spelt **chassya*. The word is after all spelt <chassya> at CW 1823. Or are we to assume the vowel is half-long? If half-long, why is the vowel of *passya* not half-long also?

13.13 The proponents of Kernowek Kemyn, apparently unhappy with some aspects of the original version, introduced a number of modifications. The first group of reforms, which included the removal of /tʲ/ and /dʲ/, appeared in *Carn* 68 (Winter 1988/90). By the spring of 1990 some further emendations were required. The editors of *Carn* were not pleased it seems, because in *Carn* 69 under the heading "LANGUAGE CORRECTION" they said:

> Since the article headed *Kernewek Kemmyn Up-Date* appeared in *Carn* 68, we have been informed that there were one or two errors in the original 'Up-date' document. No doubt along with these errors, there will be further modifications to *Kernewek Kemmyn* in the future. Therefore, rather than fall into the habit of continually printing corrections and up-dates, we suggest *Carn* readers accept the article as a general insight into the work of those involved in remodeling the pronunciation of *Unified Cornish* and contact the language organisations (via the League's Cornish branch) for details of minor changes.

A fundamental question remains: if Kernowek Kemyn were scientifically based on a thorough study of Middle Cornish, why should it need periodic modifications at all?

13.14 The most serious fault of Kernowek Kemyn is that it attempts to impose an artificial twentieth-century standardized spelling and phonology upon an extinct medieval language. As far as Kernowek Kemyn is concerned we have a parallel in Manx. Manx too is a Celtic language without traditional native-speakers. The case is not exactly comparable with Cornish inasmuch as many native-speakers have been recorded in phonetic script and on ediphone, tape and film. All the same Manx is like Cornish a linguistic orphan. Worse still its orthography is a nightmare. Although Manx is Gaelic and closely related to Ulster Irish and Scottish Gaelic, it has always been written since it first appeared as a separate language in the seventeenth-century in a semi-phonetic orthography based on Scots and English. Such a spelling system is inconsistent, misleading and extremely difficult to learn. Like Cornish, Manx has pre-occlusion. *Keayn* 'sea' is pronounced [kiᵈn] for example and *trome* 'heavy' is [troᵇm]. Pre-occlusion in Manx, however, is seldom written.

Manx would seem to be an ideal candidate for spelling reform and such a course of action has sometimes been mooted. I do not believe it will happen, however. Academic Manx revivalists would be wary of interfering with the spelling that Manx has inherited. It may have many drawbacks, but it has been

113

in place now for several centuries. The Cornish revivalists should adopt a similarly cautious approach. Revived Cornish ought as far as possible use only what is present in Middle Cornish texts. To do anything else is to invite trouble. To regularize the traditional orthography slightly, as Unified Cornish does, is justifiable. To recast it wholesale according to a questionable phonology is illegitimate.

Orthographical problems in Kernowek Kemyn

13.15 Although the orthographical defects of Kernowek Kemyn are less serious than some of its other shortcomings, one suspects that they more than anything else have lost it goodwill among Cornish-speakers.

In the Middle Cornish texts /k/ is represented in three ways. Before the back vowels *a, o, u* and before consonants it is normally spelt as <c>, before the front vowels it appears mostly as <k>, while before /w/ it is <q> and the /w/ itself is written <u>. This set of conventions was adopted by Unified Cornish. Thus one has *cara* 'to love', *kerys* 'loved' but *quyt* 'free, clear'. The threefold representation of /k/ is, of course, exactly parallel with English conventions, as for example in *cat, kitten* and *quick*. To spell /k/ in three different ways, as Unified Cornish does, is not economical, perhaps. It does have the two merits, however, of being similar to English practice and—more importantly—of reflecting the habits of the Middle Cornish scribes themselves.

It should be pointed out here in mitigation that <k> before back vowels and consonants is certainly not unknown in the texts. Note for example *kref* OM 687, *kres* BM 946, *karrek* BM 1024. On the other hand <c> for /k/ before front vowels also occurs on occasion, for example, *cemeres* OM 1123, *cen* PC 1994. For the most part, however, in Middle Cornish literature /k/ is <c> before back vowels and consonants and <k> before front vowels.

In Kernowek Kemyn the phoneme /k/ is always spelt <k> irrespective of position. Thus Kernowek Kemyn has *karrek* 'rock', *koth* 'old', *kulyek* 'cock, male bird' and *klav* 'ill' where UC has *carrek, coth, culyek* and *claf*. Similarly Kernowek Kemyn has *kwit* 'free', *kwestyon* 'question' and *skwith* 'tired' where UC has *quyt, questyon* and *squyth*.

Since the devisers of Kernowek Kemyn wanted their orthography to be as consistent as possible they adopted the expedient of making the one-to-one correlation <k> = /k/. Understandable this decision may have been, but it was, perhaps, not a wise one.

Let us look for a moment at the matter through the eyes of someone living in Cornwall who decides to take up the study of Cornish. He is no doubt delighted when he learns that in the place-names all around him he is seeing the living evidence of the original language of Cornwall. Names that were once mere utterances now have a meaning. *Carn Glaze* is 'grey rock', *Coosebean* is 'small wood', *Camborne* is *Cambron* 'the oblique hill'. Imagine then how he feels when he is told that in Cornish these names are *Karn Glas, Koes Byghan* and *Kammbronn*. Their Kernowek Kemyn representations look quite unlike the

114

everyday forms. The names on the map and on the signpost bear no resemblance to the words in the grammar-book. Not only is the connection between Cornwall's past and her present broken by these arbitrary spellings, but worse still the new spellings look bizarre. The unfamiliar nature of Kernowek Kemyn spelling and in particular the use of <k> has led Pool to observe with some justification:

> To those accustomed to Unified, as indeed to those who prefer Kernuak [Revived Late Cornish], [Kernewek] Kemyn has an alien and somewhat sinister appearance, as if the language had somehow been taken over by robots and reduced to the status of a code (1995: 6).

If *Kammbronn* is strange, *kwestyon* is even more so. It is true that the *Ordinalia* have one example of <kw>: *skwych* at RD 2595. Even so, there is little case to be made for <kw> as a graph in revived Cornish. <Qu> would have been more native and preferable for that reason alone.

13.16 The model for <k> before back vowels and consonants and <kw> was of course Breton. Since the spelling reforms introduced by Le Gonidec into his Breton dictionary of 1820, Breton has spelt /k/ as <k> in all positions. In a sense, the Bretons had no choice but to generalize <k> everywhere. The situation in Middle Breton was confused in the extreme. /k/ was frequently spelt <c> before back vowels and consonants. Before front vowels, however, it was either <ch> or <k> or in accordance with French conventions <qu>. On occasion <q> and <k> were used before back vowels also. Since <qu> meant /k/ it could not be used for /kw/. Breton scribes had to use combinations like <kou> or <cou>. In short the orthography of Breton was in this respect a mess. Le Gonidec's solution was simple. /k/ was to be <k> everwhere and /kw/ was to be spelt /kou/. Cornish is quite different. The threefold representation of /k/ in the texts as <c>, <k> and <qu> though not absolutely universal is fairly consistent. It is unambiguous and in its way elegant. There was no conceivable reason to replace *claf* and *antyquary*, for example, with *klav* and *antikwari*. Revived Cornish should spell /k/ as <c>, <k> or <q> according to position. Anything else is inauthentic and does violence to the orthographical traditions of the language.

The corollary of using <k> where Unified Cornish used <c>, is that <c> cannot be used for /s/. Instead, therefore, of *cider, certan, Cesar* Kernowek Kemyn writes *sider* 'cider', *serten* 'certain' and *Sesar* 'Caesar'. Although such spellings look a little odd, Kernowek Kemyn in this instance can cite the texts in justification. Notice *syder* 'cider' at BM 4451, *serten* [sic] at CW 1619 and *Sesar* at PA 146d. I have no example of *sita* for *cyte, cyta* 'city' from the texts, however.

13.17 A further practice in Kernowek Kemyn is the respelling of <wh> as <hw>. Since this graph is not discussed separately in PSRC but is subsumed under the heading of <h>, <x> (PSRC: 181), it must be that the author analysed the <wh> of the Middle Cornish scribes as [h] + [w] rather than a single voiceless /w/, that is, [ʍ]. The acoustic reality would have been identical. The respelling of <wh> as <hw> was presumably prompted by the Welsh and Breton equivalents: /xw/, spelt <c'hw> in Breton and <chw> in Welsh. Cornish is neither Welsh nor Breton, however, and the scribal practice makes it abundantly clear that Middle Cornish <wh> was the only graph used for the voiceless w: [ʍ].

In Standard English (though not in Scottish or Irish English) <wh> and <w> have fallen together and are both pronounced [w]. The same phenomenon was clearly occurring in Middle Cornish as well. Middle Cornish /ʍ/ was only weakly devoiced and tended to lose the devoicing on occasion. Note, for example, the following spellings from BM: *wek* 'sweet' for *whek* BM 87, 114, 286; *wy* 'ye' for *why* BM 89, 115, 325; *wath* 'still' for *whath* BM 337, 421, 499; *dywy* 'to you' for *deughwhy* BM 484, 575, 587; *wethugh wy* 'blow ye' for *whethugh why* BM 276, etc. The same voicing of <wh> is common in PA and TH also. In view of all this it seems sensible to retain the spelling of the Middle Cornish texts and to spell *why*, *whetha*, *whath* with <wh> and not <hw>. Kernowek Kemyn's <hw> for <wh> is unjustified and unnecessary.

Phonological Objections

13.18 These are by far the most serious objections to Kernowek Kemyn and in the light of the discussion of Cornish phonology at 2.1-12.7 above they will have to be dealt with at some length. George lists the deficiencies of Unified Cornish and says:

> Errors made by Nance and Smith include the following:
> 1) Failure to recognize the phonemic differences between /o/ and /ɔ/, and /y/ and /œ/
> 2) Failure to recognize the existence of the phonemes /œ/, /tʲ/ and /dʲ/
> 3) Misidentification of phonemes in certain words
> 4) Incorrect pronunciation of /a/ when long
> 5) Confusion of the pronunciation of <ay> and <ey>
> 6) Failure to recognize three degrees of vowel length
> 7) Failure to recognize the quantity rules
>
> (PSRC: 25).

Only the first two of these have any validity and even then neither is more than half true. 1) It is fair to say that Unified Cornish does not distinguish between /y:/ in *tus*, for example, and /œ:/ in *dus* 'come'. On the other hand it is clear from the texts that Middle Cornish did not always keep them separate either (see 3.15). 2) By /e/ I assume George means what in the body of his work he refers to as /ɪ/. He is right in saying that Unified Cornish does not recognize the difference between /ɪ:/ and /i:/, i.e. it does not distinguish therefore between *prys* /pri:z/ 'price' and *prys* /prɪ:z/ > /pre:z/, /pri:z/ 'time'. But then neither did the Middle Cornish scribes distinguish between them consistently. If they had done so, Unified Cornish would have distinguished them also. The 'error' in (3) above is too unspecific to need answering. As far as the other 'errors' are concerned Nance was, I believe, correct and Kernowek Kemyn is correspondingly incorrect.

Notice also that George has already admitted that he was mistaken about /tʲ/ and /dʲ/ and no such items ever existed in Cornish. He has nonetheless confidence in his own construct, for he says:

> I can therefore state with confidence that Revived Cornish [Kernowek Kemyn], as exemplified by the phonological base described in this chapter, is closer to the Cornish of 1500 than were either OldC or LateC. What is more, it is closer to the Cornish of 1500 than is, say, the "Geordie" dialect to standard English. I therefore suggest that, were a Cornish speaker from Tudor times suddenly to materialize, present-day speakers would, after some initial adjustments and probably a few laughs, be chatting together without difficulty by the end of the day (PSRC: 91).

13.19 George believes that the Cornish of our texts had three vowel-lengths, long, half-long and short. He also believes, as I do, that the quantity system changed in Cornish to one more similar to English. He says:

> Circa 1600, the Cornish quantity system changed, so as to conform mor[e] to the English system. The half-long vowels were eliminated, usually becoming short (PSRC: 68).

The only reason that George can have for dating the prosodic shift *c.* 1600 must be the prevalence of spellings like <gollan> 'heart' and <ballas> 'dig' in CW. Yet spellings like <y thadder> 'his goodness' already occur regularly in the *Ordinalia*. Moreover—and this is the most significant point—the whole batch of phonetic developments listed at 12.1 above are unintelligible unless the prosodic shift had already occurred before our earliest Middle Cornish texts. Furthermore there is every reason to believe that stressed vowels were actually lengthening *c.* 1600 (12.5).

George is, I believe, right in saying that the inherited prosodic system of Cornish was replaced by one closer to that of English. By dating the shift *c.* 1600 he is at least three hundred and fifty years too late. As a result much of his analysis of Cornish phonology is, I believe, rather wide of the mark.

The loss of half-length really means the shortening of long vowels to half-long and the shortening of half-long to short. It can hardly mean anything else. Such a shift when it occurred was bound to cause huge disruption in the sound system of Cornish. If it occurred *c.* 1600 as George claims, we can legitimately ask why CW shows no signs of the recent prosodic cataclysm. For all that the orthography is slightly more Anglicized than that of TH or BM, there is little

117

otherwise to suggest a major shift in the phonology has occurred. The reason is simple: the cataclysm occurred over three hundred years before.

13.20 We have seen that /iː/ in final position tended to diphthongize in Middle Cornish and that this was reflected in rhymes (3.5). Kernowek Kemyn ignores this development. George believes that the diphthongization of /iː/ > /ej/ occurred between *c.* 1525 and *c.* 1625 and was the result of the English Great Vowel Shift. I have pointed out above the difficulty of ascribing the phonetic developments of one language to the sound-changes of another. The diphthongization of /iː/ in Cornish occurred as a direct result of the Cornish prosodic shift. It had nothing to do with anything happening in English and was earlier than the Great Vowel Shift.

George mentions the diphthongization of /yː/ in final position. He says that /yː/ became /ɪuː/ in final position and before /x/ 'as in English, possibly *c.* 1625'. It seems that he believes that the diphthongization of /yː/ was in imitation of English. The date of *c.* 1625 is mistaken. *Dew* 'God' is spelt <du> as early as PA. This can only mean that *du* 'black' and *Dew* 'God' were pronounced identically already in the fifteenth century. The shift of /yː/ written <u> to /ɪw/ must then be at least as old as that. It can hardly have occurred '*c.* 1625'. The shift of /yː/ > /ɪw/ also explains the variation in the spelling of the word for 'spear': <gu>, <gew>, <gyw>. GKK says:

> It is difficult to arrive at a satisfactory spelling for this word...; either the [w] has become vocalized, or the word has been influenced by B *goaf*, itself influenced by F *gaffe* (GKK: 121).

There is no need to adduce contamination by Breton. The word was pronounced /gɪw/ and written <gu> (see 3.14) exactly as *Dew* was pronounced /dɪw/ and written <du>.

13.21 George mistakenly believes that Cornish originally had both /oː/ and /ɔː/. In fact it only ever had /oː/ and /oˑi/ and by the time of BM the two had fallen together (as a result of the prosodic shift) as /oː/, written <o> or <oy>. George claims that Nance's "long o" in fact comprised two different phonemes /oː/ and /ɔː/. George continues:

> Thus *trōs* 'noise' and *trōs* 'foot' were not homophones, but minimal pairs [*read*: a minimal pair]. There are so many such pairs, that it is difficult to believe that Nance was unaware of this difference; and one suspects that he deliberately over-simplified the language to make it easier to learn (PSRC: 126).

It is unfair to accuse Nance in this way. Far from simplifying Cornish, Nance, if anything, made it unnecessarily complex. The reason that Nance did not distinguish between /oː/ and /ɔː/ in Unified Cornish was that he believed they were the same. He had looked closely at the rhymes of the plays, in particular of BM (cf. 3.11), and realized that /o:/ and /o·i/ had fallen together.

Because George believes that /o:/ and /ɔ:/ were different he is compelled to find a spelling for /o:/. His solution is <oe> as in *boes* 'food', *goedh* 'goose', *loes* 'grey', etc. <oe> is a largely unhistorical graph and is quite unnecessary.

Ken George also believes that /o:/ > /u:/ '*c.* 1625'. As I have pointed out above, I think this is unlikely. It is more probable that Old Cornish /ui/ became /u:/ in western Cornish and remained as /u:/ in such words as *lûz* 'grey', *kûz* 'wood', *gûdzh* 'blood'. In more easterly Cornish, the standard dialect, /u:/ from Old Cornish /ui/ was lowered to /o:/. The evidence of the texts and of place-names corroborates this view (see 3.8, 3.10).

13.22 George appears to believe that /ɪ:/ fell together with /e:/ '*c.* 1650' (PSRC: 112). In view of spellings like <beth>, <veth> for *byth, vyth* in PA and OM and the virtually universal <beth>, <veth> in BM, it is likely that /ɪ:/ > /e:/ is much earlier than the early seventeenth century (see 3.6). In fact /ɪ:/ > /e:/ was a direct consequence of the prosodic shift and there is no reason to keep /ɪ:/ in revived Cornish at all. Jenner had already replaced Middle Cornish /ɪ:/ with /e:/ as early as 1904. Moreover, in some words, *deth* 'day' and *cref* 'strong', for example, /e:/ replaces /ɪ:/ in UC.

On occasion George seems to entertain doubts on this matter. Under <krev> 'strong', for example, GKK says "N.B. The /ɪ/ in OldC *crif* /krɪv/ seems to have changed abnormally early to [ɛ]". The shift /ɪ:/ > /e:/ is no earlier than the comparable shift in *gweth* 'trees' PA 16b; *pref* 'reptile' PA 122c, etc.

13.23 In Kernowek Kemyn 'I' and 'thou' are /mɪ:/ and /tɪ:/ respectively. These forms cannot possibly be right but are based on a misunderstanding of the evidence. Because the texts exhibit both <my>, <ty> on the one hand and <me>, <te> on the other, George assumes that the pronouns had the vowel /ɪ:/. I have indicated that /ɪ:/ in final position became /i:/ early. If so, then /mɪ:/, /tɪ:/ would have been impossible. In fact Middle Cornish had two forms for both pronouns: /mi:/ and /me/ and /ti:/ and /te/ (for a discussion of this question see 18.2 below). If Kernowek Kemyn had wished to be authentic it would have allowed both *me, te* and *mi, ti*. My /mɪ:/ and *ty* /tɪ:/ are fictions.

13.24 George admits that the word for 'to thee' is a problem and he gives an insight into his working methods when he says:

> The spelling of this word is not certain [read: pronunciation]; it could be *dhys*, as in Nance's spelling. In MidC, it was spelled *thys* or *ȝys*, and rhymed consistently with words in /-ɪs/. <i> is used in *Kernewek Kemmyn* because <i> is found in Breton (GKK: 72).

It is perhaps not wise to base the pronunciation of Cornish on that of Breton here, particularly since Breton has no /ɪ/. The problem with <thys> is actually more imagined than real. The texts seem to show two separate forms, one with a long vowel /ði:s/ and one with a short vowel /ðɪs/ (for a discussion of this question see 18.8 below). If Kernowek Kemyn wished to be authentic here it would allow both *dhys* and *dhis*.

13.25 Kernowek Kemyn spells the word for 'right hand; south' as *deghow* on the basis of Breton *dehou* and Welsh *dehau*. I have pointed out that the texts invariably spell the word with <y> (8.3). The spelling in Kernowek Kemyn is without foundation.

13.26 We saw at 5.1-4 that Middle Cornish originally had the alternation *y ~ e* in such etyma as *byth/bethaf, gwyth/gwethen, pryf/prevyon, prevas*, etc. Kernowek Kemyn is largely devoid of this alternation even though it maintains /ɪ:/. As a result in Kernowek Kemyn one finds such completely unhistorical forms as *gwydhenn* 'tree' for *gwedhen* (GKK: 130) and *bydhav, bydhydh, bydhons* [read *bydhon*], *bydhowgh, bydhons* (GMC2: 129) for the disyllabic future forms of *bos*. The reason that *bydhav, bydhydh* occur in Kernowek Kemyn is quite simply that Unified Cornish has *bydhaf, bydhyth* (Nance 1949: 24).

Kernowek Kemyn is not consistent, however. British /i/ in originally unstressed syllables gives *y* in Welsh, pronounced /ə/ and /e/ in Cornish written <e> (2.2). Kernowek Kemyn usually opts for unhistorical <y> (by false analogy with Welsh) but not consistently so, since one also finds <e> on occasion. Look at the following examples:

English	Welsh	Kernowek Kemyn
'I shall be'	byddaf	bydhav (*bethaf* OM 596)
'island'	ynys	ynys (*enys* OM 2592)
'Shrovetide'	Ynyd	Ynys (*enez* AB: 46b)
'tree'	gwydden	gwydhenn (*gwethen* OM 167)
'vomit'	chwydu	hwyja (*huedzha* AB: 177b)
'blow'	chwythu	hwytha (*wethugh*! 'blow!' BM 4563)
'be ye!'	byddwch	bedhewgh
'drink'	yfed	eva
'wide'	llydan	ledan
'grow'	tyfu	tevi

It is not clear by which criteria Kernowek Kemyn opts for <y> or <e> in such items.

From time to time George indicates that he has misgivings about his recommended forms. Under *prys* 'time, meal' GKK gives the plural as *prysyow* but adds a note: "N.B. pl. written as *preggyow* in MidC." *Preggyov* (BM 1972) is of course the expected form by *y ~ e* alternation. Similarly under the word *tevi* 'to grow' GKK says: "the cognates suggest that *tyvi* might be more correct." In fact /tevi/ and /tɪːv/ were in alternation with each other before the prosodic shift (see 5.4). GKK is also perplexed by <ledan> and ascribes it to "limited textual evidence" (GKK: 197). The lack of *y* ~ *e* alternation is particularly striking in Kernowek Kemyn with the diphthongs *yw* ~ *ew* (see 13.28 below).

13.27 George denies that /aː/ was ever pronounced [æː] in Middle Cornish. He says of the question of fronted /aː/ and the pronunciations that have been recommended for it:

> The dispute can now be settled: as far as Cornish /aː/ is concerned, [eː], [eːə], [ɛː] and [ɛə] are inappropriate realizations; for this phoneme they are English not Cornish sounds, and should not be used (PSRC: 124).

The phraseology here is a little confused but the meaning is clear: a fronted pronunciation of /aː/ is wrong for Middle Cornish, because such a pronunciation comes from English. How, then, is one to explain the fronted pronunciation of /aː/ in the Welsh of Glamorgan and of Mid-Wales? Is such a pronunciation in Welsh also to be ascribed to English influence? As I have pointed out above place-names with -*praze* and -*glaze* are inexplicable unless /aː/ was [æː].

I have also indicated above (3.17) that Lhuyd's *gêst* 'bitch' for expected *gast, can only be understood if /aː/ was originally [æː] in the word. Under the headword *gast (a form unattested in Cornish) George says: "N.B. spelled *gêst* by Lhuyd" (GKK: 106), yet he does not seem to have realized the full implications of Lhuyd's form.

13.28 Kernowek Kemyn has three diphthongs /iw/, /ɪw/ and /ew/ even though it is absolutely clear that /iw/ and /ɪw/ had fallen together as a direct result of the new prosodic system. Forms in Kernowek Kemyn like *liw* 'colour', *piw* 'who' and *gwiw* 'worthy' are without justification.

/ɪːw/ had a tendency to fall together with /ew/ after the prosodic shift, whereas original /ew/ in disyllabic words became /ow/. In Cornish before the prosodic shift one would have had /bɪːw/ <byw> 'alive' but /bewnans/ <bewnans> 'life'. After the shift these would have become /bew/ <bew> and /bownanz/ <bewnans>, <bounans> respectively (6.6). *Byv* occurs on occasion in Middle Cornish, at BM 4352, PC 847, for example. <Byv> is less common than <bew>, <bev> and is a spelling from before the prosodic shift, that has persisted after it. In the light of Middle Cornish <byv> Kernowek Kemyn's *byw* is perhaps justified. There is no possible warrant for the spellings *bywnans* and *bywa* 'to live', however. Similarly *klywes* 'to hear' and *klywav* 'I hear' are completely without basis. These should be spelt <klewes>, <klewav> or <klowes>, <klowav>. George claims to have based Kernowek Kemyn most closely on BM (PSRC: 60), yet this common verb almost always has *ou* in BM and there are only two or three instances of *eu*. There are none with *yw*. Since,

121

then, in Middle Cornish 'to live' and 'life' are always *bewe, bewa* and *bewnans* and 'to hear' and 'I hear' are either *clewes, clewaf* or *clowes/clowas, clowaf*, there can be no justification for either *bywa, bywnans* or *klywes, klywav*. I believe that these two forms, *klywes* 'to hear' and *bywnans* 'life' are by themselves quite enough to undermine any claim that Kernowek Kemyn has to acceptability.

We saw at 13.24 above that Kernowek Kemyn spells *dhis* 'to thee' with /i/ because Breton has /i/ in the corresponding word *dit* 'to thee'. George also informs me that he spells *byw* 'alive' and *bywnans* 'life' with <yw> because Welsh has *byw* 'alive': *Ny welav travith kamm gans* byw; *yndelma yth yw skrifys yn Kembrek... ytho y skrifav* Bywnans Meryadjek 'I see nothing wrong with *byw*; it is so written in Welsh... therefore I write *Bywnans Meryadjek*.' (correspondence, September 1987). There is no hint in George's remarks that he is aware of the alternation *y ~ e*, i.e. *byw* but *bewnans*.

Cornish has its own unique history and phonology. Yet Kernowek Kemyn spells parts of Cornish as though they were Breton and other parts as though they were Welsh. Welsh and Breton are useful for comparision. They should not be allowed to replace the Cornish texts as the chief source for the phonology and spelling of Neo-Cornish. Yet this seems to have been done in the case of Kernowek Kemyn. Is it any wonder that Kernowek Kemyn is so mistaken?

Kernowek Kemyn is not even consistent in the matter of *yw/ew* in disyllables/polysyllables. Usually Kernowek Kemyn has <yw> as in Welsh— but not always:

English	Breton	Welsh	Kernowek Kemyn
'hear'	klevout	clywed	klywes
'live'	bevañ	cf. bywyd	bywa
'drive'	leviañ	llywio	lywya
'Cornish'	kernevek	Cernyweg	Kernewek

If Kernowek Kemyn can write *klywes, bywnans* with <yw> as in Welsh, why does it not also write *Kernywek*? It cannot be because *ew* in *Kernewek* contains Proto-British *ow* and not *iw*, for *lywya* < **lowi-* (WG: 107) has historically the same vowel as the word for 'Cornish' < **Kornowika* (cf. HPB: 298). The vowel /ew/ in Middle Cornish *kewsel* (later *cowsel*) is the reflex of original /ow/ with *i*-affection. If Kernowek Kemyn were consistent, it would spell the word as **kywsel*.

13.29 George criticizes Nance for not distinguishing /aj/ from /ej/, i.e. the vowel of *payn* [aj] from the vowel of *dreyn* [ej]. As we have seen (6.8) from spellings like *gwaile* 'rods', *tayr* 'three' and *trailia* 'to turn' on the one hand and the complete confusion of *paynys, peynys* in Middle Cornish, the two diphthongs fell together early as a result of the new prosodic system. If Nance was right, and I believe he was, criticism of him in this matter is unfounded.

13.30 In Kernowek Kemyn inherited stressed /i/ remains in words like *mires*, *hwilas*, *gila*, etc. I have indicated at 4.2 above that in such words the texts regularly write <e> not <y> or <i> and that it seems therefore that 'look', 'search for' and 'other one' were /mɪrəz/ or /merəz/, /ʍɪləz/ or /ʍeləz/ and /ɡɪlə/ or /ɡelə/ in the period of our texts. The reason that Kernowek Kemyn maintains /i/ is simply the belief that Middle Cornish is close to Breton. Even a cursory glance at the texts would have shown that stressed /i/ in open syllables had become /ɪ/ or /e/. In BM, for example, one always finds *myr* 'look!' (singular) but *merugh* 'look!' (plural). The alternation <y> in monosyllables and <e> in disyllables ought to have provoked the realization that half-length no longer existed in Middle Cornish.

George is aware of the difficulty, because he spells 'to dwell' as <tryga> and says: "One would expect /trig/, but the word and its compounds behaved as if they contained /ɪ/ instead of /i/" (GKK: 321). Yet he does not appear to have realized that stressed /i/ in disyllables has everywhere become /ɪ/. George has understood the problem but his mistaken belief in half-length prevents his seeing the solution.

13.31 We can be completely certain that the opposition /o/ ~ /ɔ/ did not exist in the short vowels. Moreover we have seen that /o/ and /ʊ/ are often in free variation in the texts (4.4). Any attempt to keep these three sounds [ɔ], [o] and [ʊ] as separate phonemes is futile. There can be no possible justification for attempting to distinguish the vowels of /kɔθə/ 'older' and /koðə/ 'to fall'. Kernowek Kemyn does, however: <kottha> and <koedha>.

13.32 Kernowek Kemyn writes *breusi* 'to judge', *beudhi* 'to drown', *anfeusi* 'disaster', *anfeusik* 'unfortunate' and *feusik* 'fortunate', as though the stressed vowel in them all was /œ/. We have seen at 4.8 above that the evidence suggests the vowel was /y/ > /ɪ/ in all these items. Unified Cornish is probably correct, therefore, in spelling these words with <ü> /y/. The Kernowek Kemyn forms are correspondingly mistaken.

13.33 The treatment of unstressed vowels in Kernowek Kemyn is particularly at variance with the evidence. As far as /i/ and /y/ are concerned George admits (see 13.10) that both when unstressed are identical with /ɪ/, yet he seeks to maintain the vowel quality in other places where the vowel is clearly /ə/. Even a cursory look at the texts would show that the unstressed vowel in words like <onan>, <onen>, <onon>, <onyn> and <flehas>, <flehes>, <fleghys>, <flehys> was schwa (see 7.7). To attempt to maintain distinctions of quality in the pronunciation of words like *onan, benen, colon* cannot be justified.

As I mentioned above at 7.14 there is some slight evidence that the unstressed vowel in *cafos, eglos, arluth, gallos* maintained a rounded quality for a period. It is quite apparent, however, that the final vocalic segment was /ə/ in these words in everyday speech at least as early as PA and that spellings like

123

<arluth>, <gallus> were graphemic only. The attempt by Kernowek Kemyn to maintain a separate rounded vowel in unstressed position in words like *arloedh* 'lord', *galloes* 'power', *kavoes* 'to get' is as inauthentic as it is futile. George says of <kavoes> :

> The spelling <oe> in the unstressed syllable is justified by the very common spelling *cafus* in MidC (GKK: 157).

One must always remember that spellings in Middle Cornish are often a matter of scribal tradition rather than phonetic reality. In the case of the verbal noun 'to get' other spellings like *cawys, cawes, cawas* and *kafas* imply that there were two forms: /ˈkawəz/ and /ˈkafəz/ < /ˈkaɸǫz/. Kernowek Kemyn's unstressed <oe> in every instance is without foundation. Indeed one can legitimately ask of the proponents of Kernowek Kemyn the following question: if <cafus> is so common in Middle Cornish, why not spell it <cafus>? If the orthography does not allow such a spelling, perhaps the orthography needs revision.

Ray Edwards, although a user of Kernowek Kemyn, has his doubts about unstressed syllables in the system. Speaking of *honan* and *onan* in PA he says:

> Ken George has come to the conclusion that these words were written with *-yn*, *-an* or *-on* endings depending on the words with which they were set to rhyme. In almost every case the rhyming words in the Poem end in *-on* so that *onon/honon* do likewise in the MS, implying, I would think, that these final rhyming syllables are *just neutral vowels* [my emphasis]. Out of the three, the ending *-an* was chosen in imitation of Welsh and Breton forms with the unfortunate result for this Poem that these syllables will appear not to rhyme and the reader will have to treat them as neutral vowels for them to do so. The MS seems to use *e* most commonly to indicate a neutral vowel as does modern French (Edwards 1993: 20).

Edwards is a perspicacious editor of PA and his observations in the above paragraph deserve attention. In fact he is making two separate points. The first is that Middle Cornish texts really ought not to be respelt. The second is that as far as unstressed vowels are concerned, Kernowek Kemyn is mistaken.

13.34 In pursuit of non-existent half-length Kernowek Kemyn is led to an unhistorical gemination of consonants. George, imitating Breton, wants every short vowel to be followed by a geminate consonant. If a vowel is followed by a single consonant, then it is long in monosyllables and half-long elsewhere. Thus Kernowek Kemyn writes <penn> 'head', <mamm> 'mother' and <toemm> 'hot'.

Kernowek Kemyn also, however, has to double <gh> to distinguish *sygha* 'to dry' from *syggha* 'drier'. There is no need to mention that the normal Middle Cornish spelling of 'dry' is <segh>, for example, at OM 757, 1100, 1116,

1120, 1147; <sygh> does occur at OM 1131. The point at issue here is that the bizarre and unnecessary graph <ggh> in *seggha* is quite without warrant in the texts.

Kernowek Kemyn also writes consonants double before <y> as for example in the title *Passhyon agan Arloedh*. The gemination in *passhyon* is redundant because syllables were shortened before /j/. This is quite obvious from spellings like <cosullyow> 'counsels' TH 1, <pleynnya> 'plainer' TH 1a, <gwyrryan> 'righteous' TH 7a. Yet we have already seen how inconsistent Kernowek Kemyn is with gemination, for instance with <chasya> on the one hand and <passya> on the other. There is much inconsistency in Kernowek Kemyn in this respect. With <passhyon> constrast <nashyon> and <eksamnashyon> (all in GKK). In Middle English *passion* would have had a short stressed vowel and *nation* and *examination* long ones. In Cornish before /j/, however, all would have been /a/. Notice also the inexplicable variation in Kernowek Kemyn <plotya> 'to plot' but <pottya> 'to put'.

In Kernowek Kemyn *amanenn* 'butter', *gwydhenn* 'tree', *towlenn* 'programme' all have <-enn>. The geminate <nn> is to show that the final vowel is short. It is not to indicate a long /n:/, since the opposition between long and short consonants in Kernowek Kemyn is lost in unstressed syllables. On the other hand *meppik* 'little boy' and *rudhek* 'robin' have a single <k>. This seems somewhat inconstent given that Kernowek Kemyn has no objection to <kk> in *gokki* 'absurd', for example. Presumably Kernowek Kemyn did not want to spell words in *-ek* with <-ekk> since the ending is to be "realized" as /eg/ before vowels (13.10). In fact the geminate <nn> in *amanenn*, etc. is unnecessary since *all unstressed vowels are short*. The doubling of *n* in these words is not merely unhistorical, it is redundant.

Yet Kernowek Kemyn is inconsistent when it comes to doubling *n* after an unstressed vowel. It is not clear, for example, which criteria have been used to spell the words in list A with <nn> and in list B with <n>:

A
kalann '1st day of month' (Breton *kalan*)
kolonn 'heart' (Breton *kalon*)
morhwynn 'sand-hoppers' (Breton *morc'hwen*).

B
melyn 'yellow' (Breton *melen*)
lovan 'rope' (Breton *louan*)
sebon 'soap' (Breton *soavon*).

Most words with unstressed *-en* in Unified Cornish have *-enn* in Kernowek Kemyn: *gwedrenn* 'glass', *kribenn* 'comb', *glasenn* 'greensward', etc. *Reken* 'bill' and *blydhen* 'year' are spelt with a single <n>, presumably because the ending is not a diminutive. Yet in Kernowek Kemyn unstressed *-en* and *-enn* are pronounced identically. Such a difference of spelling in Kernowek Kemyn

125

without a difference in pronunciation is a further repudiation of the phonemic principle.

Here is a further list of spellings involving geminates which caught my eye as I browsed through GKK:

dryppynn 'little drop';
okkashyon 'occasion';
kwoffi 'to overeat';
krakkya 'to crack';
kommyttya 'to commit'.

Although *okkashyon* looks odd, one should remember that CW has <oblashyon> at line 1068. Note, however, the following inconsistent forms in Kernowek Kemyn: *preshyous* not **presshyous* 'precious', *skwatya* not **skwattya* 'swat' and *skitya* not **skittya* 'squirt'.

13.35 Although /dʲ/ and /tʲ/ have been removed from the latest hypostasis of Kernowek Kemyn, they were present in the earliest version (cf. 23.13). I have already mentioned how George in his paper in Ottawa referred to /dʲ/ as "this alien sound". When in PSRC he elaborated his hypothesis concerning /dʲ/ George clearly anticipated resistance. Having described /dʲ/ he says:

> Before the reader used to Unified Cornish becomes too outraged, let him study the following spellings from the texts, which show clearly that the phoneme in these words is /ð/ [i.e. /dʲ/] and not /s/ (PSRC: 166).

Since he was claiming to have solved the problem of *s/g* in the texts and in place-names, it is strange that he was expecting so much scepticism. As I have suggested above, it almost seems that he may not actually have believed the /dʲ/ hypothesis himself, but could see no alternative.

In the "Kernewek Kemmyn Up-Date" three years later (*Carn* 68: 16) George, writing under the aegis of the Cornish Language Board, declared:

> Nicholas Williams, in a … paper to be published later this year, has put forward strong arguments to show that the phonemes /τ/ and /ð/ never existed. Close examination of his evidence confirms this.… To everyone's relief, this will mean the disappearance of the corresponding graphemes <tj> and <dj>. This should remove the chief obstacle to adoption of Kernewek Kemmyn by the supporters of Unified Cornish.

George's relief signifies again that he was not convinced by his own hypothesis. It was certainly unwise of him to criticize Nance for not recognizing /tʲ/ and /dʲ/, when in his own mind he was less than happy about the two "phonemes".

13.36 In Kernowek Kemyn there is a conflict as we have seen between the desire to show that the final syllable in *medhyk* 'doctor', for example, is short and the requirement that it be pronounced as /ɪg/ before vowels.

Kernowek Kemyn assumes that Cornish operates like Breton in this matter. Final /g/, /b/, /v/, /ð/ are voiceless in final position in pausa and before consonants; before vowel they are voiced. As we have seen at 8.8-13 this is not in agreement with the evidence of the texts. Middle Cornish appears to have a developed a rule after the prosodic shift that historic voiced stops and continuants are voiced after a stressed vowel and voiceless after an unstressed one: *gwag ~ gwarrack*; *mab ~ morrap*. Although Kernowek Kemyn assumes that *gwag* and *mab* are [gwaːk] and [maːp] in pausa, it nonetheless spells them as <gwag> and <mab>. On the other hand *g/k* and *b/p* after an unstressed vowel are spelt <k> and <p> respectively: <medhyk> 'doctor' and <morrep> 'littoral', even though they are in Kernowek Kemyn to be pronounced ['meðeg] and ['morreb] before vowels.

Although Kernowek Kemyn is, I believe, not accurate as far as the pronunciation of final *g/k* and *b/p* in Cornish is concerned, by chance its spelling in this matter does correspond closely with the phonetic reality of the language.

Some etymologies in *Gerlyver Kernewek Kemmyn*

13.37 Since Kernowek Kemyn is sometimes prepared to spell etymologically rather than on purely phonemic grounds, perhaps we might digress here to examine some of the etymologies that appear in GKK.

Milliga 'curse'

This is described on page 221 as being from an 'unidentified root'. The spelling *mellyga* would be preferable (cf. 7.8 above). The origin is immediately identifiable as Vulgar Latin *mal'dico* 'curse'. The long *i* in the penult has caused *i*-affection of the first syllable of *a* to *e*.

Tesenn 'cake'

The Cornish word for 'cake', *tesenn*, is derived on page 308 from *tes* 'heat, warmth'. Cornish *tesenn*, like Welsh *teisen* 'cake', is related to the word for 'dough', Cornish *tos*, Welsh *toes* < **taisto-* ; cf. Old Irish *taís* 'dough'. *Tesen, teisen* are from **taist + ina* and show *i*-affection in the root syllable.

Cowses 'mind, thought'

GKK gives the word *kowses* 'inward thought' and suggests it may be derived from *kows* 'speech' + the abstract suffix *-ses*. The etymology is well known, however, for *kowses* is identical with Welsh *ceudod* 'cavity' > 'stomach' > 'heart, mind'. The word is a borrowing from Latin *cauitat(em)* 'cavity'.

Bolonjedh 'will, wish'
GKK does not give an etymology for the word *bolonjedh*. It merely compares Breton *bolontez* and adds "cf. W[elsh] *bodlonedd*". Welsh *bodlonedd* is a derivative of *bodlon* 'willing', which itself is a variant of *boddlon* < *bodd* 'wish'. With *bodd* compare Middle Cornish *both* 'wish'. Cornish *bolongeth, blonogath* like Breton *bolonte(z)* is derived from Latin/ French *volont-* + the native suffix *-eth/ez*. It has nothing whatever to do with Welsh *bodlonedd*. It is curious that *bolonjedh* should be compared with *bodlonedd*, because *bolonjedh* was originally spelt as *bolontjedh*. According to PSRC: 157 /ntʃ/ was the normal reflex in Middle Cornish of British /nt/, for example, in *kerentja* 'love', *syntji* 'to hold', *kyntjes* 'rather than', *gantjo* 'with him', *gantja* 'with them', *gentji* 'with her'. Clearly *bolonjedh* was originally understood to contain the group /nt/. Since *bodlonedd* never contained such a group, it is irrelevant for the purposes of comparison.

Fatell 'how' and *kettell* 'as soon as'
Under the word *fatell* 'how' GKK offers the etymology given by Williams in LCB < Old Cornish *pa delw*? 'which form?' This etymology, which originated with Lhuyd, is a most curious one for GKK to espouse. In the first place the Cornish interrogative 'which' is *py* not *pa*, as for example in *py lyes* 'how many?', *py tyller* 'which place?', etc. Secondly one would expect Old Cornish **pa delw* to result in **padelow* in Middle Cornish not *fatel*. The etymology suggested for *kettel* 'as soon as' is equally odd. *Kettell* (to give the Kernowek Kemyn spelling) we are told is from *keth dell* 'the same as'. Semantically this is a long way from 'as soon as' and on those grounds alone the etymology must be rejected.

I take *fatel* to be a reduced form of **forth del* 'the way that, the way which'. The collocation of /θ/ + /t/ has naturally enough resulted in /t/; cf. *totta* < *toth da*. The /r/ has been lost in the new cluster, but its erstwhile presence is apparent from the lowered vowel /a/ < /o/. The expression *forth del* > *fatel* was originally used, I believe, in indirect speech: *me a welas forth del ova* 'I saw the way he was' > 'I saw how he was'. As an interrogative adverb *fatel* is either an extension of this conjunction or an aphetic form of *py forth del* 'which way that?' *Kettel* similarly as a conjunction originally contained *del(l)*. I take *kettel* to be a reduced form of **ken toth del* 'as soon as', where *ken* 'as' is the equivalent of Welsh *cyn*, and has been replaced for the most part in Middle Cornish by *mar* 'as'. *Ken* survives in such expressions as *kemmys* 'how much' < **ken myns* and *kenyver* 'how many?' < **ken nyver*.

Both *fatel* the conjunction, and *kettel* were pronounced with the stress on the second syllable. In the case of *fatel* this can be guaranteed by two observations. In the first place *fatel, fatell, fetel* is always spelt with <e> in the second syllable, never with <a>. This means the second syllable is /e/ and not the neutral vowel /ə/. It must consequently always have been stressed. In the second place in Late Cornish *fatel* as a conjunction introducing indirect speech appears as *'tel* or *'ter* (see 21.17 below). This can only mean that the word was *fa'tel* and not *'fatel*. The variant *fatla* 'how', by the way, is from *forth del ha*; compare *kepar ha* 'like as'.

The interrogative adverb *fatel* 'how?' has the stress on the first syllable; cf. *fatl* 'how?' (AB: 248c).

Denythy 'give birth to'
The compiler suggests that this verb is a derivative of the word *neyth* 'nest' and means literally 'to emerge from a nest'. The reality is much more mundane, however. We have to start with the Indo-European root $*genH_1$ 'produce, give birth' that is seen, for example, in *genys* 'born' and *genesygeth* 'birth'. Proto-Celtic $*di\text{-}gn\text{-}akt\text{-}a$ would give $*dyneth$ 'act of giving birth' from which the verb *denythy* is derived.

It might be argued that mistaken etymologies do not vitiate an orthography. In themselves they do not, but there is always the risk that if we spell etymologically we will make mistakes and spell wrongly. The spelling of English contains many false etymologies, *island, hiccough,* for example. The case of Cornish is unique in that we are attempting to revive a language that we know only imperfectly. The safest course is to spell as the original speakers of the language spelt. Then we cannot possibly go wrong.

Middle Cornish, Unified Cornish and Kernowek Kemyn contrasted
13.38 Before concluding I give overleaf the same portion of *Pascon agan Arluth* in three versions the original spelling, Unified Cornish and Kernowek Kemyn. The reader can judge for himself which of the two modern orthographies looks the more authentic.

The original text:

Camen pylat pan welas
  na ylly crist delyffre
ma nan geffo ef sor bras
  ʒeworth ol an goweʒe
rag henna ef a iuggyas
  Ihesus ʒeʒe ʒy laʒe
the ves y a thelyffras
barabas quyth mayʒ elle.

Pan o Ihesus cryst dampnys
  aberth yn crows may farwe
haccra mernans byth ordnys
  ʒe creatur ny vye
en grows whath nyn io parys
  nan eʒewon ny woʒye
an prennyer py fens kefis
  ʒe wuʒyll crous aneʒe.

In Unified Cornish

Cammen Pylat pan welas
  na ylly Cryst delyfra
ma na'n jevo ef sor bras
  dhyworth oll an gowetha
raghenna ef a jujjyas
  Jhesus dhedha dh'y ladha
dhe ves y a dhelyfras
Barabas, quyt mayth ella.

Pan o Jhesus Cryst dampnys
  aberth yn crows may farwa—
haccra mernans byth ordnys
  dhe greatur ny vya
an grows whath nyns o parys,
  na'n Edhewon ny wodhya
an prenyer py fens kefys
  dhe wuthyl crows anedha.

In Kernowek Kemyn

Kammenn Pilat pan welas
  na ylli Krist delivra
ma na'n jevo ev sorr bras
  dhiworth oll an gowetha
rakhenna ev a jujyas
  Yesus dhedha dh'y ladha
dhe-ves i a dhelivras
Barabas kwit mayth ella.

Pan o Yesus dempnys
  a-berth yn krows may farwa,
hakkra mernans bydh ord'nys
  dhe greatur ny via,
an grows hwath nyns o parys,
  na'n Edhewon ny wodhya
an prennyer py fens kevys
  dhe wuthyl krows anedha.

Kernowek Kemyn: conclusion

13.39 Kernowek Kemyn is very unsatisfactory. Among the more serious errors and defects one should include the following at least:

C1) Kernowek Kemyn insists on three vocalic lengths: long, half-long and short but Middle Cornish had only long and short (2.4; 13.8).

C2) Kernowek Kemyn distinguishes /iː/ and /eː/ although the two had fallen together as /eː/ in Middle Cornish (3.6; 13.22).

C3)[15] Kernowek Kemyn distinguishes /ɔː/ and /oː/ although in standard Middle Cornish the two had fallen together (3.11; 13.21).

C4) Kernowek Kemyn is unaware that /iː/ had become /ej/ in final position in Middle Cornish (3.5; 13.8).

C5) Kernowek Kemyn is unaware that original /ej/ and /aj/ had fallen together as /aj/ in Middle Cornish (6.8; 13.29).

C6) Kernowek Kemyn is unaware that /ow/ and /aw/ were falling together as /aw/ in Middle Cornish (6.7).

C7)[16] Kernowek Kemyn is unaware that final /yː/ had become /ɪw/ in Middle Cornish and that final /uː/ had become /ew/ (3.13; 3.9; 13.20).

C8) Kernowek Kemyn distinguishes /i/ and /ɪ/, though the two had fallen together as /ɪ/ in Middle Cornish and /ɪ/ alternated with /e/. Kernowek Kemyn therefore spells 'look', for example, as <mires> with /i/ although it is most frequently *meras* in the texts (4.1-3; 13.30).

C9) Kernowek Kemyn incorrectly pronounces long /aː/ as [aː] and not [æː] (3.17; 13.27).

C10) Kernowek Kemyn is ignorant of the vocalic alternation *y ~ e* and as a result posits such non-existent forms as *gwydhenn* 'tree', *hwytha* 'to blow', *ynys* 'island' (5.1-4; 13.26).

C11) Kernowek Kemyn posits three diphthongs /iw/, /ɪw/ and /ew/, when Middle Cornish had two only (or in some cases only one) (6.2-5; 13.28).

---

15 Since the publication of the first and second editions of *Cornish Today* I have revised my view on this criticism. It should now read:

C3) KK mistakenly believes that MidC had two long vowels /ɔː/ and /oː/. MidC originally had /oː/ and /oːj/ but during the MidC period these two fell together as /oː/ except in final position where /oːj/ remained a diphthong, e.g. *moy* 'more'.

For further discussion see *Towards Authentic Cornish*, Chapter 7.

16 I have likewise revised my view on this criticism. It should now read:

C7) Kernowek Kemyn is unaware that final /yː/ had become /ɪw/ in Middle Cornish (3.13; 3.9; 13.20).

For further discussion see *Towards Authentic Cornish*, Chapter 1 and §13.06.

C12) Kernowek Kemyn has *klyw, klywes* and *byw, bywnans* when Middle Cornish had *clew, clewes/clowes* and *byw/bew, bewnans/bownans* (6.6; 13.28).

C13) Kernowek Kemyn attempts to distinguish quality in unstressed vowels even though all unstressed vowels are schwa from the Middle Cornish period onwards (7.2-15; 13.33).

C14) Kernowek Kemyn posits the impossible /mɪː/ and /tɪː/ for 'I' and 'thou' respectively (3.4; 13.23; 18.2).

C15) Kernowek Kemyn is unaware that 'to thee' was both /ðɪz/ and /ðiːz/ in Middle Cornish (13.7; 18.8).

C16) Kernowek Kemyn spells and pronounces *deghow* 'right, south' with an unhistorical /e/ (8.3; 13.25).

C17) Kernowek Kemyn posits a whole series of geminate consonants in Cornish: /pː/ <pp>, /tː/ <tt>, /xː/ <ggh>, etc., none of which existed in the Middle Cornish period (8.1; 13.34).

C18) Kernowek Kemyn has no voiceless sonants /rh/, /lh/, /nh/, even though such items were a feature of Middle Cornish (8.4).

C19) Kernowek Kemyn is unaware of the rule that *deg* 'ten', *gwreg* 'wife' always have final /g/ but *medhek* 'doctor' and *gowek* 'mendacious' always have /k/ and that the same voice/voicelessness operates with *b/p* (8.8-14; 13.10; 13.36).

C20) Kernewek uses graphs that are at variance with medieval and modern practice, e.g. <k> before back vowels as in *Kammbronn*; <kw> for <qu> and <hw> for <wh> (13.15-17).

C21) Because Kernowek Kemyn has half-length, which was absent from Middle Cornish, the system is compelled to geminate letters unhistorically in *mamm* 'mother', *gwann* 'weak', for example (13.34).

C22) Kernowek Kemyn is inconsistent with respect to the gemination of consonants: *Kalann* 'Calends' but *lovan* 'rope', *blydhen* 'year' but *kribenn* 'comb' (13.34).

C23) Kernowek Kemyn is inconsistent using <oe> for /oː/ in *moes* 'table', for example, but /o-e/ in *aloes* 'aloes' (13.11; 13.21).

C24) Kernowek Kemyn inconsistently uses <sh> to mean /ʃ/ in *shap* 'shape' but /sh/ in *leshanow* 'nickname' (13.11).

C25) The etymologies underlying Kernowek Kemyn are often wrong and the orthography is inconsistent as well as being mistaken (13.11; 13.37).

C26)[17] The database upon which Kernowek Kemyn was constructed is defective; as result GKK is replete with omissions and misinformation (13.3-4).

---

17 Since the publication of the first and second editions of *Cornish Today* I would now add five additional criticisms, which I give below. For further discussion see *Towards Authentic Cornish*, Chapter 1.

Cornish revivalists must not be misled by geography. Simply because Cornwall is approximately mid-way between Wales and Brittany, it does not follow that the phonology of Cornish is in a similarly intermediate position. The sound-system of medieval Cornish, unlike that of Welsh and Breton, was heavily influenced by English. The assibilation of dentals in Cornish as seen, for example, in *tas* 'father' where both Welsh and Breton have *tad*, should be sufficient to alert researchers to the unique nature of the Cornish sound-system. An excessive reliance on Welsh and Breton comparisons distorts our perception of Cornish since it pays insufficient attention to the Cornish texts themselves. These are without question our most important source for knowledge of the language.

The orthography or spelling-system of Cornish must also be treated quite differently from that of Breton. Breton has thousands of native-speakers, many of whom have never learnt to write the language. A spelling-reform in Breton therefore is of relatively limited importance, since it does not affect the way in which the language is pronounced. The case of Cornish is quite different. Here we are dealing with the resuscitation of a language, whose speakers will also be writers of it. As a result there is inevitably a close interdependence between orthography on the one hand and pronunciation on the other. There is only one legitimate spelling for Cornish, namely, that which is to be found in or is directly derived from the Cornish texts themselves. If we impose a modern orthography on Cornish, we cannot claim to be reviving the medieval or Tudor language.

In conclusion it has be restated that Kernowek Kemyn takes no note of Brythonic vocalic alternation (5.1-9) nor of the prosodic shift (12.1). Yet both

C27) Although it ignores the Prosodic Shift, KK allows pre-occlusion in pronunciation which is itself a direct consequence of the shift.

C28) The allophone [m:] of /m/ was entirely determined by position. Spellings like <kemmer> and <kemmyn> in KK are therefore unnecessary. KK, however, believes that /m/ and [m:] were phonemically distinct in Middle Cornish. In which case to spell them identically e.g. in <kemmeres> and <kemmer>, is a repudiation of the phonemic principle, which KK claims to espouse.

C29) The proponents of KK because they are unaware that the Prosodic Shift is early, misunderstand the function of <nn> in words like *crenna* 'to tremble', *pre(n)na* 'to buy', and *ale(n)na* 'hence'. In consequence discussion of these items in the handbooks of KK is mistaken and misleading.

C30) Even if the phonology underlying KK could be shown to be correct, the spelling system of KK is artificial, arbitrary and quite out of keeping with the orthography of the traditional language. Cornish people are attempting to revive their ancestral language because they value their traditions. In which case using such an unhistorical orthography is illegitimate.

C31) George has now admitted that the database on which he based his *Gerlyver Kernewek Kemmyn* was faulty. Perhaps George could be asked to correct his database and then rewrite KK accordingly.

phenomena are crucial to traditional Cornish. The absence of both vocalic alternation and the effects of the prosodic shift from the phonology of Kernowek Kemyn vitiate the entire system. Indeed these two omissions are the immediate reason for most of the errors listed above.

If, however, the above errors and omissions were removed from Kernowek Kemyn, it would cease to be Kernowek Kemyn.

CHAPTER 14
Revived Late Cornish[18]

14.1 Revived Late Cornish is the variety of Cornish promoted by Richard Gendall and *Teere ha Tavaz*. Unlike Unified Cornish Revived Late Cornish is based on the later texts, in particular the work of Nicholas and John Boson, Edward Lhuyd and their contemporaries. The accidence of Revived Late Cornish is more advanced than that of Unified Cornish and the orthography is a regularized form of the English-based spelling of the seventeenth and eighteenth centuries. The great merit of Revived Late Cornish is that, in theory, it does not edit its sources but presents them exactly as they are.

While I have the highest regard for Gendall's aims, it seems to me that Revived Late Cornish does not, and cannot, live up to the intentions of its proponents. Although Revived Late Cornish has brought the later texts into the public eye and has shown that to a degree Late Cornish is a viable medium of expression, I find the whole enterprise to be misconceived. The rest of this chapter will deal with my objections to Revived Late Cornish.

14.2 Gendall speaks of Late Cornish as though it were a completely different language from Middle Cornish. Middle Cornish, especially of BM, TH and, if one considers it Middle Cornish, CW, is much more racy and colloquial than the Unified Cornish norm to which we have grown accustomed. The real difference between those three texts on the one hand and Late Cornish on the other is the orthography.

If one looks at the chronology of Middle and Late Cornish one can see clearly that the division is without foundation. I list here the remains of Cornish literature and the dates of the individual texts. For the medieval literature the dating is of the earliest manuscripts and is of course highly tentative.

The Charter Fragment	mid to late 14th century
The Passion Poem	early 15th century
The Ordinalia	mid 15th century
Beunans Meriasek	1504
Tregear's Homilies	1555-58 [19]
Creation of the World	1611
Nicholas Boson	1660-1700
John Boson	1700-1725.

---

18 In the first and second editions of *Cornish Today* I used the term "Modern Cornish" in inverted commas for the variety of Neo-Cornish developed by Richard Gendall, in order to distinguish it further from "Neo-Cornish" which might also be called "Modern". More recent discussion has settled on the term "Revived Late Cornish" for *Kernowek Noweja* or *Kernowek Dewedhes*, and I have used that term here.

19 The recently-discovered play *Bewnans Ke* belongs between Tregear and the *Creation of the World*.

Starting from the Charter Fragment in the late fourteenth century and ending with John Boson in 1725 we have some kind of writing for every 50 or so years. There is no gap anywhere, nor is there any reason to draw an imaginary linguistic line between Tregear and CW or CW and Nicholas Boson. Indeed it is probable that William Jordan, the scribe of CW, was a younger contemporary of John Tregear and that Nicholas Boson was a younger contemporary of William Jordan.

We have little Cornish from the period between CW and Nicholas Boson. One fragment from that period is preserved by Davies Gilbert (1838: ii 31-2), namely the words of administration of Holy Communion used by the Reverend William Jackson, vicar of St Feock, until about 1640. The text reads as follows:

An Gorfe ay agan Arluth Jesus Chrest toan fe ry rag thy, gwetha tha gorfe hag eneff, warthe Ragnaveffera kemera ha dybbery henna en predery may Chrest marnas rag thy hag be grassylen.

An goyse ay agan Arluth Jesus Chrest toan the fowle rag thy, gwetha tha gorfe hag eneff warthe Ragnaveffera: eva henna in prederry may Chrest's goyse be towle rag tha, hag dybbery wor ren en tha gollon ryb creignans hag grassylen

[The body of our Lord Jesus Christ, which was given for thee, preserve thy body and soul unto everlasting life: take and eat this in remembrance that Christ died for thee and be thankful.

The blood of our Lord Jesus Christ, which was shed for thee, preserve thy body and soul unto everlasting life: drink this in remembrance that Christ's blood was shed for thee and feed on him in thy heart by faith with thanksgiving].

The text here is clearly very corrupt, and Jenner believed that it was a forgery on the part of Hals in whose history (1750) it first occurred (JRIC 19: 169). This seems very unlikely indeed to me. A forger would surely have produced a much less corrupt text and if active in the middle of the eighteenth century would have almost certainly betrayed himself by using Late Cornish spelling. I am convinced that the words of administration are in origin genuine, though they have been corrupted in transmission.

The orthography is substantially that of John Tregear. Notice, for example, *agan Arluth* 'our Lord', *eneff* 'soul', *henna* 'that', *tha gorfe* 'thy body', *goyse* 'blood', *tha gollon* 'thy heart'. This piece is later than CW but the spelling is more archaic than that of CW and suggests that the literary standard may have survived well into the seventeenth century.

14.3 Linguistically speaking the great change in Cornish came in the 13th–14th century when Cornish lost half-length, began to untense its long vowels, to reduce its unstressed vowels to schwa and to strengthen its nasal sonants by pre-occlusion. If we attempt to itemize the features normally associated with Late Cornish, we might get a list something like the following:

a) pre-occlusion of *n* > *dn* and *m* > *bm*
b) the prevalence of *g* or *j* where Middle Cornish has *s*, e.g. in *me a alja* for *my a alsa*
c) diphthongization of long *y* > *ey*
d) loss of *th* after *r* in *forth, horth*, etc.
e) rhotacization of *esa, esof* > *era, eram*, etc.
f) use of *angy* as a third plural pronoun
g) *-ans* in the third plural of the prepositional pronouns
h) the use of *-m* as the ending of the 1st person singular
i) use of *del/dr, fatel/tel* to introduce indirect speech
j) falling together of *ny(ns)* and *na(g)* as *na(g)*
k) periphrastic present *yma ow cregy* 'he believes'
l) *men* for *myn* 'wishes'
m) periphrastic future with *my a vyn*, etc.
n) periphrastic conditional with *my a vynsa*, etc.
o) the replacement of infixed by suffixed pronouns
p) the substitution of possessive adjectives by suffixed pronouns
q) prepositional pronouns replaced by preposition + independent pronoun
r) plurals of native words in *-s*
s) the use of *tereba* 'until'
t) distinctive vocabulary: *pecar* 'like', *bus* 'but', etc.

All these features are to be found in Cornish before the Late Cornish period. Some are as old as the *Ordinalia*, some occur in PA, still others are attested in BM or the Tregear manuscript. Let us look at them in detail.

a) **Pre-occlusion** was a direct result of the new prosodic system. Although not normally written until the sixteenth century it was probably present in the language well before then. Pre-occlusion occurs in BM as well as SA. Since pre-occlusion is a largely western phenomenon (9.5), its absence from the standard language is not astonishing.

b) /dʒ/ for /z/ is not a specifically late feature, since *woge, ege* for *wosa, esa*, etc., are well attested in the *Ordinalia*. Late Cornish exhibits /dʒ/ in the conditionals *menja* and *galja*, where more literary Cornish has /z/: *mynsa, galsa*. It is clear to me that /dʒ/ is not a reflex of /z/ but a dialectal variant that is as old as /z/. We can be sure that *mynsa, galsa* were pronounced /mendʒə/ and /galdʒə/ in western Cornish in the medieval period, but the spelling did not show the pronunciation. The /dʒ/ is sometimes shown in Middle Cornish after /n/ and /l/, e.g. *falge, polge*.

c) I have already pointed out that the diphthongization of /iː/ > /ej/ is as old as PA and the *Ordinalia* (3.5). Moreover the spellings *whay* 'you' in Tregear and *tray* 'three' in Borde indicate that by the sixteenth century the diphthongization of /iː/ was written on occasion. *Kei* for *ky* 'dog' is not, then, a Late Cornish phenomenon, but is much older.

d) **Forth, kerth, etc., > for', ker',** etc. It has been pointed out above (8.6) that the loss of /θ/ through the stage /ð/ after /r/ is already present in the *Ordinalia*. It also occurs in early place-names. This is one feature which can be clearly dated several centuries before the Late Cornish period.

e) The **rhotacization of intervocalic** /z/ > /r/ is widespread in SA, as for example in *neg eran cregy* 'we do not believe' SA 59. This again would seem to be a phenomenon that is at least as old as the sixteenth century. One suspects it is much older but was not reflected in spelling until the weakening of the scribal tradition at the Reformation.

f) **-ans** in prepositional pronouns: this feature is already well established in TH: *thethans, ynnans,* etc. (see 18.3).

g) One of the most distinctive features of Late Cornish is the use of the 3rd plural personal pronoun **angye** 'they, them'. This already occurs in embryo in TH and SA (see further 18.3). Since *anjy* probably occurred already in the sixteenth century, it cannot be thought of as a distinctively Late Cornish phenomenon.

h) **-m as a first singular ending**: Late Cornish *gellam* 'I can' etc is from *gylla(f)* + *ma*. The emphatic pronoun was necessary since the final /v/ of the ending had been lost. The use of *-ma* as a virtual ending of the first singular is already well established in the *Ordinalia* (19.2 and cf. 12.4).

i) **Fatel** and **del** to introduce indirect speech are already present in PA and BM (see 21.17).

j) **Na(g)** for **ny(ns)**: the earliest examples known to me are to be found in SA: *na illen denaha* 'we cannot deny' 66, *na illansy bos seperatis* 'they cannot be separated' SA 61.

k) The **periphrastic present** is already to be found in BM, for example: *nyns esos ow attendya an laha del vya reys* 'thou dost not consider how the law had to...' BM 848-49 (see 21.7).

l) **Men** for **myn** occurs in BM: *gul gueres dymo mar men* 'if he will help me' BM 734; *gasa crystyen byv ny ven* 'will not leave a Christian alive' BM 1327; and in TH: *mar men an cristonnyan* TH 19a.

m) The **periphrastic future** with *mynnes* is already common in the *Ordinalia*, for example, *me a vyn aga sywe* 'I will follow them' OM 1630 (see 21.9).

n) The **periphrastic conditional** with *me a vynsa*, etc. is of course related to m) above. The use of *mynsen* to form the conditional is a regular feature of Middle Cornish: *certan feryov in breten cafus y fensan certen ow gueres mara mynneth* 'I would have certain fairs in Brittany indeed if you will help me' BM 206-68.

o) The **replacement of infixed by suffixed pronouns** is a feature already present in PA: *arluth pragh y hysta vy* 'Lord, why hast thou forsaken me?' PA 201c. It is attested in SA as well (21.5).

p) The **replacement of possessive adjective by suffixed pronouns**: although *kar ve* 'my friend' looks like a distinctively Late Cornish syntax, examples are to be found earlier, notably at SA 61: *dir faith da ny* 'by our good faith'.

q) Forms like **tha ve** 'to me', **tha ge** 'to thee' may seem to be distinctively Late Cornish, but there are parallels already in SA: *the gee* 'to thee' SA 62, for example.

r) **Plurals in -s** occur in TH: *awaylers* 'evangelists' TH 53a, *aweylys* 'gospels' TH 52a.

s) **Tereba** 'until' is used, for example, by Rowe: *En wheeze tha godnatalle che ra debre tha vara, tereba tha traylyah tha noare* 'In the sweat of thy brow thou shalt eat thy bread until thou return to the earth' RC 23: 182; cf. *trebe* 'until' (AB: 249a). *Treba* is not properly a conjunction at all but a verbal phrase: Rowe's *tereba tha traylyah* < *tere ba tha traylya* 'until there shall be thy returning'. The verb in *terebah* is patent in Rowe's *terebah mernaz Herod* 'until Herod's death' RC 23: 198 (lit. 'until there was the death of Herod'). *Tere* is identical with Lhuyd's *try* 'dum, whilst' (AB: 56a, 249a). These are related to Middle Cornish *hedre* 'until', itself probably a development of Old Cornish **hid del* 'as long as' or something similar. Whatever the origin of *hedre*, it is clear that it had two forms: *hedre* and **heder*. It is also apparent from the reduced vowel in CW, that *hedre, heder* was stressed on the second syllable /hə'dre/, /hə'der/. *Hedre, *heder* is most commonly used with the subjunctive of

139

bos: *hadre von bew* 'as long as we live' CW 1258, *hadre von omma* 'as long as we are here' CW 1425. A reduced form of **heder* occurs in *dirr vo an enef in kigg mab deane* 'as long as the soul is in the flesh of mankind' SA 60a. In later Cornish the lenition of *bo/be* is omitted and /h/ in the reduced first syllable devoices *d* to *t*: *h(a)'dre* + *bo* > *te'reba, trebe* 'until'. Rowe's *tereba* and *dirr vo* in SA are thus variants of the same form.

t) **Distinctive vocabulary**:
The usual word for 'but, unless' in Late Cornish is *buz*: *buz me a aore* 'but I know' (BF: 31). *Bus* 'but' is attested in SA: *bus e dochya, not only touchya, bus e thibbry...* 'but to touch him, not only to touch him but to eat him...' (SA 60a).

The Late Cornish for 'also' in *aweeth* < Middle Cornish *ynweth*, as for example, in *m'ala ve moaze ha gortha thotha aweeth* 'that I may go and worship him also' RC 23: 196. This form occurs in SA, for example, *ha e weth, e thesan ny o recevia* 'and also we receive...' SA 61. The earliest example of 'also' without *n* is probably *y weth* RD 837.

The normal word for 'like, as' in Late Cornish is *pecar* or its reduced form *car, kar*. This is a metathesized variety of *kepar* 'like'. *Pecar* is attested in SA: *pecar a ruk an ethewan e sensy* 'just as the Jews seized him' SA 61.

The commonest word for 'all' in Late Cornish is *kaniver* < Middle Cornish *kenyver* 'as many', as for example in, *ha kanifer tra es guaya... ha kanifer hethen...* 'all things that move... and all birds...'. This occurs in SA in just this form: *the Canevar den gwyrrian* 'to all righteous men' SA 60.

In Late Cornish *golsowes* 'to listen' is simplified to *gosowes*, for example in *ev a gyzyuaz* 'he listened' JCH § 26. There are two examples of this simplified form in SA: *gosoweth* 62a, *gosough* 63, both the 2nd plural imperative.

14.4 It is quite apparent that most of the distinctive features of Late Cornish are already present in the sixteenth century. Many others are as old as the *Ordinalia* and PA. Yet Gendall has been insisting since the publication of KB in 1972 (KB: 118-19) that Medieval and Late (Modern) Cornish are different forms of the language. To attempt to amalgamate them, he says, would result in "an unreal alloy with no historical basis" (SGMC: 1). To underline his point Gendall quotes two passages, one from *Nebbaz Gerriau* and the other from BM. The reader is to be struck by how dissimilar the two forms of Cornish are. Yet the difference is only one of orthography.

Instead of a passage from BM Gendall might have used CW. The following passages, for example, look sufficiently medieval:

Lowena thewhy ow thas
   devethis a paradice
yth of lemyn tha thew gras
   ow negyssyow yth ew gwryes
   par dell wrussowgh thym orna

[Joy to you, my father.
   Come from paradise
I am now, thanks to God.
   My errand is accomplished
   as you enjoined upon me] (CW: 1880-84).

or

An chorll adam y drygva
   a vyth abarth awartha
in onyn an clowsters na
neb na vyth tam lowena
mes in tewolgow bras ena
   ow kelly presens an tase

[The churl Adam—his dwelling-place
will be on the upper side
in one of those cloisters,
who will have no whit of joy
but in great darkness there
   losing the presence of the Father] (CW: 2024-29).

The reason Gendall does not cite such passage from CW is that he uses CW as one of the chief sources for Revived Late Cornish. Although CW was written by William Jordan in 1611, Jordan was not the author. The original text of CW dates from before the Reformation and the author was almost certainly a younger contemporary of the author of BM. If BM is medieval Cornish, then CW is medieval Cornish as well. The two plays, BM and CW, are effectively written in the same kind of Cornish. To describe one as medieval and the other as modern is specious.

In fact CW is in a number of ways more archaic than BM. CW distinguishes the present subjunctive *bo* from past subjunctive *be* better than does BM; is without examples of the later Cornish *men* for *myn* 'wishes' and unlike BM has no examples of indirect speech introduced by *fatel*. CW also maintains the opposition *byth ~ bethough* far better than BM. Gendall himself admits that CW is "typical of the Mediaeval Cornish Drama" (SGMC: vii). One wonders, then, why he presses CW into service as a source for Revived Late Cornish.

14.5 As I have suggested above the difference between BM and CW on the one hand and the later writers on the other is one of spelling. Nonetheless the difference between the traditional orthography and the later English-based one is considerable and is likely to confuse beginners. Because Gendall is apparently reluctant to respell his sources, the forms he cites in SGMC exhibit three different spelling systems: traditional from CW, English-based from Boson, Tonkin, Rowe, etc., and semi-phonetic from Lhuyd. Let me give just a few examples from SGMC. I should point out that the following are taken not from the actual quotations from authors but from lists of vocabulary that are presumably to be memorized by students.

Under the incorrect heading "Nouns in Ap[p]osition" (SGMC: 3) we read *mab Noah* 'Noah's son' but *mabe cotha Adam* 'Adam's oldest son'. Later (ibid.: 33) we find *blethan* 'year' but *cansbledhan* 'century', *meeze* 'month' but *hanter mees* 'fortnight'. Yet all the months of the year are given in Lhuyd's spelling with *mîz* for 'month' not *meeze* or *mees* (ibid.: 35). 'Daybreak' (ibid.: 35) is *terri an dzhêdh* but 'mid-day' is *hanter dydh*. 'Good day', however, is *deeth dah* (ibid.: 36). The same mixture of orthographies is noticeable in Gendall's dictionary (SDMC) where, for example, 'true' is given as *guîr, gweer, gwyre, gweare, gwyer, gwear,* 'speak' is variously *cowse, kouz, cowz, cooz, cows,* 'men' is *teeze, teez, tees, tîz* or *tues* and 'strong' is *krêv, creve, creav, creeve, creaf, creyf, creif* or *kref.* The heterogeneity of spelling systems used is of the essence in both SGMC and SDMC.

Gendall's justification of his mixed orthography might be as follows: his books are a counterblast to the excessive respelling of Unified Cornish and its successors. By giving the students the various forms as they actually occur in the sources, Revived Late Cornish suppresses nothing and invents nothing. It may be slightly confusing at first but it is up to the students to decide how to spell the Cornish they learn. In the light of a close reading of SGMC, however, this argument is not compelling.

The morphology of Revived Late Cornish

14.6 Gendall describes his method of producing verbal and other paradigms in the following terms:

> The orthography used in paradigms is a standardisation taken from the *most suitable examples* [my emphasis]. It has seemed best to do this in the paradigm because of the great variety of forms available, which if all shown, would render the presentation of the material difficult (SGMC: vi).

The operative expression here is "most suitable". The suitability has less to do with frequency than extraneous factors. I have space here to deal with a very few of the paradigms. Others are open to the same kind of analysis.

14.7 Let us start with the future of *boaz* 'to be' (SGMC: 44). Of 10 examples of the 3rd singular given in the original spelling we have the following: *vêdh* x 3, *vyth* x 3, *veth* x 2, *vith* x 1 and *veath* x 1. In the list of attested forms at SGMC:

154 *veath* is not cited. *Veath*, however, is the form chosen for the paradigm. By what criterion is this "the most suitable"? The answer is obvious. *Vêdh* could not be chosen, because it contains <dh> and in Gendall's view <dh> is alien to Cornish of all periods (this is an erroneous view; see 17.12 below). Nor could *vyth*, *veth* or *vith* be selected, because they all occur in Middle Cornish, which Gendall believes is a completely different language from Late Cornish. There was therefore only one choice: *veath*. Now it is true that *veath* is attested, but to promote it over the head of more frequently attested forms is arbitrary. Nor is *veath* a wise choice phonologically. The vowel in *veath* 'will be' is /e:/ but the graph <ea> might suggest /i:/ (cf. English *heath*, *sheath*, *beneath*).

Gendall's conditional of *menna* 'wish' is also somewhat curious. If we count all the examples of all persons given we find that various forms are as follows (I ignore initial mutation) *mendzha* x 5; *mendzhia* x 1; *menja* x 5; *mengha*, *menya*, *mynsa*, *menga* all x 1. Yet *menga* is the form on which the paradigm is based. Similarly with the conditional of *gallus*. The attested forms used in examples at SGMC: 157 are (*k*)*aldzha* x 7; *olga* x 2; *algia* x 1; *allja/alja* x 2; *alga* x 1. Yet *alga* is the form on which the entire paradigm is reconstructed: *algam*, **alges*, *alga*, **algan*, **algo*, *algen* (forms with an asterisk are not attested in any spelling).

In both these instances it is clear how the choice has been made. The forms with <dzh> could not be used, because they were from Lhuyd and Lhuyd's <dzh> is alien to Cornish. The forms *menja*, *alja* with their <nj>, <lj> looked too much like something in Unified Cornish, therefore *menga* and *alga* were selected.

14.8 The verb *methes* 'to say' occurs in its entirety in Lhuyd and in the list of attested forms the whole paradigm is given from Lhuyd as *medhav*, *medhyz*, *medh e*, *medhon*, *medhoh*, *medhanz* (SGMC: 157). The third singular and third plural *meth*, *metha an chei* do occur in the fragment in Nicholas Boson's hand of JCH (BF: 16). As we have seen Gendall has rejected the use of <dh>. In the body of his grammar therefore (SGMC: 68) he respells the entire paradigm as follows: *metham*, *methez*, *meth e*, *methon*, *metho*, *methans*, where only two of six forms are attested with <th>. Gendall would no doubt criticize Nance for having respelt Middle Cornish <th> whenever it meant /ð/ as <dh>. Here Gendall himself when confronted with verbal forms containing <dh> has respelt them with <th>.

14.9 Not infrequently also Gendall is compelled to introduce forms for which there is no warrant at all. He says for example: "the form *valsa* from the CW would have become *valga* and in *sewya* to follow the form *sewsya* from the CW would have become *sewgya* or *sewja*" (SGMC: 72). If he means that students are to use such forms, he is recommending items for which we have no evidence.

Gendall does not hesitate to admit that many of his forms are hypothetical. He has but one example each of the past subjunctive and conditional of *gothaz* 'to know' (*cuffan*, *uffya*) and both come from CW—an essentially medieval text.

He says of these isolated instances "it can be seen that they are in typical Modern form. The paradigms can be confidently reconstructed as..." and he proceeds to set out the full paradigm of both tenses (SGMC: 63). Gendall's reconstructions may well be right, but they cannot legitimately be described as "traditional" or "authentic".

14.10 In his list of attested forms Gendall cites the verbal noun of 'to say' as *lavarall* (SGMC: 151). In his dictionary his first entry is *lavaral* (SDMC: 86). The commonest form of the verbal noun in Late Cornish, however, has /e/ and not /a/ in the stressed second syllable. I have collected the following examples: *laveral* BF: 15, 18 (Boson); *leverol* BF: 31, 31, 31 (Boson); *laverel* AB: 222, 2nd para., l. 2; 223, para 2, l. 12; para. 4, l. 4 (Lhuyd). The only forms known to me that have /a/ in the stressed syllable are *lavarel* BF: 16 and *lavaral* RC 23: 194.

It seems that Gendall prefers *lavaral* to *laveral/leverol* since the latter is too close to Middle and Unified Cornish *leverel*.

14.11 Gendall is apparently not aware that the present and past subjunctive are falling together in Cornish from the earliest period. The present subjunctive survives best in the third singular of *bos*. Gendall has 27 examples (SGMC: 49-50). Four of these contain the fossilized expression *pan vo > po* 'whenever'. Of the twenty-two remaining examples twenty-one are from CW, eloquent testimony to the limited nature of Late Cornish proper! So limited is it that there are virtually no examples of the present subjunctive to be found in it. Gendall says:

> The forms [of the unbound subjunctive] are only known from the "Creation", but are included here for the sake of the extra examples from the play that help to clarify the usage of the subjunctive.

Since Late Cornish proper hardly knows the subjunctive at all, there is surely little need for clarification. Late Cornish on which Revived Late Cornish is based is exiguous even by Cornish standards.

Speaking of the past subjunctive Gendall says: "This tense is used... in indirect negative commands introduced by phrases such as 'be careful that' etc." and he cites as an example *Gwayt na fe gansy mellyes* 'Mind that it is not meddled with' CW 373. Yet under the present subjunctive he cites the example *bythware na vova dean* 'mind that it is not a man' CW 1551. This latter example would surely class as 'an indirect negative command' of the sort mentioned by Gendall. Yet the subjunctive is present, not past. SGMC would seem, then, to be teaching students of Revived Late Cornish to distinguish two tenses that cannot be distinguished (see 19.6 below) and uses Middle Cornish sources to do so.

144

The subjunctive almost certainly existed in Late Cornish. Unfortunately the dilettante linguists to whom we owe such fragments of Late Cornish that we possess, do not seem to have been able to use it (see 14.23 below).

14.12 According to Gendall there are two attested forms of the subjunctive of *gul* 'to do' in Late Cornish: the third singular *reffa* (*Dewe reffa e sowia* 'God save him') and the second plural *reffo* (*Pa reffo why doaz* 'When ye come'). We have seen that from the period of the *Ordinalia* onwards final unstressed /o/ has become schwa, usually written <a>. Thus *reffa* is to be understood as /refə/. It should also be remembered that as a result of the falling together of final /o/ and /a/ there is confusion between present and past subjunctive in Middle Cornish at least as early as PA. The final vowel in *reffo* cited by Gendall is the Late Cornish reflex of earlier /owx/ of the 2nd person plural < *reffough*. Gendall, however, knowing that the 3rd singular of the present subjunctive in Unified Cornish ends in <o>, has erroneously taken the <o> of *reffo* to be a third singular ending rather than a second plural, and has generalized it throughout the paradigm: *reffo ve, reffo che, reffo e, reffo hye*, etc. He says: "*reffo* is strictly speaking present, and *reffa* past" (SGMC: 56). He is mistaken here and is introducing into Late Cornish a distinction largely absent from Middle Cornish.

I do not believe that *reffa* is part of the verb *gweel* 'to do' at all. It was Jenner misreading Lhuyd who first suggested that it was when he cited *gwreffa* as an alternative to *gwrello* (HCL: 131). The productive stem of *gweel* is *gwrell-*, which has already by the time of John Tregear spread from the subjunctive to the plural imperative (see 20.28 VII).

Gendall cites only three examples of *reffa* in the third person singular, one from Thomas Tonkin and two from John Tonkin. In each case the verb occurs as a jussive with the subject *Dewe* 'God' and the verbal noun *sowia* 'save':

Dewe reffa sowia an Egles ni 'May God save our church'
Dewe reffa gun sowia ni 'May God save us'
Dewe reffa e sowia 'May God save him'.

In Cornish the jussive subjunctive is preceded by the leniting particle *re*, for example in *re dheffo dha wlascor* 'thy kingdom come' in UC. The verb *dos, doaz* 'come' is used as an auxiliary in the subjunctive (see 21.12 below), a point which Gendall himself has noticed for he cites such non-jussive examples as *a theffa scullya* 'whoever sheds' (SGMC: 82). In later Cornish lenited *d* has a tendency to disappear between vowels. This is the origin of such forms as *kerengeek* 'loving' in TH < *kerengethek*. Behind *Dewe reffa sowia* 'May God save...' lies **Dewe re theffa sowia* 'God, may he come and save...' for in the fossilized phrase the lenited /ð/ between vowels has been lost.

The jussive nature of *reffa* was lost sight of and *reffa* itself became an unmarked form of the auxiliary. It is this development that lies behind *Pa reffo why doaz* 'When you will come', literally 'When you will come and come' quoted by Gendall from Gwavas and also Lhuyd's *pan* *'urvffo* 'when I shall do' (AB: 246a). Lhuyd gives *huarfo* 'happen' as a variant of *'urvffo*, which indicates that his informants believed *'urvffo* to mean 'happen to' rather than 'do'. Lhuyd cites *'urvffo* in the first person only. The other persons of the subjunctive of *gul* have the stem *'urell-*.

Reffa/reffo is not part of *gul* and should not be revived as such. Gendall mentions that the subjunctive of *gweel* 'to do' is *(w)rella* in CW. This is Lhuyd's *'urello*, *'urellon*, *'urelloh*. In the interests of authenticity, this genuine tense of the verb 'to do' should replace the interloper *reffa/reffo* < *doaz* in Revived Late Cornish.

14.13 Although Gendall's treatment of *doaz* as an auxiliary is illuminating, his discussion of it as a full verb is not satisfactory. In the list of attested forms of *doaz* (SGMC: 148), he makes no mention of the 1st person singular pres.-fut. *y teaf* (CW 1760). In his list Gendall has no provision for tabulating the forms of the subjunctive, yet the subjunctive of *doaz* as a full verb is not uncommon in CW: 2nd sing. *pan deffasta* CW 1752, 3rd sing. *pan defa*, *pan deffa* CW 1893, 2075. Ironically his only reference to *deffa* is in a corrupt form as the putative subjunctive of *gweel* (see previous section).

Gendall discusses the way in which the verb *boaz* 'to be' has possessive sense under the heading "the Idiomatic Possessive" (SGMC: 66-67). He does not mention, however, that the idiomatic use of *boaz* is a development of the verb *y'm bus* in which personal forms of the verb 'to be' are preceded by a particle + infixed dative pronoun. Forms of *y'm bus* are well attested in CW: *nym beas* 'I have not' CW 1966, *am bef* 'I had' CW 1979, *my am be* 'I had' CW 1986.

In the case of *doaz* as a full verb and *y'm bus* 'I have' Gendall seems, then, to have suppressed the evidence from CW. Since such forms do occur in CW, however, they should perhaps have been mentioned. On the other hand, as we have seen, Gendall admits that CW is largely medieval. He says:

> The grammar of the 'Creacion' is useful to the study of Modern Cornish inasfar as it corroborates or supplies extra examples for rules, but has features that only belong to the Mediaeval Period, but the orthography, although still largely mediaeval, shows Jordan experimenting with new spellings which are typical of the Modern Period. Furthermore, and just as the later writers, he uses more than one way of writing particular words, even to the extent of giving some in both mediaeval and modern styles; this is a great help when it comes to considering the pronunciation system (SGMC: vii).

Gendall begins the preface to his grammar by emphasizing the great gulf fixed between Middle and Late Cornish. To attempt to synthesize them would be unwise. Yet he uses for Revived Late Cornish—itself based on Late Cornish— a text that by his own admission is Middle Cornish.

Gendall has omitted some of the inflection of *doaz* and *y'm bus*. The same is true of other verbs. The omission is not accidental. Gendall seeks to give the impression that Revived Late Cornish is inherently simpler than Middle Cornish. Since grammatical complexity is "medieval" and not "modern", it must be kept to a minimum—by suppression if necessary.

14.14 Gendall gives the first person singular of *gen* 'with' as: *gennam, genama* or *gena ve* (SGMC: 104). *Gennam* is the apocopated form of *genama*, which occurs, for example, in *yn paradis genama* PA 193d. In the examples quoted by Gendall, however, there are no fewer than five examples of *genaf* 'with me', a form which is not cited in the preceding paradigm: *marth ew genaf, shame ew genaf, genaf lower y a sorras, mall ew genaf, prag y whreth genaf flattra* (ibid., 105). These are all from CW. Here the distance between the standardized paradigm and the examples is so great that the term "unreal alloy" again comes to mind.

Gendall standardizes the paradigm of the personal forms of *thort/durt* 'from' as follows: *thurtam, thurtez, durta, durte, thurtan nye/thort nye, thort why, thoranze* and he adds:

> It is quite possible that the extended form with separately expressed pronouns is usable for all persons, but the preposition is so individualistic that it is wiser to leave the paradigm simple (SGMC: 109).

This statement is obscure. Gendall appears to be saying that **thurt ve, *thurt che, *thurt eve, *thurt hye, *thort angye* may have existed in Late Cornish, but there is no evidence for them. He also seems to be recommending that speakers confine themselves to the standardized paradigm because the attested forms are difficult to systematize.

The attested forms are cited by Gendall (SGMC: 160). If we add to them those omitted by him from CW we get the following:

1 *thurtam, dhortam*
2 *ʒawortes, thaworthis, ʒuwortes, ʒaworthys sche*
3m *durta, ʒawarta, thaworta, odhiuorto*
3f *diuorte*

1 *theworth ny, the worthan, adhorton nei*
2 *thort why*
3 *thoranze*

The best attested person is the second singular with /ðe'worθəz/ and /ðə'wortəz/. Gendall, however, uses the unattested **thurtez*. Here it might be argued that *thurtez* is a later reflex of *thawortes*. This may be true, but it does not actually occur. In the third singular the best attested form is /ðə'wortə/. This is not allowed, but instead *durta* is recommended. The only attested form of the 3rd singular feminine is *diuorte* from Lhuyd, which Gendall respells as

147

durte. Diuorte is probably not feminine anyway. In the first plural he does not allow *theworthan* at all. His own form *thurtan* is not actually attested, being a respelling of Lhuyd's *adhorton (nei)*. In a word Gendall's standardized paradigm is very different from the forms that actually occur in the Late Cornish texts.

14.15 Under *war* 'upon' the third person plural inflected form is cited as *warnothans* only. The list of attested forms, however, also gives *warnanz* and *uarnedhe* from Lhuyd (SGMC: 159). These forms are ignored in the standardized paradigm, presumably because they look too much like Middle Cornish. In the standardized table *warnam* and *wara ve* are given for the first person singular. *Warnaf* occurs in CW (CW 1530, 1616) and *uarnav* is used by Lhuyd. It occurs three times, for example, in the first paragraph of the preface to his *Cornish Grammar* (AB: 222). I do not know the origin of *warnam*, for I can find no example of it. It would seem to be an invention.

Gendall gives the inflected first person singular of *worth/orth* 'on, about' as *(w)ortham* (SGMC: 108). In the list of attested forms (SGMC: 160) no inflected variant of the first person is cited, for only the analytical *urta ve, ortha vy, ortha vee* are given, the last two being from CW 214 and 193 respectively. The absence of an inflected first person singular of *(w)orth* in the list is perplexing. CW has *orthaf* CW 544, 547, 823, 2143, 2526, *orthaf vy* CW 232, *orthaf ve* CW 1432 and *worthaf ve* CW 1619. Moreover Lhuyd cites *orthiv* (AB: 244b). The actual forms that are attested in Late Cornish, then, are *orthaf/orthav* and *worthaf*. *(W)ortham* seems again to be an invention. Given that the analytical *ortha vy* is in origin *orthaf vy < orthyf vy*, it is very unlikely, I think, that a form in -*m* < -*ma* ever existed in Late Cornish. *(W)ortham* is not merely a construct, it is an unlikely construct as well.

In the preface to his Cornish grammar Lhuyd writes: *a 'ryganz skrefa ragov lîaz gerrio* 'who wrote many words for me' (AB: 222, 2nd para., line 6). This solitary instance of *ragov* 'for me' is probably the only attested example in Late Cornish of the first person singular of *rag* 'for'. Gendall incorrectly asserts that no example of the first person singular is forthcoming (SGMC: 159). As a result in his standardized paradigm Gendall gives *ragam* 'for me' (SGMC: 106), a form apparently of his own devising.

14.16 The standardized paradigm given by Gendall for the prepositional pronoun 'in' is particularly interesting. The forms that are actually attested in the texts are as follows (I have added items from SA not given by Gendall):

1   *unnaf, ynaff, yneff ve*
2   *ynnos, unas sche*
3m *itna, it an, etten, eta, ena, unna, ynna, ynno, in ef*
3f *yny, inhy, ynny, unny, unhy*

1   *ynnon*

2   —

3   *ettanz, ittanz, ettans, ynna, unna, in ansy*

Forms in *et-*, *ett-* are attested only for the 3rd singular masculine and 3rd plural. It is likely that *t*-forms were not found outside these two persons. The simplex *et* 'in' occurs in *et a phokkat* 'in his pocket' JCH § 35. *Et* 'in' I take to have been based upon the third singular masculine *eta*. This is probably to be explained as a reshaping of Middle Cornish *ynno/ynna* by analogy with *orta* and *theworta* (cf. *ughta* 'above him' TH 40, *a ught* 'above' TH 21a, 26). In both 3rd singular masculine and 3rd plural, however, *n*-forms also occur. SA's *in ansy* /in ən'dʒiː/ in particular looks very advanced.

In the standardized paradigm the *n*-forms have been ignored. The following are given: *ettam; ettas, etten, eta, ena; ette; etton; etto; ettanz/et angy* (SGMC: 107). No second plural form is attested in the sources. For the other persons, that is to say, *ettam* 'in me', *ettas* 'in thee', *ette* 'in her' and *etton* 'in us', the prepositional pronouns in *n* that actually occur, have been suppressed and have been replaced by invented forms. In fairness to Revived Late Cornish it should be pointed out that the prepositional pronouns *ettov* 'in me', *ettos* 'in thee', *etton* 'in us' and *etto* 'in you' were first suggested by Jenner in 1904 (HCL: 108). That does not, however, make them authentic.

Gendall gives the pronominal forms of the preposition *dre* as *dretham, drethas, dretha, drethe, drethon, dretho, drethans* (SGMC: 111). He cites no textual examples at all in support, though 'through it' is *tardha* at AB: 117c. It seems that Gendall's entire paradigm is an invention.

14.17 The textual basis of Revived Late Cornish is so meagre that hypothetical reconstruction is frequently necessary. I have already given some examples of both implicit reconstruction, that is, where the fact of reconstruction is not actually alluded to, and explicit reconstruction, where the hypothetical nature of the forms is admitted. Among other statements in SGMC acknowledging that forms or paradigms are conjectural one might cite the following:

> While there is no textual evidence for the Ordinals beyond this [i.e. 20th], they are likely to continue as… (SGMC: 29).

> There are no other examples of fractions but the Ordinal Numbers were probably used for the rest (SGMCL: 30).

> No other examples are known, though it is likely that 'hundreds' had a similarly based form to the above [*milliaw* 'thousands', *copplow* 'couples'] (SGMC: 30).

> There is no textual example for this [i.e. expression of depth], but by comparison with the method of expressing other measurements it is safe to say that **'en downder'** (> L: *dounder*) would be used (SGMC: 32).

Though the tense [compound future of *boaz*] is only found used in the Affirmative, any other use will be as explained in Section **22 A** and **23 A** (SGMC: 45).

Rowe's **mala ve** indicates that it [compound pres. subj. of *boaz*] is used as a Monoform but Borlase supplies **mollough** for the 2nd pl. **malasta** is likely for the 2nd sing (SGMC: 50).

The only part of this paradigm actually found in Modern Cornish is **dresta why**, supplied by Gwavas. The 3rd pers. singular masc. is certain to be **dresta**. The other parts are likely but conjectural (SGMC: 111).

From the one example of this preposition's combining with a pronoun, in **rebbam**: beside me, it is clear that a paradigm should exist; this can conjecturally be reconstructed as **rebbam, rebbas, reptha, repthe, rebbon, rebbo, repthans** (SGMC: 114).

The two examples of this preposition in combination suggest the following conjectural paradigm: **aveza ve, aveza che, avesta, aveste, aveza why, avestans** (SGMC: 114).

However, by comparison with **reb**: beside for which there is one example of its prepositional use in **rebbam**: beside me, it is possible to give a conjectural paradigm as **hebbam, hebbas, heptha, hepthe, hebbo, hepthans** (SGMC: 113).

Many of the conjectural forms posited in the above quotations may well be correct. I have strong misgivings about some of the prepositional pronouns, the feminine 3rd singulars in particular. It must be emphasized that the forms alluded to are reconstructions for which there is no direct evidence. They may or may not correspond to forms current in Late Cornish but one thing is certain: they cannot possibly be described as "authentic".

Before we leave the question of conjectural forms in Revived Late Cornish, it is instructive to compare the equivalents in Middle Cornish. Norris, for example, cites from the *Ordinalia* alone virtually complete paradigms of prepositional pronouns for *the* 'to', *gans* 'with', *war* 'upon', *orth* 'upon', *worth* 'upon', *yn* 'in', *rag* 'for', *a* 'from' and *dre* 'through' (1859: ii 246-48).

14.18 Gendall makes much of the relative simplicity of Revived Late Cornish when compared with Middle Cornish. He says:

No longer influenced by Glasney, and presently deserted by the educated, Cornish remained the vehicle of the working people: farmers, fishermen, tinners and traders. These, ever practical, simplified both grammar and vocabulary, introducing into the latter a rich store of technical terms many of which survived into the local English... (SGMC: 1).

Since linguistic change occurs spontaneously and without speakers' either intending or realizing it, the down-to-earth approach of the fishermen and tinners of Cornwall is irrelevant. Gendall's remarks are also rather dismissive of the countless people, clerical and lay, who were sufficiently practical to write and stage the mystery plays year after year for several centuries.

Gendall's statement also ignores the most significant fact about Late Cornish: it was written entirely by the educated. Nicholas Boson went to school in France and quotes Horace, Ausonius and Montaigne. John Boson had a copy of Lhuyd's *Archaeologia Britannica* by him as he worked and uses words from the *Old Cornish Vocabulary*. Ustick was the vicar of Breage, Borlase was rector of Ludgvan and later vicar of St Just. Tonkin was a historian who wrote a Cornish-Latin-English dictionary. Keigwin knew Latin, Greek and Hebrew and provided translations of Middle Cornish for the Bishop of Exeter, Sir Jonathan Trelawny. Lhuyd was the leading Oxford scholar of his day and keeper of the Ashmolean Museum. Gwavas was a barrister (see further Pool 1982).

The "working people" had little to do with Late Cornish. If they had, perhaps it would have been a richer and more natural idiom than it is. It was precisely because the Late Cornish antiquarians were educated that they were not prepared to learn from the unlettered—the only people who still spoke Cornish fluently. The attempt to link Late Cornish and therefore Revived Late Cornish with the the simple fisher and farmer folk of Cornwall is misleading. Yet Gendall says of his dictionary of Revived Late Cornish:

> This is a source dictionary that aims to present to the public the native language of my Cornish ancestors, the farmers, fishermen, miners and traders of Penwith and Kerrier, during the last centuries of its life (SDMC: 1).

It is the Middle Cornish texts themselves which were directed at the illiterate. As a result the Middle Cornish plays, *Pascon agan Arluth* and Tregear's sermons are closer to the common people than virtually all the meagre remains of Late Cornish.

As far as simplicity is concerned, one should remember that the loss of inflection almost always leads to a greater complication in syntax and thus the overall complexity of the language is not lessened. This is the case with Revived Late Cornish. Here, for example, is the "present locative" of the verb 'to be' as given by Gendall (SGMC: 42):

particular	combined particular	simple	combined simple	special
theram	*thera ve/therama*	*eram*	*erave*	
theze	*thera che/thesta*	*eze*	*esta*	
ma/ema	*ma/mava*	*igge*	*iggeva*	*eze*
ma/ema	*ma hye*	*igge*	*igge hye*	
theren	*thera nye*	*eren*	*era nye*	
thero	*thera why*	*ero*	*era why*	
mownz	*ma'ngye/ma gye*	*igganz*	*igge angye.*	

151

The equivalent paradigm in Unified Cornish (Nance 1949: 24) is:

esof
esos
us, usy   *yma, 'ma*
eson
esough
esons, usons *ymons, 'mons.*

The lexicon of Revived Late Cornish

14.19 When discussing the numerals Gendall says: "1,000,000 *myl vyl* is known from RD 132" (SGMC: 29). This word has been adopted by Revived Late Cornish users and they respell it as *meelveel*, as for example, *dro da* £3.6 *meelveel* 'about £3.6 million' (*Carn* 69: 16). Oddly enough Gendall has not noticed that *mylyon* 'million' occurs in the *Ordinalia*: *try mylyon our* 'three million of gold [coins]' RD 2258. This would be a better word to adopt into Revived Late Cornish because it would not need to be respelt.

In his discussion of grammatical gender in Cornish Gendall includes the word *portheress* 'female porter' which he glosses 'concierge' (SGMC: 1). *Portheress* is from Lhuyd's *portheres* (AB: 241a) and the spelling indicates that Lhuyd got the word from PC 1225: *Portheres gentyl mar sos.*

In SDMC no plural of the word for 'sister' is given. In SGMC: 11, however, we are told that the Cornish for 'sisters' is *wheryth.* As far as I am aware, the plural of the word for 'sister' is attested nowhere in Cornish, Old, Middle or Late. *Wheryth* is Nance's coinage on the basis of Welsh *chwiorydd* and has been taken by Gendall from Nance.

Under 'authority' SDMC cites *othoredzhek* from Gwavas. The spelling shows that this was one of Lhuyd's coinages. It was almost certainly a calque on Welsh *awdurdodol* and was intended to mean 'authoritative, authorized'. In current Revived Late Cornish the word is used adjectivally to mean 'authentic' as an epithet of Revived Late Cornish itself: *Ma an grammatek ma provya mean-lear seer than tavaz othoredgack* "This grammar provides a sure foundation for the authentic language" (*Carn* 74: 16).

Revived Late Cornish then borrows from Middle Cornish when it is convenient, and if a word is not forthcoming from those sources will use an invented one. Revived Late Cornish will also use coinages by Lhuyd, a Welshman who spent only months in Cornwall. No matter where the words in Revived Late Cornish come from, they can all be respelt in Anglicized orthography and treated as "traditional".

The poor quality of Late Cornish

14.20 A further reason for not using Late Cornish as a basis for the revival is that much of the remains of the later language are poor Cornish. This point was first made by Henry Jenner. In a telling passage Jenner says:

But it is to be remembered that a great proportion of the remains of Modern Cornish consists of translations and a few original compositions by persons whose own language was English, who had in some cases learnt Cornish very imperfectly. This would apply to most of the translations of passages of Scripture, to Lhuyd's Preface (though, of course, *his* own language was Welsh), and to Gwavas's attempts (HCL: 51).

14.21 One of Gendall's main sources for his grammar and vocabulary is Edward Lhuyd. Yet Lhuyd was a Welshman and spent only a short time in Cornwall. Although Lhuyd's *Cornish Grammar* is of inestimable value in the study of Cornish, it must be admitted that Lhuyd's grasp of the language was understandably not perfect. In his treatment of the Cornish verb in particular Lhuyd shows that he did not really know the language. For example Lhuyd never really got the hang of relative sentences in Cornish. He writes: *lîaz gêr syl nag idzhanz lebmyn en pou Kernou* and this sentence is quoted by Gendall as an example of the negative relative particle (SGMC: 25). Cornish would not naturally use the pronoun *suel* in this position. It is a calque on Lhuyd's part of *y rhai* in literary Welsh. Worse still the verb because it is relative ought to be singular, but Lhuyd has it in the plural. Good Cornish would have been (and I retain Lhuyd's spelling): **lîaz gêr (neb) nag ez lebmyn en pou Kernou.*

The so-called "abnormal word order" of sentences like *my a wel* 'I see', literally 'it is I that sees' involves a relative verb. Lhuyd did not understand the syntax of such sentences in Cornish any more than he understood ordinary relatives. Lhuyd always inflects the verb for person instead of leaving it in the 3rd person singular. Thus he writes *mi a 'urâv* 'I do', *ti a 'urei* 'thou dost', *huî a ureuh* 'you do' (AB: 246a) instead of the correct *mi a 'ura, ti a 'ura, huî a 'ura* and *mi a bernav* 'I will buy' for *mi a bern* (AB: 247a). Since Lhuyd never learnt the correct syntax, this elementary mistake occurs again and again in the verbal paradigms cited in his grammar and in his own Cornish prose: *en della huei a ureuh euna enuêdh an ragskrefyz Legradzho* 'so you will correct the above mentioned corruptions' (AB: 223, para. 6, line 5).

Lhuyd has mistaken views about Cornish inflection. He believes, for example, that the preterite of *gul* 'to do' in the plural is *gureithon* 'we did', *gureitho* 'you did', *gureithonz* 'they did' and he gives the example *gzhyi a 'ureithonz* 'they did' (AB: 246a), which is Cornish neither in morphology nor syntax. He also mistakenly believes that the infixed masculine pronoun is *i* as in Welsh and not *'n*, so he writes *Mi ai guerha* 'I will sell it' instead of **Mi a'n guerh* (AB: 246c). Lhuyd is also mistaken about the syntax of the autonomous forms of the verb. He cites such un-Cornish forms as *Henuir vî* 'I shall be called', *Henuir di* 'Thou shalt be called' (AB: 247ab) instead of **y'm henwir, *y'th henwir*. In fact in the Cornish of his day the autonomous verb was a dead letter and Lhuyd's whole section on the "passive" is therefore largely unnecessary.

Many people have criticized the poor quality of Lhuyd's Cornish. The first was probably Oliver Pender, who, writing to Gwavas in 1711, says: *Rag na algia ev clappia na screffa Curnoack peccara why. Thera moy Gembrack peath rig ea gweele* 'For he could not speak nor write Cornish like you. What he did was more Welsh' (Ellis: 104).

14.22 Nicholas Boson knew Cornish fairly well although he did not start learning it until he was six years or so. His idiom is often more English than Cornish. *Nag u an pobel coth tho bose skoothez war noniel* 'nor are the old people to be relied upon either' (BF: 25) in *Nebbaz Gerriau* is most un-Celtic in idiom. Similarly his *an skauoll crackan codna iggeva setha war* 'the break-neck chair he sits on' (BF: 9) with *war* for **warnotha* is a calque on English. Such Anglicisms are no doubt a fair reflection of the attenuated and de-Celticized Cornish of the late seventeenth century. Boson's vocabulary was limited as well. He wanted to say 'layman's effort/attempt' but he had no word for 'attempt' and thus was compelled to use *bonogath* 'will, wish' instead. He borrowed the word for 'lay' from the Old Cornish Vocabulary (BF: 33). Not astonishingly Boson recognized that the Cornish of his own day was impoverished:

> Gun tavas Carnoack eu mar pu gwadnhez, us na ellen skant quatiez tho e wellaz crefhe arta, rag car dreeg an Sausen e thanen en pow idden ma an kensa, an delna ema stella teggo warnotha hep garra thotha telhar veeth buz dro tho an aulz ha an more... en telhar idden ma hag ul ma mouy Sousenack clappiez dre eza Curnooack, rag radden el bose keevez na el skant clappia, na guthvas Curnooack, bus skant denveeth buz ore guthvas ha clappia Sousenack; rag hedna hevol den kallisk eue tho gweel dotha gurtaz ha dose a dro arta, rag ugge an teez goth tho merwal akar, ny a wele an teez younk tho e clappia le ha le ha lacka ha lacka.

> [Our Cornish tongue is so far weakened, that we can hardly expect to see it grow again, for as did the English send it into this narrow land at first, thus it is still bearing upon it without leaving to it any place but about the cliff and the sea; ... in this narrow place also there is more English spoken than there is Cornish, for some can be found that cannot scarcely speak nor understand Cornish, but scarcely anyone but knows to understand and speak English; therefore, it seems to me, it is hard to make it to stay and come back again, for after the old people to die away, we see the young people to speak it less and less and worse and worse.] (BF:25).

14.23 If Nicholas Boson's language was impoverished, the Cornish of his relative, John Boson, was worse still. When John attempted to translate the couplet 'If thou wilt go to live without end/keep God's ten commandments' he had great difficulty. His own notes show that he really wanted to say 'enter heaven' but could not think of the word for 'enter' in Cornish. He looked up the word in Lhuyd's AB but could find only Welsh words. In the event he had to paraphrase his English original because his knowledge of Cornish was inadequate (BF: 50-1). Similarly when he began to translate the first chapter of Genesis, John Boson had no word for 'image' and had to borrow from Old

Cornish. Moreover he confused the word for 'wing' (*asgal*) with the word for 'bone' (*azgran*) (BF: 52, 54).

In good Cornish if one wants to say 'speaking' as a participle one uses the verbal noun with either *ow* or *yn un*: *ow leverel, yn un leverel*. John Boson did not know that simple fact and instead tried to introduce into Cornish a present participle based on Latin. He writes *guayans* for 'moving' and *laverans* for 'saying' (BF: 54). These forms are the most outrageous solecisms and only strengthen our conviction that John Boson, one of Gendall's most important sources, did not know Cornish properly. We are to believe that the handbooks of Revived Late Cornish give a true picture of Late Cornish, yet in his discussion of the present participle Gendall fails to mention John Boson's "present participles" in *-ans* (SGMC: 84-5).

Bad Cornish is also to be noted from the hand of Thomas Boson. In his version of the Lord's Prayer for example he says *Benegaz eu de Hanou* 'hallowed is thy name' with the indicative instead of the jussive subjunctive. Presumably he did not know how to say 'hallowed be'. 'Thy kingdom come' he renders as *grua de guelaze dose* 'make thy kingdom come'—not an accurate translation at all (BF: 41). As we have seen above, the subjunctive is hardly attested at all in Late Cornish. This can be ascribed to the ignorance of the late writers. To translate properly both 'hallowed be thy name' and 'thy kingdom come' a jussive subjunctive is required. If Thomas Boson did not use the subjunctive, it was because he did not know how.

In his Cornish version of the creed Thomas Boson is at a loss to translate 'suffer' or 'judge'. The first he renders as *gath dar e galarrou* 'he went through his griefs' and the second as *do gule compuster do* 'to do correctness to' (BF: 41). Let nobody pretend that either is good idiomatic Cornish. Yet these very texts are central to Revived Late Cornish.

Gendall has in his grammar a section on what he refers to as the "Simplified Present". This curious construction consists of the personal pronoun used with the verbal noun: *Me ri marci* 'I thank you' (from John Boson); *Della pidzha JB* 'Thus prays JB' (from John Boson); *gerriow remma an tis en Loundres a credgi bos gwir* 'the Londoners believe that these words are true' (from John Boson); *me tôz* I come' (from Borlase) (see SGMC: 73). Now it is quite obvious that these pidginized sentences have their ultimate origin in the periphrastic present: *me ew ow cregy 'I believe' (better *yth esoma ow cregy*) has first become *me ew cregy in which the particle *ow* has been omitted. With this compare: *e thesta eva e presius gois* 'thou art drinking his precious blood' SA 63. Subsequently the inflected form of the verb 'to be' is elided and we are left with a construction devoid of verb. The syntax in question should not be imitated because it is not Cornish. Notice, incidentally, how many of the examples of the "simplified present" come from John Boson, whose knowledge of Cornish was so very uncertain.

14.24 An English version of Lhuyd's *Preface* to his *Cornish Grammar* from AB was published by Pryce in ACB. Although Pryce gave to understand that the translation was his own, it was really a joint effort by Gwavas and Tonkin of over 50 years previously. Norris draws attention (1859: ii 314) to one sentence from the translation that is particularly badly rendered:

> Mi a uon pordhâ try kaldzha uynyn tibiaz, a hedda gen moy 'uîrhevelepter tr'el an gerlevran bîan Brethonek-ma boz Arvorek po Brethonek Pou Lezou en Vrink (Lhuyd, AB: 222)

> I know very well that some may conjecture with greater probability, that this little book may be Armoric, or the British of Lezou in France (Norris's translation)

> I know full well that I could produce one, and that with more true likeness, than can the small vocabulary of the British Armoric, or British of the country of Lezou in France (Gwavas & Tonkin's attempted translation)

Norris observes:

> This sentence was translated by the joint effforts of Gwavas and Tonkin, and printed in Pryce's book.… A better evidence of the loss of the Cornish language in 1700 can hardly be found than in the utter misunderstanding of this easy passage, composed too, as it was, intentionally in the corrupted idiom and spelling of the time.

Gwavas and Tonkin are among the most important sources for Revived Late Cornish.

14.25 Listening to fluent native-speakers is obviously the best way of learning a language. Cornish unfortunately has no traditional speakers. We have, therefore, to rely on written remains. It is only sensible in the case of Cornish to go to those documents that contain the richest, the most native and idiomatic Cornish. Lhuyd had no native knowledge of Cornish at all. Few, if any, of the late writers were really fluent and at ease in the language. It is surely neither wise nor even morally justifiable to expect learners to acquire their Cornish from such poor sources as Lhuyd, Borlase, John Boson, and the rest, especially when the Cornish of a slightly earlier period is rich and idiomatic.

These men were not even scientific observers of native-speakers. They had all round them people whose knowledge of the language was far greater than their own but for reasons of class and education they ignored them. Nance has cogently written of the eighteenth-century Cornish antiquarians:

It maddens one to think of these learned laborious Cornishmen, misprinting earlier collections, misreading ancient manuscripts, fumbling their few Celtic or West Country English words with an indiscriminate hurling together of Cornish, Welsh, Breton and Irish from Lhuyd's Archaeologia Britannica, compiling dictionaries and making cryptograms for Cornish students that take ten times as long to unravel as they did to write, while all the time the language itself was being spoken by the poor old 'backjowster' bringing fish round to the back door, or even by the bent old gardener mowing the grass from whom— alas!—it would be infra dig to learn (quoted in Ellis: 107-08).

The phonology of Revived Late Cornish

14.26 One of the least satisfactory aspects of Revived Late Cornish is its phonology. Gendall has done his best with disparate sources but he has not attempted to systematize the results. In addition he has an uncertain approach to the relation between spelling and sound. He appears to believe that Late Cornish had both a single and a geminate /t/ and /k/. Speaking of the variation in spelling between <k> and <ck> in Late Cornish sources he says:

> A possible answer may be found in the way that final **t** is still pronounced traditionally in W[est] P[enwith] where the letter is almost spat out, and given far more prominence than in SE. As another plosive consonant, **k** might well have been treated in a similar way wherever the letter is found as part of the adjectival ending (SDMC: xv).

When talking about phonology one should be careful to distinguish *sounds* from *letters*.

At 8.4 above I suggested that Cornish had both a voiced and an unvoiced *l*. Gendall is also of the opinion that Cornish has two separate *l*-sounds since he says of "the letter *l*":

> As a final it is pronounced with the tip of the tongue against the hard palate and slightly dwelt upon. Within a word, when next to a consonant other than another **l**, it is pronounced as in English. A single or double **l** (sometimes written as **lh** or **llh**) between vowels resembles a modified version of the Welsh **ll**, but less harsh and more like a cross between this and the Spanish **ll** (SGMC: 145).

This description is detailed in its impenetrability. To arrive at such detail one would need a visitation from the spirit of Dolly Pentreath. Dolly's ghost would have to have suitably unreal organs of articulation. The Spanish *ll* is a voiced palatal [ʎ] whereas the Welsh *ll* is a voiceless lateral [ɬ]. A combination of the two is phonetically impossible. In fact Cornish /lh/ was neither palatal nor lateral but retroflex [ɭ] (8.4).

14.27 I have insufficient space here to attempt an analysis of Gendall's treatment of the phonology of Late Cornish. I shall confine myself therefore to some brief observations on his description of the vowels. Gendall uses an inverted *a* as a phonetic symbol which from his description of it appears to mean either [ɑ] or [ɔ]. Gendall appears to believe that Late Cornish had the following vowels and diphthongs (SDMC: x-xv): [a, ɑ, o, u, ɪ, e, y, ɛː, ɑː, eː, iː, uː, əː, iːə, ia, iɑ, iu, iːa, ou, ɑu, eu, eːa, eːu, eːau, ɛːu, əi]. Two things are immediately apparent. First, that the spelling of Late Cornish must be very misleading if such an unconvincing inventory of vowel sounds could be deduced from it. Secondly that a rigorous systematization would almost certainly indicate that a number of items are allophonic variants of other vowels.

This is certainly the case in the diphthongs. It is difficult to believe for example that the [eu] of *bew* 'alive' and *Deu* 'God' is different from the diphthongs [eːau] in *reaw* 'frost' and [eːu] in *pleaw* 'parish'. I assume also that the vowel [eː] in *gwreze* 'made' and the 'diphthong' [eːa] in *gwreag* 'wife' are one and the same also. As far as the short vowels are concerned it seems clear that the vowel [ɑ] in *por(th)* 'harbour' and [o] in *pobel* 'people' are members of the same phoneme. Doubtless further conflation could be achieved by phonemicization.

One of the main defects of Gendall's phonology is that he does not distinguish between stressed an unstressed syllables. In consequence there is no hint of the neutral vowel (schwa) in his description. Since the prosodic shift, however, schwa has been the dominant vowel of unstressed syllables. There is no doubt that Gendall's unstressed diphthong [ia] in *helfia* 'hunt' and *contravagian* 'neighbours' is really the consonant /j/ followed by /ə/. As has been noted above schwa in auslaut has a tendency to be realized as [a].

It is in his "supplementary note" on page xx that Gendall gives us, almost as an afterthought, an insight into the role of schwa in Late Cornish. He says: "The unstressed endings s *az/as* & *oz/os*, variously used should probably also be given the value [ɒ]." This seems to be in agreement with my own conclusion at 7.15 above, namely that in unstressed syllables in Late Cornish [ə] and [ǫ] are in free variation.

As far as the phonology of Late Cornish is concerned Gendall's discussion has some useful insights. It would be immeasurably improved by a trained phonologist. Gendall's description itself is not yet unambiguous enough to be of definitive value to the students at whom SDMC is aimed.

14.28 Gendall, like several before him, has suggested that the English dialect of Cornwall is a source for the phonology of Cornish. Others are sceptical. Wakelin, after an exhaustive study of the phonology of Cornish English, has concluded that the English of Cornwall absorbed very few words from Cornish

and received no phonological influence from it, as far as can be ascertained. This is shown both by a study of the M[iddle] E[nglish] documents, and from the present, more detailed, study of some aspects of the present-day dialects (Wakelin 1975: 205).

Where Cornish may have left its mark is on intonation of Cornish English. To describe intonation accurately, however, is very difficult and no-one, either revivalist or professional linguist, has yet attempted the task. Generally speaking much more can be deduced about the phonology of Cornish from Lhuyd and the surviving texts than from the most extensive analysis of Cornish English.

In his still unpublished Cornish-English dictionary Gendall has provided his headwords with phonetic renderings. The phonology behind these representations is apparently based upon the English speech of Cornwall. The results are not compelling.

The phonetic rendering given by Gendall for *colomman* 'dove', for example, is [kölob'mon]. The symbol <'> for stress is more usually placed before the syllable involved, not after it. A more conventional rendering would be [kö'lobmon] rather than [kölob'mon]. I find it difficult to believe that in /bm/ < /m/ by pre-occlusion the first element [b] is in one syllable and the second [m] is in the next. Yet this is implied by Gendall's phonetics. I also find Gendall's analysis of schwa as [ö] or [o] perplexing. We have seen that schwa in Cornish has a rounded allophone (7.15), but to equate this with /o/ can hardly be justified, since in auslaut schwa is frequently [a].

The most disturbing feature of Gendall's phonetic renderings involves his treatment of /r/ in unstressed syllables. He renders the word *cofar, kophor* 'coffer, chest' as [ko'fö] (read: ['kofö]). This is the form in which the word occurs or would occur in Cornish English. There is no evidence whatever that unstressed /ər/ in Cornish ever became /ö/. Lhuyd is always careful to write final <r>, for example in the following from JCH: *teller* 'place' §1, *guber* 'wages' §4, *vêster* 'master' §5, *kebmer* 'take!' §8, *lavar* 'says' §10, *nehuer* 'last night' §30, *bad-ober* 'evil work' §32.

The shift /ər/ > /ö/ is a remarkable one. If it had been apparent in the Cornish of his day, Lhuyd would surely have alluded to it somewhere. He is completely silent on the matter. If such a sound-change had been a feature of Late Cornish, one might also expect Boson in *Nebbaz Gerriau* to write *telho* 'place', *hanto* 'half', *Gevo* 'goat', *composto* 'accuracy', etc. The fact that he and all late authors write such words with a final <r>, indicates that the final segment was /r/ in Cornish until the language died.

Gendall has, I fear, been led astray by the English dialect of Cornwall and phonetic representations like [ko'fö] 'coffer', [koga'zo] 'priest', [ko'lo] 'strap' are fictions.

The orthography of Revived Late Cornish
14.29 Gendall claims that Revived Late Cornish is not a system like the other forms of Neo-Cornish but rather presents learners and other speakers with

what is to be found in the Late Cornish sources themselves. Gendall says of his dictionary, for example, that its purpose "is not to tell people what to say, but to show them what they **can** say" (SDMC: v). This *laissez-faire* approach to orthography was until recently noticeable in Revived Late Cornish texts. Here is a very short selection of spelling variants to be observed in Revived Late Cornish:

'CORNISH PEOPLE': **Kernowion** (*Carn* 57: 16); **Curnowean** (*Carn* 82: 16); **Kernowian** (*Carn* 87: 17)

'ENGLISH': **Zowsnack**(*Carn* 60: 15); **Sousenack** (*Carn* 81: 15); **Sousnack** (*Carn* 86: 17); **Sausnack** (*Carn* 87: 17)

'WELSH': **Kembrak** (*Carn* 69: 16); **Kimbrack** (*Carn* 86: 17); **Kembrack** (*Carn* 82: 16)

'AGE': **ooz** (*Carn* 57: 16); **oze** (*Carn* 85: 16); **oydge** (*Carn* 65: 15); **oodg** (*Carn* 74: 16)

'LIFE': **bounas** (*Carn* 60: 15); **bownaz** (*Carn* 82: 17)

'HOLD, CONSIDER': **zenjy** (*Carn* 57: 16); **zenge** (*Carn* 60: 15); **sendga** (*Carn* 74: 16)

'KNOW': **guthvos** (*Carn* 57: 16); **guthaz** (*Carn* 75: 17); **gothaz** (*Carn* 85: 16)

'SEE': **gweles** (*Carn* 60: 15); **gwellaz** (*Carn* 69: 16); **gwellhaz** (*Carn* 82: 17).

14.30 As we saw at 12.5, by the Late Cornish period vowels in stressed monosyllables had again lengthened. It is for this reason that Lhuyd writes the monosyllabic *plêu* 'parish' with a long vowel (AB: 113b) but the disyllabic *dho beua* 'to live' with a short one (AB: 175b). The difference between the Late Cornish long diphthong in /ple:w/ and the short one in /bewə/ is determined by the environment: stressed monosyllable vs. stressed vowel of polysyllable. There is no need, therefore, to mark *pleu* for length.

Gendall and his associates, however, lacking any theoretical understanding of Cornish phonology, have recently decided that the word for 'parish' must be written in Revived Late Cornish <pleaw> and the word for 'to live' as <bewa>. They informed their followers of the decision in an article in *Carn* entitled "Spell It!" (87: 18).

It was suggested above (6.2-3) that the two diphthongs /ɪw/ and /ew/ are only partially distinguished from the 15th century onwards. Nonetheless Gendall and his associates have decided that the two must be kept separate in Revived Late Cornish, as <yw> and <ew> respectively (ibid.).

It is apparent from these directives that the creators of Revived Late Cornish have now determined to tell the users of their system how they are to spell. A *laissez-faire* approach to orthography has apparently been superseded by a more dirigiste one. "Spell It!" in *Carn* is analogous with the "Kernewek Kemmyn Up-Dates" of some years ago. If Revived Late Cornish were merely the sum of the possibilities allowed by Late Cornish sources, the devisers of the system would not now be issuing instructions about how to spell. Moreover the creators of Revived Late Cornish do not appear to understand the inherent contradictions in what they are doing. Gendall apologizes to his followers for having introduced changes to the "recommended standard orthography" of his system and says:

> [I]t can be frustrating to relearn what may have taken you so much trouble to learn; yet if we can all be patient we are all playing our part in evolving a sounder system of spelling that will not only be of advantage to future generations of learners(…) but will also be something of which we can be proud, and can use with confidence, knowing that we are spelling the language as it was spelt traditionally (ibid.).

Gendall, then, is asserting on the one hand that he and his associates are "evolving a sounder spelling system" and on the other that his orthography is merely the spelling used by the writers of Late Cornish. This is a contradiction in terms. If Gendall's spelling is still evolving it cannot be a pre-existing orthography. If it is the "traditional" spelling of Late Cornish, it does not require further refinement. Indeed to attempt to refine it, would be to introduce into the "traditional" language non-traditional and therefore inauthentic elements. We should remember that those who favour Revived Late Cornish do so because they believe it to be the most authentic form of Cornish available.

Gendall's admission that his spelling system is still under construction is clearly at variance with the claims of Revived Late Cornish to be authentic. His admission may also act as a deterrent to prospective learners of his system. If the orthography of Revived Late Cornish is still evolving, how can students have any faith in it? How can they be sure that what they learn today will not be changed in a month or two?

As we have seen, two edicts have been issued to date; one concerns <ew> and <eaw>, the other <yw> and <ew>. Neither is justified.

14.31 Gendall has pointed out to me that had English died out, we would revive it from the works of Defoe rather than Chaucer and from Dickens rather than Defoe. His observation is correct as far as it goes, but as far as Cornish is concerned the analogy is false.

Chaucer, Defoe, and Dickens all wrote at different stages of the development of English. Their orthographies are historically linked to one another because they are in an unbroken tradition. In Cornish the orthography of PA, the *Ordinalia*, BM and TH are all closely related. CW exhibits essentially the same orthography although some Anglicizing features are also present in the spelling. When we come to Nicholas Boson, however, there has clearly been a complete break. No longer using the traditional orthography of Cornish, Boson bases his spelling on English.

Nicholas Boson wrote in an English-based orthography not because it suited him better than the old one, nor because it reflected the pronunciation of his dialect closely, nor because he was opposed to medieval obscurantism. Boson spelt as he did because he knew nothing else. He says: *rag na rigga ve beska gwellaz skreef Bretton Coth veeth* 'for I never saw any old British writing' (BF: 27). In the context of his remarks about Cornish orthography, this can only mean that he has never even seen a document in traditional Cornish, let alone learn how to read and write the language. Boson was well educated and could read English, French and Latin. We can be sure that if he had learnt to write Cornish in traditional orthography, he would have done so.

An orthography based on ignorance is not a suitable foundation for the Cornish revival. If Late Cornish were all we had, to use it exclusively might be intelligible. Since, however, we have BM, Tregear and CW, to use Boson and his younger contemporaries as our main source for revived Cornish is unwarranted. This is particularly true when we realize just how close sixteenth-century Cornish was in inflection and syntax to the Cornish of the Bosons, etc. (see 14.3 above).

A far more accurate parallel for Revived Late Cornish is available to us in Ireland. Irish has an unbroken literary tradition that started with the coming of Christianity in the fifth century. Of course Irish has changed radically over the centuries. Yet we still use an orthography that goes back to the beginnings. There have been two major reforms. One in the so-called classical period when scribes started to use vowels consistently to show consonantal quality (palatalized versus velarized). The second reform occurred in this century when quiescent letters were removed. Thus *comhnaidhe* has become *cónaí*, for example, and *athchuinghe* has been respelt as *achainí*.

Throughout its history Irish has had a vigorous manuscript tradition. It was strongest in relatively recent times in south-eastern Ulster and in Munster. Connaught was in the eighteenth and nineteenth centuries largely illiterate in Irish. Hedge-schoolmasters could always write English, however. As a result there grew up a practice in counties Galway and Mayo of writing down the songs of the folk-poets in an *ad hoc* orthography based on English. Such a spelling was very unsuitable because it was unable to show some of the important distinctions in Irish phonology. This English-based orthography is sometimes called "English character" and without it important parts of the poetic tradition would not have survived. The English character in Ireland is exactly parallel with Late Cornish orthography. It existed because people knew no other and because of it much has survived that would otherwise have perished. That is not the same as saying that it is preferable to the traditional orthography.

When the Irish revival began in earnest at the end of the nineteenth century, no one thought for an instant of using anything other than the traditional orthography, even though it did not entirely reflect the spoken language. It was the inherited system and by and large was suited to Irish. If it had deficiencies, they could be remedied. It has subsequently been revised and simplified—but it is in the same unbroken tradition. The English Character of

Connaught is now rightly forgotten. If Cornish could be successfully revived with the traditional orthography, then the spelling of Late Cornish could be forgotten except by those who are interested in the history of the language.

14.32 I said that by the time of Nicholas Boson knowledge of traditional Cornish spelling had been lost. This is not entirely true, I think. It is apparent from the fragment of ecclesiastical Cornish preserved by Gilbert (see 14.2) that traditional Cornish orthography survived until the Civil War. There is some evidence that it survived even longer. We know, for example, that a manuscript of sermons preached in 1680 exists but has gone missing. The manuscript was almost certainly written in an orthography akin to the traditional one. There is further indirect evidence for the survival of traditional spelling, and here I must digress and speak of Ireland again.

In eighteenth and nineteenth century Ireland there were men called in English *Irishians*. They could not only speak Irish but read and write it. They were repositories of traditional learning and it is to them that we owe many of our later Irish manuscripts. These traditional scholars not infrequently had other skills as well as the ability to copy and read manuscripts. Many, for example, because they could read Irish, had knowledge of traditional medicine and were able to work cures. There is no doubt that something similar obtained in all the Celtic countries, Cornwall included.

The traveller John Ray writing in 1662 says of Dickon Gwyn (Dick Angwyn) of St Just in Penwith that he "is the only man we could hear of that now writes the Cornish language". Nicholas Boson mentions the same man in *Nebbaz Gerriau* where he calls him *an Empack Angwin an brossa ha an cotha Fratier mesk ul an clappiers Carnoack* ['the Sieur Angwyn, the greatest & the eldest of the late Professors of our Cornish Tongue' in Boson's translation] (BF: 24-25). The word *Empack* has given much trouble. It is almost certainly a scribal misreading of the English word *empiric(k)*. This term was frequently used in the seventeenth and eighteenth centuries to describe healers and herbalists who had not had academic training. Outside observers in the Celtic countries did not understand that there was a native tradition of healing and consequently assumed that traditional healers learnt on the job, empirically, as it were. It is very likely that Dickon Gwyn was one such traditional healer, that the term *empiric* had been applied to him (possibly by an outsider) and that it had stuck.

Boson also calls Angwyn the greatest and oldest *Fratier*. This word has also given much trouble, though its general sense is clearly that of a traditional scholar of Cornish. I should like here to suggest an etymology. We start with the form **screffager/*screffader* < *screffa* 'to write'. Though not otherwise attested, **screffager* would be indentical in formation with *poscader* 'fisherman' (Rowe) and *deskadzher* 'teacher' (Lhuyd). **Screffager* originally meant 'writer, scribe, copyist'. I assume that metathesis of the /r/ gave a form **skeffrager*. With this compare Tregear's *blonagath* 'will, wish', a metathesized form of *bolongeth*; cf. Breton *bolonte*(z). The unstressed initial syllable of *skeffrager* was dropped; compare Late Cornish *tel* < *fatel* and *car, kar* 'like' < *pecar* < *kepar*. The resulting form *frager* then would have meant 'copyist of manuscripts, traditional scholar'. It is this form and sense that lies behind *Fratier* in *Nebbaz Gerriau*, the <ti> being an attempt to render /dʒ/.[20]

Richard Angwyn may have been both a healer and a native scholar of Cornish. He died *c.* 1675 and it is likely therefore that he was born in the early years of the seventeenth century. He almost certainly could write Cornish in the traditional spelling and if he had seen Boson's work it is probable that he would have been scandalized by it.

Given that traditional Cornish spelling probably survived until the late seventeenth century, it seems to me that there is even less reason to use an English-based orthography as a basis for the revival. Nor am I the first observer to criticize Nicholas Boson's orthography. In fact Boson was very unhappy about it himself. In *Nebbaz Gerriau* Boson speaks of Mr Keigwin who taught Lhuyd Cornish and says: *Mar kressa an dean deskez feer na gwellaz hemma [ev] a venya kavaz fraga e ouna en screefa composter* 'If that learned and wise man were to see this he would have reason to correct its orthography' (BF: 27).

If we really want to revive Cornish, Nicholas Boson's spelling should not be our model. His orthography is difficult to decipher because it is unsuitable to Cornish. It is far better to take the literary spelling of rich, idiomatic Tudor Cornish and to revive that. It should be remembered that there is no passage anywhere in Medieval or Tudor Cornish that is as difficult and as obscure as *Nebbaz Gerriau*. The reason is simple. Medieval and Tudor Cornish are written in an orthography that was developed for the language and is thus suited to it. *Nebbaz Gerriau* on the other hand is an orphan dressed in borrowed clothes that do not fit.

Gendall believes that Boson's spelling gives a good picture of his pronunciation. I cannot agree, for I find Boson's spelling misleading. It is Lhuyd's phonetic renderings of Boson's JCR that elucidate Boson's own orthography (see the following sections).

Late Cornish orthography

14.33 Gendall says of Late Cornish:

> [It has] a spelling system that not only already goes a long way to tell us how to pronounce our Cornish but was also the way in which those who lived while the language was still a vernacular, if restricted one, wrote down what they thought they heard (*Carn* 60: 15).

The view that Late Cornish orthography reflects the pronunciation well is not borne out by close examination. Late Cornish spelling seems to me to be extremely misleading. I should therefore like to look in detail at some aspects

---

20 I am no longer convinced—if ever I was—by this etymology of mine for *fratier*.

of the orthography of Late Cornish and in particular at the spelling system used for the works of Nicholas Boson.

The first thing to notice about Boson's writing and indeed about Late Cornish generally is that there is very little of it. Boson has left us the Cornish sentences in the Duchess of Cornwall's Progress, the tale *Jowan Chy an Horth* (14 sections in his own hand) and *Nebbaz Gerriau dro tho Carnoack*. That is all.

Secondly I am tempted to ask the following question: if the orthography of Late Cornish is such a fine reflection of the pronunciation, why is the phonological system given by Gendall in SDMC: ix-xxi, so unconvincing? (see my comments at 14.27 above). Jenner says of Nicholas Boson: "Boson knew the colloquial Cornish of his time very well, and wrote it idiomatically, *though his spelling was wild*" [my emphasis] (RC 24: 156).

Thirdly it is impossible to call the spelling of Late Cornish a system, since it is so completely unsystematic. Nowhere is this as obvious as in the spelling of the word for 'Cornish'. In BF one finds the following variants: *Carnoack* BF: 25; *Curnooack* BF: 25; *Curnoack* BF: 31; *Kernuak* BF: 46; *Kornooack* BF: 48; *Kernooak* BF: 48; *Kernuack* BF: 49. Other Late Cornish spellings quoted by SDMC include: *Kernowak* and *Cornoack*.

I use below for the most part those writings ascribed to Nicholas Boson that appear in "traditional orthography", not those in Lhuyd's phonetics. I am fully aware that the scribes may have altered the original spelling but there is no way of reconstructing Boson's original orthography, if it was different from what remains.

14.34 Boson uses <gg> to mean /dʒ/ in *iggeva* 'he is' (BF: 9) and *ugge* 'after' (BF: 25) but /g/ in *teggo* 'bearing', *iggans* 'twenty' (BF: 25), *rigga* 'I did' (BF: 27). Nor is it possible to claim that the difference in the pronunciation is a function of the following vowel, since *dismiggia* 'devise' (BF: 25, 29) and *tegge* 'bearing' (BF: 27) have <gg> before a front vowel but must contain /g/ not /dʒ/.

The same ambiguity is to be seen with single <g>: *meskeeges* 'confused' (BF: 25), *na gez* (BF: 27, 29) and *Contravagian* (BF: 29 x 2) all have <g> before a front vowel which must be pronounced /g/, whereas <g> before a back vowel in *na olgama* 'I could not' (BF: 27), *suppoga* 'suppose' (BF: 29), *bonogath* 'wish' (BF 27) and *crenga* 'love' (BF: 29) is to be pronounced /dʒ/. In Late Cornish *lagagow* 'eyes' (RC 23: 176) the first <g> is /g/, the second /dʒ/; but we know that from comparison with Middle Cornish only. The Late Cornish spelling in itself is misleading.

Initial /g/ is itself problematical. One finds both *gweel* BF: 8, 9 and *geeal* 'to do' BF: 15. It is not clear whether the second form represents /giːl/ or is a mistake for /gwiːl/ or represents a weakly labialized /g/.

14.35 Cornish has two dental continuants /ð/ and /θ/. The representation of them in Late Cornish orthography is confusing in the extreme.

In initial position Late Cornish writes <d> where Lhuyd has <dh>. Notice the following from JCH (I ignore Lhuyd's inverted letters): *da* 'to' (Lhuyd's *dha*) §§ 2, 3, *dotha* 'to him' (Lhuyd's *dhodho*) §, *dem* 'to me' (Lhuyd's *dhem*) § 9, *deez* 'to thee' (Lhuyd's *dhîz*) §§ 5, 7, 8. On the other hand Boson also writes *tha* 'to' §§ 11, 12, *them* 'to me' §§ 8, 10, *thoaz* 'go' (Lhuyd's *dhoz*) § 11, *tha tha'n* 'to carry' (Lhuyd's *dha dhon*) § 12.

There are several explanations for the variation between initial <d> and <th> in Boson's spelling. Quite possibly there were two forms of 'to' and 'to him': /də/, /doðə/ and /ðə/, /ðoðə/. It is also possible that the variation <d> ~ <th> represents an allophonic difference between an interdental pronunciation [ð] and an alveolar one [d̪]. Given that Lhuyd always writes <dh> this may be the more likely explanation. Such an affricated pronunciation is probably related to the pronunciation of <th> in Cornish English, which has been described as being "not like a *d*, or like *th*, but in a manner half between the two" (Jago 1882: 57). Without Lhuyd we would not be able to reach even this tentative conclusion.

Since <th> in Boson's orthography represents both /ð/ and /θ/ we are again dependent upon Lhuyd to determine which of the two is meant. Boson writes *eneth* 'once' and *meth* 'said' (JCH § 10) and it is only Lhuyd's *enueth* and *medh* that tells us one <th> is voiceless and the other voiced. Final /ð/ or /θ/ is one of the most vexed questions of Cornish phonology and without Lhuyd it could not be answered. Boson's spelling is misleading here. English frequently writes /ð/ in word final as <the>, in *scythe*, *withe*, *loathe*, for example. It is a pity that in long monosyllables Boson did not spell final /ð/ in the same way.

Gendall in his dictionary sets out the rules for determining whether <th> represents /ð/ or /θ/. He says:

> **th** occurring within a word of more than one syllable is nearly always pronounced as [ð], but in **whetha**: to blow, and **tethan**: teat, the value is [θ], as in 'think' (SGMC: xix).

Unfortunately there are many other disyllables and trisyllables in Gendall's dictionary that have medial /θ/ and not /ð/. Here are a few of them: *bothack* 'hunchback', *bothan* 'swelling', *brethal* 'mackerel', *cotha* 'oldest', *cotheneb* 'antiquity', *cowethyans* 'companionship', *crothacke* 'complaining', *dewetha* 'last', *ethas* 'eighth', *eithack* 'eighteen', *eithin* 'furze', *fetha* 'defeat', *gruthick* 'potbellied', *gothys* 'proud, *gudrathes* 'curdled', *guthell* 'do', *gwethe* 'worse', *gweetha* 'keep', *kaithes* 'bondage', *kuthu* 'pods', *lether* 'letter', *molithees* 'cursed', *morethack* 'sad', *noothe* 'nakedness', *plethan* 'plait', *progather* 'preacher', *quetha* 'clothe', *rag nevera venitha* 'everlasting', *seithack* 'seventeen', *seithas* 'seventh', *skatho* 'boats', *skethan* 'long strip', *terwithyaw* 'sometimes', *uthicke* 'frightful', *zethan* 'arrow', *zithen* 'week'. One pities the poor learners of Revived Late

Cornish who will have to remember that in each of these words <th> is to be pronounced /θ/ and not /ð/.

14.36 The question of the lenition of initial /s/ > /z/ is a difficult one and there is, as far as one can see, no satisfactory answer. It is not certain whether /s/ is lenited to /z/ in those positions when, for example, /b/ is lenited to /v/, or whether initial /s/ is always /z/ in Late Cornish. Lhuyd sometimes writes initial <z> when grammatical lenition would not be expected, for example in such words as *Zouznak* 'English', *Zanz* 'a saint'. Elsewhere he writes initial <s>, for example, in *sendzhyz* 'beholden' and *mi a savaz* 'I stood'.

Boson's spelling is of no assistance in the matter at all. Although he writes <z> internally, *tezan* 'cake' JCH § 12, and finally, *trigaz* 'dwelling', *creiez* 'called' JCH § 1, *kothaz* 'fell', *moze* 'go' JCH § 2, *looez* 'grey' BF: 25, *aulz* 'coast' BF: 25, he never writes <z> in initial position. In view of Lhuyd's renderings, we cannot be sure that Boson's *Sausen* 'English (people)', *Sousenack* 'English (language)' are to be read with initial /s/ rather than /z/, particularly since Boson often writes final /z/ as <s>, for example in *brose* 'great' BF: 29, *mose* 'go' BF: 27 and *bose* 'be' BF: 27. We find *setha* 'sit' BF: 9 but *zetha* RC 23: 190. Is the initial segment different or not? The spelling of Late Cornish does nothing to answer that question.

The users of Revived Late Cornish are apparently as perplexed as anybody. In Revived Late Cornish the word for 'English', for example, is spelt both with an initial <z> and with an initial <s> (14.29).

14.37 One apparent merit of Late Cornish spelling is that it shows pre-occlusion. One finds, therefore, *radden* < *ran* 'share' (BF: 25), *pedden* 'head' < *pen* (BF: 27), *lebben* 'but' < *lemen* (BF: 27). Some etyma, however, are written both with pre-occlusion and without it. Note for example that *hebma* 'this' with pre-occlusion occurs at CW 2493: *hebma ythew sawer wheake* 'this is a sweet smell', but is always spelt *hemma* in *Nebbaz Gerriau* (BF: 25, 27 x 3). Does this mean Late Cornish was less prone to pre-occlusion than CW, or is *hemma* merely a spelling that conceals /heᵇmə/? The first alternative is the more likely, since Lhuyd only ever writes *hemma* and not **hebma*. Again we are indebted to Lhuyd for a decision in the matter, since the other sources are ambiguous.

14.38 If the consonants of Late Cornish are obscured rather than elucidated by the spelling, the vowels are equally confusing. I have space here to deal with only one aspect of the vowels: the reflex of Old Cornish /iː/.

We have seen at 3.6 above that as a result of the prosodic shift /ɪ/ fell together with /eː/ in the Middle Cornish period.[21] Thus *bys* 'world' becomes /beːz/ and is consequently often spelt *beys*. In Late Cornish 'world' is *bes* (BF: 13) or *bez* (BF: 29). Yet on occasion the word is spelt *beez* (BF: 12) or *bees* (BF: 8).

---

21 Though in some cases it appears to have fallen together with /iː/.

<ee> as an English-based graph would seem to mean /iː/. One might think, then, that Late Cornish had both /beːz/ and /biːz/ (see 3.7). This may be the case, but it is also possible that the double *ee* in *beez, bees* is a way of showing length and that the vowel was /eː/.

Gendall himself, for all that he espouses Late Cornish spelling, had such difficulty distinguishing /eː/ and /iː/ that he gave up the unequal struggle and merely tabulates the attested spellings (SDMC: xxi).

14.39 It is almost impossible for someone who has learnt Revived Late Cornish only to read either Middle or Unified Cornish. He can therefore read *Nebbaz Gerriau, John of Chyanhor,* Lhuyd's *Preface,* parts of CW, some Late Cornish passages of scripture and some other fragments but nothing else. The Middle Cornish texts and the wealth of Neo-Cornish literature must remain closed to him. What a wretched situation in which to find oneself! Revived Late Cornish is hardly worth the effort. Such a plight is the inevitable result of resurrecting the English-based orthography of Late Cornish. The history of the revival is littered with imprudent choices. The attempt to revive Boson's and Rowe's spelling is possibly the most unwise to date.

The historic orthography of Cornish is preserved to us in an unbroken tradition from the Charter Fragment in the fourteenth century to the Words of Administration of Holy Communion in the mid-seventeenth. I can envisage neither unity nor success for the Cornish revival until all *Kernowegoryon* return to that historic orthography in one form or another.

Further observations on the lexicon of Revived Late Cornish
14.40 Revived Late Cornish does not use new coinages. Nowhere in SGMC is there any discussion of suffixation, prefixation, and compounding of words as ways of expanding the vocabulary. Instead it would seem that the devisers of Revived Late Cornish hope to apply pre-existing words to new uses. When judiciously applied, this method can be successful in some contexts. Unfortunately it is not always done well by the proponents of Revived Late Cornish.

In Revived Late Cornish, for example, 'language rights', that is to say 'the language rights of linguistic minorities' has been rendered as *lahez an tavaz* 'the laws of the language'. Not only is the use of the article incorrect here, but the whole phrase can only refer to 'sound laws' or 'phonetic laws'. The translation is inadequate.

SDMC cites two words for 'pronunciation', *ganau* and *laverianzo* (pl.). The first of these is the term preferred by the users of Revived Late Cornish. *Ganau* 'pronunciation' in Revived Late Cornish is based on Lhuyd's *Comparative Vocabulary* (AB ii), where the head-words are Latin. Under *os* 'mouth' Lhuyd cites the following senses: *The mouth, the visage, countenance, language, pronunciation; Also a mouth, passage or entrance of a river; also the outmost part of a thing, brim or edge; The beak or bill of a bird* (110a). These are the meanings and metaphorical meanings of the Latin *os* only. They are not to be understood as referring to the various meanings of the Celtic items. This is clear from the Welsh etyma cited by Lhuyd which include: *y genae* 'mouth', *savan* 'mouth', *uynebpryd* 'countenance', *edrychiad* 'appearance', *iaith* 'language', *tafodiaeth* 'dialect' and *ymadrodh* 'expression'. There is not the slightest evidence that Lhuyd understood the Cornish *ganau* to mean 'pronunciation'. Indeed in his Cornish *Preface* he always uses *laveryanz, laverryanz*, (pl.) *laverianzo* to mean 'pronunciation' (AB: 223, para. 4, line 7 (x2), para. 5, lines 3-4, 6, 7, 7-8, 8). *Ganau* 'pronunciation' is fantasy.

SDMC cites the word *ampassy* with the sense 'et cetera'. *Ampassy* is a common West-Country variant of the Standard English word *ampersand*. *Ampersand < and per se and*, is a printer's term and refers to the symbol *&* 'and', in origin a ligature or joined version of *et*, the Latin word for 'and'. Ampersand was formerly written at the end of the alphabet in school-books. *Ampassy* does not mean 'et cetera'; it is the name of the symbol for 'and'. It is not a Cornish word, nor is there any evidence that it was ever employed by Cornish speakers. Its use in Cornish for 'et cetera' is inadmissible.

Under SDMC *nation* is translated as *tîz* (from Lhuyd). *Tus, tîs* is the plural of *den* and properly means 'people'. There are occasions when 'people' and 'nation' are synonymous, but there are many others when they have quite dissimilar meanings, for example in the sentence: 'Not all the people of Cornwall form part of the Cornish nation'. Unified Cornish distinguishes *kenethel* from *tus*. Revived Late Cornish is quite simply inadequate.

Peter Wills, a Revived Late Cornish user, writes *ouge perhi co cressians an mona* 'taking inflation into account' (*Carn* 69: 16). 'Inflation' means the increase in monetary units or the corresponding decrease in value of each unit. *Cressians an mona* 'the increase in money' is a makeshift translation of 'inflation' that is very wide of the mark. Nance's *whethfyans* 'inflation' is a far better rendering.

The absence from Revived Late Cornish of any mechanism for adopting new terminology is remarkable. Given that new words are crucial in giving a minority language credibility, it is a very serious defect indeed. In this respect Unified Cornish is vastly superior.

14.41 I suggested above (14.32) that the expression *Empack* used by Boson to describe Richard Angwyn was in all probability a misreading of the English word *empirick*. Gendall prefers to understand *empack* as being an adjective derived from the word *empynyon* 'brains' < *in* 'in' + *pen* 'head' + the plural marker *-yon*; cf. Irish *inchinn* 'brain' < *in* + *cenn* 'head'. By the seventeenth century the Cornish for 'brains' was *pidnian* (AB: 47b). If an adjective had been derived from this item, one would expect it to be something like **pidniak*. *Empack* lacks the root syllable *pyn* < *pen*. Whatever the origin of the word *Empack*, one thing is certain: it cannot be connected with the Cornish for 'brains'. Revived Late Cornish nonetheless uses *empack* as an adjective meaning 'intelligent'. Speaking of Edward Lhuyd, for example, Merfyn Phillips says: *Thova dean empack* 'he was a clever man' (*Carn* 82: 16).

Boson says that English is spoken as well in Cornwall as anywhere in the country, 'the Towns & the Cities only excepted'. The Cornish for this phrase of Boson's is *evez an metherwin an* * * * *, where the last word is wanting in Ustick's copy (BF: 24-6). The text is obviously defective and it is clear that we must somehow analyse *metherwin* as containing the word for 'towns'. The text probably originally read somethig like the following: **evez an inick e therwin ha e...* 'apart only [from] its towns and its...' where 'it' is feminine after *wollaz < wlas* 'country, kingdom'. I take *therwin* to be a metathesized form of *threven* 'towns'; cf. *perna < prena* 'buy'.

Nance was perplexed by the passage and understood *metherwin* as **medheryon* 'speakers', an agent-noun based on *yn medh* 'he says/said'. The best that can be said for this suggestion of Nance's is that it is not convincing. Revived Late Cornish has adopted Nance's explanation, and uses *metherwin* to mean 'community'. Phillips says, for example, that the Cornish recognize Edward Lhuyd in particular for his work in recording the Cornish language *potherava cowsez whathe vel tavas an metherwin gen an deeze pleaw en Penwith ha Kerrier* 'when it was still spoken as the language of the community by the common people (lit. parishioners) of Penwith and Kerrier' (*Carn* 82: 16).

The meaning of *empack* is at best uncertain. Whatever its sense, it does not mean 'intelligent'. *Metherwin* is not a word at all but has arisen by false division. It almost certainly contains the Cornish word for 'towns'. The use of *empack* and *metherwin* in Revived Late Cornish to mean 'brainy' [sic SDMC, page 13, column 2, line 14] and 'community' respectively cannot possibly be justified.

14.42 Lhuyd used his thorough knowledge of Welsh to construct Cornish neologisms for the preface to his Cornish Grammar (AB: 222-24). The proponents of Revived Late Cornish have a curious ambivalence to such Welsh-based words from Lhuyd. Those in list A below are included in SDMC, those in list B do not seem to be:

A
anuezek, enuedzhek, hanuidzhek 'particular'
arbednek 'special' (glossed as 'customary')
argrafa 'print' (vb)
bolondzhedhek 'voluntary'
Brethonek 'British'
dazargrafa 'reprint' (vb)
dialek, (pl) *dialeksho* 'dialect'
gerlever 'dictionary'
gerlevran 'vocabulary'
kesson 'consonant'
laveryanz 'pronunciation'
levarva 'library'
otheredzhek 'authoritative' (glossed 'authority')

B
antikueryo (pl.) 'antiquaries'
arverezek 'customary'
Arvorek 'Breton'
eneredzhek 'honoured'
kevarvoz 'meet'
kenezl 'nation'
kollek 'college'
koth-skreforyon 'historians'
lenner 'reader
Lezauek 'Breton'
odzhedzhek 'characteristic'
tavazeth, tavadzheth 'dialect'

It is not clear by what criteria words have been admitted or disallowed. Many of those in list A are also to be found in John Boson, Gwavas, and Pryce. This was probably a factor in their inclusion. None of the items in either list seems to have existed in Cornish before Lhuyd.

14.43 The Revived Late Cornish name for 'Modern Cornish' is *Curnooack Nowedga*. *Nowedga* is the same as *nouedzha* 'fresh, new' in ACB, which has been respelt and given an extended sense, 'modern'. *Nouedzha* 'new' itself results from a misunderstanding of Lhuyd's verb *nouedzha* 'to change, to alter', seen, for example, in *ny vendzha vi rag tra vêth kemerez warnav hy nowedzha* 'I would not wish for anything in the world to take it upon myself to alter it' (AB: 223, para. 5). *Nouedzha* is Lhuyd's Cornicization of the now obsolete Welsh verb *newidio* 'change, alter'.

Nouedzha 'new' probably originated with Gwavas (SDMC: 130). The misunderstanding occurred, first because *nouedzha* (< Welsh *newidio*) was erroneously taken to be related to Cornish *noweth* 'new', and secondly, because Gwavas knew Cornish so imperfectly that he could not distinguish verbs from adjectives. Gwavas's *nouedzha* 'new', *nowedga* in Revived Late Cornish is therefore a ghost-word without basis in either Cornish or Welsh. Yet the proponents of Revived Late Cornish do not hesitate to use the word (for 'Modern Cornish'), while simultaneously claiming that their system is authentic.[22]

14.44 Instead of adopting neologisms based on Breton or Welsh, Revived Late Cornish seeks to recycle words already available. It also uses words from the English dialect of Cornwall, perhaps on the grounds that such distinctively local words were probably Cornish anyway.

---

22 It should be noted that in recent times Neil Kennedy at least has tended to use the term *Kernuak Dewethas* (UCR *Kernowek Dewedhes*) for Revived Late Cornish.

SDMC contains many such dialect words and some obviously have every right to be there. *Tullalulla* for 'dusk' is patently the Cornish **tewlwolow*. The word is already in Nance's dictionary, since Nance quite properly included dialect words when they could be reasonably shown to be Cornish. Other entries in Gendall's dictionary are much less happy. I have already discussed *ampassy* (14.40). Here are a few further examples.

afterclapses 'post-scriptum'. This is a double plural of *after-clap* 'an unexpected sequel'. The second element has nothing to do with *clappya* 'speak' as suggested by Gendall. *Afterclapses* is widely used in dialect English, as for example in "We mert a catched zom arterclapses" quoted by EDD from P. Pindar, *Middlesex Election*.

ale-hoot 'ground ivy'. This must be a misprint. Ground ivy (*Glechoma hederacea*) was formerly universally known as 'ale-hoof' because it was used to clarify ale. The word is attested everywhere in England from Yorkshire to Sussex.

aptycock 'intelligent person'. According to EDD this word is also attested from Dorset. It derives from English *apt* + *cock* 'person, fellow'.

ballyrag 'abuse'. The OED spells this word as *bullyrag* and says it is 'widely diffused in dialect'. The OED defines it thus: 'to overawe, intimidate; to assail with abusive language'.

brash 'acne'. This word is very common in English dialect. The EDD defines it as 'a rash or eruption of the skin' and cites, inter alia, the following: "He's aal come oot iv a brash like mizzles" from Northumberland.

caboose 'cooker, stove'. This is a word in Standard English derived from the Dutch *kabuis*. It originally had the meaning 'a small kitchen on the deck of a ship' OED.

clyders, clythers 'goosegrass'. This word is a West Country variant of *cleavers*, one of the vernacular names of *Galium aparine*. The EDD s.v. *cliders* tells us that the word is widespread in Hampshire, Isle of Wight, Dorset, Somerset and Devon.

cock's eye 'halo'. The EDD quotes the word *cock's eye* with the sense 'halo round the moon' from Banffshire and adds that it was considered by the local fishermen to be a sign of good weather.

dumbledory 'cockchafer, coward'. The basic meaning of *dumbledore, dumbledory* is 'bumble-bee, drone'. The EDD cites examples from Gloucestershire, Berkshire, Kent, Surrey, Sussex, Hampshire, Wiltshire, Dorset, Somerset, Devon and Cornwall. It is also applied to people; cf. "Get 'long, ya gurt dumbledary" quoted by the EDD from Somerset.[23]

fellon, fellen, vellon 'abscess'. This is a word in Standard English: 'a small abscess or boil, an inflamed sore' is the definition given by the OED.

foo'ty 'affected (in manner)'. Examples of *footy* with the sense 'mincing, affected or ridiculous' are according to EDD attested from Sussex, Hampshire and Devon.

grandge, grindge 'grind the teeth'. This is very widespread in English dialect. EDD quotes the following from the West Riding of Yorkshire: "To masticate tough substances as celery is called 'grandging'".

joram 'large cup'. This is a word in Standard English. It is spelt *jorum* by OED and defined as 'a large drinking-bowl or vessel'.

---

23 The word is, of course, now known to millions as the name of the headmaster of Hogwarts in K. D. Rowlings' *Harry Potter* series of books.

REVIVED LATE CORNISH

keamy 'mouldy (of cider)'. This is derived from *keam* 'scum on liquid'. Both the noun and its derivative adjective are common in dialect English. EDD cites examples from Herefordshire, Gloucestershire, Somerset and Devon.

kibe 'chilblain'. This is a word in Standard English. The OED defines *kibe* as 'a chapped or ulcerated chilblain, *esp.* one on the heel'.

mogget '(bib of) apron'. With this word in the English of Cornwall compare "*mugget*: the bosom ruffles of a shirt" quoted by the EDD from Devonshire.

nuddick 'back of the neck'. This is often *niddick* and *neddick*. EDD cites examples from Pembrokeshire, Somerset and Devon.

quignogs 'absurdity'. Gendall suggests that this is derived from Cornish *gokyneth*. It is more likely to be a corruption of the plural of *quidnunc* 'a gossip, tale-bearer'. *Quidnunc* was common in eighteenth- and nineteenth-century English.

rory-tory 'loud, garish'. Compare "Of all the rory-tory bonnets you ever zeed..." quoted by EDD from Somerset.

shoal 'sponge, cadge'. In origin this is a variant of the word *shovel* used as a verb. It is often spelt *shool*: "He'll shool in onnywhere, whear there's owt to be gotten" quoted by EDD from the West Riding of Yorkshire.

skeets 'cow-parsnip', *skit* 'alexanders'. In English dialect *skeet*, *skite* means 'to shoot, to squirt, to spurt'. Hence any umbelliferous plant whose stem can be fashioned into a rudimentary pea-shooter can be called *skeet* or *skit*. Compare: "*skeet*: a squirt or syringe, a water- or pea-shooter made from the stems of umbelliferous plants" quoted from Caithness by SND.

skinomalink 'lively person'. The word is more usually spelt *skinnamalink* or *skinnymalink* and properly means 'a skinny person'. Compare, for example, "Wee skinnamalink craturs dottin' up the passages in U[nited] F[ree] kirks carrying the books" quoted by SND. I have heard "Skinnymalink, melodeon legs and big sla feet" in a children's rhyme from County Armagh.

slotter 'filth'. The word *slotter* is widely used in England, Ireland and Scotland as a verb with the meaning 'bespatter' and as a noun meaning 'mess, filth'. Compare "*slotter*: a nasty mess, a filthy disgusting mass" from Banffshire, Scotland (quoted by SND s.v.).

smeech, smitch 'smell of burning'. This is quoted by EDD as *smeech* and the dictionary gives the following quotation from Somerset: "The smeech was awful—'nough to knock anybody down".

tiflings 'cotton ends'. This word, common in English dialect, is more usually spelt *tifflings*. EDD defines the word as meaning 'the thread drawn from any textile fabric; a small thready fragment; an unravelling shred' and they quote the following example from Somerset: "I could not get any cotton to match, so I was obliged to hem it with tifflings".

towser 'apron'. This is described as dialectal by OED and is defined as 'a large coarse apron'.

trim-tram 'kiss-gate'. According to EDD *trim-tram* 'lich-gate' is attested from Devonshire and Wiltshire.

wisht 'off-colour'. This is more usually spelt *wished* and properly refers to the belief that a person smitten with a sudden illness had been elf-shot. In some places the word means 'unlucky, uncanny, eerie'. In Devon as in Cornwall it meant 'sickly', though the fairies were believed to be the cause of sickness: "In Devonshire to this day all magical or supernatural dealings go under the common name of *wishtness*", quoted by EDD from a text of 1849.

It is legitimate to include a dialect word in a dictionary of Cornish if it satisfies one of two criteria: 1) it is derived unambiguously from a Cornish (Celtic) word; 2) it can be shown to have formed part of the vocabulary of native speakers of Cornish. If an item surviving in the English dialect of Cornwall satisfies neither of these criteria, it does not belong in a dictionary of Cornish.

Revived Late Cornish treats many Standard English and dialectal English words as though they were genuine Cornish. The proponents of Revived Late Cornish cannot therefore claim that this aspect of their lexicon is in any sense authentic. Nor can they answer the charge of inauthenticity by pointing to the large number of English loan-words in the Middle Cornish texts. John Tregear in particular is prone to use English borrowings, few of which have been assimilated to the phonology and morphology of Cornish. We do know, however, that all the English words used by the authors of the Middle Cornish texts from the *Ordinalia* to CW formed part of the native Cornish vocabulary. If an English word appears in the *Ordinalia*, BM or Tregear's homilies, then we know for certain that it was used in Cornish by native speakers of the language. The same cannot be said of the English words aspiring to be Cornish in SDMC.

14.45 The attitude of Revived Late Cornish to neologisms is contradictory. Lhuyd, who was not a native-speaker, adapted to Cornish a number of Welsh words—not always very successfully. If such coinages by Lhuyd are also used by Gwavas, Pryce or John Boson, none of whom was a native-speaker, they are admitted into Revived Late Cornish. On the other hand Revived Late Cornish repudiates twentieth-century neologisms based on Welsh and Breton on the grounds that they are inauthentic. Instead the gaps are filled with items from English dialect, even though there is no evidence that the bulk of them ever formed part of the lexicon of Cornish.

14.46 The approach of Revived Late Cornish to modern terminology has something in common with the views of one group of Irish-revivalists at the beginning of this century. Among educated Irish-speakers there were two schools of thought. On the one hand there were those who believed that the Irish Revival should draw on all the resources of Irish of whatever period in order to refashion the language into an instrument capable of dealing with the modern world. On the other side there were people who espoused *caint na ndaoine* 'the speech of the people'. If a word was not one of the three thousand items commonly in use in this or that parish in County Cork or Kerry, then it should not, indeed could not, be used.

Revived Late Cornish clearly reflects the *caint na ndaoine* school of thought. If a word was not current in Cornish in the seventeenth/eighteenth century or does not survive in the English dialect of Cornwall, then it cannot be used. Fortunately in Ireland *caint na ndaoine* was defeated not by argument but by necessity. When the independent Irish state was founded and Irish was used for writing the constitution, drafting laws and teaching the sciences in the universities, the vocabularies of the fishermen of Ballinskelligs and the small-holders of Ballyvourney were shown to be inadequate for a modern language and the idea of *caint na ndaoine* as the final arbiter of the lexicon died an unlamented death. Perhaps when the Cornish revival has advanced a stage further, the approach of Revived Late Cornish to the vocabulary of the language will be seen in retrospect to have been short-sighted.

Revived Late Cornish: conclusions

14.47 Richard Gendall and his associates were understandably impatient with the quaintness and the preciosity of Unified Cornish. Unified Cornish was the central element in what Tim Saunders perceptively calls the "Nancean synthesis" (see 15.3). Gendall did not want some elfish jargon, written in ornamental blackletter and enunciated only at the *Gorseth* and in the annual Cornish evensong. They wanted a language that could be used, speech that smacked of the quayside, the pub and the street. It was for this reason they based their Cornish on "Late" sources and on the writings of people who could be identified historically.

It is easy to understand the motives of the proponents of Revived Late Cornish and indeed to applaud their enterprise. Misgivings remain, however. If Tudor Cornish is effectively the same language as the Cornish of the Bosons and Lhuyd, then it seems to me that Revived Late Cornish as a separate system loses much of its *raison d'être*. Not only have we a vibrant and colloquial idiom in Tudor Cornish but we have more of it too. Much has been made of the considerable extent of Late Cornish, but this is special pleading. John Tregear's homilies by themselves are longer than all Late Cornish put together. Without forcing the Middle Cornish text CW into service as proto-Late-Cornish, Revived Late Cornish would hardly be possible.

The attempt to revive Late Cornish as "Modern Cornish" seems to me to contain serious internal contradictions. In the first place when one sets about reviving a moribund or extinct language, one is effectively proclaiming to the world that the external history of a language can be rewritten. Cornish died for historical reasons: the Reformation, the lack of the Prayer-Book and Bible in Cornish, the breaking of the links with Brittany, etc. The Cornish Revival seeks to undo the linguistic consequences of past events. But one of those consequences was the demise of the Cornish literary tradition in the sixteenth century. It is illogical to revive Cornish in an attenuated and sub-literary form. If the language can be brought back, so can the native and traditional spelling.

Had even one native-speaker survived, the revival would have used him or her as its basis. With no traditional speakers we start from scratch. That means, I believe, reviving the latest period at which Cornish was vigorous. I suggested that the original inspiration for Modern Cornish was a desire to find a colloquial and racy language, far removed from the medieval quaintness of Nance's Unified Cornish. Such a Cornish is as I have emphasized to be found in BM, TH and CW.[24] I hope that my chapter on syntactical reforms will highlight some of the colloquial resources of the language. We can certainly use Late Cornish to assist us with pronunciation and syntax. But to confine ourselves to it as a basis for the revival is, I believe, to do Cornish itself an injustice.

14.48 Gendall observes that over 56% of all Cornish literature postdates BM, which was written in 1504 (1993-94: 17). The reason for such an apparent imbalance is the relatively large amount of Cornish in the Tregear manuscript. Gendall also acknowledges that the language of the manuscript is very advanced in places, though he does not appear to realize that it is the work of two separate hands. In order to exemplify the advanced nature of the language of the manuscript Gendall quotes *Rag neg eran cregy nanyle regardia gerryow Dew* 'For we neither believe nor regard the words of God' from SA 59.

The Tregear manuscript exhibits almost all the features usually associated with Late Cornish (14.3). In many respects TH and SA are closer to Late Cornish than the *Creation of the World*, upon which Revived Late Cornish is in part based. The Tregear manuscript also provides us with by far the longest Cornish text we have. I calculate that together TH and SA contain over 35,000 words of Cornish. If one adds CW to that total one obtains approximately 46,000 words. This compares with about 3,000 words from Nicholas Boson, just under 1,700 from Rowe and 91 from Bodinar.

TH and SA are modern in language and CW is already the most extensive single source for Revived Late Cornish. It is curious, therefore, that Gendall has not taken the obvious course and based his system on TH, SA and CW together, rather than respelling CW—and effectively ignoring Tregear. It cannot be that he wishes to draw Revived Late Cornish from as narrow and uniform a series of texts as possible. Revived Late Cornish is based on CW, that was composed *c.* 1530-50 and on all Late Cornish from Nicholas Boson, *c.* 1660, to William Bodinar's letter of July 1776. This represents a time-span of approximately 240 years. Had Gendall used TH, SA and CW for his Neo-Cornish, he would have confined himself to texts separated by less than seventy years and the risk of creating an "unreal alloy" would have been considerably reduced.

14.49 I have great admiration for the proponents of Revived Late Cornish and the way in which they have resurrected a most neglected phase in the language's history. Nonetheless I believe that their enterprise is unworthy of the effort. Revived Late Cornish claims to be taking Cornish up where the language left off. This seems initially to be reasonable if rather fatalistic. When one reflects for a moment one realizes that it is deeply illogical. If fate

---

24 *Bewnans Ke* can now be added to these three texts as dating from the sixteenth century.

determined that Late Cornish was the last stage in the history of Cornish, fate has also decreed that the language of Cornwall is now English. If we are to be cowed by a crude historical determinism, then we ought not to be reviving Cornish at all.

It is quite mistaken anyway to say that Late Cornish was the latest phase of the language. Our meagre remains of Late Cornish are what we know of the seventeenth- and eighteenth-century language, but they are not co-terminous with that form of Cornish. If a modern linguist or folklorist could be transported back into the Penwith of let us say 1705, we can be sure that he could with his modern methods acquire a picture of later Cornish that would belie the bastardized fragments we have from the Bosons, Lhuyd and the others. The Medieval and Tudor Cornish texts are much closer to their contemporary language than the "pitiful fragments" (BF: 5) of Late Cornish to theirs.

Revived Late Cornish is as every bit as artificial as Unified Cornish, without the advantages of traditional spelling and relatively extensive sources. Much of Revived Late Cornish inflection has been invented. It might be answered that Revived Late Cornish merely regularizes the spelling of Late Cornish but does not invent anything. Nance said exactly the same thing about his own system: *Unified Cornish aims at using all the resources of Cornish at its richest period and spelling it only a little more consistently than anyone in the 15th century thought necessary* (Nance 1949: vii).

I have not done any statistical analysis of Revived Late Cornish as compared with Nance's system. It is clear from SGMC, however, that there is proportionally a higher degree of conjectural reconstruction in Revived Late Cornish than in Unified Cornish. This is not astonishing in view of the very limited sources used by Gendall. Unified Cornish is based on the *Ordinalia*, PA and BM, three texts that are very similar in spelling. Because Revived Late Cornish derived from texts that exhibit three different spelling-systems, medieval (CW), modern (Boson, Rowe, etc.), phonetic (Lhuyd), the degree of respelling required when writing Revived Late Cornish seems to me to be greater than that required for writers of Unified.

The Cornish revival requires an injection of new life and vitality. Cornish needs to be spoken continually and fluently. Revived Late Cornish will be of great use here, but its three major drawbacks, namely limited vocabulary, unsuitable spelling and highly conjectural inflection, lessen its value considerably.

Some commentators believe that "Modern Cornish" is the most authentic form of Neo-Cornish:

> Modern Cornish appears, therefore, to be overwhelmingly the most acceptable version of the language for the revival, not least because of its strict adherence to the principle of authenticity (Penglase 1994: 106).

Authenticity in the context of an artificially reconstructed and resuscitated language is at best a relative term. One criterion is the degree to which inflection has been derived from the texts themselves rather than being conjecturally reconstructed. Another is the extent to which the inflection is that of the sources rather than a modern simplification. A third is how far the orthography is faithful to the texts and not standardized according to extraneous preconceptions. A fourth is whether all the sources are idiomatic and native Cornish. A fifth is how far the phonology has been deduced systematically from the texts, etc., rather than from a unproven continuity between Cornish and Cornish English. A sixth is to what extent the lexicon consists of indigenous or naturalized roots. If we test Revived Late Cornish for authenticity by any of these criteria, it is found wanting.

Revived Late Cornish cannot claim to be more authentic than Unified Cornish. In fact it is more artificial. The texts on which Revived Late Cornish is based are so meagre that Revived Late Cornish is not a complete language. The phonology of Revived Late Cornish is uncertain; the orthography is unsuitable and separates the users of Revived Late Cornish from all other forms of the language. Moreover the spelling is still being "evolved" so that students cannot be sure that what they learn today will not be changed tomorrow. Much of the lexicon of Revived Late Cornish is not even Cornish and the resources that Revived Late Cornish has to create new words are inadequate. It is difficult to believe that the majority of revivalists will opt for Revived Late Cornish as their preferred system.

CHAPTER 15
Unified Cornish

15.1 Unified Cornish, or *Kernewek Unyes*, is the system of Neo-Cornish devised by Robert Morton Nance. Unified Cornish was based on the Middle Cornish texts and in particular the *Ordinalia* and PA. The first handbook of UC was Nance's *Cornish for All* which first appeared in 1929. A second edition was published in 1949. The most important book for learners was Smith's *Cornish Simplified* of 1939. A second edition was published in 1955 and reprinted in 1965, 1972 and 1981.

Unified Cornish was the only variety of Neo-Cornish from the 1930s until the 1970s. Writing in 1973 Pool says of Nance: "[He] evolved a system of spelling known as 'Unified Cornish' which is used by all modern students of the revived language, and is based on the dramas of Middle Cornish, but with most of the inconsistencies and variations of spelling removed" (PNWP: 9).

Unified Cornish has produced an extensive corpus of literature—some of it of high quality. The two longest texts are Smith's narrative poem, *Trystan hag Ysolt*, (1951) and Bennetto's novel, *An Gurun Wosek a Geltya* (1984). The most important periodical of Unified Cornish is *An Lef (Kernewek)*, founded by Richard Gendall in 1952. Gendall has to his credit many works in Unified Cornish, both translations and original compositions in prose and verse. His two learner's handbooks in Unified Cornish, KB (1972), and *Cornish is Fun* (1978), are also worthy of note.

15.2 Unified Cornish takes the Cornish of the richest period, spells it slightly more regularly than was customary at the time, adding only the graph <dh> to distinguish /ð/ from /θ/. The wide body of revived Cornish from the first appearance of Nance 1949 until the 1970s is eloquent witness to the viability of Unified Cornish as a system.

Unified Cornish has, nonetheless, a number of defects. Among them I should include the following:

1) It is based on too early a form of Cornish and prefers the old and quaint form to the more modern and simplified one. This is true of inflection, syntax and vocabulary alike.
2) Unified Cornish was produced in an *ad hoc* fashion without any thorough attempt to analyse the phonology of Middle Cornish on which it was based. As a result Unified Cornish is mistaken in spelling and pronunciation in a number of significant ways.

3) UC suppresses variation in Middle Cornish. Where several forms are attested of a morphological item, Unified allows one only and thus gives a false picture of the variety of the Cornish language.

4) UC was not used simply as a standard form of speech for learners and revivalists. It was imposed upon the Cornish texts themselves. Since Unified Cornish was itself based on the *Ordinalia* and PA, respelling either in Unified Cornish, as has been done, was unnecessary on the one hand and unwise on the other.

15.3 Speaking of Unified Cornish as part of the "Nancean synthesis", that cluster of cultural and nationalist assumptions associated with Robert Morton Nance, Tim Saunders observes:

> Cornish has a symbolic rôle in this synthesis. It plays the part of an unrecoverable past through its own impenetrability. Its written appearance, especially in a half-uncial or a blackletter script, lends the past venerability and strangeness. Where Jennery [*sic*] would have refined and codified the most recent varieties of Cornish, Nance withdrew into a remoter past for his standards of style and vocabulary. Jenner's chaste prose style was replaced by a simplistic diction drawn from poetic figures and inversions, all left ambiguous and unsystematized, [which] made approaching a Cornish text more of an exercise in puzzle-solving than an attempt at understanding. Speech was restricted to oracular ceremonial utterances. Where Mistral at least slowed the decline in Occitan and Tagore caused a new flowering of Bengali, Nance succeeded in paralysing Cornish for over forty years (Ó Luain 1983: 257).

This criticism is unfair on Nance, who was a dedicated scholar and an inspiring teacher. As far as the speaking of Cornish is concerned, however, there is a grain of truth in it. I remember in the late 1950s and early 1960s, when I started learning Unified Cornish, how disappointed I was to find that hardly anybody could actually converse in the language. It is of course difficult to speak any foreign language and particularly so when there are no natives to imitate. If a whole generation of Cornish learners were mute, much of the blame must be laid at the door of Unified Cornish itself. Had the form of the language not been so quaint and so archaic, possibly many more might have attained a degree of fluency in it.

15.4 A.S.D. Smith (Caradar) was also a significant factor in the dominance of Unified Cornish. Smith was a far abler linguist than Nance and a better writer of Cornish as well. Caradar's Cornish style was simple, idiomatic and readable. Nance's Cornish tended to be convoluted, difficult and rather precious (cf. Saunders's remarks quoted above). One has only to compare Smith's *Nebes Whethlow Ber* with Nance's *Lyver Pymp Marthus Seleven* to see which of the two was the better stylist. As far as versification was concerned

Caradar was unequalled. Indeed as a work of literature his *Trystan hag Ysolt* is in some ways preferable to *Beunans Meriasek*.

Caradar had his disagreements with Nance over Unified Cornish, but it seems that Nance's opinions won the day. Caradar's main function was to take Unified Cornish as a *fait accompli* and make it work. Caradar was a fine teacher. His *Cornish Simplified* gave the impression that Unified Cornish was a practical system. Because he could write and speak Unified Cornish and was able to present it simply and coherently, Caradar paradoxically was a regrettable influence upon the Cornish revival. Without Caradar's abilities as writer, translator, poet and teacher, dissatisfaction with Unified Cornish would have come much sooner.

15.5 I do not believe that Unified Cornish was mistaken in principle. It could, however, have been easier to learn and speak and altogether a more practical system if only Nance had been more of a linguist and less of a romantic. I believe that Nance's greatest mistake was to select the earlier rather than the later period of Middle Cornish as the model for Neo-Cornish. When Nance set about devising his system, Tregear was yet to be discovered and Nance cannot be criticized for not using him. Nance can, however, be faulted for the way in which he deliberately suppressed the modernizing aspects of his texts in favour of archaisms. Let me give a few examples.

It is quite apparent that from the *Ordinalia* onwards the present and past subjunctive are falling together (see 19.6). Yet Unified Cornish insists on keeping them apart. Similarly as early as the *Ordinalia* the future is made with the verb *mynnes*: *my a vyn mos* 'I will go', etc. Unified Cornish knows nothing of such a periphrastic formation. Correspondingly the conditional is from the early period constructed with the pluperfect/conditional of *mynnes*: *ef a vynsa leverel* 'he would say'. Unified Cornish ignores such a development. As a result unreal conditions in Unified Cornish are more difficult than they need be. It is also apparent from the texts that the periphrastic present was customary in spoken Cornish, for example, *yth esof ow crejy* 'I believe'. Unified Cornish does not allow it.

As we shall see below (21.5), the infixed pronouns were disappearing from spoken Cornish to be replaced by post-posited pronouns. A good example is to be found at CW 345: *me a wra ge, dean, a bry* 'I make thee, man, from clay'. This was a feature that should have been seized upon as facilitating the speaking of the language. Instead Unified Cornish ignores it. As early as PA indirect speech is introduced by *del* and *fatel* (see 21.17). Unified Cornish does not allow this construction. Instead speakers are compelled to use much more difficult syntax involving the verbal noun or finite verbs introduced by the particle *y*.

As far as vocabulary is concerned Unified Cornish is distinguished by a high degree of archaism. In the Middle Cornish texts the regular words for 'money', 'animal' and 'flower' are *mona*, *best* and *flowren*, yet Unified Cornish insists upon the purisms *arghans*, *myl* and *blejen*.

If Nance had reproduced the Cornish of the Tudor texts, he would have provided learners with a more vital and less quaint language. As it is Unified Cornish, in spite of the efforts of excellent teachers and some first-class materials, has failed to take off as a spoken language.

15.6 Nance was not a professional linguist and had a somewhat amateurish approach to the phonology and accidence of Cornish. He says, for example, of the graph <ow>: "when long [it] has the sound of **aou** or **eow**… a shorter **ow** is heard in **Jowan, lowen**" (Nance 1949: 4). One can legitimately ask what exactly this statement means. Is Nance talking of vocalic length or of vocalic quality? Too much of his linguistic analysis demonstrates this same vagueness.

Nance frequently shows great erudition coupled with an astonishing naivety. It is apparent in Tudor Cornish that the second person singular ending -*yth* is yielding to an analogical -*ys* (based on the second singulars of *bos: os* and *esos* 'thou art'). Either Nance knows nothing of these or he prefers to ignore them. In his Unified Version of *Jowan Chy an Horth* Nance renders Boson's *Panna weale 'lesta geeal?* (JCH § 4) as *Pana whel a yllysta gul?* and he suggests that *(g)yllysta* is the imperfect indicative used for the present-future (Nance 1949: 37). It is better understood as an analogical present-future *gyllys* 'thou canst' < *gyllyth*. Nance's failure to recognize it as such is a natural consequence of his tendency to dismiss what he did not like.

Discussing the use in Unified Cornish of <gh> in words like *byghan, lorgh*, etc., Nance says:

> Its omission in these would suggest that where it is always spelt, as in *maghteth, marghas, myghtern, segh*, etc., the guttural sound of *ch* is intended, though actually the sound, or lack of it, is the same in all, and never fully guttural (Nance 1955: v).

Two questions arise here. If <gh> is pronounced the same in the two sets of etyma, why was it not always written similarly? Secondly what exactly is meant by "never fully guttural"? Does Nance mean $/x/$, $/h/$, $/\emptyset/$ or something else? Does Nance really know what he is saying?

15.7 Nance believed, mistakenly in my view (10.1-5), that *g/j* in words like *kerenge* 'love', *pejadow* 'prayer', etc., was a "softened form of *s*" (Nance 1949: 1). He also apparently believed that such 'softening' was late and corrupt and should be kept to a minimum in revived Cornish. As a result he constructed forms like **crysyans* 'faith, belief', that are found nowhere in Cornish—*crejyans, cryjyans* being the attested forms (Williams 1990: 262). Nance also disallowed variants like *woja* 'after', *tryja* 'third', *ujy* 'is', etc., even though such variants are common in the *Ordinalia*, one of the texts on which Unified Cornish is based.

Nance obviously disliked pre-occlusion for the same reason. He regarded it as late, corrupt and to be avoided. He says:

m, n in late pronunciation when following a stressed short vowel developed a **b** and **d** before them, as **pedn, tabm**; this is not adopted in unified Cornish (Nance 1949: 1).

Nance's uncompromising refusal to countenance pre-occlusion in Neo-Cornish is inadmissible for several reasons. In the first place it occurs in BM, one of the foundation texts of Unified Cornish. Secondly, it is widespread in CW, which also provided some of the foundation of Unified Cornish. Thirdly, the phonology of Unified Cornish is based as much as anything upon Lhuyd's phonetic renderings and Lhuyd not only indicates pre-occlusion everywhere but actually alludes to it as a distinguishing feature of Cornish phonology (AB: 223, para. 3). Lastly, pre-occlusion occurs widely in western place-names and is particularly frequent in the toponyms of Penwith, whose English dialect Nance studied thoroughly for the light it could shed on the pronunciation of Cornish

15.8 At no point did Nance attempt to elaborate a scientific basis for the phonology of Unified Cornish. Indeed it is doubtful whether he could have done so, even if he had wished. Instead he let the phonology of Unified Cornish emerge piecemeal and in an *ad hoc* fashion. His system is saved quite simply by the way that for the most part he adhered to the spelling of the texts. If we measure the phonology of Unified Cornish and of Kernowek Kemyn against the yardstick of Middle Cornish, we have to acknowledge that Unified Cornish is by far the more accurate of the two.

After a detailed analysis of Middle Cornish phonology (2.1-12.7), I can find only four serious errors in Nance's phonology. They are as follows:

(a) Unified Cornish does not distinguish the vowel in *prys, preys* 'time' from that of *mys* 'month'. In view of the spelling this was understandable, but it is likely that *mys* had /iː/ whereas *prys* has /ɪ/ becoming /eː/.[25]

(b) Unified Cornish does not distinguish the vowel of *luen* 'full', *due* 'comes' from that of *tus* 'people', *ruth* 'red'. It is true that *us* 'is' and *mur* 'great' may have been both /yːz/ and /myːr/ as well as /œːz/ and /mœːr/. Nonetheless the analogy with Breton ought to have alerted Nance to the existence of /œː/ in Middle Cornish. Jenner as early as 1904 was well aware of /œː/ in Cornish; speaking of the differences between Middle and Late Cornish he says: "*eu, ue,* with the French sound of *eu,* or the German *ö,* become *ê* (= *ay* in *may*)" (HCL: 51).

(c) Unified Cornish invariably spells *kewsel* 'speak', *clewes* 'hear', etc., with <ew> even though it is obvious that from the period of the earliest texts stressed /ew/ in disyllables is becoming /ow/. The very term *Kernewek* 'Cornish', used by Nance, is first attested in LCB (1865) and is historically unwarranted. From the first recorded instance of the word in the sixteenth century the word has /ow/ in its stressed syllable, not /ew/.

---

25 *Prys* 'time' also probably had a variant in /iː/.

(d) Unified Cornish never really decided how to pronounce final stops and continuants. Nance suggests in (Nance 1949: 1) that <k> should be /k/ finally except before a vowel, where it should be /g/. He apparently believed that the Cornish of the texts resembled Breton in alternating /k/ with /g/ according to position. As we have seen at 8.19 above, this may have been the case before the prosodic shift; afterwards it was not so. The other plosives were similar. Although /ð/ and /θ/ originally alternated according to position, it is apparent from Late Cornish evidence that the final consonant of *deth* 'day' and *lath* 'kill!' was always /ð/ (8.15). In this respect Unified Cornish is, I fear, at variance with the evidence.

Although these are palpable errors, they are intelligible in the light of the Middle Cornish texts. Let us look at a) and b) first:

We know from Late Cornish that in stressed monosyllables /e:/ had a tendency to fall together with /i:/ (3.7). Similarly /œ:/ in stressed monosyllables sometimes became /y:/ and unrounded to /i:/ (3.15). These two phenomena were a result of the prosodic shift and reflect the opposition long/tense ~ short/lax which is fundamental to Middle Cornish. They also meant that /e:/ and /i:/ on the one hand and /œ:/ and /y:/ on the other were not always kept separate. Nance's failure to distinguish either pair is therefore intelligible and indeed not in every case at variance with the phonetic facts. The shift of /ɪ:/ > /i:/ was probably commoner before /z/ (see 3.7).

c) <ew> for <ow> is less easy to justify, since it is obvious that /ew/ was already becoming /ow/ in stressed disyllables by the period of the *Ordinalia* and PA. It must be admitted, however, that <ew> much commoner in both than <ow>. Some words, *beunans*, *bewnans*, for example, continued to be written with <eu>, <ew> long after the stressed diphthong had become /ow/.

d) Spellings like <whek>, <map>, <deth> are in the light of the texts perfectly understandable. The Middle Cornish scribes used the spelling and rhyming conventions of a period before *wheg*, *mab*, *dedh* became generalized in all positions. Unified Cornish is at variance with the phonology of Middle Cornish in this matter. It is not entirely at variance with scribal practice.

Taken together, then, the phonetic errors in Unified Cornish can be justified. I prefer to correct them, but acknowledge that they do not in themselves vitiate Unified Cornish completely. Unified Cornish is therefore quite unlike Kernowek Kemyn, whose phonology bears little resemblance to the sound-system of the texts on which it is based.

Nance, for all his erudition, had the humility of the scholar. He saw that all Middle Cornish literature from the Charter Fragment to the Creation of the World was written essentially in the same orthography. There were differences in the various texts and Nance did not always grasp the full import of the differences. Yet he realized that the Middle and Tudor Cornish scribes were not fools. They spelt as they did because their orthography had developed as

Cornish had developed. Moreover Nance understood that the Cornish scribes knew the language far better than he himself. He therefore did his best in Unified Cornish to regularize the spelling of the texts without reading into it what was not there. The wonder is not that he is sometimes mistaken, but that his mistakes are so few.

15.9 Objections have been made to the way in which UC regularizes Middle Cornish spelling and introduces the unhistorical graphs <dh> and extends without warrant the use of <j>. My own view is that Nance was right in this aspect of his system (see 17.11-12 below).

15.10 Cornish is a Celtic language and like all Celtic languages it seems to have had a pronounced tendency to dialectal variation. We have already noted some dialectal features: the distribution of *s* and *j* in such words as *wosa, woja* 'after' and *bohosek, bohojek* 'poor'; the presence or absence of pre-occlusion is words like *gwyn/gwydn* 'white' and *cam/cabm* 'bent'. Unified Cornish allows a little variation, but not enough. We have seen that it disallows pre-occlusion and is reluctant to allow some *g/j* variants. There are many other legitimate forms that Unified Cornish ignores.

Nance 1955, for example, cites both *crysy* and *cryjy* 'believe'. On the other hand it cites *pysy* 'to pray' but not the variant **pyjy*. In fact the more usual forms of these verbs are *cresy/crejy* and *pesy/pejy*, with historic /e/ as the stressed vowel. Unified Cornish ignores them. Again in the verb *mynnes* 'to wish' Nance allows only one form of the 1st person singular: *mynnaf*. In the Middle Cornish texts, as we have seen, *mennaf* and *mannaf* are both commoner than *mynnaf*. Throughout the inflection of Unified Cornish we find that Nance allows only one form (or grudgingly two), although the texts themselves exhibit greater variety.

Among other features ignored by Unified Cornish one might cite the following:

a) prepositional pronouns like *anothans* 'from them', *thothans* 'to them'
b) pronominal forms in *eff, thotheff*
c) *dym, dys, dotho* alongside *thym, thys, thotho*
d) personalized forms of *y'm bus* like *a's tefons, ma'm boma*
e) *me, te* alongside *my, ty*
f) 2nd singulars in *-s* rather than *-th* /θ/, e.g. *gwres* for *gwreth* 'thou dost'
g) subjunctive 2nd singular of *bos* in *-s* rather than *-y*: *bos/bes* not *by*
g) plurals in *-s*, for example, *aweylers* 'evangelists'.

In my suggested revision to Unified Cornish which I outline in Part III of this book, I cite variations in inflection where they occurs. Any form which is to be found in native Cornish should be allowed as a possible variant in the revived language (16.3 (7)).[26] The remains of Cornish are fragmentary enough without our reducing them still further.

15.11 The absence of variants in Unified Cornish would have been a trivial enough failing, had the system been confined to Neo-Cornish texts. It was quite a different matter when the *Ordinalia*, PA and CW were published in the straightjacket of Unified Cornish. In fact Nance seems to have been so confident of his system that he forced everything from the Charter Fragment (*c.* ?1350) to *Nebbaz Gerriau* (*c.* 1690) into Unified Cornish. This might have been tolerable as a help to learners, but it deprived revived Cornish of any claim that might have had to academic respectability. In future if any text is respelt in a revised orthography, the version of the manuscripts should appear alongside. Anything else is indefensible.

15.12 It will be seen from Part III of this book that my suggested reforms for Unified Cornish will among other things bring UC closer to Late Cornish— without abandoning the traditional orthography of the language. My suggested emendations are by no means the first time that a modernized Middle Cornish has been proposed as the basis for Neo-Cornish. Jenner's own system of 1904 was an amalgam of Middle and Late Cornish features. So indeed is Revived Late Cornish, though it unwisely, in my view, adopts the unsuitable orthography of Boson, Rowe, etc.

Another modernizing form of Unified Cornish was devised by Rod Lyon and published, for example, in his book *Everyday Cornish* (1984). Among the Late Cornish features discernible in the book one might cite the following:

1) pre-occlusion in such words as *kebmer* 'take', *pedn mousak* 'rascal', *ydn* 'one', *ydnek* 'eleven', *warbydn* 'against', etc.
2) rhotacism of *esof* 'am', etc. > *eram* 'I am', *erosta* 'thou art', *erony* 'we are'
3) *jy* for the second person singular pronoun
4) *an jy* as the third person plural pronoun
5) /dʒ/ in the conditionals *menja* 'would wish', *galja* 'could'
6) widespread use of *-ma* as the first singular ending: *gwrama* 'I do', *bema* 'I was'
7) *tel/tre/dr* to introduce indirect speech: *an jy wruk gweles tel era an jy ow muvya* 'they saw they were moving'
8) enclitic pronouns as possessives: *ny vedn'ma gweles jy obma namoy* 'I don't want to see you here again'
9) analytical forms of the preposition pronouns: *dhe vy* 'to me', *dhe why* 'to you', etc.

---

26 This principle of allowing any form found at any period of the language I call *tota Cornicitas*.

There are a number of ways in which *Everyday Cornish* could be criticized. Some of its prepositional pronouns are unlikely reconstructions, for example, and its phonology and lexicon exhibit some of the less satisfactory features of Unified Cornish. Nonetheless *Everyday Cornish* adopts the kind of system that the revival needs. It maintains the traditional spelling while modernizing and simplifying the morphology and syntax. Part III below is an attempt to modernize and simplify in a systematic fashion.

The varieties of Neo-Cornish: conclusions

15.13 None of the three varieties of Neo-Cornish currently in use is satisfactory. Aspiring students of Neo-Cornish are therefore confronted by a choice of evils.

Unified Cornish is by far the least unsatisfactory. Since learning materials and dictionaries are readily available, Unified should for the time being be the system of choice.

Kernowek Kemyn is faulty from the phonetic point of view and its orthography is artificial. Although Kernowek Kemyn will ultimately be abandoned, it does bear some resemblance to the bulk of Cornish literature, traditional and revived. Handbooks in Kernowek Kemyn can be used for the time being, albeit with the utmost caution.

Somebody learning **Revived Late Cornish** only will find reading any other system virtually impossible. Unless one already has a working knowledge of another system, Revived Late Cornish is best avoided.

PART III: UNIFIED CORNISH REVISED

CHAPTER 16
General remarks

16.1 This book is intended as an academic analysis of the varieties of revived Cornish. I have been critical of all the major systems currently in use. It would not be right to let the matter rest there. Since I believe that Unified Cornish is the best system available at the moment and is susceptible of being revised, I set out in the following pages how such a revision might be accomplished. I will give this revision of Unified Cornish the title **Unified Cornish Revised** or **UCR**.

In Unified Cornish the word for Cornish is *Kernewek*, a form invented by Robert Williams. The earliest reference we have to the language is from 1572 which spells the word <Cornowok> (Wakelin 1975: 89). In Late Cornish the name is variously *Kernuak, Kernuack, Kernooak, Kernowak, Kornooack, Carnoack, Curnoack, Curnooack*. In these forms the stressed syllable is clearly /ow/ and not /ew/. Lhuyd spells the names of several languages with <ek>: *Brethonek, Arvorek, Lezauek, Godhalek* and *Kelezonek* (AB: 222-24). I therefore recommend spelling the word for 'Cornish' as <Kernowek> as pronouncing it /kər'nowək/. **Kernowek** can be used to refer to UCR itself.

16.2 UCR takes as its starting point the three 'Tudor' texts BM (1504), TH (*c.* 1555) and CW. Although CW was transcribed in 1611 it is a copy of a pre-Reformation original and is believed to date from *c.* 1530-50 (Murdoch 1993: 75). These three texts taken together form something of a unity as far as pronunciation and spelling are concerned. They have the further advantage that their grammar is more advanced and less medieval than that of the *Ordinalia* and PA. UC was largely based on the *Ordinalia* and is accordingly somewhat quaint and medieval in diction. By using the Tudor texts UCR can escape from the archaism of Medieval Cornish without embracing the poor and attenuated language of the seventeenth and eighteenth centuries. Tudor Cornish is modern enough to give us contemporary diction, but still sufficiently rich and idiomatic to be a complete language.

Of the three texts Tregear is in some ways the most important: first because he is extensive, secondly because he writes in prose and thirdly because of his date, namely *c.* 1555. This is very close in time to the Prayer-Book Rebellion of 1549. If instead of rejecting the Book of Common Prayer outright, the rebels had been granted a Cornish version of it, the prayer-book would have been published in Cornish—and in the orthography of the period. The bible would

188

almost certainly have followed and Cornish, like Manx, might have survived into the nineteenth and even the twentieth century. The universally accepted orthography for Cornish would now be essentially that of John Tregear.

It may be objected that Tregear's language is too full of English to be really useful as a model. One suspects, however, that Tregear's use of English was a feature of sixteenth century Cornish preaching and that it was analogous with priests' Breton in Brittany. This homiletic dialect of Breton was deliberately larded with French words to give the language authority and the appearance of being learned. Tregear's Cornish is similar except that the intrusive language is English and not French. Close reading of Tregear's shows that his language is much less Anglicized than appears at first sight. His style is always idiomatic, his Cornish vocabulary is wide and his grammar perfect. The suggestion that Tregear was not a native-speaker of Cornish (0.1) is mistaken.

16.3 Before setting out my recommended revision of UC, I should like to list here the principles upon which the revision is based.

1) The spelling, pronunciation, inflection, syntax and vocabulary of UCR are to be based upon the three foundation texts BM, TH and CW.

2) Where the pronunciation and orthography differ from UC, UCR should use the texts as its guarantee of authenticity. Failing which it is legitimate to go outside our foundation texts both backward to the *Ordinalia* and PA and forward to Late Cornish sources.

3) Although the orthography is to be based on the three Tudor texts, UCR will respell <th> as <dh> where /ð/ is intended. The graph <dh> is already in UC and is as old as Cornish itself. I give my reasons for using <dh> at 17.12 below. In UCR <dh> occurs in final position (see 8.15-16).

4) UCR will also respell <g>, <dg> and <gg> of the basic texts as <j> or <jj> when the sound is /dʒ/. This practice is also to be found in UC. For a full discussion, see 17.11.

5) In order for the orthography of UCR to differ as little as possible from UC, I shall apply a number of spelling rules to the forms in the three foundation texts. For example, final <al(l)>, <a(c)k> in the texts may be respelt in UCR as <el> and <ek> respectively even if such variants are not attested in the texts themselves. Similarly I shall remove a final mute <e>, so as to bring the spelling close to UC. Since *os* 'thou art' alternates with *oys* and *gos* 'blood' with *goys* in the texts, I shall spell *oys* 'age' as <os> even though such a spelling does not occur in BM, TH or CW.

6) In the light of the discussion at 8.8-14 above final *g/k* will be spelt <g> after stressed vowels and <k> after unstressed ones.

7) Cornish, like the other Celtic languages, exhibits wide variation in its inflection. When teaching Cornish to beginners it is probably advisable to confine oneself to a standardized grammar and to avoid alternative forms. Where variants occur in the traditional texts, however, they

should be tolerated from experienced speakers. A learner would, for example, be taught *dhedha* 'to them' only. A more experienced speaker might use any one of the traditionally occurring variants, *dhedha, dedha, dodhans, dhodhans, dhodhanjy*.

8) In syntax and vocabulary I recommend following BM, TH and CW closely. I suggest, for example, replacing *blejyow* 'flowers' and *arghans* 'money' with the more authentic *flowrys* and *mona* (see 22.3-4). The UC forms should perhaps be preferred in certain more literary contexts.

9) Since the entire remains of Cornish are so limited, it is legitimate to obtain vocabulary from a variety of sources (see 22.11). Words should, however, conform to UCR phonetic type and orthography.

10) UCR is a variety of Neo-Cornish. It is not designed for the respelling of historical Cornish texts, Old, Middle or Late. Editions of Cornish literature should always provide the text of the manuscript(s) alongside any version in modern orthography.

CHAPTER 17
The phonology and orthography of UCR

17.1 UCR, like UC, bases both its spelling and pronunciation upon the language of the Middle Cornish texts. Unified Cornish represents a regularized form of Cornish based for the most part on the language of the *Ordinalia* and PA. Dissimilarities between UC and UCR are largely a result of the differences between the *Ordinalia* and PA on the one hand and BM and TH on the other.

Although UCR like UC has normalized the orthography of the texts, there are two significant ways in which both differ from medieval and Tudor orthography. In the first place UC and UCR both extend the use of <j> for /dʒ/ to situations where Middle Cornish normally wrote <g>. Moreover, both replace <th> and <ʒ> by <dh> when the etymology suggests /ð/ rather than /θ/. The practice of UCR is in addition different from that of UC in the use of <dh>, since UCR uses <dh> in word final position where UC has <th>: UC *deth* 'day', *scoth* 'shoulder', *lath* 'kills' but UCR *dedh, scodh, ladh* (see 17.4 below).

17.2 Traditional Cornish orthography does not indicate the place of the accent. Neither therefore does UCR. Although the penultimate syllable is usually stressed, in *awher, bysmer,* for example, the final is stressed but the anomalous accent is not shown in writing. In Unified Cornish in some words the position of the accent is indicated by the use of the hyphen: *a-jy, a-van,* etc. This practice can be continued in UCR.

Vowels and diphthongs
17.3 We have seen that in classical Middle Cornish half-long vowels were shortened. Thus the stressed vowels of *tasow* 'fathers', *gweles* 'see', *palas* 'dig', *govyn* 'ask' are all short. This shortening operates throughout the entire phonological system of Cornish. *Treth* 'passage', *us* 'use', *tros* 'foot', *squyth* 'tired' have long stressed vowels, but *tretha* 'to ferry', *usya* 'to use', *trosya* 'to plod', *squytha* 'to weary' have short ones. This was a feature of Middle Cornish that Nance does not appear to have understood. As a result he marks the root vowel in *tretha, usya, trosya* as long. I recommend pronouncing such vowels as short in UCR.

17.4 Traditional Cornish orthography on occasion (but by no means always) distinguishes long *a* and *o* from their short equivalents by inserting *y* or *i* after the long vowel. Thus one frequently finds such spellings as <tays> 'father', <grays> 'grace', <goys> 'blood', <boys> 'food', etc. <ey> is also used to indicate /eː/ from earlier /iː/: <beys> 'world', <wheys> 'sweat'. <y> is not normally used with long /iː/ and indeed there is no way of distinguishing

191

gwyn 'white' with /ɪ/ from *gwyn* 'wine' with /iː/. The disadvantage of using <y> as a marker of length is as follows: <ay>, <ey> and <oy> as graphs for the long vowels are likely to be confused with the same graphs used for the diphthongs /aj/ and /oj/ in *payn, seythen* and *moy*, for example.

Unified Cornish does not use <y> as an indicator of length. Instead it writes the long vowels as <a>, <o>, <e> and marks them long only in dictionaries. The lack of a method for indicating length is perhaps a weakness in Unified orthography, but it cannot be remedied without doing violence to the spelling of the texts. To spell *gwyn* 'white' with <y> and *gwin* 'wine' with <i>, for example, is a solution to the problem that has does not occur in Middle Cornish. It is attested in Old Cornish, however, since OCV writes *guin* 'wine' but *guyn* 'white'. Since we have no Middle Cornish warrant for such spellings, it seems wisest not to introduce them.

In UCR I recommend spelling the long vowels in accordance with traditional orthography as follows:

/aː/ as <a>: *tas* 'father', *gras* 'thanks', *can* 'song', *tal* 'forehead'
/oː/ as <o>: *bos* 'be', *bos* 'food', *bodh* 'wish', *ol* 'track'
/eː/ as <e>: *bedh* 'grave', *ken* 'other', *gwedh* 'trees'
/iː/ as <y>: *gwyn* 'wine', *tyr* 'land', *hyr* 'long', *fyn* 'fine'.

One should remember that /aː/ is normally [æː], but [ɑː] in *bras* 'great' and before /l/ in *tal* 'forehead', for example. In word final position it is permissible to replace /iː/ with /ej/, and to pronounce *chy, ky, try*, etc. as /tʃej/, /kej/, /trej/, etc. (3.5)

17.5 Where /eː/ is the reflex of earlier /ɪː/ we should spell it as <e> if we have a warrant in the texts. Thus we can write *pref* 'reptile', *cref* 'strong', *fedh* 'faith' and *dedh* 'day'. Two of these etyma already have <e> in UC. In some cases, *beys* 'world' and *preys* 'time', for example, our foundation texts have <ey> but not <e>. Since Lhuyd and other Late Cornish texts have <e> in these and other etyma, we are justified in spelling them with <e> in UCR.

The words in which <y> of UC may be respelt <e> or <ey> and to be pronounced /eː/ include the following:

Unified	UCR
brys 'mind'	*bres* (cf. *brêz* AB: 3a)
bys 'world'	*bes* (cf. *bes* BF: 13)
byth 'will be; be!'	*bedh*
fyth 'faith'	*fedh*
gwyth 'trees'	*gwedh*
norvys 'world'	*norves* (cf. *norvese* SA 60)
pryf 'reptile'	*pref*
ys 'corn'	*eys*
prys 'time'	*pres* (cf. *prêz* AB: 161c).

and the derivatives of *prys*: *kefrys, kekefrys* 'also' > **kefreys, kekefres; solabrys* 'already' > *solabreys*.

Where we have evidence for /iː/ in some of these etyma, e.g. *bys* 'world', *prys* 'time', *ys* 'corn' (3.7) and *kefrys* 'also', such spellings and pronunciations should be allowed in UCR.

17.6 /uː/ is variously spelt in the texts. In *tour* 'tower' and *gour* 'husband' it is spelt <ou> whereas *dowst, flowr* have <ow>. <ow> is also used for the diphthong /ow/ in *owr* 'gold', *dowr* 'water' and *down* 'deep'. We cannot alter the practice of the medieval scribes and are therefore compelled to accept such inconsistencies in UCR.

The central vowels /yː/ and /œː/ are special cases. Users of Unified Cornish are used to <u> for /uː/ in *gun* 'moor' and /yː/ in *hus* 'magic', *tus* 'people'. The form *gun* is nowhere attested in Middle Cornish, however, and may not be correct—though that is not important here. In those words in which <u> occurs finally or before <gh> the vowel is not /yː/ but the diphthong /ɪw/. I recommend that we spell such words as they are attested, but pronounce them with the diphthong: *du* /dɪw/ 'black', *bugh* /bɪw/ 'cow'.

Frequently Middle Cornish has <u> or <ue> where Breton has /œː/ and Welsh /aw/. UC interprets the vowel as /yː/ and recommends pronuncing it either as /yː/ or /iː/. The vowel is in fact different from /yː/ (Breton /yː/, Welsh /ɪː/) and should be treated differently. I should recommend that wherever UC has <ü> for /œː/ we should spell the vowel with <ue>, and pronounce the vowel as /œː/. We should therefore write *luen* 'full', *cuen* 'dogs', *luef* 'hand', *luer* 'floor', etc.

It is clear that /œː/ was unrounding to /eː/ already as early as PA. It is for this reason one finds such spellings as <len(e)> 'full' alongside <luen>, <skesse> 'shadow' as well as <schus>, <leff> 'hand' as well as <luef>, etc. As far as UCR is concerned, spellings with either <ue> or <e> are acceptable. It is also legitimate to spell <luen, scues, luef> but to pronounce them with /eː/.

UC does not distinguish /œː/ from /yː/. The reason is that in some words, in which /œː/ would have been expected, the vowel was in later Cornish unrounded to /iː/, spelt <ee>, rather than to /eː/. This suggests that the vowel before unrounding was /yː/ rather than /œː/. Among such etyma one can include some of the most frequent, for example, *dues* 'come', *ues* 'is', *mur, muer* 'great'. Unrounding to /eː/ is also attested in such words, however. I should therefore recommend spelling these items as <dues>, <ues>, <muer>, etc. but pronuncing them with /iː/ or /eː/ as desired.

Among the etyma in which <ü> of UC will become <ue> in UCR one should include the following:

Unified	UCR
a-drüs 'athwart'	*a-drues*
brüs 'judgment'	*brues*
cün 'dogs'	*cuen*
dü, de 'finished, done'	*due*
dür 'concerns'	*duer*
lüf 'hand'	*luef*
lün 'full'	*luen*
lür 'floor'	*luer*
mür 'great'	*muer*
namür 'many'	*namuer*
pup ür 'always'	*pub uer*
(py) sül 'how many'	*(py) suel*
scüs 'shadow'	*scues*
trüs 'contrary'	*trues.*

Monosyllabic forms of *dos* 'to come' are also to be included here: *düs, dün >* *dues, duen* and the preterite of *bos: büf, bü > buef, bue.* See under the verbs at 19.13. It is worth noting *en passant* that Caradar thought *bu/be*, etc. should be spelt with <ue>. In 1945 he wrote,

> Yn kever an lytheren *u*: esya dhe dhallethoryon hep mar-vyth vya scryfa "ue", kepar del yu gwres y'n textow. Mordon a scryf *bu* yn pup text; mes gwell martesen vya scryfa *bue* y'n Ordinalia ha Meryasek ha gwytha *be* in M[ount] C[alvary] (i.e. PA), ha C.W. le mayth yns-y kefys, hep un sompel a *bue* ynna. Trueth yu na wruk Mordon dewys "ue" y'n kensa le rag an geryow a un syllaben

> [About the letter *u*: it would undoubtedly be easier for learners to write "ue" exactly as is done in the texts. Mordon (i.e. R.M. Nance) writes *bu* in every text; but it would be preferable perhaps to write *bue* in the Ordinalia and Meryasek and keep *be* in M.C. and C.W. where they are found without a single example of *bue* in either. It is a pity that in the beginning Mordon did not choose "ue" for monosyllables] (*Kemysk Kernewek* 1964: 40).

Pub 'every, everyone' is a special case and I discuss it at 18.4.

17.7 The word *puscas* 'fishes' almost certainly contained /œ/, which was later unfronted to /o/. Since the spelling <puscas> is universal, I recommend retaining it but pronouncing the vowel either as /œ/ or /o/. *Üsy/üjy* is a special case (see 19.12).

It would seem in the light of 4.8 above that *brusy* 'to judge', *budhy* 'to drown', *anfusy* 'misfortune' and *anfusyk* 'unfortunate' should be pronounced with /y/ or /ɪ/ in the stressed syllable. There is no need, therefore, to respell the UC forms.

The weakly-stressed *re* and *the* were pronounced with /œ/ (later /o/) before /m/ in Middle Cornish (4.5). Perhaps, then, the spelling of the revived language ought to allow such forms as *ef ru'm gwelas/ef ro'm gwelas* 'he has seen me'; *dhu'm mab/dho'm mab* 'to my son'.

Words like *tryga, myras, gyla*, etc. should perhaps be spelt with <e> rather than <y> or at least a variant with <e> should be tolerated: <trega>, <meras>, <whelas>, <gela>, etc. (see 4.2). The monosyllabic forms with /i:/ must, of course, have <y>: <tryg!>, <myr!>.

17.8 Unified Cornish has <clewes>, <kewsel>, <tewlel>, <Kernewek>, etc. when it is apparent from the sources that the diphthong was /ow/ and not /ew/ (6.6). I therefore recommend respelling such disyllables and trisyllables as <clowes>, <cowsel>, <towlel>, <Kernowek>. This revision will bring the orthography of UCR closer to the spelling of the foundation texts. *Rowlya* 'to rule' and *rowlyer/rowlyas* 'ruler' can be spelt with <ew> or <ow>, though they are all best pronounced with /ow/. In theory the word *bewnans* 'life' ought to become *bownans*, but this latter spelling is unknown outside Late Cornish. I therefore recommend leaving the spelling of UC unchanged and writing <bewnans>, since this is also the spelling of the texts. The word should, however, be pronounced /ˈbownənz/.

It may legitimately be asked why we should change the diphthong <ew> in *clewes*, etc. to <ow> at all. The answer is simple. In Middle Cornish the diphthong /ew/ in such words had already become /ow/, even though the scribes continued to write <ew> for a while. The *Ordinalia* usually, but not always, have <ew>, PA has both <ew> and <ow>. By the time of BM <ow> predominates. If we wish to be authentic we will say /ˈklowəz/ not /ˈklewəz/. We might just as well then write as we speak—as indeed the later scribes did.

17.9 In view of the practice of the texts, I recommend spelling *deu* 'two' as <dew>, exactly as *Dew* 'God', except for the lower-case initial. Given that /ɪw/ and /ew/ are only imperfectly differentiated, it seems unlikely that Middle Cornish really kept *dew* 'two' (masculine) and *dyw* 'two' (feminine) apart. UC's *dywla* 'two hands' is regularly spelt <dewla, dula, dowla> in the texts. I therefore recommend replacing the feminine form of the numeral 'two', i.e. *dyw* with the masculine *dew*. UCR will therefore write <dewlagas> 'eyes' and <dewla> 'hands'. <dew-> here is to be pronounced /dew/ or /dow/.

A further minor change involves the spelling of *yu* 'is'. Nance, following Jenner, believed that the diphthong in *yu* was a rising one: /ju:/. This was an understandable misreading of Lhuyd, but it was, I believe, mistaken. The diphthong is /ɪw/. UCR therefore spells the word as <yw>. Similarly *pyu* 'who' should be <pyw> /pɪw/. The unstressed syllable of UC's *hedhyu* 'today' should also be spelt <yw>: *hedhyw*.

It should also be noted that *yl* 'one of two', *nanyl* 'neither' and *tyr* 'three (f.)' in UC should really have the diphthong /ej/ > /aj/. For these three items, therefore, I use spellings with <ey> (cf. *han neill, an neyl* TH 24a, 51a), <naneyl> (cf. *naneyll* TH 52a), <teyr> (cf. *tyyr* OM 1729, *tayre* CW 1845). Similarly the verb for 'to turn', *trelya* in UC, almost certainly contains the diphthong /ej > aj/ as does UC's *tythy* 'faculties'. I accordingly spell these two items as <treylya>, <teythy> respectively. Both spellings are warranted in the texts: *treylys* TH 4, *treylyes* CW 2085, *trailia* AB: 172c; *teythy* BM 2644.

17.10 Since unstressed *e, a, o* and on occasion *y* were indifferently pronounced /ə/ in Middle Cornish, how one spells unstressed vowels is not important. I have followed UC for the most part, spelling etymologically and/or as the texts do. Thus UCR has <colon> 'heart', <godhvos> 'know', <gortos> 'wait'; <gweles> 'see', <clowes> 'hear' but <pehas> 'sin', <gallas> 'has gone'. The spellings <gallus> 'can' and <cafus> 'get' are preferred to <gallos>, <cafos>, as being much commoner in the texts.

One should also note that in UCR final unstressed <a> and <o> are not differentiated, both being pronounced /ə/. *Ganso* 'with him' and *gansa* 'with them' must be pronounced the same way, as must *dyworto/dyworta, ragtho/ ragtha, ynno/ ynna*, etc. One might either write <ganso> but say /ganzə/ or write <gansa> 'with him' and use *gansans* only for 'with them'. In view of present practice in UC, I recommend maintaining the final <o> in *ganso, dhodho*, etc. but pronouncing it /ə/.

Since *gwrello* and *gwrella, deffo* and *deffa* are identical in pronunciation, the present subjunctive is being absorbed into the past subjunctive in Middle Cornish. This practice is followed in UCR (see 19.6 below).

Consonants
17.11 For the most part the consonants of UC will remain unchanged in UCR. UC, following Jenner, extended the use of <j> and used <dh> as a graph to represent /ð/. It is clear that Jenner and Nance were amply justified in both matters. Perhaps an explanation of the merits of both <j> in all positions and of <dh> is in order here.

17.12 First it should be observed that the texts do not distinguish <j> from <i>. I write both as <j> in the following discussion.

<j> as a graph to represent /dʒ/ is widespread in Cornish literature. It is used universally initially before a back vowel in loan-words: *jaudyn* 'knave' PC 367, *jolyf* 'jolly' RD 2013, *joy* 'joy' OM 154, 306, 359, 517, etc., *joul* 'devil' PA 16c, 18a, 57b, 62b, 115a, *jugge* 'judge' (vb) PC 815, 1333, 1344, 1979, *justys* 'justice' PC 370, 1795, 1920, 1984, 2049, *jugleer* 'juggler' BM 921, *jardyn* 'garden' TH 2, *jarden* 'garden' CW 1801, *jorna* 'day' CW 2531.

<j> is also used internally before back vowels, for example, *conjor* 'conjure' PC 1321, *venjons, vynjons, venjans* 'vengeance' RD 2260, PA 122d, 123d, 149b, 149c, OM 1498, PC 2501, *enjoya* 'enjoy' TH 16a, *rejosya* 'rejoice' TH 1, 14a, *rejoycya* CW 1272.

In TH and CW <j> is frequently used in loan-words before a front vowel: *jentyll* 'gentle' TH 6a, *jewall* 'jewel' 54a, *jestia* 'jest' TH 55a, *jyn* 'engine' CW 483, *jystes* 'joists' CW 2268.

<J> is also widely used in proper names both biblical and secular. In all the following cases we can be certain that the inititial consonant is /dʒ/:

Jafet OM 1054
Jamys RD 1375, TH 48
Jacobe RD 698
Jenkyn BM 1417
Jesmas PC 2505
Jheremy, Jheremye, Jheremyas TH 7a, 6a, 43a
Jherusalem TH 27a, *Jerusalem* OM 1928, 1948
Jhesus OM 2841, PC 160, *Jhesu* OM 2721, PC 297 (8.20)
Job TH 6a
Jonas TH 45a
Joseph RD 22
Josue TH 55a
Jovyn PC 2989, BM 43406
Jowan PA 53a, TH 37a, *Johan* RD 1363, TH 8 (8.20)
Judas PA 36a, TH 44a
Jude RD 1448
Judy RD 10.

It has been pointed out at 8.20 above that Cornish *Jhesus* and *Jowan* are not comparable with Welsh *Iesu* and *Ieuan* but are medieval borrowings from French and /or Breton.

<j> is used in native words before a back vowel in *pejadow* 'prayer' SA 62, BM 132, 3624, 2189, *pijadou* BM 560. <j> is also used in native words after <n> in the particles *ny(ns)* and *na(ns)*: *nynj o* PA 10b, 151c, 167d, 187c, 214d, 233a, 233b, 234b, *nynj ough* PA 47b, *naunj o* PA 160b, *nynj ew* CW 263.

<j> is also frequently used with third singular masculine forms of the verb *y'm bus*: *mara jeves* PC 47, *nyn jeves* PC 66, 862, *an jeves* PC 1776, *an jevas* TH 17, *nan jevas* TH 18. Note also *an fals jevan* PC 154 where *jevan* 'devil' < *devan 'demon' originally after the article, and *an jeth* 'the day' TH 47, *hethew in jeth* 'nowadays' TH 48.

<j> is not uncommon in Late Cornish. In his discussion of the Cornish numerals Nance cites *nounjack* 'nineteen' from 1644 (JRIC 21: 316). Other examples of <j> include: *jorna* 'day' (BF: 52), *crenjah* 'love' (RC 23: 182), *bewjah* 'living things' (RC 23: 183), *menja, venja* 'would' (SGMC: 59), *maljama geel* 'that I might do' (SGMC: 61). Gendall also cites *anjy* 'they' from Rowe (SGMC: 22), though the text in RC 23 has *angye* not *anjy*. Borlase in his vocabulary of 1754 usually spells /dʒ/ as <dzh> in imitation of Lhuyd. He does, however, give *denjack* 'hake-fish', *gajah* 'daisy' and *menjam* 'I will' (Borlase 1754: 383, 388, 399). He also says of *niedga* 'fly': 'pronounced as *ja*' (ibid.: 401).

<j> is widely used in place-names. The form *Trevajegmur* (*tre* + the personal name, *Masek* + *muer* 'great') is attested as early as A.D. 1300 (CPNE: 22). Note also *Aja-Bullocke, Aja-Gai* (< **aswa* 'gap'), *Adjawinjack* (< *gwynsek* 'windy'), *Pedn Tenjack* (< *denjak* 'hake'), *Bosoljack* (< **solsek* 'full of cattle/wealth'), *Clijah* (**cleysyow* 'trenches'), *Cowyjack* (< **kewesyk, *cowejyk* 'enclosed'), *Joppa* (< **shoppa* 'shop'), *Nanjizal, Nanjewick, Nanjulian, Nanjarrow* (< *nans* 'valley'), *Park an Jarne* (< *jarden* 'garden'), *Pedn Bejuffin* (< *mydzhovan* 'ridge'), *Ponjeravah, Ponjou* (< *pons* 'bridge'), *Bowjey* 'cow-shed' (< *bo* + *chy*; see JRIC 7: 279). The term *dijey* 'small farm' (**dy* + *chy*) is attested in the English dialect of Cornwall (CPNE: 84).

In view of the occurrence of <j> for /dʒ/ in so many contexts in Cornish from the medieval period onwards, it seems only sensible in revised Cornish to use the graph <j> everywhere to represent /dʒ/. We have no warrant for <j> in certain words, for example, in *chanjya, charj, mynj, ajy, cryjy/crejy*. This may be largely a result of the very limited nature of the remains of the language. It should be noticed, however, that spelling 'believe' as *crejy* is a useful way of distinguishing it from *cregy* 'hang'. If <j> is not used everywhere for /dʒ/, other inconsistencies would arise, for example in *hangya* 'hang' with /ŋj/ but *changya* 'change' with /ndʒ/.

Since it is clear that *j* is not a later reflex of *s* but a dialectal variant of equal antiquity (see 10.4-5 above and Williams 1990), it seems advisable to extend the use of <j> in UCR to places where UC writes <s>. *Cryjyans, crejyans* 'belief' should certainly replace the unhistorical **crysyans* of UC. Similarly spellings like *pejadow, cryjyans, nynj, nanj, mynj, woja* occur in the texts and should be allowed in UCR.

At the moment Gendall does not use <j> except in initial position in words like *jarden, jornah* and *judgia*. He prefers to spell items like *sengy* 'hold', *vengam* 'I should like', *angye* 'they' with <g>. A few years ago, however, he was using <j> medially before front vowels in such words as *anjye* 'they', *skianjack* 'wise', *ejy* 'is', *zenjy* 'hold, consider' (*Carn* 57: 16), that is to say, in exactly those positions in which I am recommending <j>.[27]

17.13 Gendall in his search for authenticity has abandoned the use of <dh> when spelling Cornish. He writes both /ð/ and /θ/ alike as <th>. Gendall says of the sound /ð/: "Mediaeval texts as well as modern use *th* for this sound, *dh* being foreign to the historical language of whatever period" (SDMC: xvi). It is true that Middle and Late Cornish both prefer to spell /ð/ as <th>. <dh> is well attested nonetheless.

---

27 The recently discovered play *Bewnans Ke* often uses <j>. Among instances in the play one might cite: *jangyas* 'changed', *jasty* 'chastise' (< *chastya*), *javal* 'scoundrel', *lagajak* 'observant', *marthojek* 'miraculous', *pejadow, pejadaw* 'prayer', and *rajak* 'gracious' (< **rasek*).

OCV usually spells /ð/ as <d>, for example in *arluides* 'lady', *alwed* 'key', *bleid* 'wolf', *ford* 'way', *grud* 'jaw', *guedeu* 'widow', *scuid* 'shoulder', *sened* 'synod' and *kerd* 'journey'. <d> is also used to represent /ð/ in place-names, for example, *Penmened* (< *pen meneth)* from 1261 and *Trembedou* (< *tre an bethow)* from 1293 (PNWP: 63, 73). Occasionally, however, <dh> is used for /ð/ in Old Cornish, for example, in the words *medhec* 'doctor', and *medhecnaith* 'medicine' in OCV and the place-name, *Trembedhou* (< *tre an bethow* 'farm of the graves') from *c.* 1200 (PNWP: 73). The name *Medhuil* occurs in the Bodmin Manumissions, though <dh> may well represent /ð/ + /h/ rather than /ð/.

Middle Cornish orthography follows Middle English in writing both /θ/ and /ð/ as <th>. On occasion, however, <d> is used for /ð/, for example, in *herdya* 'evict' PA 221a, *ynweyd* 'also' PC 425, *arlud* 'lord' BM 36, 142, 144, 184. Notice also *medel* 'soft' at BM 2979 as against *methel* at OM 928. We have seen above (8.6) that final /rθ/ seems to have become /rð/ in the early Middle Cornish period. In *ord* for *orth* at PA 179b, therefore, the final segment is probably /ð/. Spelling /ð/ as <d> in Middle Cornish is a continuation of the Old Cornish scribal practice seen in *arluides*, *bleid*, etc. On occasion <dh> is found in Middle Cornish for /ð/, usually after /r/, for example in *yn kerdh* PA 123b, *hardh* PA 84a, 215b, 234b, 250d.

The Middle Cornish shift /rθ/ > /rð/ in final position is noticeable in placenames containing the element *porth* 'harbour'. One finds *porth* spelt with <d> for /ð/ in *Pordye* (1300), *Pordmenster* (1301) and with <dh> in *Pordhenes* (1301), *Pordhunes* (1313) (PNWP: 40, 65). There are a few other examples of <dh> in place-names, for example, in *Poldhu* near Altarnun and *Poldhu Cove*, Mullion. *Pol* is usually masculine, but there are enough examples to show that it was feminine on occasion, e.g. *Polvean Wood* (Duloe) < *pol* + *byan*, *Polvellan* (Fowey), *Polly Vellyn* (St Gluvias) both < *pol* + *melyn*, *Polgath* (1502, Towednack) < *pol* + *cath*, *Polgassick Cove* (St Ives), *Polgazick* (Lansallos) both < *pol* + *casek*, *Polgear* (Wendron) < *pol* + *ker*, *Polwrath* (St Cleer) < *pol* + *gurah*. *Poldhu* is late and may well ultimately derive from Lhuyd's orthography. Nonetheless it would seem that the graph <dh> in these toponyms may stand for original /ð/. The modern pronunciation of *Poldhu* with /d/ is not conclusive evidence against such a view for two reasons. In the first place Cornish English has a tendency to shift /ð/ to /d/ in syllable initial (WHLC: 159) and in the second place Boson often writes <d> where Lhuyd has <dh> (14.35). Notice also that there are three places called *Baldhu* 'black mine' (CPNE: 16). Whatever the origin and significance of <dh> in such toponyms, it cannot be denied that <dh> is a well-attested graph in Cornish place-names. I have no doubt that a close examination of Gover's unpublished work (to which unfortunately I have no access) would reveal further examples of <dh> /ð/ in the toponymy of Cornwall.[28]

---

28 Craig Weatherhill has provided me with the following list of Cornish toponyms containing <dh> from the twelfth to the fourteenth century: *Boneydhon;*

In Old and Middle Cornish alike the sound /ð/ is often represented by a special symbol. In the Old Cornish period the graph used is the Anglo-Saxon <ð> or *eth*. This is ultimately the origin of the phonetic symbol <ð> itself. Since <ð> is used for Cornish place-names in Anglo-Saxons charters one finds such spellings as *beð* 'grave', *beðow* 'graves' and *pen hal weðoc* 'the end of the wooded moor' in local names in pre-Norman documents (CPNE: 21, 122). <ð> is also used for Cornish personal names in the Bodmin Manumissions, for example in *Wenceneðel, Grifiuð, Bleyðcuf* and *Meðwuistel*. Jenner when discussing the manumissions transcribes <ð> of the manuscript as <dh> (JRIC 21: 260).

OCV uses the Anglo-Saxon letter *thorn*, <þ>, for /ð/ on occasion, for example, in the words *bliþen* 'year' and *heþeu* 'today'. Four of our surviving Middle Cornish texts, the Charter Fragment, PA, BM and CW, use another symbol for /ð/, namely *yogh* <ȝ>. The use of yogh for /ð/ in these texts is not consistent, for the symbol on occasion stands for *th, y* or *s*. Nonetheless its main use in all four texts is to represent /ð/. Here are some examples:

ȝymo 'to me' CF 4
ȝys 'to thee' CF 6
ȝoȝo 'to him' CF 33, PA 11d, 5ib
ȝe 'thy' CF 5, 22
ȝe 'to' CF 20, 24, 35
ȝe eseȝa 'to sit' PA 13c
beȝens 'let there be' PA 24d
yntreȝa 'among them' PA 45a
ȝen eȝewan 'to the Jews' PA 62c
aȝesympys 'straightway' PA 84b
a ȝyghow 'on the right' PA 97c
arlyȝy 'lords' BM 8
dyȝyyow 'days' BM 48
ny veȝaf 'I shall not be' BM 109
heȝyv 'today' BM 120
ȝawarta 'from him' CW 266
ȝeso 'to thee' CW 50
ȝa 'to' CW 542, 571, 603, 808
ȝym 'to me' CW 657, 703, 774.

When dealing with this symbol editors often quite sensibly transcribe it as <dh>. Thus Stokes in his notes on BM uses <dh> where the text has <ð>; on page 132, for example, he renders *ȝe uȝyll* of the text as *dhe udhyll*. Similarly Jenner when transcribing part of the Charter Fragment for his discussion of

Boswydhegy, Gludholgan, Godholkan, Godholgan, Midhyan; Pordhenes; Pordhunes mur/byan; Treludhas bighan; Treneydhyn; Tredhac; Trewydhosa; Tredheuergy, Tredhevergy; Trevardhian; Wydhyel. It will be seen that Gendall is mistaken when he says that <dh> is "foreign to the historical language of whatever period".

Cornish prosody uses <dh> for <ð> when it means /ð/ but <th> when /θ/ is intended. Jenner's text begins:

> Golsow, ty *cowedh*,
> Byth na borth *medh*,
> Dyyskyn ha powes
> Ha *dhymo* dus nes,
> Mar *codhes* dhe les
> (HCL: 181).

The *Ordinalia* almost invariably use <th> for both /θ/ and /ð/. On occasion, however, *thorn* is used for /ð/, both in English: *þey* 'they' PC 2526 and Cornish *þe* 'thy' RD 1562, *þ'y* 'to his' RD 2189. No editor has, to my knowledge, expanded this to <dh>.

<dh> was first used as the sole graph for /ð/ in Cornish by Edward Lhuyd with the publication of AB in 1707. Lhuyd used <dh> as a graph to represent /ð/ in Welsh. It is possible, however, that he was partially motivated to use <dh> for /ð/ in Cornish by such forms as *medhec* in the OCV. It must be remembered that Lhuyd was the first scholar to realize that the Vocabulary was Cornish and not Welsh. Moreover he published selections from the Vocabulary in the preface to his *Cornish Grammar* (AB 222–53). Lhuyd's understanding of Brythonic orthography is acute for he says:

> *D* in Old Manuscripts whether Welsh or Cornish has two pronunciations; for besides the common Reading as in the English and other Languages, it serves in the Midst and Termination for *dh* or the English *th* in *this, that,* &c. So *medal* [soft] is to be pronounced *medhal*, *Echvyd* the Evening, *echuydh*; *hurᵭ* a ram, *hurdh*; and *heid*, barley, *haidh*. *dd* was introduced to express this sound about the year 1400; and in the time of H[enry] 8, &c. *d* pointed at the top or underneath by H. Lhuyd, and W. Salisbury at home, and by Dr Gryffydh Roberts and Roger Smyth in the Welsh Books they printed beyond Sea. In the Reign of Q Elizabeth Dr J. D. Rhys, Dr D. Powel and others used *dh*, which was afterwards rejected by Dr Davies and *dd* restored (AB: 227a).

The reference to J.D. Rhys is to the *Institutiones* of 1592 where <dh> was first used for Welsh /ð/.

In the preface to his *Cornish Grammar*, which is addressed to the gentlemen of Cornwall, Lhuyd feels bound to explain the peculiarities of his own orthography, <dzh> for /dʒ/ for example, and to mention some of the ways in which Cornish and Welsh spelling differ (AB: 223). Nowhere does he allude to <dh> for /ð/. Either Lhuyd forgot to mention <dh>, which is highly unlikely, or he thought that it was not necessary to allude to <dh> at all. If explanation of <dh> was unnecessary, it can only be that the native writers of Cornish were already familiar with the graph. I think it is reasonable to assume, therefore, that Lhuyd had seen <dh> in use in Cornish manuscripts apart from OCV, and assumed that *Tiz hegaraz ha pednzhivik Pou Kernou* were already familiar with <dh> for /ð/.

After the publication of AB Lhuyd's <dh> was widely adopted by the native writers of Cornish. John Boson, for example, writing in 1709-10, has *dydh* 'day', *neudhou* 'news', *dha* 'to', *triuadh* 'pity', *diuadh* 'end', *dh'eu* 'to you', *hydhou* 'today' (BF: 46). In a letter to Thomas Tonkin dated 1736 William Gwavas writes *dydh* 'day', *Kevardhiu* 'December', *dho ve* 'to me' (JRIC 21: 430). Tonkin himself used <dh> in his Cornish-Latin-English dictionary. On the first page, for example, he has *adhysempyz* 'immediately', *adhelar* 'behind', *adhart* 'from'. <dh> is used by William Borlase in his vocabulary of 1754, for he writes *bardh* 'mimic', *bedh* 'grave', *guedhan* 'tree', *ladh* 'kill' and *guredhan* 'root', for example.

William Pryce, who plagiarized Lhuyd, Gwavas and Tonkin, uses <dh> for /ð/ in ACB (1790), for example in *nowydh* 'new', *kledh* 'left', *pemdhak* 'fifteen', *dedh* 'day', *idhio* 'ivy', *tardhak* 'thirteen'. Norris also wanted to use <dh> in his 'Sketch of Cornish grammar' to represent Middle Cornish /ð/, but was uncertain on occasion whether /ð/ or /θ/ was intended. As a result he adopted the less drastic device of writing a point under the t of <th>, if /ð/ appeared to be the sound intended (1859: ii 222). Robert Williams used the graph <dh> in LCB (1865) and spelt every <th> /ð/ in the medieval texts as <dh>, even in word-final position. Williams, following Norris, believed that the final segment in *noweth, deth, deweth, arluth*, etc. was /ð/ and not /θ/. Thus he writes *dhymmo* 'to me', *dhodho* 'to him', *kerdhes* 'walk', *gordhyans* 'glory', *ladhas* 'killed', *warnedhy* 'upon her', *goydh* 'goose', *bodh* 'wish', *bydh* 'will be'.

As we have already seen, Stokes uses <dh> to transcribe <ȝ> in his notes to BM. In CG (1868-69) he changes <th> to <dh> when /ð/ is meant. Thus he writes *fydhye* 'trust', *Budhek* 'Budock', *pûr-dhal* 'very blind', *pûr-dhyogel* 'very certain', etc. Stokes says of his orthography:

> In inlaut I have written *dh* for *th*, where the change is justified by the etymology or the authority of the *Passion*, in which poem 3 is, as a rule, written for *dh* (ð). (CG: 138).

Stokes also represents *methel* of OM 928 as *medhel* (1900: 126). Jago has many examples of <dh> in ECD not only where he quotes from Lhuyd, Pryce and Williams, but also in material of his own.

The French Celticist, Joseph Loth, does not use <dh>. Instead he rewrites <th> of the Middle Cornish texts as <ð> when the voiced spirant is required. Loth therefore writes *kerðes, guða, me a ðueth, yntreðo, gweðan, eðen, ða'n dor, diwað*, etc. (RC 23: 178-85 fnn). These spellings are unobjectionable from the academic point of view, even though <ð> does not occur in the manuscripts . When Loth spells <th> as <ð> his main concern is to keep /ð/ separate from /θ/. In this respect his practice is similar in intent to that of Williams, Stokes and Jenner, though he uses <ð> where they prefer <dh>.

Jenner, as has been observed, used <dh> for both <ð> in the Bodmin Manumissions and <3> in his edition of the Charter Fragment. In fact in HCL Jenner uses <dh> for /ð/ everywhere. From there the graph <dh> for /ð/ made its way into Unified Cornish.

Gendall says: "th was always used by native writers, whether in Medieval or Modern Cornish, for both the voiced and the unvoiced values of the letters" (SDMC: xviii). This is not so. Not only was <dh> used on occasion for /ð/ in Old, Middle and Late Cornish, but the scribes of CF, PA, BM and CW repeatedly use <3> for /ð/ (see above). Because Gendall cites Late Cornish in its original spelling and because Lhuyd is such an important source of Late Cornish, Gendall's own handbooks (SGMC, SDMC) are themselves replete with examples of <dh>. The full paradigm of the defective verb *medhes* 'to say' is attested in post-Tudor Cornish only from Lhuyd, who spells it with <dh> throughout. Even though the 3rd singular and 3rd plural only are attested with <dh>, Gendall generalizes <th> throughout: *metham, methez, meth, methon, metho, methans*. Since Gendall changes <dh> to <th> in this verb and in other places, he cannot argue that respelling <th> as <dh> in UC is in any sense illegitimate.

Old and Middle Cornish could and frequently did distinguish /ð/ from /θ/ in writing. The graph <dh> to represent /ð/ is attested in Old, Middle and Late Cornish. <dh> is also used by some modern scholars to indicate /ð/, whether the original texts have <ð>, <3> or <th>. In addition <dh> for /ð/ was used in Cornish by **Lhuyd** (1707), **John Boson** (1709-10), **Gwavas** (1736), **Tonkin** (*c.* 1730), **Borlase** (1754), **Pryce** (1790), **Robert Williams** (1865), **Stokes** (1872, 1868-69, 1900), **Jago** (1887) and **Jenner** (1904). There is no reason to reject <dh> on the grounds that it is somehow alien. If we are to pronounce /ð/ and /θ/ differently in revived Cornish , it is sensible to spell them differently (for the problem in Revived Late Cornish see 14.35). Since we spell /θ/ as <th>, there is every reason to use <dh> for /ð/.

17.14 Unified Cornish hesitates between <p> and <b> and <k> and <g> in word final position. As has been suggested above (8.19) it is likely that etymological /b/ and /g/ were [b] and [g] after stressed vowels but were replaced by /p/ and /k/ after unstressed ones. In UCR therefore the following are recommended: <ryb> 'beside', <gleb> 'wet', <mab> 'son', <rag> 'for', <gwreg> 'wife', <teg> 'beautiful' but <morrap> 'littoral', <gorthyp> 'answer' (but see 8.14), <enep> 'face', <medhek> 'doctor', <meppyk> 'little boy', <uthyk> 'dreadful'.

Final <f> should probably be pronounced /f/ after unstressed vowels, as far as it occurs, for example in *enef* 'soul'. Spellings like *genaffa* 'with me' (< *genef-vy*) CW 271 and *ny sewenaffa* 'I shall not prosper' (< *ny sowenaf vy*) CW 1285 suggest that *f/v* was [f] when unstressed. Usually final /f/ has been lost as in *ena* 'soul', *gene* 'with me', etc. <f> must be pronounced as /v/ after stressed vowels, however: *ef* /e:v/ 'he', *nef* /ne:v/ 'heaven', *gof* /go:v/ 'smith', *lef* /le:v/ 'voice', *luef* /lœ:v/ 'hand', etc.

In UCR also it is recommended that all instances of final <s> whether after stressed or unstressed vowels be pronounced as /z/.

17.15 Unified Cornish assumed that in word final position /ð/ was devoiced to /θ/. As has been suggested above (8.15-16) there is reason to believe that after the prosodic shift etymological /ð/ was no longer devoiced in final position. This means that unlike UC, UCR will have many instances of <dh> finally, for example in the following words:

UC	UCR
beth 'grave'	*bedh*
byth 'be; will be'	*bedh*
both 'wish'	*bodh*
cleth 'left'	*cledh*
cleth 'ditch'	*cledh*
coth 'falls, befits'	*codh*
deth 'day'	*dedh*
fyth 'faith'	*fedh*
forth 'way'	*fordh*
goth 'goose'	*godh*
gwyth 'trees'	*gwedh*
kerth 'walk'	*kerdh*
meth 'said'	*medh*
ruth 'red'	*rudh*
scoth 'shoulder'	*scodh*
soth 'employment'	*sodh*
ynweth 'also'	*ynwedh.*

It is probably unnecessary to spell *dewethfa* with <dh> since it is likely that the devoicing of /ð/ to /θ/ in syllable-final position was maintained by the adjacent voiceless consonant /f/ even though the /f/ was voiceless only because the final segment in /deweθ/ was voiceless. In view of Lhuyd's *guodhaz, gydhaz* 'to know' it is probable that *gothvos* in UC should be emended to *godhvos* /goðvoz/.

Although respelling of UC *deth* 'day', *byth* 'be!', *gwyth* 'trees', *lath* 'kill!' as UCR <dedh>, <bedh>, <gwedh>, <ladh> looks like a major change, it should be remembered that such spellings were the norm in both LCB (1865) and HCL (1904).

17.16 Pre-occlusion is a feature of BM, SA and CW. There is consequently an argument for writing it where it occurs in UCR. Since, however, it does not occur in John Tregear, the longest of our basic texts, it seems to me wiser not to indicate pre-occlusion, but to pronounce it, if desired. I therefore recommend writing <gwan> 'weak', <gwyn> 'white', <pen> 'head', <benneth> 'blessing', <mam> 'mother', <tom> 'hot', <omma> 'here' but pronouncing them as [gwaᵈn], [gwɪᵈn], [peᵈn], ['beᵈnəθ], [maᵇm], [toᵇm], ['oᵇmə] if one wishes.

17.17 Some varieties of Cornish probably had the three voiceless sonants, /rh/, /nh/ and /lh/ (8.4). In the revised language *gwertha* 'sell', *hartha* 'bark' on the one hand and *ynny* 'in her/it' on the other, can be pronounced with /rh/ and /nh/ respectively. Similarly *pella* 'further', *tyller* 'place' (*telhar* BF: 25) and *collan* 'knife' may be pronounced with medial /lh/. There is no need, however, to introduce special graphs for the voiceless sonants in these items. /nh/ should, of course, be written in *glanhe* 'cleanse' and *lowenhe* 'gladden'.

17.18 Unified Cornish uses <gh> both internally as in <fleghes>, <peghas>, <nagha>, <golghy>, <myrghes> and finally as in <flogh>, <pegh>, <nagh>, <golgh>, <myrgh>. It has been pointed out above (8.2) that the texts themselves more usually write <h> at the beginning of a syllable but <gh> finally: <flehes> but <flogh>, <pehas> but <pegh>, etc. Since the difference is almost certainly a phonetic one rather than a mere scribal convention, I recommend replacing the <gh> of UC by <h> at the beginning of a syllable. UCR then will write: *flehes, peha, naha, golhy, kerhes* but *flogh, pegh, nagh, golgh, kergh*. The practice of writing <h> internally and <gh> finally was adopted by Jenner, who wrote *flogh* 'child', *mergh* 'girl', *margh* 'horse' but *flehes* 'children', *merhes* 'girls', *porhel* 'pig' (HCL: 87).

One exception to the rule of *gh/h* alternation is the word for 'small'. UC writes <byghan> (cf. *beghan* PA 166b). and according to the rule just enunciated this in UCR spelling ought to be **byhan*. <byhan> was the spelling used invariably by E.G.R. Hooper when editor of *An Lef Kernewek*. I have no example of <byhan> from BM, TH or CW with an internal <h>, however, since all three texts spell the word without any medial consonant. This is a well-established spelling; cf. *byan, vyan* PC 2082, 2643, 3004 and the place-name *Drefvyan* '[the] small homestead' from 1398 (CPNE: 228). I therefore recommend writing the word for 'small' as <byan>.

The Middle Cornish word for 'king' is sometimes spelt with <gh> and sometimes without. We thus find both *myghtern* and *mytern*. I recommend that either be acceptable in UCR.

17.19 Unified Cornish spells 'beauty' as <tekter> and 'ugliness' as <hakter>. There is nothing inherently unsatisfactory with these spellings. In our three texts, however, the medial consonant group is more frequently <ct> than <kt> (e.g. *tectar* CW 288, *hacter* CW 289). Similarly 'blessedness' is spelt by the scribes as <benesycter>, <benegycter>. There is no need to respell as UC does to <benesykter>, <benejykter>. As a general rule it seems reasonable to keep <c> before <t> if such is the spelling of the texts. I should therefore prefer *tecter, hacter, benejycter*.

The same applies to loan-words in <(i)ction>. The word for 'benediction' is variously spelt <benedyccon> or <benediccon> in BM. Unified Cornish respells it as <benedyksyon>, where the <s> is required to indicate the pronunciation and to assimilate the word to *nasyon, oblasyon*, etc. If we are to render the second <c> by <s>, perhaps we should leave the first intact and spell the word as <benedycsyon>.

CHAPTER 18
The accidence of UCR

18.1 There are three aspects of the inflection of UC that require revision: 1) pronouns, 2) prepositional pronouns, and 3) verbs. These I shall deal with in turn.

Pronouns
18.2 In Unified Cornish *the* 1st and 2nd singular pronouns are *my* and *ty* respectively. In Middle Cornish there were two forms of both pronouns: *my* and *me*, *ty* and *te*. If we exclude the 3rd singular masculine personal pronoun *ef*, *eff*, the personal pronouns in Middle Cornish seem to form a series: *my*, *ty*, *hy*, *ny*, *why/wy*, *y*. Since these all have a long vowel, and since Middle Cornish has a dislike of /ɪː/ in auslaut, we can assume that they were all pronounced with /iː/. That *my* and *ty* were /miː/ and /tiː/ respectively is guaranteed by such spellings as *tha vee* 'to me' CW 889 and *ha tee* 'and thou' CW 914. The first and second singular pronouns have variants that have to be accounted for, namely, *me* and *te*. This is not true of the rest of the series, since **he*, **ne*, **whe* and **e* are unattested.

The CC reflex of the IE first person pronoun was **mi*. This was inherited by British as **mi*, whence it was lengthened by the new quantity system to **/miː/* (LHEB 339). Thereafter it appears that the Brythonic languages developed two separate forms. The first as an independent pronoun and in slow speech, the pausa form, remained as *mi*. In proclitic position an unaccented or allegro variant lost its length and became *me*. In Welsh the long form was generalized, since *mi* only is found. In Breton the short form, *me*, was generalized and is found both as a proclitic and as an independent stressed pronoun. In Cornish both /miː/ written <my>, and /me/ <me> are attested.

The second person pronoun *te*, *ty* is similar in origin to *me*, *my*. It derives from CC **tu* > **tü* > **ti* and also the oblique form **t(w)e*. The second person pronoun seems to have developed in Welsh, Cornish and Breton in parallel with *mi*, *me*. Note however that Old Breton has both *ti* and *te* (HMSB: 69). In Cornish both *ty* and *te* occur, although *ty* is the only form attested in some texts.

It is apparent that *me/my* and *te/ty* in the texts are not merely graphic variants. The evidence of the Middle Cornish texts makes it clear that *me/my* and *te/ty* are not in free variation. The distribution of the two forms is briefly as follows: everywhere *me* is commoner than *my*. In some texts, RD, PC and BM, instances of *me* outnumber those of *my* by four or five to one. In OM *me* predominates, but *my* is two-thirds as frequent. I have no examples of *te* from OM, PC, RD or BM. In PA however *te* is the only form. Lhuyd corroborates the view that there were two separate forms of both pronouns. For the first person pronoun Lhuyd cites both *mî* and *me* (AB: 244a). For the second person he gives *ti, tî* (AB: 252a), i.e. /ti:/ and *ta* (AB: 167b), which represents /tə/.

The origin of *me* and *te* as unaccented allegro forms is incidentally corroborated by the reduplicated pronouns; *tegy* < British **ti'ti,* where the unaccented *ti* has developed as *te.*

Originally *me* and *te* were allegro forms to be used in conjunction with a verb, for example in *me a vyn.* On the other hand *my* and *ty* were the fully stressed forms that could be used when the pronoun stood alone: *Pyw? My ha ty.* This difference of function is no longer operative in Middle Cornish, but there is every reason to allow both *my* and *me, ty* and *te. Me, te* when unstressed should be pronounced /mə/, /tə/ and /me:/, /te:/ when stressed.

Late Cornish also has a 2nd singular personal pronoun *che* (RC 23: 174, 181, 183) and *chee* (RC 23: 180, 181, 182). The initial segment /tʃ/ clearly results from the affrication of earlier /t/; cf. *chy* 'house' < *ty.* The variants <che> and <chee> suggest /tʃə/ and /tʃi:/. There is no need to introduce these forms into UCR, but *te, ty* can be pronounced with initial /tʃ/ if desired.

18.3 In Late Cornish *angye, gye* is used as a third person plural pronoun. *Angye* /ən'dʒei/ as a pronoun is based on *-ans* the 3rd plural ending of verbs and it arose through false division. When the enclitic pronoun *y* 'they' was added to the inflected 3rd plural of verbs, the whole complex of ending + *y* acquired the nature of a pronoun. Thus parallel with *ny yll e(f)* 'he cannot' one has *ny yllansy* /ɪl ən'dʒi:/. Because *ny yll ef* seems to consist of *ny + yll +* pronoun *ef,* speakers analysed *ny yllanjy* as *ny + yll +* pronoun *anjy.* In this way *anjy* acquired status as an independent pronoun.

Analogy then applied *anjy* to the prepositional pronouns. If *ynno ef* becomes *in eff* (as for example *eth ony onyn in eff* 'we are one in him' SA 61), then 'in them' should be *in anjy.* This form, spelt *in ansy* is found at SA 59a: *fatla vgy faith an tasow coth a vam egglys in an sy* 'that the faith of the ancient fathers of mother church is in them' SA 59a. Compare *the wortans y* 'from them' TH 23 and *ragthans y* 'for them' TH 23. Notice first of all that although the text has *the wortans y, ragthans y* these were almost certainly pronounced *thewortanjy, ragthanjy.*

It is clear, then, that *anjy* began as a verbal ending, *-ans + y,* and was at first bound to its verb. It was only in the later Middle Cornish period that it became detached from the verbal stem. It is worth noting, nonetheless, that as a bound morpheme *-anjy* is already present in the *Ordinalia.* The opening section of OM, lines 1-48, consists of a majestic soliloquy by God the Father as he creates the universe. The language of the passage is ornate, though not regularly so. It contains much internal rhyme, alliteration and consonantal assonance both within the line and across line boundary. Lines 37-40 read as follows:

my a set ahugh an gweyth
   yn creys a'n ebron avan
   an lor y'n nos, howl y'n geyth
   may rollons y golow splan

[I will set above the trees
   in the midst of the heaven above
   the moon in the night, sun in the day,
   that they may give brilliant light]

Here *ahugh* is probably to be pronounced /ə'ɪwθ/ to assonate with *gweyth* and *geyth; creys* probably has /θ/ as its final segment in order to rhyme with both *gweyth* and *geyth*. The unstressed syllable of *ebron* assonates with the stressed syllable of *avan*. The vowel of *nos* echoes that of *lor*, while the stressed syllables of *rollons* and *golow* rhyme. Moreover, if we read *rollons y* as *rollongy* /ˌrolən'dʒeiː/, we obtain consonantal assonance and partial rhyme between *yn geyth* and *ongy*. This would be quite in keeping with the poet's diction, and is therefore a likely reading.

In view of the above discussion I recommend allowing *anjy* alongside *y* 'they' in UCR.

18.4 Padel has shown (SC 14/15: 232-37) that there are two words *pup/pub* in Middle Cornish. When the word is used adjectivally in conjunction with a following noun, *pup tra, pup ur*, etc. and means 'every, each', *pup/pub* is almost universally spelt with a <u>. When it stands by itself as a pronoun meaning 'everybody' the word is not infrequently spelt with <o> or <e>.

It would seem that the adjective *pub* being weakly stressed has the vowel /ə/, which is written <u>. When the *pub* is a pronoun it had the vowel /œː/ also written <u>. Since /œ(ː)/ in later Cornish had a tendency to unround to /eː/ as in *len* for *luen* 'full', or to unfront, as in *poscas* for *puskas*, it seems that we can see a similar process at work here, with /pœːb/ becoming /peːb/ or /poːb/.

As far as the revived language is concerned I should recommend the following for simplicity's sake. The adjective should be written <pub> and be pronounced /pəb/. The pronoun should also be written <pub> but be pronounced /pœːb/. The difference in pronunciation is not great, and one can use *pub huny, pub onen*, etc. instead of *pub* 'everybody' if required.[29]

The prepositional pronouns
18.5 These are highly schematized in Unified Cornish and are in need of some revision. The revision will not lead to a simplification but rather a more complicated (and more authentic) picture in which variants are tolerated.

---

29 The later form *kenyver onen* 'everybody' may also be used.

Before dealing with the main prepositions in turn, I should like to make some general observations. Since final *-o* and *-a* had begun to fall together by the period of the *Ordinalia*, a process that was complete before the composition of BM, there is no difference in Tudor Cornish pronunciation between *ynno* 'in him' and *ynna* 'in them', *ganso* 'with him' and *gansa* 'with them', *dretho* 'through him' and *dretha* 'through them'. If we do not revise the Unified Cornish forms of these and other prepositional pronouns, yet attempt to pronounce them authentically, that is with final /ə/, then we will run into difficulties—as indeed the speakers of Cornish did until they found a solution to the problem.

The method by which the 3rd singular masculine was differentiated from the 3rd plural was by the addition of an enclitic personal pronoun. When *ganso* and *gansa* fell together in pronunciation, *gansa* < *ganso* was recharacterized as *gansa eff* or *ganseff*. Similarly *gansa* 'with them' became at first *gansa y* > *gansy* and later *gansans, gansansy*. This strategy should be adopted in UCR.

18.6 Let us now look at the inflected forms as they actually occur in our three basic texts. The numerals 1, 2, 3, 3a, 4,5, 6 refer to the 1st, 2nd, 3rd masc., 3rd fem., 1st plural, 2nd plural and 3rd plural respectively. Any form cited without one may for emphasis be used with an enclitic pronoun.

The references are as follows: M = *Beunans Meriasek*; T = Tregear; A= *Sacrament an Alter*; C = *Creation of the World*.

18.7 *Gans* 'with'

1 geneff, gena, gene, genevy, genavy M; genaf, genaff, genaf ve C
2 genes, genas M; genas T; genas ge A; genas sche C
3 ganso M; gonsa, gansa, ganso eff, gansa eff T; ganso, gonȝa, ganȝa C; gonz eve Rowe
3a gensy M; gynsy T; gansy, gensy C
4 genen M; genyn, genan ny T; genan A; genan C
5 genough, genogh, genogh why M; genowgh, genowgh why, genowhy T; genogh A; genawhy C
6 ganse, gans y M; gansa, gansans, gansansy T; ganssy C

Note also that *genama* 'with me' occurs at PA 193d. In the light of that and the above forms I should recommend the following paradigm for UCR:

genef /genə/, *genef vy* /genə viː/, *genama* /ˈgenəmə/
genes
ganso /ganzə/ and *ganso ef* /ganz ev/
gensy
genen
genough
gansa y /ˈganziː/, *gansans* /ˈganzənz/ and *gansans y* /ˈganz ənˈdʒiː/

210

18.8 *Dhe* 'to'

1 3ym, thym, dym, 3ymmo, thymmo, dymo, dymmovy, dymovy M; thym, thymo, thymmove T; 3ym, thyma, thema, themma, 3ymmo, thymove, thyma ve, 3a ve, the vy, tha ve C
2 3ys, dys, dis, thyso, 3iso, dyso, dysogy, 3ysogy, thysogy M; this theso ge T; thees, the gee A; 3es, theis, thys, thyes, theys, 3ysa, 3esa, thysa, 3eso, 3eso gy, tha ge, tha gye C
3 dotho, dotha, dothe, thotho, dotho eff M; thotha, thotha eff, thotheff, thetho T; thotheffe A; 303a, dotha, tho3o, thothef C
3a dethy M; 3ethy, thethy C
4 dyn, 3yn, dynny, 3ynny, thynny, thenny M; thyn, thin, then, thynny, thyny, thenny T; then A; theyn, theny C
5 dyugh, 3yugh, thyugh, dywy, dywhy, thywhy M; theugh, thewgh, thewhy T
6 dethe, detha, dethy M; thetha, thethy, thethans y T; thethans A; thethy, dethy, thothans, dothans C; tho angye Rowe.

Several things should be noted about these forms. Firstly, forms with initial <d> are common in BM and in CW. This may represent a dental [d] (14.35). Secondly, it is apparent from the spelling of the 3rd singular masc. that the final vowel is /ə/.

There appear to have been two forms of the second singular, one with /iː/ and the other with /ɪ/. The long vowel appears to be the commoner and is guaranteed by spellings like *they's* (rhyming with *beys*) OM 329, and the almost universal spelling in CW *theis* (CW 204, 265, 289, 557, 627, 792, 818, 903).

The origin of the word is pre-British *di+te*. This would have given *dit* /diːd/ in Old Cornish and *dys* /diːz/ in Middle Cornish; cf. Middle Breton *dit*. The Middle Cornish reflexes with initial *d* are not infrequent. Equally common, however, are forms with initial /ð/, where the initial has been analogically extended from the 3rd masculine /ðoðo/ from earlier */deðo/. The first person singular was *thym*, emphatic *thymmo* (with *thym* cf. Middle Welsh *ym*, Middle Breton *din*). By analogy with *thymmo, thotho* the second singular *thys* acquired an emphatic variant *thyso*. Because the vowel in *thyso* was short < half-long, it was frequently lowered to *e*, for example, *3eso* PA 116a, CW 1279, 2379, *deso* PA 99b, *theso* CW 2075. The alternation *thymmo ~ thym*, both with a short vowel provided the basis for an analogical *thys* /ðɪz/: /ðizə/ ~ /ðiːz/ > /ðizə/ ~ /ðɪz/.

Thus classical Middle Cornish has two forms of the unmarked lexeme for 'to thee'. One has /iː/, the other /ɪ/. Because the commonest spelling of both is <thys> it is difficult to distinguish them in the texts. One possible example of /ðɪs/ may be seen at PC 2256-57 where *thy's* 'to thee' rhymes with Middle English *wagys* 'wages'. Since the English word must be pronounced /waːdʒəz/, it is likely that *thy's* was /ðɪz/ to rhyme with it. Similarly *des* at BM

211

2593 (rhyming with *nes*) is for /dez/ < /dɪz/. Notice also *ʒeth* 'to thee' at BM 150. This is a variant /ðeð/ of /ðez/ for /ðɪz/.

There can be no doubt that the two forms existed side by side in Cornish, however, for both are attested in the later language: the long form is seen in *dîs* (BF: 16-17 x 4), *theeze, theese* (RC 23: 179, 182), and the short form, *dez, des, dhiz, dhyz* (SGMC: 159).

In view of the above discussion I should recommend the following paradigm for UCR:

dhym, dym, dhymmo /ðɪmə/, *dymmo* /dɪmə/
dhys /ðɪz/ and /ði:z/, *dhyso, dyso*
dhodho /ðoðə/, *dodho* /doðə/, *dhodho ef* /ðoð ev/, *dodho ef* /doð ev/
dhedhy
dhyn, dhynny
dheugh, deughwhy, deuwhy
dhedha, dedha, dhedhans, dhodhans, dodhans, dhodhanjy.

18.9 *Rag* 'for'

1 ragovy M
2 ragos M; ragas, ragas sche C; ragez NBoson
3 ragtho M; ragtha T; ragtho, ractha C; ragta AB
3a —
4 ragon, ragonn, ragoen, ragon ny M; ragan, ragan ny T
5 ragogh M; ragow why T
6 ragtha M; ratha, ragtha, ragthans, ragthans y T; ractha C.

The third feminine is wanting from our foundation texts. SGMC cites *ragthe* as the 3rd singular feminine from Lhuyd, but Lhuyd reads: 'Ragta *and* ragthe, *For him or it*' (AB: 244c), where *ragthe* is probably masculine. Norris gives *ragthy* without citing his source. Jenner's *ragdhi* (HCL: 107) is not convincing. The only Middle Cornish example known to me is *rygthy* at PA 184b, and I advise using that here to complete the paradigm. I should standardize the whole as follows:

ragof /ragə/, *ragof vy*
ragos
ragtho
rygthy
ragon
ragough
ragtha, ragthans, ragthanjy.

18.10 *Dherag* 'in front of'

1 therago, theragoff, theragovy M
2 —
3 theragtho M; deracta TBoson
3a ȝerygthy PA 226c
4 theragon, theragon ny M; deragen A
5 [aragogh M]
6 deractanze Rowe; derarta enge (*read.* deracta enge) NBoson.

This can be standardized:

dheragof
dheragos
dheragtho
dherygthy
dheragon
dheragough
*dheragtha, dheragthans, dheragthanjy.

18.11 *A* 'from'

1 ahaneff M; ahanaf C
2 ahanas, ahanes gy M; ahanas, ahanes C
3 anotha, annotha, annotho M; anotha, anotho eff, anotheff, anetha T; annotha C
3a anythy, anethy, anethe hy T; annethy, anothy C; anothe Rowe
4 ahanan M; ahanan, ahanan ny T
5 ahanowgh, ananowhy, ahanow T
6 annetha M; anetha, anotha, anethy, anetha y T; anothans y C; nonge Rowe; anetha NBoson.

Although 6 is *anetha, anothans(y)*, there seems to have been in Late Cornish a form *ahanjy*. At all events *ahanjy* is the form I understand in JCH §25. Lhuyd's text reads: *hei a kynsiliaz gen nebyn vanah a erra en tre, a dha destrîa an den koth en guilli en termen an noz, a resta an dzhyi syppozia.* This I think should be slightly emended to: *hei a kynsiliaz gen nebyn vanah a erra en tre dha destrîa an den koth en guilli en termen an noz ha'n rest a'andzhyi 'ryppozia* 'she conspired with a certain monk that was in the town to murder the old man in bed at night-time and the rest of them reposing'. My restored *a'andzhyi* would be *ahanjy* in UCR.

I should standardize the whole paradigm for UCR as follows:

ahanaf
ahanas
anodho
anedhy, anodhy
ahanan
ahanough
*anedha, anodha, anedha y, anodhans, anodhanj, anodhanjy, *ahanjy.*

18.12 *Orth* 'upon, against'

1 orthef, ortheff vy M; warthave T; orthaf, worthaf, orthaf ve, orthaf vy, ortha vee C
2 orthys M; worthys C
3 orto M; worto, worta T; orta C
3a worty, ortye, orty hy C
4 orthen ny M; worthan ny T
5 orthugh, orthogh M; worthow T
6 —.

The third plural is wanting but cf. *worte* OM 2476. The whole paradigm could be standardized as follows:

orthyf, worthyf
orthys, worthys
orto, worto
orty, worty
orthyn, worthyn
**orta, worta, *wortans, *wortanjy.*

18.13 *Dheworth* 'from'

1 theortheff vy M; theworthave T; thurtam Rowe
2 theorthys M; theworthas A; thaworthis ge, ʒuwortes, ʒaworthys sche C
3 theworto, theworth eff, theworta T; thaworta A; ʒawarta C
3a theworty T
4 theorthen, theworthen, theworthan, theworthan ny T
5 theorthugh M
6 theworta, theworthansy T; thoranze Rowe.

In the first singular of both *orth* and *deworth* one might equally write *orthyf* and *dheworthyf* as *orthef* and *dheworthef*. I am reluctant to recommend <e> in the ending, however, because <y> occurs in the 2nd singular of both prepositional pronouns: *orthys, deworthys.*

In the light of the above forms I should recommend the following paradigm for UCR:

dheworthyf, dhewortama
dheworthys, dhewortys
dheworto, dheworth ef
dheworty
dheworthyn, dheworthyn
dheworthough
dheworta, dheworthans, dheworth anjy.

18.14 *Yn* 'in'

1   innove, innave T; innef ve S; unnaf, ynaf C
2   unas sche C
2   inno M; inna, ynna, in eff T; in ef A; unna C; ynno C
3a   inhy T; ynny, unhy C
4   innan, ynann, innan ny, ynnan ny T
5   innowhy, innow why T
6   inna M; ynna, inna, innans, ynnansy T; inansy A; unna C.

Late Cornish also has *etta* 'in him' and *ettanz* 'in them'. These could be used as permitted variants, though there is no warrant for forms in *et-* outside the third singular masculine and the third plural (14.16).

The paradigm could be standardized as follows:

ynnof, ynnof vy
ynnos, ynnos jy
ynno, ynno ef, etta
ynny
ynnon
ynnough why
ynna, ynnans, ynnanjy, ettans.

18.15 *War* 'upon'

1   warnaf, warnaff, warnavy M; warnaf C
2   warnes M; warnas C
3   warnotho, warnotha M; warnotho, warnotha T
3a   —
4   warnan M; warnan, warnan ny T
5   warnogh M; warnough C
6   warnetha M; warnetha T; warnothans C.

The third singular feminine is wanting, but cf. *warnethy* OM 775. The paradigm could be standardized as follows:

warnaf, warnaf vy
warnas
warnodho / war'noðə /
warnedhy
warnan, warnan ny
warnough
warnedha, warnodhans, *warnodhanjy.

18.15 *Dre* 'through'

1   drethaf C
2   drethos M; drethas sche C
3   dretho M; dretha, dretha eff, dretho eff T; tardha Lhuyd
3a —
4   drethon M; drethan T
5   drethogh M; drethowhy T
6   drethe M; dretha T.

The third singular feminine is wanting, but cf. *drythy* OM 1668. The paradigm could be standardized as follows:

dredhof
dredhos, dredhos jy
dredho / dreðə /, *dredho ef*
dredhy
dredhon
dredhough, dredhough why
dredha, *dredhans, *dredhanjy.

Ynter 'between, among' is similarly conjugated to *ynter*: *yntredhof, yntredhos*, etc.

18.16 There are other prepositional pronouns not included above, for example *heb* 'without', *ryb* 'beside' and *dres* 'across'. The first two conjugate like *rag*, the third is similar to *dre* except that the feminine is *dresty*.

A *ugh* 'above' also possesses pronominal forms. In Tudor Cornish the third singular masculine is *a ughta* TH 40 for earlier *a ugho*.

It must be admitted that the differences between the paradigms recommended above and UC is very slight. The greatest difference is the use of the suffixes *-ans* and *-anjy* in the third plural.

18.17 Since we are discussing inflected prepositions here, it is perhaps worth pointing out that Tudor Cornish prefers *warbyn* to *erbyn* for 'against'. I should therefore recommend that both *warbyn* and *erbyn* be permitted variants in UCR. We would thus write *war ow fyn* or *er ow fyn*, *war dha byn jy* and *er dha byn jy*, etc.

CHAPTER 19
The verbs of UCR

General remarks about verbs

19.1 Before dealing with the individual verbs in detail, something must be said about verbs in general.

In Middle Cornish (and therefore in UC) the present future indicative ends in -*af*, -*yth*, -Ø in the singular. Moreover the second and third persons frequently have *i*-affection in UC. Thus one finds *lavaraf* 'I say' but *leveryth* 'thou sayest', *lever* 'he says'. Tudor Cornish has a tendency to present an analogically altered picture of all three persons.

19.2 Since the -*af* of the 1st person pres.-fut. was reduced to -*a* in later Middle Cornish, for example in *caraf* 'I love' > *cara*, it became indistinguishable from a number of other endings, in particular the 3rd singular imperfect in -*a* and the 3rd singular present subjunctive in -*a* < -*o*. In verbs like *gwraf* 'I do' and *whylaf* 'I seek' the 1st singular pres-fut. and the 3rd singular were identical in speech: *gwra'*, *gwra*; *whyla'*, *whyla*.

In order to avoid confusion the spoken language recharacterized the 1st singular pres.-fut. by the addition of the enclitic pronoun -*ma*. This occurs in BM and CW (12.4). It is also attested on occasion in the *Ordinalia: a dev ker assoma squyth* 'dear God, how tired I am!' OM 1009; *pedra wrama thys* 'what shall I do to thee?' PC 856, *pendra wrama* 'what shall I do?' RD 2219 .

I would suggest therefore that alongside the literary -*af*, -*of*, UCR should use the colloquial -*ama*, -*oma*. It should be pointed out that these forms are neutral rather than emphatic. *Ythoma* means 'I am' not '*I* am' and *ny allama* 'I cannot' rather than '*I* cannot'. Students could also be taught that UCR *ny allama* and Late Cornish *na ellam* are the same form differently spelt.

Forms in -*af* do occur in Tudor Cornish also, for example, *fatell caraff ve ge* 'that I love thee' TH 43.

19.3 The ending of the second person singular in UC is -*yth*. This corresponds exactly with Middle Welsh -*yd* (<d> = /ð/) and Middle Breton -*ez* /eð/ (CCCG: 278-79) and was almost certainly pronounced /əθ/ in Middle Cornish.

The commonest second person singular form in the language is *os, oys* 'thou art'. By analogy with this the second person singular of other verbs in later Cornish replaces -*th* /θ/ with -*s* in the second singular. Thus in CW we find *wres* 'thou dost' CW 160, 214; *ny vynnys* 'thou wishest not' CW 665; *ny vethys, ny vethis* 'thou wilt not be' CW 1178, 1183. Where -*s* forms are attested in the 2nd singular UCR should allow them.

19.4 Although Middle and Unified Cornish both have 1st person sing. *lavaraf* but 3rd singular *lever*, for example, there is a strong tendency in Tudor Cornish to simplify the paradigm and to replace *lever* 'says' with *lavar*. I have noted the following examples: *dell lavar an abostyll* 'as the apostle says' TH 3a; *ny lavar* 'he does not say', *Pew a laver* 'Who says?, *te a lavar* 'thou wilt say' SA: 59, 59, 62a; *a lavar gow* 'who tells a lie' CW 184, *why a lavar* 'you say' CW 588, *me a lavar* 'I say' CW 1839. The Middle Cornish form *kyf, keyf* 'gets' was assimilated to the first singular *cafaf* to give **caf* /kaːv/. This form occurs in *ti an kav* 'you will find him' in JCH § 22.

Where forms without *i*-affection are attested in the third singular of any verb, UCR should certainly allow them as variants.

19.5 We saw at 7.10 above that there were two 3rd preterites of the verb *kewsel, cowsel*, namely *kewsys/cowsys* and *cowsas*. Similarly *dybrys* 'he ate' of the *Ordinalia* corresponds to Tregear's *debras* (cf. *dhabraz* JCH § 46). My view is that *cowsas* and *debras* are not analogical formations on the basis of verbs in -*as*; they are rather phonetic developments of the earlier *y*-preterites. I should therefore recommend that in a colloquial context the forms *ef a gowsas, ef a dhebras* could be used in preference to the more literary *ef a gowsys, ef a dhybrys*. Other similar preterites might include *savas* 'stood' (JCH § 26), *prederas* (JCH § 40).

I should also recommend that for colloquial style the -*ys* of the preterite, both 1st and 3rd singular, should be pronounced as /əz/. We cannot legitimately write *me a *leveras*, for example, since such a form is unsupported by the Middle Cornish evidence. There is, however, every reason to allow the pronunciation /me ə ləˈverəz/.

Where there is any likelihood of confusion between 1st and 3rd singular in such expressions as *ny leverys travyth* 'I/he said nothing' the preterite of *gul* marked for person can be used (see 21.11 below): *ny wrugavy leverel travyth ~ ny wrug ef leverel travyth*.

19.6 Because final -*a* and -*o* were falling together in the period of the *Ordinalia*, the distinction in Cornish between *gwello* (present subjunctive) and *gwella* (past subjunctive) had already started to disappear in our earliest texts. As a result there was a tendency to conflate the two tenses, by using the past subjunctive instead of the present. This feature is already noticeable in PA (Edwards 1993: 14) and in the *Ordinalia*:

> *ov dywluef colm ha'm garrow gans louan fast colmennow na allan seuel am saf* 'bind my hands and legs with a fast rope of knots so that I cannot stand up' OM 1346-48
>
> *dry den the vos dampnys the ponow na fe sylwys henna ol yw y thysyr* 'to bring a man to be damned to pains so that he be not saved, that is all his desire' PC 16-8

ol del vynny arluth ker my a wra yn pup tyller hedre veyn bev yn bys ma 'all thou wishest, dear lord, I will do in all places as long as I live in this world' PC 113-15.

On occasion the present is used for the past subjunctive:

rak na wrello dasserghy neffre nygen byen ny ioy hep thyweth 'for were he not to rise again we should not have everlasting joy' RD 1028-30.

Past for present subjunctive is particularly common in BM. The present subjunctive of *bos*, for example, survives in the Tudor period in set expressions, *may fo, re by, re bo,* etc., but for the most part the imperfect subjunctive replaces the present subjunctive. Note, for example, the following:

Me a vyn moys then guylfoys
ena ermet purguir boys
    may hallen gorthya ov du
na ven temptis
gans tus an beys
    hedre ven byv

[I will go to the wilderness,
there be hermit indeed
    so that I may worship my God,
lest I be not tempted
by the people of the world
    as long as I live] (BM 1132-37).

In that passage *hallen* has replaced *hyllyf* and *ven* has replaced *vyf* twice. Further examples of the past for the present subjunctive include: *eff a ra prest the golhy may festa sav eredy* 'he will readily wash thee, that thou mayst be whole indeed' BM 1716-17; *Set ow seth the denewhan may hallan tenna thotha* 'Set my arrow to one side that I may fire at it' CW 1553-54; *lead ve quycke besyn thotha may hallan ve attendya pan vanar lon ythewa* 'lead me quickly to it that I may consider what kind of beast it is' CW 1567-69.

I should recommend that the present subjunctive should be replaced by the past subjunctive in UCR. Not only would that simplify the language, but it would be in keeping with the usage of our texts. UCR, then, unlike UC, *has only one subjunctive tense and that is identical with the past subjunctive.* We should therefore say *hedre ven bew* 'as long as I live', *pan dheffes adre* 'when you come home', *pan wella dha vam henna* 'when your mother sees that', etc. The only place where the old present subjunctive is to be retained is in 2nd singular jussives: *re wrylly* 'mayst thou do', *byner re wylly* 'may thou never see' and 3rd singular jussives with *bos: re bo* 'may he be'.

19.7 Unstressed *-eugh, -ewgh, -(o)ugh, -owgh* are not phonetically different in the second person plural since they are all /owx/ or /ǫx/. As a result the second person plural of the various tenses are indifferently written in the texts. UCR must, however, make some kind of choice of spelling which will by its very nature be arbitrary.

I suggest using *-ough* for present and preterite but *-eugh* elsewhere: *kerough* 'you love', *carsough* 'you loved' but *kereugh!* (imperative) 'love'; *carreugh* 'you love' (subjunctive) and *carseugh* 'you would love' (pluperfect/conditional).

19.8 When the third person plural ending is unstressed, since the vowel is /ə/, it is indifferently written <-ens>, <-ons> and <-ans> in the texts. For simplicity's sake I should recommend that two spellings be generally used in UCR: *-ons* in the present and preterite; but *-ens* elsewhere. Thus UCR will write *carons* 'they love', *carsons* 'they loved' but *carens* 'let them love', *carrens* 'they love' (subj.) and *carsens* 'they would love' (pluperfect/conditional). The ending *-ens* could also be used for the unstressed ending of the third singular imperative: *degens* 'let him bear', *bedhens* 'let him be', etc. If the tense has <y> throughout, then *-yns* should remain in the 3rd plural, for example in *gyllyns*.

19.9 Autonomous forms are fairly well attested in the *Ordinalia* and PA. They are rare thereafter, being replaced by *bos* + past participle. Note the difference between *En tas a nef y'm gylwyr* 'I am called the Father of Heaven' OM 1 and *Me yw gylwys duk bryten* 'I am called Duke of Brittany' BM 1. The imperative autonomous of *godhvos* may have survived in Late Cornish (21.17). I recommend using the later syntax of *bos* + past participle in UCR to make any kind of passive.

19.10 BOS 'to be'. The short form of the present of *bos* in UC is conjugated as follows: *of, os, yu, on, ough, yns*. I have already suggested that the first singular could also be *oma* in colloquial contexts. Similarly *os* could be replaced in spoken Cornish by *osa, oja* or *osta*. All forms are attested in Middle Cornish.

The 3rd singular *yu* /ju:/ is, I believe, a mistake (see 6.3; 17.8). The error seems to have originated with Henry Jenner who first used the form (HCL: 124). His source was Lhuyd who wrote <yu> with a point under the *u* (AB: 251c). This variety of *u* is Lhuyd's way of showing /w/ in other contexts, as for example in *glyuaz* 'heard', *uar* 'upon' (AB: 252a), *Goruedh* 'Lie down', *uorfenna* 'finish' (AB: 250a) [where the semivocalic *u* has a point under it in every case, though it is not shown here]. Lhuyd also spells 'is' as <eu> with a point under the *u* (AB: 246a). Since <e> cannot be a semivowel in *eu*, *y* is unlikely to be a semivowel in *yu* either. It seems probable, therefore, that the third singular present of the short form of *bos* was in the spoken Cornish of Lhuyd's day either /ɪw/ or /ew/.

One cannot, I think, escape the conclusion that Unified Cornish has been wrong in this matter. The word for 'is' should never have been spelt <yu> nor pronounced /juː/. In this word it is the *y* that is the vowel and the *u/w* is the semivowel. <Yu> should be a falling diphthong not a rising one. I strongly recommend that <yu> /juː/ should be replaced in UCR by <yw> /ɪw/. In view of the spellings listed at 6.3 above, I would further suggest that <ew> be accepted as a permissible alternative, though <ew> should be pronounced /ew/ and not /juː/.

A sentence of spoken Cornish from Ludgvan that survived orally for over a hundred years was discussed at length by Nance in JRIC 22: 281-87. It runs *Jee an jee wopen ha gessa boo catter*. This was reconstructed by Nance as *Ajy hens yu open ha geses ow bugh ater* 'the road gap is open and my cow let out'. Here Nance's *yu* 'is' appears as *ee w*, i.e. /iːw/. If Nance's reconstruction is correct, and it probably is, then we have incontrovertible evidence that *yu/yw* was /iːw/ < /ɪw/ and not /juː/. Curiously, Nance did not realize the full import of his brilliant reconstruction.

Yw/yu is such a basic word that it will take time to remove the less authentic form. I remember when I used to write <yw> for <yu> in my entries for the *Gorseth* competitions in the early 1960s, I was criticized for spelling the vowel /uː/ as a consonant. I tried to explain to my critics that I wrote <w> in *yw* because it was a consonant and not a vowel at all. I convinced nobody.

To spell 'is' as *yw/ew* will not only correct a long-standing error, it will also bring Neo-Cornish closer to the scribal practice of the manuscripts where *yw* is as common as *yv/yu* and where *ew/eu* is not infrequent. Before I proceed to my next point, may I appeal to all users of Unified Cornish. If you have been using <yu> /juː/ till now, please think seriously about adopting the historically justifiable form *yw* /ɪw/. *Yu* was a mistake, albeit an understandable one. The time has come to correct it.

19.11 The long present of *bos* in Unified Cornish is *esof, esos, us/usy, eson, esough, usons*. The third singular with its two forms is particularly troublesome and I shall have to deal with it at length. The rest of the paradigm of UC seems to accord with the evidence of the texts. I have no example of **esoma* for *esof* but it is apparent from Late Cornish *eram* (< **esoma* < *esof* + *ma*) that such a form existed. I can see no real objection to using it at least in conversation in UCR. It should be noted, however, that *esof-vy* does occur in Tudor Cornish, at SA 64a, for example: *Eth esa ve ow covyn* 'I ask'. *Esta*, the second person + enclitic pronoun, is well attested.

The last sermon SA in the Tregear manuscript is not the work of Tregear himself and its dialect is different from his. SA exhibits many examples of /-r-/ for /-s-/ in the long present of *bos*: *neg eran cregy* 'we do not believe' SA 59, *ne geranny ow kemeras* 'we do not take' SA 63a, *an bara erany ow tyrry* 'the bread which we break' SA 65. Because of the subject matter, instances are forthcoming only in the 1st person plural. It is likely, however, that *r*-forms occurred elsewhere in the paradigm. We should therefore allow permit rhotacism in this verb at least as a possible variant. If so, UCR can legitimately pronounce *esof vy / esoma, eson ny, esough(-why)* as /'erəvi/, /'erəmə/, /'erəni:/, /'erəwhi:/.

19.12 In the long form of *bos* Unified Cornish has *üs, üsy* in the third singular. *Esof* is simply the short form *of* preceded by the formant *es-* (< **ed-* < **ita-*); compare Welsh *ydwyf, ydwyt* and Breton *edoun, edout*, etc. *Us, usy* do not contain **ita-*, though *usy* has been analogically assimilated to the forms that do.

Proto-Celtic seems to have had three forms of the present of the verb 'to be', **esti, *est* and **estiyo*. **Esti* was the absolute form used originally by itself at the head of a clause. **est* was the conjunct form, used after a preverbal particle. **Estiyo* was relative. **Est* developed regularly: **est* > **ēss* > **uis* > **ui* in Primitive Cornish, where it was metathesized to **iu* before the vowel could monophthongize to /u:/ or /o:/. Old Cornish **iu* appears in Middle Cornish as *yw, ew*.

*Esti seems to have developed regularly in Welsh: **essi* > **uissi* > *oes*. In Cornish and Breton, however, the vowel is /œ:/, Breton *eus*, Cornish *us, ues* (CCCG: 321). This can probably be best explained as the generalizing of a weakly stressed form */əs/* > /œs/; compare Breton *eun* 'one' with /œ:/ as against *un* in Welsh with /y:/ < Proto-Celtic **oino-*.

The relative form **estiyo* > **essiyo* > **uissið* gave Middle Welsh *yssyd* > Modern Welsh *sy(dd)* quite regularly. In Cornish, however, **uissið* was analogically assimilated to those parts of the paradigm that contained *es-* (< **ed-*). At the time that the analogical reshaping took place, however, /d/ appears to have been in the process of assibilating to /s/ or /dʒ/ and the ensuing form was **udzið*. With *i*-affection the result was either *usy* /yzı/ or *ugy* /ydʒı/ in Middle Cornish.

There can be no doubt that the vowel of *us, ues* is different in Middle Cornish from the vowel in *usy, ugy*. *Us* occurs in the verb *y'm bus* and when unstressed in the 3rd singular *us* appears as /ez/, *a'n geves, a's teves*. Similarly after *nyns* already in Middle Cornish *us* appears frequently as *es*. This means that the vowel in *us* was a rounded mid-high front vowel /œ:/. In Late Cornish *us* appears usually as *es, ez*, which is further evidence that was usually /œ:z/ in Middle Cornish.

On occasion the vowel of *us* appears as /i:/ spelt <ee>, for example *mars ees* 'if there is' SA 62a, which implies that in some forms of Cornish it was sometimes /y:z/ > /i:z/. There can be little doubt on the other hand that the vowel in *usy, ugy* was always /y/ since in Late Cornish it unrounds to /ı/, for example in *iggeva* < **ugyva* 'which he is' (BF: 9) and *idzha* 'which is' (AB: 245a).

The consonantal segment in *usy, ugy* is either /z/ or /dʒ/ and both should be allowed in UCR. The final <y> should be pronounced /ı/. In view of such forms as *vge* SA 59, 61 bis, 62c, however, the final segment might also colloquially be pronounced /ə/.

In the light of the above discussion I should make the following recommendations. It is probably more authentic to replace *üs* /y:z/ 'is' in

Unified Cornish with /œ:z/ or /e:z/. Since I also recommend that /œ:/ be spelt as <ue>, it would be helpful to emend the spelling of *üs* to <ues>. It is likely, however, that *üs* /y:z/ did occur in Middle Cornish and its continuation in UCR can be defended.

The long form *usy* should retain /y/, spelt <u>. *Usy* can also have a variant *ujy* < Middle Cornish *ugy*. *Usy* should be pronounced /'yzɪ/ or /'ɪzɪ/. *Ujy* should be /'ydʒɪ/ or colloquially, especially with the enclitic pronoun -*va*, /'ɪdʒə/. SA writes *neg esa o gwell* for *nynj usy ow cul* 'he does not, is not doing' (SA 59a). It might also therefore be legitimate to pronounce *usy* as /ezə/, but only if *esa* 'he was' is rhotacized to *era*. Otherwise there will be no difference between present and imperfect.

The third plural *usons* should remain as it is in UC and should be pronounced /'yzənz/ or /'ɪzənz/. We can also spell Tregear's *ugens* 'they are' as <ujons>.

19.13 The preterite of *bos* in Unified Cornish is *büf, bes, be, ben, beugh, bons*. On occasion the 3rd singular is written <bu> or <bue>. Apart from in the 3rd plural the vowel was probably /œ/ and could be written <ue>: *buef, bues, bue, buen, beugh, bons*. /œ:/ in this word had been unrounded to /e:/ as early as PA: *tergweyth y fe convyctiis* 'thrice he was convicted' PA 18b, *an neff y fe danvenys* 'from heaven was sent' PA 18d. BM on the other hand prefers <ue>: *my re bue* BM 3056, *re bue* BM 3356, *fue* BM 3416, *ny vue* BM 3468. Either should be allowed. UC's *büf* 'I was' is not authentic. Indeed <ue> or <e> should occur through the whole paradigm except the 2nd and 3rd pl.

19.14 In UC the conditional/pluperfect of *bos* is *byen, byes, bya*, etc. (CS: 53). The use of this tense as a conditional is quite in accordance with the texts. It should, however, be noted that the imperfect *bethen, bethes, bethe* (UC *bedhen, bedhes, bedha*) is usually used as a conditional in indirect speech:

> *an el a bregewthy a'n wethen hag a'y vertu a'y frut a wrello dybry y fethe kepar ha dev* 'the angel preached of the tree and its virtue, whoever should eat of its fruit would be like a god' OM 229-32
>
> *hy leuerys kepar ha dev y fethe* 'she said [he] would be like a god' OM 289-90
>
> *ha thym y a worthebys y fethons myttyn parys* 'and they answered me that they would be ready in the morning' OM 2306-07
>
> *hag a cousis donfon warlergh seluester hag y fethen… a oll ou cleves sawys* 'and said to send for Silvester and that I would be cured of all my disease' BM 1729-32
>
> *leskis glan ny a vethe pur dyson* 'utterly burnt we would have been right truly' BM 2150-51.

19.15 Y'M BUES 'I have'. Although *y'm bues* 'I have' is very useful, it is not well attested in the later language. I have noted one example in JCH and that is a result of an emendation (see 21.12 below).

Noteworthy is the way in which the verb has been recharacterized by the addition of personal endings or enclitic pronouns: *an tekter a's betheugh why* 'the pleasure you will have' PC 33, *benytho arluth ath par... nygyn bethen* 'never will we have a lord equal to thee' BM 4267-68, *am bef* 'I had' CW 1978, *kyn na'm boma lowena* 'though I have not joy' CW 928, *bythqwath me nyn beys moy dewan* 'never had I more sorrow' CW 1393. Enclitic pronouns characterize the verb for person in such a way that the infixed pronoun can become the object rather than the datival subject: *yn pan vanar y'n bema* 'in which way I had it' CW 756.

John Tregear and CW use the 3rd singular masculine and feminine for each other and for the other two persons. I have noted the following examples:

rag an re ew claffe an gevas othom ay elyow 'for those who are sick have need of medicine' TH 8a

mas an catholyk eglos an jevas an gothfas a pub tra oll necessary rag salvacion 'but the Catholic Church [fem.] has the knowledge of all things necessary for salvation' TH 17

ny an gevith ganso eff eternall bewnans 'we with him will receive eternal life' TH 26

ha ny an jeva promes a brassa royow 'and we had the promise of greater gifts' TH 28

neb astevas spot vith a gras 'anyone who has any grace at all' TH 30a

An dadder han mercy a thu why an jeva sufficient declaracion anotha 'The goodness and mercy of God, you have had sufficient declaration of them' TH 30a

why as tevith sufficient instruccion 'you will have sufficient instruction' TH 31a

ny an gevyth sure droke lam 'we will surely have a mishap' CW 806

me an gevyth oll an blame 'I'll get all the blame' CW 809

ef astevyth vij plague moy 'he will have sevenfold more' CW 1378.

A further stage is reached when the verb *y'm bues* is actually replaced by *bos* itself with possessive sense:

pana rewarde a vethow why? 'what reward will you have?' TH 22

pana commodite a vethyn ny dretha 'what advantage do we get through it?' TH 22a

mar ny vethaf ow desyre 'If I do not get my wish' CW 824

yn pub otham a vesta 'in every need thou mayst have' CW 1948

grace na vo 'mayst thou not have grace' CW 874

may fetha paynes ragtha 'that he would have pains for it' CW 1002.

This construction is described by Gendall as the 'idiomatic possessive' (SGMC: 66).

It is also to be noted that *y'm bues* is sometimes used with a past participle to express the perfect or pluperfect: *flehys am bef denethys* 'I had produced children' CW 1979, *ty a vyth mabe denethys* 'thou shalt have borne a son' CW 1323. Nance (Nance 1949: 26) and George (1990: 239) are mistaken, therefore, when they say that *y'm bues* is not used as an auxiliary.

It is probably best not to confuse *y'm bues* with *bos* as is done in CW, since this might lead to ambiguity. *Why a vedh gour* might either mean 'You will have a husband' or 'You will be a husband', which are not the same thing at all. There is however no reason for proscribing Tregear's syntax. I should therefore recommend that expressions like the following be allowed in UCR:

Plesour a'gan bedh orth agas gweles 'We will have pleasure in seeing you'
Why a's bedhough mona lowr 'You will have enough money'
Drog vos a'gan bedhen 'we used to have poor food'
Ef a'n jeva an markys uhella 'He had the highest marks'
Ny a'n jevyth chy nowedh 'We will get a new house'.

Since the final vowel in *y'n gevo* (imperfect) and *y'n geve* (preterite) is /ə/ in both cases, they are not kept separate in Middle Cornish, except for the sake of rhyme. In UCR both forms should be *y'n jeva*.

19.16 CAFUS 'to get'. The verbal noun is *cafos* in Unified Cornish. As has been suggested above (7.14) this may have been pronounced with *o*-colouring in the unstressed vowel, /kaɸǫz/, in the earliest Middle Cornish but by the period of our texts it was almost certainly /ˈkafəz/ or /ˈkavəz/. *Cawas* /ˈkawəz/ is also attested from RD, BM and CW. This latter form is in Nance 1955, and I recommend that it should be allowed, not to say encouraged, as a colloquial variant.

There is something of a problem with this verb inasmuch as it is not certain whether the root is /kaf-/ or /kav-/. Some parts of the verb would have certainly had /f/ in all dialects, for example the 3rd plural preterite *caffsons* at PA 142a; the subjunctive *keffen* BM 2740, *a'n caffans* PA 67c, etc. Indeed PA seems to have /kaf/ throughout, as is apparent from such forms as *caffos* 'to find' PA 148d, *ny gaffe* 'I do not find' PA 142d, *ny gaffas* 'he did not find' PA 116d, *keffys* 'got, found' PA 119c, 128d, *gyff* PA 37c. Other texts prefer /kav-/, /kev-/. Note for example *ny gavas* 'I did not get' CW 1464, *kevys* 'found' CW 1496, 1745, 1896, 2366. *Kevys* in CW is identical with Nicholas Boson's *kevez* (BF: 31). Notice the third singular pres.-fut. *kav* in Late Cornish (19.4).

The only legitimate procedure here is to accept that both stems were attested in Middle Cornish and to allow both *cafaf, kefyth*, etc. and *cavaf, kevyth* etc. in Neo-Cornish.

19.17 DOS 'to come'. The root vowel of this verb should be /œː/ <ue> in most parts of the paradigm, since it is derived from British **do-ag-*, which would regularly give *aw/o* in the root in Welsh and /œː/ in Breton and Cornish. The pres.-future paradigm in Unified Cornish is *dof, düth, de, dün, deugh, dons*. The <ü> in the 2nd singular and 1st plural should be replaced by <ue> /œː/. *Duen* 'we come' and 'let us go' is common in the texts, as, for example, at BM 2800,

2848, 3426, 3434. The 3rd singular *de* with /e:/ < /œ:/ is unobjectionable, but *due* /dœ:/ also occurs, for example, *a thue* 'comes' BM 2803, 3375.

The 1st singular *dof* of UC is based on *ple tof* RD 1665 and Lhuyd's *dhôv* (AB: 247b). This form is by analogy with *of* 'I am'. The expected form < British **do-agami* would be *duef*; this occurs as *mar tuff* 'if I come' BM 3365 and unrounded to *def* as *y teaf* 'I shall come' CW 1760.

19.18 GALLUS 'be able'. The usual 3rd singular of the present-future in Tudor Cornish is almost certainly *gyll* /gɪl/ but Lhuyd gives *tî a îl* (AB: 247c), which implies a variant *gyl* with a long vowel. *Gyl* is the form in the *Ordinalia*, for example at OM 157, 162, 670, 1717, and it is difficult not to understand it as /giːl/. Notice further that *gyl* 'can' rhymes with *vyl* /viːl/ 'vile' at BM 461-62. Lhuyd's *îl* may be the reflex of *gyll* with vowel lengthening before /ll/. Both *gyll* /gɪl/ and *gyl* /giːl/ should be allowed in UCR.

In the light of Late Cornish forms it is likely that *galsa* was also pronounced /galdʒə/ as well as /galzə/. The *galj-* stem should therefore be permissible in this tense in UCR.[30]

19.19 MYNNES 'to wish'. The pres.-fut. of *mynnes* was widely used in Middle Cornish as an auxiliary verb to form a periphrastic future (21.9 below). If this useful syntactical feature is adopted into the revived language, then *mynnes* will be an even more important verb than it is at present.

In Unified Cornish at the moment the pres.-fut. has <y> throughout the paradigm. Although this can be justified, it is something of an over-simplification. A more authentic paradigm would be: *mannaf/mennaf*, *mennydh*, *myn*, *mennyn*, *mennough*, *mennons*. In view of *men* in BM and TH, *men* as well as *myn* could usefully be allowed in the 3rd singular. It should be noted also that *mynnes* has a historically geminate /n:/ not /n/. A pre-occluded pronunciation of the entire paradigm (and indeed of all forms, including the verbal noun) should be permitted: /madnə/, /'mednəð/, /medn/, /'mednən/, etc.

Notice, incidentally, that there is no need to add *-ma* to the 1st singular, since the root vowel marks the form adequately for person. It is for this reason that *madna* < *mannaf* survives in Late Cornish: *ybma na vadna vi ostia* 'here I will not lodge' JCH §24.

I should also recommend that the stem with /e/ be allowed elsewhere in this verb. We would then have forms like *mennes* 'to wish' and pluperfect/subj. *mensen* 'I should like' (cf. *mensen* BM 3069, *y fensen* BM 2864).

19.20 CLOWES 'hear, feel, taste'. This verb is regular except that it also has a special compound future made with *bos* 'to be': *clowvyth* 'will hear'.

---

30 A future form *gylvyth* '(he) will be able' is now attested from *Bewnans Ke*.

The root vowel in Tudor Cornish is /ow/ and not /ew/ (6.6). In view of Tregear's *clew* 'hears' alongside *clow* at SA 60, we should allow both *clew* and *clow* as the imperative and 3rd singular pres.-fut.

19.21 COWSEL 'to speak'. This verb is regular. As is clear from the texts the vowel of the root is /ow/ throughout. A further example of the verbal noun is in the sentence preserved by Carew from 1602: *meea na uidna cowza sawsneck* 'I won't speak English' (Jago 1882: 5). The preterite 3rd singular is either *cowsys* or *cowsas*.

19.22 CREJY 'believe', PESY 'pray'. Etymologically both verbs have *e*, not *y* in the root. *Pesaf* and *cresaf* are much commoner than forms with *y* and should be the regular forms. I also prefer /dʒ/ before /ɪ/ in the verbal noun and the past participle of *crejy*.

I should recommend a pres.-fut. paradigm *pesaf, pesyth, peys, pesyn, pesough, pesons*, where *peys* = /peːz/ (cf. *peys* BM 296, 546, 667, 1436, 3135).

Notice also that *pejadow* (*peyadow* BM 128, 143, *peiadow* BM 132, *peiadov* BM 2189, 3624, 4015), *pesadow* (*pesadow* TH 6a) 'prayer' is as common as *pysadow, pyjadow*.

19.23 GASA 'leave, allow'. This verb is used as an auxiliary to form the imperative (21.15). The medial /z/ is often rhotacized to /r/, for example *gerys the vois* 'allowed to go' TH 25c, *na reo garra* 'do not leave' BF: 25 and *hep garra thotha* 'without allowing it' BF: 25. It is probably better to allow rhotacism is speech but not to write it.

CHAPTER 20
The verbal paradigms of UCR

UCR verbal paradigms

20.1 I list below the various forms as they are attested in our texts and give thereafter in italic type the reconstructed paradigms or portions of them as I would recommend them. The Roman numerals are to be interpreted as follows: I = verbal noun; II present-future (IIa future); III imperfect; IV preterite; V subjunctive; VI pluperfect/conditional; VII imperative; VIII verbal adjective. I start with *bos* and *y'm bues*. It will be noticed in connection with *bos* that the verb has more than one present/future and imperfect tense and these are listed as II, IIa, IIb, IIc, IId, III, IIIa and IIIb respectively. Forms of *y'm bues* have been culled from the *Ordinalia* and PA as well as the Tudor texts. *Dos* 'come' and *mos* 'go' also have separate perfects; these are listed under IVa. Notice the following abbreviations below: M = BM, T = TH, A = SA, C = CW

20.2

I bos, boys, boas, bones M, bos, bois, bose T, bos, boese, boos, bose A, bonas C

II 1 of, off, ovy, oma M, off T, of, ove, oma, ama C; 2 oys, os, ote, ota M, os, osta, osta ge, ota T, ose, osta, es, oes C; 3 yw, yu, ew, ywa, ywe, ewe M, ew, ewa T, yw, ywe, ow C; 4 on, onn, onny M, one, one, ony, oneny T; 5 ough, ogh, owhy M, owgh, owhy, ewhy T; 6 yns, ens, ens y M, yns, ensy, engy, ons T, ens A

IIa 1 eseff, ese M, esoff, esaff T, esaf, esave C; 2 eses, esos, esta M, esos, esas, esta, esta se T; 3 us, ues, uys, os, es M, us, es, ues T, ees A, eus Borde; 4 esen M, eson, esan, essan T, eran, esyn A; 5 esogh M, esogh, esow, egow T, 6 usons M, usans, ugens T

IIb 3 usy M, usy, ugy, esy, uga, usa, ussy T, use, uge, egy, ugy A

IIc 3 yma, ima, ymae M, yma, ima T, ema A; 6 ymons M, ymons, ymowns, mowns T

IId 1 beȝaf, bethaff, bethe, betha, bethevy M, bethaf C; 2 betheth M, bethys, bethis C; 3 byth, beth, bethe, betha M, beth, byth, bith T, bethe C; 4 bethen, bethenny M, bethyn T; 5 bethugh, bethogh M, bethowgh T; 6 bethens M, bethans, bethens T

III 1 en vy, eva M; 2 es, este, esta M; 3 o, ove M, o, ova T; 4 en T, ene C; 6 ens T

IIIa 1 esen M; 2 eses M; 3 ese M, esa, essa, ega T; 4 esen M; 6 esans T

IIIb 1 bethen M; 3 betha, bethe M, betha T; 6 bethans T

IV 1 buf, bef, bueff, buff, buma M, bef, bema C; 2 bus, bys, busta M, besta T; 3 bue, bua M, be, beva T; 4 buen M, bene T; 6 bonsy T

V 1 ben, beva M, bon, bone C; 2 by, besta, beste M, by, beys, bota, boes, bosta C; 3 bo, bove, be, by M, bo, bova, be T; 4 benny, beny M, bon, ben, benny T, bon C; 5 bugh, begh, bewhy, bewy, bowhy M; 6 bens, bensi M, bons T, bowns C

VI 1 byen M; 3 bye, bya M, bea T; 4 byen M

VII 2 beth M, byth C; 3 bethyns, bethens M, bethans C; 4 bethen M; 5 bewhy M, bethow T, bethowgh, bethowh C; 6 bethens M, bethans, bethance C.

I *bos, bones*

II 1 *of, oma;* 2 *os, ota, osta;* 3 *yw, ywa, ew;* 4 *on;* 5 *ough;* 6 *yns, ens, enjy*

IIa 1 *esof, esof vy;* 2 *esos, esta;* 3 *ues, es;* 4 *eson, eson ny;* 5 *esough, esough why;* 6 *usons, ujons*

IIb *usy, ujy, usa, uja*

IIc *yma; ymons, ymowns*

IId 1 *bedhaf;* 2 *bedhyth, bedhys;* 3 *bedh;* 4 *bedhyn;* 5 *bedhough;* 6 *bedhons*

III 1 *en;* 2 *es;* 3 *o;* 4 *en;* 5 *eugh;* 6 *ens*

IIIa 1 *esen;* 2 *eses;* 3 *esa;* 4 *esen;* 5 *eseugh;* 6 *esens*

IV 1 *buef, bef;* 2 *bues, besta;* 3 *bue, be;* 4 *buen, ben;* 5 **beugh;* 6 *bons*

V 1 *ben;* 2 *bes, besta;* 3 *be;* 4 *ben, benny;* 5 *beugh;* 6 *bens, bensy* + 1 *beva;* 2 *by, bosta;* 3 *bo, bova;* 4 *bon;* 5 *bough;* 6 *bons, bowns*

VI 1 *byen;* 3 *bya;* 4 *byen*

VII 2 *bedh;* 3 *bedhens;* 5 *bedheugh; bedhens.*

20.3

II 1 y'm bes, y'm bus OM, y'm bues PC, y'm bues RD, y'm bus M, y'm beas, y'm bes C; 3m y'n gefes OM, y'n jeves PC, y'n gefes RD, y'n geuas PA, y'n geves M, y'n gevas, y'n gefas, y'n jevas, y'n sevas T, y'n gevas C; 3f ys tevas T

IIa 1 y'm byth, y'm beth OM, my a'n byth PC, y'm byth RD, y'm byth PA, y'm beth M; 2 y 'fyth, y 'fet OM, y 'fyth PC, y fyth, y vyth, y veth RD, y feth, y fyth PA, y feth M, y fyth C; 3m y'n gevyth, y'n gefyth OM, y'n gevyth PC, y'n gevyth, y'n gefyth RD, y'n geuyth PA, y'n geveth M, y'n gevith, y'n sevith T, y'n gevyth C; 3f y's tevyth OM, y's tevith T, y's tevyth C; 4 y'gen byth PC, y'gyn bethen M, y'n bythe C; 5 y'gys byth OM, y's betheugh why, y's byth PC, y's byth RD; y'gys beth M, y's byth C, 6 y's

tevyth, y's tefyth, y's tevyt OM, y's teveth, y's tevyth M

III 1 y'm bo PC; 3m y'n gefo RD, y'n geue, y'n geve, y'n gevo PA

IV 1 y'm buef OM, y'm buevy, y'm bue M, y'm be C; 2 y' fue M; 3m y'n geve OM, y'n geve PC, y'n gefe RD, y'n jeva T, y'n geva C; 6 y's teve OM, y's teve PC

V 1 y'm boma, y'm bo OM, y bome, y ben, y ben vy, y'm bo RD, y'm beua M, y'm boma, y'm bome C; 2 y'th fo OM, y'th fo PC, y'th fo RD, y'n festa, y'th vo, y fy M; 3m y'n geffo (past sense), y'n geffe OM, y'n geffo PC, y'n geffo, y'n jeffo RD, y'n geffo (present and past sense) PA, y'n geffa, y'n geffo M, y'n geffa T, y'n geffa; 4 y'n beny, y'gan bo OM, y'gen bo, y ben RD; 5 y'gas bo OM, y'gas bo PC, y'gas bo RD; y's tefo PC; y's teffo RD, y's tefe, y's tefons, y's tufons M

VI 2 y vea PA, y'm bethe M; 4 y'gen byen RD.

(For the sake of simplicity the preverbal particles *y, a, na* and *ma* in this verb have been standardized to *y*).

II 1 *y'm bues;* 2 *y'th ues;* 3m *y'n jeves;* 3f *y's teves;* 4 *y'gan bues;* 5 *y'gas bues;* 6 *y's teves*

IIa 1 *y'm bedh;* 2 *y fedh;* 3m *y'n jevyth;* 3f *y's tevyth;* 4 *y'gan bedh;* 5 *y'gas bedh, y'gas bedhough;* 6 *y's tevyth*

III 1 *y'm bo;* 3m *y'n jeva*

IV 1 *y'm buef;* 3m *y'n jeva;* 3f *y's teva;* 6 *y's teva*

V 1 *y'm bo, y'm boma, y'm ben;* 2 *y'th fo;* 3m *y'n jeffa;* 3f *y's teffa;* 4 *y'gan bo, y'gan ben;* 5 *y'gas bo;* 6 *y's teffa, y's teffons*

VI 1 *y'm bya;* 3 *y'n jevya;* 4 *y'gan byen.*

20.4

I ankevy M, ankevy T

VIII ankevys C

I   *ankevy*
IV 3 **ancovas*
VIII *ankevys.*

20.5

I   aswen M, aswon, aswan, asswon T
II   3 aswon T
III 3 aswonna T
IV aswannas T
VIII aswonys T.

I   *aswon*
II   3 *aswon*
III 3 *aswona*
IV 3 *aswonas*
VIII *aswonys.*

20.6

I   cara M, cara T
II   1 cara, care M, caraff T; 2 kerte M; 3 car M, kare C, carr T; 5 kerowgh C
III 3 cara T; 4 keryn C
IV 1 kerys C
V   2 kerry M; 3 carra M, carra T
VI 1 karsen, carsen M; 3 carse, carsa M
VIII kerys, keris M, kerys T.

I   *cara*
II   1 *caraf;* 2 **keryth, kerta;* 3 *car;* 4 **keryn;* 5 *kerough;* 6 **carons*
III 3 *cara;* 4 *keryn*
IV 1 *kerys;* 3 **caras*
V   2 *kerry, *carres;* 3 *carra*
VI 1 *carsen;* 3 *carsa*
VIII *kerys.*

20.7

I   cawas, cafus M, cafus, kafus, kafas T, gawas, cawas, cavos C
II   1 cafa M; 2 kefyth M; 3 kyff M, kef OM, kav AB; 4 keuyn M, kefyn, keffyn T
III 1 kefen M
IV 1 cavas C; 3 cavas M, cafas T, cavas C
V   1 cafen, caffen M; 2 kyffy M; 4 keffen M; 5 caffough M
VI 1 caffsen M
VIII kefis, kefys M, keffys, kyffys, kyfys, kyffes T, kevys C.

I   *cafus, cawas*
II   1 *cafaf;* 2 *kefyth;* 3 *kyf, kef, caf;* 4 *kefyn, kevyn*
III 1 *kefyn, kevyn*
IV 1 *kefys, kevys;* 3 *cavas, cafas*
V   1 *caffen;* 2 *kyffy, *caffes;* 3 *caffa;* 4 *caffen;* 5 *caffeugh;* 6 *caffens*
VI 1 *cafsen*
VIII *kefys, kevys.*

20.8

I   cloweys, clowas, clowes M, clowes, clowas T, clowaz Rowe
II   1 clowa, clowevy M, clowaf C; 2 clowyth M; 3 clou M, clew, clow T, clow A; 5 clowugh, clewugh M
IIa 3 clowyth M, clowith T
IV 1 clowys M; 2 clowses C; 3 clowes, clowas, cloways M, clowas, clowes T; 5 closugh, clousugh M
V   3 clowe M, clowa T
VII 2 clew OM, clow ge C; 5 clowugh M
VIII clowys M.

I   *clowes*
II   1 *clowaf;* 2 *clowyth;* 3 *clew, clow;* 4 **clowyn;* 5 *clowough;* 6 **clowons*
IIa 3 *clowyth*
IV 1 *clowys;* 2 *clowsys;* 3 *clowas;* 4 **clowsyn;* 5 *clowsough;* 6 **clowsons*
V   3 *clowa*
VII 2 *clew, clow;* 5 *cloweugh*
VIII *clowys.*

20.9

I   cows, cousel M, cowse T, cowsall C
II   1 couseff M, cowsaf C; 3 cous M; 5 cousugh, cousughwy M, cowsow C
III 3 cousy M
IV 3 cousis M, cowsis, cowses, causis, cowsys T, cow3as C, cowzas Rowe
V   1 cousen M; 5 kewsoughwy M
VII 2 cous, cows M, cowse, cowes C, 5 cousogh, cousugh M, cowsow C
VIII cowsys, cousis M, kewsys, kowsys, kewses, kowses, cowsys, cowgys, cowses T.

I   cows, cowsel
II   1 cowsaf; 3 cows; 5 cowsough
IV   3 cowsys, cowsas
VII 2 cows; 5 cowseugh
VIII cowsys, cowjys.

20.10

I   cresy M, cresy, crege, cregye T, cregy C
II   1 crese, creseff M; 3 creys M, crys, crise T, creys C
VI   3 cresse M, crissa T
VII 2 creys M, creys, creis C; 5 cresugh M, cressowgh, creseugh, cresowgh, cresowh C
VIII cryses, cregys T.

I   cresy, crejy
II   1 cresaf; 3 creys, crys
VI   3 cressa, cryssa
VII 2 creys; 5 creseugh
VIII cresys, crejys.

20.11

I   don M, done, don T, doen C
II   3 dek M, deyg, deke, deg, deige, dog C; 4 degen C
IV   3 duk M
V   3 doga M, docka C; 6 dockans C
VII 2 doag C; 3 degens M; 4 degen M; 5 degogh, degeugh M, degow T, degowhe C, doga ACB; 6 degens M.

I   don
II   1 *degaf; 3 deg, dog; 4 degyn
IV   3 dug
V   3 docca; 6 doccans
VII 3 dog; 4 degyn; 5 degeugh, dogeugh; 6 degens.

20.12

I   doys, dos, dones M, dos, doys, does T, doos C
II   1 dof RD, duf, duff M, dema A, deaf C; 2 deth, dethe, deta C; 3 due, dua, due-a M, de, deva T, defa C; 4 duen, dun, duny M, den, deneny T; 5 dewgh, dewhy T, dewh C; 6 downs C

IV   1 duth, duthe M, deth ve C; 3 duth, dueth, deth, duthe M, deth, duth T; 4 duthen M
IVa 3 deve, deva, dufe, dufa M, defa T
V   1 deffen M; 2 deffes, defes M, dyffy, deffasta T; 3 deffo M, deffa T; 4 deffan, deffen T; 6 deffons M, deffans, deffens T
VII 2 dus, duys M, des, deas C; 3 dens M; 5 dugh M, dewh C; 6 dens M
VIII devethys M, devethis T, devethys C.

I   dos, dones
II   1 duef, dof, dema; 2 dedh, deta; 3 deu, deva; 4 duen, den, den-ny; 5 deugh, deugh why; 6 downs
IV   1 dueth, deth; 3 dueth, deth; 4 duethen
IVa 3 dueva, deva
V   1 deffen; 2 deffes, deffesta; 3 deffa; 4 deffen; 5 *deffeugh; 6 deffens
VII 2 dues, des; 3 dens; 5 deugh; 6 dens
VIII devedhys.

20.13

I   dry, drey M, dry T
II   1 droff M; 2 dreythe C; 3 doro M, dora, dro T; 4 dryn
IV   3 dros, droys M, dros T
V   3 drolla T
VI   3 drossa T
VII 2 dro M, dro C; 3 drens M; 5 drewhy M, drewhy C
VIII dreys M, drys, dris, dres C.

I   dry
II   1 drof; 2 dredh; 3 dora, dro; 4 dryn
IV   3 dros
V   3 drolla
VI   3 drossa
VIII dreys, drys.

20.14

I   dybry, dybbry M, dybbry, dibry, debry T, dibbry, dybbry A, debbry C
II   3 debbyr, debyr T
IV   3 debbras T
V   5 depprow T
VI   3 depse M
VII 2 debar T, 5 debrogh, debbrogh T
VIII dibbris T, debbrys C.

I   *dybry, debry*
II   3 *debyr*
IV   3 *debras*
V   5 *deppreugh*
VI   3 *depsa*
VII   2 *deber;* 5 *debreugh*
VIII   *debrys, dybrys.*

20.15
I   setha M, setha T, setha C
II   3 esa M, ysa, sethe, seathe C
VII   5 sethoug, esethugh M
VIII   ysethys, sethys C.

I   *esedha, sedha*
II   3 *esedh, esa*
VII   5 *esedheugh, sedheugh*
VIII   *esedhys, sedhys.*

20.16
I   fyllall, fillall T, fyllell C
II   1 falla M; 2 fylleth, fellyth, fyllyth M; 3 fyl M, fyll T
IV   3 fyllys T, fyllas, fylles C.

I   *fyllel*
II   1 *fallaf;* 2 *fyllyth;* 3 *fyll*
IV   3 *fyllys, fyllas.*

20.17
I   gallus M, gallus T
II   1 galla M, galla T, gallaf, gallaff C; 2 gylleth, gyllyth, gylta gy, gelta gy, gelte gy M, gylleth C, 'lesta NBoson; 3 gyl, gyll M, gyll, gill, gylla T; 4 gyllen, gyllyn M, gyllyn, gillyn T, gellyn C; 5 gyllogh M, gillowgh T; 6 gyllons M, gyllans, gillans, gellans T
III   1 gyllan C; 3 gylly M, gylly T; 6 gallans T
V   1 gallen M, gallen T, gallan C; 2 gylly M, gallas C; 3 galla, gallo, galho, gala M, galla T; 4 gallen, gyllyn, gyllen M, gallan, gallon T; 5 gallogh M, gallowgh, gallogh, gallow T; 6 gallons M
VI   1 galsan C, golgama (*golgan + ma) NBoson; 2 galses M; 3 galse M, galsa, galse T, golga NBoson, galdzha Lhuyd; 4 galsan T; 6 galsons M, galsans T.

I   *gallus*
II   1 *gallaf;* 2 *gyllyth, gylta, gyllysta;* 3 *gyll, gyl;* 4 *gyllyn;* 5 *gyllough;* 6 *gyllons*
III   1 *gyllyn;* 3 *gylly;* 6 *gyllyns, gallens*
V   1 *gallen;* 2 *galles + gylly;* 3 *galla;* 4 *gallen + gyllyn;* 5 *galleugh;* 6 *gallens*
VI   *galsen, galjen;* 2 *galses, galjes;* 3 *galsa, galja;* 4 *galsen, galjen;* 6 *galsens, galjens.*

20.18
I   gase, gasa M, gara T
II   3 gas, gays M
IV   2 gyssys M; 3 gases M, gasas, gassas T, gasas A
VII   2 gays M, gas T, gas A; 4 gesyn, gesen A; 5 gesugh M, gesowgh, gesow T
VIII   gesys M, gesis, geses, gerys T.

I   *gasa*
II   3 *gas*
IV   2 *gyssys;* 3 *gasas*
VII   2 *gas;* 4 *gesyn;* 5 *geseugh*
VIII   *gesys.*

20.19
I   gava M, gava T
IV   gawas C
VIII   gevys T.

I   *gava*
IV   *gavas*
VIII   *gevys.*

20.20
I   gylwall T, gyllwall C
II   3 gylwe T
III   3 gylwy M
IV   3 gelwys M, gylwys, gilwis T
V   3 galwa T
VII   2 galwy 'call them' M
VIII   gylwys, gelwys M, gylwys, gyllwis, gylwis T.

I   *gylwel, gelwel*
II   3 *gylow*
III   3 *gylwy*

IV   3 *gylwys*
VII 2 *galow, galw* before vowels
VIII *gylwys.*

20.21
I   golsowes, golsowas T
VII 2 golsou M, golsow C; 5 golsowugh, golsovugh M, gosoweth A, golsowowh, golsowogh C.

I   *golsowes*
VII 2 *golsow;* 5 *golsoweugh, gosoweugh.*

20.22
I   gorra, gora, gore M, gora T, gorra C
II   3 gor, gorr M, gore, goer T
IV   3 gores M, goras T, gorras C
VII 2 gor M, goer C; 4 goren M, gorryn C; 5 gorowgh, gorrowgh C
VIII gorrys M.

I   *gorra*
II   3 *gor*
IV   3 *gorras*
VII 2 *gor;* 4 *gorryn;* 5 *gorreugh*
VIII *gorrys.*

20.23
I   gortays, gortes M, gortas C, gurtas T
II   3 gorte, gorta M, gorta T
VII 2 gorta M; 4 gorten M; 5 gurteugh T.

I   *gortas, gortos*
II   3 *gorta*
VII 2 *gorta;* 4 *gortyn;* 5 *gorteugh.*

20.24
I   gortheby M, gortheby T, gweryby C
II   3 gorthyb M; gorryb T, gorthib C
IV   3 gorrebys, gorrybys, gorthebys, gurthebys T; gwerebas Rowe
VII 5 gorthebugh M, gorrybowhe C.
VIII gorthebys M

I   *gortheby*
II   3 *gorthyb*
IV   3 *gorthebys, gorthebas*
VII 5 *gorthebeugh*
VIII *gorthebys.*
234

20.25
I   gothfos, gothvos, gothvas gothfes M, gothfas, gothfes T, gothevas, gothvas C
II   1 gon M, gon C; 2 gothes M; 3 gor, gour M, gor, gore T; 4 gothen M, gothyn, goryn T; 5 gothogh M; 6 gothens M
III 1 gothyan M, gothyan C; 3 gothya M, gothya, gothia T; 6 gothyans T
V   1 guffan C; 2 gothves, gothfes M, goffas C; 3 gothfa T; 5 gothow T
VI   3 guffya C
VII 2 gothveth, gothfeth M; 5 gothvethugh M, gothvethow T
VIII guthvethis, gothvethis T.

I   *godhvos*
II   1 *gon;* 2 *godhes;* 3 *gor;* 4 *godhyn;* 5 *godhough;* 6 *godhons*
III 1 *godhyen;* 3 *godhya;* 6 *godhyens*
V   1 *gothfen;* 2 *gothfes;* 3 *gothfa;* 5 *gothfeugh*
VI   3 *gothfya*
VII 2 *godhvydh;* 5 *godhvedheugh*
VIII *godhvethys.*

20.26
I   goven, govyn M, gophen Lhuyd, gofen Rowe, gofyn OM 1481
II   2 govynnyth M
IV   3 govynnys T
VII 2 govyn M, goven T
VIII govynnys M, govynnys T.

I   *govyn, gofyn*
II   2 *govynnyth*
IV   3 *govynnys*
VII 2 *govyn*
VIII *govynnys.*

20.27
I   gu3yll, guthel, gul M, gul, gull, gyll, gwiell T, gwiell, gwyell, gweill A, gwyle, gwyl, gwyll, gwethill, gweyll C
II   1 gruaff, guraf, *gurama M, gwra ve T, gwraf, gwraff, gwrama C; 2 gureth M, gwreth, gwrethe, gwreta, gwres,

gwreas C; 3 grua, gureva M, gwra T, gwra C; 4 guren, gureny M, gwren T, gwreen C; 5 guregh M, gwrewgh T; 6 gurons M, gwronns, gwronsy, gwrowng, gwrongy T

III 1 gwre T; 4 gwrean C; 6 gwrens T

IV 1 guruk M, gwrugaf, gwregaf C; 2 gurussys, gurussis, guruste, gurusta M, gwrusta T, gwresta, gwressys C; 3 guruk M, gwrug, grug, gwruga, gruge, gwrege T; gwruck, gwruk A, gwruge, gwrega C; 4 gurussyn M, gwrussyn T, gwressan C; 5 gurussugh M, gwrussough T, gwressowh C; 6 gurussons M, gwrussans, gwrussens T, gwressans C

V 1 gurellen M, gwrellean ve T, gwrellan C; 2 gurelles, gurylly M; gwrylly T; 3 gurelle, gurella M, gwrella T, gwrella C; 4 gwrellan T, gwrellan C; 5 gurellogh M, gwrellowgh T; 6 gwrellens T

VI 1 gurussen M, gwressan, gwrussen C; 3 gurussa, gurusse M, gwrussa T, gwressa C; 6 gwressans C

VII 2 gura, grua M, gwra ge T, gwra C; 3 gruens M; 4 gruen M, gwryn T, gwren C; 5 gruegh, grugh, grueghwy, gureugh M, gwrewgh, gwregh, gwrellowgh, gwrellogh, gwrellow T, gwrewh, gwrewgh, growgh C

VIII gwrys, grueys M, gwrys, gwres T, gwreis A, gwryes, gwrres, gwrez C

(In this paradigm forms with lenited initial r- have for simplicity's sake been standardized to begin with gru-, gwr-, not gr-).

I *gul, guthyl, gwyll*

II 1 *gwraf, gwrama; 2 gwredh, gwreta, gwres; 3 gwra, gwrava; 4 gwren; 5 gwreugh; 6 gwrons, gwrowns, gwrownjy*

III 3 *gwre; 4 gwren; 6 gwrens*

IV 1 *gwrug, gwrugaf; 2 gwrussys, gwressys, gwrusta, gwresta; 3 gwrug,*

gwruga, gwreg; 4 gwrussyn; 5 gwrussough; 6 gwrussons

V 1 *gwrellen; 2 gwrelles + gwrylly; 3 gwrella; 4 gwrellen; 5 gwrelleugh; 6 gwrellens*

VI 1 *gwrussen; 3 gwrussa; 6 gwrussens*

VII 2 *gwra, gwra jy; 3 gwrens; 4 gwren; 5 gwreugh, gwrelleugh, gwreugh why*

VIII *gwreys, gwres.*

20.28

I guelas, gueles, gueleys M, gwellas T

II guelaff, guela M, gwelaf, gwellaf C; 2 guelyth M, gwelyth, gwelleth, gwelta, gwelta ge C; 3 guel, gueyl, gueyll, guyl M, gwell, gwele T, gweall, gweel C; 4 gwelyn M, gwelyn T; 5 gwelogh M, gwelowgh C

III 1 gwellyn C; 4 gwyllyn T

IV 1 gwelys M, gwelys C; gwylste gy M; 3 gwelas M, gwellas T; 4 gwylsyn T; 5 gwelsowgh C

V 3 guelle M, gwella C; 5 gwella why C

VIII guelys M, gwelys T, gwellys C.

I *gweles*

II 1 *gwelaf; 2 gwelyth, gwelta; 3 gwel, gweyl, gwell; 4 gwelyn; 5 gwelough; 6 gwelons*

III 1 *gwelyn; 4 gwelyn*

IV 1 *gwelys; 2 gwelsys, gwelsta; 3 gwelas; 4 gwelsyn; 5 gwelsough*

V 3 *gwella; 5 gwelleugh why.*

20.29

I henwall T

II 1 henwaf C

VII 2 hanw M

VIII henways, henwys M, henwis, henwys C.

I *henwel*

II 1 *henwaf*

VII 2 *hanow, hanw* before vowels

VIII *henwys.*

20.30

I hevely T

II 3 havel, hevel M, hevall T, havall C

III 3 hevely M, fylly C
VI 3 hevelsa M, falsa, valsa C; 6 havalsens M
VIII hevelys T.

I *hevelly*
II 3 *hevel*
III 3 *hevelly*
VI 3 *hevelsa, havalsa*; 6 *havalsens*
VIII *hevelys.*

20.31
I kylly M, kelly C
II 3 kyll C
IV 3 collas T
V 2 kelly T
VIII kellys, kyllys M, kellys C, kyllys T.

I *kelly*
II 3 *kyll*
IV 3 *collas*
V 2 *kylly*
VIII *kellys.*

20.32
I kemeres M, kemeres, kemeras T, kemeras A, kameras C
II 3 kemer M, kymmer T, kemar A, kymmar C
IV 1 kemerys M; 2 kemercys M; 3 kemerays M, kemeras A
V 3 kemerre M, kemera T
VI 3 kemersa M
VII 2 kemer, kymmer, kemmer M, kemmar T, kemer A, kymar, kymmar, kemer C; 3 kemerens M; 5 kemerugh, kemerogh M, kemmerogh, kemerogh T
VIII kemerys M, kemerys T.

I *kemeres*
II 3 *kemer*
IV 1 *kemerys*; 2 *kemersys*; 3 *kemeras*
V 3 *kemerra*
VI 3 *kemersa*
VII 2 *kemer*; 3 *kemerens*; 5 *kemereugh*
VIII *kemerys.*

20.33
I leferel M, leverel, leverell, leverall T, leverall A
II 1 lefara M, lavaraf C; 2 leueryth M; 3 lever, leuer, lefer M, lever, lavar T, lavar, laver A, lavar C; 5 leverough T
III 3 levery T
IV 3 leferys, leferis M, leverys, leveris, lyverys T, leveris A, laverys C, laveraz JBoson, lavarraz Rowe
V 3 lavarra T, lavara C
VII 2 laver, lafar, lafer M, lavar, lavare T; 4 leferyn, leveryn M; 5 leferugh M
VIII leferys M, leveris A.

I *leverel*
II 1 *lavaraf*; 2 *leveryth*; 3 *lever, lavar*; 5 *leverough*
III 3 *levery*
IV 3 *leverys, laveras*
V 3 *lavarra*
VII 2 *lavar*; 4 *leveryn*; 5 *levereugh*
VIII *leverys.*

20.34
I lesky, leskye, lysky, lyskye C
II 3 loske C
IV 3 loskas C
VIII leskys, leskis M, leskys C.

I *lesky*
II *losk*
IV *loscas*
VIII *leskys.*

20.35
I myras, merays, meres, meras M, meras T
V 1 merhan T
VII 2 myr M, meir, meer, meere, mere, meyr, myer C; 4 myryn M; 5 merough, merugh M, merogh, merow, merowgh T, merowgh C.

I *myras, meras*
V 1 *merren*
VII 2 *myr*; 4 *myryn*; 5 *mereugh.*

20.36

I   merwel M, merwell, merwall T
II   3 myrwe M, merwe T, merve C
IV   3 myrwys M.

I   *merwel*
II   3 *merow*
IV   3 *merwys.*

20.37

I   mos, mois, moys, mones M, mos, mois T, mose C
II   1 aff, ama M, ama C; 2 eth M; 3 a M, a T; 4 en M; 5 egh M; 6 ons M
III   3 e M, e T
IV   1 eth C; 3 eth, etha, ethe M, eth T
IVa   3 galles, galleys M, gallas C; 6 galsons M
V   1 ellen M; 2 ylly M, ellas T; 3 ella M, ella C; 4 ellen M; 6 ellens M
VII   2 ke, kea, keʒegy M, ke C; 3 ens M; 4 duen M, den, dune, deen, deun, dewne C; 5 eugh M, kewgh C; 6 ens M
VIII gyllys, gylles M, gyllys T.

I   *mos, mones*
II   1 *af, ama*; 2 *edh*; 3 *a*; 4 *en*; 5 *eugh*; 6 *ons*
III   3 *e*
IV   1 *eth*; 3 *eth*
IVa   3 *gallas*; 6 *galsons*
V   1 *ellen*; 2 *elles* + *ylly*; 3 *ella*; 4 *ellen*; 6 *ellens*
VII   2 *ke, ke dhejy*; 3 *ens*; 4 *duen*; 5 *eugh, keugh*; 6 *ens*
VIII *gyllys.*

20.38

I   mynnes, mennes M, mynnas T
II   1 manna, menna, mannaf, manneff, maneff, manaff, mannaff, mannafi, mannavy M, manna, manna ve T, mannaf, mannaff, manaf, mydnaf, midna C; 2 mynnyth, mynneth, mennyth M, mynyth, mynnys, mynta C; 3 myn, men, mynna M, myn, men T, mydn, midn, mynna C; 4 mynen, menyn, menen M, mynnyn, menyn T; 5 mynnogh M, mynnough, menow T, mennow ACB; 6 mynnons M

III   1 mennen M; 3 mynna T
IV   1 mynnys M; 2 mynsys M; 3 mynnas M, mennas T, mydnas C
V   1 mennen, menen M; 2 mynny, mynnes, mynneys M, mynny, mennas C; 3 mynne, mynna M, mynna T; 5 mynnogh M; 6 mynnans M
VI   1 mensen M, mynsan T, mensan C, menjam (< menjen + ma) ACB; 2 mynses C; 3 mynsa M, mynsa T, mengha NBoson, mendzha Lhuyd, menja, menjah ACB; 4 mensyn M; 6 mynsans T.

I   *mynnes, mynnas, mennes*
II   1 *mannaf, mennaf*; 2 *mennyth, menta, mynnyth*; 3 *myn, men*; 4 *mennyn, mynnyn*; 5 *mennough, mynnough*; 6 *mynnons*
III   1 *mynnen*; 3 *mynna*
IV   1 *mynnys*; 2 *mynsys*; 3 *mynnas, mennas*
V   1 *mennen*; 2 *mynnes* + *mynny, mennes*; 3 *mynna, menna*; 5 *mynneugh*; 6 *mynnens*
VI   1 *mensen, menjen*; 2 *menses, menjes*; 3 *mensa, menja*; 4 *mensyn, menjyn*; 6 *mynsens, menjens.*

20.39

I   perthy M, perthy C
II   1 perraf C; 3 perth M
IV   3 porthes, porthas M
V   3 portho RD
VII   2 porth OM, perth C, per ACB; 5 perthugh, perthuth M.

I   *perthy*
II   1 *perthaf*, **porthaf*; 3 *perth*
IV   3 *porthas*
V   3 *portha*
VII   2 *perth, porth*; 5 *pertheugh.*

20.40

I   prevy M, prevy T
II   3 preif C
IV   1 provas C; 3 proves M
VI   3 proffse M
VIII prevys M, provys T, prevys C.

I   *prevy*
II   3 *pref*
IV   1 **prevys, provys*; 3 *provas*
VI   3 *profsa*
VIII *prevys, provys.*

20.41

I   pysy, pesy M, pegy C
II   1 pesef, peseff, pesa M, pydgyaf C; 3 pys, peys M, pys C
IV   3 pesys, pegis T
VI   3 pesse, pysse M
VII   2 peys M; 5 pesough T.

I   *pesy, pysy, pejy, pyjy*
II   1 *pesaf, pyjaf*; 3 *peys, pys*
IV   3 *pesys, pejys*
VI   3 *pessa, pyssa*
VII   2 *peys*; 5 *peseugh.*

20.42

I   ry M, ry T
II   1 rof, roff M, rof, roof C; 2 reyth M; 3 ree M, ro C; 5 regh M
IV   3 ros, roys M, ros T, rose C
V   3 roy M; 4 rollen M
VI   1 rosen M; 3 rose M
VII   2 roy M, ro, roy C; 5 regh M, rewhy C
VIII   res, reis T.

I   *ry*
II   1 *rof*; 2 *reydh*; 3 *re, ro*; 5 *reugh*
IV   3 *ros*
V   3 *roy*; 4 *rollen*
VI   1 *rosen*; 3 *rosa*
VII   2 *roy, ro*; 5 *reugh, reugh why*
VIII   *res, reys.*

20.43

I   sensy M, singy, syngy T, sensy A
II   1 senseff, sense, sensa, sensevy M, sensaf C; 3 sens M, syns C
IV   3 synges C
VII   2 sens M
VIII   sensys, senses, sensis M, sengys C, sendzhyz AB.

I   *sensy, synsy, synjy*
II   1 *sensaf*; 3 *sens, syns*

IV   3 *synjas*
VII   2 *sens*
VIII *sensys, senjys.*

20.44

I   sevell, sevel M, sevall T
II   3 seff M
IV   3 sevys T, savaz AB
VII   2 saff, sa M, save, saf C; 5 sevugh M
VIII   seuys, sevys M, sevys C.

I   *sevel*
II   3 *sef*
IV   3 *sevys, savas*
VII   2 *saf, sa'*; 5 *seveugh*
VIII *sevys.*

20.45

I   terry M, terry, tyrry T
IV   3 torras C
VIII   terrys C.

I   *terry*
IV   3 *torras*
VIII *terrys.*

20.46

I   tevy C
II   3 teyf, teff T, teiff C
VIII   tevys T.

I   *tevy*
II   3 *teyf, tef*
VIII *tevys.*

20.47

I   toulel M, tewlell, towlell T, towlall C
II   3 towle C
IV   3 towlas T
VII   2 toul M
VIII   teulys M, towlys, towlis T, towles C.

I   *towlel*
II   3 *towl*
IV   3 *towlas*
VII   2 *towl*
VIII *towlys.*

CHAPTER 21
The syntax of UCR

Mutation

21.1 In UC lenition (the soft mutation) operates upon *b, d, g, gw, p, t, k/c, qu, ch* and *m*. The result in each case is shown in writing: *v, dh, –, w, b, d, g, gw, j* and *v*. F and *s* are also lenited to /v/ and /z/ although the mutation is not shown in writing (CS: 14).

There can be no doubt that the mutation of /f/ > /v/ is regular in Cornish. Lhuyd expressly mentions that the feminine noun *fordh* or *forh* 'a way' is lenited after the article > *an vordh* 'the way' (AB: 241c). Moreover Lhuyd is consistent in writing *an vor* in JCR §§ 6, 16. It seems also that lenition in Late Cornish sometimes occurred after *agas* 'your' because Lhuyd also writes: *Fordh* 'a way' but '*gyz vordh* 'your way' (AB: 230c). The mutation of *f* > *v* is a simple process of voicing and as such is similar to the lenition of *p* > *b, t* > *d, k* > *g* and /tʃ/ > /dʒ/.

The lenition of /f/ > /v/ in Cornish may not always be the cause of *v* for *f* in place-names, particularly in the more easterly half of Cornwall. The initial *v* in *Venton Ends* (St Issey), for example, is probably due to the shift in SW English of *f* > *v*. This sound-change is seen for example in standard English word *vixen* < OE *fyxen*, which is a distinctively western form.

21.2 The lenition of /s/ > /z/ as in *my a sew* 'I follow' is regular in UC in speech, though it is not shown in writing. The evidence for this mutation is unfortunately very uncertain. Caradar cites *Penzance* < *pen sans* as evidence (CS: 14), but this place-name is hardly relevant since there is no reason to lenite the adjective *sans* 'holy' after a masculine noun, *pen* 'head'. Moreover /s/ was often voiced to /z/ after /n/ as is obvious from Late Cornish forms like *karenza* 'love'. It would seem historic /s/ at the beginning of some words was always voiced. Lhuyd writes *zêh* 'dry' (AB: 150a s.v. *siccus*) and John Boson writes *zeth* 'dry' with initial <z> (BF: 52). *Sans* 'holy' is both *sanz* and *zanz* in Late Cornish, irrespective of lenition (AB: 144a). Note *an zanso* 'the saints' (BF: 41), *en Zanz Garrack* (BF:44) where grammatical lenition might be expected and *gerriow zans* (BF: 60) where lenition would be unmotivated. *De'Zîl* 'Sunday' has /z/ unexpectedly (BF: 55). Nicholas Boson writes *an Sausen, Sousenack* with <s> (BF: 25), while Lhuyd writes *Zouz, gerrio Zouznak* (AB: 223, 224). On the other hand the spelling *ny zensen* 'I would not consider' (OM 2358) might suggest that /s/ was lenited in initial position after leniting particles. Given the uncertainty of the alleged grammatical lenition of /s/ > /z/, it is probably sensible not to make it a rule in UCR.

21.3 The so-called 'mixed mutation' or 'fifth state' of Middle Cornish is somewhat anomalous. Particles like the adverbial *yn* and *maga* provect /d/ to /t/ but both provect and spirantize /b/ and /m/ to /f/, and /g/ and /gw/ to /h/ and /ʍ/ respectively. Thus one finds *yn ta* 'well', *magata* 'as well, also' but *yn few* 'alive', *yn harow* 'roughly'. According to Lhuyd, however, *yn* is followed by lenition, for example in *yn vêu* 'alive' (AB: 227c).

It is unlikely that *yn few* in Middle Cornish is merely a graph for **yn vew*, which comes to light fully only in the Late Cornish period. It is much more likely that *yn vêu* is a Late Cornish replacement of *yn few*. When a Celtic dialect is in severe decline, the initial mutations are always among the first part of the system to suffer. There is certainly good evidence that lenition itself was in retreat in Late Cornish. It is likely, therefore, that *yn vêu* is a Late Cornish replacement of the earlier *yn few*.[31]

Pronouns

21.4 The probable origin of the pronoun *anjy* has been discussed at 18.3 above. In Late Cornish *angye* (*anjy*) is used not merely as a pronoun but as a quasi-possessive adjective, for example *lagagow angie ve 'gerres* 'and their eyes were opened' (RC 23: 177) and *mesk angy* 'among them' for *y'ga mesk* (BF: 27). This construction is similar to *dir faith da ny* 'through our good faith' SA 61, for **dir agan faith da ny*, where the suffixed pronoun *ny* is used possessively. Cf. such Late Cornish examples as *Kar ve* 'My friend', *canow vee* 'my song', *haval ni* 'our likeness', *egles nei* 'our church' (BF: 43, 52, 57). The beginnings of the construction are seen in such forms as *an mammeth nyy* 'our nurse' SA 59a and *hem ew ow corff ve* 'this is my body' SA 62a. In the second example the mutation after *ow* is suppressed and the possessive is reinforced by suffixed *ve*.

The suffixed possessive is commoner with the first person singular than with other persons, presumably because *ow* 'my' was reduced to *a* in rapid speech and had a tendency to be lost completely. I should be reluctant to recommend such expressions for everyday use in UCR. There is a difference between *ow mab* 'my son' and *ow mab vy* '*my* son' and it would be foolish to lose that distinction. Nonetheless variants of the kind *chy vy* 'my house', *myrgh ny* 'our daughter' could be used colloquially or for substandard registers.

Rowe's *lagagow an gie* 'their eyes' (RC 23: 177) may be due to the awkwardness of the alternative **aga lagagow*. Revived Late Cornish uses *angye* as a post-positive possessive regularly, in *tavas angye* 'their language', for example, and *vreage angye* 'their mind' (*Carn* 60: 15). Such expressions are best avoided in UCR. I should, therefore, prefer *aga mebyon* or *aga mebyon anjy* 'their sons' to *mebyon anjy*.

---

31 Note that in the expression *yn gwyr* 'truly' in the text the second element is a noun meaning 'truth'. Nance's *yn whyr* is spurious and is never found in traditional Cornish.

21.5 With inflected forms of the verb the personal object is indicated by an infixed pronoun. This is the rule in both Middle Cornish and UC. Yet from an early period it seems that a simplification was taking place in the spoken language. The double marking of the object by infixed pronoun + (optional) suffixed pronoun was giving way to an obligatory suffixed pronoun without the infixed pronoun: *me a'th car gy* 'I love thee' was yielding to *me a gar gy*. This syntax is not frequent in the texts, but it may well have been common in speech. Note the following examples:

arluth pragh y hysta vy 'Lord, why hast thou forsaken me?' PA 201c

Ea, arluth, te a wore henna, fatell caraff ve ge 'Yea, Lord, thou knowest that, that I love thee' TH 43

Me a wra ge dean a bry havall thagan face whare 'I will make thee, O man, of clay anon like unto our face' CW 345-46

An hager-breeve a thullas ve 'The evil serpent deceived me' RC 23: 180

Rag hedda an Arleth Deew devanas ea arage thoro paraves 'Therefore the Lord God sent him forth from paradise' RC 23: 184

Ha Deu goras gi en ebron neve 'And God put them in the firmament of heaven' BF: 52

Rag hedda an Arleth benaz an sithas dêth ha sonaz a 'Therefore the Lord blessed the seventh day and hallowed it' BF: 55.

Even so, the infixed object pronoun survived into Late Cornish, for example:

ti an kav 'you will find him' JCH § 22

rag tha hannen te yn gura 'for thyself thou doest it' JRIC 1866: 10

Ha e ez devannaz tha Bethalem 'And he sent them to Bethlehem' RC 23: 190

an jowle an comeraz e man... ha en zettyaz 'the devil took him up... and set him' RC 23: 186-87

angee arass go rôza ha an suyas 'they left their nets and followed him' RC 23: 191

Rag e theuaz eave gon kibmeare 'He takes us for his sheep' BF: 39.

In view of the relative simplicity of *me a welas why* 'I saw you', *y a ladhas anjy* 'they killed them', etc., I recommend that the suffixed object be allowed in UCR, at least in colloquial registers.

Verbal syntax

21.6 In Cornish there are two chief ways of constructing non-negative clauses. The first of these is the so-called 'normal word-order' of Welsh. It involves in Cornish the verbal particle *y* and the inflected form of the verb. The following are examples:

Yth henwaf bewgh ha tarow 'I shall name cow and bull' CW 403

i rof hewyn than puskas 'I will give names to the fish' CW 409.

The so-called abnormal order also occurs, that is to say the subject + *a* (leniting verbal particle) + lenition + the third singular of the verb:

> *an tas a usias solempnyty bras* 'the Father used great ceremony' TH 1
>
> *an venyn a welas y bos an frut da the thybbry* 'the woman saw that the fruit was good to eat' TH 3a
>
> *in tyrmyn na eff a gemeras bara in y thewla* 'at that moment he took bread in his hands' TH 52
>
> *honna a vythe ow skavall droose* 'that will be my foot-stool' CW 20.

Two things should be noted about the abnormal order. First, comparison with other Celtic languages makes it clear that the verb is really relative and that there is an implied copula ('is, it is') at the head of the clause. When Cornish says *Du an formyas han shappyas* 'God made and shaped him' the underlying syntax is really 'It was God who made and shaped him', even though the initial copula is always suppressed. It is because the abnormal order contains an implied copula and involves a relative clause that it cannot be negative. Normal order must be used. *Me a's gwelas* 'I saw her' but *ny's gwelys* or *ny wrugavy hy gweles* 'I did not see her'.

The second thing to notice about the abnormal order is that in positive sentences it is by far the commonest syntax in Middle Cornish. In the discursive prose of John Tregear the normal order with *y(th)* occurs only with the verb *bos: yth ew, yma, yth esaf*, etc. The normal order does not occur with other verbs.

In UC it has been customary to use *y whraf, y whruk* with normal word-order as everyday auxiliaries. For example in *Kernewek Mar Plek*—an otherwise excellent book—one finds such sentences as:

> *Y whruk vy gweles droklam hedhyu*
> *Y whruk gorror dos adro dhe elyn an forth re scaf*
> *Y whruk vy pellgewsel orth an creslu*
> *Y whruk an gwythyas govyn lyes govyn* (KMP: 18).

These sentences are not ungrammatical but in the light of the syntactic practice of Middle Cornish, they would have been better phrased as follows: *My a wruk gweles droklam…, Nep gorror a wruk dos…, My a wruk pellgewsel…, An gwythyas a wruk govyn…*, etc. In UCR moreover one will say *droglam, a wrug* and *pellgowsel.*

Normal word-order with *y(th)* should be used only with the verb 'to be'. Normal order is correct also in negatives: *nynj eth ef* 'he did not go', *ny welas hy ow hath* 'she did not see my cat'. Normal word-order without preceding particle is also correct with *gallas* 'has gone': *gallas ow mona* 'my money has gone' and optionally with *duefa* 'has come': *Duefa an pres dhe leverel Dew genough* 'The time has come to say goodbye'. One can also say *Re dhuefa an pres* or *An pres re dhuefa.*

21.7 The standard way of forming the present in Unified Cornish is by use of the present-future tense of the verb. Thus *Pyu a gows* is taken to mean 'Who is speaking?' and 'Who speaks?' as well as 'Who will speak?' There is considerable evidence that by the Tudor period the present-future had been largely confined to future sentences. Instead of the present-future a periphrastic tense with *bos* and the verbal noun was used. TH and SA in particular have many examples of this construction, which continued into the seventeenth and eighteenth centuries:

in crist ihesu caradov yth eseff prest ov cresy 'in beloved Christ Jesus I believe always' BM 833-34

nyns esos ow attendya an laha del vya reys 'thou dost not consider how the law had to…' BM 848-49

Ima an profet Dauit in peswar ugans ha nownsag psalme ow exortya oll an bobyll 'The prophet David exhorts all the people in the 99th psalm' TH 1

yma an scriptur ow leverell in ii-de Geneses 'the scripture says in the 2nd chapter of Genesis' TH 2

kepar dell vgy an profett ow prononcia 'as the prophet pronounces' TH 7a

Arluth, esta ge ow jugia mett the veras war onyn an parna 'Lord, dost thou judge me meet to look upon one like those?' TH 7

y thesan ow desyvya agan honyn 'we deceive ourselves' TH 8

Yma tus an parna ow trelya an scriptures thega distruccion aga honyn 'Such people turn the scriptures to their own destruction' TH 18a

ken nyns ugens y ow regardya du nan re usy in dan aga governans 'otherwise they do not regard God nor those who are under their rule' TH 25

fatell essan ny ow deservia le gyvyans theworth du 'that we deserve less forgiveness from God' TH 24a

nena yma crist ow promysya ha ow assurya thyn fatell usy eff worth agan cara ny 'then Christ promises and assures us that he loves us' TH 26

kyn nag esogh why ow consyddra an plag a behosow 'though you do not consider the plague of sins' TH 40a

Ith esaff ow supposya na veva heb cowse bras an ii the suffra in un dith 'I suppose that it was not without much talk of the two's having suffered on the same day' TH 47

ew ascendis then nef ha ynweth ow gwelas pew uge ow despisea ha gwetha y erriow benegas ef 'who is ascended into heaven and also sees who despises and keeps his blessed words' SA 59

an kethsam tra ugy an elath ow gwelas ha ow trembla 'the very same thing that the angels see and tremble' SA 59

rag neg yns abell the welas heb mere a own rag an golowder use ow tos thaworta 'for they cannot see without great fear because of the brilliance that comes from him' SA 59

Indella emay Christ urth agyn maga ny gans e kiyg ha gos 'Thus Christ feeds us with his flesh and blood' SA 59

mas Christ, an mammeth nyy, neg esa ow gwell indella genan. Insted rag henn a boos, ema ef agyn maga gans e kegg e honyn ha eweth insted a thewas, emay urth agan maga gans e woos 'but Christ, our nurse, does not deal thus with us. Therefore instead of food he feeds us with his own flesh and likewise instead of drink he feeds us with his blood' SA 59a

Ima lowarth onyn o bostia 'Many a one boasts' SA 59a

O mirkell ha blonogath da a thew…ugy setha in gwlas neff 'O miracle and goodwill of God… that sits in the kingdom of heaven' SA 60

neg esa ow desuethas theugh elath nanyle arthelath 'he shows you neither angels nor archangels' SA 60

Tee a ill percevia pavaner a sort esta o quelas agen saviour Christ 'Thou canst perceive in what kind of sort thou seest our Saviour Christ' SA 60a

an kigg yma causya an ena the vos junys the dew an neff 'the flesh causes the soul to be joined to the God of heaven' SA 60a

indelma ema ef o tisquethas kepar a rug Judas betraya e arluth Dew 'thus he shows just how Judas betrayed his Lord God' SA 61

Indella emowns y o dishonora Christ 'So they dishonour Christ' SA 61

eth esan ny o recevia dan an lell mystery kigg ay corf benegas 'we receive under the true mystery the flesh of his blessed body' SA 61

rag henna gere Christ ema gwiell an keth sacrament ma 'therefore the word of Christ effects this same sacrament' SA 62

Gosoweth pandr' uge S. Ambrose ow leverall 'Listen to what St Ambrose says' SA 62a

indella eth esta eva e presius gois 'thus thou drinkest his precious blood' SA 63

Neg eran ny ow kemeras henna rag commen bara ha dewas 'We do not take this for common bread and drink' SA 63a

eth esa ve ow menya… 'I mean…' SA 64

Eth esa ve ow covyn (mith ef) pandr' ew an scavall e drys eff 'I ask, he says, what is the foot-stool of his feet' SA 64a

eth esa ow trylya ow honyn then Arluth Christ 'I turn myself to the Lord Christ' SA 64a

Nyng us denvyth ow tybbry an kigg na arrna theffa ha e worthia 'No man eats that flesh until he come and worship him' SA 64a

fatla ew sittis onne Dew war an alter benegas, uge ow kemeras e ker pegh an bobell 'that the lamb of God sits upon the blessed altar, who takes away the sin of the people' SA 65a

ema Christ corporally ow trega innan 'Christ bodily dwells in us' SA 66

yn defyth yn myske bestas yma ef prest ow pewa 'in the desert among animals he lives continually' CW 1481-82

mere yth esaf ow towtya y vedna ʒym ny vyn ef 'I greatly fear that he will not grant me his blessing' CW 1540-41

bewa yth esaf pub eare in tomdar ha yender reaw 'I live all the time in heat and the chill of frost' CW 1667-68

mes pub eare ma ow crya warlerth an oyle a vercy 'but always he cries after the oil of mercy' CW 1795-96

urt an hagar auall iggeva gweel do derevoll warneny 'because of the storms he makes to rise' BF: 9

Theram ry do why an bele ma 'I give you this ball' BF: 12

therama suppoga andelna 'I suppose so' BF: 29

a vedden pedeere dr' erama creege hedna tho bose gweer 'who will think that I believe that to be true' BF: 31

ma eaue gon maga 'he feeds us' BF: 39

E wreeanath ol termen ma seval kreaue 'His truth at all times stands firm' BF: 39

ma an mableean ni e gana terwitheyaw war an zeell 'our clerk sometimes sings it on Sunday' BF: 39

pecare ter erany gava an pehadurrian war agen pedne 'as we forgive the trespassers against us' BF: 41

ha enna ma setha war dorne dyhou an Taz Ulnerth 'and there sits on the right hand of the Father Almighty' BF: 41

Thera ve crege en Speres Zance 'I believe in the Holy Spirit' BF: 41

ha deskeutha trueth da milliow vor'n gi es kara vê ha gwitha gerria vê 'and show mercy to thousands of them that love me and keep my words' BF: 55

Theram credia en Deiu Tâz Olner 'I believe in God the Father Almighty' BF: 56

kenefra geer eze toaze meez meaz a ganaw Deaw 'every word that comes out of the mouth of God' RC 23: 186

An lyzûan bîan gen i'ar nedhez, ez a tivi en an halou ni, ez kreiez plêth Maria 'The small plant with the twisted stem that grows on our hills is called lady's-tresses' AB: 245a

Thera tshi a guelez 'Thou seest' AB: 246b

Patl [sic] *yzhi a kylyui ha trenna!* 'How it thunders and lightens!' AB: 248a

Thera ve cara why en colon 'I love you in my heart' ACB

En metten pan a why sevel, why rez cawse tha guz taz 'In the morning when you rise, you must say to your father' ACB

ema angye suyah hâz go honnen 'they follow their own nature' ACB

rag henna theren ry agan mighterneth gorseans then pow na 'therefore we give our royal thanks to that country' Keigwin

A mean ez a rhyllio 'The stone that rolls' Lhuyd.

It should be noticed further that the Cornish periphrastic presents *Thera vi kouz, thera vi lâol* are used by Lhuyd to translate English 'I say', Latin *inquam* (AB: 71b).

The periphrastic present need not always be used. *Me a greys* means 'I believe' as well as 'I shall believe'. Periphrastic and simple present occur together in *Neb a rella agys clowes why, eff am clow ve, ha neb a rella agys despisia why, yma worth ow despisia ve* 'Whoever hears you, hears me and whoever despises you, despises me' TH 41a. The periphrastic present is not used with *bos* or the other auxiliaries *mynnes* or *gallus*. Nonetheless it seems to me that UCR should use the periphrastic construction for the unmarked present and should reserve the pres.-future for future sense. Thus we should say: *Yth esoma ow queles* 'I see', but *me a wel* 'I shall see'.

A periphrastic imperfect is also found, for example, in *han re esa ow pewa in tyrmyn coth in dan an la* 'and those who in ancient times lived under the law' TH 27 and *an poble erra zetha en tulgo a wellaz gullow braze* 'the people that sat in darkness saw a great light' RC 23: 190.

21.8 We have already noted at 21.6 the use of the preterite of *gul* as an auxiliary for sentences expressing past time. This usage is very common indeed in Tregear:

Rag Du a rug declarya yn kythsame parabill ma 'For God declared in this same parable' TH 40

so an auctorite an egglos a rug amyttya an peswar aweylar only 'so the authority of the church allowed the four evangelists only' TH 37a

Y a rug vrsurpia ha kemeres thetha y an henow an lell egglos 'They usurped and took to themselves the name of the true church' TH 31a

ny a rug disky pe ma an egglos 'we learnt where the church was' TH 32.

It should be noted that *gwrug* as auxiliary is pronounced /grɪg/. On occasion the preterite of *gul* is used as a full verb meaning 'made':

han venyn an tas as grug perfect 'and the woman the Father made perfect' TH 2a

Eff agan grege ny in dede in hevelep thy ymag eff y honyn 'He indeed made us in the image of his own likeness' TH 1a.

In view of *grege* in the above quotation it would seem that the full verb in the preterite is /griːg/ not /grɪg/.

21.9 In Unified Cornish future time is frequently indicated by the pres.-fut. of *gul*: *my a wra scryfa lyther* 'I shall write a letter', *ty a wra redya lyver* 'you will read a book' (CS: 19). Nowhere in Unified Cornish is *mynnes* used as the future auxiliary even though it is very widely used in Cornish of all periods. Note for example:

mos the wolhy ow dule a thesempes my a vyn omma yn dour 'I will go immediately to wash my hands here in the water' RD 2202-04

pur wyr my a vyn mones the geusel sur orth moyses 'truly I will go to speak surely to Moses' OM 1582-83

me a vyn aga sywe 'I will follow them' OM 1630

ny vynna streche pella 'I will not delay further' OM 2166

ny a vyn polge avodya 'we will go away for a while' BM 1338

mannaff gueles agys dour 'I will look at your urine' BM 1440

me a vyn gul drynk dywhy 'I will make a drink for you' BM 1462

me a vyn pesy cumyes rag mones dre 'I will ask permission to go home' BM 1470-71

mar mynnyth oma latha flehys 'if you will kill children here' BM 1592-93

Me a vyn dewose myl 'I will bleed a thousand' BM 1619

My a vyn settya envy intre te ha haes an venyn 'I will set enmity between thee and the woman's offspring' TH 13

sur rag henna theth honora me a vyn uhan drenges 'surely therefore will I honour thee above the Trinity' CW 153-54

me a vyn towlall neb gyn the dulla mar callaf 'I will devise some stratagem to deceive him if I can' CW 441-42

me a vyn mos tha wandra omma yn myske an flowrys 'I will go to wander here among the flowers' CW 538-39

hag a honna pur serten my a vyn gwyll theis pryas 'and of that will I very certainly make thee a wife' CW 386-88.

Notice further that *me a vyn govyn* at TH 36 translates the Latin future *rogabo* 'I shall ask'.

In all the above examples there is still a hint of volition. Yet there are other instances where there is no trace of intention:

> *ny vyn mernans ov gueles* 'death will not see me' BM 3070
> *mar myn ov descans servya* 'if my learning will be adequate' BM 524.

Brown says of *mynnes* as an auxiliary verb that it is 'only applicable to sentient beings or to personalized objects' (GMC1: 209). My last example contradicts that statement.

Lhuyd expressly mentions the use of *mynnes* as a future auxiliary when he says: 'Another auxiliary verb in the Cornish is *Menni* To will; which they use as in the English, before the future tense of the Indicative Mood, and as would in the Optative, &c.' (AB: 246b). Lhuyd cites such forms as *Mi a vedn guelez* 'I will see', *Ti a ven guelez* 'you will see', etc. (ibid., 246c). Compare also John Boson's usage: *boz oun dha ve na vedn an tavaz ma beska bos kavaz arta en uz ni* 'but I fear this language will never be found again in our age' (BF: 46), *en marhaz gwella gy vedn guerha* 'in the market they will sell best' (BF: 44).

In view of the universality of *mynnes* to make the future in Tudor and Late Cornish, I strongly recommend that in UCR this be the main future construction. UCR will say *Me a vyn scryfa lyther avorow* 'I shall write a letter tomorrow', *Ow gwreg a vyn bos plesyes pan wella hy an flowrys* 'My wife will be greatly pleased when she sees the flowers', etc.

21.10 Just as a periphrastic future can be formed with the pres.-fut. of *mynnes*, so can the conditional be made with the conditional or the imperfect subjunctive of the same verb. The texts have many examples:

> *my a vynsa the pysy* 'I should ask you' OM 2140
> *ef a vynse gul deray* 'he would have made a disturbance' OM 2223
> *my a vynse y wythe* 'I would have saved him' PC 3125
> *the pygy certan mensen* 'I would indeed pray thee' RD 444
> *y fense bos dre vestry* 'he would have been [so] by violence' PA 188c
> *the radn an ry-na ef a vynsa disclosya an distructyon* 'to some of those he would have disclosed the destruction' CW 2356-58
> *certen feryov in breten cafus y fensen* 'I would have certain fairs in Brittany' BM 2066-67
> *Rag crist a promysyas fatell vynna eff bos gans y egglos rag neffra* 'For Christ promised that he would be with his church for ever' TH 20
> *ny vynsa Pedyr kemeras* 'Peter would not have accepted' TH 44a
> *e ne vendzha servia... bez a vendzha moz* 'he would not serve... but would go' BF: 17.

21.11 *Gul* 'to do' is used as an auxiliary in Cornish from the earliest Middle Cornish texts onwards. It is particularly common in OM with all tenses:

> *Awos travyth ny wrussen benytha the guhuthas* 'Not for anything would I denounce thee' OM 163-64
>
> *ef a ruk agan dyfen aual na wrellen dybry* 'he forbade us to eat an apple' OM 182-84
>
> *lauar thymmo… an frut ple russys tyrry* 'tell me… where thou didst pluck the fruit' OM 209-10
>
> *a'y frut a wrello dybry y fethe kepar ha dev* 'whoever should eat of its fruit would be like a god' OM 231-32
>
> *a ros thyn defennadow frut na wrellen the thybry* 'gave us prohibition that we should not eat any fruit' OM 238-39
>
> *gans deyl agan cuthe guren* 'with leaves let us hide ourselves' OM 254
>
> *y'th whys lavur the thybry ty a wra bys y'th worfen* 'in the sweat of thy labour thou shalt eat until thine end' OM 273-74
>
> *omma ny wreugh why tryge* 'here you shall not dwell' OM 317
>
> *may whrussons camdremene* 'so that they transgressed' OM 337
>
> *Ellas gueles an termyn ou arluth pan wruk serry* 'Alas, to see the time when I angered my Lord' OM 351-52
>
> *ou ertech gruk the gylly* 'I lost my inheritance' OM 354
>
> *mar quren flogh vyth denythy* 'If we produce any child' OM 390
>
> *daggrow tyn guraf dyvere* 'I shall weep bitter tears' OM 402
>
> *nethe dyllas my a wra* 'I shall spin clothes' OM 416.

Gul can be used as an auxiliary with any tense in UCR.

21.12 *Dos* 'to come' may also be used as an auxiliary verb in Cornish although its use is more restricted. Here are some examples:

> *aspyugh lemmyn bysy mara tue the thylyffre* 'watch intently whether he happen to deliver' PC 2960-61
>
> *mar tufe ha datherghy* 'if he happen to rise' RD 7
>
> *may teffans y haga thowllell in mes* 'so that they should throw them out' TH 35a
>
> *mar teva ha folya henna* 'if he follow that' TH 20
>
> *I wysce ath face te a thebbyr the vara, bys may tyffy arta ha trelya the thore ha pry* 'In the sweat of thy face thou shalt eat thy bread till thou come and turn again to earth and clay' TH 6
>
> *mar ten ny ha gurtas in Catholik egglos* 'if we happen to stay in the Catholic Church' TH 39a
>
> *mar te an bys ha durya mar bell* 'if the world happen to last as long' TH 50a
>
> *neb a theffa dibbry ow kig ha eva ow dewas, ema ef ow trega inneff ve* 'whoever eats my flesh and drinks my drink, he dwells in me' SA 61
>
> *An bara a theffan ry, ew ow kigg ve* 'The bread I give, is my flesh' SA 66
>
> *dew a ornas contrary na thesan* [leg. *thefan*] *tastya henna* 'God decreed on the contrary that we should not taste that' CW 630-31
>
> *me a vidn ye requyrya a thewla an kethe dean-na y woose a theffa scullya* 'I will require it from the hands of that same man who sheds his blood' CW 2520-22.

Note that *dos* is sometimes followed by *ha* + the verbal noun and on occasion by the verbal noun without *ha*.

Dos as an auxiliary occurs in the story JCH. At § 32 Lhuyd's text reads: *mar nyz medra dheffa previ peu a 'ryg an bad-ober, mî a vedn kreg ragta*. Lhuyd clearly did not understand what lay behind *nyz medra dheffa* and it would appear that he emended to obtain the word *medra*. This he thought was the same as Welsh *medra(f)* 'I can'. The Cornish verb, however, means 'aim, notice' not 'be able to'. If we transpose the *me* of *medra* and the *z* of *nyz* and divide the words differently, we get: *mar nymez 'dra dheffa previ peu a ryg an bad-ober, mî a vedn kreg ragta*. In UCR spelling this would read: *mar ny'm bes 'dra 'dheffa prevy pyw 'wrug an bad-ober, me a ven cregy ragtho* 'If I have not got the thing that would prove who did the crime, I'll hang for it'. Jowan is talking about the *pîs pyr-round* 'the circular piece' that he secretly cut from the monk's habit. If this interpretation of the text is correct and it does make perfect sense, it would not only give us a further example of *dos* as an auxiliary, it would also provide an instance of *y'm bues* in Late Cornish.

As is clear from some of the examples given above, *dos* as an auxiliary is often used in conditional sentences. Here are some further examples of conditional sentences that use *dos*:

> *mar teffa tus ha gweӡe bos ӡe ӡu ӡe wull gynsy* 'should people come to restrain you [say] that God has need of her' PA 27
> *Cryst kymmys payn yn geve…ma teth an goys ha dropye war y fas* 'Christ had such pain…that the blood actually dripped on his face' PA 59ab
> *myrugh mar te drehevell* 'see whether he happen to rise' PA 203
> *mar tewgh why ha cara an re vsy…* 'if you love those who…' TH 22
> *Mar teneny* [read *tuen-ny*] *comparia an gyrryow… ny res thynny dowtya…*'If we compare the words… we need not fear' TH 52
> *ha mar ten ny y folya ha sewya, ny ren fyllall the vnderstondaya an scriptur* 'and if we follow and obey him, we will not fail to understand the scripture' TH 17a

21.13 This is a suitable place to discuss unreal conditions in general. In Unified Cornish unreal conditions are expressed as follows: the *if*-clause (protasis) takes the imperfect subjunctive and the other clause (apodosis) takes the conditional, for example, *hedhyu a trykes yn tre, dheragos ty a-n-gwelsa* 'to-day hadst thou stayed at home, thou shouldst have seen him before thee'. In that example *a trykes* is the past subjunctive of *tryga* and *gwelsa* the conditional of *gweles*. This example was taken word for word from *Cornish Simplified* (CS: 54). If this is Cornish simplified, one dreads to contemplate Cornish unsimplified. Is it any wonder that Unified Cornish has remained unspoken for so long?

The doctrine in Unified Cornish is certainly based on authentic Middle Cornish syntax.[32] Colloquial Cornish clearly found such constructions too

---

[32] The example above given by Caradar is a respelling of *hythew a tryckes yn tre thyragos ty a'n guelse* at RD 1381–82.

difficult for everyday use and preferred to use auxiliary verbs. The most frequent auxiliary in the clause without *if* (apodosis) is *mynnes* (see above) though *gul* is also used. Often *dos* 'to come' is the verb employed in the *if*-clause, a point well described by Gendall (SGMC: 82). Look at the following examples:

> *mar teffa du aga suffra the vsya aga naturall powers y a vynsa optaynya salvacion in ta lovr heb gweras vith arell in party du* 'had God suffered them to use their natural powers, they would have wanted to obtain salvation easily enough without any other help on the part of God' TH 13a

> *Mar teffa den vith ha pregoth thyn kythsame barbarus nacions ma in aga eyth y aga honyn… y a vynsa stoppya aga scovurnow* 'If anyone were to preach to these same barbarous nations in their own language… they would stop up their ears' TH 19

> *Rag mar teffa crist ha dos in dalleth an bys… tus a russa supposia…* 'For if Christ had come in the beginning of the world… people would have supposed…' TH 13a

> *ny vynsan cresy an aweyll, na ve an Catholyk egglos the ry thym experiens* 'I would not believe the gospel, were the Catholic Church not there to give me experience' TH 37a

> *mar teffa an epscobow ha'n brontyryan in tyrmyn passis… dysky ha practysya aga duty… surly ny russa an egglos a crist dos then dishonor han disordyr a wylsyn ny* 'if the bishops and the priests in time past… had learnt and practised their duty…surely the church of Christ would not have come to the dishonour and chaos that we have seen' TH 39

> *mar teffa an holl brodereth obeya…ny vynsa den vith styrrya na gwaya warbyn an colleges* 'if all the brothers had obeyed…no one would have agitated or moved against the colleges' TH 42a

> *An kyth office ma ny vynsa pedyr kemeras na ve crist the ry thotha an auctorite* 'This same office Peter would not have accepted had Christ not given him the authority' TH 44a

> *mar pe an holl fraternity…obedient, ny vynsa den vyth gwaya na styrrya warbyn an bredereth a crist* 'had the entire fraternity been obedient, no one would have agitated or moved against the brethren of Christ' TH 48a

> *Mar kressa an dean deskez feer na gwellaz hemma [eve] a venya kavaz fraga e ouna en skreefa composter* 'If that learned and wise man were to see this, he would have reason to correct its orthography' BF: 27.

In view of the prevalence of *dos, mynnes* and *gul* as auxiliaries in Tudor and later Cornish, I would recommend most strongly that students be taught to express unreal conditions, both (A) positive and (B) negative, as follows:

> A1 PROTASIS: *mar* + imperfect subjunctive of *dos* (+ *ha*) + verbal noun + APODOSIS: conditional of *mynnes* + verbal noun

> A2 PROTASIS: *mar* + conditional of *gul* + verbal noun + APODOSIS: conditional of *mynnes* + verbal noun.

B1 PROTASIS: *na* + (past) subjunctive of *bos* + APODOSIS: conditional of *mynnes* + verbal noun

B2 PROTASIS: *mar ny* + Auxiliary (as in A) + APODOSIS (as in A).

This would give us in UCR sentences like the following:

Mar teffa Kernowek ha bewa, ny vynsen-ny cafus caletter gans an leveryans 'If Cornish had survived, we wouldn't have difficulty with the pronunciation'

Mar teffen ha redya an lyver-na, ny vynsen understondya tra vyth anodho ef 'If I were to read that book, I wouldn't understand any of it'

Me a vynsa ry gweres dhothans, na venjy mar dygortes 'I would give them help, if they weren't so rude'

Mar qurusseugh why gweles an den-na, a vynseugh why y aswon? 'If you saw that man, would you recognize him?'

Na ve Jowan, an vowes a vynsa bos budhys 'Had it not been for John, the girl would have been drowned'

Mar ny wrusseugh why leverel henna, ny vynsa agas dyscajor bos mar serrys 'If you had not said that, your teacher would not have been so annoyed'

Na vesta why dhe ry an mona dhedhy, me a wrussa y leverel dhe'th das 'Were you not to give her the money, I should tell your father'.

21.14 The verb *gallaf* 'I can' is by its very nature a modal auxiliary. In Cornish, however, its use is sometimes extended to introduce final clauses. Thus the present or imperfect subjunctive of *gallos* is used after *rag may* 'so that' to express the meaning 'in order that':

3eworte un lam beghan y 3eth pesy may halle 'he went a little way from them in order to pray' PA 53cd

yndella ef a vynne may halle dre baynys bras merwel rag 3e gerense 'thus he wished so that he might die for love of thee' PA 70cd

3e scole lemmyn y worra me a vyn… dysky dader may halla 'I will now send him to school… in order to learn goodness' BM 11-13

an corf ema tibbry rag malla [may halla] an enef bos megys 'the body eats that the soul may be nourished' SA 61

an parna a vo myt rag mabden the wothfas rag may hallans dretha attaynya an bewnans heb deweth 'such as may be meet for mankind to know in order that they may through them attain eternal life' TH 17

Me a vyn govyn worth ow thas, hag eff a re thewhy conforter erell, may halla eff gortas genowhy rag neffra 'I shall ask my father and he will give you another comforter so that he may remain with you always' TH 36.

This last example is a translation of the Latin sentence: *Ego rogabo patrem et alium paraclitum dabit vobis ut maneat vobiscum in eternum* 'I will ask my father and he will give you another comforter that he may remain with you for ever.' The expression *may halla* occurs in Late Cornish also: *dro geere tha vee arta, m'ala ve moaze ha gortha thotha aweeth* 'bring word to me again so that I can go to worship him also' (RC 23: 196) and *Gura worry de taz ha de vam mol* (< *ma halla*)

de dethyo boz pel 'Honour thy father and thy mother that thy days may be long'
BF: 42

There is also an instance of the phrase *may halla* 'in order that' in the story JCH, though it is clear that Lhuyd did not understand it. At JCH § 39 the text reads: *ev a dhelledzhaz an termen mal dha va prev erra e wreg guitha kympez et i gever*. The crux is in *mal dha va* which is Lhuyd's attempt to make sense of the passage. He presumably understood *mal dha va* as **mal dho va* 'desire to him', i.e. 'he wanted'. If so, we should probably emend *mal dhava* to *mallava < may hallava* 'that he might' and assume that *prev* is a verbal noun. It is either Lhuyd's emendation for **previ* 'prove' or it is a variant **prev*, cf. *kreg* 'to hang' at § 32. The text then reads: *ev a dhelledzhaz an termen mallava prev erra e wreg guitha kympez et i gever* 'he span out the time in order to prove whether his wife was staying faithful to him'.

21.15 In Unified Cornish the usual way of making the first person plural imperative is by use of a special form, as for example *gwelyn* 'let us see', *bedhen* 'let us be', *gwren* 'let us do' (CS: 33). From the Middle Cornish period onward, however, it is common also to use a periphrastic construction with the verb *gasa* 'leave, let'. Note the following examples:

> *gesough ov thus us gene the ves quyt the tremena* 'let my people who are with me
>   depart away PC 1122-23
> *geseugh y the thysplevyas* 'let them spread out' PC 2832
> *gas ny tha vos alemma* 'let us go hence' CW 1333
> *gas an haneth ma a virnans the vos the wortha ve* 'let this cup of death pass from me'
>   TH 22a
> *Gesyn ny the consyddra an circumstans an dra* 'Let us consider the circumstances of
>   the matter' TH 4
> *Gesow ny the wull den* 'Let us make man' TH 1a
> *gesow ny the venegas agan honyn the thu* 'let us confess ourselves to God' TH 9
> *gesow ny the repentya* 'let us repent' TH 9
> *gesow ny oll the confessia* 'let us all confess' TH 9a
> *gesow ny the aswon agan oberow agan honyn* 'let us acknowledge our own deeds'
>   TH 9a
> *gesow ny oll the leverall* 'Let us all say' TH 9a
> *gas an mynd confessia da achy* 'let the mind confess well inside' SA 61a
> *gas an golan percyvia da* 'let the heart perceive well' SA 61a
> *gesen confirmia henna* 'let us confirm that' SA 62
> *gero ni guil dean en avain ni* 'let us make man in our own image' BF: 52.

Gasa is also used with the first person singular:

> *gas vy the thehesy* 'let me strike!' OM 2703
> *gesough vy the wortheby* 'let me answer' PC 2493
> *gesough vy th'y handle* 'let me touch him' PC 3165
> *gays thym the ombrene* 'let me redeem myself' BM 1252

THE SYNTAX OF UCR

gas ve the wellas 'let me see' CW 741
gas vy the dava 'let me feel him' CW 1591.

Such constructions should certainly be allowed in UCR.

21.16 In Unified Cornish indirect statement, when the verb is positive, can be expressed with the verbal noun. This is either governed by a noun or possessive adjective or preceded by the subject + *the* 'to'. One can say, for example, *my a wor agas jarden bos tek* 'I know your garden is beautiful' or *ef a breder ow bos y'n chy* 'he believes that I am in the house' or *my a lever ty dhe gows yndella* 'I will say that you spoke thus'. These constructions are all based upon the Middle Cornish texts. Here are some examples with the verbal noun A) + noun/possessive adjective; B) + noun/pronoun + the preposition *the* 'to':

A
y a leuer ol ynweth y vos daserghys a'n beth 'they will all say also that he has risen from the grave' RD 357-58
ty a yl y atendye bos guyr ow cous 'thou canst rely upon it that my speech is true' RD 477-78
a'n beth the vos datherghys y luen crygy me a wra 'I will fully believe it, that thou art risen from the tomb' RD 481-82
na greseugh bos treyson gures 'do not believe that treason has been done' RD 640
na gresough a luen golon bos an tas dev hep parow 'that you do not believe with full heart that the Father is a peerless God' OM 1857-58.

B
y grassaf lemmyn an cas ty the vynnes thy'm danfon thu'm confortye 'I am now grateful for the case that thou shouldst wish to send to me to comfort me' RD 508-10
saw pyw a vyn leuerel the vewnans ef the seuel 'but who will say that he has risen to life?' RD 589-90
ha lauar my th'y warnye 'and say that I am warning him' OM 1423.

Both A and B are to be seen in the following:

ef the seuel a'n beth men ha'y vos datherys certen y gous ny dal thynny ny 'certainly it behoves us not to declare that he has risen from the tomb and that he is arisen' RD 566-68.

In TH and CW the construction with the verbal noun is taken a little further. In CW, for example, the verbal noun after the possessive adjective is itself marked for person by the addition of an enclitic pronoun:

cresowh ow bosaf prince creif 'believe that I am a strong prince' CW 116
why a wore ynta henna ow bosaf gwell es an tase 'you know that full well, that I am better than the Father' CW 122-23

splanna es an howle deverye why a yll warbarthe gwelas ow bosaf sertayn pub preyse
'You can all together see that I am certainly more resplendent than the sun ever' CW 131-33.

In TH the possessive adjective before the verbal noun is fossilized as *y* which causes no mutation. Instead of pronouns/possessive adjectives the various persons are indicated where necessary by suffixes attached to the verbal noun. Note the following examples:

In nena an venyn a welas y bos an frut da the thybbry 'Then the woman saw that the fruit was good to eat' TH 3a

Ith ew the vos cresys gans oll cristonnyan heb dowt vith y bos in sacrament an aulter an very corfe ha gois a crist 'It is to be believed by all Christians that without any doubt the very body and blood of Christ are in the sacrament of the altar' TH 54

yma ow settya in mes very notably an primasie... y bosans an successors, hennew an sewysy, a pedyr 'he sets out very notably the primacy... that they are the successors, that is the followers, of Peter' TH 49

whath dre reson y bosa gwrys dre an blonogeth a thu 'further since it was created through the will of God' TH 50a

A te dore, remember y bosta, dore, dore 'Thou earth, remember that thou art, earth, earth' TH 7a.

It is doubtful whether either the syntax of CW (*ow bosaf*) or of TH (*y bosta*) should be introduced into the revived language.

21.17 There does, however, exist a much easier way of introducing indirect statement and one which is as old as the Middle Cornish texts themselves. It is particularly frequent in Tudor Cornish. The construction involves using the words *del* 'as' and *fatel, fatla* 'how' in the same way that English uses 'that'. Here are some examples with *del*:

yn ur na y fyth clewys del ony ganse brewys hag elf at es 'in that hour it will be heard that we are wounded by them and ill at ease' RD 572-74

par del won lauaraff 3ys yntre du ha pehadur acordh del ve kemerys 'as best I can I will tell thee that a covenant was made between God and the sinner' PA 8ab

te a leuerys del yw 'thou saidst that it is' PA 129d

un venyn da a welas dell o Jhesus dystryppijs 'a good woman saw that Jesus had been stripped' PA 177a

lemmyn ny a yll gwelas lauar du maga del wra neb a vynno y glewas 'now we can see that the word of God nurtures all who will hear it' PA 12cd

Yma an profet dauid ow allegia helma kepar dell ewa sufficient cawse agan redempcion 'The prophet David alleges this that it is sufficient cause of our salvation' TH 1.

Examples with *fatel* are more numerous. We may see the beginnings of the usage in such sentences as the following:

fatel fue cryst mertheryys rak kerenge tus a'n beys why a welas yn tyen 'you have seen completely how / that Christ was martyred for the people of the world' PC 3220-22

the welas fetel sevys cryst mes a'n beth 'to see how / that Christ rose from the tomb' PC 3241-42

ty a wor yn pup maner fatel fue ow map lethys 'thou knowest in every way how / that my son was slain' RD 427-28.

The fully developed construction with *fatel* is to be seen in these examples:

ny a fyn leuerel ol yn pow sur the pub den ol fatel wrussyn ny keusel orth an arluth ker 'we will tell everybody in all the country that we spoke to the dear lord' RD 1339-42

Arluth me ages guarnyas fetel ese turant brays er agis pyn drehevys 'Lord, I warned you that a great tyrant had risen against you' BM 3444-46

yma ree ov leferel... delyfrys der varia fetel ywa dyogel 'some are saying that he was certainly delivered by Mary' BM 3739-41

Gothvethow fatell ew du agan arluth ny 'Understand that God is our lord' TH 1

pendra alsan ny predery fatell ylly du gull moy ragan in agen creacion dell ruga gull 'how could we think that God could have done more for us in our creation than he did?' TH 2a

Du a commondyas an profet Ysay the wull proclamacion the oll an bys fatell ew mabden gwels ha fatell ew oll an glory an broghter han lowender a vabden kepar ha flowres in prasow 'God commanded the prophet Isaiah to proclaim to all the world that man is grass and all the glory, splendour and joy of man is like the flowers of the fields' TH 6a-7

Rag an understonding a henna why a ra perfectly done in agys remembrans fatell ve an holl nature a then kyffrys in corffe hag in ena defoylys ha kyllys dre originall pegh 'For the understanding of that you will perfectly bear in remembrance that the entire nature of man both in body and soul was defiled and lost through original sin' TH 12

may hillyn gwelas ha percevya fatell esa the crist mer a garensa worthan 'that we may see and perceive that Christ had great love for us' TH 15a

Rag henna gesen confirmia hemma: fatla ew an bara corf Christ dir consecration an girreow 'Therefore let us confirm this: that the bread is the body of Christ through the consecration of the words' SA 62

Ima lowarth onyn o bostia fatla vgy faith an tasow coth a vam egglys in an sy 'Many a one boasts that the faith of the ancient fathers of mother church is in them' SA 59a.

Not surprisingly this construction continued into Late Cornish, where the conjunction varies in form: *fatal, tr, tel, ter* (all < *fatel*); *dr* (< *del*). The forms *tr* and *dr* are normally attached to the following verb.

Pe reg e gwellaz fatal o geaze gwreaze anotha gen an teeze feere 'When he saw he was
   mocked by the wise men' RC 23: 199
ha an gie oyah tel er an gye en hoath 'and they knew that they were naked' RC 23:
   177
pu reg laule theese tell estah en hoath? 'who told thee thou wast naked? RC 23: 179
Leben pe reg Jesus clowaz 'ter o Jowan towlaz tha bressen 'Now when Jesus heard
   that John was thrown into prison RC 23: 189
*Pe reege an vennen gwellas tro an an wethan da rag booze ha der o hi bleck tha'n
   lagagow* 'When the woman saw that the tree was good for food and that it
   was pleasing to the eyes' RC 23: 176
ha Deu gwellas tro vo da 'and God saw that it was good' BF: 52.
eue levarraz droua Gever ul 'he said it was Goat-All' BF: 25
buz Me a aore hemma... druava talvez buz nebbaz 'but I know this... that it is
   accounted but little' BF: 31
drolga tavas an Brittez cooth tose 'that the language of the ancient Britons could
   come' BF: 31.

Jenner was aware of the indirect statement with *fatel, del,* although he believed
that the conjunction was *tre, tro* or *dro* (HCL: 162, 164). Nance also knew of the
construction and he realized that *fatel* was the chief origin of the conjunction.
In JCH § 28 Lhuyd's text reads: *hei a dhalasvaz dhe 'wîl krei ter dha a thermaz hei
deztrîez.* Nance in his Unified versions renders this: *hy a dhallethas dhe wul cry
fatel o hy dremas-hy dystrewys* (Nance 1949: 43). Here the *ter* of the original has
been rendered by Nance as *fatel.* A second instance of *ter* introducing indirect
speech occurs at JCH § 40: *Bez e brederaz ter gotha dhodho boz aviziyz diueth ken
guesgal enueth* 'But he considered that he should be advised twice before
striking once'. In his normalized text Nance renders this: *Mes ef a brederys fatel
gotho dhodho bos avyses dywwyth ken gweskel unwyth* (Nance 1949: 45), where *ter*
is again rendered by *fatel.*

There is another instance of *ter < tel* in JCH, however, that has gone
unnoticed. At § 31 Lhuyd's text reads: *Huei òl? mer a huei an Iustîziou (a medh
Dzhuan) gyr tero an dhis rag riman a 'ryg an bad-ober?* Lhuyd did not understand
this and his text and word-division are faulty. I would emend *riman* to *haman*
and redivide the words to give: *Huei òl? mera-huei, anjustîz iou (a medh Dzhuan);
gyr ter o an dhis-rag ha mana 'ryg an bad-ober* [*Why oll? Merough-why, anjustys yw
(y' meth Jowan). Godhyr 'ter o an dhewas-wreg ha managh 'wrug an bad-ober*] 'You
all? Look now, it's an injustice (said Jowan). Be it known that it was the ale-
wife and a monk who committed the crime'. *Gyr = godhyr* is a fossilized
passive imperative of *godhvos* 'to know' with the sense 'be it known, I'll have
you know'.[33] Jowan's listeners are amazed at his accusation and their response,
naturally enough, is *Piua... pîu a 'ryg an bad-ober?* 'Who? Who did the crime?'

In view of the ease with which the construction with *fatel, 'tel, del, der, dr,*
can be used and in view of its frequency in Tudor and Late Cornish, I would

---

33 The form *gyr* may simply be the 2nd singular imperative *gor* 'know!' formed on the
   basis of *gor* 'he knows'.

strongly recommend that it be adopted as soon as possible into UCR as well. In UCR, then, we would get sentences like these:

Me a wor fatel dhethons a-dhewedhes 'I know they arrived late'
Hy a ujas fatel wrug nebonen ladra hy fors 'She screamed that someone had stolen her purse'
Ny wrussons convedhes fatel vedha res dhe janjya pub tra 'They did not understand that everything would have to be changed'
Ef a leverys del ova medhek 'He said he was a doctor'.

Since *fatel* is stressed on the second syllable (13.37), it can be reduced to *'tel* in speech. Similarly *del* could be reduced to *dl > dr* before stressed vowels.

21.18 In Middle Cornish a verb is rendered reflexive by the use of the leniting prefix *em-, ym-* or *om-*:

ragon ny wor omweʒe 'he cannot protect himself from us' PA 194c
mar ny wreth ymamendye 'if you do not improve yourself' OM 1527
yth emwyskys yn golon 'he stabbed himself in the heart' RD 2067
omgolhough in age goys 'wash yourself in their blood' BM 1642
omconfortya may hylly 'so that you can comfort yourself' BM 3080.

In Tudor and Late Cornish this syntax yields to a construction with the possessive adjective + *honen, honyn* 'self' after the verb:

yth esan ow desyvya agan honyn 'we deceive ourselves' TH 8
ha joynyas y honyn then dusys 'and joined himself to the godhead' TH 12a
mar lyas del ra devydya aga honyn theworth an kysam egglos ma 'as many as divide themselves from this same church' TH 17a
Hag indelma eff a vsyas y honyn 'And thus he conducted himself' TH 22a
eth esa ow trylya ow honyn then Arluth Christ 'I turn myself to the Lord Christ' SA 64a
towle tha honnen doore 'throw yourself down!' RC 23: 187
dre vengama gweel a hunnen tho bose devethez drez maur 'that I would make myself to be come over the sea' BF: 31.

This syntax can be imitated in UCR.

CHAPTER 22
The lexicon of UCR

22.1 It was suggested above (15.5) that Nance had a predilection for the quaint over the modern. Nowhere was this so apparent as in the vocabulary of Unified Cornish. Nance, perhaps unconsciously, suppressed various words in Middle Cornish and replaced them with items that were poorly attested in the language or not at all. In the following sections I should like to look in some detail at a few of Nance's words and the commoner words that should perhaps now take their place.

22.2 The UC word for 'river' is *avon*. *Auon* 'flumen' [river] occurs in OCV and this entry was probably the origin of Lhuyd's *auan bras* 'flumen, a river' (AB: 60b). Note also Lhuyd's *auan 'rivus*, a river, a brook' (AB: 141b). *Auon* is the Common Celtic word for 'river' seen also in Welsh *afon*, Breton *aven*, Irish *abhainn*, etc.

Avon 'river' is attested nowhere in the Middle Cornish texts. Padel suggests that Lhuyd's *torneuan an auan* 'ripa, a bank of a river' (AB: 141a) may be genuine. It is more likely to be Lhuyd's own coinage. Padel says of *avon*: 'The word is virtually unknown in Cornish place-names, as well as in the language' (CPNE: 14). The plural *avenow* in UC is completely hypothetical. The only toponym that can be shown to contain *avon* is *Awen Tregare* for *Tregear Water* (ibid.). It is to be noticed also that both this toponym and Lhuyd's form show /w/ and not /v/ as the medial consonant. *Avon* in UC should therefore be *awon*.

Commoner words for 'river, stream' in Cornish are *gover* 'stream' and *dowr* 'water'. OM refers to the biblical brook Kidron three times and on each occasion it is known as *dour cedron* OM 2804, 2811, 2815. Compare also

> *yn dour tyber ef a fue yn geler horn gorrys doun* 'into the River Tiber he was put deep in the iron coffin' RD 2319-20.

and the toponym *Dour Conor c.* 1540 = the Connor River (CPNE: 262). *Gover* occurs in the expression *erbys an goverow* 'herbs of the streams' BM 1971 and in *kepar dell ra lyas govar resak thea un kenegan* 'as many streams flow from one boggy place' TH 8a. The expression *stremys bras* 'great streams' occurs at OM 1083.

There are two further references to 'river(s)' in Middle Cornish literature and in both instances the word is the English borrowing:

> *hag orth an ryuer surly a josselyne* 'and surely upon the river of Josseline' BM 1141-42
> *ryvars a thowre a ra resek in mes anetha y* 'rivers of water will run out of them' TH 53

It seems, then, that the normal word for 'river' in Middle Cornish was either *dowr* or *ryver*, (pl.) *ryvers*.

22.3 The word *arhans, arghans* is well attested in Cornish at all periods. The first reference is in OCV where *gueidvur arghans* means 'silversmith'. Other instances include the following:

fenten bryght avel arhans 'a spring as bright as silver' OM 771

my a vyn bos garlont gureys a arhans adro thethe 'I will that a garland of silver be made around it' OM 2096-97

a arans pur ha fyn 'of silver pure and fine' OM 2100

saw un pren gans garlontow a arhans adro thotho 'but one tree with garlands of silver about it' OM 2499-500

en arhans me a gymer hagh a's guyth kettep dyner 'the silver [i.e. the 30 pieces given to Judas Iscariot] I will take and keep every penny of it' PC 1537-38

awos cost arhans nag our greugh y tenne mes a'n dour 'for the cost of silver or gold drag him out of the water' RD 2231-32

owr hag arghans gwels ha gweth 'gold and silver, grass and trees' PA 16b

Henna Iudas pan welas crist an bewnans na sawye, an arghans a gemeras rag corf crist ʒe rysseve 'When Judas saw that Christ would not save his own life, he took silver for handing over Christ's body' PA 103ab

An pelle Arrance ma ve resse 'This silver ball was given' BF: 38

lavar war Cota Dean brauze en Arganz 'a motto on a great man's coat of arms in silver' BF: 27

forh arhans 'a fork of silver' AB: 242a

Kymero 'wyth goz lavrak pouz, goz argan, ha guz aur 'Take care of your heavy trousers, your silver and your gold' BF: 58.

Also relevant are the toponyms *Wheal Arrans* 'silver mine' and *Venton Ariance* 'bright spring' (CPNE: 11). First, one should note that in Middle Cornish the commonest spelling for the word is <arhans> not <arghans>. The second point to notice is that the word usually means 'silver' and not 'money', though the case of the thirty pieces of silver given to Judas is ambiguous. The usual Middle Cornish word for 'money' is *mona*:

ow box mennaf the terry a dal mur a vone da 'I will break my box that is worth much good money' PC 485-86

dek warn ugens a mone 'thirty [coins] of money' PC 593

xxx a vone 'thirty [coins] of money' PA 39d

an guella us dascor myns mone yu pys 'the best thing is to hand over all the money that has been paid' PC 1507-08

otte an mone parys 'behold the money ready here' PC 1556

Iudas fals a leuerys: trehans dyner a vone 'False Judas said: "300 pence of money!"' PA 35a

ha me a vyn then benenes ry mona 'and I will give money to the women' BM 1671-72

due yv an mona rum fay 'the money is all gone, by my faith' BM 1873

yma mona gans henna 'that one has money' BM 1904
dascor ol the vona 'hand over all your money' BM 1917
I costyans showre a vona 'They cost a lot of money' CW 2445
Ha an mona an dzhei a gavaz 'And the money they found' JCH § 46
Dry dre an mona ha perna muy 'Bring home the money and buy more' ACB: Efe
ha Mona lour ganz goz Gureg 'and enough money with your wife' BF: 45.

Lhuyd gives *Pecunia* [money] *monnah* AB: 115c.

Perhaps, then, *mona* should replace *arhans* as the word for 'money' in revived Cornish.

22.4 The standard word in Unified Cornish for 'flower' is either *blejen*, (pl.) *blejennow*, or *blejyowen*, (pl.) *blejyow*. Compare, for example, the title of Mary Mills's satire on tourism in Cornwall, *Kernow a'gas Dynergh gans Blejyow Tek* 'Cornwall greets you with beautiful flowers' (Mills 1980). In fact neither *blejen* nor the singular *blejyowen* is attested in Middle Cornish. *Blejen* is based on Lhuyd's *bledzhan* 'flos' [flower] (AB: 60b). Lhuyd implies (AB: 223) that *bledzhan* 'flower' was the current form and that *blesen* was the Middle Cornish variant. Since *blesen* is unattested, Lhuyd's *bledzhan* may well not be authentic. It is even possible that *bledzhan* itself is Lhuyd's modernization of *blodon* 'flos' in OCV. It is perhaps more likely that *bledzhan* survived in Late Cornish in plant-names but was no longer used as an unbound form. The form *blejyowen* is based on the collective plural *blegyow* which occurs in the phrase *Dewsull blegyow* 'Palm Sunday' at PA 27a.

In the Middle Cornish texts themselves the only word for 'flower' is *flowr*, *flowren*, (pl.) *flowrys*. I have collected the following examples:

ny dyf guels na flour yn bys yn keth forth na 'no grass nor flower at all grows in that same way' OM 712-13

a frut da ha floures tek 'of goodly fruit and fair flower' OM 769

Yma gynef flowrys tek 'I have fair flowers' PC 258

ow tos yn onor thymmo gans branchis flourys kefrys 'coming to honour me with branches and also flowers' PC 266-67

palm ha floris kekeffris er y byn degis a ve 'palm and flowers also were brought to meet him' PA 29d

ha doen dellyow teke ha da ha flowres wheag in serten 'and bring forth leaves fair and good and sweet flowers indeed' CW 94-5

lower flowrys a bub ehan yn place ma yta [sic] *tevys* 'behold growing in this place many flowers of every kind' CW 363-64

me a vyn mos the wandra omma yn myske an flowrys 'I shall go to wander here among the flowers' CW 538-39

ena yth esa flowrys 'there were flowers there' CW 1050

eff a deffe in ban kepar ha flowren 'he grows up like a flower' TH 7

an flowre a glomder 'the flower withers' TH 7

an flowre a ra clamdera 'the flower withers' TH 7

kepar ha flowres in prasow 'like flowers in the meadows' TH 7.

In view of these examples I strongly recommend that in revived Cornish the word 'flower' be translated as *flowr* /fluːr/, *flowren* /ˈfluːrən/, (pl.) *flowrys* /ˈfluːrəz/.

22.5 Nance 1952 cites three words for 'animal': *myl, mylas; eneval, enevales; lon, lonnow* or *lothnow*. *Mil* 'animal' occurs in OCV and may also be what is meant in two places in the *Ordinalia* with the expression *myl dyawl* 'devilish beast':

> *Mar ny'n gorraf an myl dyaul* 'If I take him not, the devilish beast' PC 1618
> *re thueth the vyl deaul* 'hath come to the devilish beast' RD 2505-06.

In neither quotation is it certain that *myl* 'animal' is intended. *Myl* also occurs as an element of the word *mylgy* 'hunting dog'; see, for example, *mylguen* 'hunting dogs' BM 3166. *Mil* from OCV is also used by John Boson in his version of Genesis i:

> *Ha do ol mil en aor, ha do kanifer hethen en ebron* 'And to all the beasts of the earth and to all the birds of the air' BF: 53.

Boson has almost certainly got *mil* from Lhuyd. Lhuyd cites *mîl* and *gurthvil* under *Bêstia* 'beast' (AB: 44c) with an obelus in front of them to indicate that they are archaisms. *Eneval* is attested in the *Ordinalia*:

> *pragh yth hembrenkygh ov enevalles the ves* 'why do you lead away my animals?' PC 204-05.

Lon occurs in OM and CW:

> *ha thotho agan lothnow warnethy sacryfye* 'and sacrifice on it our bullocks to him' OM 1175-76
> *na a veast na lodn in beyse* 'or of beast or animal in the world' CW 1471-72
> *me a weall un lodn pur vras* 'I see a very great animal' CW 1546.

Lhuyd cites *lodn* under Latin *juvencus* 'a steer' (AB: 74c).

By far the commonest word for 'animal' in Middle Cornish is *best*, (pl.) *bestas*. Apart from the first quotation above from CW, I have noted the following instances:

> *me a vyn may fo formyys dre ov nel bestes puskes hag ethyn* 'I wish that through my power be created animals, fish and birds' OM 41-3
> *bestes puskes golowys* 'animals, fishes, lights in the sky' OM 52
> *otte an puskes ythyn a'n nef ha'n bestes* 'behold the fish, the birds of the heaven and the animals' OM 117-18
> *margh yw best hep parow* 'a horse which is beast without equal' OM 124
> *best uthek hep falladow* 'a monstrous beast without fail' OM 798

a bub eghen best yn wlas gor genes dew annethe 'of every kind of animal in the country take with you two of them' OM 977-78

rag den ha best magata 'for man and beast as well' OM 995

a pup best kemmyr whare gorow ha benow 'take immediately of every animal male and female' OM 1021-22

ha pup best warbarth buthys 'and every animal drowned together' OM 1044

kefrys bestes hag ethyn 'also animals and birds' OM 1051

the'n bestes us omma 'to the animals that are here' OM 1059

ethyn bestes ha prevyon 'birds, animals and reptiles' OM 1160

bestes ynweth magata 'and animals also as well' OM 1182

war ethyn bestes pop prys 'upon birds, beast always' OM 1213

kynyver best us yn tyr 'as many animals as are in the land' OM 1215

mur a tus dyswreys ha bestes certan y'th wlas 'many people destroyed and animals in thy country' OM 1560-61

may hallo tus ha bestes ha myns a vynno eve 'that people and animals and as many as desire may drink' OM 1847-48

gour gruek na best 'man, woman nor beast' RD 2227

noth off avel best oma 'I'm naked here like an animal' BM 4217

hag oll an bestas yn beyse 'and all the animals in the world' CW 110-11

ethen in ayre ha bestas 'the birds of the air and animals' CW 398

ha dreis preif ha beast yn bys 'and beyond reptile or animal in the world' CW 909

na susten moy es bestas 'nor food more than beasts' CW 1046

an oblashyon war an beastas ha'n (n)ohan 'an oblation of the animals and oxen' CW 1068-69

ha latha an strange bestas 'and to kill the strange animals' CW 1469

a us kyck an bestas na 'is there flesh of those animals...' CW 1470

gans krehen an bestas na me a ra dyllas thyma 'with the skins of those animals I make myself clothes' CW 1477-78

yn defyth yn myske bestas yma ef prest ow pewa 'in the wilderness among animals he lives always' CW 1481-82

me a vyn mos the wandra bestas gwylls tha asspeas 'I will go to wander to aspy wild animals' CW 1489-90

avell beast prest ow pewa 'always living like an animal' CW 1521

yn myske an bestas 'among the animals' CW 1548

ken es beast nag ew henna 'that is not other than an animal' CW 1557

hag a lathas moy es myell a vestas 'and killed more than a thousand animals' CW 1562-63

han beast sure yma gweskes 'and the animal has surely been struck' CW 1565

ow karma yma an beast 'the animal is crying out' CW 1581

marses den po beast bras 'if thou art man or large animal' CW 1594

rag dean ba beast magata 'for man and beast alike' CW 2276

a bub ehan a vestas 'of every kind of animal' CW 2411

nynges beast na preif in beyse 'there is no animal nor reptile in the world' CW 2415

pub beast oll ymma gyllys 'every single animal has gone' CW 2433

chattall ethyn ha bestas 'cattle, birds and animals' CW 2482

keffrys bestas hag ethyn 'both animals and birds' CW 2489

pub ehan ha beast in byes 'every species and animal in the world' CW 2512

an nore a thros in rag bestes peswar trosek 'the earth brought forth four-footed animals' TH 2 *ha war oll an bestas in nore* 'and over all the animals of the earth' TH 2

an brut beastas heb reason 'the brute beasts without reason' TH 5

pobill discrysik ha bestas gwyls 'unbelieving people and wild animals' TH 24

Lebben an hager-breeve o moy foulze avell onen vethell an bestaz an gweale a reege an arleth Deew geele 'Now the serpent was more treacherous than any of the beasts of the field that the Lord God had created' RC 23: 174

derez kenefra bestaz an gweal 'beyond all the beasts of the field' RC 23: 180.

To these should be added *bêst* with which Lhuyd glosses *Animal* (AB: 3a).

In view of the overwhelming preponderance of *best, bestas* 'animal' over any other word, perhaps we should accept *best, bestas* as the normal term for 'animal' in revived Cornish.

22.6 The customary word in UC for 'room' is *stevel*. This is attested only from OCV where it is cited as *steuel* 'triclinium' [dining-room]. Nance adopted the word into Unified Cornish and gave it the plural *stevelyow*. *Stevel* is a borrowing from Latin *stabellum* and appears in Welsh as *ystafell*, (pl.) *ystafelloedd*. Nance's plural *stevelyow* is as good a guess as any. It is presumably by analogy with other UC plurals of words in *-el*: *bresel* 'war', *breselyow*; *gevel* 'tongs', *gevelyow*, etc.

In fact the regular word for 'room' in Middle Cornish is either A *rom*, (pl.) *romys* or B *chambour*. A. is variously used:

hag ynno lues trygva romes y a vyth gylwys 'and in it many dwellings: rooms they shall be called' OM 951-52

thega movya y the thewys onyn rag bos in rome esa Judas ynna 'to urge them to elect someone to occupy the room [place] Judas had been in' TH 44a

fatell rug agan savyoure appoyntya pedyr in brassa rome ys onyn vith an abosteleth erell 'that our Saviour appointed Peter to a greater room [place] than any other of the apostles' TH 47a

rag collenwall an romes a vyth voyd yn nef 'to fill up the rooms in heaven that will be vacant' CW 241-42

occupya rage sertayne ow rome ve nagevas peare 'to occupy my room indeed who am without equal' CW 256-57

the golenwall an romys 'to fill up the rooms' CW 463

hag vnna leas trigva rowmys y a vythe henwys 'and in it many dwellings: rooms they shall be named' CW 2256-57.

B is apparently a bedroom:

rof thys ov thour hel ha chammbour 'I'll give thee my tower, hall and chamber' OM 2110.

With this compare Lhuyd's *tshombar* glossing *Cubiculum* 'bedroom' (AB: 52c) and the toponyms *Chamber Byan, Chamber an Tresousse, Park and Chamber* (CPNE: 76). In the *Ordinalia* the word *skyber* is used for the 'upper room' of the

263

last supper. *Skyber* really means 'barn' (cf. Irish *scioból* 'barn' borrowed from Brythonic) being a derivative of a hypothetical Late Latin **scoparium*:

> *hag ef a thyswe thywhy un skyber efan yn scon* 'and he will straightaway show you a capacious room' PC 637-38
> *otte omma skyber dek* 'here is a fair chamber' PC 679.

In view of the two words *rom* and *chambour*, using *stevel* for 'room' in general seems indefensible. For everyday use the word *rom* /ro:m/, *romys* /ro:məz/ would be more authentic for a room in general and *chambour* /'tʃombər/ or /tʃam'bu:r/ (cf. 3.8) for a bedroom.

22.7 Unified Cornish has two ways of saying 'use': *gul defnyth a* and *usya*. The first of these is attested only once in Middle Cornish, as far as I am aware:

> *rak ny allas den yn beys anotho gul defnyth vas* 'for no one in the world could make good use of it' PC 2547-48.

The usual Middle Cornish word for 'use' with both the sense 'employ' and 'be accustomed to' is *usya*. Here are some examples:

> *rag an arlont a usye* 'because of the crown he was using/wearing' PA 205b
> *newyth parrys nyn io usijs* 'newly ready, it had not been used' PA 233b
> *ha re usias hager gas raffna, ladra pur lues feyst* 'and have used to—an ugly case—rob and plunder very many indeed' BM 2143-44
> *drok hag anfusy inweth guetyogh usia* 'be sure to use evil and wickedness' BM 3421-22
> *bredereth usyogh dader* 'brethren, use goodness' BM 4260
> *guyn na syder ny usya* 'he used neither wine nor cider' BM 4451
> *na gwyne ny usyan badna* 'nor do we use a drop of wine' CW 1474
> *an tas a usias solempnyty bras* 'the Father used great ceremony' TH 1
> *I a usse crafft ha deceyt* 'They practise/use craft and deceit' TH 7a
> *ha the usya agan honyn jentyll the pub den* 'and use ourselves [i.e. behave] kindly to all men' TH 21a
> *hag usya inta y tavas* 'and use his tongue well' TH 23a
> *ha'n thew ew necessary the vos gwris ha the vos ussyys* 'and the two are necessary to be done and practised/used' TH 24a
> *ha hemma ew the vos usiis warbyn an drog pobill* 'and that is to be used against miscreants' TH 25
> *unworthy the usya an hanow a egglos* 'unworthy to use the name of "church"' TH 33
> *ny ren ny redya fatell rug S paule usya an kythsame auctorite ma* 'do we not read that St Paul used this same authority?' TH 39
> *ny rug an espscob benegas S Ambros usya an auctorite ma in pub poynt* 'the blessed bishop St Ambrose did not use this authority in every point' TH 39
> *ny vea vices ha drokoleth mar fre usyys* 'vices and wickedness would not be so freely used' TH 39

henna a ve gesys ha na moy usyys 'that was abandoned and no more practised/used' TH 52a

nena ne ra an pronter usya girreow e honyn 'then the priest does not use his own words' SA 62

Na esyn usya argumentys, mas usya exampels Christ 'Let us not use arguments but let us use the examples of Christ' SA 61a

syl nag idzhanz iuzyz lebmyn en pou Kernou 'which are not in use now in Cornwall' AB: 223.

Lhuyd also gives *Dho yuzia* as the Cornish for *soleo* 'be accustomed to or wont' (AB: 151c).

Usya is from Middle English *use*, itself from French. The English vowel /juː/ in /juːz/ is for earlier /yː/. One might therefore expect /'yzjə/ rather than /juzjə/. The quotation from Lhuyd shows that by the late 17th century the word was indeed /juzjə/.

22.8 The customary expression for 'remember' in UC is *perthy cof a*. This expression is attested in the texts:

arluth porth cof yn geyth dyweth am enef vy 'Lord, remember my soul at the last day' OM 1272-73

pertheugh cof ol an tokyn 'do you all remember the sign' PC 1081

ahanaf may portho cof 'that he might remember me' RD 272

ahanan y a perth coff 'they will remember us' BM 2486

hag arta perthugh cof guel 'and again remember better' BM 1064

Perh co t' ra te guetha a' Suile begenas 'Remember that thou shalt keep Sunday holy' BF: 41

En hav per kou gwav 'In summer remember winter' (Gwavas's motto) ACB.

The English borrowing *remembra*, however, becomes increasingly common:

hav remembra in plasma 'and remember me in this place' BM 1002

remembrogh agis sperys 'remember your spirit' BM 1250

ha remembrogh agis du 'and remember your God' BM 2161

ny remembrons y an charych 'they do not remember the injunction' BM 2831

remembrogh helma lemen 'remember this now' BM 2835

an patriark benegas Abraham a remembras ay thalleth 'the blessed patriarch Abraham remembered his origin' TH 6a

ha remembra agan mortall genesegeth 'and remember our mortal birth' TH 6a

fatell russens remembra aga henwyn 'that they remembered their names' TH 6a

pan rellans remembra ha lamentya aga pehosow 'whenever they remember and lament their sins' TH 6a

Remymbrow fatell rug pegh agan dry ny in kynsa thea an favour a thu 'Remember that sin first brought us from the favour of God' TH 16

an gabmthavas in teffry pesqwythe mays gwella why hy remembra ahanaf why 'the rainbow indeed, whenever you see it, remember me' CW 2501-03.

Lhuyd and Nicholas Boson use the Late Cornish equivalent of *yma cof dhym* for 'I remember':

> *Ma ko dho vî* 'I remember' AB: 138b
> *may ko them penag oma buz dro tho wheeath bloah coth* 'I remember when I was only about six years old' BF: 27
> *nag ez ko them tho guthva[z] meer en tavaz Curnooack* 'I do not remember to know much of the Cornish language' BF: 29
> *Ma kothem cavaz tra an parma* 'I remember finding something similar' BF: 29.

Almost certainly Boson knew the word *remembra* but preferred not to use it for purist reasons. He says: *buz thera ma wheelaz en skreefma (mar mere dr elama) tho gurra an geerna a treneuhan ra dismiggia gun tavaz ny senges tho re 'rol* 'but I seek in this writing (as much as I can) to put to one side that word which suggests that our language is indebted to others' (BF: 29).

In view of the prevalence of *remembra* in Tudor Cornish, perhaps it should be allowed in UCR alongside *perthy cof a, yma cof dhym a*.

22.9 The chief word for the noun 'promise' in Unified Cornish is *dedhewadow*. This is attested in Middle Cornish as far as I am aware only in the expression meaning 'promised land' which occurs twice in OM:

> *the'n tyreth a thythwadow* 'to the promised land' OM 1624
> *the'n tyr a thythewadow* 'to the promised land' OM 1871.

A more frequently attested word in the texts is *promys, promes*, (pl.) *promysyow, promyses*:

> *oll the promes hath teryou* 'all thy promise and thy lands' BM 2594
> *ha'y bromas o mar wheake* 'his promise was so sweet' CW 776
> *ha'y bromas ytho largya* 'and his promise it was larger' CW 780
> *an promas me ny roof oye* 'I don't give a fig [egg] for the promise' CW 1379
> *wos an promes na* 'in spite of that promise' CW 1539
> *may halla an promys dre an feth a Jhesu crist bos res the oll an re na* 'so that the promise may be given to all these through faith in Jesus Christ' TH 7a
> *fatell ew an promys ny colynwys* 'how is our promise fulfilled?' TH 13
> *Arta yma du ow kull an second promys* 'Again God makes the second promise' TH 13
> *oll an promysyow ma a thu* 'all these promises of God' TH 13a
> *dre reson du the wortas mar bell heb colynwel an promyses* 'because God waited so long without fulfilling the promises' TH 13a
> *ha then kythsam eglos ma crist a rug promys* 'and to this same church Christ made a promise' TH 17
> *ha ny an jeva promes a brassa royow* 'and we had a promise of greater gifts' TH 28
> *Ow kull an promys eff e leverys* 'Making the promise he said...' TH 51a
> *pan rug eff gul an promes* 'when he made the promise' TH 52.

The verb 'promise' is usually *dedhewy* in Unified Cornish. This verb is attested in the literature:

> *hen eu an oel a versy o dethywys dyso sy* 'that is the oil of mercy that was promised thee' OM 841-42
> *del thethyusys thymmo vy* 'as thou didst promise me' RD 450
> *thymmo why a thethywys* 'to me you promised' RD 623
> *par del dythywys thethe* 'as he promised them' RD 797
> *henna o poynt a falsury deʒewys heb koweras* 'that was a stroke of treachery promised but unfulfilled' PA 83d
> *y tethewys nans yu meys* 'I promised a month ago' BM 3918
> *mi ai didhiuys dhodho* 'I promised it to him' AB: 242a.

The verb *promysya* 'promise' is attested in Tudor Cornish:

> *hag y promysyas tha vee y fethan tha well nefra* 'and he promised me that I should always be the better' CW 889-90
> *a rug du promysya wosa an towle agan hendasow* 'which God promised after the fall of our first fathers' TH 13
> *eff a promysyas fatell vetha onyn genys* 'he promised that one would be born' TH 13
> *Eff a promysyas the viterne Dauid* 'He promised to King David' TH 13a
> *kepar dell rug crist promysya in xvi chapter a mathew* 'just as Christ promised in the 16th chapter of Matthew' TH 17
> *nena yma crist ow promysya* 'then Christ promises' TH 26
> *in mar ver dell rug crist promysya an conforter* 'inasmuch as Christ promised the Comforter' TH 36
> *eff a ve promysiis thethans y* 'it was promised to them' TH 36a.

It might be sensible in UCR to use *promys, promysya* as everyday words in preference to or alongside *dedhewadow, dedhewy*.

22.10 Other doublets of native word-borrowing include *brusy/juggia* 'judge' and *gothaf/suffra* 'suffer'. Either can be used in the revived language.

There are a number of other words that are now customary in Unified Cornish, but which are poorly attested in the texts. *Cannas* 'messenger' does occur in Middle Cornish but it is much less common than *messeger*. *Durdala thewhy* 'thank you' is attested in Late Cornish sources. The usual way of saying 'thank you' in Middle Cornish is *gromercy (the)*. In Middle Cornish the word for 'face' is invariably *fas, face, fath; bedgeth, budgeth* 'visage' occurs in Late Cornish, but *enep* 'face' is attested only by Lhuyd, as far as one can see. The Middle Cornish for 'receive' is almost always *receva* rather than *degemeres*.

The usual word for 'city' in revived Cornish is *cyta*, which is well attested in the literature. The native word *dynas* is not used in the sense 'city'. Nance's dictionary glosses it as 'hill-fort, earthwork camp'. The lexeme is common in place-names, *Dynas Ia, Dennis Head, Dennis Point, Hall Dinas*, for example.

Padel explains it as 'fort'. It has not generally been realized, however, that Lhuyd, who cites the word in the form *dinaz*, glosses it 'urbs; a city, a wall'd town' (AB: 177c). *Dynas* 'city' would be a useful item in the revived lexicon, since it would provide such derivatives as **pendhynas* 'capital city' and **mamdhynas* 'metropolis'. **Pendhynas* is not the same as *Pen Dynas* seen, for example, in *Pendennis Castle* and *Pendinas* = St Ives Head (CPNE: 85).

The expansion of the revived Cornish lexicon

22.11 Since the remains of Cornish of all periods are so meagre, it seems to me quite legitimate for the revived language to obtain its words from any of the following sources:

1. Middle Cornish
2. Old Cornish
3. Late Cornish
4. placenames
5. dialect survivals
6. analogy with Welsh and/or Breton
7. international roots
8. English

There should however be three basic rules for the adoption and spelling of new words. First, they should be respelt according to the principles laid down at 16.3. In the case of international borrowings we should not necessarily replace <i> with <y>. *Universita* (see BM 78) is preferable to *unyversyta*. Secondly, the adoption of new terms should be done in a disciplined way and not by individuals who believe that this or that dialect word may possibly be of Cornish origin. Thirdly, Welsh and Breton parallels or international/ English words should be adopted only when the native resources of the language are wanting.

For an excellent statement of the principles of creating neologisms in Cornish see Snell and Morris (1981: 3; 1984: 3).

The next step

22.12 It remains only to give texts in the various orthographies that have been used until now for Cornish and Neo-Cornish, and a vocabulary of UCR. Before that some observations are in order about the future of Neo-Cornish itself.

If the revised phonology, orthography, accidence and syntax of Neo-Cornish sketched above are valid, then UCR is likely wholly or in part to be accepted by Cornish revivalists as an acceptable variety of Neo-Cornish. Though it is to be hoped that nothing in UCR will be accepted without detailed discussion and full consultation.

The next stage will be to prepare and publish text-books and dictionaries. Since UCR is based as much as anything on John Tregear, I should also recommend that an adequate edition with a full glossary be prepared and published as soon as possible.

The first priority for the revival itself will be a learner's handbook on the lines of *Cornish Simplified* or *Kernewek Bew*. Longer term desiderata will be a descriptive grammar and a full Cornish-English/ English-Cornish dictionary. Any complete dictionary of Neo-Cornish should embrace all periods and forms of Cornish including toponyms and survivals in dialect. Nance's dictionaries use a variety of symbols to indicate when words have been respelt from Old Cornish and Late Cornish, or have been borrowed from Breton, Welsh or Middle English. This was questionable methodologically speaking, since the attested forms were not actually cited. An adequate dictionary of Neo-Cornish would give not only the standard spelling but also the form or forms in which the etymon is attested and the text or toponym in which it occurs. In this way neologisms could be included without prejudice to the academic integrity of the dictionary. Since Neo-Cornish orthography cannot be phonetic, the dictionary should also show the recommended pronunciation of every headword.

CHAPTER 23
Texts

1: Traditional Cornish

23.1 From the Charter Fragment, ed. Campanile, 1963 (CF)

Golsoug. Ty, cowe3,
by3 na bor3 me3,
dyyskyn ha powes
ha 3ymo dus nes.
Mar co3es 3e les,
ha 3ys y rof mowes,
ha fest vnan dek;
genes mara plek,
ha, tanha y,
kymmerr y 303 wrek.
Sconye 3ys ny vek
ha ty a vy3 hy.

Hy a vy3 gwreg ty da
3ys 3e synsy;
pur wyr a lauara,
ha, govyn worty.

23.2 From *Pascon agan Arluth*, 217-19

In aga herwyth y3 ese. un marreg Longis hynwys
dal o ny wely banna. ef rebea den a brys
gew a ve yn y 3ewle. gans an E3ewon gorris
ha pen lym rag y wane. 3e golon Jhesus hynwys.

Longis sur an barth dyghow. 3e grous Jhesus y3 ese
3en marreg worth y hanow. y a yrhys may whane
yn corf Jhesus caradow. en gew lym ef a bechye
pur ewn yn dan an asow. dre an golon may3 ese

An golon y3 eth stret bras. dour ha goys yn kemeskis
ha ryp an gyw a resas. 3e 3ewle neb an gwyskis
y wholhas y 3ewlagas. gans y eyll leyff o gosys
dre ras an goys y whelas. Jhesus crist del o dy3gtis.

23.3 From *Resurrexio Domini*, 2571-2606

Myghtern of guyron ha cref
    kyns pegh map den a'm sorras;
er ow fyn travyth ny sef.
    Porth yfarn me a torras
hag a thros lyes enef
    a ver drok, tervyns ha cas.
the ioy y tethons gynef
    kemmys a wruk both ow thas.

Ow stons a fue crous a pren
    kyns en myghtern, den ha Deu,
yn le basnet war ow fen
    curyn a spern lym ha gleu
ol ou ysyly yn ten
    hag a wel the lyes plu
y'n golon dre'n tenewen
    the restye syngys ow gu.

Dre ow thrys y tuth un smat
    gans kentrow d'aga gorre;
y fue ow manegow plat
    spygys bras dres ow dywle.
Yth o ou fous ha'm brustplat
    purpur garow thu'm strothe;
dre an gos a-rak Pylat
    worto an kyc a glene.

Pan fue an purpur war skwych
    kychys the ves gan dywthorn,
worto y glynes hardlych
    ran a'n kyc bys y'n ascorn.
Woge ow da oberow
    dywes y yrhys dethe.
Thym rosons bystyl wherow—
    byth ny fynnys y eve.

Gans gu guenys ha marow
    dre an golon me a fue.
An tryge deth sur hep gow
    y whruk dasserghy arte.

23.4 From *Beunans Meriasek,* 4269-4301

Yma an preys ou nesse
the Crist me a vyn grasse
    thym y thadder in bysma
ʒesseys unctis communijs
off lemen the Jhesu grays
the orth Crist lel map guirhas
rag ow servesy in beas
    war Thu pesy me a ra.

Neb am gorth vy in bysma
    Jhesus arluth gront dethy
gallus boys ʒesseys oma
    kyns es merwel eredy
corff Crist inweth receva
    ungijs gans henna defry
then vlas neff age ena
    mayth ella purguir then ioy.

In le may feva gorthys
    peseff rag an keth rena
may's tefons y luen ʒeheys,
    pesy warnaff a rella,
ha sawys a pup cleveys
    aberth an corff ha'n ena;
susten may's tefons kefrys
    ha lor pegans the vewa.

In Kernou me a'm beth chy
    ryb Maria a Cambron.
Thu'm wyles neb a thue dy
    me a's aquit pur dyson
        kyn fo ou corff in ken le.
In keth plas-na neb a beys
gans Jhesu y feth clowys
ha'y petyconn colenwys,
    lafyll pur guir mar peth e.

23.5 From John Tregear, 24a-25

Rag an declaracion a hemma, why a ra understondia fatell us the charite ii office, ha'n neill ew contrary thy gela ha'n thew ew necessary the vos gwris ha the vos ussyys war an re ew contrary in aga disposition. An neill office a charite ew the wull merechesya a'n dus tha ha'n dus innocent ha na vons y oppressys gans fals accusacion; 'ma the ry thetha corag the wull da ha the contynewa in dadder ha'ga defendya dre gletha theworth aga yskerens.

Ha'n office a epscobow ha'n re a'n jeffa cure a enevow ew the ry laude ha preise the oll an dus da rag aga oberow da, may hallans contynewa in dadder; ea, ha the rebukya ha correctia dre an gere a Thu an offences ha fawtys an drog-pobill. An office arell ew the rebukya, correctya ha punsya vicys, heb exception a then vith ha hemma ew the vos usiis warbyn an drog-pobill only. Rag yth ew an office a charite magata the rebukya, punsya ha correctia drog pobyll magata dell ewa the chesya, rewardia ha defendia an re-na ew da ha innocent. Yma S Poule indelma ow declaria thy'n Romans: An uhall powers ew ordeynys gans Du, not the vos dowtys gans an re ew da, mas the punsya an drog-pobill gans an gletha ha the gemeras vingians a'n drog-pobill. Inweth [ima] S Paule the Tymothe ow rebukya pegh constantly ha vehemently dre an gere a Thu.

Indelma an ii office a vynsa bos diligently executys rag avoydya gwlaskur an teball el, an pregowther gans an gere ha'n governor gans an cletha; ken nyns ugensy ow regardya Du na'n re usy in dan aga governans, mar townsy ha suffra Du the vos offendys rag lak a correccion ha'n re usy in aga governans the vos perisshys kepar del ra pub naturall tas ha correctia y naturall flogh pan deffa ha gull amys; ken nyns ugy worth y gara.

23.6 From *The Creation of the World*, 1965-91

Coth ha gwan yth of gyllys.
       Ny'm beas bewa na fella.
Ankaw yth ew devethys;
       ny vyn omma ow gasa
the vewa omma udn spyes.

Me a'n gweall prest gans gew
parys thom gwana pub tew.
       Nyg eas scappya. Deva
       an preys; mall ew genaf.

Me a servyas pell an beyse
       aban vema kyns formys.
Naw cans bloth of, me a gryes,
       ha deakwarnegans recknys,
          mayth ew pryes mos alema.

Flehys am bef denethys
       a Eva, ow freas, mear,
dewthack warnygans genys
       a vybbyan, hemma ew gwyre,
heb ow mabe Cayne hag Abell.

Ynweth dewthack warnugans
a virhas in pur thibblans
       me a'm be heb tull na gyll
       a thalathfas an bys ma.

Ha'n bys yth ew incresshys
drethaf-ve hag ow flehys
       heb number tha vos comptys;
       tha Thew y whon ras ractha.

23.7 From Edward Lhuyd, AB: 222

Mi a uon pordhâ try kaldzha trigerio an dhêau ulâz-ma gurèiz an ober-ma pylta guèl tro yu gurèiz geno vi. Mez huâth mi brediraz try peva guèl neb riu guerraz vel guerraz veth; ha kekeffryz try kaldzha an huêl bohodzhak-ma piga erel am'àn dho dallah ydn dâ. Ha en kettermen-na ma neb esperans dhebm try veddons en lennerio pednzhivik ha maz-brezek geffya e foto dhe estren pel-pou, neb mar peue gerlevar &c. Kernûak ha Godhalek skrefyz arâg, ny vendzha vesga argrafa an papyrio hemma; ha py ny kouze mèz nebaz bîan adrô'n tavazo raglaveryz en an levar-ma py kèn e vendzha dazargrafa hy grammatekio ha gerlevro e honan, mar venz guesgez a vêz; andella 'ryg me (gen an trayllyanz reizyz) dazargrafa an raggorryz 'rammatek ha'n gerlevran Arvorek py Gal-Vrethonek.

Mez huâth (uar an parh aral) del ny vendzha vi rag tra vêth, kemerez uarnav dho gîl ydn bennag dra ez a uartha ma alloz; endella mi rakemera kibmiaz obba dho laveral uorth an lenner, trez el bôz rez y vî kevarvoz uorth nebaz brederyanzo adrô'n tavazeth Kernûak dre uerraz an tavaz Kembrîan, a aldzha neb bennak na odhe dravêth anydha drizlebmal.

23.8 From Nicholas Boson, BF: 15

En termen ez passiez thera trigaz en St. Levan dean ha bennen en tellar creiez Chei a Horr. Ha an weale a kothaz scant ha meth a dean da an wreag, "Mee a vedn moze da whelaz weale da weele; ha whi a el dendal gose bounans obba."

Kibmiaz teag ev a komeraz ha pel da east ev a travaliaz ha uor an duath e a reeg thoaz da chei teeack ha reeg whelaz ena weale da weele. "Panna weale 'lesta geeal?" meth an teeack.

"Pob weale oll," meth Jooan. Ena chei a varginiaz rag trei penz an vlethan gubber.

Ha pa thera duath an vlethan e vaster thesguethaz dotha an trei penz. "Meer, Jooan," meth e vaster, "obba tha gubber. Buz mar venta ri them arta, mee a deska deez point a skeeans."

"Dreu hedna," meth Jooan.

"Na," meth an vaster. "Ri them ha mee a vedn laveral deez."

"Komeroe than," meth Jooan.

Nenna meth an vaster, "Komeer weeth na reo gara an vorr goeth rag an vorr noueth."

Nenna chei a varginiaz rag vlethan moy rag pokaar gubber ha po thera duath an vlethan e vaster a droaz an trei penz.

"Meer Jooan," meth e vaster, "obba tha gubber buz mar venta ri them arta, mee a deska deeze point a skeeans."

23.9 From William Rowe, RC 23: 193-97

Leben po ve Jesus gennez en Bethalem a Judeah en dethyow Herod an matern a reeg doaze teeze veer thor an Est tha Jerusalem, lavaral: peleah ma e yw gennez matern an Ethewan? Rag ma gwellez genani e steran en Est, ha tho ni devethez tha gorthe thotha. Pe reeg Herod an matern clowaz hemma, e ve toublez ha oll Jerusalem gonz eve. Ha pe reeg e contell oll an cogazers euhall ha'n screffars a'n bobel worbarth, e avednaz thoranze; pelle ve Chreest gennez. Ha engye lavarraz thotha: en Bethalem a Judea: râg andellma math ewa screffez gen an prophet: Ha che, Bethalem, en pow Judah, neg ooz an bethathna amisk maternyow Judah; rag ames a che e ra doas matern rag rowlia tha pobel Ezarel. Nena Herod, pe reeg e prevath crya an deese feere, e avednyaz thoranze seer pana termin reeg an steere disquethaz. Ha e ez devannaz tha Bethalem ha reege laule thonz: gworeuh whellaz seere râg an flô younk, he pe rewe why e gavaz, dro geere tha ve arta, m'ala ve moaze ha gortha thotha aweeth. Pe rêg angye clowaz an matern, y eath caar, ha an stearan a reeg angye gwellhaz en East geeth deractanze 'ne rege hi doaze ha zavaz derez leba era an flô yonk. Pe rêg angye gwellaz an steran, thonge loan gen meare a loander. Ha po tho angye devethez en an choy, y a wellaz an flô yonk gen Mareea e thama, ha angye a cothaz en doar ha gorthaz tha eve; ha pe reg angye gere go throzor, y a rooz thotha awr ha frokensence ha mere.

23.10 From Robert Williams, LCB: 396

Dew a gewsys an gerryow-ma ha leverys: Me yw an Arluth dhe Dhew, nêb a's drôs dhe vês a'n Tŷr Misraim, dhe vês a'n chy gwasanaeth.

1. Te ny's bŷdh dewyow erell mês ve.

2. Na wra dhys honan nêp del gravys na havalder tra vŷth ûs yn nêf awartha po yn nôr a woles po yn dour yn dan an nôr. Na wra ty plegy dhe remma na 'ga wordhyé; râg me an Arluth dhe Dhew yw Dew a sor hag a vyn dry pechasow an tasow war an flechys bys an tressa ha'n pesweré denythyans a'n nêb na'm pertho ve; hag a vyn dyscudhé trueth dhe milyow a'n nêb ûs ow caré hag ûs ow gwythé ow gorhemmynadow.

3. Na wra cemeres hanow an Arluth dhe Dhew dhe scul, râg an Arluth dhe Dhew ny vyn sensy e dipêh, neb ûs cymeres y hanow ef dhe scul.

4. Perth côf dhe gwythé sans an dŷdh Sabboth; whêh dydhyow te wra whêl hag a wra myns ûs dhys dhe wûl, mês an sythves dŷdh yw an Sabboth an Arluth dhe Dhew. Yn dŷdh-na te nyn wra echen a whêl; te na dhe vâb, na dhe verch na dhe dhên whêl na dhe vôs whêl na dhe lodnow na'n dên uncouth ûs aberth dhe dharasow. Râg yn whêh dydhyow Dew a wrûg an nêf ha'n môr ha myns ûs ynné y ha powesas an sythves dŷdh hag a'n uchellas.

2: Neo-Cornish

23.11 From Henry Jenner, *Handbook of the Cornish Language*, 1904

> Kerra ow holon! Beniges re vo
> gans bennath Dew an dêdh a'th ros dhemmo,
> dhô whelas gerryow gwan pan dhetha vî,
> tavas dha dassow, ha dhô'th drovya dî.
> En cov an dêdh splan-na es pel passyes;
> en cov idn dêdh lowenek, gwin 'gan bês,
> war Garrack Loys en Côs, es en dan skês
> askelly Myhal El, o'gan gwithes;
> en cov lîas dêdh wheg en Kernow da,
> ha ny mar younk—na wekkah vel êr-ma
> dhemmo a dhîg genev an gwella tra,
> pan dhetha vî en kerh, en ol bro-na;
> dheso mî re levar dha davas teg,
> flogh ow empinyon vî, dhô'm kerra gwrêg.

23.12 Unified Cornish, R.M. Nance, *Lyver an Pymp Marthus Seleven* 1939: 9-10

Synta Brek a-drussas yn-ban hy breghellow hep ynnyadow, ow hedhes collel ha'y lemma orth an truthow, hag a-dhallathas gonys a-dro dhe wolghy ha glanhé an puscas. An re-erel ynweth eth yn-un-fysky dhe gunyssa, Sen Seleven y-honen dhe derry prenyer eythyn ha dreyn segh a-dro dhe'n keow, ha'n dheu vaw byghan dhe guntell glos y'n parcow a-dre-dro rag y weres ow-cul tan whyflyn kepar ha gelforn yn-dan an chek war an men-olas, scon mayth o cowl-barusys an dheu sew ha gorrys tom-bros war dallyour-pren yn cres an vos.

Kens dhe dybry, bytegens, an dheu Sans eth war ben aga deulyn, degés aga lagasow, hag a-ros grassys dhe Dhew Ollgallosek gans pysadow hyr dres kynda a'y dhader mur dh'y servyjy ow-ry dre varthus dhedha an dheu sew. Mar res leverel gwyryoneth, nebes stryf a-sordyas martesen yntredha y'n ur-na, pynyl a-alsa dysquedhes moy sansoleth dre wortos pella ow-pysy; saw boghes cows a henna a-vyth an gwella, an pyth a-won yu, pynagoll a-ve dhe'n Syns, nyns-o dhe'n dheu flogh yeunadow-vytholl a bysy wosa mar bell lafurya, lemen awell cref dhe dhybry, mayth ethons ha mos ogas fol rak nown ow-clewes eth whek an puscas tom a-dhuth dh'aga deufryk-y. Cowl-ygerys aga deulagas y a-sevys dyson ha clor, whath pan esa an dus da war bendeulyn, hag a-settyas dalghen warbarth y'n puscas hep na hyrra gortos, ow-kemeres pup y bysk oll yn-tyen yn y vesyas ha'y dhybry, hep holan, hep bara, hep meth, ogas mayth o hep dynsel, na scantlowr tenna anal drefen bos dhedha mar vur own a'n dheu Sans, y dhe ygery aga deulagas martesen kens bos gansa dybrys an sewyon yn kettep tam.

Yn ketelma y-wharfa, lowr del yllyr y waytya, an vebyon grefny dhe omdaga, an dheu sew orth aga-hollenky mar arow, gans dreyn lym an puscas fast gwenys y'ga bryansen, hep bos avysyes an dheu Sans a'n droklam a-s-darfa; ha pan o dewedhys aga fysadow ha'ga deulagas arta ygerys, y-whelsons, soweth, a-dheragtha war an vos tallyour gwak ha war an lur an dheu omdhevas a-hes a'ga groweth, y'ga dywla grom remenantys squerdys an puscas!

CORNISH TODAY

23.13 Kernowek Kemyn [first form], Wella Brown, *Carn* 60: 15

Yn pub sorn a Vreten Veur yma trevow yw gevellys gans trevow erell tramor, trevow yw kehaval po gohaval an eyl dh'y ben war neb kor. Homm yw an kas omma yn Kernow ha'n brassa rann a'n trevow ma yw gevelly gans trevow yn hons dhe Vreten Vyghan.

Yndella mardj yw hi, res yw traweythyow mires orth an dra yn un omwovynn pana dhader a'gan beus adhiworth an gevrenn ma. Wostalleth ha'n towl nowydh venegys yma kolonnekter ha nerth a du an tybyans. Bagas bras a dus a dheu warbarth yn pub a'n dhyw dre ha "Kowetha Gevellyans" yw drehevys yn skon. Wodja misyow a ober uth yw ordenys "Dydh an Solempnita" ma fo dustunys an Chartour-Gevellyans. Hemm yw an kynsa poynt a strif traweythyow. Py yethow ynna y fydh skrivys an Chartour—Frynkek po Bretonek, Sawsnek po Kernewek? Po martesen y'n peder yeth.

Gwynn agan bys klywes bos usys an dhyw keltek aden[e]wan an yethow erell yn lies le.

Ena, an dhew Jartour dustunys, pandr'a siw? Gwaryow peldroes, kuryow, fleghes ow mos dhe bedja seythyn yn tjiow aga gevel-dre. Vyajyow gans bagasow unwyth y'n vlydhen?

Nyndj eus diank a leverel bos chons da a wodhvos meur adro agan kendrewi ha kenitterywi geltek, aga bywnans ha'ga huddenow. An gwella fordh oll a vydh tus dhe vos onyn orth onyn rag keskewsel yn town, dhe gonvedhes an eyl y gila. My a vynsa klywes hemma gwrys yn neb yeth keltek kyns y vos gwrys po yn Sawsnek po yn Frynkek.

23.14 Kernowek Kemyn [second form], G.S., *Carn* 87:17

Byttegyns, trist yw yn lyver da yn pub tremmyn arall bos an dhew skrifer mar bell diworth bys an Gernowyon ma na wodhons skant vyth oll an pyth usi ow hwarvos; poken gweth, awos aga skila pynag aga honen, i a vynn pesya liwya delinyans kamm. Rag ensampel i a vynn previ dell hevel bos avonsyans an yeth ow fyllel hag i a wra dewis aga niverennow yndellma; dre dhiskwedhes bos an niver a dus owth ombrofya rag apposyansow an Gesva nebes isella, i a lever bos an yeth ow hokya yn neb fordh; mar mynnsens dos ha kewsel orth soedhogyon an Gesva po an Gowethas i a dhysksa distowgh bos an klassow brassa ha kreffa es bydhkweyth, saw ny vynn an dus ow studhya holya apposyansow. Yn hwir hemm yw arwoedh pur dha awos bos movyans dhe-ves diworth studhyans skolheyjek war-tu ha'n yeth kewsys avel kynsa kostenn.

Ynwedh i a vynn leverel bos an niver a dus ow tos dhe'n Bennseythun Gernewek ow tiynkresya; kamm arta. Prag na vynn an skriforyon dos ha gweles mar mynnons pregowtha war studh an yeth? Ena i a wrussa godhvos bos moy a dus ow tos dres an jydh—tus yowynk heb lowr a arghans dhe dylly kost tryga pub nos, ha tus nowydh pub blydhen.

Diwettha rann an chaptra yw pur wann yn y dhevnydh owth assaya previ nebes poyntow yn kever gnas an dus a dhysk Kernewek ha heb dustuni vydh oll. Arta gwell via omgusulya gans an re a woer an pyth usi ow hwarvos. Wosa dyski kansow a dus dres an blydhynyow my a lavarsa bos tus a bub oes, soedh, kryjyans ha galloes ow tos dhe'n klassow; mes gwell yw godhvos bos tus yowynka ha krev y'ga mynnas ow tos ha tenkys an yeth ynter aga diwleuv yn le an re akademek a hevel tryga war gen planet.

23.15 Revived Late Cornish, Richard Gendall, *Carn* 75: 17 [UCR version by NJAW]

En termen ew pell passyez an Curnowean alga boaz guthvethez heb calletter dreffen gye tha cowz an Cornoack. Hethow nag ewa louare tha usya an tavaz rag gweel onen Cornoack: boaz Cornoack, thew mouy vel [boaz] treegaz en Kernow, ha thew kene vel cawas passport Cornoack. Me a fangaz lether athewethaz thurt Sawz younk o kebmys comerez gen Kernow dro mal dotha trailya tha Curnow e honen; alga ve gweras dotha? Soweth, na ell hedda boaz, namoy es drell Sawz trailya tha Cathay po enwethan tha elan.* Na ednack oll e vownaz vea louare tha gweel notha Curnow.

Della, fatel ellen nye guthaz edn Curnow? Fatel ell brane guthaz brane? Der leeaz seen na ell boaz guthvethez boz gen Curnow... der e ganaw,** e gowz, an vor leb mava gwereby, e vreaz war an beaz, e deez, ha rina eze cooth dotha. Edn Curnow ell adgan orrol skone louare der tedna meaz notha e story. E vedn guthaz boree ewa Curnow po nag ewa....

Enurma ma an Curnowean devethez mar nebbaz uz thysompyas gye reeg dalla tha guthaz dren'gye an radn vehatna et ago powe go honen; Deew a ore rag fra na riganz guthaz hedna kens. Boz lebben ma zoer dothans, ha thew hedda an gwella esperans ellen nye cawas rag termen vedn doaz an bobel nye. Whathe rag dirrya an Curnowean a dale boaz callatsha, garowa, tumba; na vedn nye moaz pell pothera nye gara tha gon egary the voaz nevra an kensa tha gweskall... "Bethez gweskez duath ken gweskall eneth" thew lavar coath leb ve comerez ree than colan gen an Curnowean: nye reez pedeery droan gweskez eneth kenzemmyn... nessa, thew nye leb dale gweskall.

[Y'n termyn yw pell passyes an Kernowyon a alja bos godhvedhys heb caletter drefen anjy dhe cows an Kernowek. Hedhyw nag ywa lowar dhe usya an tavas rag gul onen Kernowek: bos Kernowek yth yw moy 'vel [bos] trygys yn Kernow, ha yth yw ken 'vel cawas passport Kernowek. Me a fangyas lyther adhewedhes dywort Sows yowynk o kemmys kemerys gans Kernow del o mal dodho treylya dhe Kernow y honen: 'alja vy gweres dodho? Soweth, na yll henna bos, namoy es del yll Sows treylya dhe Cathay po onnwedhen dhe el'en.* Na unyk oll y vewnans 'vya lowar dhe gul anodho Kernow.

Yndella fatel yllyn ny godhvos un Kernow? Fatel yll bran godhvos bran? Der lyes syn na yll bos godhvedhys bus gans Kernow... der y ganow,** y gows, an for' le mava gortheby, y vrues war an bes, y dus ha'n re-na ues coth dodho. Un Kernow a yll ajwon aral scon lowar der tenna 'mes anodho y story. Ef 'ven godhvos whare ywa Kernow po nag ywa....

Y'n eur ma yma an Kernowyon devedhys mar nebes *as* adhesempys anjy a wrug dalleth dhe godhvos del enjy an ran vyhanna et 'ga pow 'ga honen. Dew a wor rag fra' na wrugons godhvos henna kens. Bus lemmyn yma sor dodhans ha yth yw henna an gwella esperans 'yllyn ny cawas rag termyn 'ven dos agan pobel ny. Whath rag durya an Kernowyon a dal bos calessa, garowa, tomma. Ny 'ven ny mos pell pa 'th eson ny 'gasa dha'gan *egary* [escar] dhe vos nefra an kensa dhe gweskel... "Bedhys gweskys dewweyth kens gweskel unweyth" yth yw lavar coth neb 've kemerys re dhe'n colan gans an Kernowyon: ny a res pedery del on gweskys unweyth kens lemmyn... nessa, yth yw ny neb 'dal gweskel.]

Notes: *elan = elowen 'elm tree'; **ganow 'pronunciation' in Revived Late Cornish is based on a misreading of Lhuyd (14.40)

23.16 Tim Saunders, *The Celtic Pen*, 1 ii: 24

Yn gworor gwlazgordh ann gwolow
y'ma dowr ow' kana dhy'nn grow;
Le pawes ann gwynz ry'n trovyas
Ym mysk ann gwleuth yr ha'nn deil glas:
Ow' c'hwystra c'hwath y'ma gwreidhenn
Avorow yn gweryz ow phenn;
Yn gworor gwlazgordh ann gwolow
Y'ma dowr owth amma dhy'nn grow.

Yn gworor gwlazgordh ann gwolow
Y'ma gwiwer ow' chwiliaz know;
Le pawes ann skeuz ry'n trovyas
Yn mysk tonnow rewyz gwelz bas;
Ow' c'hwystra c'hwath y'ma lanwez
Bloedh c'hwath y'm gwoez sal, lez ha' lez;
Yn gworor gwlazgorh ann gwolow
Y'ma gwiwer ow' kyntell know.

Yn gworor gwlazgordh ann gwolow
Y'ma gwas ow' trec'hevyl krow;
Le pawes ann dyn ry'n trovyas
Yn mysk magoer lomm ann hen blas:
Ow c'hwystra c'hwath y'ma oerwynz
Deg mil oes na' vu byth gweith kynz;
Yn gworor gwlazgordh ann gwolow
Y'ma flammow war oelez grow.

23.17 From Lewis Carroll, *Through the Looking Glass,* translated into UCR by NJAW

"Na saf stag ena yndella ha te ow clappya genes dha honen," yn medh Bothan-Crothan hag ef ow meras orty rag an kensa treveth, "mes lavar dhym dha hanow ha'th neges."

"Me yw gylwys Alys, mes—"

"Hanow goky lowr ywa!" yn medh Bothan-Crothan nebes dygortes heb gasa dhedhy gorfenna. "Pandr' usy ow styrya?"

"A res dhe hanow styrya travyth?" a wovynnys Alys yn un hokkya.

"Res yw porres," yn medh Bothan-Crothan gans wharth cot: "ow hanow avy, ymava ow styrya an shap usy dhym—hag shap fest teg ywa ynwedh. Te a alja bos ogasty a shap vyth oll ha'n hanow na dhys."

"Prag esough why owth esedha yn mes omma agas honen oll?" yn medh Alys rag nynj o whensys dhe dhalleth stryf.

"Drefen nag ues den vyth oll genama," a gryas Bothan-Crothan. "A wrusta predery nag o genef an gorthyp ewn rag henna? Govyn questyon pella."

"A nynj esough ow crejy y fedheugh why moy dyogel yn nans omma war an grond?" yn medh Alys ha hy ow contynewa an kescows. Nynj esa man ow tesyrya govyn desmyk aral mes cuf o hy hag y's teva fyenasow rag sawment an creatur coynt. "Pur gul yw an fos na!"

"Ass yw sempel an desmygow esta orth aga govyn!" yn medh Bothan-Crothan yn un romyal. "Ny hevel dhym man y vos cul. Dar, mar teffen ha codha—ha nyns ues peryl vyth oll a henna—mes mar teffen ha codha—" Ena ef a wrug pors a'y dheuweus hag mar sevur ha ryel o y semlant, ma na alla Alys omwetha orth wherthyn. "Mar teffen ha codha," ef a leverys pella, "an Mytern re bromysyas dhym—ty a yll omwana, mar menta! Ny wrusta predery me dhe leverel henna, a wrusta? An Mytern re bromysyas dhym gans y anow y honen, ef dhe— dhe—"

"Dhe dhanvon y vergh ha'y soudoryon oll," yn medh Alys adhesempys, heb muer a furneth.

"Wel! Me a lever dhys, hen yw lacka oll!" a gryas Bothan-Crothan dystough hag ef serrys bras. "Te re be ow coslowes a dryf dhe dharrasow ha wor tu delergh gwedh—ha chymblas war nans—boken ny aljesta y wodhvos!"

"Na vuef man!" yn medh Alys yn purra clor. "Me a'n redyas yn lyver."

"Dar! Y a alja scryfa taclow a'n par-na yn lyver," yn medh Bothan-Crothan hag ef moy whar. "Henna yth yw an dra yw gylwys an Ystory a Gernow, yth yw yn gwyr. Lemmyn myr orthyf vy yn ta! Nebonen oma a wrug cowsel orth Mytern. Ny venta martesen gweles nebonen a'n par na arta bys vycken. Ha rag ma halles godhvos nag oma gothys, te a yll shakya ow luef!" Hag ef a vynwharthas ogasty dheworth scovarn dhe scovarn hag ef owth omblegya yn rag (ha namna wruga codha adhywar an fos pan wrug ef yndella) ha offra y luef dhe Alys. Hy a veras orto yn prederys pan wrug hy hy senjy. "Mar teffa ha mynwherthyn bohes moy, y fensa tuyow y anow omvetya wor' tu dhelergh," hy a brederys: "hag y'n uer na ny wodhfyen man pandra wrussa wharfos dh'y ben! Own a'm bues an top dhe dhos dheworto ha godha dhe'n dor."

"Ea, oll y vergh ha'y soudoryon oll," a sewyas Bothan-Crothan. "Y a vensa ow drehevel kens pen mynysen, mensens yn certan! Byttegens bohes re scaf yw an kescows ma. Gesough ny mos dhelergh bys dhe'n lavar dewetha marnas un."

"Dowt a'm bues na won y remembra," yn medh Alys yn pur gortes.

"Y'n cas na res yw dhyn dalleth a-noweth," yn medh Bothan-Crothan, "ha my a'm bues cumyas dhe dhowys devnyth a'n cows—" ("Ymava prest ow cowsel adro dhodho kepar ha gwary!" yn medh Alys dhedhy hy honen) "Rag henna ottomma questyon ragos. Pygemmys blodh a wrusta leverel dha vos?"

Alys a wrug amontyans cot yn hy fen ha leverel: "Seyth blodh ha hanter."

"Dygompes," a gryas Bothan-Crothan yn fudhygel. "Ny wrusta leverel travyth a'n par na!"

"Yth esen ow crejy why dhe venya 'Pygemmys blodh osta?'" yn medh Alys.

"Mar teffen ha menya henna, me a vensa y leverel," yn medh Bothan-Crothan.

Ny's teva Alys whans vyth oll a dhalleth argyans noweth. Rag henna hy a wrug tewy.

"Seyth blodh ha hanter!" yn medh Bothan-Crothan. "Bohes confort usy y'n os na. Mar teffes ha govyn orthyf vyvy, my a vensa cusulya dhys cessya ha ty seyth blodh—mes re adhewedhes yw y'n uer ma."

"Nyns oma usyes dhe whelas cusyl ow tuchya tevy," yn medh Alys ha hy nebes serrys.

"Re wothys?" yn medh an den aral.

Moy serrys whath ve Alys pan glowas henna. "Yth esof ow menya," yn medh hy, "na yll un den vyth oll omwetha orth tevy."

"Na yll un den," yn medh Bothan-Crothan, "mes y halja deu dhen martesen! Mar questa cafus an gweres ewn, martesen ty a alja cessya ha ty seyth blodh."

"Ass yw teg an grugys esough why ow quysca!" yn medh Alys yn sodyn. (Y re's teva lowr adro dhe'n mater a os, yth hevelly dhedhy, ha mars ens y dhe dhowys devnyth a'n kescows an eyl warlergh y gela, hy chons hy ova lemmyn). "Dhe'n lyha," yn medh hy yn un janjya hy breys, "ass yw teg agas cravat—na, agas grugys, hen yw dhe styrya—geveugh dhym!" yn medh hy yn amays.

A short dictionary of UCR

24.1 This glossary of words has been excerpted from BM, TH, SA, CW, AB, ACB and selectively from and elswhere. It is not intended as a full vocabulary. Its purpose is to give some idea of the orthography recommended for UCR.

The order of items in each entry is as follows: the UCR variant in bold type, the English meaning, the attested forms from the various texts in italics and lastly in curled brackets the Unifed Cornish spelling.

References different from elsewhere in this book are as follows: M = BM; T = TH; A = SA; C = CW.

a of: *a* T {a}
a byle: whence: *a py le* M; *a by le* C {a ble / a byla}
(a-)dherag: before (prep.): *therag* M; *therag* T; *derag* A {adherag / a dherak}
a'y saf upright: *ay saff* M; *ay save* C {ay saf}
a berth: within: *berth* M; *aberh* AB {a berth}
a der dro: around about: *ader dro* C {a dre dro}
a-dhelergh: behind: *athellargh* C; *adhelar* AB; *a theller* ACB {adhelergh}
a-dhewedhes: recently: *athewethas* T; *a theweʒas* C; *a dewethaz* NBoson {a-dhewedhes}
a-dro: about (adv.): *adro* M; *adro* T; *adro* C; *adro* AB {a-dro}
a-drues: athwart: *adrus* M {a-drus}
a-hes: at length: *aheys* C {a hes}
a-jy: within: *achy* M; *agye, agy* C; *adzhyi* AB {a-jy}
a-les: wide open: *aleys* M; *ales, a leis, a leys* T; *a lees* C {a les}
a-rag: before: *arak, arag* M; *a râg* ACB; *a raage* Rowe {a rag, a rak}
a-rag dorn / derag dom: beforehand: *arag dorne* T; *derag dorn* A {a rag dom, derag dorn}
a-ugh: above: *a ugh, ugh* T; *a uhe, a ughe* C {a-ugh}
a-van: up above: *avan* M; *avadn* C {avan}
a-ves: outside: *a vez* AB {a- ves}
a-west: to the west: *awest* {awest}
a-woles: below (adv.): *awoles; awolas* A; *awollas, awolas* C; *a wollas, a wollaz* ACB {a-woles}
aban: since: *aban* T; *aban* C {aban}
abarth: on behalf of: *abarth, aberth* M; *abarth* C {abarth}
abarth a-woles: below (adv.): *abarth wollas* C {abarth awoles}
abel: able: *abel* M; *abyll, abill* T; *abel* A {abel}
aberveth: inside: *aberveth* M; *abervath, abervathe* C; *abervedh* AB {aberveth}
abostel, abosteleth: apostle: *abostel* M; *apostle,* (pl.) *abosteleth* T; (pl.) *abostolath,* (pl.) *aposelath* A; *abosdol,* (pl.) *abesdel,* (pl.) *abesteledh* AB {abostel, abesteleth}
abrans: eyebrows: *abrans* AB {abrans}

acompt / acont: account (n.): *acompt* T {acont}
acomptya / acontya: account (vb): *acontya* M; *accomptya* T; *accomptya* C {acontya}
acordya: agree: *acordya* M {acordya}
adar / ater; apart from: *adar, ater* M {adar / ater}
affyrmya: affirrn: *affirmya, affyrmya* T {—}
afynys: refined: *afynes* C {afynya}
aga: their: *age* M; *aga* T; *go* AB; *go* ACB {aga}
agan: our; *agen* M; *agan* T; *agyn, agen* A; *agen, agan* C; *gen* AB {agan}
agas: your: *agis, agys* M; *agys* T; *ages* C; *gyz, goz* AB; *agaz* ACB {agas}
agolen: whetstone: *agolan* AB {agalen}
agrya: agree: *agrya* T {agrya}
alejya: allege: *alegya* T {alejya}
alemma: hence: *alemma, alema, aleme* M; *alemma* T; *alemma, alebma* C; *alebma* AB {alemma}
alena / alenna: thence: *alena* C; *a lena* AB; *alenna* Rowe {alenna}
alowa: allow: *alowe* M; *allowa* T {alowa}
als: cliff: *alz* AB; *aulz* NBoson {als}
alter: altar: *aulter, alter* T; *alter* A; *alter* C {alter}
alusyen, alusonow: alms: *alusyon, alusyen,* (pl.) *alesonou* M {alusen, alusonow}
alwheth / awhel, alwhedhow: key: (pl.) *alwethow* M; (pl.) *alwetho* T; *aluedh, ahuel,* (pl.) *alwedhou* AB {alwheth, alwhedhow}
alwhedha: lock (vb): *alwetha* M; *lyhuetha* AB {alwhedha}
alyon: alien: *alyon, allyon* M {alyon}
amanyn: butter: *amanyn* Borde; *amman, manyn* AB {amanyn}
amaya: perplex: *ameya* M {amaya}
amendya: improve: *amendie* M; (pp.) *amyndys* T; *amendya, mendya* C {amendya}
amma: kiss (vb): *amma* M {amma}
amontya: avail, count: *ammontya* M; *amowntya* C {amontya}
amuvya: disturb: *amuwya* M {amuvya}
an Deg Gormynadow: the 10 Commandrnents: *An Deg Gormynadow* T {An Dek Gorhemmynadow}

an pyth awartha a-woles: upside down: *an pith awartha the wolas* T {an pyth awartha a-woles}

an re-ma: these (pron.): *an rema* M; *an ryma* C {an re-ma}

an re-na: those (pron.): *an rena* M; *an re na* T; *an ryna* C {an re-na}

an Werhes Marya: the Virgin Mary: *an wyrhes maria* T; *an worthias marya, an werthias marya* A {an Werghes Marya}

anal: breath: *anel* M {anal}

ancledhyas: bury (vb); funeral (n.): *anclethias, anclethyes* M; *anclythyas* C; (pp.) *enkledhyz* AB {encledhyas}

ancow: death: *ancou* M; *ankaw, ankowe, ankow* C; *ankou* AB {ancow}

ancumbra: encumber: *ancumbra* M {ancombra}

anella: breathe: *anella* T {anella}

aneth: wonder: *aneth* T {aneth}

anfusy/anfujy: misfortune: *anfusy* M; *enfugy, anfugye* C {anfusy/anfujy}

anger: anger (n.): *anger* A {anger}

angra: anger (vb): *angra* T; *angra* C; (pp.) *engrez* Rowe {angra}

anhedhek: diseased: *anhethek* M {anhedhek}

anken: misery: *anken* M; *anken, ankyn* T {anken}

ankevy: forget: *ankevy* M; *ankevy* T; *ankevy* C {ankevy}

annya: disturb: *annya, annye* M; *anya, unya* T; *nea* C {annya}

anowy: light (vb): *annowy* T {enawy}

antarlyk: interlude, comedy: *antarlick* AB {ynterlut}

antel, antylly: snare: (pl.) *antylly* T; *antal, antoll* JBoson {antel, antylly}

anteythy: incapable: *antythy* M {antythy}

anvoth: reluctance: *anvoth* M {anvoth}

anwan: anvil: *anuan* AB {anwan}

anwhek: unpleasant: *anwek* M {anwhek}

anwys: cold (illness): *anwous* PC; *anwys* M; *annez* AB {anwos}

aperya: damage (vb): *aperya* M {aperya}

apperya: appear: *apperya* T {—}

apposya: examine: *apposia* M {apposya}

appoyntya: appoint: *apoyntya* T; *apoyntya, poyntya* C {appoyntya}

apron, apronyow: apron: *apparn* AB; *aprodnieo* Rowe {aparn, apronyow]

aquytya: recompense (vb): *aquytya* M; *acquyttya* C {aquytya}

aral, erel: other: *arall, arel, areyl* M; *arell*, (pl.) *erell* T {aral, erel}

aras: plough (vb): *araz*: AB; *aras* ACB {aras}

ardar: plough: *ardar* AB; *arder* ACB {ardar}

arf, arvow: weapon: (pl.) *arvow* M; *arv* AB {arf, arvow}

argh: chest: *argh* M {argh}

arghel, argheleth: archangel: (pl.) *arthelath* A; (pl.) *arthelath* C; *archail* AB {arghel, argheleth}

argya: argue: *argya* M {argya}

arhadow: command (n.): *arhadowe, aradowe* C {arghadow}

arlodhes: lady: *arlothes* M; *arlothas* NBoson {arlodhes}

arluth, arlydhy: lord: *arluth, arlud*, (pl.) *arlyзy*, (pl.) *arlythy* M; *arluth* T; *arluth, arluthe* C; *arleth, arludh*, (pl.) *arlydhi*, (pl.) *arlodho* AB; *arleth* Rowe {arluth, arlydhy}

art: art: *art* C {art}

arta: again: *arta* M; *arta* T; *arta* AB {arta}

artykel: article: *artickell* A {artykyl}

arveth: wages: *arveth* M {arfeth}

ascallen, ascal: thistle: *askallan, askallen*, (pl.) *askal* AB; (pl.) *askal* Rowe {ascallen}

ascendya: ascend: *assendia* M; *assendia* T; *ascendia* A {ascendya}

ascor: offspring: *ascore* C {ascor}

ascorn, eskern: bone: (pl.) *escarn* OM; *ascorn* RD; *askern* C; *asgarn, asgorn* AB; *askern* NBoson {ascorn, eskern}

ascra: bosom: *ascra* M; *ascra* T {ascra}

ascusya: excuse: *ascusia* M; (cf. *esgyzianz* AB) {ascusya}

asen: donkey: *asan* C; *asen* AB {asen}

asen/asowen, asow: rib: *asowen*, (pl.) *assow* T; *asan, asen*, (pl.) *assow*, (pl.) *asow* C; *azan* AB {asen/asowen, asow}

askel, askelly: wing: *askal*, (pl.) *skelli* AB; *asgal, askal*, (pl.) *askelli*, (pl.) *skelli* ACB {askel, askelly}

askelly grehyn: bat (mammal): *asgelli grehan* AB {askelly greghyn}

aspya/aspyas: spy (vb): *aspya* M; *aspeas* C {aspya}

assaya: try: *assaya* M; *assaya, saya* C {assaya}

assentya: agree: *assentya* M; *assentya* T; *assentya* C {assentya}

astranj/stranj: strange, foreign: *astrange* M; *strang, strayng* T; *strange* C {astranj/stranj}

aswon/ajwon/aswonvos: recognise: *aswen, aswonfos* M; *aswon* C; *adzhan, adzhuonfaz* AB; *adzhan* JBoson {aswon/aswonvos}

atla/adla, atlyan: villain: *athla*, (pl.) *atlyan* M; *addla* T; *adla* C {atla, atlyon}

atomma: behold here: *awot omma* OM; *atoma* M; *tomma* C {ot omma}

atta: behold: *ate* M; *atta* T; *yta* C {atta/otta}

attendya: attend: *attendia, attendya* M; *attendya* C {attendya}

aval, avallow: apple: *avall* T; *avall*, (pl.) *avallow* C; (pl.) *avalou*, (pl.) *lavalou* AB {aval, avallow}

avel: like (prep.): *avell, avel* C {avel}

avlavar: dumb: *avlavar* AB {aflavar}

avorow: tomorrow: *avorow* M; *avorowe* C; *avuru, avorou, y vuru* AB; *avorou* ACB {avorow}

avowtrer adulterer: *avouter* T {avowtrer}

avowtry: adultery: *advowtry* {avowtry}

avowa: admit: *vowa, advowa* C {avowa}

avoydya: avoid, go away: *avodya, avodia* M; *avoydia* T; *voydeya* A; *avoydya, voydya* C {avodya}

avys: advice: *avys* M {avys}

avysya: advise: *avysya* M; *avycya, avysshya* C {avysya}

awan: river: *auan* AB {awan}

awartha: above (adv.): *awartha* M; *awartha* A; *awartha* C; *uarrah* AB; *avorra* JBoson {awartha}

awayl, awaylys: gospel: *awell* M; *awelle, aweyll*, (pl.) *aweylys* T; *awaile* A; *awell* C {awayl, awaylow}

awaylor, awaylors: evangelist: *aweylar*, (pl.) *aweilers*, (pl.) *aweylers*, (pl.) *aweylors* T {awaylor, awayloryon}

awel: weather: *awell, auel* ACB {awel}

awher: sorrow: *awer* M {awher}

awos: because of: *awos, awoys* M; *awois* T; *awos, awoos* C; *auôs* AB {awos}

ayr: air: *eyer* T; *ayre* C; *air* AB {ayr}

baby, babyow: baby: *baby*, (pl.) *babyou* M {baby, babyow}

bacheler: bachelor: *bagcheler, bakcheler* M {bacheler}

bagas: bush: *bagaz* AB {bagas}

bagyl: staff: *bagyl* M {bagyl}

balyer: barrel: *balliar* AB; *balliar* ACB; *balliar* JBoson {balyer}

ban: high: *ban* AB {ban}

banallen, banal: broom: *bynollan*, (pl.) *banal* AB; (pl.) *banal*, (pl.) *bannel* ACB {banalen, banal}

banken: bank, dyke: *bankan* AB {banken}

banket: banquet: *banket, bankat* T {banket}

banna: drop: *banna* T; *banna, badna* C; *banne, badna* AB {banna}

bar: top: *bar* AB {bar}

***bar, barrow**: branching bough: (pl.) *barrow* T {bar, barrow}

bara: bread: *bara* T; *bara* C; *bara* AB; *bara* Bilbao MS; *bara* ACB {bara}

bardh: bard, mime: *barth* OCV; *bardh* AB {barth}

barf, barvow: beard: (pl.) *barvou* M; *bar', barev* AB; *baref, barf, bar* ACB {barf, barvow}

bargyn: bargain (n.): *bargyn* M; *bargayn, bargayne* C; *bargen* ACB {bargen}

bargynya: bargain (vb.): *barginia, bargidnia* AB; *bargidnia* ACB {bargenya}

barlys: barly: *barlys* C; *barliz* AB; *barles* Bilbao MS {barlys}

basket: basket: *basket* AB; *basket* ACB {basket}

batalyas: battle (vb): *batalyays* M {batalyas}

batel, batalyow: battle (n.): *batel* OM; *batel* M; (pl.) *batallyow* T {batel, batalow}

bath: bath: *bath* M {bath}

bay, bayow: kiss (n.): *bay* PC; *bay* M; (pl.) *baiou* AB {bay}

baya: kiss (vb): *baye* ACB {baya}

bedh, bedhow: grave: *beth*, (pl.) *bethow* M; *beth* C; *bedh*, (pl.) *bedhou* AB; *bedh*, (pl)} *bedhou* ACB {beth, bedhow}

bedha: dare: *betha* M; *betha* C {bedha}

bedhgyla: bellow (vb): *bedhigla* AB {bedhgyla}

bejeth / beseth: baptism: *begeth, beseth* T {byjyth}

bejeth: face: *bedgeth* ACB; *budgeth* JBoson {bejeth}

bejydhya / besydhya: baptise: *bygithia, begethya, begythya* M; *besythia, besitthia* T {bysydhya / byjydhya}

bejydhyans: christening: *bedzhidhian[z]* AB {bysydhyans}

benary: ever: *benary* M; *benary* C; *benary* AB; *benary* ACB {bynary}

benedycsyon: benediction: *benedycconn, benedicconn* M {benedyksyon}

benejycter / benesycter: blessedness: *benegycter, benesygter* M; *benegitter* T; *benegicter* A {benesykter / benejykter}

benen, benenes: woman: *bynen, benen*, (pl.) *benenes* M; *benyn*, (pl.) *benenes* T; *benyn* C; *bennen, banen*, (pl.) *benenez* AB; *bennen* ACB {benen, benenes}

benewen: wench: *benewen* M {benewen}

benneth / banneth, bannothow: blessing: *beneth, benneth, bennath, bedneth, banneth*, (pl.) *bannothou* M; *bannath, bannethe, bedna, banneth* C; *bednath, bedneth* ACB {bennath, bennothow}

benowes: bradawl: *beneuez* AB; *beneuez* ACB {menowes}

benow: female (n.): *benaw* C {benow}

benyga: bless: *benyga* M; *benigia* AB; (imp.) *beniggo* TBoson {benyga}

benygys / benegas: blessed: *benyges* M; *benegas, benegys* T; *benegys* A; *benegas* C; *benigaz* AB; *benigas* NBoson {benygys}

benytha: ever: *benyꝫa* M {bynytha}

ber: short: *bur* M; *ber* AB {ber}

ber-anal: asthma: *ber-anal* AB {ber-anal}

bern: concern (n.): *bearn* C {bern}

berya: pierce: *berya* M {berya}

bes / bys: world: *bys, beys* M; *bys, bis* T; *beise, beyse, bys, byes, beys* C; *beyz* AB; *beys, bez, biz* ACB; *beaze* Rowe {bys}

bes, besyas: finger: *bêz*, (pl.) *boziaz* AB {bys, besyas}

besken: thimble: *besgan* AB; *besgan* ACB {bysken}

besow: ring: *bezau* AB; *besau* ACB {bysow}

best, bestas: animal: *best* M; *best*, (pl.) *bestas*, (pl.) *bestes* T; *beast*, (pl.) *bestas* C; *bêst*, (pl.) *bestez* AB {best, bestas}

besy: busy: *besy* M; *besy* T {bysy}

besyon: vision: *besyon* M {vesyon}

bew: alive: *byu, beu* M; *bêu* AB {bew}

bewa: live: *bewe* M; *bewa* C; *beua* AB; *bowa* Rowe {bewa}

bewek: lively: *bewek* T {bewek}

bewnans: life: *beunans* M; *bewnans* T; *bewnans, bewnas* C; *bounaz* AB; *bownans* JBoson; *bowngas* Rowe {bewnans}

blam: blame (n.): *blame* C {blam}

blamya: blame (vb): *blamya* M; *blamya* C {blamya}

bledhen, bledhynnyow, blodh: year: *blethen, blyꝫan*, (pl.) *blethynnyou* M; *blethan*, (pl.) *blethynnyow* T; *blethan*, (pl.) *bloth*, (pl.) *blethydnyow*, (pl.) *blethydnyowe* C; *bledhan*, (pl.) *bledhynno* AB; (pl.) *blethanniou* JBoson; (pl.) *blouth* TBoson; *blouth* Bodinar {bledhen, bledhynnyow, bloth}

blejen: flower: *bledzhan* AB {blejen}

blew: hair: *blew, bleaw, bleawe* C; *blêu* AB; *blew* ACB {blew}

blewak: hairy: *blewake* C; *bleuak* AB {blewak}

blues/bles: flour. *blez* AB; *blease* Bilbao MS {bles}

bleydh, bleydhas: wolf: *blyth* M; (pl.) *blythes* T; *blygh* C; *blaidh* AB; *blaidh* ACB {blyth, blydhas}

blonojeth, bolunjeth: will, wish (n.): *blonogeth, bolnogeth* M; *blonogeth, blonogath* T; *blonogath, blanogathe* C; *bolonegeth, bolyndzheth* AB; *bonogath* NBoson {bolunjeth}

blow: blue: *blou* AB {blou}

bo/po: or: *bo* M; *bo* T; *po* C {bo/po}

bocla: buckle (vb): *bocla* T {bocla}

bodh: wish (n.): *both* M; *both* T: *bothe, both* C {both}

bodhar: deaf: *bother* M; *bothar* T {bodhar}

body: body: *body* M; *body* C {body}

bogh: buck: *bogh* M {bogh}

bogh, bohow: cheek: *bogh* AB; *boh*, (pl.) *bohow* ACB {bogh, boghow}

bohes: little: *bohes* M {boghes}

bohes venough: seldom: *bohes venogh* M {boghes venough}

bohojogneth: poverty: *bohogogneth* M {boghojogneth}

bohosek/bohojek, bohosogyon/bohojogyon: poor (adj.); poor person (n.): *bohosek, bothosek*, (pl.) *bohosogyan*, (pl.) *bohosogyon*, (pl.) *bohogogyon* M; *bohosek* T; *bohodzhak* AB; *boadjack* Bodinar {boghosek, boghosogyon/boghojogyon}

bol: axe: *bool* OM; *boell* C {bol}

bolla: cup, bowl: *bolla* AB; *bolla* ACB {bolla}

bom: blow (n.): *bum* M {bom}

boneyl: or: *bonyl* {bonyl}

bos: food: *boys, bos* M; *bos* T; *boos* C; *bûz* AB; *booz* ACB; *booze* Rowe {bos}

bos/bones: be: *bos, bois, bones* M; *bos, bois* T; *boos, bonas* C; *bôz* AB; *bonas, bones, bôs, bôz* ACB {bos/bones}

***bost, bostow**: boast: (pl.) *bostou* M; (pl.) *bostow* T {bost, bostow}

bostya: boast: *bostya* M; *bostya* T; *bostya, bostia* A {bostya}

bowjy: cowshed: *boudzhi* AB; *boudzhi* ACB {bowjy}

bowyn: beef: *bowyn* M; *bouin* AB {bowyn}

boya: boy: *boya* C {boya}

bragya: threaten: *braggye, bragya* M {bragya}

bram: fart (n.): *bram* C; *brabm* AB {bram}

bran: raven: *bran* M; *brane* C; *bran* AB {bran}

bras, brasyon: great (adj.); great person (n.): *brays*, (pl.) *brosyen* M; *bras* T; *bras, braes* C; *braoz* AB; *broas* NBoson; *braos, brawse* ACB {bras, brasyon}

braster: greatness, firmament: *braster* T; *broster* C; *braozder* AB {braster}

brathky: cur: *brathky* M; *brathkey* ACB {brathky}

bregh, dewvregh: arm: (dual) *deffregh* PA; (dual) *ij vregh* M; *bregh* C; *brêh*, (dual) *dibreh* AB; *breh* ACB {bregh, dywvregh}

brehal: sleeve: *brehal* AB; *brehal* ACB {breghal}

brehy: dandruff: *brehy* M {breghy}

brennygen, brennyk: barnacle: *bernigan*, (pl.) *brennik* AB; *brenigan, bernigan*, (pl.) *brennik* ACB {bernygen, bernyk}

brentyn: noble: *brentyn* M; *brentyn* C; *bryntyn* ACB {bryntyn}

bres/brys: mind: *brys, breys* M; *brys* T; *breis* C; *brêz* AB; *brez* NBoson; *brez, brys* ACB {brys}

brethel: trout: *brethal* AB; *brethal* ACB {brythel}

breys: womb: *breys* M; *breis* T {brys}

broder, breder/bredereth: brother: *broder*, (pl.) *bredereth*, (pl.) *breder* M; *brother*, (pl.) *bredereth*, (pl.) *brederath* T; *brodar* C; *bredar*, (pl.) *brederedh* AB; *broder*, (pl.) *broderath* Rowe {broder, breder/bredereth}

brogh: badger: *brogh* M; *broch* AB {brogh}

bron, dewvron: breast: *bron* M; (dual) *defran* C; *brodn* AB; *bron* ACB {bron, dywvron}

bronnen, bronn: rush (= plant): *bronnen* RD; *brydnan*, (pl.) *brydn* AB {bronnen}

browy: crush (vb): *browi, brewe* Rowe; *brewy* ACB {brewy}

brues: judgment: *brus, brues* M {brus}

brusy: judge (vb): *brusy, brusi* M {brusy}

bry: regard (n.): *bry* M {bry}

bryansen/bryanjen: throat: *bryonsen* M; *beransen* T; *brandzhan* AB {bryansen}

brybour: vagabond: *brebour* M {brybour}

bryjyon: boil, seethe: *bridzhan* AB; *bridzhan*, (pp.) *bridzhiez, brudzhiaz* ACB {bryjyon}

bryk: brick: *bryck, bricke* C {bryk}

bryttel: brittle: *brytyll* T; *bruttall, brotall* C; *brettal* AB {brottel}

bryvya: bleat: *priva* AB {bryvya}}

bucca: goblin: *bucka* C {bucca}

budhy: drown: *buthy* M; *buthy* T: *bethy* C; (pp.) *bidhyz* AB {budhy}

bugel, bugeleth: shepherd: *bugel* M; (pl.) *beguleth*, (pl.) *bugula* T; *bugell* A; *bigal* AB {bugel, bugeleth}

bugh: cow: *bugh* OM; *bewgh* C; *biuh* AB; *beu* ACB; *bew* Bilbao MS {bugh}

buk: buck goat: *byk* AB {buk}

bulhorn: snail: *bulhorn* AB {bulhorn}

burluan: morning star: *burluan* T; *byrlûan* AB; *byrluan* ACB {berlewen}

busel: dung (as fuel): *buzl* AB; *buzl* ACB {busel}

bush, bushys: bush, crowd: *busche* T; *bushe, bush*, (pl.) *bushes* C {bush, bushys}

byan: small: *byen, byan* M; *bean* T; *bean* C; *bian, bihan* AB {byghan}

byldya: build: *buldya, byldya* T; *buyldya* C {buyldya}

bylen: villain: *byleyn, belan, belen* M; *byllan* C {bylen}

bylyny: villainy: *belyny* M {bylyny}

byner: never: *bener* M; *bydner* C {byner}

byrla: embrace (vb): *byrla* AB; *byrla* ACB {byrla}

bys may: until (conj.): *bys may* T {bys may}

bys vycken: ever: *bys vyckan* T; *bys vyckan* C {bys vvken}

bys yn: until: *bys yn* M; *bys in* T; *bez yn, bes yn* C {bys yn}

bysmer: injury: *bysmer* M {bysmer}

bytegens: nonetheless: *bitegyns* RD; *bytegyns* M {bytegens}

byteweth: to the end, after all: *byteweth* M {byteweth}

byth moy: never more: *byth moy* M {byth moy}

bythqueth: ever (in the past): *bythqueth* M; *bythqueth* T; *bythquath, bythquathe* C; *bysqueth, besga* AB; *beska* NBoson; *besga* ACB; *biscath* Bodinar {bythqueth}

byttedhewetha: nonetheless: *bette thewetha* T {bytedhewetha}

byttele: nonetheless: *bytte le* T {bytele}

caken: cake: *kakan* AB {caken}

cachya: catch: *catchah* ACB {cachya}

caf: cave: *caff* M {caf}

cafus / cawas: get: *cafus, cawas* M; *cafus, kafas* T; *cowis* A; *cawas* C; *kauaz, kavaz* AB; *cafus, cawas, gawas* ACB {cafos / cawas}

cala: straw: *cala* M; *cala* C; *kala* AB {cala}

Calan Gwaf: All Saints Day: *kalan gwâv* AB {Calan Gwaf}

Cala' Me: Mayday: *calame* M; cf. *kalan* AB & *Calan* ACB {Cala' Me}

cales / calys: hard: *cales* M; *calys, calis* T; *callys* C; *kalliz, kallish* AB {cales}

caletter: hardness: *kaletter* AB; *kallater* ACB {caletter}

cals / calj: much: *cals* PA; *calge* M {cals / calj}

cam: bent; wrong (n.): *cam* M; *cam* T; *cam, cabm* C; *kabm* AB; *cam, cabm* ACB {cam}

cam: step: *cam* M {cam}

camlagajek: cross-eyed: *kabmlagazdzhak* AB {camlagajek}

cammenseth: injustice: *cammenseth, kamynsoth* T {camhenseth}

camneves / camdhavas: rainbow: *camnevet* OCV; *cabmthavas* C; *kamdhavas* AB; *cabm-thavaz, kabm-thavaz* ACB {camneves / camdhavas}

campolla: mention (vb): (imp.) *campol*, (pret.) *campollys* M {campolla}

camscodhek: humped, round-shouldered: *kabm-sgudhak* AB {—}

can, canow: song: *can* M; *cane*, (pl.) *canow* C {can, canow}

cana: sing: *cana* C; *kana* AB; *kana*, (imp.) *keno* TBoson {cana}

canker, kencras: crab: *kankr, kankar*, (pl.) *kenkraz* AB {canker, kencras}

cannas, cannasow / cannajow: messenger: *cannas* M; (pl.) *canhasawe*, (pl.) *canhagowe* C {cannas, cannasow}

cans: hundred: *cans* M; *cans* T; *cans* C; *kanz* AB {cans}

cantol, cantolyow: candle: *kantyll* T; *kantl*, (pl.) *kyntulu* AB {cantol, cantolyow}

cantolbren / coltrebyn: lampstand: *cantulbren* OCV; *coltrebyn* T {cantolbren}

capel: cable: *capel* M {capel}

car, kerens: friend, relative: *car*, (pl.) *kerens* M; *car*, (pl.) *kerens* T; *car*, (pl.) *kerens* C; *kar*, (pl.) *keranz* AB {car, kerens}

cara: love (vb): *kara, cara* M; *cara* T; *cara* C; *kara* AB {cara}

caradewder loving-kindness: *caradeuder* M {caradewder}

caradow, caradowyon: beloved (adj. & n.): *karadow, caradou* ; *caradow, caradowe*, C; (pl.) *kardouion* AB; (pl.) *cardowyon* ACB {caradow}

caretys (pl.): carrots: *karetys* AB {caretys}

carhar, carharow: prison, fetter: (pl.) *carharou* M; *karhar* AB {carghar, cargharow}

carhara: imprison, shackle: *carhara* M {carghara}

carow: stag: *carow* PA; *carou, karou* M; *karo* AB {carow}

carrek: rock: *carrek* M; *carrak, carrak* T; *karrak, karak* AB; *karrack* NBoson; *carak, carrik* ACB {carrek}

carya: carry: *cariah, coria* ACB {carya}

cas: case: *cas, cays* M; *cas* T; *case* C {cas}

casa: hate: (3sg.) *cays* M; *casa* T {casa}

casadow: hateful: *casadowe* C {casadow}

casek: mare: *casak* C; *kazak* AB; *casek* Bilbao MS {casek}

casel: armpit: *casel* M; *kazal* AB {casal}

castel, castylly: castle: *castel, castell*, (pl.) *castylly* M; *kastal* AB; (pl.) *castilly* Scawen; *kastal*, (pl.) *kestell* ACB {castel, castylly}

cath: cat: *cath* M; *kâth* AB {cath}

caudarn: cauldron: *kaudarn* AB {caudarn}

caus: cause (n.): *caus* M; *cawse* T {caus}

cavach: cabbage: *kavatsh* AB {cavach}

cavow: grief: (pl.) *cavow* C {cavow}

certan: certain: *certan, certyn, certen* M; *certan* T; *certyn* A; *sertan, serten, sertayne* C {certan}

cessya: cease: *cessya* T {cessya}

challa: jaw-bone: *chala* C {challa}

chalynj: challenge: *chalyng* M {chalynj}

chamber: bedroom: *chammbour* OM; *tshombar* AB; *chumber* place-names {chambour}

chanel: channel: *chanel* M {chanel}

chanj: change (n.): *change, chang* T {chanj}

chanjya: change (vb): *changya* A {chanjya}

chapel: chapel: *chappell* M {chapel}

charjya: charge (vb): *chardgia, chargya* M; *chardgya, charrdgya* C {charjya}

charych / charj: charge (n.): *charg, charge, charych* M; *chardg, chardge* C {charych / charj}

chassya: chase (vb): *chassya* C {chassya}

chastya: chastise: *chastya* M {chastya}

chattel: cattle: *chattall, chattell* C; *tshatttal* AB; *chattoll* JBoson; *chattel* Rowe {chattel}

chayn, chaynys: chain (n.): (pl.) *chaynys* PC; *chayne* C {chayn}

chaynya: chain (vb): *chenya, cheynya* M {chaynya}

cheften: chieftain: *cheften* M; *cheften* C {chyften}

cher: cheer, demeanour: *cheare* C {cher}

cherya: cherish: *cherya* M {cherya}

chesya: cherish: *chesya* T {chersya}

cheyr, cheyrys: chair: (pl.) *cheyrys* PC; *cheer* M {chayr, chayrys}

chons: chance: *chaunce* T {chons}

chorl: churl: *chorle, chorll* C {chorl}

chy, trevow/treven: house: *chy*, (pl.) *trefou* M; *chy, chi*, (pl.) *trevyn* T; *tshyi*, (pl.) *treven* AB; (pl.) *treven* ACB; *choy* Rowe {chy, trevow/treven}

chyf: chief: *chyff* M; *chyff, chiff* T: *cheif* C {chyf}

chymbla: chimney: *tshimbla* AB {chymbla}

clabyttour: bittern: *klabitter* AB; *clabitter* ACB {clabytttour}

claf, clevyon: sick (adj.); sick person, patient (n.): *claff*, (pl.) *clevyen, clevyon* M; *claff* T; *clave* C; *klau, klav*, (pl.) *klevion* AB; (pl.) *glevyan* Rowe {claf, clevyon}

clappya: talk (vb): *clappia* NBoson; *clapia* JBoson; *clapier* ACB {clappya}

cos, cosow wood: *coys* M; (pl.) *cosow, cossow* C; *kûz* A B; *cos, coys, cus, cooz*, (pl.) *cosow* ACB {cos, cosow}

coscar: company: *cosker* M; *koskar* AB; *cosgar* ACB {coscar}

cosel: quiet, peaceful: *cosel* M; *kuzal, kozal* AB; *cosel, cusal* ACB {cosel}

cosoleth. quiet, peace: *cosoleth* T; *kyzalath* AB; *cosoleth, cosolath* ACB {cosoleth}

coselhe: quieten: *coselhe* M {coselhe}

cost: expense: *cost* M {cost}

costen: target: *kostan* AB; *costan* ACB {costen}

costya: cost (vb): *costya* C {costya}

cot: short: *cot* M; *cut* T; *cutt* C; *cot, cut* ACB {cot}

coth: companion: *coth* T; *cooth* C {coth}

coth: old: *coth, coeth* M; *coth, coith* T; *cooth, cothe* C {coth}

cothman, cothmens: friend: *cothman*, (pl.) *cothmans*, (pl.) *cothmens* M; *cothman*, (pl.) *cothmans* T; (pl.) *cuthmans* A; *cothman* C; *kydhman* AB {cothman, cothmens}

coveytys: covetousness: *coveytes* C {covaytys}

covya: cherish: *covya* M; (pp.) *covys* T {covya}

cowal/cowl: completely: *cowel* M; *cowl* C {cowal/cowl}

cowargh: hemp: *kûer* AB {kewargh}

cowas: storm, squall: *cowas* T; *kûas* AB {cowas}

cowel: pannier: *kaual* AB; *kawal, kawall* JBoson {cowel}

coweth, cowetha: companion: *cowyth*, (pl.) *coweʒa*, (pl) *cowethe* M; (pl.) *cowetha* C; *kyuedh* AB; *coweth* ACB {coweth, cowetha}

cowethas: company: *cowetheys, cowethes, cowethas* M; *cowethas* C {cowethas}

cowethes: female companion: *cowethes* OM; *cowethes* ACB {cowethes}

cowl: broth: *coule* M; *kaul, kowl* AB {cowl}

cows/cowsel: speak: *cous, cousel* M; *cows* T; *cowse, cowsall* C; *kouz* AB {cows, kewsel}

cowsys, cowjejyow: thought: *cousys*, (pl.) *cowgegyow* M {cowsys, cojejyow}

coynt: clever: *coynt* M; *coynt* C {coynt}

crackya: crack (vb): *crakkya* M; (imp.) *crack* NBoson {crakkya}

craf: covetous: *krâv* AB {craf}

crambla: climb, scramble: *krambla* AB {crambla}

creacyon: creation: *creacion, creasion, creacyon* T; *creacon* C {creasyon}

creatya: create: *creatya* T; *creatya* C {creatya}

cref: strong: *cref* OM; *creffe, creff* M; *cryffe, creffe* T; *kref, creif, creyf* C; *krêv* AB; *creve, kreaue* TBoson {cref}

crefder: might: *creffder* M; *crefter* A; *krevder* AB {crefder}

crefhe/crefya: strengthen: *creffe*, (pp.) *crefeis* T; *creffya, creffe* A; *crefhe* NBoson {crefhe}

crefny: avaricious: *crefnye* C {crefny}

cregy: hang: *cregy* M; *cregy, kregy* C; *kregi* AB; *cregi, cregy* ACB {cregy}

crehy: scurf, dandruff: *crehy* M; *krehy* C {creghy}

crejyans/cryjyans: belief: *cregyans* M; *crygyans, cregyans* T; *crydgyans, cregyans* C; *kridzhans, kredzhans* AB; *credzhyans, credgyans* ACB {crysyans, cryjyans}

crenna: tremble: *crenna* M; *kerna, krenna* AB {crenna}

cres: middle: *kres, creys* M; *cres* T; *creys* C; *krêz* AB; *kreis* JBoson {cres}

cres: peace: *cres, creys* M; *cres, cresse* T; *cres, creez* NBoson; *cres, creez* ACB {cres}

cresy/crejy: believe: *cresy* M; *crege, cresy* T; *cregye* C; *kredzhi, kridzhi* AB; *crege* TBoson; *credzha* ACB {crysy/cryjy}

creven: scab, scurf: *krevan* AB {creven}

croder: sieve: *krodar* AB {croder}

crodra: winnow, sieve (vb): *kroddre* PC; *kroddre* ACB {crodra}

crogen, cregyn: shell: *crogon* M; *krogen*, (pl.) *kregin* AB {crogen, cregyn}

crohen, crehen: skin: *cron* M; (pl.) *crehyn* T; *crohan*, (pl.) *krehen* C; *krohan* AB; *crohan* Rowe; *crohen* ACB {croghen, creghyn}

cromman: hook: *krobman* AB; *crobman* ACB {cromman}

cronek: toad. *cronek* OM; *kranag* AB; *cranag* ACB {cronek}

cronkya: hit, strike: *cronkye, cronkya* M; *cronkya* T; *crownkya* C; *krongkia, kronki* AB {cronkya}

crothak: fault-finding (adj.): *crothake* C {crothak}

crow: hut, eye (needle): *crou* M; *krou* AB; *crou, crow* ACB {crow}

crowd: fiddle: *kroud* AB; *crowd* ACB {crowd}

crows: cross: *crous* A; *krouz* AB {crows}

crowspren: cross: *crowspren* T {crowspren}

crullyes: curied: *krylliaz* AB {crullyes}

cruppya: crawl (vb): *cruppyia* C {cruppya}

crya: cry (vb): *crya* M; *crya* T; *crya* A; *crya* C; *kreia, kriha* AB; *crya* Rowe {crya}

cryb an chy: roof ridge: *krib an tshyi* AB {cryb an chy}

cryba/crybas: comb (vb): *kriba, kribaz* AB; *criba, cribaz* ACB {cryba/crybas}

cryben: crest, comb: *kriban* AB; *criban* ACB {cryben}

cryben mel: honeycomb: *kriban mel* AB {cryben mel}

cryf: raw: *kreff* A; *kriv, criv* AB; *criv* ACB {cryf}

Crystones: Christian woman: *crystones* T {crystyones}

Crystyon, Crystonyon: Christian: *cristyan, crystyan*, (pl.) *crustunyon* M; *cristian, krystyan*,

A SHORT DICTIONARY OF UCR

(pl.) *cristonyan*, (pl.) *cristonyon* T; (pl.) *krestudnian* AB {Crystyon, Crystonyon}

cudha: hide, cover: *cutha, cuthe* M; *cutha* C; *kidha* AB {cudha}

cuf, cuvvyon: dear (adj.); dear one (n.): *cuff*, (pl.) *cufyon* M {cuf, cuvvyon}

cuhudha: accuse: *kyhydha* AB; *cuhuthe* ACB {cuhudha}

culyek: cock: *kullyek* PC; *kulliag* AB {culyek}

culyek godhow: gander: *kulliag godho* AB {culyek godhow}

cumyas: permission: *cumyes, kumyas, cumyys* M; *kymmyas* C; *kibmiaz* AB; *kibmiaz* NBoson; *cummyas, kibmias, kibmiaz* ACB {cumyas}

cuntell/cuntelles: gather (vb); gathering (n.): *kuntel* M; *contylles* C; *kyntl* AB; *cuntle* ACB; *contell* Rowe {cuntell/cuntelles}

cuntullva: assembly: *contulva* T {cuntellva}

cunys: firewood: *kunys* OM; *kinnis* AB; *cunys, kunys, kinnis* ACB {cunys}

curun: crown (n.): *curyn* PC; *curen* M; *curyn* T {curun}

curuna: crown (vb): *curuna* M {curuna}

cusk: sleep (n.): *kusg* AB; *cusg* ACB {cusk}

cusca: sleep: *cosca* M; *cuske* C; *kusga, kysga* AB {cusca}

cussya: curse: *cussya* C; (pp.) *cushez* Rowe {cussya}

cusul, cusulyow: counsel: *cusel* M; *cusyll*, (pl.) *cosullyow* T; *kusell, cucell* A; *cusyll* C; *kyssyl*, (pl.) *kysylgou* AB {cusul, cusulyow}

cusulya: advise: *cusullya* M; *cosylllya* C {cusulya}

cuth, cuthow: husk, pod: *kuth*, (pl.) *kuthu* AB {cuth, cuthow}

cyder: cider: *cydyr, syder* M {cyder}

cyta: city: *cyte* M; *cyte, cyta, cita* T; *cyte* Rowe; *cytè* ACB {cyta}

da: good: *da* M; *da* T; *da* C; *da* AB {da}

dader: goodness: *dader, dadder* M; *dadder, daddar* T; *dadar* C {dader}

dagren, dager, dagrow: drop, tear: (pl.) *daggrow* PC; *dagren* M; *dagar*, (pl.) *dagrou* AB {dagren, dager, dagrow}

dalhenna: grasp, seize: *dalhenna* M {dalghenna}

dall: blind (adj.): *dal* PC; *dal* M; *dal* AB {dall}

dalla: blind (vb): *dalla* T {dalla}

dalleth: begin: *dalleth* M; *dallath, dalleth* T; *dalleth* C {dalleth}

dallethfos: beginning: *dallathvas* T; *dallathfas* C {dallethfos}

dama: mother: *dama* M; *dama* C; *dama* AB; *damma* ACB; *damah* Rowe {dama}

dama wyn: grandmother: *dama widn* AB {dama wyn}

damach: damage: *damach* M {damach}

dampnya: damn: *dampnya* M; *dampnya* C {dampnya}

danjer: domination, danger: *daynger, danger, daunger* T {danjer}

dans, dens: tooth, tine: (pl.) *dyns* M; (pl.) *dens* A; *danz*, (pl.) *denz* AB; (pl.) *dens* ACB {dans, dyns}

*dans a-dhelergh, dens a-dhelergh: molar: (pl.) *denz dhelhor* AB {dans a-dhelergh}

dans rag: incisor: *danz rag* AB {dans a-rak}

danvon, danvenys: send: *danvon* OCV; *donfon, donfen*, (pp.) *danvenys* M; *danvon, denvon, dynvon, dynwyn, dynvyn* T; (pp.) *danvenys* C; *danyn* AB; *danen* ACB; *danen* NBoson {danvon, danvenys}

*darbary: provide: (imp.) *darber*, (subj.) *darbara* M {darbary}

darras, darrasow/darrajow: door: *dares*, (pl.) *darasou* M; *daras* C; *darraz* AB; (pl.) *derggawe* TBoson; (pl.) *darazow* ACB {darras, darrasow}

darras rag: front door: *darraz rag* AB {darras a-rak}

dascor: relinquish: *dascor* M {dascor}

dasserhy: rise again: (pp.) *daserrys*, (pp.) *dasserrys* M; *dasserghy, datherghy* ACB {dasserghy}

dasserhyans: resurrection: *dethyrryans* T; *dasserghyans* ACB {dasserghyans}

dasvewa: revive: *dasvewa* M; *dazveua* AB {dasvewa}

davas, deves/devysyow/devyjyow: sheep: (pl.) *dewysyou* M; *davas*, (pl.) *devas, deves* T; (pl.) *devidgyow* C; *davaz*, (pl.) *devez* AB; (pl.) *deuas* TBoson {davas, deves, devysyow}

de: yesterday: *dê* AB {de}

de Gwener, Gwener: Friday: *dugwener, guener* M; *guenar, De guenar* AB {de Gwener}

de Lun: Monday: *Delin* AB {de Lun}

de Mergh: Tuesday: *De merh* AB {de Mergh}

de Merher: Wednesday: *dumerher* M; *De Marhar* AB {de Mergher}

de Sadorn: Saturday: *De Zadarn* AB {de Sadorn}

de Sul, Sul, Sulyow: Sunday: *sul* M; *Dezil* AB; *zeell* TBoson; *da zeel* JTonkin; (pl.) *Zelio* ACB {de Sul}

de Yow: Thursday: *deth you, deyou* M; *De Ieu* AB {de Yow}

de Yow Hablys: Maundy Thursday: *Deow Habblys* A {de Yow Hablys}

debatya: strive: *debatya* M {debatya}

debron: itch: *debron, debren* M; *debarn* AB {debron}

decernya: discern: *decernya* M; *decernya* C {decernya}

decevya: deceive: *desevia, desyvya* T; *decevia* A {—}

declarya: declare: *declarya* T; *declarya* A {—}

dedh, an jedh, dedhyow: day: *deth, an geth*, (pl.) *dyʒyou*, (pl.) *dethyou* M; *dith, an jeth* T; *deth* A; *dyth, an gyth, an geth*, (pl.) *dethyow*, (pl.) *dythyow* C; *dedh, an dzhêdh* AB; *deth* TBoson; *deeth*, (pl.) *dethyow* Rowe {deth, an jeth, dedhyow}

dedhewy: promise (vb): *dethewy* M; (pret.) *didhiuys* AB {dedhewy}

dedhweyth: daytime: *dethwyth* M {dedhwyth}

defollya: violate: *defollya, defoylya* T {deffola}

defry/pur dhefry/yn tefry: indeed: *deffry, devrey* M; *defry, devery, in teffrye, pur thefry* C {defry/pur dhefry/yn tefry}

289

CORNISH TODAY

defya: defie: *defya, deffya* M {defya}
deg: ten: *dec* Borde; *dêg* AB; *dêg, dêk, dêag* ACB {dek}
degves: tenth: *dekfaz* AB; *deagvas* ACB {degves}
deg warn ugans: thirty: *deakwarnegans, deagwarnygans* C; *deg uar niganz* AB {dek-warn-ugans}
***degea**: close: (pp.) *degeys* M; (pp.) *degys* C {degea}
degemeres: accept: *degemores* M {degemeres}
degensete: the day before yesterday: *degenzhete* AB {degensete}
deglena: shudder (vb): *deglynna* C {deglena}
degoth. behoves: *degoth* M {degoth}
degol Myhal: Michaelmas: *dugol myhal* M {degol Myghal}
degol Stul: Epiphany: *degl stûl* AB {degol Stul}
degre, degres: degree: *degre, degry,* (pl.) *degreys* T; *decree, degre, degree* C {degre, degres}
dehesy: hurl: *dehesy* M; *dehesy* T {deghesy}
del: as: *del* M; *dell* T; *del, der* C {del}
delen, del/delyow: leaf: (pl.) *deel,* (pl.) *dellyow* C; *delkian, delk,* (pl.) *delyou* AB; (pl.) *delkiow* ACB; (pl.) *delkiow* Rowe {delen, del, delyow}
delycyous: delicious: *delicius* T; *delicyous, delycyous* C {delycyous}
delyvra: deliver: *delyfra* M; *delyvera,* (pp.) *delyuerys* T; *delyvera* C {delyfra/delyfrya}
demandya: demand (vb): *demandea* A; *dymandia* AB {demondya}
demedhy: marry: *domethy* M; *dimedha* AB; *demithe* ACB: (pp.) *demithez* NBoson {demedhy}
den, tus: man: *den,* (pl.) *tus* M; *den,* (pl.) *tus* T; *deane* A; *dean,* (pl.) *tues* C; *dên,* (pl.) *tiz* AB {den, tus}
dena: suck (vb): *dena* M; *tena* AB {dena}
denaha: deny: *denaha* M; *denaha* T {denagha}
dendyl/dyndyl: earn: *dendyl, dendel, dyndyl* M; *dendyll* C; *dendle* ACB; *dendal* NBoson {dyndyl}
denethy: give birth: *denethy* C; *denethy* Keigwin {denythy}
denlath: murder (n.): *denlath* T {denlath}
denledhyas: murderer: *denleythyas* T {denledhyas}
dens clav: toothache: *denz klav* AB {—}
densa: goodman: *densa* M {densa}
densys: humanity: *densis* M; *densys, dynsys* T {densys}
denty: dainty: *denty* C {denty}
deragla: scold: *deragla* AB {deraylya}
derfyn: deserve: *derfen* M; *dyrfyn* T; *derfyn* C {dervyn}
deryvas: declaration: *daryvays, deryvas* M; *daryvas* C {deryvas}
descendya: descend: *desendya* T {descendya}
desedha: sit down: *desetha* M {desedha}
desempys/a-dhesempys: straightway: *desempys* M; *athesempys, desempys* C; *adhysempyz* AB; *thosympyas* Rowe {desempys/a-dhesempys}
desmygy: conjecture, suspect: *dismigo* AB; *dismiggia* NBoson {desmygy}
desta: attest: *dysta* C {desta}

destrya: destroy: *distruya* M; *dystrya* T; *destrya, destrea* C {—}
desyr: desire (n.): *desyr* M; *desyre* T; *desyre* A; *desyre* C {desyr}
desyrya: desire (vb): *desyrya, deserya* M; *desyrya* T; (pp.) *desyryes* Rowe {desyrya}
devar: duty: *dufer* M; *dewar* C {devar}
devedhyans: origin: *devethyans* M {devedhyans}
devera: drip (vb): *deverra* M {devera}
devergy, dovergy: otter: *devirgi, dour-gi* AB {dowrgy}
devorya: devour: *deworia* M; *devorya, devourya, devowrya* T {devorya}
devys: device: *davys, devyse, devise* C {devys}
dew: two: *deu, dyu* M; *dew* T; *deow* A; *dow* Borde; *deow, dew, deaw* C; *deau* AB {deu, dyw}
Dew, dewow: God, gods: *du,* (pl.) *dewou* M; *du, dew,* (pl.) *duow* T; *dew,* (pl.) *dewyow* C; (pl.) *deuon,* (pl.) *deuou* AB; *dieu* NBoson {Dew, dewow}
dewas, dewosow: drink (n.): *dewes, deves,* (pl.) *dewosou* M; *dewas* T; *dewas* A; *deuaz, dewas* AB {dewas, dewosow}
dewdhek/dowdhek: twelve: *dowʒek* PA; *dewthack* C; *dowthack* ACB; *douthack* Bilbao MS {deudhek}
dewdhek warn ugans: thirty two: *dewthack warnugans, dewthack warnygans* C {deudhek-warn-ugans}
dewedha: finish (vb): *diuadhe* AB {dewedha}
dewedhes: late: *dewethaz* NBoson {dewedhes}
deweth: end (n.): *dyweth* M; *deweth* T; *dewathe, dewath* C; *diuadh, dûadh, diuedh* AB; *duah* Rowe; *duath* NBoson; *duath* Gwavas {deweth}
dewetha: last: *dewetha* T; *dewetha* A; *dyuetha* AB; *dewetha* NBoson {dewetha}
dewethva: end (n.): *dewethfa* T; *dowethva* C {dewethva}
dewgans: forty: *dew ugens* PC; *duganz* AB; *doganze* Rowe {deugans}
dewglun: haunch: (dual) *duklyn* M {dywglun}
dewhans: forthwith: *dewhans, dewans* C {dewhans}
dewhelyans: atonement: *dewelyans* M; *dewhillyans* C {dewhelans}
dewlujy: devilry: *deulugy* M {dewlujy}
dewlyn: knees: *dewleyn* PA; *deu lyn* M; *dewglyen* C; *dowlin* ACB {dewlyn}
dewsys/dewjys: deity: *deugys, deusys* M; *dusys, dugys* T; *dewges* C {dewsys}
dewys/dowys: chose: (pp.) *dewesys* M; *dewys,* (pp.) *dewesys* T; (pp.) *dowesys* C {dewys}
dha: thy: *ʒe, ʒeth* M; *the* T; *ʒa, theth* C; *dha* AB {dha}
dhe: to: *ʒe, the* M; *the* T; *ʒa, tha* C; *dho, dha, do* AB {dhe}
dhe stray: astray: *the stray* T {dhe stray}
dhe ves: away: *the ves* T; *the veas* C {dhe ves}
dhe'n dor. down: *then dor* M; *then dore* T {dhe'n dor}
dhya: from: *thea* T {dhya}
dhywar: from off: *thewar* M {a-dhywar}

A SHORT DICTIONARY OF UCR

dhyworth / dheworth: from: *theorth* M; *theworth* T; *thyworth* A; *adhort, adheuorth, dhort, dho ort* AB; *adheworth* Gwavas {a-dhyworth}

doctour, doctours: doctor: *doctor*, (pl.) *doctours* M; *doctour, docture*, (pl.) *doctours* T; (pl.) *doctors* A {doctour, doctours}

dof: tame: *dof, doff* M {dof}

dohajedh. afternoon: *dohadzhedh, dyhodzhadh* AB {dohajeth}

don: carry: *don* M; *done, don* T; *dûn* AB {don}

donsya: dance (vb): *donsia* M; *downsya* C {donsya}

dor, an nor: earth: *doyr, an nor, an nour* M; *dore, an nore* T; *dor, door, dore, doer, an noer* C; *dôr, an aôr* AB {dor, an nor}

dorn, dornow: hand: *dorn*, (pl.) *dornow* T: *dorn, doarn* C; *dorn* AB {dorn, dornow}

doryen: east: *thuryan* ACB; *thorians* Borlase {—}

dos: come: *doys, dos* M; *dos* T; *dose* A; *doos* C {dos}

dotya: dote: *dotya* M {dotya}

dova: tame (vb). *dova* AB {dova}

down: deep: *down* M; *downe* C; *doun* AB {down}

downder. depth: *dounder* AB {downder}

dowr, dowrow: water: *dour, dovyr* M; *dowre* T; *dowr* A; *dower*, (pl.) *dorrowe* C; *dour* AB {dowr, dowrow}

dowst: dust: *dust, dowst* T; *dowst* C; *douste* Rowe {dowst}

dowt: fear, doubt (n.): *dout, dowte, dowt* C {dowt}

dowtya: fear (vb): *doutya* M; *dowtya* T; *dowtya* C {dowtya}

dragon: dragon: *dragan, dragon* M; *dragun* AB {dragon}

dre, a-dre: homewards: *dre, adre* M; *a dre* AB {dre, a-dre}

dre / der: through: *der, dre* M; *dre* T; *der* C {dre, der}

drefen: because: *drefen* M; *drefan, drevan* C; *dreffen* Rowe {drefen}

dregyn: harm (n.): *dregyn, dregen, dregan* M {dregyn}

drehevel: lift, raise, rise: *derevel, drehevel* M; *drehevall, drehevell* T; *dreval, dereval* AB; *derevoll* NBoson; *direvall* ACB {drehevell}

dremas: goodman: *dremas* M; *dremas* C; *dermâz* AB {dremas}

dres: over: *drys* M; *drys* T; *dryes, dres* C; *drêz* AB {dres}

dreyn: thorn: (pl.) *dryn*, (pl.) *dreyn* M; (pl.) *dreyn* C; *drên* AB {dreyn}

dreysen: bramble: (pl.) *dreys* T; *dreizan* AB; (pl.) *drize* ACB {dreysen}

drocoleth: wrong, harm (n.): *drokcoleth* M; *drockoleth, drogkoleth, drokolleth, drocoleth* T {drocoleth}

drog: evil (n. & adj.): *drog, drok* M; *drog* T; *droke, droog, drog* C; *drôg* AB; *droag* Rowe {drok / drog}

droghandla: mistreat: *drokhandla* M {drok-handla}

drushyan: thresh: *drushen* ACB {drushya}

dry: bring: *dry* M; *dry* T; *dry* C {dry}

du: black: *du* RD; *diu* AB {du}

due: finished, over: *due* M; *de* C {du / de}

duer concerns: *duer* M {dur}

duhan: sorrow: *duen, duwon, dewen* M; *duwhan, dewan, dewhan* C; *dewhan* Rowe {dughan}

duhanhees: grieved: *dewhanhees* C {dughanhees}

duk, dukys: duke: *duk*, (pl.) *dukis* M; *duke* C {duk, dukys}

Dursona d(h)eugh(-why): God bless you: *Dorsona dywy, Dorsona dyugh* M; *Durzona dewhi* Borde {Dursona dheugh-why}

durya: last (vb): *durya* M; *durrya, durya* T; *dirria* JTonkin; *dirra* ACB; *dyrria* Keigwin {durya}

dustuny: witness: *dustuny* M; *distuny* A; *destinye* C {dustuny}

duta: duty: *dute* M; *duty* T; *dewty* C {duta}

dy / dhy: thither: *dy* M; *thy* C {dy / dhy}

dyal: revenge, vengeance: *dyel* M; *deall* C {dyal}

dyalar: healthy: *dealer* M {dyalar}

dyank: escape (vb): *dyank* M {dyank}

dybarth: separate (vb): *dybarth, dyberth, dybert* M; (pp.) *deberthis*, (pp.) *debyrthys* T; *diberh, barri* AB {dybarth, dyberthys}

dybarthva: separation: *deberthva* C {dybarthva}

dybenna: behead: *debynna* M {dybenna}

dyber: saddle: *dibre, diber, debre* AB {dyber}

dyblans: clearly: *dyblans* M; *dybblance, dibblance* C {dyblans}

dybry / debry eat: *dybry, dybbry* M; *debbry, dybbry* T; *debbry, dybbry* C; *debbry* AB; *debre* Rowe {dybry}

dybyta: pitiless: *debyta* M; *dibitti* AB {dybyta}

dyegrys: shocked: *dyegrys* M {dyegrys}

dyek: lazy: *dyek* M; *dyag* T {dyek}

dyeskynna / skynnya: descend, fall: *skynnya, deyskynna* M; *skynnya* T; *diskynnya, dyiskynnya, yskydnya, skydnya* C {dyeskynna / skynnya}

dyeskys: barefoot, shoeless: *diesgiz* AB {—}

dyfacya: deform: (pp.) *defashes* C {dyfacya}

dyfelebys: deformed: *defalebys* C {dyfelebys}

dyfen: prohibition (n.); forbid (vb): (pres.) *dufen* M; *defen* T; *defan*, (pp.) *defednys* C {dyfen}

dyffrans: difference (n.); different (adj.): *dyfferens, defferance* T; *deffrans, defrans, diffrans* C {dyffrans}

dyfun: awake (adj.): *dufen, dyvune* M {dyfun}

dyfuna: wake: *dufuna* M {dyfuna}

dyfygya: tire, become exhausted: *tefigia* AB {defygya}

dyfyth: desert (n.): *devyth, defyth* C {dyfyth}

dygelmy: unbind. *degelmy* M; *degylmy* T {dygelmy}

dyghtya: treat (vb): *dyghtya* M {dyghtya}

dyg'lon: discouragement: *dyglon* M {dyg'lon / dygolon}

dyheras: apologise: *deheras* M {dyharas}

dyhow: right hand: *dyou* M; *dyghow, dyhow* C; *dyhou* AB; *dihow* ACB {dyghow}

dylla: release: (imp.) *dulle* M; *dylla* C {dvllo}

dyllas: clothes: *delles* M; *dillas, dyllas* T; *dyllas, dillas* C; *dillaz* AB {dyllas}

dynar, dynerow: penny: (pl.) *denerou* M; *dinar* Borde; {dynar, dynerow}

dynas: city, fortress: *dinaz* AB {*in UC* dynas = hill fort}

dynerhy: greet: *dynerhy* AB {dynerghy}

dynnya: urge: *dynnya* M {dynnya}

dynyta: dignity: *dynyte, dynnyte* M {dynyta}

dyogel: certain: *dyogeyl, dyogel* M; *dyhogall, dehogall* C; *diougel* AB {dyogel}

dyowl, an jowl, dewolow: devil: *deule, an ioul, an joule*, (pl.) *dewolow*, (pl.) *dewolou* M; *dyowle* T; *jowle, an joule*, (pl.) *devollow*, (pl.) *dewollow* C; *dzhiaul* AB; *an jowle* Rowe {dyawl, an jawl, dewolow}

dyowles: she devil: *dzhoules* AB {dyawles}

dysawor: unsavoury: *desawer* M {dvsawor}

dyscajor: teacher: *deskadzher* AB {dyscajor}

dyscans: teaching: *dyskans, discans* M; *discans, diskans, dyscans* T; *dyskans, discans* C; *deskans* AB; *deskanz* NBoson {dyscans}

dysclosya: disclose: *disclosya, dysclosya* C {dysclosya}

dyscor: teacher: *dysker* T {dyscor}

dyscrassya: afflict: *dyscrassya* M {dyscrassya}

dyscrejyans: disbelief, unbelief: *dysgregyans* M; *discregyans* T {dyscryjyans}

dyscrysyk: unbelieving: *discrysik* T {dyscryjyk}

dyscudha: reveal: *descotha* C {dyscudha}

dysdayn: disdain: *dysdayne* T {dysdayn}

dysert: desert: *dysert* M {dysert}

dysesya: vex: *desesea* M {dysesya}

dyskevera: uncover: *dyskevera, dyskevra* C {dyskevera}

dysky/desky: teach, learn: *dysky, desky* M; *disky, dysky* T; *desky* C; *deski, desgi, desga* AB; *desga, desgy* ACB {dysky}

dyskybel: disciple: *dissipill*, (pl.) *discabels* T; *desgibl* AB {dyskybel}

dysobaya: disobey: *dysobaya, dysobeya, disobeya* T {dysobaya}

dyson: forthwith: *dyson* M {dyson}

dysplesur, dysplesurs: displeasure: *despleasure, displesure*, (pl.) *displesurs* T; *dyspleasure, dysplesure* C {dysplesour}

dysplesya: displease: *dysplesya, displesya* M {dysplesya}

dyspletya: display (vb): *dyspletya* M {dyspletya}

dysprevy: disprove: *disprevy* T {dysprevy}

dyspuyssant: powerless: *dyspusant* M {dyspuyssant}

dysquedhes: show, appear: (pp.) *disquetheys* M; *disquethas, desquethas, desquethes* T; *dysqwethas* C; *dizkuedha* AB; *disquethaz* Rowe {dysquedhes}

dysquedhyans: demonstration: *dyswythyans* T; *desquethyans* C; *diskuedhyans* AB; *diskuethians* ACB {dysquedhyans}

dyssembla: pretend: *dyssymbla* T; *dissembla* AB {dyssembla}

dystempra: vex: *dystempra* M {dystempra}

dystough: immediately: *dystogh* M {dystough}

dystrowy: destroy: *destrowhy* M; *destrowhy, destrowy* C {destrowy}

dyswar: unaware: *dyswar* M {dyswar}

dyswul/dyswuthyl: undo, destroy: *dyswul, dyswuthel* M; *diz'il, dizurythyl* AB {dyswul/ dyswuthyl}

dyvres: banished, exiled: *diures* AB {dyvres}

***dyvunya**: mince: (pp.) *devenys*, (pp.) *dufunys* M {dyvynya}

dyvydya: divide: *devydya* T {—}

dywosa/dywoja: bleed: *dewosa, dewose*, (pp.) *dewogys* M {dywosa/dywoja}

ea: yea: *ea* M; *ea* T; *yea* C; *îa, yea* AB {ya/ye}

ebol: colt: *eball* C; *ebol, ebal* AB: *eball* Bilbao MS {ebol}

cbren: sky: *ybbern, yborn* C; *ebron* A {ebron/ebren}

edhen, edhyn/ednhow: bird: *ethen*, (pl.) *ethyn* T; *ethan*, (pl.) *ethyn, ethen* C; (pl.) *idhen*, (pl.) *ednhow* AB {edhen, ydhyn}

edrega: regret (n.): *edrega* M {edrega}

edrek. regret (n.): *edrek* M; *yddrag, yddrage, yddrack, eddrack* C; *edrak* AB {edrek}

edrygys: regretful: *eddryggys* T {edrygys}

ef: he, him: *ef, eff* M; *eff* T; *eve, ef* C; *eve, e* AB {ef}

efan: wide: *efan* C {efan}

efredhek/efre'g. crippled: *efrethek* M; *effreg* T {efredhek, efre'k}

egery: open: (pres.) *ugoreff*, (pret.) *egoras* M; *agery, egery* T; *ageri*, (imp.) *agerou* AB; (pp.) *geres, gerres* Rowe {ygery}

egor/egor Dew: daisy: *êgr, egr deu* AB {ygor/egor Dew}

eglos, eglosyow: church: *eglos*, (pl.) *eglosyou* M; *egglos, eglos*, (pl.) *egglosyow* T; *egglos, egglys* A; *egliz* AB; *eglez* NBoson; *eglez*, (pl.) *eglezow* Rowe {eglos, eglosyow}

ehen: kindred: *ehen* M; *ehan* C {eghen}

el, eleth: angel: (pl.) *eleth* M; *ell* T: *eall*, (pl.) *elath* C; (pl.) *elath* A; *el, eal*, (pl.) *eladh, eledh* AB; (pl.) *elez*, (pl.) *eelez* Rowe {el, eleth}

element: element: *elyment* A {element}

ellas: alas: *ellas* M; *ellas, ethlayz, aylas* C; *ellaz* AB {ellas}

***elowen, elow**: elm tree: *elaw, elau* AB {elowen, elow}

elyn: elbow: *ilin, gelen* AB {elyn}

embrassya: embrace (vb): *ymbracya, ymbrasia* T {—}

emperour: emperor: *emperour* M; *emperowre* T {emperour}

empynyon: brains: *ompenyon, ompynyon, ompynnen* M; *ampydnyan* C; *empynion, pidnian* AB {ympynyon}

ena: then, there: *ena* M; *ena* C {ena}

encressya/cressya: increase: *cresyae* M; *cressya, incressya, incresshya* C; *kressia* JBoson; *cressha* Rowe {encressya/cressya}

enef/ena, enevow: soul: *ena, enaff, eneff*, (pl.) *enevou* M; *ena*, (pl.) *enevow* T; *enaff* A; *ena* C; *ena*, (pl.) *anevou* AB; *ena* ACB {enef/ena, enevow}

enep: face: *enap* AB; *enap, enep* ACB {enep}

Enes: Shrovetide: *enez* AB; *enez* ACB {enes}

enjoya: enjoy: *enjoya, injoya* T {—}

enora: honour (vb): *enora* M; *onora* T; *honora* C; (pp.) *onerez* TBoson {enora}

enos: yonder: *enos* M {enos}

ensampel: example: *ensampill* T {ensompel}

entra: enter: *entra* T; *entra* C {entra}

envy: enmity: *envy* T; *envy* C {envy}

envyes: envious: *envyes* C {envyes}

enys: island: *enys* ÔM; *enys, ennis* AB; *enys* NBoson; *ennis,* (pl.) *enesou* ACB {enys}

epscop, epscobow: bishop: *epscop,* (pl.) *epscobou* M; *epscop, epscob,* (pl.) *epscobow* T; *ispak,* (pl.) *epskobou* AB {epscop}

equal: equal (adj. & n.): *equall, egwall* C {equal}

er, eryon: heir: *er,* (pl.) *erryan* T; *heare* A; *heare* C {er, eryon}

erbyn / warbyn: against: *erbyn* M; *warbyn* T; *warbyn* A; *warbyn, warbydn* C; *bidn* AB; *warbedden* Gwavas {erbyn / warbyn}

erbys: herb: (pl.) *erbys* M; (pl.) *earbes* C {erbys}

erhy: command (vb): *erhy* M {erghy}

ermyt / hermyt: hermit: *hermyt, ermet* M {ermyt / hermyt}

erna: until: *erna* T; *arrna* A; *ne* Rowe {erna}

errour: error: *error, erroure, errar* T {—}

errya: err: *errya* T {—}

ervyrys: determined: *erverys* M {ervyrys}

ervys: armed: *eruys* M {ervys}

erytons: inheritance: *eretons, hertons* M; *herytans* T {ertons}

es / ages: than: *es* M; *agys* T; *agis* C {es / ages}

escar, eskerens: enemy: *escare, escar,* (pl.) *eskerans* M; *iskar, yskar, yskyr, eskar,* (pl.) *yskerens* T {escar, eskerens}

esel, esyly: member: *esel,* (pl.) *esely* M; *esall,* (pl.) *esylly,* (pl.) *eyssely,* (pl.) *esyly* T {esel, ysyly}

eskys, eskysyow / eskyjyow: shoe: (pl.) *skygg-yow* T; *esgiz, eskaz,* (pl.) *eskizou* AB {eskys, eskyjyow}

esperans: hope: *esperans* AB {—}

est: east: *east* NBoson; *est* Rowe; *est* AB {yst}

esy, (comp.) **esya**: easy: *esey* T; (comp.) *esya* C {es, esya}

esya: ease (vb): *esya* M {esya}

etek: eighteen: *eitag* AB; *eatag* ACB {etek}

eth: eight: *eth* Borde; *êath* AB {eth}

ethes: eighth: *ethaz* AB; *eathas* ACB {ethes}

eva: drink (vb): *eva* M; *eva* T; *eva* AB; *evah* ACB {eva}

evreth, evredhyon: maimed person: (pl.) *evrethyon* M {evreth, evredhyon}

ewhyas: ride forth: *ewyas* M {ewhyas}

ewn: right: *ewne* M {ewn}

ewna / owna: correct, mend: *euna, ouna* AB; *ouna* Rowe; *owna* ACB {ewna}

ewnadow: desire: *ewnadow* M {yeunadow}

ewyn / ewynas: nail (of hand, etc): *winaz* AB {ewyn, ewynas}

exaltya: exalt: *exaltya, exaltye* M {exaltya}

examnya: examine: *examnya* C {examnya}

exampyl, examplys: example: *exampyll, exampil, exampill,* (pl.,) *examplys,* (pl.) *examplis* T; (pl.) *exampels* A {—}

experyans: experiment: *experyans* M {experyans}

eys, esow: corn: *eys* T; *eys, yees,* (pl.) *esowe* C; *îz* AB; *isse* ACB {ys, ysow}

eys du: whortleberries: *iz diu* AB {ys du}

eyth / *yeth: language: *eyth* T {yeth}

eythyn: furze: *eithin* AB; *ithen* ACB {eythyn}

fall: fail (n.): *fal* M; *fall* C {fall}

falladow: fail (n.): *falladou, ffeladou* M; *falladowe* C {falladow}

fals / falj: false: *fals* PA; *fals* PC; *falge, fals* M; *fals* T; *foulz* AB; *foulze* Rowe {fals / falj}

fals: sickle: *voulz* AB {fals}

falsury: falsehood: *falsury* M; *fallsurye, falsurye* C {falsury}

famya: starve: *famya* T {famya}

farwel: farewell: *farwel, farwell* M; *farewell* C {farwel}

fas: face: *fays* M; *face* T; *face* C; *fas* ACB {fas}

fast: fast: firm: *fast* M {fast}

fatel / fatla: how: *fetel, fetla* M; *fatell, fatla* T; *fatla, fetla* C {fatel, fatla}

faven: bean: *faven* M; *favan* AB; *favan,* (pl.) *fave* ACB {faven}

favera: favour (vb): *favera* M {favera}

favour: favour (n.): *favor, favore, favowre, favoure* T; *favoure, favour* C {favour}

faytour: swindler: *feytour* M {faytour}

fedh: faith: *feth* PA; *feth, feith* T; *faith* A; *feth* ACB {fyth}

fedhya: trust (n.): *fethye* M {fydhya}

felja: split: (pres.) *felge* M; *feldzha* AB {falja}

fenten, fentynyow: spring (of water): *fenten* M; *fentan, fyntan* T; *fentan* AB; *venton,* (pl.) *fentiniow* ACB {fenten}

fer, feryow: fair: *fer,* (pl.) *feryou* M; *fer* ACB {fer, feryow}

fest: certainly: *fest* M; *fest* ACB {fest}

fethy: vanquish: (pp.) *fethys* C; *fethy* ACB {fethy}

fevyr: fever: *fevyr* M {fevyr}

flam: flame: *flam* M; *flam* T {flam}

flattra: beguile: *flattra* M; *flattra* C {flattra}

fleyrys: fetid: *flayrys* C {flerys}

flogh, flehes: child: *flogh,* (pl.) *flehys,* (pl.) *flehas,* (pl.) *flehes* M; *flogh,* (pl.) *flehes,* (pl.) *flehys,* (pl.) *fleghys* T; *flogh, floghe,* (pl.) *flehys,* (pl.) *flehis* C; *flo* AB; *floh,* (pl.) *flehez,* (pl.) *fleâz* ACB; *flô,* (pl.) *flehas* Rowe {flogh, fleghes}

flok: flock: *flok, flocke* T {flok}

flowren / flowre, flowrys: flower: *flour* M; *flowren, flowre,* (pl.) *flowres* T; (pl.) *flowrys,* (pl.) *flowres* C {flowren, flowr, flowrys}

fo: flight: *fo* M {fo}

fol: fool (n.), foolish (adj.): *fol, foyl* M; *foole* C {fol}

folen: page: *folen* A {folen}

folneth: foolishness: *folneth* M; *folneth* ACB {folneth}

foly: folly: *foly* M; *foly, folly* C {foly}

folya: follow: *folya* T {folya}

folyer, folyers: follower: (pl.) *folyars* T {—}

fordh, fordhow: way: *ford* OCV; *forth, for,* (pl.) *forthou* M; *forth,* (pl.) *forthow,* (pl.) *furrow* T; *for*

293

C; *fordh, for*, (pl.) *furu* AB; *vor* Rowe; *for, vor*, (pl.) *furu* ACB {forth, fordhow}

forgh: fork: *vorh, forh* AB; *vorh* ACB {forgh}

form: form (n.): *forme* M {form}

formya: create, form: *formya* M; *formya, furmya* T; *formya* C {formya}

formyer: creator: *formyer* M; *formyer* C {forrnyer}

forn: oven: *forn* AB; *vorn, foarn* ACB {forn}

forsakya: forsake: *forsakya* M; (pret.) *forsakiaz* AB {forsakya}

fortyn: fortune: *fortyn, forten* M {fortyn}

fos: wall: *fôz* AB; *fôz, fôs, vôs, vôz*, (pl.) *fosu, fusu* ACB {fos};

fowt, fowtys: fault, lack: *fout* M; *foude, fowt, fawt*, (pl.) *fautes*, (pl.) *fawtys* T; *faut*, (pl.) *foto*, (pl.) *fotou* AB {fowt, fowtow}

frut: frutys: fruit: *frut*, (pl.) *frutys* T; *frute*, (pl.) *frutes* C {frut, frutys}

frya: fry: *fria* AB {frya}

frygow, dewfryg: nostrils, nose: *frygou* M; *dywfridg, dewfreyg, fregowe* C; *frigau* AB {deufryk, frygow}

Frynk: France: *Vrink, Frenk* AB; *Frenk* NBoson; *Frink* JTonkin {Frynk}

Frynkek: French (language): *Frenkek, Vrinkak* AB; *Frenkock* NBoson {Frynkek}

fundya: found (vb): *fondya, fundia* M; *foundya* T {fundya}

fur: wise: *fur* M; *fur* T; *fuer, fure* C; *ffeere, fyr* ACB; *feere* Rowe {fur}

fust: flail (n.): *vyst* AB; *fust*, (pl.) *fustow* ACB {fust}

fusta: thresh, flail: *fysta* AB {fusta}

fya: despise: *fygha* M {fya}

fya: flee: *fya, feya* M; *fya* T; *fye* ACB {fya}

fygur: figure: *fugur* T; *fygur* A; *fegure* C {fygur}

fyllel: fail (vb): *fyllel* M; *fillall* T; *fyllall* C {fyllel}

fyn: fine, astute: *fyne* C; *fin* AB {fyn}

fyn: fine (n.): *fyne* C {fyn}

fynsya: finish (vb): *fynsya* M {fynsya}

fysek: medicine: *fysek* M {fysek}

fysky: hurry: *fesky* M {fysky}

fysmant, fysmens: appearance: (pl.) *fysmens* M; *fysment* C {fysmant, fysmens}

fystena: hasten: *ffystena* M; *fystena* C; *festinna* AB {fystyna}

fysycyon: physician: *fecycyen, fecessyon* M; *phisicion* T {fesycyen}

gal: rascal: *gal* M {gal}

galar, galarow: affliction, disease: *galer*, (pl.) *galarow* M; (pl.) *gallarowe*, (pl.) *golarowe*, (pl.) *galarow* C; *galar*, (pl.) *galarow*, (pl.) *galarou* ACB {galar}

gallosek: powerful: *galosek, gallosek* M; *golosek, galosek* T {gallosek}

gallus: power: *gallus, galloys* M {gallos}

gam: game (hunt): *game* M; *game* C {gam}

ganow, ganowow: mouth: *ganou* M; *ganow*, (pl.) *ganowow* T; *ganow, ganaw* A; *ganow, ganaw* C; *genau*, (pl.) *genauo* AB; *ganow* JBoson; *gannaw*

TBoson; *genau*, (pl.) *genuow* ACB {ganow, ganowow}

gans: with: *gans* M; *gans* T; *gan, gen* AB {gans}

gar, garrow: leg: (pl.) *garrou*, (pl.) *garou* M; *garr, gar* AB; *gar*, (pl.) *garrow* ACB {gar, garrow}

gargam: bandy-legged: *gargabm* AB; *gar cam* ACB {gargam}

gargasen: glutton: *gargasen* M {gargasen}

garget: garter: *gargat* AB; *garget*, (pl.) *gargettow* ACB {garget}

garma: call (vb): *garma* C; *garma* Rowe; *garmi* ACB {garma}

garow: rough: *garou* M; *garow* T; *garow* C; *garo* AB; *garo, garow* ACB {garow}

gasa: leave: *gasa, gase* M; *gasa*, (pp.) *gerys* T; *gasa* C; *gara* AB; *garra* NBoson; *garah* Rowe; (pp.) *gerres* ACB {gasa}

gava: forgive: *gava* T; *gava, gawa* C {gava}

gavar, gever / gyfras: goat: *gaver* M; (pl.) *gyffras* T; *gour, gavar*, (pl.) *gever* AB; (pl.) *gever* NBoson; (pl.) *gever* Bilbao MS {gavar, gever / gyfras}

gawl: vocation: *gawle* T {galow}

gedya: guide: *gedya, gyydya* M {gedya}

geler: coffin, bier: *geler* M; *elar* AB {geler}

gelvynak: curlew: *golvinak* AB; *gelvinak, gylvinak* ACB {gelvvnak}

gelwel: call: *gelwel* M; *gylwall, gylwell* T; *gyllwall* C; *gelwel* ACB {gelwel}

gen: wedge: *gedn* AB {gen}

genesygeth: birth: *genesygeth* M; *genesegeth* T; *genegegath* A {genesygeth}

genesyk: native: *genesek, genesyk* M {genesyk}

genys: born: *genys* M; *genys* T; *genys* C {genys}

ger, geryow: word: *ger, geer*, (pl.) *geryou* M; *ger*, (pl.) *gerryow* (pl.) *gyrryow* T; (pl.) *girreow* (pl.) *girrow* A; *geare*, (pl.) *gyrryow*, (pl.) *gyrryaw* C; *gêr*, (pl.) *gerrio* AB {ger, geryow}

ges: mockery: *geas* C; *geaze* Rowe; *ges, geys* ACB {ges}

gest, gesty: bitch: *gêst*, (pl.) *gesti* AB; *gest, gyst* ACB {gast, gysty}

gesya: mock: *gesia* M {gesya}

gew: spear: *gu* M; *gew* C; *geu, gew, gu, guu* ACB {gew}

gew: woe: *gew* C {gew}

glan: clean: *glan, glane* T; *glan* C; *glan, glane* ACB {glan}

glander: cleanliness: *glander* M {glander}

glanhe: cleanse: *glanhe* M; *glanhe* T; (pp.) *glanhis* A {glanhe}

glanyth: neat, clean: *glannith* AB; *glaneth* JBoson {glanyth}

glas: green, grey: *glas* OM; *glays* M; *glase* C; *glase, glaz, glaze* ACB {glas}

glaw: rain: *glaw* T; *glawe* C; *glau, glaue, glawe* ACB {glawl}

gleb: wet: *glêb, gleab* AB; *gleab, gleb* ACB {glyp}

glebya: wet (vb): *glebya* M; *glybye* ACB {glybya}

glena: stick (vb): *glena* T; *glena* AB; (pp.) *glenaz* ACB {glena}

glew: sharp: *gleu* PC; *gleu* RD; *glu* OM; *glu* M; *glew* ACB {glew}

gloryes: glorious: *glorijs* M; *gloryes* C {gloryes}
glos: pain: *gloys* M {glos}
*****glosen, glos**: dung for fuel: (pl.) *glose* C; *glose, gloas* ACB {glosen, glos}
glow: coal: *glou* AB; *glow* ACB {glow}
glusa: glue (vb): *glusa* M {glusa}
gober, gobrow: wage: *gober*, (pl.) *gobrou* M; *gober* T; *gober* A; *gubar, guber* AB; *gubber* NBoson; *gubar, gobyr* ACB {gober, gobrow}
gocky: foolish: *goky* M; *gucky, gockye* C; *goky* ACB {goky}
godh, godhow: goose: *goyth, goth* OM; *gûdh, guydh*, (pl.) *godho* AB {goth, godhow}
godhaf: suffer: *gothe* M; *gothef* ACB {godhaf}
Godhalek: Irish, Gaelic (n.): *Godhalek* AB; *Godhalek* ACB {Gwydhalek}
godhas: dregs, sediment: *godhaz* AB {godhas}
godh 'or: mole (mammal): *godh 'or* AB; *godh dhâr* ACB {godhor}
godhvos: know: *gothvos, gothfes, gothfos, gothfas* M; *gothfas, gothfes* T; *gothvas* C; *guodhaz* AB; *godhaz* ACB {gothvos}
godra: milk (vb): *gudra* AB; *gudra* ACB {gudra}
godreva: three days hence: *gydreva* AB; *gydreva* ACB {godreva}
gof: smith: *goff, goyff* PA; *gof* PC; *gôv* AB; *gof, gove* ACB {gof}
gogleth: north: *gogleth* ACB {—}
goheles: avoid: *goheles, gohelas* M {goheles}
gojogen: black pudding: *gydzhygan* AB {gosogen}
gol: holiday: *gol* M {gol}
gol: sail (n.): *goyl* RD; *goyl, gol* M; *gôl* AB; *goil, gol* ACB {gol}
goles: bottom, base: *golas* AB; *golas, gullas* ACB {goles}
golhy: wash: *golhy* M; *golhy* T; *golhe* A; *golhya, gulhi* AB; *golhya, golhy* ACB {golghy}
golok: sight: *golek* M; *golok* C; *golok* ACB {golok}
golow, golowys: bright (adj.), light (n.): *golou* M; *golow* T; *golow, golowe, gollowe*, (pl.) *gullowys* C; *gulou* AB {golow, golowys}
Golowan: Midsummer: *goluan* Ustick {Golowan}
golowys: brilliance, lightning: *golouaz* AB; *golouas, golowas* ACB {golowys}
golowder brilliance: *golouder* M; *golowder* A {golowder}
golowy: shine (vb): *golowhy* M; *gollowye* C; *gylyui, gylyua* AB; *goloua* ACB {golowy}
golowyjyon: radiance: *golvygyen* M {golowyjyon}
golsowes / gosowes: listen: (imp.) *golsou* M; *golsowes, golsowas* T; (imp.) *gosoweth* A; (imp.) *golsow* C; *gazowaz* Rowe; *gasawaz* TBoson; *gasowas* JTonkin; *gozowaz* ACB {golsowes}
golvan: sparrow: *golvan* OCV; *gylvan* AB; *golvan, gylvan* ACB {golvan}
goly, golyow: wound (n.): (pl.) *golyou* M; *guli*, (pl.) *gollyou* AB; *guli*, (pl.) *gullyou* ACB {goly, golyow}
golya: wound (vb): *golya* M {golya}
golyas: watch (n. & vb): *golyas* M; *gollyaz* AB {golyas}

gon: gown: *gon* M; *gûn* AB {gon}
gon: scabbard: *gûn* AB {gon}
gonys: cultivate, sow: *gonys* OM; *gonys* M; *gonys* T; *gonys* A; *goneth, gones* C; *gynez* AB; *gunnes* ACB; *gones* Rowe {gonys}
gora: hay: *gorha* AB; *gorra* ACB {gora}
gordhewer: evening: *gurthuwer* OCV; *gorʒewar* M; *gydhiuhar, gydhiuhar, godhihuar* AB; *gethihuer, gethihuar* JBoson; *godhihuar, gothuar, gorthuer* ACB {gorthewer}
gordhya: worship (vb): *gorthye, gorthia* M; *gorthya* T; *gwerthya, gorthya* C; *gurria* AB; *gorthi, gordhy, gorthya* ACB; *gortha, gorthi* Rowe {gordhya}
gordhyans: glory: *gorthyans* M: *gordhyans* AB; *worriance* TBoson; *worriance* Rowe; *gordhyans* ACB {gordhyans}
gorfen: end (n.): *gorfen* M; *gorfan, gorfen* T; *gorfan, gorvan, gorffan, gorffen* C; *gorfen* AB {gorfen}
gorfenna: finish (n.): *gorfenna* AB {gorfenna}
gorhel, gorholyon: ship: *gorhel, gorel* M; *gorthell* C; *gurhal* AB; *gurroll* NBoson; (pl.) *gorrollion* JBoson; *goral* Rowe; *gurhal, gorhel, gorhal* ACB {gorhel}
gorhemmyn: command (n. & vb): *gorhemmyn* M; *gorhemyn, gorhemen, gorwmyn* C; AB; (pl.) *garebma* JBoson; *gurhemmyn* ACB {gorhemmyn}
gormel: praise (vb): *gormel* M; (imp.) *gormall*, (imp.) *gormollow* TBoson {gormel}
gormola: praise (n.): *gormola* AB {gormola}
gormynadow: commandment: *gormenadou, gormennadou* M; *gormynadow* T; *gormenadow* C {gorhemmynadow}
gorow: male (n.): *gorrow, gorrawe, gorawe* C; *gurow* ACB {gorow}
gorra: put, send: *gorra, gora* M; *gora* T; *gorra* C: *gora* AB; *gora, gorah* ACB {gorra}
gorryth: male (n.): *gorryth* M {gorryth}
gorth: perverse: *gorth* M {gorth}
gortheby: answer (vb): *gortheby* M; *gorreby, gortheby* T; *gweryby* C; *gorthebi* AB; (pret.) *gwerebas*, (pret.) *worebaz* Rowe {gortheby}
gorthyb, gorthebow: answer (n.): *gorthyb*, (pl.) *gorthebou* M; *gurryb, gorrub* T; *gorthib* C; *gorthyp* ACB {gorthyp, gorthebow}
gortos: wait (vb): *gortes* M; *gortas, gurtes* T; *gortas* C; *kyrtaz, kyrtez* AB {gortos}
gos: blood: *goys* M; *gosse, goos, goys, gois* T; *gois, gos, gose* A; *gûdzh* AB; *gois, goos, gûdzh* ACB {gos}
gostyth: obedient: *gustith* T; *gostyth* C; *gosteyth, gustyth* ACB {gostyth}
gosygen: bladder: *gyzigan* AB {gusygen}
goth: pride: *goth* T; *goth* C {goth}
*****gothyen, gothy**: vein: (pl.) *guthy* M {gwythyen, gwythy}
gothys: proud: *gothys* C; *gothus, gothys* ACB {gothys}
gouman: seaweed: *gubman* AB; *gubman* ACB {goumman}

CORNISH TODAY

gour, gwer busband: *gor* M; *gore, gwerrer*, (pl.)
gwer T; *gûr* AB; *goore* Rowe {gour, gwer}
gourty: husband: *gorty* C {gourty}
govenek: hope: *govenek* M; *govenek* T; *govenek*
AB; *govenek* ACB {govenek}
gover, goverow: stream: *gover*, (pl.) *goverou* M;
govar T; *gover* ACB {gover, goverow}
governa: govern: *governye* OM; *governye* PC;
governa T; *governa* C; *govarna* AB {governya}
governans: government: *governens* M;
governans, gevernans T {governans}
governour, governours: governor: *governer,*
governour M; *governor, governer*, (pl.) *governors*
T {governour, governours}
govyn / gofyn: ask: *gofyn* OM; *govyn, goven* M;
goven C; *govyn, gofen, gophen* AB; *gofen*
Gwavas; *gofen* Rowe; *gophen, gophidn, gofen,*
gofyn, goven ACB {govyn}
govys: behalf: *govys* OM; *govys* M {govys}
gow: lie: *gou* M; *gow, gowe* C; *gou* AB; *gou, gow*
ACB {gow}
gowek: mendacious: *gowak* T; *goacke* C; *gûak,*
guěk AB {gowek}
grammer: grammar: *grammer, gramer* M
{grammer}
***grappa, grappys**: grape: (pl.) *grappys* T
{grappa, grappys}
gras, grassow: grace, thanks: *grays, gras, grath,*
grac M; *grace* T; *grase, grace, grasse*, (pl.) *grassow*
C; *gras* AB; *gras, grass* ACB {gras, grassow}
grassa: thank: *grassa* M {grassa}
grassyes: gracious: *gracyus, grassijs* M {grassyes}
gravar dewla: wheelbarrow: *gravar dula* AB;
gravar dula, gravar dhula ACB {grava dywla}
gref: grief: *greff* M {gref}
grevons: grievance: *grefons* M {grefons}
grevya: grieve: *grefia* M; *grevya* C {grevya}
gromercy: thank you: *gromersy* OM; *grantmercy*
PC; *gramercy, gromercy* M; *gramercy* C
{gromercy}
grond: ground: *grond* M; *grownd, grownde* T;
grond A {grond}
grondya: ground (vb): *grondya* M; *groundya* T
{grondya}
grontya: grant (vb): *grontya* M; *grantya* T;
grontya, grauntya, granntya C {grontya}
growedha: lie, lie down: *growetha* M; *growetha* T;
growetha C; *guruedha, goruedha* AB; *gorwetha*
ACB {growedha}
grugys: belt: *grigiz* AB {grugys}
grysla: grin, show the teeth: *grizla* AB {grysla}
gul / guthyl / gwyll: do: *gul, guȝyll, guthel* M;
gull, gul T; *gwiel, gule* A; *gwyll, gwyell, gule,*
guythyll, gwethill C {gul / guthyl}
***gulla, gullys**: sea gull: (pl.) *gullez* AB {gulla,
gullys}
gun, gonyow: down (n.): *gon*, (pl.) *gonyou* M;
gûn, (pl.) *guniau* AB; *goon*, (pl.) *gunneau*
NBoson; *goon* Scawen {gun, gonyow}
gwaf: winter: *gwaf, gwave* C; *guâv* AB; *guâv,*
gwâv, gwaf ACB {gwaf}
gwag: empty, hungry: *guak* M; *gwag* C; *gwage*
Rowe; *guag, gwag* ACB {gwak / gwag}

gwan: weak: *gwan, guan* M; *gwan* T; *gwadn,*
gwan C; *guadn* AB; *guadn, gwan* ACB {gwan}
gwana: wound (vb). *guana* M; *gwana* T; *gwana* C;
guana AB {gwana}
gwandra: wander: *guandra* M; *gwandra* T;
gwandra C; *guandre* AB; *gwandra* Rowe
{gwandra}
***gwandryas, gwandrysy**: wanderer: (pl.)
gwandresy T {gwandryas, gwandrysy}
gwanegreth: weakness: *gwanegreth, gwann-*
ygreth T {gwanegreth}
gwaneth: wheat: *gwaneth* C; *guanath* AB;
guanath ACB; *gwanath* Bilbao MS {gwaneth}
gwanhe: weaken: (pp.) *gwadnhez* NBoson
{gwanhe}
gwarak, gwaregow: bow, arc: *guarak* OM; (pl.)
guaregou M; *gwaracke, gweracke* C; *guarrak* AB
{gwarak, gwaregow}
gwarnya: warn: *guarnya* M; *gwrnya* T; *gwarnya*
C; (pp.) *gwarnez* Rowe {gwarnya}
gwarthek: cattle: *guarthek* OM; *guarthek* M;
guarrhog AB {gwarthek}
gwarthevyas: overlord: *guarthevyas* M
{gwarthevyas}
gwary: play (n. & vb): *guary* M; *gwary* C; *guare*
AB; *guare, guary, gwary* ACB {gwary}
gwas, gwesyon: fellow: *guas*, (pl.) *guesyen*, (pl.)
guesyon M; *gwase* C; *guâz* AB {gwas, gwesyon}
gwaya: move (vb): *guaya* M; *gwaya* T {gwaya}
gwayn: gain (n.): *gwayne* C; *gwayn* Scawen
{gwayn}
gwaynya: gain (vb): *guaynya* M; *guaynia* AB;
gwaynia ACB {gwaynya}
gwaynten: spring (= season): *guainten* AB;
gwaynten Scawen; *guainten, gwainten* ACB
{gwaynten}
gwetyas: expect: *gwettyas, gwetias* T; *quatiez*
NBoson; *quachas* JTonkin {gwaytya}
gweder: glass: *gueder* M; *gwedyr, gweder* T;
gueder AB {gweder}
gwedhen, gwedh: tree: *guethen* OM; (pl.) *gweth*
PA; *gwethan*, (pl.) *guyth* T; *gwethan*, (pl.) *gwyth*
C; *guedhan*, (pl.) *gueidh* AB; *gwethan* JBoson;
gwethan, (pl.) *gweth* Rowe; *gwethan, gwyth*
ACB {gwedhen, gwyth}
gwedhra: wither: *guedhra* AB {gwedhra}
gwedhves: widow: *gwethfas* T; *gwethvas* A
{gwedhowes}
gwedren: glass, tumbler: *guedran* AB {gwedren}
gwel: field: *gweall* C; *gweale* Rowe {gwel}
gwelen, gwelynny, gwel: rod: *guelen, guelan,*
(pl.) *guelynny* M; (pl.) *gwaile* C; *guelan* AB
{gwelen, gwelynny, gwel}
gwelen gol: sail-yard: *guelan gôl* AB {gwelen
gol}
gweles: see: *guelas, guelays, gueles* M; *gwelas,*
gwellas T; *gwellas* C; *guelaz, guellaz* AB; *guelaz,*
gwellas ACB; *gwellas* Rowe {gweles}
gwelf: lip: *guelv* AB {gwelf}
gwelhevyn: superior (n.): (pl.) *guelhevyn*, (pl.)
guelheven M {gwelhevyn}
gwell: better: *guell, guel* M; *gwell* C; *guel, guell*
AB {gwell}

296

gwella: best: *guella* M; *gwella* T; *gwelha* C; *guella, guelha* AB {gwella}

gwella: improve: *gwella* C; *guelha* AB {gwella}

gweljow: scissors, shears: *gueldzhou* AB {gwelsow}

gwels: grass: *gwels* T; *guelz* AB {gwels}

gwelsen: blade of grass: *gwelsan* T {gwelsen}

gwely, gwelyow: bed: *guely* M; *gwely* A; *guili, guilli*, (pl.) *gueliau* AB {gwely, gwelyow}

gwelyvedhes / glyvedhes: midwife: *glyvedhaz* AB {gwellyvedhes}

gwelyvos / golovas: confinement: *golovas* AB {gwelyvos / golovas}

gwenenen, gwenyn: bee: *guenenen* OCV; *guanen*, (pl.) *guenyn* AB; *guenen* ACB {gwenenen, gwenyn}

gwer: green (adj.): *guer* AB {gwer}

gweras: soil: *gweras, gwyras* C {gweras}

gweres: help: *gueras, guereys, gueres* M; *gweras* T; *gweres, gweras* C; *gwerras* TBoson; *gwerras* ACB {gweres}

gwergh: innocent: *gruegh, gruergh* M {gwergh}

gwerhes: virgin: *guirhays, gwerhes, guirhes* M; *gwyrhes* T {gwerghes}

gwern, gwernow: mast: *guern* OCV; (pl.) *gwernow* C; *guern* AB {gwern, gwernow}

gwernen: alder tree: *guernen* OCV; *guernan* AB {gwernen}

gwerrya: wage war: *guerrya* M {gwerrya}

gwertha: sell: *guertha* M; *guerha* AB; *wharra, guerha* JBoson; *gwarra* ACB {gwertha}

gwerwels: grassland, pasture: *gueruelz* AB {gwerwels}

gweth: worse: *gueyth* M; *gwethe* C {gweth}

gweus, gwessyow: lip: (pl.) *gwessyow* T; *gueus* AB {gweus, gweusyow}

gwewen: heel: *gueuan* AB; *gwewan* Rowe {gwewen}

gweyth: occasion: *guyth* M; *gweith* T; *gwyeth* A; *gwyth, gwythe* C; *guêth* AB {gwyth}

gweyth: work, working day: *guyth* M {gwyth}

gwlan: wool: *glân, gluan* AB; *glân* ACB {gwlan}

gwlas, gwlasow: country: *gluas* M; *gwlas*, (pl.) *gwlasow* T; *gwlase* C {gwlas, gwlasow}

gwlascor: kingdom: *gwlascur, gulascor, gluascor* M; *gwlascur, gwlaskur, gwlascor* T; *glaskor* AB; *gulasketh* Rowe; *glasgar* JBoson {gwlascor}

gwrannen: wren. *guradnan* AB {gwrannen}

gwredhen, gwredhow: root: *gwrethan, gwrethyan* T; (pl.) *gwrethow*, (pl.) *gwreythow* C; *guredhan*, (pl.) *guredhiou* AB {gwredhen, gwrydhyow}

gwreer: creator: *gwrer* T; *gwerer* A; *gwrear* C {gwryer}

gwreg, gwrageth / gwregeth: wife: *gruek* M; *gwreg*, (pl.) *gwregath* T; *gwreag, gwreak, gwreage*, (pl.) *gwregath* C; *gurêg*, (pl.) *guragedh* AB {gwreg, gwrageth}

gwreghty: housewife: *guregty* CF; *gwrethtye, gwreghty* C; *gyrti* AB {gwre'ty}

gwryans: doing: *guryans* M; *gwrythyans* T; *gwreans* C {gwryans}

gwya: weave (vb): *guîa* AB {gwya}

gwyador: weaver: *gueiadar* AB; *gweader* ACB {gwyador}

gwyban: fly (= insect): *guiban* AB {gwyban}

gwycor: dealer: *gwicker* C {gwycor}

gwyw: worthy: *guyf, guyff* M; (comp.) *gweffa* C {gwyw / gwyf}

gwyhen: periwinkle (= mollusc): *guihan* AB {gwyghen}

gwylfos: wilderness: *guelfos, guylfoys, guylfos* M {gwylfos}

gwyls: wild: *guyls* M; *gwyls* T; *gwylls* C; *guelz* AB {gwyls}

gwyn: white: *gwyn, guyn* M; *gwyn* T; *gwyn* C; *guidn* AB; *guidn, guydn, gwin, gwyn* ACB {gwyn}

gwyn: wine: *guin* OCV; *guyn, gwyn* M; *gwyn, gwyne* T; *gwyn* A; *gwyne* C; *gwin* Borde; *guîn* AB {gwyn}

gwynder: whiteness: *guynder* M {gwynder}

gwynnak: whiting: *guidnak* AB {gwynnack}

gwyns: wind: *guyns* M; *gwyns* T; *guenz, guinz* AB; *guenz, gwenz* ACB {gwyns}

gwynsell: fan: *guinzal* AB {gwynsell}

gwyr: right (n.), true (adj.): *guyr, guir* M; *gwyre, gwyr* T; *gwyre, gweare* C; *guîr* AB {gwyr}

gwyryon: righteous: *guyryon* M; *gwyrryan* T; *gwyrryan* C {gwyryon}

gwyryoneth / gwyroneth: truth: *gueroneth, gwryoneth* T; *gweranath, gwreonath, gwryonath* A; *gwreanathe* C; *guironeth, gwyroneth* AB; *gwiranath* ACB {gwyryoneth}

gwysk: raiment: *guyske* M {gwysk}

gwysca: wear (vb): *gwyska* T; *gwyska* C; *guesga* AB {gwysca}

gwyskel: strike: *gwyskall* T; (imp.) *gwysk*, (pp.) *gwyskes* C; *gueskal* AB {gwyskel}

gwyth: keeping: *gwith* T {gwyth}

gwytha / gwetha: keep (vb): *guytha, guythe* M; *gwetha* T; *gwetha* C; *guitha* AB {gwytha}

gwythres: work (n.): *guythres* M {gwythres}

gwythyas, gwythysy: keeper: *gwothyas, gwethyas* C; (pl.) *kuithizi* AB {gwythyas}

gyk na myk: least sound: *gycke na mycke* C {gyk na myk}

gyl: guile: *gyll* C {gyl}

gyrr: gripes: diarrhoea: *girr* AB {gyrr}

gys: guise: *geys* C {gys}

gyvyans: forgiveness: *gyvyans, gevyans* T; *gevyans* C {gyvyans}

ha(g): and: *ha(g)* M; *ha(g)* T; *ha(g)* C; *ha, a* AB {ha(g)}

hacter: ugliness: *hacter* C; *hactar* ACB {hakter}

hadre: while: *hedre* PA; *hedre* OM; *hedre* M; *dirr* A: *hadre* C; *try* AB {hedra}

haf: summer: *haf* OM; *have* C; *hâv* AB; *hâv, hâff* ACB; {haf}

hager, haccra: ugly: *hager* M; *haker* A; *hager, hagar*, (comp.) *hackra* C; *hagar* AB {hager, haccra}

hager-awel: bad weather, storm: *hagar-aual* AB; *hagar awell* ACB; *hagar-awal* NBoson {hagar-awel}

hager-bref: serpent: *hager-breeve* Rowe {—}

hal, hellow/**hallow**: moor: *hal, haal* OM; (pl.) *hellou* M; *hâl*, (pl.) *halou* AB; *hal* ACB {hal, hallow}

hanath: cup: *haneth* T; *hanath* AB {hanaf}

handla: handle (vb): *handla* M {handla}

haneth: tonight: *haneth* RD; *haneth* M {haneth}

hangya: hang: *hangya* M; *hangya* T {hangya}

hanow, henwyn: name: *hanow, hanou* M; *henow, hanow*, (pl.) *henwyn* T; *hanow*, (pl.) *henwyn* C; *hannawe* TBoson; *hanno, hannow* ACB {hanow, hynwyn}

hansel: breakfast: *hansell, honthsel* M; *haunsel* AB; *haunsell* ACB {hansel}

hanter: half: *hanter* C; *hanter* AB {hanter}

hantercans: fifty: *hantercans* C {hantercans}

harber: lodging. *harber* M {harber}

harlych: strictly: *harlych* M {hardlych}

hartha: bark (vb): *hartha, harthy* AB {hartha}

has: seed: *hays* M; *has, haes, hasse* T; *hays* C; *hâz* ACB; *haaze, haage* Rowe {has}

hast: haste: *hast* C {hast}

hasteneb: haste: *hasteneb* T {hastenep}

haval: like (adj.): *havall* T; *havall* C; *havel* AB; *haval, havel* ACB {haval}

hayl: hail (= greeting): *heyl* OM; *heyl* PC; *heyl, heyll* M {hayl}

heb: without: *heb* M; *heb* T; *heb* C; *heb* AB; *heb* ACB {heb/hep}

hebasca: relief: *hebasca* M {hebasca}

hedhes: fetch: *hethes* M; *hethas* C; *hedhaz* AB {hedhes}

hedhy: cease: *hethy* C; *hethy* ACB {hedhy}

hedhyw: today: *heჳyu, hyჳyu, hythyu, hythou, hethow* M; *hethew, hethow* T; *hythew* C; *hedhyu, hidhu* AB; *hithew, hithow* ACB {hedhyu}

hedhyw y'n jedh: nowadays: *hethew in jeth* T: *hidhu yn dzhêdh* AB {hedhyu y'n jeth}

helghya: hunt: *helghya* M; *hellya* C; *helfia*, (pp.) *helhyz* AB; (pret.) *hellas* Rowe; *helfia, helhia* ACB {helghya}

helygen, helyk: willow: *helagan*, (pl.) *helak* AB; *helagan*, (pl.) *helak*, (pl.) *helik* ACB {helygen, helyk}

hemma: this (pron.): *helma* M; *helma* T: *helma* C {hemma}

hen, henna: that: (masc. pron.): *hen, henna* M; *henna* T; *hena, hedna* C; *hedda, hana* AB {hen, henna}

hendas, hendasow. grandfather, ancestor: *hendas, hyndas*, (pl.) *hendasow*, (pl.) *hyndasow* T; *hendas*, (pl.) *hendasow* C {hendas, hendasow}

hengok: ancestor: *hengyke* C; *hengog* AB {hengok}

hensa: fellow: *hense* M; *hensa, hynsa* T {hynsa}

hensy: ruin (= building): *hensy* M {—}

henwel: name (vb): *henwall* T; (pres.) *henwaf*, (pp.) *henwys* C; *henual, honua* AB; *hanwelle, hanwall* TBoson {henwel}

henys: old age: *henys* M {henys}

hernen, hern: pilchard: *hernan* AB; (pl.) *hern* JBoson; (pl.) *hearne* ACB {hernen, hern}

hernessya: harness (vb): *hernessya* M {hernessya}

hernya: shoe (vb): *herniah* ACB {hernya}

herwyth: according to, about: *hyrwith* T; *heruydh, heruedh* AB {herwyth}

hes: length: *heys* C; *hêz* AB; *heys, hês, hêz* ACB {hes}

hes: swarm: *hêz* AB {hes}

hevelep: likeness, similarity: *hevelep* M; *heveleb* T; *hevelep* ACB {hevelep}

hevelly, hevel: seem: (pluperf.) *hevelsa* M; (imperf.) *hevely*, (pres.) *hevall* T; (pres.) *havall* C {hevelly}

hevys: shirt: *hevys* M; *heves, hevez* AB {hevys}

heweres: helpful: *heweres* M {heweres}

hogen: still, yet: *hogan* C {hogen}

hogh: pig, sow: *hôh* AB {hogh}

holan: salt: *holan* AB; *holan* JBoson; *hollan* Gwavas {holan}

holma: this (f. pron.): *holma* M; *holma* T; *holma* C {homma}

honen: self: *honan, honyn* M; *honyn* T; *honyn, hunyn* C; *honyn* AB; *honnen* ACB {honen},

honna: that (f. pron.): *honna* M; *honna* T; *honna, hona* C; *honna, hodda* AB {honna}

hordh: ram: *hordh* M; *hordh, hurdh, hor* AB; *horr* NBoson; *hor* Bilbao MS {horth}

horn: iron: horne: *horne* T; *hoarn* AB: *horen* Keigwin {horn}

horsen, horsens: whoreson: *horsen*, (pl.) *horsens* M; *horsen* C {horsen, horsens}

hos: duck: *hos* OM; *haz* AB {hos}

hos: hoarse: *hôz* AB {hos}

hot: headgear, hat: *hot* M; *hat* AB {hot}

hothfy: swell: *hothfy* M; *huedhi* AB {hothfy}

howl: sun: *houle* M; *howle* T; *howle* C; *houl* AB {howl}

howlsedhas: sunset, west: *houlzedhas* AB; *houlzethas* ACB {howlsedhas}

humbrank: lead (vb): *hembronk* OM; (pret.) *hembroncas* PC; *humbrag, humbrak, humbrynk* T; (pp.) *humbregez* Rowe {hembronk}

hunros: dream (n.): *hunrus* OM; *hendrez* Rowe {hunros}

hunrosa: dream (vb): (pret.) *henrosas* RD; *henrosa* ACB {hunrosa}

hurtya: hurt (vb); *hurtya* T; *hertia* AB {hurtya}

hus: magic: *hus* M {hus}

hy: she: *hy* M; *hai* AB; *hy, hye* ACB {hy}

hyr: long: *hyr* M; *here, hyre* T; *hîr* AB; *hîr* ACB {hyr}

hyreth: yearning, longing: *hereth* M; *hyrathe* C; *hirrath* JBoson {hyreth}

hyrethek: wistful: *herethek* M {hyrethek}

hyrneth: long time: *hyrenath* C {hyrneth}

jardyn: garden: *jardyn* T; *jarden* C; *dzharn* AB {jardyn}

jaudyn: knave: *iouden* M; *jawdyn* C {jaudyn}

jentyl: gentle: *gentyl* M; *jentyll* T; *gentill, gentell* C; *gentle* TBoson {jentyl}

jewal: jewel: *jewall* T {jowal}

A SHORT DICTIONARY OF UCR

*jeyler, jeylers: jailer: (pl.) *geylers* M {jayler, jaylers}

jorna: day: *jorna, jorne* C; *jurna, dzhyrna* AB; *journa* TBoson; *jorna* JBoson; *jorna* Rowe {jorna}

joy, joyes: joy: *joy*, (pl.) *joyes* T; *joye, joy*, (pl.) *joyes* C {joy, joyes}

joynya/jonnya: join (vb): *jonya, joynya, joynea* T; *junya* A; *dzhunia* AB {junnya}

jugler: trickster: *jugleer* M {juglour}

jujya: judge (vb): *jugia, judgia* T; *judgia* A {jujja}

junt. joint: *junt* M {junt}

justya: joust (vb): *iustya* M {justya}

justys: justice: *justus, justice, justyce* T {justys}

jyn: engine: *gyn, jyn* C {jyn}

jyst, jystes: joist: *gyst* OM; (pl.) *jystes* C {jyst, iystys}

ke, keow: hedge: *kee* M; *kee, ke* T; *kea* C; *kê*, (pl.) *kêau* AB; (pl.) *keaw* ACB {ke, keow}

kefrys, kekefrys: also: *kefrys, kekyfrys* M; *kyffrys* T; *keveris* A; *keffrys, kekeffrys, kekefres* C {kefrys, kekefrys}

kegyn: kitchen: *kegyn* M; *kegen* C; *kegen* AB; *kegin* ACB {kegyn}

kegys: hemlock: *kegaz* AB {kegys}

kehaval: similar: *kehavall* C {kehaval}

keheja: retch (vb): *kehedzhe* AB {keheja}

keher: flesh: *keher* M {keher}

keles: conceal: *kelas, kellas* C {keles}

kelynen: holly-bush: *kelinen* AB {kelynen}

kelly: lose: *kelly* M; *kylly* T; *kelly* C; *kelli, kolli* AB {kelly}

kelmy: bind (vb): *kelmy* M; *kylmy* T; *kelmy* C; *kelma* AB; *kelmy* ACB {kelmy}

kemeres: take: *kemeres* M; *kemeras, kemeres* T; (imp.) *kymar*, (imp.) *kybmar* C; *kymeraz, kemeraz* AB *komeraz* Rowe {kemeres}

kemmynna: commend: *kemynna, kemena* M; *comena* C {kemynna}

kemmys: as much: *kemys* M; *kemmys, kebmys, kybmys* C {kemmys}

kemyn: common (adj.): *kemyn* M {kemyn}

ken: other: *ken* M; *keyn* T; *keen* C {ken}

ken: reason (n.): *ken* M {ken}

kendon: debt: *kyndan* AB {kendon}

kenkya: contend, dispute: *kennkia* AB {kenkya}

kennyn: wild garlic, leek: *kinin* AB {kennyn}

kensowha: forenoon: *kenzhoha* AB {kensewha}

kensa: first: *kensa, kynsa* M; *kensa, kynsa* T; *kensa, kynsa* C; *kensa* AB; *kensa* TBoson; *kenza* JBoson; *kensa* ACB {kensa}

kenter, kentrow: nail (n.): *kenter*, (pl.) *kentrow* PA; (pl.) *kentrow* PC; (pl.) *kyntrou* T; *kentar* AB; (pl.) *kentrow* Bilbao MS {kenter, kentrow}

kentrevak, kentrevogyon: neighbour: (pl.) *kentrevogyan* M; *kentrevak, kentrevek*, (pl.) *kentrevogyan* T; *kontrevak* AB; (pl.) *contravagian* NBoson; *contrevak*, (pl.) *contrevogion* ACB {kentrevak, kentrevogyon}

kentrevoges: neighbour (f.): *kentrevoges* M {kentrevoges}

kentrewy: nail (vb): *kentrewy* M; *kyntrewy* T {kentrewy}

kenyver: as many, all: *kenever* M; *kenever* T; *kenever, canevar* A; *kinever* JBoson; *kaniffer* JTonkin; *kenifer* AB; *kenefra* Rowe {kenyver}

kenyver onen: every one: *kyniver uonan* AB {kenyver onen}

kepar/pecar: like, as: *kepar* T; *pecar* A; *pekare* C; *pokâr* AB; *pokaar* NBoson {kepar}

kepar del: as (conj.): *kepar del* M; *kepar dell* T; *pare dell, par dell* C {kepar del}

ker: dear: *ker* M; *ker* T; *kear, kere* C; *kear* Gwavas {ker}

kerdh: expedition: *kerth* M {kerth}

kerdhes: walk: *kerthes* M; *kerthes* T; *keras* C; *kerdhez, karras* AB; *kerras*, Rowe {kerdhes} .

*keredhy: chastise: (pp.) *kerethys* M {keredhy}

*kerenje'ek/kerense'ek: loving: *kerengeak, kerngeek, kernsyak* T {kerensedhek}

kerensa/kerenja: love: *kerensa, kerense* M; *kerensa, carensa, carenga* T; *carensa, carenga* C; *crenga* NBoson; *crensa* TBoson; *crenjah* Rowe; *karensa, karenza, karendzhia* ACB {kerensa}

kergh: oats: *kerth* C: *kerh* AB; *keer* Bilbao MS {kergh}

kerhes: fetch: *kerghes, kerhes* M; (pp.) *kerrys* C {kerghes}

Kernow: Cornwall: *kernou* M; *Kernou* AB; *Kernow, Curnow* NBoson; *Cernow* TBoson; *Kernow* ACB {Kernow}

Kernowek: Cornish (language): *Cornowok* 1572; *Carnoack, Curnooack* NBoson; *Carnoack, Karnooack, Kernuak, Kernooak, Kornooack* JBoson; *Kernuack* Gwavas; *Curnoack* Pender; *Kernûak* AB; *Kernuack* ACB; *Cornoack* Bodinar {Kernewek}

kerys: beloved: *kerys* M {kerys}

kes/cues: cheese: *kêz* AB; *kêz, keas* ACB {kes}

kescolon: unanimous: *kescolon* M {kescolon}

kesen, kesow: turf: *kezan* AB; (pl.) *kesow* ACB {kesen}

keser: hail (= weather): *kezzar, kezar* AB; *kezer* ACB {keser}

kesky: admonish: *keskey* M; *kesky* C {kesky}

keskyans: conscience: *keskians* AB {—}

kestalkya: converse: *kestalkye* M {kestalkya}

kesvewa: cohabit: *kesvewa* C {kesvewa}

keth: same: *keth* M; *kyth* T; *keth* A; *keth* C {keth}

kevelek: woodcock: *kyvelak* AB {kevelek}

kevelyn: cubit: *keuelyn* OM; *kevellyn, kevellen* C {kevelyn}

kevrennek: participating: *kevrennak, keverennak, kevrennek* T {kevrennek}

kewer: weather: *keuar* AB; *kuer* ACB {kewer}

keyn: back (n.): *keyn* M; *kyen* C; *kein* AB; *kein* JBoson {keyn}

knak: snap (n.): *knak* M {knak}

knava: scoundrel: *knava* T; *kynava* AB {knava}

knesen, knes: skin: *knesen*, (pl.) *kneys* M {knesen, knes}

knevya/knvvyas: shear (vb): *knevya* T; *kyniviaz* AB {knyvyas}

knew: fleece: *knew* T; *knêu* AB {knew}

knofen: nut: *knyfan; kynyphan* AB; *kynyfan* ACB {knofen}
ky, cuen: dog: *ky*, (pl.) *kuen* M; *ky* C; *kei*, (pl.) *kên* AB; *ki, kei*, (pl.) *kên* ACB {ky, cun}
kyffewy: guests: (pl.) *kyffuywy* M {kvffewy}
kyfyans: reliance: *kefyans* M {kyfyans}
kyg: flesh: *kyke, kyk* M; *kyge, kyk* T; *kyg, kig, kigg, kegg* A; *kyke, kycke* C {kyk/kyg}
kyg porhel: pork: *kyge porrell* T {—}
kylben: occiput: *kylban* C {kylben}
kyn: although: *kyn* M; *kyn* T; *kyn* C {kyn}
kynda, kyndes: kind (n.): *kynda*; (pl.) *kyndes* T; *cunda, kynda* C {kynda}
kyns: before (adv.): *kyns* M; *kyns* T; *kins* A; *kyns* C; *kenz* AB {kens}
kyny: lament (vb): *kyny* C {kyny}
kynyaf. autumn, harvest: *kynyaf* OCV; *kidniath, kidniaz, kidniadh, kyniav* AB {kynyaf}
kynyow. dinner: *kidniau, kidnio* AB {kynyow}

lacka: worse: *lakka* M; *lacka* T; *lacka* C; *laka* AB; *lacka* NBoson; *lacka* ACB {lacca}
lader, ladron: robber: *lader*, (pl.) *ladron*, (pl.) *laddron*, (pl.) *laddren* M; *ladyr*, (pl.) *laddron* T; *lader* C; *ladar*, (pl.) *leddarn*, (pl.) *ledran* AB; (pl.) *ladran* JBoson {lader, ladron}
ladha: kill: *latha* M; *latha* T; *latha* C; *ladha* AB; *latha* Rowe; *latha*, (pp.) *ledhaz* ACB {ladha}
ladra: rob: *ladra, laddra* M; *laddra* TBoson; *laddra* JBoson; *laddra* ACB {ladra}
lafyl: lawful: *lafyll* M; *leafull* T {lafyl}
lagas, deulagas, lagasow: eye: *lagas*, (pl.) *lagasow* T; (dual) *dewlagas*, (pl.) *lagasowe* C; *lagaz*, (dual) *dealagaz* AB; (pl.) *lagagow* Rowe {lagas, deulagas, lagasow}
lagasek/lagajek: observant: *lagasek* M; *lagadzhek* AB {lagasek/lagajek}
laha, lahys/lawys: law: *laha, latha* M; *la*, (pl.) *lawys, lawes* T; *laha* AB; (pl.) *lahes* ACB {lagha, laghys}
lak: lack: *lak, lake* T {—}
lantern: lantern: *lantern* M; *lantorn, lanthorn* C {lantern}
larj/larjy: generous: (comp.) *larchya* M; *largy* T; *largya* (not comp.) C; *lardzh* AB {larch/larj}
Latyn: Latin: *laten* M; *latyn* T; *Latten* NBoson {Latyn}
lavar, lavarow: expression, utterance: (pl.) *lafarow* M; *lavar* C; *lavar* AB; *lavor, lavar* ACB {lavar, lavarow}
lavrak: trousers: *lavrak* AB; *lavrak* JBoson {lavrak}
lavur: labour: *lavyr, laver* M; *lavure* T; *lavyr, lavyer, lyvyer* C {lafur}
lavurya: travel (vb), labour (vb): *lafuria* M; *lavyrrya* C; *laviria* AB {lafurya}
lavuryans: travelling: *lafuryans* M {lafuryans}
lawa: praise (vb): *lawe* OM; *lawe* PC; *lawe* M {lawa}
le: less: *lee* M; *le* T; *lê* AB; *lê, lêa* ACB {le}
le: place: *lee* M; *le* C; *le* AB {le}
lecyans: license: *lessyans, lescyens* M {lecyans}
ledan: broad: *leden* PA; *ledan* AB {ledan}

ledya: lead (vb): *ledya* M; *ledia* T; (pres.) *ledia* AB {ledya}
lef: voice: *leff* PA; *lef* OM; *leaf* C; *leauve* Rowe {lef}
leg: lay (adj.): *lek, leyk* M; *leg* T {lek}
legessa: catch mice: *legessa* M {legessa}
leghya: lessen: *leghya* M {lehe}
lehen: slate: *lehan* AB {leghen}
lejek: heifer: *ledzhek* AB; *leoyock* Bilbao MS {lejek}
lel: loyal: *lel* M; *lell* T: *lell* A; *leel, leall* C; *leal* AB; *leal* ACB {lel}
leldury: sincerity: *lelldury* T {leldury}
lemma: sharpen: *lemma* C; *lebma* AB; *lebma* ACB {lemma}
lemmel: jump: *lebmal* AB; *lemmell* Scawen {lemmel}
lemmyn: now: *lemmyn, lemmen, lemman, lemen* M; *lemmyn, lymmyn* T; *lemyn, lebmyn* C; *lebben* AB {lemmyn}
len: trusty, true: *len* M {len}
lendury: honesty: *lendury* T {lendury}
lenky: swallow (vb): *lenky* M {lenky}
lent: slow: *lent* M {lent}
lenwel, lenwys: fill: (pp.) *lynwys* T; (pp.) *lenwys* C; *lenal* JBoson {lenwel, lenwys}
les: advantage: *lees, les* M; *leas, les* C; *lêz* AB {les}
les: breadth: *les* M; *leas* C {les}
lesky: burn (vb): *lesky* M; *lesky, lyskye* C; *loski* AB {lesky}
lesson, lessons: lesson: *lesson*, (pl.) *lessons* T {—}
lester: vessel: *lester* M; *lester* T; *lysster, lester, lesster* C {lester}
let: hindrance: *let* M {let}
leth: milk: *leth* M; *leath* A; *lêath* AB; *leath* ACB {milk}
lettrys: lettered: *lettrys* PC; *letrys* M {lettrys}
lettya: hinder: *lettya, letya* M; *lettya* T {lettya}
leven: even, level: *leven* AB {leven}
leverel: say: *leferel* M; *leverall, leverell, leverel* T; *leverall* C; *laveral, lâol* AB; *lavarel, leverol* NBoson; *lavaral, lawle* Rowe {leverel}
levryth: fresh milk: *leverith* AB {levryth}
lo, loyow: spoon: *lo* M; *lo*, (pl.) *leu* AB {lo, loyow}
loder, lodrow: stocking: *lodr*, (pl.) *lydrau* AB {loder, lodrow}
logosen/logojen, logas: mouse: *logosan* C; *lygodzhan*, (pl.) *logaz* AB {logosen}
lon: bullock: *lodn, lon* C; *lodn* (pl.) *ludnu* AB {lon, lonnow}
londya: land (vb): *londia* M {londya}
longya: belong: *longia, longya* T {longya}
lor: moon: *lor* M; *loer, loor* C; *lûr* AB {lor}
lorden: blockhead, clown: *lorden* M {lorden}
lordya: lord (vb): *lordya* C {lordya}
los: grey: *loys, los* M; *loose* C; *lûdzh* AB {los}
losel/lorel: rascal: *losal, lorel, lorel* M {losel/lorel}
losowen, losow: herb: *losouen*, (pl.) *losou* M; (pl.) *losowe* C; *lyzuan*, (pl.) *luzu* AB; (pl.) *lozo* Rowe {losowen, losow}

lost, lostow: tail: (pl.) *lostou* M; *lost* T; *lost* AB {lost, lostow}

lovan, lovonow: rope: (pl.) *lovonow* T; (pl.) *lavonowe* C; *lôvan* AB {lovan, lovonow}

lovanen: cord, twine: *lovannan* AB {lovanen}

lovryjyon: leprosy: *lovrygyan* M {lovryjyon}

lowar/low: enough: *lour, lor* M; *lowre, lowar* T; *lowarth, lowr* A; *lower, lowar* C; *laur* AB {lowr}

lowarn: fox: *lowern* M {lowarn}

lowarth: garden: *lowarth* PA; *lûar* AB; *looar* Rowe {lowarth}

lowen: glad: *lowen* M; *lowan* C; *lûan* AB; *looan* NBoson; *loan* Rowe; *loan* ACB {lowen}

lowen, low: louse: *lûan*, (pl.) *lou* AB {lewen, low}

lowena: joy: *lowena* M; *lowena* C {lowena}

lowender: joy: *lowendar* T; *loander* Rowe {lowender}

lowenek: joyful: *lowenek* M; *lowenacke* C; *lowenycke* Borde; *loouenak, lauenik* AB; *lawannek* ACB {lowenek}

lowenhe: gladden: *lowenhe* M; *lowenhe* T {lowenhe}

lows: lax, careless: *lowse* C {lows}

lowsya/lowsel: loosen, undo: *lowsya* T; *louzall* AB {lowsya}

lowta: loyalty: *leute, louta* M; *lowta* C {leouta}

luef, dewlef/dewla: hand: *luef, luff*, (dual) *dula, dule* M; (dual.) *dewla, dewleff* T; (dual) *dowla* A; *leff*, (dual) *dewla* C; (dual) *dula* AB; (dual) *dula* NBoson {luf, dywluf/dywla}

luhes: lightning: *luehes* M; *lowas, louas* AB {lughes}

luen/len: full: *luen* M; *lene, len* T; *lean* C; *lên* AB {lun}

luer: floor: *luyr, lur* M; *lêr*, (pl.) *lerriou, lerou* AB {lur}

lugh, luhy: calf: *lugh* M; (pl.) *ley* T; *lêauh* AB; *leaw* BilbaoMS {lugh, lughy}

luk: enough: *lyk* AB; *luck* ACB {luk}

lusew/lujew: ashes: *lusu* M; *lusew, lewsew, lesew* T; *lidzhiu* AB {lusew}

lust, lustys: lust: *lust, luyst*, (pl.) *lustis* M; *lust*, (pl.) *lustys* T {lust, lustys}

lycor: liquid: *lycor* M {lycour}

lyen, lyenyow: sheet: (pl.) *lyynnyou* M; *lîan* AB {lyen, lyenyow}

lyes: many: *lues, luas, lius* M; *lyas* T; *leas* C; *lîaz* AB {lyes}

lyes huny: many a one: *leas huny* PA; *lues huny* {lyes huny}

lyf/ly: lunch: *li* ACB {ly(f)}

lyha: least: *lya, lyha* T; *leiha* AB {lyha}

lyn: liquid: *lyn* M {lyn}

lynas: nettles: *lynas* T; *linaz* AB {lynas}

lynyeth/lynyaj: lineage: *lynneth, lynyeth* M; *lynyath, lignag* T; *lydnyathe* C {lynyeth/lynaja}

lyon: lion: *lyon* PA; *lyon* T {lyon}

lyther, lytherow: letters: *lyther*, (pl.) *leʒerou* M; (pl.) *lytherau* AB; (pl.) *letherau* NBoson {lyther, lytherow}

lyven: page of book: *livan* AB {lyven}

lyver, lyvrow/lyfryow: book: *liver, lefer*, (pl.) *leffrou*, (pl..) *lyfryou* M; *lever, lyver, lyffer* T; (pl.) *leverow*, (pl.) *leverowe* C; *levar*, (pl.) *livrou* AB {lyver, lyfrow/lyfryow}

lyvya: take lunch: *lyfye, lefya* M {lyfya}

lyw: colour (n.): *lyw* RD; *lew* C; *liu* AB {lyw}

lywyer: dyer: *liuiar* AB {lywyor}

lyw/lyf, lyvyow: flood: *lewe* T; *lyw, lywe*, (pl.) *lyvyow*, (pl.) *levyaw* C; *lyv* AB {lyw, lyvyow}

mab, mebyon: son: *mab, map, mapp* M; *mab* T; *mabe*, (pl.) *mybbyan* C {mab, rnebyon}

mab den: mankind: *mab den* M; *mab den* T; *mab dene* A; *mab dean* C {mab den}

mab lyen, mebyon lyen: clerk: *mab lyen*, (pl.) *mebyon lyen*, (pl.) *mebyen lyen* M; *mab lyan* T; *mab leean* TBoson {mab lyen, mebyon lyen}

maga: as (conj.): *mage* M; *maga* C {maga}

maga: nurture (vb): *maga* M; *maga* T; *maga* C {maga}

magata: also: *mageta* M; *magata* T; *magata* C; *magatâ* AB {magata}

maghteth: maiden: *mahtheid* OCV; *maghteth* M; *mathtath* Borde; *maiteth* TBoson {maghteth}

maker: maker: *makar* C {—}

mal: willingness: *mal* M {mal}

mam, mammow: mother: *mam*, (pl.) *mammow* M; *mam* T; *mamb* A; *mabm, mamm* C {mam, mammow}

mammeth, mammethow: wetnurse, breast-feeding woman: (pl.) *mammethou* M; *mammeth* A; *mammath* AB {mammeth, mammethow}

managh: monk: *manach* OCV; *manah* AB {managh}

manek: glove: *manag* AB {manek}

maner, manerow: manner: *maner*, (pl.) *manerou* M; *maner* T; *maner, manar* C {maner, manerow}

mans: maimed: *mans* M; *mans* AB {mans}

mantel: mantle: *mantel* PC; *mantall* A; *mantel* AB {mantel}

mar(s), mara(s): if: *mer(s), mara* M; *mar* T; *mar* C {mar(s), mara(s)}

marbel: marble: *marbell* C {marbel}

marchont, marchons: merchant: *marchont* M; *marchant* T; *mertshant*, (pl.) *mertshants* (pl.) *martshants* AB {marchont, marchons}

margh, mergh: horse: *margh*, (pl.) *mergh* M; *marth*, (pl.) *merth* T; *marth, margh* C; *marh* AB; *mar* Bilbao MS; (pl.) *merh* ACB {margh, mergh}

marhak, marrogyon: knight: *marrek*, (pl.) *marrogyon*, (pl.) *marogyon* M; *marhak*, (pl.) *marregion*, (pl.) *marrogion* AB; *marrack* NBoson {marghak/marrek, marghog-yon}

marhas: market *marras* T; *marhaz* AB; *marraz* JBoson {marghas}

marnas: unless: *marnes* M; *marnas* C {marnas}

***marner, marners**: sailor. (pl.) *marners* M {marner, marners}

marow: dead: *marou, marrou* M; *marrou* TBoson; *maro* TBoson {marow}

CORNISH TODAY

martesen/martejen: perhaps: *martegen* M; *mertesyn, martesyn* T; *martesyn* A; *martezen* AB; *metessen* NBoson {martesen}

marth: wonder, astonishment: *marth* M; *marth, marthe* C {marth}

*****marthus, marthujyon**: wonder: (pl.) *marthugian*, (pl.) *marthuggian*, (pl.) *marthussyan* T; (pl.) *marugian*, (pl.) *marugion* A; *marudgyan* ACB {marthus, marthojyon}

marthys: wondrous: *marthys* M; *marthys* C {marthys}

marya: marry: *marya* M {marya}

maryach/maryaj: marriage: *maryag, maryach* M; *mariag* T {maryach}

mas: good: *mas* T; *mas* C {mas}

mata, matys: mate: *mata*, (pl.) *matis* M; (pl.) *matas* Borde {mata, matys}

mater, maters: matter: *mater* M; *mattar* T; *matter*, (pl.) *maters* C {mater, maters}

maw: boy: *mau* M; *mawe, maw* C; *mau* AB {maw}

maylya: wrap: *malya* M; (pp.) *maylyes* C {maylya}

me/my: I, me: *my* M; *me* T; *me, my* C; *mi* AB; *me* ACB {my}

mebyl: furniture, property: *mebyl* M {mebyl}

medelhe: weaken: *medelhe* M {medelhe}

medhegyeth: medicine: *methegyeth* M; cf. *medheknedh* AB {medhegyeth}

medhek. doctor: *methek* M; *metheg* T; *medhek, medhik* AB {medhek}

medhel/medel: soft: *methel* OM; *medel* M; (comp.) *medalha* T; *medall* C; *medal* AB {medhel/medel}

medhewnep: drunkenness: *methewnep* T {medhewnep}

medhow: drunk: *methou, methou* M; *medho, medhu* AB {medhow}

medra: aim (vb): *meddra* C {medra}

megyans: nurture (n.): *megyans* M {megyans}

megynnow: bellows: *miginiau, meginnu* AB {megynnow}

mel: honey: *mel* OM; *mel* RD; *mil* AB; *mêl, meal* ACB {mel}

mel, mellow: joint: (pl.) *mellou* M {mel, mellow}

melen: yellow: *melyn* OM; *melyn* M; *melen* AB; *mellyn* ACB {melen}

mellya: meddle: *melya* M; *myllya* T; *mellya* C {mellya}

melwhejen: snail, slug: *molhuydzhan* AB {melwhesen}

melyges: accursed: *mylyges* RD; *malegas, melagas, melegas* C {mylygys}

melyn: mill: *melin* OCV; *belin* AB; *melin, mellyn* ACB {melyn}

men, meyn: stone: *men* M; *mene* T; *mean* AB; (pl.) *mine* NBoson; (pl.) *mine* ACB {men, meyn}

meneges: admit, confess: *menegas, meneges* T {meneges}

meneth, menydhyow: mountain: *meneth* M; *meneth* T; *menythe* C; *menedh, menedhiou* AB; *menneth* NBoson {meneth, menydhyow}

mennas: wish (vb.): *mynnes, mennes* M; *mynnas* T; (pres.) *medn* AB {mynnes}

menough: often: *menogh* M; *manno* AB; *menough* ACB {menough}

mentenour: upholder: *mentenour* M {mentenour}

mentenya: support: *mentenya, menteyna* M; *mentanya* T; *mayntaynya* C {mentena}

mentons: maintenance: *mentons* M {mentons}

menya: mean (vb): *menya* T {menya}

menystra: administer: *menystra* M {menystra}

mercy: mercy: *mercy* M; *mercy* T; *mercye, mersy, mercy* C {mercy}

merk/mark: mark (n.): *marck, marcke, merck, merke* C {merk}

merkya: notice, mark (vb): *markya* M; *merkya* T; *merkya* C {merkya}

merkyl, merclys: miracle: *merkyl*, (pl.) *merclys* M; *myrakyll*, (pl.) *myraclis* T; *mirkell* A {merkyl, merclys}

mernans: death: *mernans* M; *mernans, myrnans* T; *mernans* C; *marnance* A; *marnans* AB {mernans}

merwel: die: *meruel, merwell* M; *merwall, merwell* T; *merwall* C; *meruel* AB; *merwal* NBoson; *merwall* Rowe {merwel}

mery: merry: *mery* M; *mery* C {mery}

mes ha chy: inside and out: *mes a chy* C {mes ha chy}

mes/mas/bus: but: *mes* M; *mas* T; *bus, mase* A; *mes* C; *buz* AB; *buz* NBoson {mes}

mesklen: mussel: *mesclen* AB {mesklen}

messejer: messenger: *meseger, messeger* M {messejer}

mester/mayster, mestrysy/mestryjy: master: *mester, mayster*, (pl.) *mestresy*, (pl.) *mestrigy* M; *mester, meister, maister*, (pl.) *meisters* T; *master* A; *mester* C; *mester, master*, (pl.) *mestrizi* AB {mester, mestrysy}

mestry: mastery: *mestry* M {maystry}

metal: steel: *metol* AB {metol}

meth: shame: *meth* M; *meth* C {meth}

methek: ashamed: *methek* T {methek}

methya: nurture (vb): *metha* AB {methy}

metya: meet: *metya* M; *mettia* AB; (pret.) *mettiaz* NBoson {metya}

mewl: disgrace: *meule* M {mewl}

meyn, meynys: means: *meen* M; *meyn*, (pl.) *menes*, (pl.) *meanys*, (pl.) *menys* T {mayn, maynys}

meyny: household: *meyny, meny* M; *mayny* C {meny}

modryp: aunt: *modrap* AB {modryp}

mog: smoke: *mooge, moog* C; *môg* AB {mog}

mogh: fruitless: *mogh* M {mogh}

moghhe: increase: *moghhe* M; *moyghe* C {moghhe}

mola dhu: blackbird: *mola dhiu* AB {molgh dhu}

moldra: murder (vb): *moldra* M {moldra}

mollath, mollothow: curse: *moleth, molleth* M; *molath*, (pl.) *molothowe* C; *moleth* AB {mollath, mollothow}

mollothek: accursed: *molothek* M {mollothek}

mollythys: accursed: *mollythys* C; *molithees* Rowe {mollythys}

302

mona: money: *mona* M; *mona* T; *mona* C; *mona, monnah* AB; *mona* ACB {mona}

mor: sea: mor M; *more* A; *more, moer, moare* C; *môr* AB {mor}

mordhos: thigh: *morras* AB {mordhos}

moren: blackberry: *moaren* AB {moren}

moren dhu: blackberry: *moran diu* AB {moren dhu}

moren cala: strawberry: *moran kala* AB {moren cala}

moreth: sorrow: *morathe* C {moreth}

morethek: sorrowful: *morethek* M; *morethack* C {morethek}

morlenwel: high tide: *morlenol* AB {morlenwel}

mornya: mourn: *murnye, mornya* C {mornya}

mos: table: *moys* M; *mois* T {mos}

mos/mones: go: *mones* OM; *mones* PC; *mos, mois, mones* M; *mos* T; *mos* C {mos, mones}

mosek: stinking: *mosek* M {mosek}

mostethes: dirt: *mostethes, mustethas* T; *mustethas* A {mostethes}

mostya: sully: *mostye* M {mostya}

mowes, mowysy: girl: (pl.) *mowysy* PC; *mowes* M; *moos*, (pl.) *mowyssye* C; *moz*, (pl.) *muzi* AB; (pl.) *muzzi*, (pl.) *musi* JBoson; (pl.) *muzi* ACB {mowes, mowysy}

moy: more: *moy* M; *moy, moye* T; *moy, moye* C; *mûy* AB; *muy* ACB {moy}

moyha: most: *moyha* T; *moygha* A; *moygha* Keigwin; *moyha* AB {moygha}

muer/mur/mer: great: *muer, mur* M; *mer* T; *meer* A; *mear, meer, mere, meare* C {mur}

muer 'ras dheuwhy: thank you: *mear a rase thewhy* C; *merastewhy* ACB {mur ras dheugh why}

munys: tiny: *munys* M; *menys* C; *minniz* ACB {munys}

muskegys: mad: *muscugys* M {muskegys}

muvya: move (vb): *muvye* M; *movia* T {muvya}

mytern, myterneth: king: *myterne, mytern, myghtern* M; *mytern*, (pl.) *myterneth* T; *mytearne*, (pl.) *meternath* A; *materen* JTonkin; *matern* AB; (pl.) *metearneau* 1660; *mitern*, (pl.) *maternyow* Rowe; *mateyrn* ACB {myghtern, myghterneth}

myternes: queen: *myʒternas, myternes* M; *myternes* AB; *maternes* Bilbao MS {myghternes}

myjer, myjoryon: reaper: *midzhar* AB; (pl.) *megouzion* [leg. megourion] ACB {myjer, myjoryon}

myjy: reap: *midzhi* AB; *medge* ACB {myjy}

myl, mylyow: thousand: *myl*, (pl.) *myllyou* M; *myll*, (pl.) *myllyow* T; *myell* C; *mil* AB; *meele* Bilbao MS; (pl.) *milliow* JBoson; *mil* ACB {myl, mylyow}

mylgy, mylguen: hunting dog: *mylgy*, (pl.) *mylguen* M {mylgy, mylgun}

mylweyth: a thousandfold: *mylwyth* M {mylwyth}

myn: by (in oaths): *men* C {myn}

myn: lip, edge: *myn* M; *mîn* AB {myn}

*****myn, menas**: kid, young goat: *menas* BilbaoMS {myn, menas}

mynen: kid, young goat: *mynnan* AB {mynen}

myns/mynj: as many: *myns, mens* M; *myng, myns* T; *myns* C; *mens, myns* ACB {myns}

mynstrel, mynstrels: minstrel: (pl.) *menstrels* M; (pl.) *mynstrels* C {menstrel, menstrels}

myras/meras: look at: *meras* PA; *myras, meras, meres* M; *meras* T; (imp.) *meer*, (imp.) *myer* C; *miraz* AB; JBoson *meraz* {myras}

myrgh, myrhas: daughter: *mergh, myrgh* M; *mirth* T; (pl.) *mirhas* C; *myrh, merh* AB; *merth* TBoson {myrgh, myrghas}

mys, mysyow: month: *mys*, (pl.) *msyou* M; *mîz* AB; *meese* Bilbao MS {mys, mysyow}

mys Du: November: *Mîz diu* AB; *Miz-Diu, Miz-du* ACB {mys Du}

mys Ebrel: April: *Miz ebral* AB; *Mîz Ebral* JBoson; *Míz-Ebrall* ACB {mys Ebrel}

mys Est: August: *mys est, meys est* M; *East* AB; *East, mys Est, mîz-east* Gwavas; *Miz-East, miz-east* ACB {mys Est}

mys Genver: January: *genvar* AB; *Miz-Genver* ACB {mys Genver}

mys Gortheren, mys Gorefen, Gortheren: July: *gortheren* M; *Miz gorephan* AB; *Gorephan, Miz-Gorephan* ACB {mys Gortheren}

mys Gwyngala: September: *mys guyngala* M; *Mîz-guedn-gala* AB; *Guedngala, Miz-Guedn-Gala* ABC {mys Gwyngala}

mys Hedra: October: *Hedra, Mîz-hedra* AB; *messe Heddra* TBoson; *myz heddra* Keigwin; *Hedra, Miz-Hedra* ACB {mys Hedra}

mys Kevardhu: December: *Mis kevardhiu* AB; *Kevardhin* [leg. *Kevardhiu*], *Miz-Kevardhin* [leg. *Kevardhiu*] ACB {mys Kevardhu}

mys Me: May: *Mîz mê* AB; *Me, Miz-Mê* ACB {mys Me}

mys Merth: March: *Miz merh* AB; *mîz-merh* Gwavas; *Merh, Mîs-Merh* ACB {mys Merth}

mys Metheven/mys Efen: June: *mes metheven* M; *Miz ephan* AB; *Ephan, Miz-Ephan* ACB {mys Metheven}

mys Whevrel: February: *Huevral* AB; *Mîs-Huevral* ACB {mys-Whevrer}

myshef/myschew: mischief: *myscheff* M; *myschyw, myshew, myshow, mysshew, myschef* C {myshyf}

mystrust: mistrust (n.): *mystrust* C {mystrest}

mystrustya: mistrust (vb): *mystrustya* C {mystrestya}

myttyn/mettyn: morning: *meten, metten* M; *myttyn* T; *metin* AB; *metten* ACB; *metten* Borlase {myttyn}

na fors: no matter: *na fors* M {na fors}

na(g): nor: *na(g)* M {na(g)}

nacyon, nacyons: nation: *nascyon* M; *nacion*, (pl.) *nacions* T {nasyon, nasyons}

Nadelik: Christmas: *Nedelic, Nadelik* AB; *Nadelik* ACB; *Nedelack* Ustick {Nadelek}

nader, nedras: viper: (pl.) *neddras* T: *nadar, nadyr, naddyr* AB {nader, nedras}

nagh: denial: *nagh* M {nagh}

naha: deny: *naha* M; *naha* T; *naha* C {nagha}

CORNISH TODAY

nahen: otherwise: *nahen* M; *nahene* T {nahen}
nam: flaw: *nam* M {nam}
namuer. not many, not much: *namur* M {namur}
na moy: any more: *na moy* M; *na moy* C {na rnoy}
na neyl: neither: *nanyl* M; *na neill, na neyll, na neil, na nell* T; *na neile* AB; *noniel* NBoson {nanyl}
namnygen: just now: *namnygen* M {namnygen}
nans/nanj: now: *nawnj* PA; *nang* M; *nang* C {nans}
nappyth/neppyth: something: *napyth* M; *nampith* T; *nappith* A; *nepeth* AB; *nepeath* TBoson {neppyth}
nasweth/najweth: needle: *nasweth* M; *nadzhedh* AB {nasweth}
natur: nature: *nattur* M; *nature* A; *natyr* AB {natur}
naw: nine: *naw* C; *naw* Borde; *nau* AB; *naw* ACB {naw}
nawnsek/nawnjek: nineteen: *nownsag* T; *noundzhak* AB; *nounjak* Jenner; *nawnzack* ACB {nawnjek}
nawves: ninth: *nahuaz* AB; *nawas* ACB {nawves}
neb: who (rel.): *neb* T; *neb* C {neb/nep}
nebes: little (pron.): *nebes* M; *nebas, nebes* T; *nebas* A; *nebas* C; *nebas, nebaz* AB; *nebbaz* NBoson {nebes}
nedha: spin: *nethe* OM; *netha* C; *nedha* AB {nedha}
nef: heaven: *nef, neff* M; *neff* T; *neff, nef, neave* C; *nêv* AB; *neeve* Rowe; *nefe* TBoson; *neue* JBoson {nef}
nefra/nevra: ever (in the future): *nefra, neffra* M; *neffra* T; *nefra, neffra* C; *nevra* AB; *nevra* Rowe; *neverah* TBoson {nefra}
negedhys: renegade (n.): *negethys* M {negedhys}
negejeth: messenger: *negegath* A {negesyth}
negys, negysyow: business: *nygys*, (pl.) *nygysyou*, (pl.) *negesyou* M; *negys, nygys*, (pl.) *negissyow*, (pl.) *negyssyow* C {negys, negysyow}
nell: might: *nel* M {nell}
nerth: strength: *nerth* M; *nerth* T {nerth}
nes: nearer: *nes* C; *nêz* AB {nes}
nessa: next, nearest: *nessa, nesse* M; *nessa* T; *nessa* AB; *nessa* ACB {nessa}
nessevyn: kinsmen: *nessevyn* M {neshevyn}
newl: fog: *niul* AB {newl}
newyth: youth: *newyth* {newyth}
neyja: swim, fly: (pret.) *nygyas* OM; *nyga* M; (imp.) *nyedge* C; *nyidzha* AB; *neidga* JBoson {nyja}
neyth, neythow: nest: *nyth* M; *neith*, (pl.) *neitho* AB; *nythow* ACB {nyth, nythow}
nobyl: noble: *nobil* M; *nobell* C; (comp.) *nobla* NBoson {nobyl}
north: north: *north* M {North}
north est: north east: *north yst* M; *Noor East* JBoson {north yst}
norves, norvys: world: *norvys* T; *norvys, norvese, norevese* A {norvys}
nos: night: *nos, noys* M; *nois, nos* T; *noos* C; *noaze* Rowe; *noz* JBoson {nos}

nosweyth: night-time: *noswyth* M {noswyth}
noth: naked: *noth* M; *noith* T; *nooth* C; *noath* AB; *en hoath* Rowe; *noath, nooth, noth* ACB {noth}
notha: nakedness: *nootha* C; *noatha, nootha* ACB {notha}
notya: note (vb): *notya, notia* M; *notya* T {notya}
nowedhys: tidings: *nowethys, nowethis* C {nowedhys}
noweth: new: *nowyth* M; *nowith, nowyth* T; *noweth* A; *nowyth* C; *noueth, neuydh* AB; *noweth* Scawen {noweth}
nowodhow: news: *newothow, nowethou* M; *nawothow, nowothow* C {newodhow}
number: number: *number* M; *number, numbyr* T; *number* C {nomber}
numbra: number (vb): *numbra* T {—}
ny: we, us: *ny* M; *ny* T; *nei* AB {ny}
ny dal: behoves not: *ny dall* T; *ny dale* C {ny dal}
ny godh: ought not: *ny goth* M {ny goth}
ny..man: at all: *ny..man* M {ny..man}
ny(ns)/ny(nj): not: *ny, nyg, nyng* T; *ny, nyng, nyg, nynj* C {ny(ns)}
ny vern: concerns not: *ny vern* M {ny vern}
nyver: number: *nyver* M; *nyver, never* ACB {nyver}
nyvera: number (vb): *neuera* PA; *nivera* AB {nyvera}

obaya: obey: *obaya* M; *abeya, obeya* T {obaya}
ober, oberow/obereth: work: (pl.) *oberou* M; *ober*, (pl.) *oberow*, (pl.) *obereth* T; *obar, ober*, (pl.) *oberowe* C; (pl.) *oberou* AB {ober, oberow, obereth}
oblacyon: oblation: *oblacion* T; *oblation* A; *oblacon, oblasshon, oblashyon* C {oblasyon}
occupya: occupy: *occupya* C {—}
offendya: offend: *offendia* M; *offendiia, offendya* T; *offendya* C {offendya}
offra: offer (vb): *offra* T; *offra* A {—}
offrynnya: offer (vb): *offrynnya* M; *offrennia* A {offrynnya}
offys: office: *office* T {offys}
offyser, offysers: officer: *officer*, (pl.) *officers* T {offyser}
ogas: near: *oges* M; *ogas* T; *ogas* C; *agoz, ogoz* AB; *ogaz* Rowe {ogas}
ogasty: nearly: *ogasty* T; *oggastigh* NBoson {ogasty}
ojyon, ohen: ox: (pl.) *oghan* T; (pl.) *ohan* C; *udzheon* AB; *odgan* Bilbao MS; *ouggan* TBoson; *udzheon, odgan*, (pl.) *ohan* ACB {ojyon, oghen}
ol, olow: track: (pl.) *olow* OM; *ooll*, (pl.) *allow* C {ol, olow}
ola: weep: *ole* PC; *ola* M; *hoalea, ola* AB; *whola* Rowe {ola}
olas: hearth: *olaz* AB; *ollaz* ACB {olas}
oll: all: *ol* M; *oll* T; *oll* C; *ôl* AB; *hole* Bilbao MS {oll}
ollgallosek: omnipotent *olgollousacke* C; *olgallouseck* Keigwin {ollgallosek}
olva: lamentation: *olva* Rowe {olva}
olyf: olive: *olyf* PC; *olyf* C {olyf}
omdenna: withdraw: *omdenna* T {omdenna}

omdowlel: wrestle: *ymdoula* AB {omdewlel}

omdowler: wrestler: *ymdoular* AB {omdewler}

omdhal: dispute, quarrel (vb): *omdhal* AB {omdhal}

omdhevas: orphan: *omthevas* M; *omthevas* T {omdhevas}

omdhon: breed (vb): *umthan* ACB; *humthan* Rowe {omdhon}

omlath: fight (vb): *omloth, ornlath, omleth* T; *hemladh* AB {omlath}

omlavar: dumb: *omlavar* T {omlavar}

omma: here: *omma, oma* M; *omma* T; *umma* A; *omma, obma* C; *omma, obma, ymma* AB; *uppa* ACB {omma}

omskemunys: accursed: *omschumunys* M; *omskemynes, umskemynes, omskemynys, skemynys* C {emskemunys}

***omwheles**: capsize: *omelly*, (1 pres.) *umhelaf* C {omwheles}

on, eyn: lamb: *on* M; *one, oyen*, (pl.) *eyen*, (pl.) *eyn*, (pl.) *eyne* T; *onn* A; *ôan, oan*, (pl.) *ein* AB {on, en}

onen: one: *onen* M; *onyn* T; *onen, onyn* A; *onyn* C; *uynyn* AB; *onen* Rowe; *onan, onen, onyn* ACB {onen}

onest: seemly, honest: *onest* RD; *onest* M; *honest* T; *onest* AB {onest}

onester: seemliness: *onester* M {onester}

onnen: ash tree: *onen* M; *onnen* AB {onnen}

onour/enour: honour (n.): *onour* OM; *honour, enour* M; *honore, honor* T; *honor, honour* A {onour/enour}

order, orders: order: *order* M; *ordyr, order*, (pl.) *orders* T; *order* C {ordyr, ordyrs}

orna: ordain, order (vb): *orna* M; *orna* C {orna}

os, oj: age: *oys* M; *oys, ois* T; *oydge* C; *ûz* AB; *oys, oydge, ooz, oze, uze* ACB {os}

ost: host, man of house: *ost* AB {ost}

ost: host, army: *ost* M {ost}

ostes: hostess: *hostes* Borde; *ostez, hostez* AB {ostes}

ostya: lodge (vb): *ostia* AB {ostya}

othem/ethom: need: *othem* M; *othom, ethom* T; *otham* C; *otham* ACB {ethorn}

othomek, othomogyon: needy (adj.); needy person (n.): *othommek, othomek* , (pl.) *othomogyon*, (pl.) *othomgyan* M {ethomek, ethomogyon}

ow: my: *ou* M; *ow* T; *ow* A; *ow* C {ow}

own: fear: *oun* M; *owne* T; *own* A; *owne* C; *oun* AB; *owne* Rowe {own}

ownek. fearful: *ownek* T {ownek}

ownter: uncle: *ounter, ountr* AB {ewnter}

owr: hour: *owre* T; *or, ower* C; *our, ouer, ûr* AB {owr}

owr. gold: *our* M; *owr* A; *awr* Rowe {owr}

owrlyn: silk: *ourlyn* M; *ourlen* AB {owrlyn}

oy, oyow: egg: *oy, wy* M; *oye* C; (pl.) *eyo* Borde; *oi* AB; *oye*, (pl.) *oyow* ACB {oy, oyow}

oyl: oil: *oel, oyl* OM; oyle C; *oel* ACB {oyl}

pab: pope: *pap* M; *pab* T {pap}

padel: dish, pan: *padal* AB {padel}

pader: paternoster: *padar, pader* ACB {pader}

pajya, pajys: page (boy): *pagya*, (pl.) *pagys* M; *pagya* C {paja, pajys}

pal: shovel: *pal* OM; *pâl* AB {pal}

palas: dig: *palas* OM; *pallas, palas* C {palas}

paljy: palsy: *palgy* M {paljy}

paljyes: paralytic, palsied: *palgeaz* Rowe {paljyes}

palys: palace: *palys* M {palys}

pan: when: *pan* T; *pen* {pan}

pan, pannow: cloth: (pl.) *pannou* M; *padn* AB; *padn* ACB {pan, pannow}

pana/pan: what kind of: *pana, pan* M; *pana* T; *pana* C {pana/pan}

pandra: what: *pandra, pendra* M; *pandra, pendra* T; *pandra* C {pandra}

panen, panes: parsnip: *panan*, (pl.) *panez* AB; *panan*, (pl.) *panez* ACB {panesen, panen}

paper, paperyow: paper: *papar*, (pl.) *papyrio* AB {paper, paperyow}

par, parow: equal (n.): *par*, (pl.) *parou* M; *par* T; (pl.) *parowe* C {par, parow}

paradys/paradhys: paradise: *parathis; paradys* T; *paradice, paradys, paradise* C; *paraves* Rowe; *parathys* ACB {paradys/paradhys}

parlet: prelate: *parlet* M {perlet}

part: part: *part, parte* M; *part* T; *part, parte* C {part}

parusy: prepare: *parusy* PC; (imp.) *parusugh* M {parusy}

parys: ready: *parys* M; *paris* T; *parys* C; *parryz, parez* AB; *parrez* NBoson {parys}

pas: pace: *pas* M {pas}

pas: cough: *pâz* AB {pas}

Pask: Easter, Passover: *pasch* PA; *pask* PC; *Pask* A; *Pask* AB {Pask}

passyes: past (adj.): *passyes* T; *passhes* C; *passiez* AB {passyes}

passyon: passion: *pascon* PA; *passyon* PC; *pascyon, passyon, pasconn* M; *pascion* T {passyon}

pastel: portion (of land): *pastel* M {pastel}

patryark: patriarch: *patriark* T {*patryargh}

paw: paw: *pau* M; *paw* ACB {paw}

payn, paynys: pain (n.): *payn, peyn*, (pl.) *paynys*, (pl.) *peynys* PA; *payn, peyn*, (pl.) *paynys*, (pl.) *peynys* PC; *peyn*, (pl.) *peynys* M; *payne*, (pl.) *paynys* T; *payn*, (pl.) *paynes* C {payn, paynys}

payntya: paint (vb): *payntya* T {pentya}

paynya: torture: *penya* C {payna}

pe: pay (vb): *pegh, pe, pee* M; *pe* T; *pea* AB {pe}

***pedren, pedrennow**: buttock: (pl.) *pedrennou* M {pedrennow}

pedrevan: lizard: *pedrevan* ACB {pedrevan}

pedry: rot (vb): *peddry* RD; *pedry* M; *peddry* C {pedry}

peg: pitch: *peyke* C; *peg* {pek}

pegans: utensils: *pegans* M; *pegans* C {pegans}

pegh: sin (n.): *pegh* M; *pegh* T; *pegh* A; *pegh, peth, peagh* C {pegh}

peha: sin (vb): *peha* M; *peha* T; *peha* C {pegha}

pehador, pehadoryon: sinner: *pehadur*, (pl.) *pehadoryon* PA; *pehadur*, (pl.) *pehadorryan* T;

305

(pl.) *pehadurrian* TBoson {peghador, peghadoryon}

pehas, pehosow: sin, offence: (pl.) *pehosow* OM; *pehas*, (pl.) *pehosou* M; (pl.) *pehosow* T; (pl.) *pehosow* A; (pl.) *pehasowe* C {peghas, peghosow}

pela: pillage, strip (vb): *pela, pyle* M; *pela* C; (pp) *pilez* AB {pylya + pylla}

pell: far: *pel* M; *pell* T; *pell* C; *pel* AB; *pell* JBoson {pell}

pellder: distance: *peldar* T; *peldar* C; *pelldar* ACB {pellder}

pemont: payment: *payment* PA; *pemont, pement* M {payment}

pen, pennow: head: *pen*, (pl.) *pennou* M; *pen*, (pl.) *pennow* T; *pedn, pen* C; *pedn* AB {pen, pennow}

pen blogh: shaven pate: *pen blogh* M {pen blogh}

pen cog: nitwit: *pedn cooge* C {pen cok}

pen pylys: bald pate: *pen pylys, pedn pylles* C; *pedn pilez* AB {pen pilys}

pen pyst: blockead: *pen pyst* M {pen pyst}

Pencast/de Fencast: Whitsunday: *Du Fencost* T; *Pencas, Penkast* AB {Pencast, de Fencast}

pengarn, pengarnas: gurnard: (pl.) *pengarnas* C; *pengarne* ACB {pengarn, pengarnas}

pengasen: belly: *pengasen* M {pengasen}

pennoth: bareheaded: *pennoth* {pennoth}

penplas: headquarters: *pen plas* M {penplas}

pensevyk: prince: *pensevyk* M; *pensevik, pensevike* A; *pensevicke* C; *pensivik*, (pl.) *pendzhivikio*, (pl.) *pendzhivigion* AB {pensevyk, pensevygyon}

penys: penance: *penys* PA; *pynys, penys* M *penes* Rowe {penys}

percevya: perceive: *percevia, percevya, persevya* T {—}

peren, per: pear (fruit): *peran*, (pl.) *pêr* AB {peren, per}

perfect: perfect: *perfect* M; *perfect* T {—}

perfeth/perfyt: perfect: *perfyth* OM; *perfyth* PC; *perfeyth* RD; *perfeth* M; (comp.) *perfetha* T; *perfyt* C {perfyth/parfyt}

performya: perform: *performya, perfumya* T {—}

perhen: owner: *perhen* AB {perghen}

perhennek owner: *perhennek* M {perghennek}

person, persons: person: *person* M; *person*, (pl.) *persons* T; *person* C {person, persons}

perswadya: persuade: *persuadya* T {—}

perthy: bear (vb): *perthy* M; *perthy* C {perthy}

peryl: danger: *peryl* OM; *peryl, perel* M; *peryll* T; *perill* C {peryl}

peryllya: risk (vb): *peryllya* M {peryllya}

peryssya: perish: *peryshya* T {persya}

pes: peas, pease: *pêz* AB {pys}

pysadow/pejadov/pyjadov: prayer: *peyadow, peiadou, piiadou* M; *pesadow* T; *peiadow, pesadow* A; *pydzhadou* AB {pysadow}

pescotter: as soon: *peskytter, pyscotter* T {—}

pesquyth: as often: *pesqueth* T; *pesqwythe* C {pesquyth}

306

---

peswar/pajer: four: *peswar* PA; *peswar* RD; *peswar* T; *peswar* Borde; *padzhar* AB; *padzar* ACB {peswar}

peswar ugans/pajer ugans: eighty: *peswar ugans* T; *padzhar iganz* AB; *padgwar iganz* ACB {peswar ugans}

peswara/pajwera: fourth: *peswara, peswora* T; *peswera* C; *pazuera, padzhuera* AB; *peswarra, padzhuera* ACB {peswara}

peswardhek: fourteen: *pazuardhak* AB; *puzwarthack* ACB; *bizwaudhak* Jenner {peswardhek}

***pesya**: last (vb): (pres.) *peys* M {pesya}

peth: riches, possessions: *pyth, peth, peyth* M; *pith* T; *pythe* C; *pêth* AB {pyth}

petycyon: petition: *petyconn* M; *peticion* T {petysyon}

pewa: possess: *pewa, peua* M; *pewa* C {pewa}

peys: peace: *peys* M {pes}

pla: plague: *pla* M {pla}

plag, plagys: plague: *plag* T; (pl.) *plagys* C {plag, plagys}

plagya: plague (vb): *plagia* T {plagya}

plank, plankys: plank: (pl.) *plankes* C; (pl.) *plankyz*, (pl.) *plankoz* AB {plank, plankys}

plans: plant (n.): *planz* AB {plans}

plansa/planja: plant (vb): *planga, plansa*, (pret.) *planges*, (pp.) *plyngys* T {plansa}

plas: place: *plass, plaes, plath* M; *plas, place* C {plas}

plattya: crouch: *plattya* C {plattya}

plegadow: agreeable; inclination: *plygadow* M; *plegadow* C {plegadow}

plegya: fold: *plegia* AB {plegya}

plekya: please: *plekya* M; *plekya* C {plekya}

plen: plain (n.): *plen* M {plen}

plen: plain (adj.): *plen, pleyn, playn* T; *playn* A {plen}

plesour: pleasure: *pleysour* M; *plesure* T; *pleasure* C {plesour}

plesya: please (vb): *plesya* M; *pleycya* C; *plezia* AB {plesya}

plew: parish: *plu* RD; *plu* M; *plew* T; *plêu* AB; *plew* TBoson; *plewe* JTonkin; *pleû, plû, plew* ACB {plu}

plom: lead: *plobm* AB {plom}

plos: dirty: *plos* M; *ploos* C {plos}

plumen: plum: *pluman* AB {plumen}

pluven, pluf: pen, feather: *pluven* M; *plyvan*, (pl.) *pliv* AB; *plyv, pliv* ACB {pluven, pluf}

plynken: plank: *plyenkyn* C; *plankan* AB {plynken}

plyt: plight: *plyt* PC; *plet* M {plyt}

pobas: bake: *pobaz, peba* AB; *pobaz* NBoson; (pp.) *pebes* ACB {pobas}

pobel: people: *pobell, pobil, pobyl* M; *pobyll, pobill* T; *pobell* A; *pobell* C; *pobl* AB; *poble* Rowe; *poble* ACB {pobell}

poder: putrid, rotten: *poder* M; *podar* AB {poder}

podh: rot (n.): *poth* {poth}

podrek: rotten (adj.), rotten person (n.): *podrek* M; *poddrack* NBoson {podrek}

podrethek: rottten: *podrethek* M {podrethek}

podryn: rotten person: *poddren* M {podryn}

A SHORT DICTIONARY OF UCR

poken: or: *poken, pokene* T; *poken, pokeean* C {poken}

pol, pollow: pool: (pl.) *pollou* M {pol, pollow}

pollen: little pool, pond: *pollan* AB {pollen}

pollat, pollatys: fellow: *polat, pullat,* (pl.) *polatis* C; *pollat* AB {pollat, pollattys}

pols/polj: distance: *pols* PA; *pols* OM; *pols* PC; *pols* RD; *polge* M {pols}

polta: long time, great amount: *polta* (< *pols da*) C; *pylta* AB; *polta* NBoson {polta}

polytyk: shrewd: *polytyk* T {polytyk}

pon: pain: (pl.) *ponow* T; *poan* AB {pon, ponow}

pondra: ponder: *pondra* T {—}

ponvos: hardship: *ponvos* RD; *ponfos, ponfeys* M {ponvos}

ponya: run: *ponya* T; (pret.) *poonias* JTonkin; *punnya* AB {ponya}

poran: exactly: *poren* M; *poran* T; *poran* C {poran}

porhel, porhelly: porker: *porhel* M; *porrell* T; *porhal,* (pl.) *porelli* AB {porghel, porghelly}

porrys: urgently: *porris* PA; *porrys* OM; *porrys* PC; *porrys* RD; *purreys* M; *purris* T {porres}

pors, porsys: purse: *pors,* (pl.) *porses* M {pors, porsys}

portal: porch: *portal* AB {portal}

porth, porthow: gate, harbour: (pl) *porthou* M; *porh, por* AB; (pl.) *porthow* ACB {porth, porthow}

pos: heavy: *pos* RD; *poys* M; *poos, pos* T; *pûz* AB; *pouz* JBoson {pos}

possessyon: possession: *poscessyon* M; *possessyon* T {possessyon}

possybyl: possible: *possibil, possyble* T {possybyl}

pottya: put: *pottya* M {pottya}

pow: country: *pow, pou* M; *pow* T; *pow, powe* C; *pou* AB; *pow* Rowe {pow}

pow ysel: plain (n.): *pou izal* AB {pow ysel}

power, powers: power: *power* M; (pl.) *powers* T; *pohar* Rowe {power}

powes: rest (vb & n.): *powas, powes* M; *powas* C; *poaz* TBoson {powes}

powesva: rest (n.): *powesva* T; *powesva* C {powesva}

pows: garment: *pows* PA; *pous* PC; *pous* M; *powze* Rowe {pows}

poynt: point: *poynt* M; *poynt* T: *poynt* C; *point* NBoson {poynt}

poyson: poison: *poyson* T {poyson}

prag/praga/pyraga: why: *pyraga* M; *prag, praga* C; *prag, praga* AB {prak/prag(a)/pyraga}

pras, prasow: meadow: *prays,* (pl.) *prasou;* (pl.) *prasow* T {pras, prasow}

prat: trick: *prat* OM; *prat* RD; *pratt* C {prat}

prays: praise (n.): *prayse, preysse, preise* T {prays}

praysya: praise (vb): *praysya* PA; *preysya* M; *presia, presya* T; *praysya* C; (imp.) *preezyo* TBoson {praysya}

precyous: precious: *precyous* OM; *precius, precyous, presyus* T; *presius* A; *presyus, precyous* C {precyous}

preder: thought: *preder* T; *preder* C {preder}

predery: consider: *predery* M; *predery* T; *prederye* C; *prediri* AB {predery}

prederys: thoughtful, careful: *prederys* M; *pryderys* AB {prederus}

pref, prevyon, prevas: reptile, insect: *preff,* (pl.) *prevyon* M; *prif, preve, preaf, preif, preyf,* (pl.) *prevas* C; *prêv* AB; *prev,* (pl.) *prêvyon* ACB {pryf, prevyon, pryves}

preferrya: prefer: *preferrya* T {—}

pregoth/pregowth: (vb & n.) preach, sermon: *pregowth, pregoth, progath* T; *boroga* Rowe; (pp.) *peregowthys* Keigwin; *pregoth* ACB {pregoth}

pregowther, pregothoryon: preacher: *pregowther,* (pl.) *pregothorryan* T; *progowther* C; *progathar* AB {pregowther, pregothoryon}

pren: tree, timber: *pren* OM; *pren* PC; *predn* AB {pren}

prena/perna: buy: *prenna, perna* M; *perna* AB; *perna* ACB {prena}

pres/prys, prejyow: time, meal: *preys, pris,* (pl.) *preggyow* M; *preis, preys, preyse* C; *prêz* AB {prys, prysyow}

presentya: present (vb): *presentya* C {presentya}

prest: continually: *prest* M; *prest* C {prest}

prevaylya: prevail: *prevaylya* T {prevaylya}

preven: small worm: *prevan* AB {preven}

prevy: prove: *prevy* M; *prevy* T; *prevy* C; *previ, preva* AB {prevy}

prof: proof: *proff, prove* T; *prof, prove* C {prof}

profet, profetys: prophet: *profet,* (pl.) *prophetes, prophettys* T; *prophet* Rowe {—}

promys, promysyow: promise (n.): *promes* M; *promes, promys,* (pl.) *promysyow* T; *promas, promes* C {promys, promesys}

promysya: promise (vb): *promysya* T; *promysya* C {promysya}

pronter, prontyryon: priest: *pronter* M; *prounter, pronter, prontyr,* (pl.) *prontiran,* (pl.) *prontyryan* T; *pronter* A; *pronter, praonter* AB; *proanter* ACB {pronter, prontyryon}

prontereth: priesthood: *prontereth* T {prontereth}

provya: provide: *profia* M; *provya* T; *profya, provya* C; *pryuia* AB {provya}

prowt: proud: *prout* PC; *prowt, prowd* T; *prowte* C {prowt}

pry: clay: *pry* M; *pry, prye* T; *pry* C; *pryi* AB {pry}

pryas: spouse: *pryas, preas* C {pryas}

pryns: prince: *prence* M; *prince,* (pl.) *princes* T; *pryns, prynce* C {pryns}

prynt: print (n.): *prynt* C {prynt}

prys: price: *prys* A; *priz* AB; *priz* ACB {prys}

prysner: prisoner: (pl.) *prysners* PC; *presner, presnour* M {prysner}

pryson: prison: *preson, pressan; prison* T; *pressen* Rowe {pryson}

prysonya: imprison: *presonya* C {prysonya}

pryveth: private: *prevath, priveth* T; *prevathe* C; *prevath* Rowe {pryveth}

pub: every: *pup* M; *pub* T; *pub* C {pub/pup}

pub huny: everybody: *pub hwny, pub huny* C {pup huny}

pub/peb/pob: everybody: *peb, pup* M; *peb, pob* C {pub/pup}
pub tra: everything: *pub tra* T; *pub tra* C {pub tra}
pub uer/pub er: always: *pub er* PA; *pup ur* M; *pub ur* T; *pub ere, pub eare* C {pup ur}
puns, punsow: pound: *puns*, (pl.) *punsou* M; (pl.) *pynsow* C; *penz* AB; *pens* ACB {puns, punsow}
punsya: punish: *punsya, punyssya* T; (pp.) *punyshes* C {punsya}
pur: nasal mucus, snot: *pûr* AB {pur}
pur, purra: very: *pur* M; *pur*, (superlative) *purra* C; *por* AB {pur, purra}
purjya: purge (vb): *purgya* T; *pyrdzha* AB {purjya}
purpos: purpose (n.): *porpos* M; *purpos, porposse* T; *purpose, purpas* C {porpos}
purposya: purpose (vb): *purposya* T {porposya}
puscador: fisherman: *puscador* T; *pysgadur* AB; (pl.) *poscaders* Rowe {pyscador}
py: which: *py* M {py}
py ehen: what kind: *pehan, pehane* T {py eghen}
py le: where: *py le* T; *py lea* C {py le}
py suel: how many: *py sul* M; *pesuell* A {py sul}
py(th): where: *py(th)* M; *py(th)* C {py(th)}
pyba/peba: pipe (vb): *pyba* M; *peba* C {pyba}
pyber, pyboryon: piper: (pl.) *pyboryon* M; *peeber* Bilbao MS {pyber, pyboryon}
pymp/pemp: five: *pemp* T; *pymp, pympe* C; *pemp* AB; *pemp* ACB {pymp}
pympes: fifth: *pempas* T; *pympas* C; *pempaz* AB; *pempaz* ACB {pympes}
pympthek: fifteen: *pemdhak* AB; *pemdhak* ACB; *pemthak* Jenner {pympthek}
pynag: whichever, whoever: *panak, penag* M {pynak/pynag}
pynag oll: whoever, whichever: *penagull* T; *pennagel, pennagle, pynagell* C {pynak oll/pynag oll}
pyneyl: whichever: *peneyl* M {pynyl}
pys: piece: *pice* C; *pîs* AB {pys}
pysas: urine: *pizaz* AB {pysas}
pysk/pesk, puscas: fish: *pysk*, (pl.) *puskes* OM; (pl.) *puscas*, (pl.) *puskas* T; (pl.) puskas C; *pêsk*, (pl.) *pysgoz* AB {pysk, puscas}
pystry: sorcery: *pystry* M {pystry}
pysy/pyjy/pesy/pejy: pray: *pysy, pesy* M; (imp.) *pesough* T; *pegy* C; *pidzha, pidzhi* AB {pysy}
pyt: pit: *pytt* C {pyt}
pyta: pity: *pyta* M {pyta}
pyteth: compassion: *pyteth* T {pyteth}
pytethus: merciful: *pytethays* M {pytethus}
pyth: pit: *pyth* C {pyth}
pyw/pewa: who: *pyu* M; *pew, pewa* T; *pew* A; *pew, pewa, pyw* C; *peu, peua, pîu, piua* AB; *pu* Rowe {pyu/p'yua}

quarel: quarrel: *quarel* M {quarel}
quary: quarry: *kuarre* AB {—}
quarter: quarter (n.): *quarter* C {quarter}

quartron: quarter (n.): *quartron, quartren* M; *kuartan* AB; *quartan* Bilbao MS {quartron}
quartrona: quarter (vb): *quartrona* M {quartrona}
questyon, questyonow: question: *questyon*, (pl.) *questonow* T {questyon, questyons}
queth, quethow: garment: *queth*, (pl.) *quethou* M; *queth* A; *queth* C {queth, quethow}
quetha: clothe: *quetha* C {quetha}
quyk: quick: *quyk* OM; *quyk* PC; *quyk* RD; *quik* M; *quick, quicke, quyck, quycke* C {quyk}
quylkyn: frog: *kuilken* AB {quylkyn}
quyt: quite: *quyt* PC; *quyt* RD; *quyte* C {quyt}

racan: rake (n.): *rackan* AB {racan}
rafna: ravage: *raffna* M {rafna}
rag: for: *rag* M; *rag* T; *rage* A {rag/rak}
rambla: ramble: *rambla* AB {rarnbla}
ran: share (n.): *ran* M; *ran* T; *ran* A; *ran, radn* C {ran}
ranna: divide: (pret.) *rannas*, (pp.) *rynnys* PA; *radna, ranna* AB {ranna}
raunson: ransom (n.): *raunson, raunsyn* T; *rawnson* C {raunson}
raynya: reign (vb): *regnya* M; *raynya* T; *raynya* C {regnya}
re/ru/ro: by (in oaths): *ru* M; *ra* C {re}
re-: too: re- T; ra- C {re }
rebellyans: rebellion: *rebellyans* C {rebellyans}
rebukya: rebuke (vb): (pp.) *rebekis* PA; *rebukya* T {rebukya}
receva/recevya: receive: *receva* M; *receva* T; *recevya, recevia, recivia* A {recevya}
recevans: reception: *recevans* T {recevans}
record, recordys: record: *record* OM; (pl.) *recordys* C {record, recordys}
recordya: record (vb): *recordya* M; *recordya* T {recordya}
redempcyon: redemption: *redempcyon, redemcon* C {redempsyon}
redenen: fern: *reden* AB {reden}
redenen: fern-brake: *redanan* ACB {redenen}
redya: read: *redye* PA; *redya* M; *redya* T {redya}
ref: shovel, oar: *rêv* AB {ref}
regardya: regard (vb): *regardya, regardia* A {—}
rejoycya: rejoice: *rejosya* T; *rejoycya, regoyssya* C {rejoycya}
reken: reckoning, account: *reken* M; *reken* T; *recken* Borde {reken}
rekna: reckon: *rekna* M; *rekenna* T; *reckna* C {rekna}
remaynya: remain: *remaynya* T; *remaynya* C {remaynya)}
remembra: remember: *remembra* M; *remembra* T; *remembra* A; *remembra* C {remembra}
remnant: remainder: *remenant* M; *remenant* T; *remnant* A; *ramenat* AB {remenant}
remocyon: removal: *remoconn* M {remosyon}
renky: snore (vb): *renki* AB {renky}
rennys: divided: *rennys* C {rynnys}
reouta: royalty: *reoute* M {reouta}
repentya: repent: *repentya* M; *repentya* T; (pp.) *repentys* C {repentya}

A SHORT DICTIONARY OF UCR

repref: reproof: *repreff* M {repref}
requyrya: require: *requiria, requyrya* T; *requyrya* C {requyrya}
res: necessity: *res, reys* OM; *reys* M; *res* T; *rêz* AB {res}
resek: run: *resek* M; *resak, resek* T; *resacke* C {resek}
resna: reason (vb): *resna* T; *resna* C {resna}
reson: reason (n.): *reson, reason* T; *reson* C {reson}
resortya: resort (vb): *resortya* M {resortya}
restorya: restore: *restoria* M {restorya}
revrans: reverence: *reverens, reuerens, reverans, reverons* M; *reverens* T; *refrance* C {revrons}
rew: frost: *reaw* C; *rêau* AB; *reu* ACB {rew}
rew: row (in a row): *rew* C {rew}
reward: reward (n.): *reward* M; *rewarde* T {reward}
rewardya: reward (vb): *rewardye* PC; *rewardya* M; *rewardia* T; *rewardya* C {rewardya}
rewl: rule (n.): *reule* M; *rulle* T; *rowle* C {rewl}
rewlya/rowlya: rule (vb): *rewlya, reulya* M; *rewlya* T; *rowlya* C; *roulia* AB {rewlya}
***rewlyas, rewlysy**: ruler: (pl.) *rewlysy* T {rewlyas, rewlysy}
ro, roow/royow: gift: *ro*, (pl.) *roou* M; *ro*, (pl.) *royow* T; *rô* AB {ro, rohow/royow}
robbya: rob: (pp.) *robijs* M; *robbya* T; *robbia* AB {robbya}
rol: roll (n.): *rol* M {rol}
rom, romys: room: (pl.) *romes* OM; *rome* T; (pl.) *romys*, (pl.) *romes* C {rom, romys}
rond: round (adj.): *rond* M; *round* AB {rond}
ros, rosow: net: *roois, ros* T; *rûz* AB; (pl.) *roza* Rowe; (pl.) *rosow* Bilbao MS {ros, rosow}
ros: wheel: *rôz, rôs* AB {ros}
rostya: roast (vb): *rostia* AB {rostya}
roweth: sway: *roweth* M {roweth}
rowtya: rule (vb): *routia* M; *rowtya* Rowe {rowtya}
rudh: red: *ruth* M; *ruth* A; *rydh* AB; *rydh, ryth* ACB {ruth}
rusk: bark: *risk* AB {rusk}
ruth: crowd: *ruth* PA; *ruth* Rowe {ruth}
ruthy: relent: *ruthy* M {ruthy}
ruttya: rub: *rhittia* AB {ruttya}
ry: give: *ry* M; *ry* T; *rhei* AB {ry}
ryal: royal: *ryal* RD; *ryel* M; *ryall, reall* C {ryal}
ryb: beside: *ryb* M; *ryb* T; *ryb* C; *reb* AB; *reb* Rowe {ryb/ryp}
rych: rich: *rych* OM; *rych* M; *rych* T {rych}
rychys, rychyth: riches: *rychys, rechys, rychyth* M; *rychis* T {rychys, rychyth}
ryder: sieve (n.): *ridar* AB {ryder}
ryelder: magnificence: *reelder* M {ryelder}
ryver, ryvers: river: *ryuer* M; (pl.) *ryvars* T {ryver, ryvers}

saben: fir tree: *zaban* AB {saben}
sacra: consecrate: *sacra* OM; *sacra* M {sacra}
sacrament, sacramentys: sacrament: *sacrament*, (pl.) *sacramentys* T; *sacrament*, (pl.) *sacramentes, sacramentys* A {sacrament, sacramens}

sacryfys: sacrifice: *sakyrfeys* M; *sacrifice* A; *sacrafice, sacrifice, sacryfice* C {sacryfys}
saf yn ban/sa' ban: get up: *saf yn ban* OM; *sa ban* M; *save in ban* C; (pret.) *e savaz am'àn* AB; *save aman* Rowe; *sâv a man* ACB {saf yn ban/sa'ban}
sagh, seghyer bag, sack: (pl.) *syeher* T; *zah* AB {sagh, seghyer}
salla: salt (vb): *zalla* AB; (pp.) *salles* JBoson {salla}
salow: whole: *salou* M {salow}
salujy: greet: *salugy* PC; *salugy, sallugye* C {salujy}
salvacyon: salvation: *salvaccon* M; *salvacion, salvacyon* T {salvasyon}
sans, sens: holy (adj.); saint (n.): *sans*, (pl.) *sens*, (pl.) *syns* M; *sans* T; *sans* A; *zance*, (pl.) *zanzo* TBoson; *sanz*, (pl.) *sanzow* JBoson {sans, syns}
sansoleth: sanctity: *sansoleth* M {sansoleth}
sarchya: search (vb): *sarchia* T {—}
savyour: saviour: *savyour, savyoure* T; *saviour* A {savyour}
saw: but: *sau* M; *saw, sow* T; *saw, sowe* C {saw}
saw: whole: *sau* M; *sowe* JTonkin {saw}
sawgh: burden: *sawe* T; *sawe* ACB {sawgh}
sawment: healing: *saument* M; *sawment* C {sawment}
sawor: fragrance: *sawor* OM; *sauer* M; *sawer* C {sawor}
Saws, Sawson: Englishman: *Zouz*, (pl.) *Zouzon* AB; (pl.) *Sausen* NBoson; (pl.) *Zowzan* ACB {Saws, Sawson}
Sawsnek: English (language): *sawsneck* Carew; *Zouznak* AB; *Sousenack* NBoson; *Zawznak* ACB; *Sowsnack* Bodinar {Sawsnek}
sawthan: confusion: *sowthan* T {sawthan}
sawya: heal: *sawya* M; *sawya* T; *sawya* C; *sawyah* Rowe {sawya}
scaf: light (adj.): *schaff* M; *scaff* T; *skave* C; *sgâv* AB {scaf}
scaldya: scald: *skaldya* M {scaldya}
scant: scant: *schant, ascant* M; *skant* C; *skent* AB; *skant* NBoson {scant}
scantlowr: hardly: *schanlour, scantlor* M; *scantlower* Bodinar {scantlowr}
scappya: escape: *schappya* M; *scappya* C {scappya}
scat: blow, box on ears: *skat* AB {scat}
scavel: stool: *skavall, scavall* A; *skaval* AB; *skauoll, skavoll* NBoson {scavel}
sclandra: offend, slander: (pp.) *sclandrys* PC; *sclandra* M {sclandra}
scodh, dewscoth: shoulder: *scouth* PC; *scoth* M; *skudh, skodh*, (dual) *diskodh* AB {scoth, dywscoth}
scol: school: *scole, scoll* M; *scool* T {scol}
scoler, scoloryon: scholar: *scholar* A; *sgylur*, (pl.) *Skolàryo*, (pl.) *skylurion* AB {scoler, scoloryon}
scon: soon: *scon* M; *skon, scon* C {scon}
sconya: refuse (vb): *sconye* PA; *sconya* M {sconya}
scoren: branch: *skoran* C; *skoren* AB {scoren}

scorjya: scourge (vb): *scorgye* PA; *scorgya* M {scorja/scorjya}

scorn: scorn (n.): *scorne* M {scorn}

scornya: scorn (vb): *scornye* PA; *scornya* M {scornya}

scovarn, scovornow: ear: (pl.) *scovurnow*, (pl.) *scovornow* T; *skavarn, skevarn* AB {scovarn, scovarnow}

scovarnak: hare: *skouarnak* AB {scovarnak}

scravynyas: scratch (vb): *skriviniaz* AB {scravynyas}

scruth: shudder (n.): *scruth* PA; *skruth* A {scruth}

scryfa, screfa: write (vb); writing (n.): *screfa, scryve* M; *scriffa, screffa, scryffa, scryfa* T; *scryfa* A; *scryffa, scryva* C; *skrefa, skrepha* AB; (pp.) *scriffez* NBoson {scryfa}

scryptur, scrypturs: scripture: (pl.) *scryptours* PC; *scryptur* M; *scriptur, scripture*, (pl.) *scripturs* T {scryptor, scryptors}

scubya: sweep: *skibia* AB {scuba}

scudel: dish: *scudel* PA; *skidal* AB {scudel}

scues/skes: shadow: *schus* M; *skesse* T; *skêz* AB {skes, scus}

scullya: shed (vb): *scollya* M; *scollya, scoyllya* T; (pp.) *skullys* A {scullya}

scurya: scour: *scurya* T {scurya}

se: (episcopal) seat: *se* M {se}

secund: second: *secund* M; *second* T {secund}

sedha/esedha: sit: *setha* M; *setha* T; *setha* A; *setha* C; *sedha* AB; *zetha* Rowe {sedha/esedha}

segh: dry: *segh* OM; *seigh* C; *zêh, zâh* AB; *zeth* JBoson {segh}

seha: dry (vb): *seeha, seha* T; *seha* AB {segha}

sehes: thirst: *zehaz* ACB {seghes}

sehor: drought: *zehar* AB {seghor}

semblans: semblance: *symblans* T; *semblanz* NBoson {—}

semly: handsome: *sembly, semely* C {semly}

sempel: simple: *sempel* M; *sempill* T; *sympell* C {sempel}

sensy/senjy: hold: *sensy* M; *sengy, sensy, singy, syngy* T; (pres.) *sensaf*, (pres.) *syns*, (pp.) *synges* C; *sendzha, sindzhza, seinzhe* AB {synsy}

serpont, serpons: serpent: *serpent*, (pl.) *serpons* T; *serpent*, (pl.) *serpentis* C {serpont, serpons}

sera, serys: sir: *sera*, (pl.) *serys* M; *sera* C; *sarra* ACB {syrra}

serrys: angry: *serrys* M; *serrys* T {serrys}

servont, servons: servant: (pl.) *servons*, (pl.) *cervons* M; *servont, servant*, (pl.) *servans* T; *servant* C {servont, servons}

servya: serve: *servye, cervya* M; *servia* T; *servia, servya* C; *servia* AB; *servya* Rowe {servya}

*servyas, servysy/servyjy: servant: (pl.) *servysy*, (pl.) *servesy* M; (pl.) *servizi*, (pl.) *servidzhi* AB {servyas, servysy}

servys: service: *servys* OM; *servys* M; *serves* Bilbao MS {servys}

seson: season (n.): *seson* M; *season* C {seson}

sesya: seize: *sesya* M; *sesia* AB {sesya}

set: seat: seat C {—}

seth, sethow: arrow: *seth, segh*, (pl.) *sethow*, (pl.) *sethaw* C; *zêath, zêah* AB {seth, sethow}

sethor: archer: *zethar* AB {sethor}

settya: set: *syttya* M; *settya* T; *settya* C; (pret.) *zettyas* Rowe {settya}

sevel: stand: *sevell, sevel* M; *sevall* T; *sevall* C; *zeval* AB; *saval* Rowe; *sevel* ACB {sevel}

sevy: strawberries: *sevi, sivi; sevi* ACB {syvy}

sevylyak: standing (adj.): *sevyllyake* C {sevylyak}

sew, sewyon: bream: (pl.) *shewyan*, (pl.) *ziu*, (pl.) *ziuion* AB {sew, sewyon}

sewajya: assuage: *sewagya* M {sewajya}

sewya: follow: *sywa* M; *sewya* T; *sewya* C; (pret.) *suyas* Rowe {sewya}

*sewyas, sewysy: follower: (pl.) *sewysy* T {sewyas, sewysy}

seyth: seven: *syth* Borde; *seith* AB; *seith* ACB {seyth}

seythen: week: *sythen* M; *zeithan* AB; *sithen* Bilbao MS {seythen}

seythpleg: sevenfold: *vii plag* C {seythplek}

seythves: seventh: *sythvas* C; *seithaz* B; *sithas, sithvas* TBoson; *sithas* JBoson; *seythaz, seithvas* ACB {seythves}

shagga: shag, cormorant: *shagga* AB {shagga}

shakya: shake (vb): *shakya* M; *shackya; shakiah* ACB {shakya}

sham: shame (n.): *schame* M; *shame* C {sham}

shamya: shame (vb): *schamya* M {shamya}

shanel: channel, gutter: *shanel* AB {shanel}

shap: shape (n.): *shap* T; *shap* A; *shape* C {shap}

shappya: shape (vb): *schappia, schappya, shappya* T; *shapya* C {shapya}

shara: share (n.): *shara* C {shara}

sherewa: scoundrel: *scherevwa* M {sherewa}

sherewynsys: wickedness: *scherwynsy* M; *sherewynsy* C {sherewynsy}

showr: shower: *showre* C {showr}

skevens: lungs: *skephanz* AB {skevens}

skyans: intelligence: *skyans* M; *skyans* T; *skeans* C; *skians* AB; *skeeanz* NBoson {skyans}

skyansek: intelligent: *skyansek* {skyansek}

skyentoleth: wisdom: *skyentoleth, skentoleth* M; *skyantoleth* T {skyentoleth}

slakya: slacken: *slackya* C {slakya}

slym: slime: *sleme* C {slym}

slynkya: crawl: *slynkya* M; *slynckya* C {slynkya}

smoth: smooth: *smoth* C {smoth}

snell: quick: *snel, snell* M {snel}

socor: succour (n.): *sokyr* M; *succur, succure* T {socor}

socra: succour (vb): *socra* M; *succra* T {socra}

sodh: employment: *soyth* M {soth}

solabreys: already: *sollebreys* M {solabrys}

soladhedh: already: *solladeth* M {soladheth}

solempnyty: solemnity: *solempnyty* T; *solempnyty* C {solempnyta}

sols: shilling: *zoulz* AB {sols}

son: sound: *sone* T {son}

sona: bless: *sona* C; *sona* JBoson {sona}

sor: anger (n.): *sorre* T; *sor* C; *zoer* Rowe {sor}

sort, sortow: sort: *sort* M; (pl.) *sortow*, (pl.) *sortowe* C; (pl.) *sorto* Rowe {sort, sortow}

sotel: subtle: *sotel* M; *suttal, sottall* C {sotel}

sotelneth: subtlety: *subtelnath* A {sotelneth}
soudor, soudrys/soudoryon: soldier: (pl.) *soudoryan*, (pl.) *soudoryon*, (pl.) *soudrys* M {soudor, soudrys/soudoryon}
soveran: sovereign (n.): *soveran* M; *soveran* T {sovran}
soweny: prosper: *soweny* M; (pres.) *sowenaf* C {sowyny}
soweth: worst luck!: *soueth* M; *soweth* T; *syueth* AB {soweth}
sowl: stubble: *zoul* AB {sowl}
sparya: spare (vb): *sparya* C; *sparria* AB {sparya}
spas: space: *spas* M; *space* C {spas}
specyal: special: *especiall, speciall, specyall* T {specyal}
speda: speed (n.): *spede* M; *speda* T {speda}
spedhes: bramble: (pl.) *spethas* T; (pl.) *speras* C {spedhes}
spedya: succeed: *spedya, spedie* M {spedya}
spena: spend: *speyna* M {spena}
spera: spear: *spera* C {spera}
spernen, spern: thorn: (pl.) *spern* M; (pl.) *sperne* T; (pl.) *spearn* C; *spernan* AB; (pl) *spearn* Rowe {spernen, spern}
speys: time: *speys* M; *spyes* C {spys}
speytya: vex: *speitia* AB {spytya}
splan: splendid: *splan* M; *splan* C; *spladn* AB {splan}
sport: sport (n.): *sport* M {sport}
sportya: sport (vb): *sportya* M {sportya}
sprusen, sprus: pip: *sprusan*, (pl.) *sprus, spruse* C {sprusen, sprus}
spyrys/sperys/spurys, spyryjyon/spuryjyon: spirit: *spyrys, sperys* M; *spuris*, (pl.) *spurugian* T; *spyrys, spiris, sperys* C; *speriz* AB; *speres* TBoson; *spiriz* JBoson {spyrys, spyrysyon/spyryjyon}
squardya: tear (vb): *squerdya, squardya* M; *squardia* A {squardya}
squattya: hit, destroy: *squattya* M; (pp.) *squattys* C; *sguattia* AB; *squatchia* JBoson {squattya}
squyer, squyeryon: squire: *squyer* M; (pl.) *skuerrion* AB {squyer, squyeryon}
squyth: tired: *squeth, squyth* M; *squyth, sqwyth* C; *skith* AB {squyth}
stak: tether (n.): *stak* M {stak}
stap: step (n.): *stap* M {stap}
stat: estate, state: *stat* M; *stat* T; *stat* A; *stat, state* C {stat}
statya: endow: *statya* M {statya}
sten: tin: *stêan* AB; *stean* ACB {sten}
stenor, stenoryon: tinner; (pl.) *stynnorian* JBoson; *stener, stênor*, (pl.) *stennerion* ACB {stenor, stenoryon}
steren, ster, sterennow: star: (pl.) *stear* C; *sterran* AB; *sterradnou* JBoson; *steran, stearan*, (pl.) *steare* Rowe {steren, ster}
stoppya: stop (vb): *stopya* M; *stoppya* T; *stoppia* JTonkin {stoppya}
stowt: stout (adj.): *stout* M; *stowte* C {stowt}
strayt: strict: *strayte* C {strayt}
strechya: delay (vb): *strechya* M {strechya}
strewy: sneeze (vb): *striui* AB {strewy}

strotha: clasp (vb): *strotha* T {strotha}
stryf: strife: *stryff* T {stryf}
stryk: quick, nimble: *strik* AB {stryk}
stryppya: strip (vb): *streppya* M {stryppya}
stryvya: strive: *stryvya* T {stryvya}
studhya: study (vb): *stuthya, stethya* M {studhya}
styrya: mean (vb): *styrrya* T {styrya}
styward: steward: *styward, stywart* M {styward}
substans: substance: *substans* T; *substance, substans* A; *substance* C {substans}
suel: whoever: *suel* PA; *seyl* C {sul}
suffra: suffer: *suffra* T {suffra}
sugan: juice: *sugan* AB {sugan}
suger: lazy, sluggish: *siger, zigir* AB {suger}
Sulgweyth: on Sunday: *Sylgueth* AB {Sulgwyth}
supposya: suppose: *soposia, seposia* M; *supposia, supposya* T; *supposya* C; *sybbosia* AB; *suppoga* NBoson {supposya}
sur: sure: *sur, suyr* M; *sur* T; *sur, sure, suer, ser* C; *seer* TBoson; *seere* Rowe {sur}
susten: sustenance: *susten* M; *susten* C {susten}
syans: whim: *seeanz* NBoson; *seeanz* ACB {syans}
syght: sight: *syght* M; *sight* T; *syght* C {syght}
sylly, syllyas: eel: (pl.) *selyas* C; *zilli* AB {sylly}
sylwador: saviour: *selwadour* M; *salvador* C {sylwador}
sylwans: salvation: *seluans* M; *sylwans* C {sylwans}
sylwel: save: *selwel* M; (pp.) *sylwys* C {sylwel}
syn: sign (n.): *syne* M {syn}
syns dha glap: shut up!: *sens the clap* M {syns dha glap}
syr: sir: *ser* M {syr}
syra: sire, father: *sira* AB; *seera* NBoson; *zeerah* Rowe; *sirra, seera* ACB {syrra}
syra wyn: grandfather: *sira wydn* AB {syra wyn}

tabel: table: *tabel* A {tabel}
tacla: furnish: *takla* M {tacla}
taga: throttle, choke: *taga* AB {taga}
tal: forehead: *tale* C; *tâl* AB {tal}
tala: tale: (pl.) *talys* T; *tallah* Rowe {tala}
talkya: talk (vb): *talkya* T; *talkya* C {talkya}
tam: bit: *tam* M; *tam* T; *tam, tabm* C; *tabm* AB {tam}
tan: fire: *tan* M; *tane* T; *tan, tane* C; *tane* Rowe {tan}
tan: take!: *tan* M {tan}
tanjys: bonfire: *tanges* M {tansys}
tanow: few: *tanou* M; *tanow* C; *tanau* AB {tanow}
taran, tarennow: thunder (n.): *taran* AB; (pl.) *tarednow* ACB {taran}
tardar: drill, auger: *tardar* OM; *tardar* AB {tardar}
tarenna: thunder (vb): *trenna, tredna* AB {tarenna}
tarosvan: phantom: *tarosvan* M {tarosvan}
tarow: bull: *tarou* M; *tarow* C; *taro* AB; *tarrow* Bilbao MS {tarow}

tas, tasow: father: *tas, tays* M; *tas* T; (pl.) *tasow* A; *tace, tas, tase, taes* C; *tås*, (pl.) *tassow* ACB {tas, tasow}

tas gwyn: granfather: *taz gwydn* AB {tas gwyn}

tastya: taste (vb): *tastya* T; *tastia* A; *tastya* C {tastya}

tava: touch (vb): *tava* M; *tava* C {tava}

tavas, tavosow: tongue: *tavas*, (pl.) *tevosow* M; *tavas*, (pl.) *tavosow* T; *tavas* A; *tavaz*, (pl.) *tavazo* AB {tavas, tavasow}

tavasek: loquacious: *tavazek* AB {tavasek}

tavern: tavern: *tavern* M; *tavarn* AB {tavern}

tavolen: dock leaf: *tavolan* AB {tavolen}

taw: be silent!: *taw*! M; *taw*! C; *taw*! Scawen {taw}

tebel: evil (adj.): *teball* M; *teball* T {tebel}

tebel-el: devil: *tebel el* M; *tebell ell* T {tebel-el}

tebelwryans: evil deed: *tebelvryans* M {tebel-wryans}

tecter: beauty: *tecter, tekter* M; *tectar* C {tekter}

tedha: melt: *tedha* AB {tedha}

teg: beautiful: *tek* M; *tege* T; *teke, teake* C; *teag* AB; *teag* ACB {tek/teg}

teken: moment, little while: *teken* AB {teken}

teleth: ought: *teleth* M {teleth}

telly: bore, perforate: *telly* PA; (pp.) *tellys* PC; (pp.) *tellys* RD; *tolla, tulla*, (pp.) *tellyz* AB {telly}

tempel, templys: temple: *tempel*, (pl.) *templys* M; *tempill* T; *tempel*, (pl.) *templys* AB {templa, templys}

tempra: temper (vb): *tempra* M {tempra}

temptacyon: temptation: *temtacyon, temptasconn* M; *temptacon* C {temptasyon}

temptya: tempt: *temptya* M; *temtia, temptia* T; *temptya, temtya* C; (pp.) *temptez* Rowe {temptya}

tenewan: side: *tenewen, tenewon* M; *tenewan* T; *tenewan, tenewhan* C {tenewan}

tenna: draw: *tenna* M; *tenna* T; *tedna, tenna* C; *tedna* AB {tenna}

terlemmel: skip (vb): *terlemel* M {terlemmel}

terlentry: shine (vb): *terlentry* C {terlentry}

termyn, termynyow: time: *termen, termyn* M; *termyn*, (pl.) *tyrmynnyow* T; *termyn* C; *termen* Rowe; *termen* ACB {termyn, termynyow}

ternos. the next day: *ternoz* AB {ternos}

terneyja: pass over: *tarneidzha* AB {ternyja}

terry: break: *terry* M; *terry* T; *terry* C; *terhi* AB {terry}

terry an jedh: dawn: *terri an dzhêdh* AB {—}

Testament Noweth: New Testament: *testament nowyth* T; *testament noweth* A {Testament Noweth}

tethen: udder, teat: *tethan* AB {tethen}

tevy: grow: *tevy* T; *tevy* C; *teva, tivi* AB {tevy}

tew: thick: *tew* OM; *teu* AB {tew}

tewl: dark (adj.): *tewl* RD; *teule* M; *tewlle* T; *teual* AB {tewl}

tewolgow: darkness: *tewolgow* T; *tewolgow, tewolgowe* C; *tulgu* AB; *tolgo* Rowe {tewolgow}

teyl: dung: *teil* AB {teyl}

teyrgweyth: thrice: *ter guyth* PC; *teir gueth* AB {tergwyth}

teythy: faculties: *teythy* M {tythy}

token: token: *tokyn* T; *token* C {tokyn}

toll: hole: *tol* M; *toll* C; *tol* AB {toll}

tollek: perforated: *tollek* AB {tollek}

tom: warm (adj.): *tum* M; *tom, tubm* AB {tom}

tomder: heat: *tomder* T; *tomdar* C; *tumder* AB {tomder}

tomma: heat (vb): *tomma* PC; *tubma* AB {tomma}

tontya: taunt (vb): *tountya* M {tontya}

top: top: *top* M; *top* T; *top, tope, toppe* C {top}

tor: womb, belly: *tor* M; *tore* T; *tor* AB; *toer* Rowe {tor}

tormentya: torture (vb): *tormontya* M; *tremowntya* C; (pp.) *tormentyaz* Rowe {tormentya}

torn: turn: *turne* T; *torn* C {torn}

torth: loaf: *torh* AB {torth}

torva: breach: *torva* T {torva}

toth da: quickly: *tota* M; *totheta, tothta* C {totta}

tour: tower: *tour* M; *tûr* AB; *tur* JBoson {tour}

towl: intent, fall (n.): *toule* M; *towle* T; *towle* C {towl}

towlel: throw: *toulel* M; (pp.) *towlys* PC; *towlall* C; *toula* AB {towlel}

tra, taclennow/taclow: thing: *tra* M; *tra*, (pl.) *taclennow*, (pl.) *tacklennow* T; (pl.) *tacclow, taglenno* A; *tra*, (pl.) *tacklow*, (pl.) *tacklowe* C; (pl.) *taklaw* TBoson; (pl.) *tacklow*, (pl.) *taklow* ACB {tra, taclennow/taclow}

tra vyth, tra veth: nothing: *travyth, travith* T; *trevyth* C; *traveth* AB {tra vyth}

transformya: transform: *transformya* C {transfomya}

travalya: travel (vb): *travalia* AB {travalya}

travla: labour (vb): *travela, trafla* T {—}

traweythyow: sometimes: *trewythyou* M; *trewethow, treweythow* T {trawythyow}

traytor, traytours: traitor: *traytor, traytour* PA; *treytour*, (pl.) *treytours* M {traytour}

tre, trevow: town: *tre* M; *tre*, (pl.) *trevow* T {tre, trevow}

trebuchya: trip (vb): *trebytchya* C {trebuchya}

treddeth: three days: *try deth* RD; *treddeth* M {treddeth}

tregereth: pity: *tregereth* OM; *tregereth* M {tregereth}

trehy: cut (vb): *trehy* OM; *trehy* M; *treghy* T; *trehe* ACB {treghy}

trembla: tremble: *trembla* A {—}

tremena: die, pass over: *tremena* M; *tremena* C; (pp.) *tremenez* AB {tremena}

tremmyl: three thousand: *tremmyl* M {tremmyl}

tremmys: three months: *tremmys* {tremmys}

trenja: the day after tomorrow: *trenzha* AB {trenja}

tresor: treasure: *treasur* M; *trozor* Rowe {tresor}

trespas, trespassys: violence, trespass: *trespas, trespys* PC; *truspys* M; *trespas*, (pl.) *trespasces* T; *trespas* C {trespas}

trest: trust (n.): *tryst, trest* M; *trest* C {trest}

trestya. trust (vb): *trestia* M; *trystya* T; *trustya, tristya* C {trestya}

treth: sand, beach: *dreath* AB; *treath* ACB {treth}

trettya: tread: *trettya* M {trettya}

treveth: occasion: *trevath* T {treveth}

A SHORT DICTIONARY OF UCR

trewa: spit (vb): *trewe* PA; *treffia* AB {trewa}

trewya: sputum: *triffia* AB {trewvas}

treylya: turn (vb): *trelya, treyla, treylya* M; *trelya, treylya* T; *trylya* A; *treyllya, traylya* C; *trailia, traylya* AB; *traylyah* Rowe {trelya}

trobel: trouble (n.): *trobel, trubell* C {trobel}

trobla: trouble (vb): *trobla* T; *troubla* A; (pp.) *troublez* Rowe {trobla}

trogh: broken: trogh M {trogh}

troha: towards: *trohe, troha* M; *troha* C; *troha* AB; *tuah* NBoson {troha}

*__trompa, trompys__: trumpet: (pl.) *trompys* M {trompa, trompys}

tron, tronys: throne: *trone, throne,* (pl.) *tronys* C {tron, tronys}

tros: noise: *tros* M; *troes* C {tros}

tros, treys: foot: *troys* M; *tros,* (pl.) *treys* T; (pl.) *tryes,* (pl.) *trys* A; *tros, trose,* (pl.) *tryes* C; *trûz,* (pl.) *treiz* AB; *trooze* Rowe; *trooze* JTonkin {tros, treys}

tru: alas, (what a) pity: *tru* M; *trew* C {tru}

truedhek: piteous: *trewethek* M; *truadhek, trauedhak* AB {truethek}

trues: contrary (adj.): *treus* PA; *trues* M {trus}

truesy: doleful: *trewesy* M {truesy}

trueth: pity: *trueth, truath* M; *trewath* C {trueth}

try, teyr: three: (m.) *try* M; *tray* Borde; (f.) *tayre,* (f.) *tayer,* (f.) *tayr* C; *tre, trei,* (f.) *tair* AB {try, tyr}

trya: try (vb): *trea* M; *trya* T; *trea* C; *tria* AB {trya}

tryga/trega: dwell: *trega, trege* M; *trega, tryga* T; *trega* C; *trigia, trega* AB {tryga}

trygva: dwelling-place: *trygva* T; *trygva, trigva* C {trygva}

trynsys/trynjys: trinity: *trensis, trensys* M; *trynsys, tringys* T; *trengys* C; *trenzhez* AB {trynsys/trynjys}

tryssa/tryja: third: *tresse* M; *trissa, tryssa* T; *tryssa* C; *tridzha, tredzha* AB; *trugga* TBoson; *tridga, tregya* JBoson; *tridga* Rowe {tressa}

tryst: sad: *trest* M {tryst}

trystyns: sadness: *trystyns* PC; *trestyns* M {trystans}

tu: side: *tu* M; *tew* C {tu}

tuchya: touch (vb): *tuchya* M; *tuchya, tochya, tochia* T; *touchia* A; *towchya* C; *totcha* Rowe {tuchya}

tull: deceit: *tull* C {tull}

tulla: deceive: *tolla* M; *tulla* C; (pret.) *tullas* Rowe {tulla}

turnypen: turnip: *turnupan* AB {turnypen}

turont, *__turons__: tyrant: *turont, turant, turent* M {turont, turons}

ty: swear: *tye* C {ty}

ty/te: thou: *ty* M; *te* T; *tee, te* A; *ty, te* C; *ta, ti* AB; *chee* Rowe; *chee* ACB {ty}

tyak: farmer: *tyack* C; *tiak* AB; *teeack* NBoson {tyak}

tyas: call someone 'thou': *tyas* T {tyas}

tyby: think: *teby* M {tyby}

tybyans: opinion: *tybyanz* AB {tybyans}

tycky Dew: butterfly: *tikki Deu* AB {tykky Dew}

tykly: tricky: *tykly* M {tykly}

tyller, tylleryow: place: *teller* M; *teller, tyllar, tyller, tellar,* (pl.) *tellyrryow* T; *tillar* A; *tellar* C; *telhar* AB; *telhar* NBoson {tyller, tylleryow}

tyn: sharp: *tyn* M; *tyn* C {tyn}

tyr, tyryow. country: *tyr,* (pl.) *teryou* M; (pl.) *tyrryow* T; *tyre, tyer* C; *tîr,* (pl,) *tirriou* AB {tyr, tyryow}

tyra: land (vb): *tyrha* M; *teera* NBoson {tyra}

tyreth: land, country: *tyreth, tereth* M; *terathe* C {tyreth}

tythya: hiss (vb): *tithia* AB {tythya}

*__uer/er__: hour, time: *eare* C {ur}

ufer: vain: *ufer* M {ufer}

ugans: twenty: *ugans, ugens* M; *egans* T; *ugans, ygans* C; *igans* AB; *iganz* ACB {ugans}

ugansves: twentieth: *iganz vath* AB; *iganz vas* ACB {ugansves}

uhel: high: *uhel, uhell* M; *uhel, uhell* T; *ughall, uhall, uhull* C; *ehual, iuhal* AB; *ewhall* NBoson; *euhall* Rowe {ughel}

uhelder: height: *uhelderT;* *uheldar* C; *hiuhelder* AB; *ughelder* ACB {ughelder}

uja/eja: shriek (vb): *uga* T; *ega* C {uja}

ula: owl: *ula* AB {ula}

ullya: howl (vb): *ullia* AB {ullya}

un: one: *un* M; *un* T; *idn, udn, un* C {un}

unlagajek: one eyed: *ydnlagadzhak* AB {unlagasek}

unnek: eleven: *unec* Borde; *idnak* AB; *ednack* ACB {unnek}

unnegves: eleventh: *ydnhakvas* AB; *eden dêgvas* ACB {unnegves}

understondya: understand: *understondia, undyrstondia* T; *understandya* A {understondya}

ungrassyes: graceless, ungracious: *ongrassys, ongrassyas* M; *ungrasshes* C {ungrassyes}

universita: university: *universite* {unyversyta}

unkynda: unnatuial: *unkynda, unkunda* T; *unkinda* C {unkynda}

unverhes: agreed: (pp.) *unferheys* M; cf. *unver* PA {unverhes}

unwodhvos: ignorance: *unwothfas, unwothfos* T {unwothfos}

unwos: related: *unwoys* M {unwos}

unweyth: once: *unwyth* M; *unwith* T; *unwith* C; *enueth* AB {unwyth}

ura: anoint: *ure* PA; *ure* PC; *ira* AB {ura}

uryn: urine: *uryn* M {uryn}

usadow: custom: *usadow* {usadow}

uskys: quickly: *uskys* M; *uskys, uskes* C {uskys}

usya: use (vb): *usia* M; *usia* T; *usya* C; *yuzia* AB {usya}

uthyk: dreadful: *uthyk* T; *uthicke, uthek* C; *eithick* ACB {uthyk}

uttra: utter: *uttra* T {—}

uvel: humble: *ufel, uvel* M; *uvell* T; *hewwal* A; *evall* C {huvel}

uvelder: humility: *uvelder* M; *uveldar, uvelder* T {huvelder}

venjans: vengeance: *venjons* PA; *venjans* PC; *vynjons* OM; *vingians* T; *vengens, vengeance* C {venjyans}

venjya: avenge: *vyngia* M {venjya}

vers: verse: *vers* M {vers}

vessyl: vessel: *vecyl* M; *vessell* T {vessyl}

vexya: vex: *vexya* M; *vexia* T {vexya}

voys, voycys: voice: *voys* OM; *voys* PC; *voyce*, (pl.) *voyses* T; *voice* C {voys, voycys}

vyaj: expedition: *vyadge, vyadg* C {vyaj}

vyajya: journey (vb): *vyaggya* C {vyajya}

vyctory: victory: *victory* RD; *vyctory* M; *victory, victuri* T {vyctory}

vyl: vile: *vyl* OM; *vyl* PC; *vyl* M {vyl}

vyrtu, vyrtuys: virtue: *virtu* PA; *virtu* M; *virtu*, (pl.) *virtues*, (pl.) *virtus* T; *vertew* C {vertu, vertuys}

vytel: food: *vytel* M; *vyctuall* C {vytel}

vyth / veth: any: *vyth* M; *vith* T; *veith* A; *vythe, vyth, veth* C; *vêth* AB {vyth}

walkya: walk (vb): *walkia* A {walkya}

war: aware: *var* M; *ware* T; *ware* C {war}

war: upon: *war* M; *war* T; *war* C {war}

war dhelergh: backwards: *war ʒellargh* PA; *war thellar* T {war dhelergh}

war jy: inside: *war gy* T {war-jy}

war neb cor: in any way: *war neb coore* C {war neb cor}

war nuk: immediately: *war nuk* M {war nuk}

war van: up: *war van* M {war van}

warbarth: together: *warbarth* M; *warbarth* T; *warbarth* C; *uarbarh* AB; *warbarth* Rowe; *varrbarr* NBoson; *warbar* ACB {warbarth}

warlergh: after, according to: *warlergh* M; *warlerth, warlyrth* T; *warlerth* C; *uarlêr* AB; *vorler* JBoson {war lergh}

wastya: lay waste: *vastya* M; *wastya* C; *guastia* AB {wastya}

welcum / wolcum: welcome (adj. & n.): *wolcom, wolcum* PC; *wolcom* RD; *wolcum, welcum* M; *welcom* Borde; *welcome* C; *uelkym* AB {wolcum}

welcomma: welcome (vb): *wolcumme* OM; (pp.) *welcummys* M; *welcomma* C; (pret.) *welcumbes* JTonkin {wolcumma}

west: west: *weyst* M {west}

whans: desire (n.): *wans* M; *whanse* T; *huanz* AB {whans}

whansek: desirous: *whansek* PC; *whansek* C {whansek}

whar: docile: *whar* M {whar}

whare: shortly: *wharre* OM; *wharee* M; *whare* T; *whare* C {whare}

wharth: laughter: *wharthe* C {wharth}

whath: still: *whath, wath, weyth* M; *whath* T; *whath* C; *huath* AB {whath}

whedh: swelling, tumour: *huedh* AB {wheth}

whedhel, whedhlow: story: (pl.) *whethlow* OM; (pl.) *whethlow* PC; (pl.) *whethlow* RD; *huedhel*, (pl.) *huedhlou* AB {whethel, whethlow}

whedhy: swell (vb): (pp.) *huedhyz* AB; *huedhi* ACB {whedhy}

wheg, whegow: sweet (adj.); darling (n.): *wek, whek*, (pl.) *wegou* M; *wheg* T; *wheag, wheake* C; *huêg* AB {whek, whegow}

***whegen, whegennow**: sweetie, darling: (pl.) *wegennou* M {whegen, whegennow}

whegh: six: *whea* C; *whe* Borde; *wheeath* NBoson; *whee'ah* JBoson; *huih* AB; *wheh* ACB {whegh}

wheghves: sixth: *wehes* M; *hueffaz, hueffas* AB; *wheythaz* ACB {wheghves}

wheja: vomit (vb): *huedzha* AB {wheja}

whel: work (n.): *weyll* M; *huêl* AB; *weale* NBoson {whel}

whensys: desirous: *wensys* T {whensys}

wher, wharfedhys: happen: (pp.) *wharfethys* OM; (pres.) *wher*, (pp.) *warfethys* M; (pres.) *wheare* C {wher, wharfedhys}

wherow: bitter: *wherow* RD; *huero* AB {wherow}

wherthyn: laugh: (pres.) *warth* M; *huerhin* AB {wherthyn}

whes: sweat (n.): *wysce* T; *wheys* C; *huêz* AB; *wheeze* Rowe {whes}

whesa: sweat (vb): (imperf.) *wese* PA; *hueza* AB {whesa}

whetha: blow (vb): *wetha* M; *whetha* C; *huetha* AB {whetha}

whethfyans an dowr: bubble: *huethvians an dour* AB {whethfyans an dowr}

whor: sister: *hore* T; *hoer* C; *hôar* AB; *hoer* NBoson {whor}

why: you: *wy* M; *why* T; *why* C; *huei* AB {why}

whylas / whelas: seek: *weles* M; *whelas, whylas* T; *whelas* C; *huillaz, huila* AB; *whelaz* NBoson; *whelas* ACB {whylas}

whylen: beetle: *huîlan* AB {whylen}

whyppya: whip (vb): (pp.) *whippys* A {whyppya}

wondrys: wondrous: *wondres* T; *wondrys, wondres* C {wondrys}

wordhy: worthy: *worthy* M; *worthy* C {wordhy}

wosa / woja: after: *woge* RD; *wosa, wose* M; *wosa, whosa* T; *osa* A; *woʒa* C; *udzha, udzhe, woze* AB; *ugge* NBoson; *ouga* Rowe {wosa}

woteweth: finally: *otyweth* M; *woteweth* T {woteweth}

y, anjy: they: *y* M; *y, ansy* T; *y, an dzhyi, dzhei, gy* AB; *angie* Rowe; *angy* ACB {y, ynsy}

y gyla / y gela: the other: *y gela* M; *y gela* T; *y gela, y gylla* C; *gele* AB {y gyla}

yagh: healthy: *yagh* M; *yagh* T {yagh}

yaghhe: heal: *yaghhe* M {yaghhe}

yar: hen: *iâr* AB {yar}

yehes / ehes: health: *yehes, ʒeheys* M; *yehas, eghas* T; *ehaz* AB; *ehaz* ACB {yeghes}

yes: confess: *ʒeys* M {yes}

yet, yettys: gate: (pl.) *yeattys*, (pl.) *yettys* T; *yet* C; *yet* AB; (pl.) *yettes* TBoson {yet, yettys}

yeyn: cold: *yeyn* PC; *yne, ʒeyn* M; *yeyne* C; *iên, iein* AB; *yein, yeine* ACB {yeyn}

yeynder: cold (n.): *yeindre* Rowe {yeynder}

yffarn, yffarnow: hell: *yfern* M; *yffarne* T; *effarn, efarn*, (pl.) *effarnow* C; *ifarn* AB; *efferne* TBoson {yffarn, yffarnow}

yly, ylyow: cure, remedy: *yly*, (pl.) *elyou* M; (pl.) *elyow* T {yly, ylyow}

ylyn: clear: *ylyn* M; *elyn* C {ylyn}

ymach / ymaj: image: *ymach* M; *ymag* T; *image* C {ymach}

ympossybyl: impossible: *impossybyl* T; *unpossyble* C {unpossybyl}

yn: in: *in* M; *in* T; *yn* C {yn}

yn: narrow: *edn* AB; *idden* NBoson {yn}

yn ban: up: *in ban* M; *in ban, in man* T; *yn ban, in ban, in badn* C; *a mann, am'an* AB {yn ban}

yn berveth: within: *en bera* AB {yn berveth}

yn cusk: asleep: *in coske* M {yn cusk}

yn dan: under: *yn dan, in dan* M; *in dan* T; *dan* A; *dadn* AB {yn dan}

y'n uer na / nena: then: *yn ur na* M; *nyna, nena* T; *in nena* C {y'n ur na}

yn gwyr: truly: *en gwyr* PA; *in guyr* OM; *en uîr* AB {Nance's *yn whyr is unattested}

yn hans: yonder: *in hans* M; *hons, in hons* C {yn hans}

yn kerdh / yn ker: away: *in kerth* M; *in kerth, yn kerth* T; *e ker* A; *in kerthe, in ker* C; *ker, kerr* AB; *a kar* NBoson; *caar, carr* Rowe {yn kerth}

yn kerhyn: around: *yn kerhyn, yn kerhen* M {yn kerghyn}

yn ketelma: thus: *in ketelma* M {yn ketelma}

yn kever: regarding, with respect to: *yn kever* M {yn kever}

yn medh: said: *in meth* M; *myth* T; *meth* NBoson; *medh* AB {yn meth}

yn mes: out: *in mes* T; *yn mes* C {yn mes}

yn mysk: among: *in meske, yn myske* M; *yn myske, in mysk* T; *yn myske* C; *amisk* Rowe; *mesk* NBoson {yn mysk}

yn rag: forward: *in rag* T {yn rak / yn rag}

yn sevureth: deliberately, as a joke: *in sevureth* M; *in sovereth* T {yn sevureth}

yn spyt dhe: in spite of: *in spyt the* M; *in spyte ʒa, yn spyta ʒa* C {yn spyt dhe}

yn ta: well: *yn ta* M; *in ta* T; *yn ta* C {yn ta}

y'n tor' ma: at the moment: *in tor ma* M; *in torn ma* C {y'n tor' ma}

yn tyen: completely: *yn tyan* M; *yn tean* C {yn tyen}

yn unyk: only: *en ednak* AB {yn unyk}

ynclynya: incline: *inclynya, inclenya* M {ynclynya}

yndella: thus: *indella* M; *indella* T; *yndella, indella* C; *an della* AB {yndella}

yndelma: thus: *indelma* M; *indellma* T; *an dellma, dellma* Rowe {yndelma}

*ynjyn, ynjynnys: contrivance: (pl.) *ingynnys* M {ynjyn, ynjynnys}

ynnocent, ynnocens: innocent (adj. & n.): (pl.) *ynocens* M; *innocent*, (pl.) *innocentys* T {ynocent, —}

ynter, yntre: between: *ynter* M; *intre* T; *intyr* A; *inter* C; *ter, tre* AB; *treeth* Rowe {ynter}

ynwedh: also: *y weth* RD; *ynweth, inweth* M; *inweth, ynweth* T; *e weth* A; *ynweth* C; *auêdh, enuêdh* AB; *aweeth* Rowe {ynweth}

ynyvry: injustice: *inivri* T {—}

yowynk / yonk: young: *yowynk* PC; *yowynk, yonk* M; (comp.) *younka* C; *iunk* AB; *younk* Rowe {yowynk / yonk}

yredy: indeed: *yredy, eredy* M; *aredy* C {yredy}

yrgh: snow: *yrgh* M; *yrth* T; *err* AB; *er* ACB {yrgh}

ysel: low: *ysel* M; *esell* T; *ysal, ysall* C; *izal* AB; *izal* ACB {ysel}

yselder: lowness: *eselder* M; *eselder* T; *yseldar* C {yselder}

yshew: issue: *ussew* T; *asshew, ayshew* C {yssew}

ystynna: stretch (vb): *ystenna* M; (imper.) *ysten* C {ystynna}

ytho: therefore: *ytho* T {ytho}

yurl, yurlys: earl: *yurl* OCV; *ʒurle*, (pl.) *ʒurlys* M {yurl, yurlys}

Glossary of symbols and technical terms

[ ] Square brackets around a set of symbols indicate that the sounds in question are to be understood as sounds (phones) only, without reference to their function in the sound system of the language.

// Slanted brackets enclose phonemes, that is to say, sounds understood as significant units in the sound system of the language in question. In Late Cornish [a] and [ɪ] in unstressed syllables are both members of the phoneme /ə/. See *phoneme*.

< > Angle brackets are used when referring to the way in which a word or sound is written rather than to the way in which it is pronounced.

: The triangular colon denotes a long vowel. In the present work a half-long vowel is denoted by a half triangular colon: [eː] is long, therefore, but [e·] is half-long.

ˈ The vertical line modifier indicates that the following syllable bears the stress, for example, in [təˈdej] 'today'.

- The hyphen is used to indicate hiatus, that is to say, a momentary stopping of the air flow between one vowel and another. If two vowels follow one another without any such break in articulation, they form a *diphthong*, q.v.

> X > Y means that X develops into Y.

< Y < X means that Y develops from X.

* The asterisk is used to indicate that a form is not actually attested but has been reconstructed on the basis of earlier or later forms or related items.

a The vowel of *hat, fat* in the English of Northern England.

æ The vowel of *hat, fat* in Standard English

316

ɑ The short equivalent of the stressed vowel in Standard English *father*.

ɛ "Open *e*": Approximately the vowel in Standard English *get, pen*.

e "Closed *e*": Similar to the first element of the diphthong in *same* [sejm] in Standard English or the *é* in French *été*.

i "Closed *i*": Approximately the short equivalent of the vowel in Standard English *screen, feed*.

ɪ "Open *i*": The vowel in Standard English *bit, sit, bin*. Open *i* [ɪ] and closed *e* [e] are very close to one another.

ɔ "Open *o*": Approximately the vowel of Standard English *hot, not*.

o "Closed *o*": The short equivalent approximately of the vowel of Standard English *law, pause*.

u "Closed *u*": Approximately the short equivalent of the vowel of Standard English *tune, moon*.

ʊ "Open *u*": The vowel of Standard English *good, hood*.

œ The short equivalent of the vowel in French *cœur* or in German *schön*.

y The vowel of German *Stück* or French *vu*.

ø Similar to [œ] but closer to [y].

ə "Schwa". This is the neutral vowel heard in the unstressed syllables of Standard English *bigot, onion, brother*, etc.

ɒ Schwa pronounced with the lips rounded as for [ɔ]. Similar to [œ] except that it occurs in unstressed syllables only.

ɨ The Welsh central *i*. A fair approximation can be got by putting the mouth and tongue in the position for [i] and attempting, to say [u].

ö This symbol is used by Gendall to represent schwa with *r*-colouring

j Similar to English *y*. [j] is used in the present work to indicate the second element in diphthongs. English *say, boy*, therefore would be represented as [sej] and [bɔj].

w The same as *w* in English *well, won't*, etc. It also occurs as the second

GLOSSARY OF SYMBOLS AND TECHNICAL TERMS

element in diphthongs. English *house*, *grown* are phonetically [haws] and [grəwn] respectively.

ʍ The voiceless equivalent of *w*. In some dialects of English, for example, *witch* [witʃ] is pronounced with initial [w] but *which* [ʍitʃ] has a voiceless initial.

n: This is used to indicate a long *n*, i.e. with twice the duration of *n*. In Cornish before the prosodic shift *benen* 'woman' had a single *n* whereas *benneth* 'blessing' had [n:].

l: This is used to indicate a long *l*, that is to say, an *l* pronounced with double the duration of *l*.

n̥ The voiceless equivalent of [n]. [n̥] is obtained by trying to say both [n] and [h] together.

l̥ The voiceless equivalent of [l]. In Cornish this consonant was probably retroflex (q.v.). The voiceless *ll* [ɬ] of Welsh in *Llanelli, Llewelyn* is a lateral (q.v.).

ɾ The voiceless equivalent of [r].

ʃ The initial consonant in English *ship* [ʃɪp], *show* [ʃow], *shack* [ʃæk].

tʃ The initial consonant of English *chip* [tʃɪp] and *choose* [tʃuːz].

ʒ The sound of *s* in such English words as *leisure, pleasure, Asian*.

dʒ The sound of *j* in the English words *jug, jam*, etc.

ð The sound of *th* in the English words *this, that, breathe*.

θ The sound of *th* in the English words *thick, thin, breath*.

x The sound of *ch* in the Scottish word *loch*, or in the German word *Achtung*.

ɸ An *f* sound produced with both upper and lower lips rounded and in contact with each other.

d̪ The kind of *d* sound produced with the tip of the tongue against the alveolar ridge. Standard English *d* is of this variety. The symbol [d] is often used to indicate a dental *d*, that is to say, a sound produced with the tip of the tongue pressed against the top teeth.

ᵈn The graphic representation of n with pre-occlusion. See 9.1.

ᵇm The graphic representation of m with pre-occlusion. See 9.1.

tj/dj These are the two graphs recommended by Ken George to spell a palatalized *t* and *d* in Kernowek Kemyn. Since neither ever existed in Cornish, their pronunciation is of academic interest only; it would be [tʲ]/[dʲ] or [c]/[ɟ].

accidence: a term used to describe the way in which nouns, verbs, etc., change according to their function. In Cornish *mab* 'son' has a plural *mebyon* 'sons'. The change of *a > e* and the ending *-yon* are part of the accidence of Cornish. See also *morphology* and *inflection*.

affricate: a sound that begins as a plosive and ends as a continuant. [tʃ], [dʒ] are affricates.

allophone: a variant pronunciation of a phoneme that does not alter the meaning of words in which it occurs. in Late Cornish *trygys* 'dwelling, resident' was either ['trɪgəz], ['trɪgɪz], or ['trɪgọz]. The phoneme /ə/ therefore had the allophones [ɪ] and [ọ].

alveolar: a consonant is alveolar when it is pronounced with the tip of the tongue against the alveolar ridge, that is, the ridge between the upper teeth and the hard palate.

analogy: the way in which one part of the sound system or grammar of a language forms a model (or the reshaping of another part. Forms in children's English like 'I throwed', 'I shooted' are by analogy with 'I showed', 'I hooted', etc.

apocopated: with a final segment removed. Late Cornish *gennam* is an apocopated form of Middle Cornish *genama* 'with me'.

apodosis: in conditional sentences, the clause that does not contain *if* (or *unless*) is referred to as the *apodosis*. See *protasis*.

317

articulation: the way in which sound are produced by the organs of speech (tongue, mouth, throat, voice box, nasal passages) is referred to as articulation.

assibilation: when plosives become sibilants, the process is known as assibilation. The final segment in Old Cornish *tat* 'father' /taːd/ was assibilated to /z/ in Middle Cornish: /taːz/.

assimilation: when a sound comes to resemble an adjacent segment, it is said to have been assimilated to its neighbour.

auslaut: a term borrowed from German that refers to final position in a word. In Middle Cornish *du* 'black' the vowel <u> [y] or [iw] is in auslaut.

auxiliary: auxiliary verbs are those that are used with main verbs in order to express various nuances of meaning. In English *have, shall, will* are common auxiliaries in such expressions as *we have seen, you shall not steal* and *I will go*. In Cornish *bos, mennas, gul* and *dos* are common auxiliaries.

back vowel: the back vowels are those that are pronounced with the tongue retracted towards the back of the mouth cavity. [u], [o], and [ɑ] are back vowels.

calque: a calque is a loan translation from one language to another. *Aval-dor* 'potato' in Nance s English-Cornish Dictionary is a calque on French *pomme de terre* 'potato' (literally 'earth-apple').

central vowel: a central vowel is one that is produced when the tongue is in the central area of the mouth cavity. [ə] and [œ] are central vowels.

closed syllable: a syllable that ends in a consonant or a consonant cluster is said to be closed. In English the word *godlessness* consists of three closed syllables whereas the word *family* has three open syllables.

cluster: a group of consonants together; *str* in the English word *strength,* for example.

coda: the less sonorous part of a diphthong that follows the nucleus. In /ej/, for example, /e/ is the nucleus and /j/ the coda.

dental: dental consonants are those that are pronounced with the tongue against or close to the teeth. [t], [d] and [n] can all be dental in pronunciation.

diphthong: a sequence of two vocalic elements pronounced as a unit. /aw/ in English *house* /haws/ and /ɔj/ in *boy* /bɔj/ are both diphthongs.

enclitic: an enclitic is a short word that cannot stand by itself but is attached to another and forms a single accentual unit with it. In Cornish *an chy-ma* 'this house' *-ma* is an enclitic.

etymon: a word, especially when thought of as a separate item in a language's lexicon.

fortis: this term refers to the vigour with which a consonant is pronounced. in Cornish before the prosodic shift there would have been a difference in pronunciation between the fortis *b* in *byan* 'small' and the lenis *b* in *mab* 'son'.

free variation: allophones of a phoneme are often in free variation with one another. That is to say either can be used without prejudice to the sense. In unstressed closed syllables in Late Cornish [ɪ], [ə] and [o̞] seem to have been in free variation.

fricative: a term sometimes used to describe those consonants that are produced by a continuous flow of air. [f], [v], [θ] and [ð] are fricatives, whereas [p], [b], [t] and [d] are stops.

front vowel: front vowels are those that are pronounced with the tongue towards the front of the mouth cavity. [i] and [e] are front vowels.

fronted: a vowel is said to be fronted when as the result of some linguistic change its articulation has moved from the central or back position to the front.

geminate: when a consonant is written or pronounced double, it may be described as geminate.

graphemic: graphemic is a term used when referring to the way that a sound is written rather than how it is pronounced. For historical reasons the schwa in English is written <o> in *cotton*, as <e> in *written* and as <a> in *Asian*. The difference is graphemic not phonetic.

Great Vowel Shift: a series of sound changes that occurred in fifteenth century English. Among other things /iː/ and /uː/ were diphthongized to /əj/ and /əw/ respectively and /eː/ and /oː/ became /iː/ and /uː/.

hiatus: when two vowels are pronounced in sequence but with a momentary stopping of the breath between them, the momentary stopping of the air flow is called hiatus.

high vowel: A high vowel is one that is produced with the tongue in a high position in the mouth cavity. /i/ and /u/ are high vowels. /a/ is a low one.

***i*-affection**: this refers to a sound shift in the history of Welsh, Cornish and Breton by which the high vowel /i/ in the next syllable has raised the low back vowels /o/ and /a/ to /e/. As examples one might cite Cornish *kegyn* 'kitchen' < Latin *coquina* and Welsh *Tegid* < Latin *Tacitus*.

indirect statement: indirect statements are ones that are reported and occur after verbs of saying, telling, believing, etc. "Cornish will be successfully revived" is a direct statement but "In 1904 few thought that Cornish would be successfully revived" is an indirect one.

infixed pronoun: a distinctive feature of Cornish grammar is that a pronoun as the direct object of a verb comes between the verbal particle *y, a, ny, na* or *may* and the verb proper. In the sentence *my a'n gwelas* 'I saw him' *a* is a verbal particle, *gwelas* is the verb and *'n* is an infixed pronoun. From the Middle Cornish period onwards Cornish had a slight tendency to replace infixed pronouns with suffixed ones, i.e.

pronouns that were placed after the verb rather than before it.

inflection: inflection is the term used to refer to the various forms taken by a word to show tense, person, gender, number, etc. Inflections are the details of accidence.

isogloss: this term refers to a line drawn on a map grouping together all the places that share a particular feature. Isogloss is frequently used by metonomy to refer to the dialect feature itself.

jussive: jussive is used to describe the subjunctive mood when used for commands. In *re dheffo dha wlascor* 'thy kingdom come' *re dheffo* is a jussive subjunctive.

labialized: a consonant is labialized when it is pronounced with rounding of the lips.

lateral: lateral consonants are produced by contact between the edge of the blade of the tongue and the side of the hard palate. The Welsh <ll> is a voiceless lateral [ɬ].

lax: lax in phonetics is a relative term and means that a vowel or consonant is pronounced with the organs in a more relaxed position than is the case with the tense equivalent. In English the short vowel in *ship* is more lax than the long equivalent in *sheep*.

lenis: lenis refers to the way in which a consonant is pronounced in a relatively unvigorous way. In Cornish before the prosodic shift /b/ from earlier /p/ between vowels was a lenis, whereas initial /b/ would have been a fortis.

lenition: a feature common to all the Celtic languages by which consonants that were originally in intervocalic position were weakened in articulation. Thus in Cornish *an margh* 'the horse' < **sindos markos* shows initial *m* unaffected by any sound change. *An vergh* 'the daughter' < **sinda merka* shows *v* as the lenition product of *m* between vowels.

low: vowels are low when they are produced with the tongue in a low position in the mouth-cavity. [a] is a low vowel.

metathesis: This refers to the spontaneous inversion of consonants around a vowel. In English, for example, *girn* ('to pull faces') and *crud* are metathesized variants of *grin* and *curd.*

mid: a mid vowel is between the high vowels and the low vowels. /e/ and /o/ are mid vowels.

minimal pair: a pair of words differentiated from each other by a single phoneme. In English *set* /sɛt/ and *sat* /sæt/ are a minimal pair, as also are *loth* /ləwθ/ and *loathe* /ləwð/.

mora: a unit of length used when discussing long/short vowels, etc.

morphology: this term refers to the inflection of a language. In some contexts morphology and accidence are synonyms.

neologism: a new word coined or borrowed to deal with a new idea or invention. Though well established in English, by now such coinages as *television, telephone, user-friendly* were originally neologisms. Minority languages have a great need of neologisms and indeed in many cases have terminological academies continuously at work.

neutralize: when a distinction between two phonemes disappears in certain environments, the distinction is said to be neutralized. In Cornish the distinction between /g/ and /k/ is neutralized before /s/, for example in *deksen*, pluperfect of *degaf* 'I carry'.

nucleus: the nucleus is the more sonorous part of a diphthong. In /aw/ in /haws/ 'house' /a/ is the nucleus, while /w/ is the coda.

obstruent: any consonant that obstructs the air-flow. A stop or a fricative.

open syllable: a syllable is open if it ends in a vowel. The English word *debility* consists of four open syllables.

orthography: the term orthography is synonymous with "spelling system". Three separate orthographies are currently in use in Neo-Cornish.

overlong: overlong refers to a vowel or diphthong that is unusually long. Since long vowels in Cornish were of two morae after the Prosodic Shift, an overlong vowel would have been one of three morae.

palatalized: consonants are said palatalized when they are pronounced with the blade of the tongue against the hard palate. In the English words *kitten, kitchen* the initial element is a palatalized allophone of /k/.

paradigm: the full list of forms of a verb for person and number in any given tense. The Cornish *ef, os, yw, on, ough, yns* constitutes the full paradigm of the short present of *bos.*

paradigmatic pressure: the tendency of an anomalous form in a paradigm to be reshaped according to the other members.

particle: in the Celtic languages a particle is a short unstressed word that precedes a verb. In Cornish *y, a, ny, na, nanj, may, re* are the main particles.

pausa: when a word comes at the end of a sentence or is uttered by itself, it is said to be in pausa.

periphrastic: tenses, etc., of a verb are said to be periphrastic when they are formed by using auxiliary verbs. Cornish *me a vyn mos* and English *I will go* are alike examples of periphrastic futures.

phoneme: the notion of the phoneme is central to modern phonology. A phoneme is the smallest unit of sound that has function. In English /kæt/ *cat* and /fæt/ *fat* are different words because /k/ and /f/ are different phonemes. In the word *cat* and the word *kitten* the initial segment is different, the *k* of *kitten* being pronounced further forward in the mouth than that of *cat.* The difference in pronunciation is entirely conditioned by the different environment, i.e before a high front vowel /ɪ/. The two different forms of *k* in *cat* and *kitten* are not therefore separate phonemes, but are allophones of the same phoneme /k/. The process of phonemicization determines which are the phonemes of a language and which sounds are allophones of others. An orthography designed to be phonemic should consistently represent one phoneme by one letter. If a spelling system uses different symbols to represent the same phoneme, it cannot be said to be phonemic.

phonetics: phonetics is that part of linguistic investigation that is concerned with the production of sounds.

phonology: phonology is the part of linguistic investigation that concerns itself with phonemes.

plosive: a stop, a consonant that stops the air-flow completely. /p/, /t/, /k/ and /b/, /d/, and /g/ are all plosives.

post-tonic: a vowel is post tonic if it occurs in a syllable that occurs immediately after the main accent.

prefix: an item attached to the beginning of a word in order to change its meaning. In English *re-* in *rewrite*, *redo*, *reshape* is a prefix with the sense 'again'.

prepositional pronoun: prepositional pronouns are a distinctive feature of all the Celtic languages. in Celtic, prepositions combine with pronouns to form a single unit. in Cornish, *dhym* 'to me' is a prepositional pronoun consisting of the preposition *dhe* 'to' and the first person pronoun. Other examples would be *orthys*, *ragtho*, *hebon*, *genough* and *warnedha*.

pretonic: a vowel or syllable is pretonic if it occurs immediately before the main accent.

proclitic: a proclitic is a short 'word' that occurs immediately before a stressed word and forms a single unit with it. The verbal particles *y*, *a*, etc. are proclitics.

Prosodic Shift: the radical change that occurred in Cornish between the Old and Middle period. As a result of the prosodic shift stressed syllables lost in length and gained in intensity. Long vowels shortened from three to two morae. Half-long vowels became short and unstressed syllables were weakened to schwa. There is no disagreement among scholars that the prosodic shift occurred. Until the present book, however, it has been assumed that the shift occurred between the Middle Cornish and Late Cornish periods.

prosody: prosody properly refers to the system of rhythm, syllabic length and rhyl me that forms the basis of verse as distinct from prose. In this book prosody is used with an extended sense to refer to the system of syllabic length and stress that obtained in Cornish.

protasis: the clause in a conditional sentence, that contains the if-word. in the English sentence *If the prayer book had been translated into Cornish, the language would have survived beyond the eighteenth century*, the clause *If the prayer book had been translated into Cornish*, is the protasis, the rest is the apodosis.

provection: the initial mutation in Breton and Cornish that converts a voiced stop into a voiceless one. Provection occurs, for example, after the particle *ow*. Thus one says *gul* 'to do' but *ow cul* 'doing', *bewa* 'to live' but *ow pewa* 'living'.

reflex: the development of an earlier form according to the expected sound changes. French *chien* 'dog' is a reflex of Colloquial Latin *canis*, for example, and Cornish *bryntyn* 'noble' is a reflex of British **brigantinos* 'royal, princely'

retroflex: a consonant is retroflex when it is pronounced with the tip of the tongue curled back against the hard palate. There is good evidence that /r/ in Cornish was retroflex [ɽ].

rhotacize, rhotacism: the root of these words is *rho*, the name of the Greek

321

letter <ǫ> *r*. When /s/ or /z/ becomes /r/ between vowels the sibilant (s or z) is said to have been rhotacized. Rhotacism is normal in Latin and its effects are seen in Latin borrowings in English, for example, *genus*, but *generic*, *pus* but *purulent*.

rounded: a vowel is said to be rounded when it is pronounced with the lips pursed. /u/ and /o/ are rounded vowels, though the degree of rounding is greater with /u/ than with /o/.

schwa: a term borrowed by the German Neo-Grammarians from Hebrew grammar. *Sheva* in Hebrew means 'nothingness'. Schwa is the mid central vowel [ə] that is neither front nor back, high nor low. In Cornish after the Prosodic Shift all unstressed vowels tended to become schwa.

segment: any discrete item in a phonological utterance can be referred to as a segment. Phonemes are segments but sounds can conveniently be described as segments before their phonemic status has been determined.

semivowel: semivowels are consonants that are phonetically very close to vowels. In English, for example, /w/ and /j/ are semivowels but they are acoustically close to /u/ and /i/. This can be seen in the way in which the phrases *you err* and *you were* are virtually indistinguishable.

sonant: next to the semivowels the sonants are the most vocalic class of consonants. They include [n], [l], [m] and [r].

spirantization: fricatives are sometimes known as spirants. As a result the initial Brythonic mutation that converts /p/ > /f/ and /t/ > /θ/ is known as spirantization. Notice, however, that in Cornish the result of the spirantization of /k/ is /h/, not /x/, since Cornish does not tolerate /x/ at the beginning of a syllable.

stop: stop is another name for the plosive consonants, [p], [t], [k], [b], [d] and [g].

stressed: a vowel or syllable is stressed when it carries more emphasis than adjacent vowels or syllables. In the English word *relation* /ri'lejʃən/ the second syllable, /lej/, is stressed. The first, /ri/, is pretonic and the third, /ʃən/, is post-tonic.

suffix: an item appended to a word to change its meaning. In English the suffix *-ly* makes adverbs of adjectives, for example, in *badly, sharply, curiously*.

tense: there are two quite different words *tense* used in linguistic discussion. The first is from Latin *tempus* and refers to those forms of verbs that refer to particular times, future tense, past tense, present tense. As an adjective *tense* applies to vowels. A tense vowel is one that is pronounced with the organs of articulation more tense than is the case with the lax counterpart. Generally speaking long vowels are tenser than short ones.

unreal condition: unreal conditions are those in which the condition expressed is more hypothetical than in a real condition. *If he comes, I'll give him his money back* is a real condition. *If he were to come, I'd give him his money back* is an unreal one.

unstressed: a vowel or syllable is unstressed when it does not carry the main emphasis in a word or accentual unit. In the English phrase *The scoundrel!* the two syllables *the* and *drel* are unstressed.

voiced: a consonant is voiced if the vocal chords are vibrating while it is being pronounced. If the vocal cords are not vibrating while a consonant is being pronounced, the consonant is voiceless. /g/ is voiced but /k/ is voiceless. /w/ is voiced but /ʍ/ is voiceless.

yod: when discussing the history of a language the phoneme /j/ is frequently referred to as *yod*.

General Index

CORNISH TODAY

Kernowek 'Cornish language'; variants of the name 7.15, 14.33, 16.1; George inconsistently spells <Kernewek> (not *<Kernywek>) 13.28
Kesva an Taves Kernewek 'Cornish Language Board'; promoting spurious Cornish (Kernowek Kemyn) for twenty years 13.1
kettel 'as soon as' 13.37
ky, kei 'dog' 3.2, 3.5, 6.8; *kuen* 3.9
kyg 'flesh' 3.3, 8.9, 8.19

Laneast 8.20
Latin 2.1, 8.8, 8.20-21, 11.4, 11.6, 14.18, 14.23, 14.31, 14.40, 17.13; Neo-Latin 0.1
Lescudjack 11.17
lesky 'burn' (vb) 20.34
leverel 'say' (vb) 14.10, 14.24, 20.34; *leverys* 7.10; *lever, laver* 7.11
Lewis, Henry 0.4
Leyowne (< *Lan Yowan*) 8.20
Lezauek 14.42, 16.1
Lhuyd, Edward 0.4, 0.5, 0.10, 2.2, 3.5, 3.7, 3.9, 3.10; pronunciation of diu 'black' 3.13; and *biuh* 'cow' 3.13; Welsh dialect spoken by 3.17; and future of *bos* 5.2; and words for 'fish' and 'finger' 5.8; and word for 'alive' 6.6; and final -*ow* 6.7; and word for 'to turn' 6.8; and final -*i* 17.12; and *hidhu* 'today' 17.13; and final -*ek*, -*ak* 7.15; describes -*ys* 7.15; and *ehual* 'high' 8.3; and *gydhihuar* 'evening' 8.3; and *delkio* 'leaves' 8.4; and voiceless *r* 8.4; final consonants and 8.8, 8.14-15; his text of JCR and *s ~ z* 8.17; and *genver* 'January' 8.21; and *alene* 9.3; and *kinin* 'garlic' 9.4; and *gudzh* 'blood' 11.16; George unaware that Lhuyd created *arbednek* 13.4; and *gest* (not understood by George) 13.27; his orthography 14.5-8; his preface 14.24; ignorance of Cornish grammar 14.21; views on <dh> 17.13; and OCV 17.14; and *Zouz, Zousnak* 21.2; and 'I say' 21.7; and *mynnes, mennas* 'wish' as an auxiliary' 21.9; did not understand *dos* as auxiliary 21.12; did not understand *may halla va* 21.14; did not understand *ter* introducing indirect speech 21.17; and *auan* 'river' 22.2; and *monna* 'money' 22.3; and *blejen* 'flower' 22.4; and *mil* 'animal' 22.5; and *lodn* 'steer' 22.5; and *best* 22.5; and *chambour* 22.6; and *usya* 22.7; and *yma cof dhym* 22.8; and *enep* 'face' 22.10; and *dynas* 22.10; passage from 23.7
logosen 'mouse' 10.5
lon 'steer' 22.5
los, loys 'grey' 3.8, 3,10, 3.11
Loth, Joseph 10.3, 11.2, 17.13; George misunderstood a point made by 10.3; erroneous "Loth-George hypothesis" 10.4

Londres 'London' 8.20, 11.13
Low Saxon 0.6
Lowarth-lavender-en-parson 13.6
Lyon, Rod 15.12
Lyver an Pymp Marthus Seleven 15.4; passage from 23.12

Madoc 10.5, 11.17
Manx 2.1, 13.14, 16.2
margh, mergh 'horse(s)' 8.7
Marghas Yow 8.20
marhak 'horseman' 8.14, 13.10
Market Jew 8.20
Maria, Marya 'Mary' 8.20, 11.13
may halla 'in order that' 21.14
medhek, medhyk 'doctor' 8.10, 13.10, 13.36, 13.39; medhec 0.7, 17.13
medhes 'speak' 14.8, 17.13
melyga 'curse' (vb) (< Latin *maledico*); George unaware of etymology 13.37; past participle *melyges* 7.8
Menheniot 11.6, 11.12
mergh 'daughter' 8.2, 8.7, 17.18
Merrasicks, Mera-jacks 10.5
merwel 'die' (vb) 20.36
metathesis; in *gul > gwel* 3.14; of /r/ and /n/ 8.4, 8.22; of diphthong in *dew* 'god' 6.4; *kepar > pecar* 14.3; *ui > yw* 'is' 19.12
metherwin (ghost word) 14.41
Middle English 0.6; borrowings from 6.8, 7.10, 8.20, 11.13; word stress in 11.10; literature of 11.3; influence on Middle Cornish 12.3; the graph <th> in 17.13; George's bizarre spellings of borrowings: *<kommyttya>, *<okkashyon>, *<preshyous>, etc. 13.34
Middle Breton 4.9; absence of vocalic alternation 5.1; borrowings from 8.20; *Jesus* in 11.13; orthography 13.16
Middle French 0.6, 8.20
Mid-Wales 3.17, 13.27
Minster 11.5, 11.7
mona 'money' 14.40; 22.3
Modern English 0.6, 11.10; quantity in 12.3
Moreman, John 11.6
mousegy 'stink' (vb); George says this attested form was "invented" by Nance 13.3; George says his spurious form *mosogi* is correct 13.3
my/me 'I, me'; George mistaken about the vowel 3.4, 13.23, 13.39; in UCR 18.2
myghtern, mytern 'king' 15.6, 17.18
myl 'animal' 15.5, 22.5
mylyon 'million' 14.19
mylvyl 'million' 0.7, 14.19
mynnes, mennas 'wish' (vb) 19.19, 20.38; *men* for *myn* 14.3; *mynnaf ~ mennaf ~ mannaf* 4.9, 5.5;

man 5.6; *menja* 14.3, 14.7; as auxiliary 15.5, 21.9-10; Wella Brown mistaken about its use 21.9

myras, meras 'look' (vb) 4.2, 20.35; George's erroneous spelling * <mires> 13.30, 13.39

Nance, Robert Morton 0.4; wrongly criticized by George 13.3, 13.18; views on Moreman 11.6; views on Late Cornish writers 14.25; as linguist 15.5-8; rejects pre-occlusion 15.7; and indirect statement 21.17; his purism 22.1

Nancean Synthesis 14.47, 15.3

nans 'valley' 8.7; *nant* 11.15

Nebbaz Gerriau dro tho Carnoack 14.4, 14.32-3, 15.11; quotation from 14.22

Nebes Whethlow Ber 15.4

Necessary Doctrine and Erudition for any Christian Man (1543) 11.6

New Prosodic System 2.4-7, 3.5; effects 12.1-2, 12.4; origins of 12.3; George mistakenly dates it to *c.* 1600 13.19; all George's many errors result from this erroneous dating 13.39

New Quantity System (in British) 2.1

Norman Conquest 11.3, 11.12, 11.13, 12.3, 12.6

norves, norvys 'world' 17.4

nowedga (ghost word) 14.43

oan 'lamb' 3.10

Old Cornish Vocabulary (OCV) 11.4, 12.6, 14.18

Old Norse 0.6

onen 'one' 7.7, 13.33; *pub onen* 18.4

Ordinalia 2.5, 6.3, 6.6, 8.6; unstressed vowels in and George's error 7.2-4, 13.19; place-names in 11.14; <g> in 11.16; George is unaware that *treveth* occurs in 13.4; apparently late features in 14.3, 14.12; dialects in 12.7; passage from 23.3

othoredzhek 'authoritative' 14.19

os, oys 'age' 3.11

owr 'gold' 3.9

Padel, Oliver 3.17, 9.4, 11.10, 11.13, 11.16, 11.17, 18.4; discusses *auan* 22.2; cites *dynas* 22.10

paradigms; alleged gaps in 0.4

Parret 11.10

Pascon agan Arluth 14.18; inadvertently omitted by George 13.5; passages from 13.38, 23.2; scribe not western 12.7

Pathada, Patrieda 11.10

Pedersen, Henry 11.16

Pender, Oliver 13.11, 14.21

Pentreath, Dolly 0.1, 14.26

periphrastic verbal forms 0.4; present 14.3, 21.7; conditional 14.3, 21.10; future 14.3, 15.5, 21.9; imperative 21.15

perthy 'bear, carry' 5.9, 8.5, 20.39

pesy, pysy 'pray' 15.10, 20.41

Phillips, Merfyn 14.41

place-names; containing *-oc/-ek/ak* 3.10, 11.9, 11.12, 11.18; without pre-occlusion 9.2; with pre-occlusion 9.5; in mid- and western Cornwall 11.7; in *Lann-* 11.10; containing *porth* 8.6; containing final *g/k* 8.10; containing <j> 17.12; containing <dh> 17.13; in *-jek/-jack* and George's error 11.17

plen an gwary; near Saltash 11.14

plew/plu 'parish' 3.9, 12.1, 13.20

pobel 'people' 7.7, 14.27

Polpidnick 9.5, 11.18

Polwhele, R. 11.6

Ponteisou 'Panters Bridge' 8.20

Pool, Peter A.S. 7.13, 9.4, 11.17, 13.9; his criticism of Kernowek Kemyn 13.15; his description of Unified Cornish 15.1

pos, poys 'heavy' 3.11

Prayer Book Rebellion 16.2

pre-occlusion 9.1-6, 14.3; as dialect marker 9.6; in Late Cornish 14.37; in place-names 9.5; absence of pre-occlusion in some words 9.2; in Manx 13.14

prepositional pronouns 18.5-16; *a* 'from' 18.11; *a ugh* 'above' 18.16; *dhe* 'to' 18.8; *tha vee, tha gee* 'to me, to thee' 14.3; *dherag* 'in front of' 18.10; *dheworth* 'from' 14.15, 18.13; *dre* 'through' 14.16, 18.15; *dres* 'over' 18.16; *gans* 'with' 14.14, 18.7; *orth* 'against' 14.15, 18.12; *rag* 'for' 14.15, 18.9; *ryb* 14.17, 18.16; *war* 'upon' 14.15, 18.15; *yn* 'in' 14.16, 18.14; *ynter* 'among' 18.15

prevy 'prove' 20.40

Price, Glanville; his views on revived Cornish 0.1-7

proper names in Cornish 8.20

profus 'prophet' 7.14

promys 'promise' (n.) 7.10, 22.9

promysya 'promise' (vb) 22.9

Pryce, William 14.24, 14.42, 14.45, 17.13

prys, preggyow 'time(s), meal(s)' 3.6, 5.4; George perplexed by the attested spelling 13.26

pub 'every(body)' 18.4

pysk, puscas 'fish(es)' 2.3, 5.8, 17.7

Ray, John 14.32

rag 'for' 0.7, 8.8-9, 13.10

re 'by' (in oaths) 4.5

re (perfective particle) 4.5

remembra 'remember' 22.8

retroflex *r* 8.4, 14.26

res 'ford' (n.) 11.5

rom 'room' 22.6

Rosecraddock 11.11

Rowe, William 14.48, 23.9

Map 1. Pre-occlusion in place-names.

Map 2. The alternation <s> ~ <g>/<j> in place-names.

Map 3. -*a*(*c*)*k* in place-names.

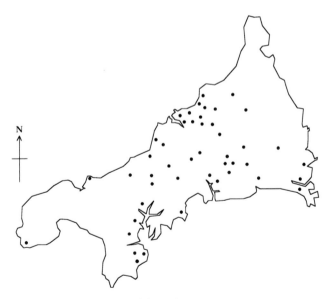

Map 4. -*oc*(*k*) in place-names.

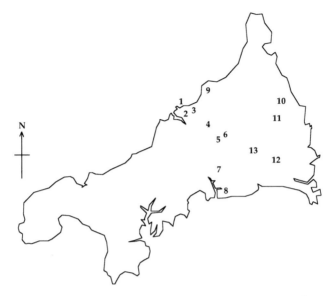

Map 5. Assibilation in place-names in eastern Cornwall.

1 *Mouls < mols* (near Pentire)
2 *Brownsue < bron du* (St Minver)
3 *Hensens < sens* (St Minver 1315)
4 *Nanceduy < nans* (St Mabyn 1302)
5 *Treslea < res* 'ford' (Cardinham)
6 *Trezance < sans* (Cardinham)
7 *Bosmaugan < bos* (Fairy Cross)
8 *Treweers < gweras* (Lansallos)
9 *Trewins < gwyns* (Trevalga)
10 *Rezare < res* 'ford' (Lezant)
11 *Coskallow Wood < cos* (South Hill)
12 *Treweese < gweras* (Quethiock)
13 *Rosecraddock < res* 'ford' (St Cleer)

RESOURCES IN UCR

Ashworth, Heather. 2006. *Whedhel Gyttern*. Ewny Redreth: Spyrys a Gernow. ISBN: 978-0-9548451-5-5

Litchfield, Jo. 2004. *Everyday Words in Cornish*. Cornish language consultants Ray & Denise Chubb. Portreath: Agan Tavas. ISBN 1-901409-08-2

Palmer, Myghal. 2001. *Rebellyans*. Ewny Redreth: Spyrys a Gernow. ISBN 0-9535975-3-9

Phillips, Andy & Nicholas Williams. 2004. *Lyver Pejadow rag Kenyver Jorna: Cornish Daily Prayer*. Redruth: Spyrys a Gernow. ISBN 0-9535975-8-X

Prohaska, Daniel. 2006. *Kornisch: Wort für Wort*. Bielefeld: Reise Know-how Verlag, Peter Rump GmbH.

Williams, Nicholas. 1997. *Clappya Kernowek: an introduction to Unified Cornish Revised*. Portreath: Agan Tavas. ISBN 1-901409-01-5

Williams, Nicholas, translator. 2002. *Testament Noweth agan Arluth ha Savyour Jesu Cryst*. Ewny Redrteth: Spyrys a Gernow. ISBN 0-9535975-4-7

Williams, Nicholas. 2005. *English-Cornish Dictionary: Gerlyver Sawsnek Kernowek*. Second edition. Redruth: Agan Tavas. ISBN 978-1-901409-09-3. Westport: Evertype. ISBN 978-1-904808-06-0

Williams, Nicholas. 2006. *Cornish Today: An examination of the revived language*. Third edition. Westport: Evertype. ISBN 978-1-904808-07-7

Williams, Nicholas. 2006. *Writings on Revived Cornish*. Westport: Evertype. ISBN 978-1-904808-08-4

Williams, Nicholas. 2006. *Towards Authentic Cornish*. Westport: Evertype. ISBN 978-1-904808-09-1

Lightning Source UK Ltd.
Milton Keynes UK
UKOW04f1851020316

269499UK00001B/70/P